MAJID. GHASSEMZADEH

ELECTRONIC FILTER
DESIGN HANDBOOK

ELECTRONIC FILTER DESIGN HANDBOOK

Arthur B. Williams

Fred J. Taylor

Third Edition

McGRAW-HILL, INC.

New York San Francisco Washington, D.C. Auckland Bogotá
Caracas Lisbon London Madrid Mexico City Milan
Montreal New Delhi San Juan Singapore
Sydney Tokyo Toronto

Library of Congress Cataloging-in-Publication Data

Williams, Arthur Bernard.
 Electronic filter design handbook / Arthur B. Williams, Fred J.
Taylor. — 3rd ed.
  p.   cm.
 Includes index.
 ISBN 0-07-070441-4 (hc)
 1. Electric filters—Design and construction—Handbooks, manuals,
etc.   I. Taylor, Fred J.   II. Title.
TK7872.F5W55   1995
 621.3815'324—dc20   95-21977
                                                                      CIP

1 2 3 4 5 6 7 8 9 0   DOC/DOC   9 0 0 9 8 7 6 5

ISBN 0-07-070441-4

*The sponsoring editor for this book was Stephen S. Chapman, the editing
supervisor was Joseph Bertuna, and the production supervisor was Suzanne
Rapcavage. It was set in Times Roman by North Market Street Graphics.*

Printed and bound by R. R. Donnelley & Sons Company.

McGraw-Hill books are available at special quantity discounts to use as pre-
miums and sales promotions or for use in corporate training programs. For
more information, please write to the Director of Special Sales, McGraw-
Hill, Inc., 11 West 19th Street, New York, NY 10011; or contact your local
bookstore.

CONTENTS

Chapter 8. Refinements in *LC* Filter Design   8.1

Chapter 9. Design of Magnetic Components   9.1

Chapter 15.   Filter Architecture   15.1

Chapter 16.   Digital Filter Technology   16.1

Chapter 17.   Switched-Capacitor Filters   17.1

Chapter 18.   Filter Design for EMI Suppression   18.1

Appendix A.   Discrete Systems Mathematics   A.1

Appendix B.   The TMS320   B.1

PREFACE

This is the third edition of the *Electronic Filter Design Handbook*. This book was first published in 1981. It was expanded in 1988 to include five additional chapters on digital filters. This revised edition contains new material on both analog and digital filters. A powerful software package has been included to allow rapid design of both analog and digital filters without the tedious mathematical computations normally encountered.

Prior to the introduction of this book in 1981, the design of LC and active filters had been reserved for specialists. The *Electronic Filter Design Handbook* treated the design of these filters in a practical manner and provided extensive tabulated data so that the average engineer with no previous experience could design passive or active filters. This philosophy was expanded to include digital filters in the second edition published in 1988. For the first time in any book, the design of all three classes of filters was covered in a practical easy-to-follow style. Now this third edition has been updated to include a number of new technologies and design methods. A powerful software package is now included to complement the material covered in the text.

Chapter 1 introduces the concept of modern network theory and discusses the tradeoffs between active and passive filter implementations.

The mathematical properties of standard filter response types are covered in chapter 2, including Butterworth, Chebyshev, Bessel, linear phase with equiripple error, transitional, synchronously tuned, and constant delay with Chebyshev stopband. Extensive normalized curves for both frequency and time-domain parameters of these standard polynomial transfer functions are provided. The highly efficient elliptic-function filter response is also discussed in this chapter and emphasized throughout the handbook.

In chapter 3 the design of both passive and active low-pass filters is covered using normalized tables. Specialized passive low-pass filter design techniques are illustrated, such as designing for unequal terminations and compensating for the effects of component dissipation (low Q). Various active low-pass filter structures are covered for both all-pole and elliptic-function types.

High-pass filters for both passive and active implementations are discussed in chapter 4.

Chapter 5 covers bandpass filters. Various passive filter transformations, approximations, and identities are shown to ensure practical element values even for extreme conditions of center frequency, bandwidth, or impedance level. New active bandpass implementations are given that exhibit low sensitivity at frequencies previously considered too high for active filters.

Techniques for band-reject filter design are presented in chapter 6. Passive and active types are covered.

Chapter 7 covers the design of networks having properties best described in the time domain. All-pass delay and amplitude equalizers are discussed in detail. Methods are shown for the design of LC and active delay lines are wideband 90° phase shift networks.

Refinements in LC filter design are covered in chapter 8. Special techniques are presented to manipulate element values so that practical values can always be obtained. Measurement techniques are shown.

Successful operation of LC filter design is highly dependent upon proper selection and manufacture of inductors. The design of magnetic components is presented in chapter 9. The entire process ranging from selection of magnetic material type and shape to coil-winding methods for optimum characteristics over the operating frequency range is detailed using a step-by-step approach.

Component selection for LC and active filters is discussed in chapter 10. Coverage includes capacitor characteristics and selection of fixed and variable resistor types. Operational amplifier theory is reviewed both from a theoretical and a practical standpoint. Expanded and updated device selection charts are provided to enable rapid choice of the appropriate operational amplifier for a given filter configuration and required operating frequency range. A new section has been added on surface-mount technology. Surface-mount (SMD) components are discussed as well as the manufacturing considerations using this technology.

Chapter 11 contains normalized tables for rapid design of both passive and active filters. In addition to the standard polynomial types, tables are provided for the unique constant-delay low-pass filters with Chebyshev stopband characteristics and elliptic-function filters up to the 17th order.

Chapter 12 introduces digital filters. Topics include the relation to analog filters and mathematical transforms.

Finite impulse-response filters (FIR) are discussed in chapter 13. The design procedure is outlined. Specialized topics such as windowing are covered. New material has been added on multirate processing and the quadrature mirror filter.

Chapter 14 covers the infinite impulse-response (IIR) filter type and the transformation of conventional analog filters into digital IIR filters.

Various forms of digital filter architecture are illustrated in chapter 15. Material has been added on fixed-point design.

Chapter 16, "Digital Filter Technology," has been rewritten to include implementation of digital filters using Texas Instruments, Motorola, Analog Devices, and AT&T DSP microprocessors.

Chapter 17 has been added and covers switched-capacitor filters. The underlying theory behind this technology is presented. Some design examples are shown using standard building-block ICs. A survey and convenient selection guide is included.

Chapter 18 is also new and discusses filter design to control conducted and radiated interference, i.e., EMI suppression. Domestic and international requirements such as the FCC rules and VDE regulations place mandatory restrictions on conducted and radiated interference. This chapter addresses these issues from a detailed design perspective and provides a guide for selecting components for these applications.

Appendix A provides a review of discrete system mathematics as applicable to digital filters. Digital filter design using the TMS320 family of DSP products is covered in appendix B.

The authors would like to thank Mike Lewis of The Athena Group, Inc., for contributing chapter 16 and for his skilled integration of the software into a cohesive package.

Arthur B. Williams
Fred J. Taylor

ELECTRONIC FILTER
DESIGN HANDBOOK

CHAPTER 1

INTRODUCTION TO MODERN NETWORK THEORY

1.1 MODERN NETWORK THEORY

A generalized filter is shown in figure 1-1. The filter block may consist of inductors, capacitors, resistors, and possibly active elements such as operational amplifiers and transistors. The terminations shown are a voltage source E_s, a source resistance R_s, and a load resistor R_L.

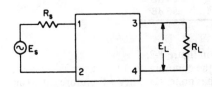

FIGURE 1-1 Generalized filter.

The circuit equations for the network of figure 1-1 can be written by using circuit-analysis techniques. Modern network theory solves these equations to determine the network values for optimum performance in some respect.

The Pole-Zero Concept

The frequency response of the generalized filter can be expressed as a ratio of two polynomials in s where $s = j\omega$ ($j = \sqrt{-1}$ and ω, the frequency in radians per second, is $2\pi f$) and is referred to as a transfer function. This can be stated mathematically as

$$T(s) = \frac{E_L}{E_s} = \frac{N(s)}{D(s)} \tag{1-1}$$

The roots of the denominator polynomial $D(s)$ are called poles and the roots of the numerator polynomial $N(s)$ are referred to as zeros.

Deriving a network's transfer function could become quite tedious and is beyond the scope of this book. The following discussion explores the evaluation and representation of a relatively simple transfer function.

Analysis of the low-pass filter of figure 1-2a results in the following transfer function:

$$T(s) = \frac{1}{s^3 + 2s^2 + 2s + 1} \tag{1-2}$$

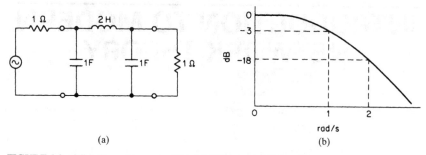

FIGURE 1-2   All-pole $n = 3$ low-pass filter: (a) filter circuit; (b) frequency response.

Let us now evaluate this expression at different frequencies after substituting $j\omega$ for s. The result will be expressed as the absolute magnitude of $T(j\omega)$ and the relative attenuation in decibels with respect to the response at DC.

$$T(j\omega) = \frac{1}{1 - 2\omega^2 + j(2\omega - \omega^3)} \tag{1-3}$$

ω	$|T(j\omega)|$	$20 \log|T(j\omega)|$
0	1	0 dB
1	0.707	−3 dB
2	0.124	−18 dB
3	0.0370	−29 dB
4	0.0156	−36 dB

The frequency-response curve is plotted in figure 1-2b.

Analysis of equation (1-2) indicates that the denominator of the transfer function has three roots or poles and the numerator has none. The filter is therefore called an all-pole type. Since the denominator is a third-order polynomial, the filter is also said to have an $n = 3$ complexity. The denominator poles are $s = -1$, $s = -0.500 + j0.866$, and $s = -0.500 - j0.866$.

These complex numbers can be represented as symbols on a complex-number plane. The abscissa is α, the real component of the root, and the ordinate is β, the imaginary part. Each pole is represented as the symbol X, and a zero is represented as 0. Figure 1-3 illustrates the complex-number plane representation for the roots of equation (1-2).

There are certain mathematical restrictions on the location of poles and zeros in order for the filter to be realizable. They must occur in pairs which are conjugates of each other, except for real-axis poles and zeros, which may occur singly. Poles must also be restricted to the left half plane (i.e., the real coordinate of the pole must be negative). Zeros may occur in either plane.

Synthesis of Filters From Polynomials

Modern network theory has produced families of standard transfer functions that provide optimum filter performance in some desired respect. Synthesis is the pro-

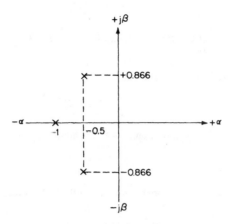

FIGURE 1-3 Complex-frequency plane representation of equation (1-2).

cess of deriving circuit component values from these transfer functions. Chapter 11 contains extensive tables of transfer functions and their associated component values so that design by synthesis is not required. However, in order to gain some understanding as to how these values have been determined, we will now discuss a few methods of filter synthesis.

Synthesis by Expansion of Driving-Point Impedance.   The input impedance to the generalized filter of figure 1-1 is the impedance seen looking into terminals 1 and 2 with terminals 3 and 4 terminated, and is referred to as the driving-point impedance or Z_{11} of the network. If an expression for Z_{11} could be determined from the given transfer function, this expression could then be expanded to define the filter.

A family of transfer functions describing the flattest possible shape and a monotonically increasing attenuation in the stopband is the Butterworth low-pass response. These all-pole transfer functions have denominator polynomial roots which fall on a circle having a radius of unity from the origin of the $j\omega$ axis. The attenuation for this family is 3 dB at 1 rad/s.

The transfer function of equation (1-2) satisfies this criterion. It is evident from figure 1-3 that if a circle were drawn having a radius of 1, with the origin as the center, it would intersect the real root and both complex roots.

If R_s in the generalized filter of figure 1-1 is set to 1 Ω, a driving-point impedance expression can be derived in terms of the Butterworth transfer function as

$$Z_{11} = \frac{D(s) - s^n}{D(s) + s^n} \tag{1-4}$$

where $D(s)$ is the denominator polynomial of the transfer function and n is the order of the polynomial.

After $D(s)$ is substituted into equation (1-4), Z_{11} is expanded using the continuous-fraction expansion. This expansion involves successive division and inversion of a ratio of two polynomials. The final form contains a sequence of terms, each alternately representing a capacitor and an inductor and finally the resistive termination. This procedure is demonstrated by the following example.

EXAMPLE 1-1

REQUIRED: Low-pass LC filter having a Butterworth $n = 3$ response.

RESULT:

(a) Use the Butterworth transfer function:

$$T(s) = \frac{1}{s^3 + 2s^2 + 2s + 1} \tag{1-2}$$

(b) Substitute $D(s) = s^3 + 2s^2 + 2s + 1$ and $s^n = s^3$ into equation (1-4), which results in

$$Z_{11} = \frac{2s^2 + 2s + 1}{2s^3 + 2s^2 + 2s + 1} \tag{1-4}$$

(c) Express Z_{11} so that the denominator is a ratio of the higher-order to the lower-order polynomial:

$$Z_{11} = \frac{1}{\dfrac{2s^3 + 2s^2 + 2s + 1}{2s^2 + 2s + 1}}$$

(d) Dividing the denominator and inverting the remainder results in

$$Z_{11} = \frac{1}{s + \dfrac{1}{\dfrac{2s^2 + 2s + 1}{s + 1}}}$$

(e) After further division and inversion, we get as our final expression

$$Z_{11} = \frac{1}{s + \dfrac{1}{2s + \dfrac{1}{s + 1}}} \tag{1-5}$$

The circuit configuration of figure 1-4 is called a ladder network, since it consists of alternating series and shunt branches. The input impedance can be expressed as the following continued fraction:

$$Z_{11} = \frac{1}{Y_1 + \dfrac{1}{Z_2 + \dfrac{1}{Y_3 + \ldots \dfrac{1}{Z_{n-1} + \dfrac{1}{Y_n}}}}} \tag{1-6}$$

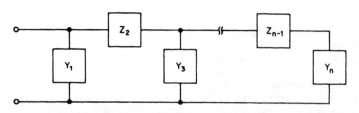

FIGURE 1-4 General ladder network.

where $Y = sC$ and $Z = sL$ for the low-pass all-pole ladder except for a resistive termination where $Y_n = sC + 1/R_L$.

Figure 1-5 can then be derived from equations (1-5) and (1-6) by inspection. This can be proved by reversing the process of expanding Z_{11}. By alternately adding admittances and impedances while working toward the input, Z_{11} is verified as being equal to equation (1-5).

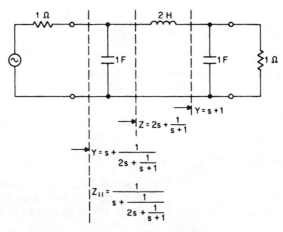

FIGURE 1-5   Low-pass filter for equation (1-5).

Synthesis for Unequal Terminations.   If the source resistor is set equal to 1 Ω and the load resistor is desired to be infinite (unterminated), the impedance looking into terminals 1 and 2 of the generalized filter of figure 1-1 can be expressed as

$$Z_{11} = \frac{D(s \text{ even})}{D(s \text{ odd})} \tag{1-7}$$

$D(s \text{ even})$ contains all the even-power s terms of the denominator polynomial and $D(s \text{ odd})$ consists of all the odd-power s terms of any realizable all-pole low-pass transfer function. Z_{11} is expanded into a continued fraction as in example 1-1 to define the circuit.

EXAMPLE 1-2

REQUIRED: Low-pass filter having a Butterworth $n = 3$ response with a source resistance of 1 Ω and an infinite termination.

RESULT:

(a) Use the Butterworth transfer function:

$$T(s) = \frac{1}{s^3 + 2s^2 + 2s + 1} \tag{1-2}$$

(b) Substitute $D(s \text{ even}) = 2s^2 + 1$ and $D(s \text{ odd}) = s^3 + 2s$ into equation (1-7):

$$Z_{11} = \frac{2s^2 + 1}{s^3 + 2s} \tag{1-7}$$

(c) Express Z_{11} so that the denominator is a ratio of the higher- to the lower-order polynomial:

$$Z_{11} = \cfrac{1}{\cfrac{s^3 + 2s}{2s^2 + 1}}$$

(d) Dividing the denominator and inverting the remainder results in

$$Z_{11} = \cfrac{1}{0.5s + \cfrac{1}{\cfrac{2s^2 + 1}{1.5s}}}$$

(e) Dividing and further inverting results in the final continued fraction

$$Z_{11} = \cfrac{1}{0.5s + \cfrac{1}{1.333s + \cfrac{1}{1.5s}}} \tag{1-8}$$

The circuit is shown in figure 1-6.

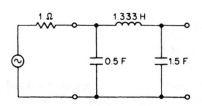

FIGURE 1-6   Low-pass filter of example 1-2.

Synthesis by Equating Coefficients. An active three-pole low-pass filter is shown in figure 1-7. Its transfer function is given by

$$T(s) = \frac{1}{s^3 A + s^2 B + sC + 1} \tag{1-9}$$

where $\quad A = C_1 C_2 C_3 \tag{1-10}$

$$B = 2C_3(C_1 + C_2) \tag{1-11}$$

and $\quad C = C_2 + 3C_3 \tag{1-12}$

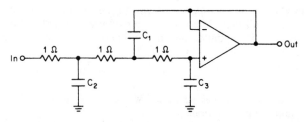

FIGURE 1-7   General $n = 3$ active low-pass filter.

If a Butterworth transfer function is desired, we can set equation (1-9) equal to equation (1-2).

$$T(s) = \frac{1}{s^3 A + s^2 B + sC + 1} = \frac{1}{s^3 + 2s^2 + 2s + 1} \tag{1-13}$$

By equating coefficients we obtain

$$A = 1$$
$$B = 2$$
$$C = 2$$

Substituting these coefficients in equations (1-10) through (1-12) and solving for C_1, C_2, and C_3 results in the circuit of figure 1-8.

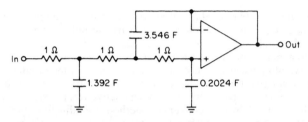

FIGURE 1-8 Butterworth $n = 3$ active low-pass filter.

Synthesis of filters directly from polynomials offers an elegant solution to filter design. However, it also may involve laborious computations to determine circuit element values. Design methods have been greatly simplified by the curves, tables, and step-by-step procedures provided in this handbook; so design by synthesis can be left to the advanced specialist.

Active Versus Passive Filters

The LC filters of figures 1-5 and 1-6 and the active filter of figure 1-8 all satisfy an $n = 3$ Butterworth low-pass transfer function. The filter designer is frequently faced with the sometimes difficult decision of choosing whether to use an active or LC design. A number of factors must be considered. Some of the limitations and considerations for each filter type will now be discussed.

Frequency Limitations. At subaudio frequencies, LC filter designs require high values of inductance and capacitance along with their associated bulk. Active filters are more practical because they can be designed at higher impedance levels so that capacitor magnitudes are reduced.

Above 50 kHz, most commercial-grade operational amplifiers have insufficient open-loop gain for the average active filter requirement. However, amplifiers are available with extended bandwidth at increased cost so that active filters at frequencies up to 500 kHz are possible. LC filters, on the other hand, are practical at frequencies up to a few hundred megahertz. Beyond this range, filters become impractical to build in lumped form, and so distributed parameter techniques are used.

Size Considerations. Active filters are generally smaller than their LC counterparts, since inductors are not required. Further reduction in size is possible with microelectronic technology. By using deposited RC networks and monolithic operational amplifier chips or with hybrid technology, active filters can be reduced to microscopic proportions.

Economics and Ease of Manufacture. *LC* filters generally cost more than active filters because they use inductors. High-quality coils require efficient magnetic cores. Sometimes, special coil-winding methods are needed. These factors lead to the increased cost of *LC* filters.

Active filters have the distinct advantage that they can be easily assembled using standard off-the-shelf components. *LC* filters require coil-winding and coil-assembly skills.

Ease of Adjustment. In critical *LC* filters, tuned circuits require adjustment to specific resonances. Capacitors cannot be made variable unless they are below a few hundred picofarads. Inductors, however, can easily be adjusted, since most coil structures provide a means for tuning, such as an adjustment slug.

Many active filter circuits are not easily adjustable. They may contain *RC* sections where two or more resistors in each section have to be varied in order to control resonances. These circuits have been avoided. The active filter design techniques presented in this handbook include convenient methods for adjusting resonances where required, such as for narrowband bandpass filters.

BIBLIOGRAPHY

Guillemin, E. A., *Introduction to Circuit Theory,* John Wiley and Sons, New York, 1957.

Stewart, J. L., *Circuit Theory and Design,* John Wiley and Sons, New York, 1956.

White Electromagnetics, *A Handbook on Electrical Filters,* White Electromagnetics, Inc., 1963.

CHAPTER 2
SELECTING THE RESPONSE CHARACTERISTIC

2.1 FREQUENCY-RESPONSE NORMALIZATION

Several parameters are used to characterize a filter's performance. The most commonly specified requirement is frequency response. When given a frequency-response specification, the engineer must select a filter design that meets these requirements. This is accomplished by transforming the required response to a normalized low-pass specification having a cutoff of 1 rad/s. This normalized response is compared with curves of normalized low-pass filters which also have a 1-rad/s cutoff. After a satisfactory low-pass filter is determined from the curves, the tabulated normalized element values of the chosen filter are transformed or denormalized to the final design.

Modern network theory has provided us with many different shapes of amplitude versus frequency which have been analytically derived by placing various restrictions on transfer functions. The major categories of these low-pass responses are:

Butterworth

Chebyshev

Linear phase

Transitional

Synchronously tuned

Elliptic-function

With the exception of the elliptic-function family, these responses are all normalized to a 3-dB cutoff of 1 rad/s.

Frequency and Impedance Scaling

The basis for normalization of filters is the fact that a given filter's response can be scaled (shifted) to a different frequency range by dividing the reactive elements by a frequency-scaling factor (FSF). The FSF is the ratio of a reference frequency of the desired response to the corresponding reference frequency of the given filter. Usually 3-dB points are selected as reference frequencies of low-pass and high-pass filters and the center frequency is chosen as the reference for bandpass filters. The FSF can be expressed as

$$FSF = \frac{\text{desired reference frequency}}{\text{existing reference frequency}} \tag{2-1}$$

The FSF must be a dimensionless number; so both the numerator and denominator of equation (2-1) must be expressed in the same units, usually radians per second. The following example demonstrates computation of the FSF and frequency scaling of filters.

EXAMPLE 2-1

REQUIRED: Low-pass filter either LC or active with $n = 3$ Butterworth transfer function having a 3-dB cutoff at 1000 Hz.

RESULT: Figure 2-1 illustrates the LC and active $n = 3$ Butterworth low-pass filters discussed in chapter 1 and their response.

(a) Compute FSF.

$$FSF = \frac{2\pi 1000 \text{ rad/s}}{1 \text{ rad/s}} = 6280 \tag{2-1}$$

(b) Dividing all the reactive elements by the FSF results in the filters of figure 2-2*a* and *b* and the response of figure 2-2*c*.

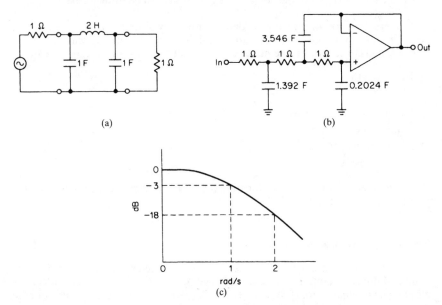

FIGURE 2-1 $n = 3$ Butterworth low-pass filter: *(a)* LC filter; *(b)* active filter; *(c)* frequency response.

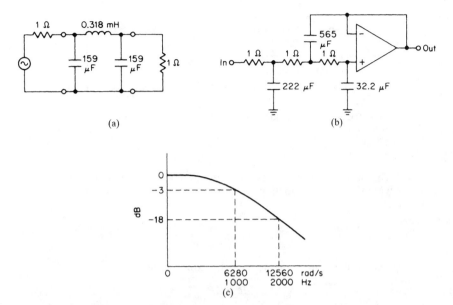

FIGURE 2-2   Denormalized low-pass filter of example 2-1: (*a*) *LC* filter; (*b*) active filter; (*c*) frequency response.

Note that all points on the frequency axis of the normalized response have been multiplied by the FSF. Also, since the normalized filter has its cutoff at 1 rad/s, the FSF can be directly expressed by $2\pi f_c$, where f_c is the desired low-pass cutoff frequency in hertz.

Frequency scaling a filter has the effect of multiplying all points on the frequency axis of the response curve by the FSF. Therefore, a normalized response curve can be directly used to predict the attenuation of the denormalized filter.

When the filters of figure 2-1 were denormalized to those of figure 2-2, the transfer function changed as well. The denormalized transfer function became

$$T(s) = \frac{1}{4.03 \times 10^{-12}s^3 + 5.08 \times 10^{-9}s^2 + 3.18 \times 10^{-4}s + 1} \tag{2-2}$$

The denominator has the roots: $s = -6280$, $s = -3140 + j5438$, and $s = -3140 - j5438$.

These roots can be obtained directly from the normalized roots by multiplying the normalized root coordinates by the FSF. Frequency scaling a filter also scales the poles and zeros (if any) by the same factor.

The component values of the filters in figure 2-2 are not very practical. The capacitor values are much too large and the $1 - \Omega$ resistor values are not very desirable. This situation can be resolved by impedance scaling. Any linear active or passive network maintains its transfer function if all resistor and inductor values are multiplied by an impedance-scaling factor Z and all capacitors are divided by the same

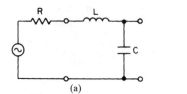 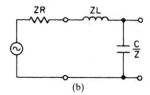

FIGURE 2-3 Two-pole low-pass *LC* filter: (*a*) basic filter; (*b*) impedance-scaled filter.

factor Z. This occurs because the Zs cancel in the transfer function. To prove this, let us investigate the transfer function of the simple two-pole low-pass filter of figure 2-3*a*, which is

$$T(s) = \frac{1}{s^2 LC + sCR + 1} \tag{2-3}$$

Impedance scaling can be mathematically expressed as

$$R' = ZR \tag{2-4}$$

$$L' = ZL \tag{2-5}$$

$$C' = \frac{C}{Z} \tag{2-6}$$

where the primes denote the values after impedance scaling.

If we impedance-scale the filter, we obtain the circuit of figure 2-3*b*. The new transfer function becomes

$$T(s) = \frac{1}{s^2 ZL\dfrac{C}{Z} + s\dfrac{C}{Z} ZR + 1} \tag{2-7}$$

Clearly, the Zs cancel; so both transfer functions are equivalent.

We can now use impedance scaling to make the values in the filters of figure 2-2 more practical. If we use impedance scaling with a Z of 1000, we obtain the filters of figure 2-4. The values are certainly more suitable.

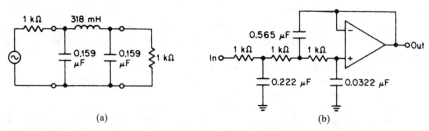

(a)   (b)

FIGURE 2-4 Impedance-scaled filters of example 2-1: (*a*) *LC* filter; (*b*) active filter.

Frequency and impedance scaling are normally combined into one step rather than performed sequentially. The denormalized values are then given by

$$R' = R \times Z \tag{2-8}$$

$$L' = \frac{L \times Z}{FSF} \tag{2-9}$$

$$C' = \frac{C}{FSF \times Z} \tag{2-10}$$

where the primed values are both frequency- and impedance-scaled.

Low-Pass Normalization

In order to use normalized low-pass filter curves and tables, a given low-pass filter requirement must first be converted into a normalized requirement. The curves can now be entered to find a satisfactory normalized filter which is then scaled to the desired cutoff.

The first step in selecting a normalized design is to convert the requirement into a steepness factor A_s, which can be defined as

$$A_s = \frac{f_s}{f_c} \qquad LPF \tag{2-11}$$

where f_s is the frequency having the minimum required stopband attenuation and f_c is the limiting frequency or cutoff of the passband, usually the 3-dB point. The normalized curves are compared with A_s, and a design is selected that meets or exceeds the requirement. The design is then frequency-scaled so that the selected passband limit of the normalized design occurs at f_c.

If the required passband limit f_c is defined as the 3-dB cutoff, the steepness factor A_s can be directly looked up in radians per second on the frequency axis of the normalized curves.

Suppose that we required a low-pass filter that has a 3-dB point at 100 Hz and more than 30 dB attenuation at 400 Hz. A normalized low-pass filter that has its 3-dB point at 1 rad/s and over 30 dB attenuation at 4 rad/s would meet the requirement if the filter were frequency-scaled so that the 3-dB point occurred at 100 Hz. Then there would be over 30 dB attenuation at 400 Hz, or 4 times the cutoff, because a response shape is retained when a filter is frequency-scaled.

The following example demonstrates normalizing a simple low-pass requirement.

EXAMPLE 2-2

REQUIRED: Normalize the following specification:

Low-pass filter
3 dB at 200 Hz
30 dB minimum at 800 Hz

RESULT:

(a) Compute A_s.

$$A_s = \frac{f_s}{f_c} = \frac{800 \text{ Hz}}{200 \text{ Hz}} = 4 \tag{2-11}$$

(b) Normalized requirement:
    3 dB at 1 rad/s
    30 dB minimum at 4 rad/s

In the event f_c does not correspond to the 3-dB cutoff, A_s can still be computed and a normalized design found that will meet the specifications. This is illustrated in the following example.

EXAMPLE 2-3

REQUIRED: Normalize the following specification:

Low-pass filter
1 dB at 200 Hz
30 dB minimum at 800 Hz

RESULT:

(a) Compute A_s.

$$A_s = \frac{f_s}{f_c} = \frac{800 \text{ Hz}}{200 \text{ Hz}} = 4 \qquad (2\text{-}11)$$

(b) Normalized requirement:
    1 dB at K rad/s
    30 dB minimum at $4\,K$ rad/s
    (where K is arbitrary)

A possible solution to example 2-3 would be a normalized filter which has a 1-dB point at 0.8 rad/s and over 30 dB attenuation at 3.2 rad/s. The fundamental requirement is that the normalized filter makes the transition between the passband and stopband limits within a frequency ratio A_s.

High-Pass Normalization

A normalized $n = 3$ low-pass Butterworth transfer function was given in section 1.1 as

$$T(s) = \frac{1}{s^3 + 2s^2 + 2s + 1} \qquad (1\text{-}2)$$

and the results of evaluating this transfer function at various frequencies were:

ω	$|T(j\omega)|$	$20 \log |T(j\omega)|$
0	1	0 dB
1	0.707	−3 dB
2	0.124	−18 dB
3	0.0370	−29 dB
4	0.0156	−36 dB

Let us now perform a high-pass transformation by substituting $1/s$ for s in equation (1-2). After some algebraic manipulations, the resulting transfer function becomes

$$T(s) = \frac{s^3}{s^3 + 2s^2 + 2s + 1} \qquad (2\text{-}12)$$

If we evaluate this expression at specific frequencies, we can generate the following table:

ω	$|T(j\omega)|$	$20 \log |T(j\omega)|$
0.25	0.0156	−36 dB
0.333	0.0370	−29 dB
0.500	0.124	−18 dB
1	0.707	−3 dB
∞	1	0 dB

The response is clearly that of a high-pass filter. It is also apparent that the low-pass attenuation values now occur at high-pass frequencies that are exactly the reciprocals of the corresponding low-pass frequencies. A high-pass transformation of a normalized low-pass filter transposes the low-pass attenuation values to reciprocal frequencies and retains the 3-dB cutoff at 1 rad/s. This relationship is evident in figure 2-5, where both filter responses are compared.

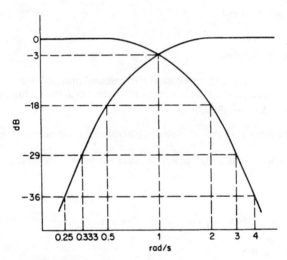

FIGURE 2-5   Normalized low-pass high-pass relationship.

The normalized low-pass curves could be interpreted as normalized high-pass curves by reading the attenuation as indicated and taking the reciprocals of the frequencies. However, it is much easier to convert a high-pass specification into a normalized low-pass requirement and use the curves directly.

To normalize a high-pass filter specification, calculate A_s, which in the case of high-pass filters is given by

$$A_s = \frac{f_c}{f_s} \qquad (2\text{-}13)$$

Since the A_s for high-pass filters is defined as the reciprocal of the A_s for low-pass filters, equation (2-13) can be directly interpreted as a low-pass requirement. A normalized low-pass filter can then be selected from the curves. A high-pass transformation is performed on the corresponding low-pass filter, and the resulting high-pass filter is scaled to the desired cutoff frequency.

The following example shows the normalization of a high-pass filter requirement.

EXAMPLE 2-4

REQUIRED: Normalize the following requirement:

High-pass filter
3 dB at 200 Hz
30 dB minimum at 50 Hz

RESULT:

(a) Compute A_s.

$$A_s = \frac{f_c}{f_s} = \frac{200 \text{ Hz}}{50 \text{ Hz}} = 4 \qquad \text{HPF} \qquad (2\text{-}13)$$

(b) Normalized equivalent low-pass requirement:
3 dB at 1 rad/s
30 dB minimum at 4 rad/s

Bandpass Normalization

Bandpass filters fall into two categories: narrowband and wideband. If the ratio of the upper cutoff frequency to the lower cutoff frequency is over 2 (an octave), the filter is considered a wideband type.

Wideband Bandpass Filters. Wideband filter specifications can be separated into individual low-pass and high-pass requirements which are treated independently. The resulting low-pass and high-pass filters are then cascaded to meet the composite response.

EXAMPLE 2-5

REQUIRED: Normalize the following specification:

Bandpass filter
3 dB at 500 and 1000 Hz
40 dB minimum at 200 and 2000 Hz

RESULT:

(a) Determine the ratio of upper cutoff to lower cutoff.

$$\frac{1000 \text{ Hz}}{500 \text{ Hz}} = 2$$

wideband type

(b) Separate requirement into individual specifications.

High-pass filter:	Low-pass filter:
3 dB at 500 Hz	3 dB at 1000 Hz
40 dB minimum at 200 Hz	40 dB minimum at 2000 Hz
$A_s = 2.5$ (2-13)	$A_s = 2.0$ (2-11)

(c) Normalized high-pass and low-pass filters are now selected, scaled to the required cutoff frequencies, and cascaded to meet the composite requirements. Figure 2-6 shows the resulting circuit and response.

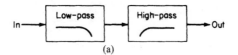

(a)

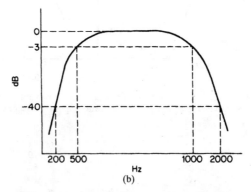

(b)

FIGURE 2-6 Results of example 2-5: (a) cascade of low-pass and high-pass filters; (b) frequency response.

Narrowband Bandpass Filters. Narrowband bandpass filters have a ratio of upper cutoff frequency to lower cutoff frequency of approximately 2 or less and cannot be designed as separate low-pass and high-pass filters. The major reason for this is evident from figure 2-7. As the ratio of upper cutoff to lower cutoff decreases, the loss at center frequency will increase, and it may become prohibitive for ratios near unity.

If we substitute $s + 1/s$ for s in a low-pass transfer function, a bandpass filter results. The center frequency occurs at 1 rad/s, and the frequency response of the low-pass filter is directly transformed into the bandwidth of the bandpass filter at points of equivalent attenuation. In other words, the attenuation bandwidth ratios remain unchanged. This is shown in figure 2-8, which shows the relationship between a low-pass filter and its transformed bandpass equivalent. Each pole and zero of the low-pass filter is transformed into a *pair* of poles and zeros in the bandpass filter.

In order to design a bandpass filter, the following sequence of steps is involved.

1. Convert the given bandpass filter requirement into a normalized low-pass specification.

2. Select a satisfactory low-pass filter from the normalized frequency-response curves.

3. Transform the normalized low-pass parameters into the required bandpass filter.

The response shape of a bandpass filter is shown in figure 2-9 along with some basic terminology. The center frequency is defined as

$$f_0 = \sqrt{f_L f_u} \qquad (2\text{-}14)$$

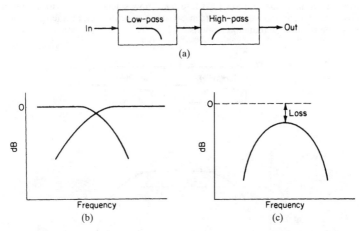

FIGURE 2-7 Limitation of wideband approach for narrowband filters: (*a*) cascade of low-pass and high-pass filters; (*b*) composite response; (*c*) algebraic sum of attenuation.

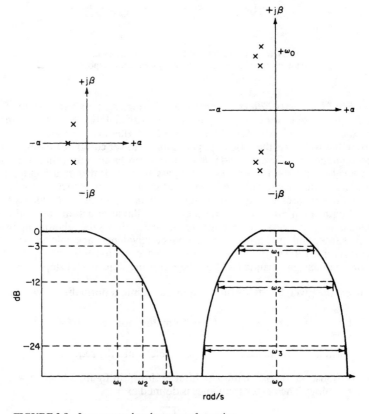

FIGURE 2-8 Low-pass to bandpass transformation.

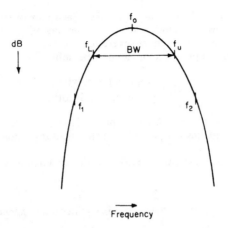

FIGURE 2-9 General bandpass filter response shape.

where f_L is the lower passband limit and f_u is the upper passband limit, usually the 3-dB attenuation frequencies. For the more general case

$$f_0 = \sqrt{f_1 f_2} \qquad (2\text{-}15)$$

where f_1 and f_2 are any two frequencies having equal attenuation. These relationships imply geometric symmetry; that is, the entire curve below f_0 is the mirror image of the curve above f_0 when plotted on a *logarithmic* frequency axis.

An important parameter of bandpass filters is the filter selectivity factor or Q, which is defined as

$$Q = \frac{f_0}{\text{BW}} \qquad (2\text{-}16)$$

where BW is the passband bandwidth or $f_u - f_L$.

As the filter Q increases, the response shape near the passband approaches the arithmetically symmetrical condition, i.e., mirror-image symmetry near the center frequency, when plotted using a *linear* frequency axis. For Qs of 10 or more, the center frequency can be redefined as the arithmetic mean of the passband limits; so we can replace equation (2-14) with

$$f_0 = \frac{f_L + f_u}{2} \qquad (2\text{-}17)$$

In order to utilize the normalized low-pass filter frequency-response curves, a given narrowband bandpass filter specification must be transformed into a normalized low-pass requirement. This is accomplished by first manipulating the specification to make it geometrically symmetrical. At equivalent attenuation points, corresponding frequencies above and below f_0 must satisfy

$$f_1 f_2 = f_0^2 \qquad (2\text{-}18)$$

which is an alternate form of equation (2-15) for geometric symmetry. The given specification is modified by calculating the corresponding opposite geometric frequency for each stopband frequency specified. Each pair of stopband frequencies will result in two new frequency pairs. The pair having the lesser separation is retained, since it represents the more severe requirement.

A bandpass filter steepness factor can now be defined as

$$A_s = \frac{\text{stopband bandwidth}}{\text{passband bandwidth}} \quad (2\text{-}19)$$

This steepness factor is used to select a normalized low-pass filter from the frequency-response curves that makes the passband to stopband transition within a frequency ratio of A_s.

The following example shows the normalization of a bandpass filter requirement.

EXAMPLE 2-6

REQUIRED: Normalize the following bandpass filter requirement:

Bandpass filter
Center frequency of 100 Hz
3 dB at ±15 Hz (85 Hz, 115 Hz)
40 dB at ±30 Hz (70 Hz, 130 Hz)

RESULT:

(a) First compute center frequency f_0.

$$f_0 = \sqrt{f_l f_u} = \sqrt{85 \times 115} = 98.9 \text{ Hz} \quad (2\text{-}14)$$

(b) Compute two geometrically related stopband frequency pairs for each pair of stopband frequencies given.

Let $f_1 = 70$ Hz.

$$f_2 = \frac{f_0^2}{f_1} = \frac{(98.9)^2}{70} = 139.7 \text{ Hz} \quad (2\text{-}18)$$

Let $f_2 = 130$ Hz.

$$f_1 = \frac{f_0^2}{f_2} = \frac{(98.9)^2}{130} = 75.2 \text{ Hz} \quad (2\text{-}18)$$

The two pairs are

$$f_1 = 70 \text{ Hz}, f_2 = 139.7 \text{ Hz } (f_2 - f_1 = 69.7 \text{ Hz})$$

and $$f_1 = 75.2 \text{ Hz}, f_2 = 130 \text{ Hz } (f_2 - f_1 = 54.8 \text{ Hz})$$

Retain the second frequency pair, since it has the lesser separation. Figure 2-10 compares the specified filter requirement and the geometrically symmetrical equivalent.

(c) Calculate A_s.

$$A_s = \frac{\text{stopband bandwidth}}{\text{passband bandwidth}} = \frac{54.8 \text{ Hz}}{30 \text{ Hz}} = 1.83 \quad (2\text{-}19)$$

(d) A normalized low-pass filter can now be selected from the normalized curves. Since the passband limit is the 3-dB point, the normalized filter is required to have over 40 dB of rejection at 1.83 rad/s or 1.83 times the 1-rad/s cutoff.

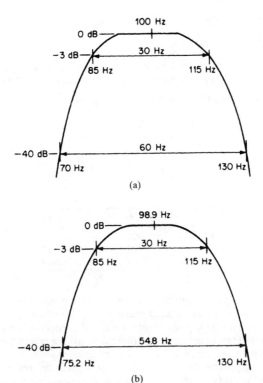

FIGURE 2-10 Frequency-response requirements of example 2-6: (a) given filter requirement; (b) geometrically symmetrical requirement.

The results of example 2-6 indicate that when frequencies are specified in an arithmetically symmetrical manner, the narrower stopband bandwidth can be directly computed by

$$BW_{\text{stopband}} = f_2 - \frac{f_0^2}{f_2} \tag{2-20}$$

The narrower stopband bandwidth corresponds to the more stringent value of A_s, the steepness factor.

It is sometimes desirable to compute two geometrically related frequencies that correspond to a given bandwidth. Upon being given the center frequency f_0 and the bandwidth BW, the lower and upper frequencies are respectively computed by

$$f_1 = \sqrt{\left(\frac{BW}{2}\right)^2 + f_0^2} - \frac{BW}{2} \tag{2-21}$$

$$f_2 = \sqrt{\left(\frac{BW}{2}\right)^2 + f_0^2} + \frac{BW}{2} \tag{2-22}$$

Use of these formulas is illustrated in the following example.

EXAMPLE 2-7

REQUIRED: For a bandpass filter having a center frequency of 10 kHz, determine the frequencies corresponding to bandwidths of 100 Hz, 500 Hz, and 2000 Hz.

RESULT: Compute f_1 and f_2 for each bandwidth using

$$f_1 = \sqrt{\left(\frac{BW}{2}\right)^2 + f_0^2} - \frac{BW}{2} \tag{2-21}$$

$$f_2 = \sqrt{\left(\frac{BW}{2}\right)^2 + f_0^2} + \frac{BW}{2} \tag{2-22}$$

BW, Hz	f_1, Hz	f_2, Hz
100	9950	10,050
500	9753	10,253
2000	9050	11,050

The results of example 2-7 indicate that for narrow percentage bandwidths (100 Hz) f_1 and f_2 are arithmetically spaced about f_0. For the wider cases the arithmetic center of f_1 and f_2 would be slightly above the actual geometric center frequency f_0. Another and more meaningful way of stating the converse is that for a given pair of frequencies, the geometric mean is below the arithmetic mean.

Bandpass filter requirements are not always specified in an arithmetically symmetrical manner as in the previous examples. Multiple stopband attenuation requirements may also exist. The design engineer is still faced with the basic problem of converting the given parameters into geometrically symmetrical characteristics so that a steepness factor or factors can be determined. The following example demonstrates conversion of a specification somewhat more complicated than the previous example.

EXAMPLE 2-8

REQUIRED: Normalize the following bandpass filter specification:

Bandpass filter
1 dB passband limits of 12 and 14 kHz
20 dB minimum at 6 kHz
30 dB minimum at 4 kHz
40 dB minimum at 56 kHz

RESULT:

(a) First compute the center frequency.

$$f_L = 12 \text{ kHz} \qquad f_u = 14 \text{ kHz}$$

$$f_0 = 12.96 \text{ kHz} \tag{2-14}$$

(b) Compute the corresponding geometric frequency for each stopband frequency given, using equation (2-18).

$$f_1 f_2 = f_0^2 \tag{2-18}$$

Figure 2-11 illustrates the comparison between the given requirement and the corresponding geometrically symmetrical equivalent response.

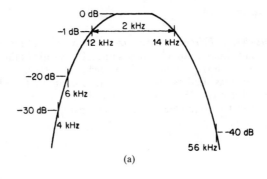

(a)

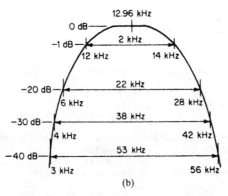

(b)

FIGURE 2-11 Given and transformed response of example 2-7: (*a*) given requirement; (*b*) geometrically symmetrical response.

f_1	f_2
6 kHz	28 kHz
4 kHz	42 kHz
3 kHz	56 kHz

(*c*) Calculate the steepness factor for each stopband bandwidth in figure 2-11*b*.

20 dB:
$$A_s = \frac{22\ \text{kHz}}{2\ \text{kHz}} = 11 \qquad (2\text{-}19)$$

30 dB:
$$A_s = \frac{38\ \text{kHz}}{2\ \text{kHz}} = 19$$

40 dB:
$$A_s = \frac{53\ \text{kHz}}{2\ \text{kHz}} = 26.5$$

(*d*) Select a low-pass filter from the normalized tables. A filter is required that has over 20, 30, and 40 dB of rejection at, respectively, 11, 19, and 26.5 times its 1-dB cutoff.

Band-Reject Normalization

Wideband Band-Reject Filters.　　Normalizing a band-reject filter requirement proceeds along the same lines as for a bandpass filter. If the ratio of the upper cutoff frequency to the lower cutoff frequency is an octave or more, a band-reject filter requirement can be classified as wideband and separated into individual low-pass and high-pass specifications. The resulting filters are paralleled at the input and combined at the output. The following example demonstrates normalization of a wideband band-reject filter requirement.

EXAMPLE 2-9

REQUIRED:

Band-reject filter
3 dB at 200 and 800 Hz
40 dB minimum at 300 and 500 Hz

RESULT:

(a) Determine ratio of upper cutoff to lower cutoff.

$$\frac{800 \text{ Hz}}{200 \text{ Hz}} = 4$$

wideband type

(b) Separate requirements into individual low-pass and high-pass specifications.

Low-pass filter:	High-pass filter:
3 dB at 200 Hz	3 dB at 800 Hz
40 dB minimum at 300 Hz	40 dB minimum at 500 Hz
$A_s = 1.5$　(2-11)	$A_s = 1.6$　(2-13)

(c) Select appropriate filters from the normalized curves and scale the normalized low-pass and high-pass filters to cutoffs of 200 and 800 Hz, respectively. Figure 2-12 shows the resulting circuit and response.

The basic assumption of the previous example is that when the filter outputs are combined, the resulting response is the superimposed individual response of both filters. This is a valid assumption if each filter has sufficient rejection in the band of the other filter so that there is no interaction when the outputs are combined. Figure 2-13 shows the case where inadequate separation exists.

The requirement for a minimum separation between cutoffs of an octave or more is by no means rigid. Sharper filters can have their cutoffs placed closer together with minimal interaction.

Narrowband Band-Reject Filters.　　The normalized transformation described for bandpass filters where $s + 1/s$ is substituted into a low-pass transfer function can instead be applied to a high-pass transfer function to obtain a band-reject filter. Figure 2-14 shows the direct equivalence between a high-pass filter's frequency response and the transformed band-reject filter's bandwidth.

The design method for narrowband band-reject filters can be defined as follows:

1. Convert the band-reject requirement directly into a normalized low-pass specification.

2. Select a low-pass filter from the normalized curves that meets the normalized requirements.

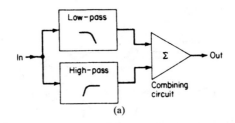

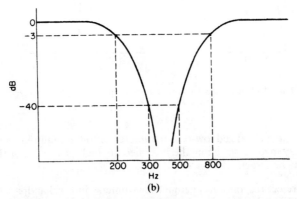

FIGURE 2-12   Results of example 2-9: (*a*) combined low-pass and high-pass filters; (*b*) frequency response.

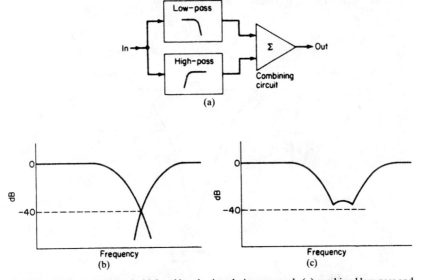

FIGURE 2-13   Limitation of wideband band-reject design approach: (*a*) combined low-pass and high-pass filters; (*b*) composite response; (*c*) combined response by summation of outputs.

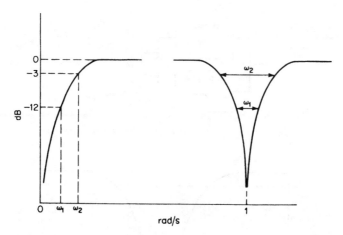

FIGURE 2-14 Relationship between band-reject and high-pass filters.

3. Transform the normalized low-pass parameters into the required band-reject filter. This may involve designing the intermediate high-pass filter, or the transformation may be direct.

The band-reject response has geometric symmetry just as bandpass filters have. Figure 2-15 defines this response shape. The parameters shown have the same relationship to each other as they do for bandpass filters. The attenuation at center frequency is theoretically infinite, since the response of a high-pass filter at DC has been transformed to the center frequency.

The geometric center frequency can be defined as

$$f_0 = \sqrt{f_L f_u} \tag{2-14}$$

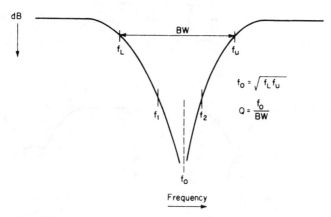

FIGURE 2-15 Band-reject response.

where f_L and f_u are usually the 3-dB frequencies, or for the more general case:

$$f_0 = \sqrt{f_1 f_2} \tag{2-15}$$

The selectivity factor Q is defined as

$$Q = \frac{f_0}{\text{BW}} \tag{2-16}$$

where BW is $f_u - f_L$. For Qs of 10 or more, the response near center frequency approaches the arithmetically symmetrical condition; so we can then state

$$f_0 = \frac{f_L + f_u}{2} \tag{2-17}$$

To use the normalized curves for the design of a band-reject filter, the response requirement must be converted to a normalized low-pass filter specification. In order to accomplish this, the band-reject specification should first be made geometrically symmetrical; that is, each pair of frequencies having equal attenuation should satisfy

$$f_1 f_2 = f_0^2 \tag{2-18}$$

which is an alternate form of equation (2-15). When two frequencies are specified at a particular attenuation level, two frequency pairs will result from calculating the corresponding opposite geometric frequency for each frequency specified. Retain the pair having the wider separation, since it represents the more severe requirement. In the bandpass case the pair having the lesser separation represented the more difficult requirement.

The band-reject filter steepness factor is defined by

$$A_s = \frac{\text{passband bandwidth}}{\text{stopband bandwidth}} \tag{2-23}$$

A normalized low-pass filter can now be selected that makes the transition from the passband attenuation limit to the minimum required stopband attenuation within a frequency ratio A_s.

The following example demonstrates the normalization procedure for a band-reject filter.

EXAMPLE 2-10

REQUIRED: Band-reject filter

> Center frequency of 1000 Hz
> 3 dB at ±300 Hz (700 Hz, 1300 Hz)
> 40 dB at ±200 Hz (800 Hz, 1200 Hz)

RESULT:

(a) First compute center frequency f_0.

$$f_0 = \sqrt{f_L f_u} = \sqrt{700 \times 1300} = 954 \text{ Hz} \tag{2-14}$$

(b) Compute two geometrically related stopband frequency pairs for each pair of stopband frequencies given:
Let $f_1 = 800$ Hz

$$f_2 = \frac{f_0^2}{f_1} = \frac{(954)^2}{800} = 1138 \text{ Hz} \tag{2-18}$$

Let $f_2 = 1200$ Hz

$$f_1 = \frac{f_0^2}{f_2} = \frac{(954)^2}{1200} = 758 \text{ Hz} \tag{2-18}$$

the two pairs are

$$f_1 = 800 \text{ Hz}, f_2 = 1138 \text{ Hz} \ (f_2 - f_1 = 338 \text{ Hz})$$

and

$$f_1 = 758 \text{ Hz}, f_2 = 1200 \text{ Hz} \ (f_2 - f_1 = 442 \text{ Hz})$$

Retain the second pair, since it has the *wider* separation and represents the more severe requirement. The given response requirement and the geometrically symmetrical equivalent are compared in figure 2-16.

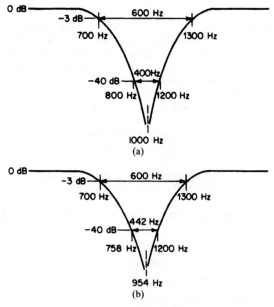

FIGURE 2-16 Response of example 2-10: (*a*) given requirement; (*b*) geometrically symmetrical response.

(c) Calculate A_s.

$$A_s = \frac{\text{passband bandwidth}}{\text{stopband bandwidth}} = \frac{600 \text{ Hz}}{442 \text{ Hz}} = 1.36 \tag{2-23}$$

(*d*) Select a normalized low-pass filter from the normalized curves that makes the transition from the 3-dB point to the 40-dB point within a frequency ratio of 1.36. Since these curves are all normalized to 3 dB, a filter is required with over 40 dB of rejection at 1.36 rad/s.

2.2 TRANSIENT RESPONSE

In our previous discussions of filters we have restricted our interest to frequency-domain parameters such as frequency response. The input forcing function was a sine wave. In real-world applications of filters, input signals consist of a variety of complex waveforms. The response of filters to these nonsinusoidal inputs is called *transient response.*

A filter's transient response is best evaluated in the time domain, since we are usually dealing with input signals which are functions of time, such as pulses or amplitude steps. The frequency- and time-domain parameters of a filter are directly related through the Fourier or Laplace transforms.

Effect of Nonuniform Time Delay

Evaluating a transfer function as a function of frequency results in both a magnitude and phase characteristic. Figure 2-17 shows the amplitude and phase response of a normalized $n = 3$ Butterworth low-pass filter. Butterworth low-pass filters have a phase shift of exactly n times $-45°$ at the 3-dB frequency. The phase shift continuously increases as the transition is made into the stopband and eventually approaches n times $-90°$ at frequencies far removed from the passband. Since the filter described by figure 2-17 has a complexity of $n = 3$, the phase shift is $-135°$ at the 3-dB cutoff and approaches $-270°$ in the stopband. Frequency scaling will transpose the phase characteristics to a new frequency range as determined by the FSF.

It is well known that a square wave can be represented by a Fourier series of odd harmonic components as indicated in figure 2-18. Since the amplitude of each harmonic is reduced as the harmonic order increases, only the first few harmonics are of significance. If a square wave is applied to a filter, the fundamental and its significant harmonics must have the proper relative amplitude relationship at the filter's output

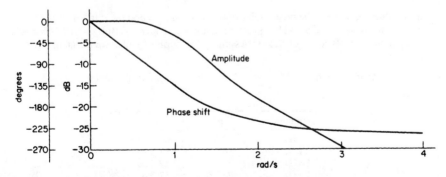

FIGURE 2-17   Amplitude and phase response of $n = 3$ Butterworth low-pass filter.

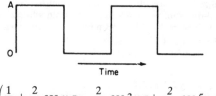

$$A(t) = A\left(\frac{1}{2} + \frac{2}{\pi}\cos\omega_1\tau - \frac{2}{3\pi}\cos 3\omega_1\tau + \frac{2}{5\pi}\cos 5\omega_1\tau + \ldots\right)$$

FIGURE 2-18   Frequency analysis of a square wave.

in order to retain the square waveshape. In addition, these components must not be displaced in time with respect to each other. Let us now consider the effect of a low-pass filter's phase shift on a square wave.

If we assume that a low-pass filter has a linear phase shift between 0° at DC and n times −45° at the cutoff, we can express the phase shift in the passband as

$$\phi = -\frac{45nf_x}{f_c} \tag{2-24}$$

where f_x is any frequency in the passband and f_c is the 3-dB cutoff frequency.

A phase-shifted sine wave appears displaced in time from the input waveform. This displacement is called *phase delay* and can be computed by determining the time interval represented by the phase shift, using the fact that a full period contains 360°. Phase delay can then be computed by

$$T_{pd} = \frac{\phi}{360}\frac{1}{f_x} \tag{2-25}$$

or, as an alternate form,

$$T_{pd} = -\frac{\beta}{\omega} \tag{2-26}$$

where β is the phase shift in radians (1 rad = 360/2π or 57.3°) and ω is the input frequency expressed in radians per second ($\omega = 2\pi f_x$).

EXAMPLE 2-11

REQUIRED: Compute the phase delay of the fundamental and the third, fifth, seventh, and ninth harmonics of a 1-kHz square wave applied to an $n = 3$ Butterworth low-pass filter having a 3-dB cutoff of 10 kHz. Assume a linear phase shift with frequency in the passband.

RESULT: Using equations (2-24) and (2-25), the following table can be computed:

Frequency	ϕ	T_{pd}
1 kHz	−13.5°	37.5 μs
3 kHz	−40.5°	37.5 μs
5 kHz	−67.5°	37.5 μs
7 kHz	−94.5°	37.5 μs
9 kHz	−121.5°	37.5 μs

The phase delays of the fundamental and each of the significant harmonics in example 2-11 are identical. The output waveform would then appear nearly equivalent to the input except for a delay of 37.5 μs. If the phase shift is not linear with frequency, the ratio ϕ/f_x in equation (2-25) is not constant; so each significant component of the input square wave would undergo a different delay. This displacement in time of the spectral components, with respect to each other, introduces a distortion of the output waveform. Figure 2-19 shows some typical effects of nonlinear phase shift upon a square wave. Most filters have nonlinear phase versus frequency characteristics; so some waveform distortion will usually occur for complex input signals.

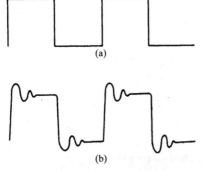

FIGURE 2-19 Effect of nonlinear phase: (a) ideal square wave; (b) distorted square wave.

Not all complex waveforms have harmonically related spectral components. An amplitude-modulated signal, for example, consists of a carrier and two sidebands, each sideband separated from the carrier by the modulating frequency. If a filter's phase characteristic is linear with frequency and intersects zero phase shift at zero frequency (DC), both the carrier and the two sidebands will have the same delay in passing through the filter; so the output will be a delayed replica of the input. If these conditions are not satisfied, the carrier and both sidebands will be delayed by different amounts. The carrier delay will be in accordance with the equation for phase delay

$$T_{pd} = -\frac{\beta}{\omega} \tag{2-26}$$

(The terms *carrier delay* and *phase delay* are used interchangeably.)

A new definition is required for the delay of the sidebands. This delay is commonly called *group delay* and is defined as the derivative of phase versus frequency, which can be expressed as

$$T_{gd} = -\frac{d\beta}{d\omega} \tag{2-27}$$

Linear phase shift results in constant group delay, since the derivative of a linear function is a constant. Figure 2-20 illustrates a low-pass filter phase shift which is nonlinear in the vicinity of a carrier ω_c and the two sidebands $\omega_c - \omega_m$ and $\omega_c + \omega_m$. The phase delay at ω_c is the negative slope of a line drawn from the origin to the phase shift corresponding to ω_c which is in agreement with equation (2-26). The group delay at ω_c is shown as the negative slope of a line which is tangent to the phase response at ω_c. This can be mathematically expressed as

$$T_{gd} = -\frac{d\beta}{d\omega}\bigg|_{\omega=\omega_c}$$

If the two sidebands are restricted to a region surrounding ω_c having a constant group delay, the envelope of the modulated signal will be delayed by T_{gd}. Figure 2-21 compares the input and output waveforms of an amplitude-modulated signal applied to the filter depicted by figure 2-20. Note that the carrier is delayed by the

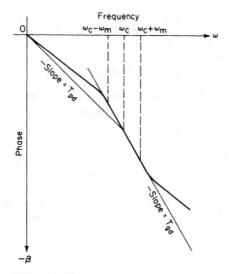

FIGURE 2-20 Nonlinear phase shift of a low-pass filter.

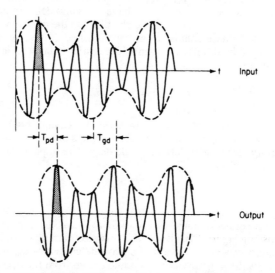

FIGURE 2-21 Effect of nonlinear phase on AM signal.

phase delay while the envelope is delayed by the group delay. For this reason group delay is sometimes called *envelope delay.*

If the group delay is not constant over the bandwidth of the modulated signal, waveform distortion will occur. Narrow-bandwidth signals are more likely to encounter constant group delay than signals having a wider spectrum. It is common practice to use group-delay variation as a criterion to evaluate phase nonlinearity and subsequent waveform distortion. The absolute magnitude of the nominal delay is usually of little consequence.

Step Response of Networks

If we were to define a hypothetical ideal low-pass filter, it would have the response shown in figure 2-22. The amplitude response is unity from DC to the cutoff frequency ω_c and zero beyond the cutoff. The phase shift is a linearly increasing function in the passband, where n is the order of the ideal filter. The group delay is constant in the passband and zero in the stopband. If a unity amplitude step were applied to this ideal filter at $t = 0$, the output would be in accordance with figure 2-23. The delay of the half-amplitude point would be $n\pi/2\omega_c$ and the rise time, which is defined as the interval required to go from zero amplitude to unity amplitude with a slope equal to that at the half-amplitude point, would be equal to π/ω_c. Since rise time is inversely proportional to ω_c, a wider filter results in reduced rise time. This proportionality is in agreement with a fundamental rule of thumb relating rise time to bandwidth, which is

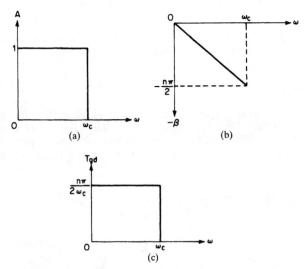

FIGURE 2-22 Ideal low-pass filter: (*a*) frequency response; (*b*) phase shift; (*c*) group delay.

$$T_r \approx \frac{0.35}{f_c} \qquad (2\text{-}28)$$

where T_r is the rise time in seconds and f_c is the 3-dB cutoff in hertz.

A 9% overshoot exists on the leading edge. Also, a sustained oscillation occurs having a period of $2\pi/\omega_c$, which eventually decays and unity amplitude is established. This oscillation is called *ringing*. Overshoot and ringing occur in an ideal low-pass filter even though we have linear phase. This is because of the abrupt amplitude roll-off at cutoff. Therefore, both linear phase and a prescribed roll-off are required for minimum transient distortion.

Overshoot and prolonged ringing are both very undesirable if the filter is required to pass pulses with minimum waveform distortion. The step-response

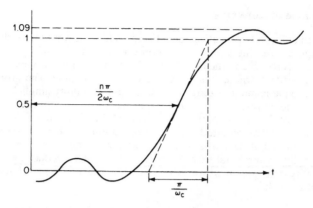

FIGURE 2-23   Step response of ideal low-pass filter.

curves provided for the different families of normalized low-pass filters can be very useful for evaluating the transient properties of these filters.

Impulse Response

A unit impulse is defined as a pulse which is infinitely high and infinitesimally narrow, and has an area of unity. The response of the ideal filter of figure 2-22 to a unit impulse is shown in figure 2-24. The peak output amplitude is ω_c/π, which is proportional to the filter's bandwidth. The pulse width, $2\pi/\omega_c$, is inversely proportional to bandwidth.

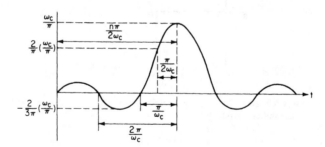

FIGURE 2-24   Impulse response of ideal low-pass filter.

An input signal having the form of a unit impulse is physically impossible. However, a narrow pulse of finite amplitude will represent a reasonable approximation; so the impulse response of normalized low-pass filters can be useful in estimating the filter's response to a relatively narrow pulse.

Estimating Transient Characteristics

Group-delay, step-response, and impulse-response curves are given for the normalized low-pass filters discussed in the latter section of this chapter. These curves are useful for estimating filter responses to nonsinusoidal signals. If the input waveforms are steps or pulses, the curves may be used directly. For more complex inputs we can use the method of superposition, which permits the representation of a complex signal as the sum of individual components. If we find the filter's output for each individual input signal, we can combine these responses to obtain the composite output.

Group Delay of Low-Pass Filters. When a normalized low-pass filter is frequency-scaled, the delay characteristics are frequency-scaled as well. The following rules can be applied to derive the resulting delay curve from the normalized response:

1. Divide the delay axis by $2\pi f_c$, where f_c is the filter's 3-dB cutoff.
2. Multiply all points on the frequency axis by f_c.

The following example demonstrates the denormalization of a low-pass curve.

EXAMPLE 2-12

REQUIRED: Using the normalized delay curve of an $n = 3$ Butterworth low-pass filter given in figure 2-25a, compute the delay at DC and the delay variation in the passband if the filter is frequency-scaled to a 3-dB cutoff of 100 Hz.

RESULT: To denormalize the curve, divide the delay axis by $2\pi f_c$ and multiply the frequency axis by f_c where f_c is 100 Hz. The resulting curve is shown in figure 2-25b. The delay at DC is 3.2 ms, and the delay variation in the passband is 1.3 ms.

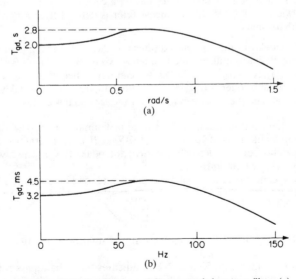

FIGURE 2-25 Delay of $n = 3$ Butterworth low-pass filter: (*a*) normalized delay; (*b*) delay with $f_c = 100$ Hz.

The nominal delay of a low-pass filter at frequencies well below the cutoff can be estimated by the following formula:

$$T \approx \frac{125n}{f_c} \qquad (2\text{-}29)$$

where T is the delay in milliseconds, n is the order of the filter, and f_c is the 3-dB cutoff in hertz. Equation (2-29) is an approximation which usually is accurate to within 25%.

Group Delay of Bandpass Filters. When a low-pass filter is transformed to a narrowband bandpass filter, the delay is transformed to a nearly symmetrical curve mirrored about the center frequency. As the bandwidth increases from the narrowbandwidth case, the symmetry of the delay curve is distorted approximately in proportion to the filter's bandwidth.

For the narrowband condition, the bandpass delay curve can be approximated by implementing the following rules:

1. Divide the delay axis of the normalized delay curve by πBW, where BW is the 3-dB bandwidth in hertz.
2. Multiply the frequency axis by $BW/2$.
3. A delay characteristic symmetrical around the center frequency can now be formed by generating the mirror image of the curve obtained by implementing steps 1 and 2. The total 3-dB bandwidth becomes BW.

The following example demonstrates the approximation of a narrowband bandpass filter's delay curve.

EXAMPLE 2-13

REQUIRED: Estimate the group delay at the center frequency and the delay variation over the passband of a bandpass filter having a center frequency of 1000 Hz and a 3-dB bandwidth of 100 Hz. The bandpass filter is derived from a normalized $n = 3$ Butterworth low-pass filter.

RESULT: The delay of the normalized filter is shown in figure 2-25a. If we divide the delay axis by πBW and multiply the frequency axis by $BW/2$, where BW = 100 Hz, we obtain the delay curve of figure 2-26a. We can now reflect this delay curve on both sides of the center frequency of 1000 Hz to obtain figure 2-26b. The delay at center frequency is 6.4 ms and the delay variation over the passband is 2.6 ms.

The technique used in example 2-13 to approximate a bandpass delay curve is valid for bandpass filter Qs of 10 or more ($f_0/BW \geq 10$). As the fractional bandwidth increases, the delay becomes less symmetrical and peaks toward the low side of center frequency as shown in figure 2-27.

The delay at center frequency of a bandpass filter can be estimated by

$$T \approx \frac{250n}{BW} \qquad (2\text{-}30)$$

where T is the delay in milliseconds. This approximation is usually accurate within 25%.

Comparison of figures 2-25b and 2-26b indicates that a bandpass filter has twice the delay of the equivalent low-pass filter of the same bandwidth. This results from

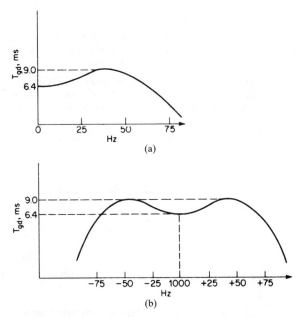

FIGURE 2-26   Delay of narrowband bandpass filter: (*a*) low-pass delay; (*b*) bandpass delay.

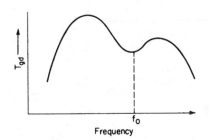

FIGURE 2-27   Delay of wideband bandpass filter.

the low-pass to bandpass transformation where a low-pass filter transfer function of order n always results in a bandpass filter transfer function having an order $2n$. However, a bandpass filter is conventionally referred to as having the same order n as the low-pass filter it was derived from.

Step Response of Low-Pass Filters.

Delay distortion usually cannot be directly used to determine the extent of the distortion of a modulated signal. A more direct parameter would be the step response, especially where the modulation consists of an amplitude step or pulse.

The two essential parameters of a filter's step response are overshoot and ringing. Overshoot should be minimized for accurate pulse reproduction. Ringing should decay as rapidly as possible to prevent interference with subsequent pulses. Rise time and delay are usually less important considerations.

Step-response curves for standard normalized low-pass filters are provided in the latter part of this chapter. These responses can be denormalized by dividing the time axis by $2\pi f_c$ where f_c is the 3-dB cutoff of the filter. Denormalization of the step response is shown in the following example.

EXAMPLE 2-14

REQUIRED: Determine the amount of overshoot of an $n = 3$ Butterworth low-pass filter having a 3-dB cutoff of 100 Hz. Also, determine the approximate time required for the ringing to decay substantially, i.e., the settling time.

RESULT: The step response of the normalized low-pass filter is shown in figure 2-28a. If the time axis is divided by $2\pi f_c$, where $f_c = 100$ Hz, the step response of figure 2-28b is obtained. The overshoot is slightly under 10%. After 25 ms the amplitude has almost completely settled.

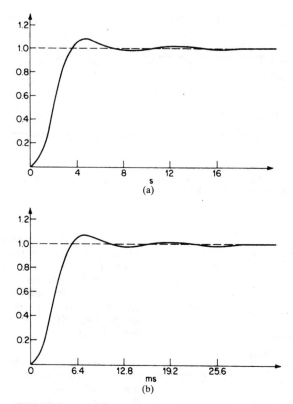

FIGURE 2-28   Step response of example 2-14: (a) normalized step response; (b) denormalized step response.

If the input signal to a filter is a pulse rather than a step, the step-response curves can still be used to estimate the transient response provided that the pulse width is greater than the settling time.

EXAMPLE 2-15

REQUIRED: Estimate the output waveform of the filter of example 2-14 if the input is the pulse of figure 2-29a.

RESULT: Since the pulse width is in excess of the settling time, the step response can be used to estimate the transient response. The leading edge is determined by the shape of the denormalized step response of figure 2-28b. The trailing edge can be derived by inverting the denormalized step response. The resulting waveform is shown in figure 2-29b.

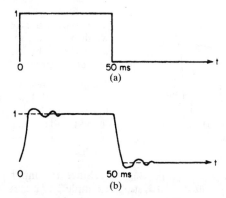

FIGURE 2-29 Pulse response of example 2-15: (a) input pulse; (b) output pulse.

Step Response of Bandpass Filters. The envelope of the response of a narrow bandpass filter to a step of the center frequency is almost identical to the step response of the equivalent low-pass filter having half the bandwidth. To determine this envelope shape, denormalize the low-pass step response by dividing the time axis by πBW, where BW is the 3-dB bandwidth of the bandpass filter. The previous discussions of overshoot, ringing, etc., can be applied to carrier envelope.

EXAMPLE 2-16

REQUIRED: Determine the envelope of the response to a 1000-Hz step for an $n = 3$ Butterworth bandpass filter having a center frequency of 1000 Hz and a 3-dB bandwidth of 100 Hz.

RESULT: Using the normalized step response of figure 2-28a, divide the time axis by πBW, where BW = 100 Hz. The results are shown in figure 2-30.

Impulse Response of Low-Pass Filters. If the duration of a pulse applied to a low-pass filter is much less than the rise time of the filter's step response, the filter's impulse response will provide a reasonable approximation to the shape of the output waveform.

Impulse-response curves are provided for the different families of low-pass filters. These curves are all normalized to correspond to a filter having a 3-dB cutoff of 1 rad/s and have an area of unity. To denormalize the curve, multiply the amplitude by the FSF and divide the time axis by the same factor.

It is desirable to select a normalized low-pass filter having an impulse response whose peak is as high as possible. The ringing which occurs after the trailing edge should also decay rapidly to avoid interference with subsequent pulses.

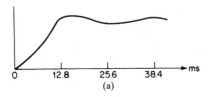

(a)

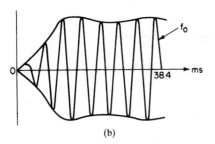

(b)

FIGURE 2-30 Bandpass response to center frequency step: (*a*) denormalized low-pass step response; (*b*) bandpass envelope response.

REQUIRED: Determine the approximate output waveform if a 100-μs pulse is applied to an $n = 3$ Butterworth low-pass filter having a 3-dB cutoff of 100 Hz.

RESULT: The denormalized step response of the filter is given in figure 2-28*b*. The rise time is well in excess of the given pulse width of 100 μs; so the impulse response curve should be used to approximate the output waveform.

The impulse response of a normalized $n = 3$ Butterworth low-pass filter is shown in figure 2-31*a*. If the time axis is divided by the FSF and the amplitude is multiplied by this same factor, the curve of figure 2-31*b* results.

Since the input pulse amplitude of example 2-17 is certainly not infinite, the amplitude axis is in error. However, the pulse shape is retained at a lower amplitude. As the input pulse width is reduced in relation to the filter rise time, the output amplitude will decrease and eventually the output pulse will vanish.

Impulse Response of Bandpass Filters. The envelope of the response of a narrowband bandpass filter to a short tone burst of center frequency can be found by denormalizing the low-pass impulse response. This approximation is valid if the burst width is much less than the rise time of the denormalized step response of the bandpass filter. Also, the center frequency should be high enough so that many cycles occur during the burst interval.

To transform the impulse-response curve, multiply the amplitude axis by πBW and divide the time axis by this same factor, where BW is the 3-dB bandwidth of the bandpass filter. The resulting curve defines the shape of the envelope of the filter's response to the tone burst.

REQUIRED: Determine the approximate shape of the response of an $n = 3$ Butterworth bandpass filter having a center frequency of 1000 Hz and a 3-dB bandwidth of 10 Hz to a tone burst of center frequency having a duration of 10 ms.

RESULT: The step response of a normalized $n = 3$ Butterworth low-pass filter is shown in figure 2-28*a*. To determine the rise time of the bandpass step response, divide the normalized low-pass rise time by πBW, where BW is 10 Hz. The resulting rise time is approximately 120 ms, which well exceeds the burst duration. Also, 10 cycles of center frequency occur during the burst interval; so the impulse response can be used to approximate the output envelope. To denormalize the impulse response, multiply the amplitude axis by πBW and divide the time axis by the same factor. The results are shown in figure 2-32.

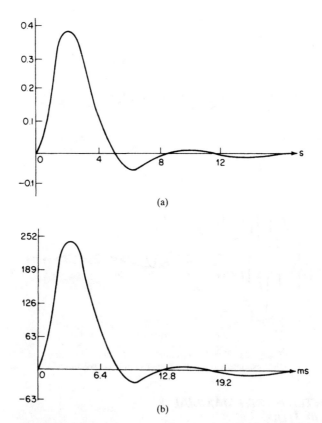

FIGURE 2-31 Impulse response for example 2-17: (*a*) normalized response; (*b*) denormalized response.

Effective Use of the Group-Delay, Step-Response, and Impulse-Response Curves. Many signals consist of complex forms of modulation rather than pulses or steps; so the transient response curves cannot be directly used to estimate the amount of distortion introduced by the filters. However, the curves are useful as a figure of merit, since networks having desirable step- or impulse-response behavior introduce minimal distortion to most forms of modulation.

Examination of the step- and impulse-response curves in conjunction with group delay indicates that a necessary condition for good pulse transmission is a flat group delay. A gradual transition from the passband to the stopband is also required for low transient distortion but is highly undesirable from a frequency-attenuation point of view.

In order to obtain a rapid pulse rise time the higher-frequency spectral components should not be delayed with respect to the lower frequencies. The curves indicate that low-pass filters which do have sharply increasing delay at higher frequencies have an impulse response which comes to a peak at a later time.

When a low-pass filter is transformed to a high-pass, a band-reject, or a wideband bandpass filter, the transient properties are not preserved. Lindquist and Zverev (see bibliography) provide computational methods for the calculation of these responses.

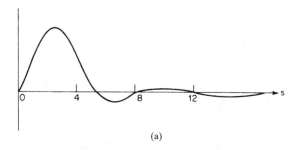

(a)

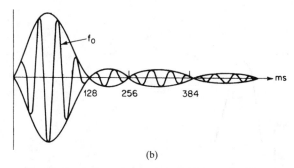

(b)

FIGURE 2-32   Results of example 2-18: (*a*) normalized low-pass impulse response; (*b*) impulse response of bandpass filter.

2.3 BUTTERWORTH MAXIMALLY FLAT AMPLITUDE

The Butterworth approximation to an ideal low-pass filter is based on the assumption that a flat response at zero frequency is more important than the response at other frequencies. The normalized transfer function is an all-pole type having roots which all fall on a unit circle. The attenuation is 3 dB at 1 rad/s.

The attenuation of a Butterworth low-pass filter can be expressed by

$$A_{dB} = 10 \log \left[1 + \left(\frac{\omega_x}{\omega_c} \right)^{2n} \right] \tag{2-31}$$

where ω_x/ω_c is the ratio of the given frequency ω_x to the 3-dB cutoff frequency ω_c and n is the order of the filter.

For the more general case,

$$A_{dB} = 10 \log (1 + \Omega^{2n}) \tag{2-32}$$

where Ω is defined by the following table.

The value Ω is a dimensionless ratio of frequencies or normalized frequency. $BW_{3\,dB}$ is the 3-dB bandwidth and BW_x is the bandwidth of interest. At high values of Ω, the attenuation increases at a rate of $6n$ dB per octave, where an octave is defined as a frequency ratio of 2 for the low-pass and high-pass cases and a *bandwidth* ratio of 2 for bandpass and band-reject filters.

Filter Type	Ω
Low-pass	ω_x/ω_c
High-pass	ω_c/ω_x
Bandpass	$BW_x/BW_{3\ dB}$
Band-reject	$BW_{3\ dB}/BW_x$

The pole positions of the normalized filter all lie on a unit circle and can be computed by

$$-\sin\frac{(2K-1)\pi}{2n} + j\cos\frac{(2K-1)\pi}{2n}, \qquad K = 1,2,\ldots,n \qquad (2\text{-}33)$$

and the element values for an LC normalized low-pass filter operating between equal 1-Ω terminations can be calculated by

$$L_K \text{ or } C_K = 2\sin\frac{(2K-1)\pi}{2n}, \qquad K = 1,2,\ldots,n \qquad (2\text{-}34)$$

where $(2K-1)\pi/2n$ is in radians.

Equation (2-34) is exactly equal to twice the real part of the pole positions of equation (2-33) except that the sign is positive.

EXAMPLE 2-19

REQUIRED: Calculate the frequency response at 1, 2, and 4 rad/s, the pole positions, and the LC element values of a normalized $n = 5$ Butterworth low-pass filter.

RESULT:

(a) Using equation (2-32) with $n = 5$, the following frequency-response table can be derived:

Ω	Attenuation
1	3 dB
2	30 dB
4	60 dB

(b) The pole positions are computed using equation (2-33) as follows:

K	$-\sin\dfrac{(2K-1)\pi}{2n}$	$j\cos\dfrac{(2K-1)\pi}{2n}$
1	−0.309	$+j\,0.951$
2	−0.809	$+j\,0.588$
3	−1	
4	−0.809	$-j\,0.588$
5	−0.309	$-j\,0.951$

(c) The element values can be computed by equation (2-34) and have the following values:

$L_1 = 0.618$ H	$C_1 = 0.618$ F
$C_2 = 1.618$ F	$L_2 = 1.618$ H
$L_3 = 2$ H or	$C_3 = 2$ F
$C_4 = 1.618$ F	$L_4 = 1.618$ H
$L_5 = 0.618$ H	$C_5 = 0.618$ F

The results of example 2-19 are shown in figure 2-33.

Chapter 11 provides pole locations and element values for both LC and active Butterworth low-pass filters having complexities up to $n = 10$.

The Butterworth approximation results in a class of filters which have moderate attenuation steepness and acceptable transient characteristics. Their element values are more practical and less critical than those of most other filter types. The rounding of the frequency response in the vicinity of cutoff may make these filters undesirable where a sharp cutoff is required; nevertheless, they should be used wherever possible because of their favorable characteristics.

Figures 2-34 through 2-37 indicate the frequency response, group delay, impulse response, and step response for the Butterworth family of low-pass filters normalized to a 3-dB cutoff of 1 rad/s.

2.4 CHEBYSHEV RESPONSE

If the poles of the normalized Butterworth low-pass transfer function were moved to the right by multiplying the real parts of the pole position by a constant k_r and the

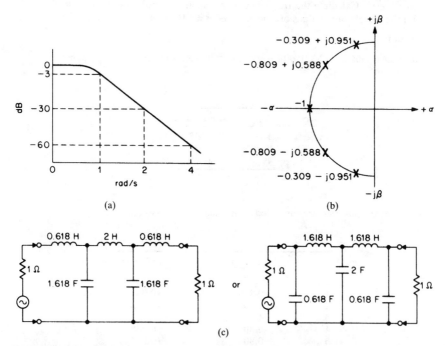

FIGURE 2-33 Butterworth low-pass filter of example 2-19: (*a*) frequency response; (*b*) pole locations; (*c*) circuit configuration.

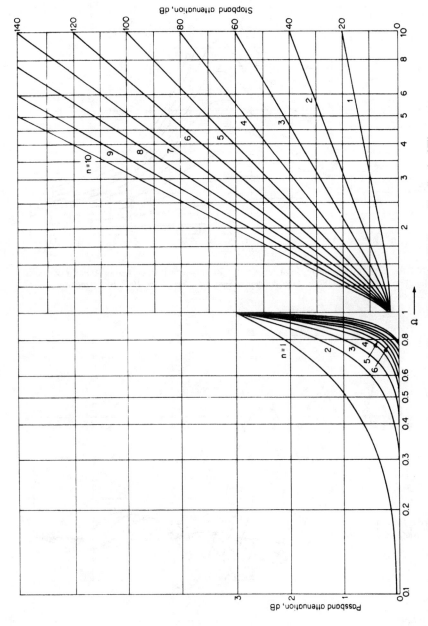

FIGURE 2-34 Attenuation characteristics for Butterworth filters. (*From Anatol I. Zverev, Handbook of Filter Synthesis, John Wiley and Sons, Inc., New York, 1967. By permission of the publishers.*)

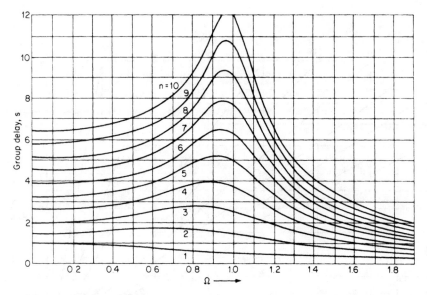

FIGURE 2-35 Group-delay characteristics for **Butterworth filters.** (*From Anatol I. Zverev,* Handbook of Filter Synthesis, *John Wiley and Sons, Inc., New York, 1967. By permission of the publishers.*)

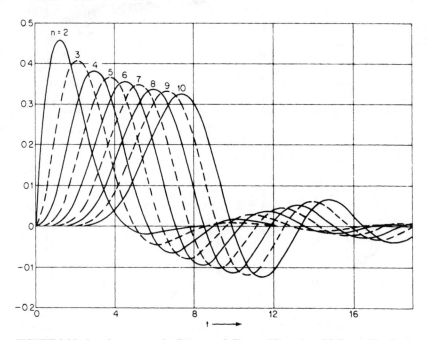

FIGURE 2-36 Impulse response for Butterworth filters. (*From Anatol I. Zverev,* Handbook of Filter Synthesis, *John Wiley and Sons, Inc., New York, 1967. By permission of the publishers.*)

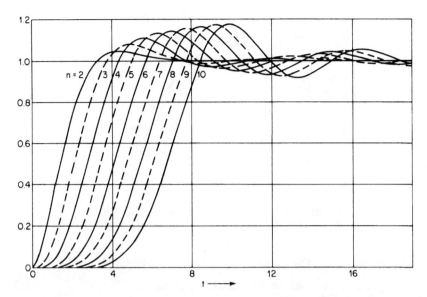

FIGURE 2-37 Step response for Butterworth filters. (*From Anatol I. Zverev,* Handbook of Filter Synthesis, *John Wiley and Sons, Inc., New York, 1967. By permission of the publishers.*)

imaginary parts by a constant k_j where both k's are <1, the poles would now lie on an ellipse instead of a unit circle. The frequency response would ripple evenly and have an attenuation at 1 rad/s equal to the ripple. The resulting response is called the Chebyshev or equiripple function.

The Chebyshev approximation to an ideal filter has a much more rectangular frequency response in the region near cutoff than the Butterworth family of filters. This is accomplished at the expense of allowing ripples in the passband.

The factors k_r and k_j are computed by:

$$k_r = \sinh A \qquad (2\text{-}35a)$$

$$k_j = \cosh A \qquad (2\text{-}35b)$$

The parameter A is given by

$$A = \frac{1}{n}\ \sinh^{-1}\frac{1}{\varepsilon} \qquad (2\text{-}36)$$

where

$$\varepsilon = \sqrt{10^{R_{dB}/10} - 1} \qquad (2\text{-}37)$$

and R_{dB} is the ripple in decibels.

Figure 2-38 compares the frequency response of an $n = 3$ Butterworth normalized low-pass filter and the Chebyshev filter generated by applying equations 2-35a and 2-35b. The Chebyshev filter response has also been normalized so that the attenuation is 3 dB at 1 rad/s. The actual 3-dB bandwidth of a Chebyshev filter computed using equations 2-35a and 2-35b is $\cosh A_1$ where A_1 is given by:

$$A_1 = \frac{1}{n}\ \cosh^{-1}\left(\frac{1}{\varepsilon}\right) \qquad (2\text{-}37a)$$

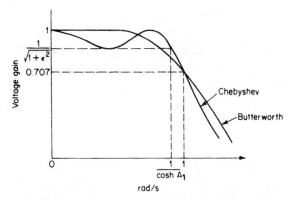

FIGURE 2-38 Comparison of Butterworth and Chebyshev low-pass filters.

The attenuation of Chebyshev filters can be expressed as

$$A_{dB} = 10 \log \left[1 + \varepsilon^2 C_n^{\,2}(\Omega) \right] \tag{2-38}$$

where $C_n(\Omega)$ is a Chebyshev polynomial whose magnitude oscillates between ± 1 for $\Omega \leqq 1$. Table 2-1 lists the Chebyshev polynomials up to order $n = 10$.

TABLE 2-1   Chebyshev Polynomials

1.	Ω
2.	$2\Omega^2 - 1$
3.	$4\Omega^3 - 3\Omega$
4.	$8\Omega^4 - 8\Omega^2 + 1$
5.	$16\Omega^5 - 20\Omega^3 + 5\Omega$
6.	$32\Omega^6 - 48\Omega^4 + 18\Omega^2 - 1$
7.	$64\Omega^7 - 112\Omega^5 + 56\Omega^3 - 7\Omega$
8.	$128\Omega^8 - 256\Omega^6 + 160\Omega^4 - 32\Omega^2 + 1$
9.	$256\Omega^9 - 576\Omega^7 + 432\Omega^5 - 120\Omega^3 + 9\Omega$
10.	$512\Omega^{10} - 1280\Omega^8 + 1120\Omega^6 - 400\Omega^4 + 50\Omega^2 - 1$

At $\Omega = 1$, Chebyshev polynomials have a value of unity; so the attenuation defined by equation (2-38) would be equal to the ripple. The 3-dB cutoff is slightly above $\Omega = 1$ and is equal to cosh A_1. In order to normalize the response equation so that 3 dB of attenuation occurs at $\Omega = 1$, the Ω of equation (2-38) is computed by using the following table:

Filter Type	Ω
Low-pass	$(\cosh A_1)\, \omega_x/\omega_c$
High-pass	$(\cosh A_1)\, \omega_c/\omega_x$
Bandpass	$(\cosh A_1)\, BW_x/BW_{3\,dB}$
Band-reject	$(\cosh A_1)\, BW_{3\,dB}/BW_x$

Figure 2-39 compares the ratios of 3-dB bandwidth to ripple bandwidth (cosh A_1) for Chebyshev low-pass filters ranging from $n = 2$ through $n = 10$.

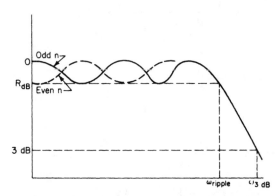

FIGURE 2-39   Ratio of 3-dB bandwidth to ripple bandwidth.

n	0.001 dB	0.005 dB	0.01 dB	0.05 dB
2	5.7834930	3.9027831	3.3036192	2.2685899
3	2.6427081	2.0740079	1.8771819	1.5120983
4	1.8416695	1.5656920	1.4669048	1.2783955
5	1.5155888	1.3510908	1.2912179	1.1753684
6	1.3495755	1.2397596	1.1994127	1.1207360
7	1.2531352	1.1743735	1.1452685	1.0882424
8	1.1919877	1.1326279	1.1106090	1.0673321
9	1.1507149	1.1043196	1.0870644	1.0530771
10	1.1215143	1.0842257	1.0703312	1.0429210

n	0.10 dB	0.25 dB	0.50 dB	1.00 dB
2	1.9432194	1.5981413	1.3897437	1.2176261
3	1.3889948	1.2528880	1.1674852	1.0948680
4	1.2130992	1.1397678	1.0931019	1.0530019
5	1.1347180	1.0887238	1.0592591	1.0338146
6	1.0929306	1.0613406	1.0410296	1.0234422
7	1.0680005	1.0449460	1.0300900	1.0172051
8	1.0519266	1.0343519	1.0230107	1.0131638
9	1.0409547	1.0271099	1.0181668	1.0103963
10	1.0331307	1.0219402	1.0147066	1.0084182

Odd-order Chebyshev LC filters have zero relative attenuation at DC. Even-order filters, however, have a loss at DC equal to the passband ripple. As a result, the even-order networks must operate between unequal source and load resistances, whereas for odd n's, the source and load may be equal. However, a mathematical transformation can alter even-order networks for operation between equal terminations (see $\theta = T$ in table 11-56). The result is a Chebyshev-like behavior in the passband and a slightly diminished rate of roll-off when compared with a comparable unaltered network.

The element values for an LC normalized low-pass filter operating between equal 1-Ω terminations and having an odd n can be calculated from the following series of relations:

$$G_1 = \frac{2A_1 \cosh A}{Y} \tag{2-39}$$

$$G_k = \frac{4A_{k-1}A_k \cosh^2 A}{B_{k-1}G_{k-1}} \qquad k = 2, 3, 4, \ldots, n \tag{2-40}$$

where

$$Y = \sinh \frac{\beta}{2n} \tag{2-41}$$

$$\beta = \ln \left(\coth \frac{R_{dB}}{17.37} \right) \tag{2-42}$$

$$A_k = \sin \frac{(2k-1)\,\pi}{2n} \qquad k = 1, 2, 3, \ldots, n \tag{2-43}$$

$$B_k = Y^2 + \sin^2 \left(\frac{k\pi}{n} \right) \qquad k = 1, 2, 3, \ldots, n \tag{2-44}$$

Coefficients G_1 through G_n are the element values.

An alternate form of determining LC element values is by synthesis of the driving-point impedance directly from the transfer function. This method includes both odd- and even-order n's.

EXAMPLE 2-20

REQUIRED: Compute the pole positions, the frequency response at 1, 2, and 4 rad/s, and the element values of a normalized $n = 5$ Chebyshev low-pass filter having a ripple of 0.5 dB.

RESULT:

(a) To compute the pole positions, first solve for k_c as follows:

$$\varepsilon = \sqrt{10^{R_{dB}/10} - 1} = 0.349 \tag{2-37}$$

$$A = \frac{1}{n}\,\sinh^{-1} \frac{1}{\varepsilon} = 0.355 \tag{2-36}$$

$$k_r = \sinh A = 0.3625 \tag{2-35a}$$

$$k_j = \cosh A = 1.0637 \tag{2-35b}$$

Multiplication of the real parts of the normalized Butterworth poles of example 2-19 by k_r and the imaginary parts by k_j results in:

$$-0.1120 \pm j1.0116; -0.2933 \pm j0.6255; -0.3625$$

To denormalize these coordinates for 3 dB at 1 rad/s divide all values by $\cosh A_1$ where A_1 is given by:

$$A_1 = 0.3428 \tag{2-37a}$$

so $\cosh A_1 = 1.0593$. The resulting pole positions are:

$$-0.1057 \pm j0.9549; -0.2769 \pm j0.5905; -0.3422$$

(b) To calculate the frequency response, substitute a fifth-order Chebyshev polynomial and $\varepsilon = 0.349$ into equation (2-38). The following results are obtained:

Ω	A_{dB}
1.0	3 dB
2.0	45 dB
4.0	77 dB

(c) The element values are computed as follows:

$$A_1 = 0.309 \tag{2-43}$$

$$\beta = 3.55 \tag{2-42}$$

$$Y = 0.363 \tag{2-41}$$

$$G_1 = 1.81 \tag{2-39}$$

$$G_2 = 1.30 \tag{2-40}$$

$$G_3 = 2.69 \tag{2-40}$$

$$G_4 = 1.30 \tag{2-40}$$

$$G_5 = 1.81 \tag{2-40}$$

Coefficients G_1 through G_5 represent the element values of a normalized Chebyshev low-pass filter having a 0.5-dB ripple and a 3-dB cutoff of 1 rad/s.

Figure 2-40 shows the results of this example.

Chebyshev filters have a narrower transition region between the passband and stopband than Butterworth filters but have more delay variation in their passband. As the passband ripple is made larger, the rate of roll-off increases, but the transient properties rapidly deteriorate. If no ripples are permitted, the Chebyshev filter degenerates to a Butterworth.

The Chebyshev function is useful where frequency response is the major consideration. It provides the maximum theoretical rate of roll-off of any all-pole transfer function for a given order. It does not have the mathematical simplicity of the Butterworth family which should be evident from comparing examples 2-20 and 2-19. Fortunately, the computation of poles and element values is not required, since this information is provided in chapter 11.

Figures 2-41 through 2-54 show the frequency and time-domain parameters of Chebyshev low-pass filters for ripples of 0.01, 0.1, 0.25, 0.5, and 1 dB, all normalized for a 3-dB cutoff of 1 rad/s.

2.5 BESSEL MAXIMALLY FLAT DELAY

Butterworth filters have fairly good amplitude and transient characteristics. The Chebyshev family of filters offers increased selectivity but poor transient behavior.

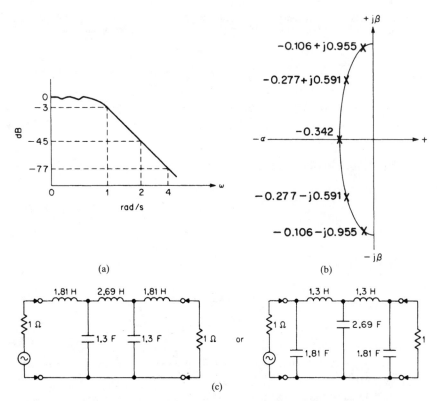

(a)

(b)

(c)

FIGURE 2-40 Chebyshev low-pass filter of example 2-20: (a) frequency response; (b) pole locations; (c) circuit configuration.

Neither approximation to an ideal filter is directed toward obtaining a constant delay in the passband.

The Bessel transfer function has been optimized to obtain a linear phase, i.e., a maximally flat delay. The step response has essentially no overshoot or ringing and the impulse response lacks oscillatory behavior. However, the frequency response is much less selective than in the other filter types.

The low-pass approximation to a constant delay can be expressed as the following general transfer function:

$$T(s) = \frac{1}{\sinh s + \cosh s} \tag{2-45}$$

If a continued-fraction expansion is used to approximate the hyperbolic functions and the expansion is truncated at different lengths, the Bessel family of transfer functions will result.

A crude approximation to the pole locations can be found by locating all the poles on a circle and separating their imaginary parts by $2/n$, as shown in figure 2-55. The vertical spacing between poles is equal, whereas in the Butterworth case the angles were equal.

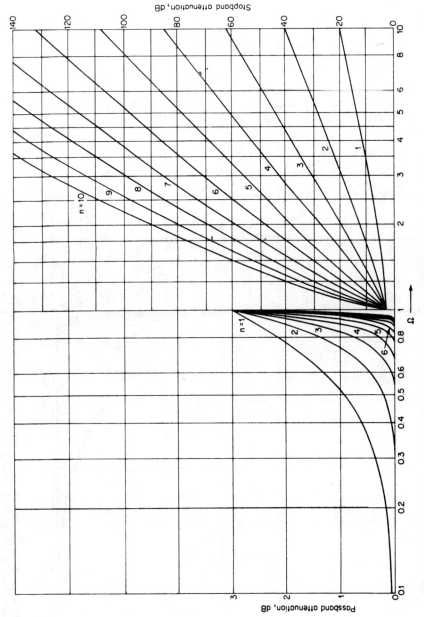

FIGURE 2-41 Attenuation characteristics for Chebyshev filters with 0.01-dB ripple. *(From Anatol I. Zverev, Handbook of Filter Synthesis, John Wiley and Sons, Inc., New York, 1967. By permission of the publishers.)*

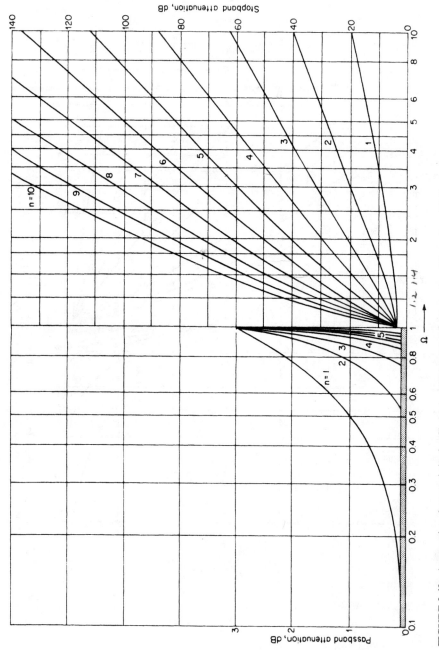

FIGURE 2-42 Attenuation characteristics for Chebyshev filters with 0.1-dB ripple. (*From Anatol I. Zverev, Handbook of Filter Synthesis, John Wiley and Sons, Inc., New York, 1967. By permission of the publishers.*)

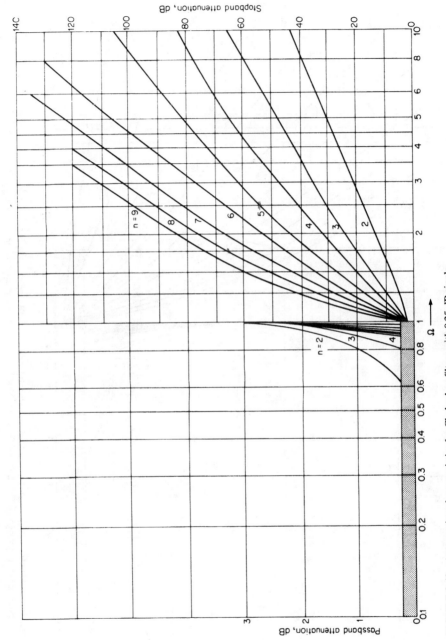

FIGURE 2-43 Attenuation characteristics for Chebyshev filters with 0.25-dB ripple.

2.47

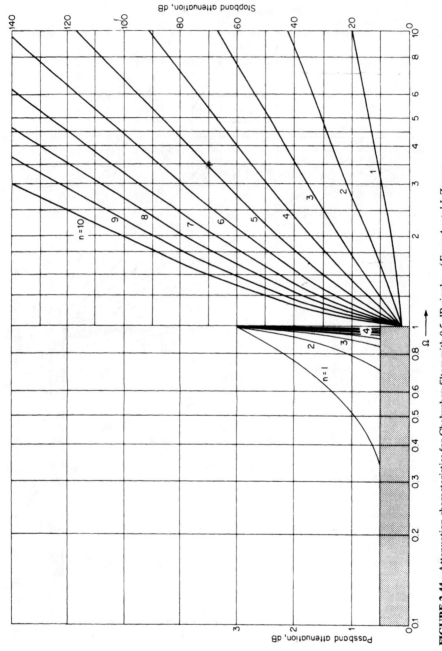

FIGURE 2-44 Attenuation characteristics for Chebyshev filters with 0.5-dB ripple. *(From Anatol I. Zverev, Handbook of Filter Synthesis, John Wiley and Sons, Inc., New York, 1967. By permission of the publishers.)*

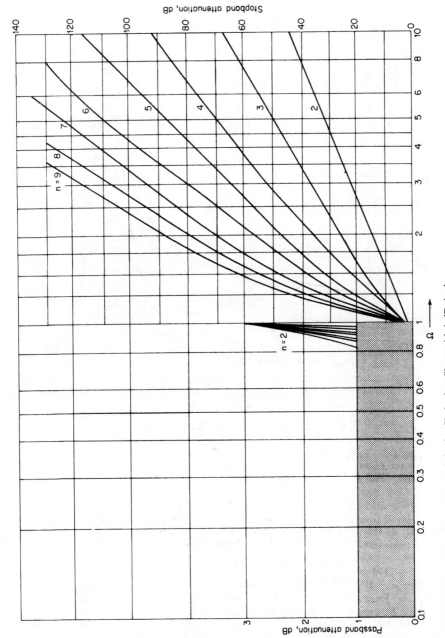

FIGURE 2-45 Attenuation characteristics for Chebyshev filters with 1-dB ripple.

2.49

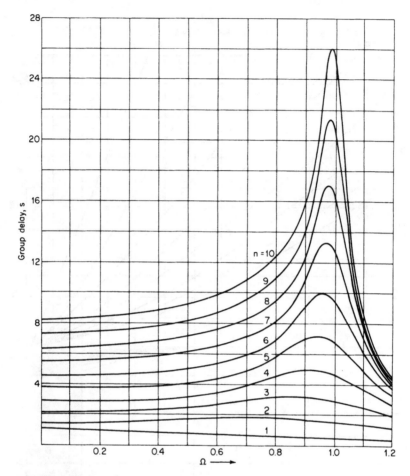

FIGURE 2-46 Group-delay characteristics for Chebyshev filters with 0.01-dB ripple. (*From Anatol I. Zverev,* Handbook of Filter Synthesis, *John Wiley and Sons, Inc., New York, 1967. By permission of the publishers.*)

The relative attenuation of a Bessel low-pass filter can be approximated by

$$A_{dB} = 3\left(\frac{\omega_x}{\omega_c}\right)^2 \tag{2-46}$$

This expression is reasonably accurate for ω_x/ω_c ranging between 0 and 2.

Figures 2-56 through 2-59 indicate that as the order n is increased, the region of flat delay is extended farther into the stopband. However, the steepness of roll-off in the transition region does not improve significantly. This restricts the use of Bessel filters to applications where the transient properties are the major consideration.

A similar family of filters is the gaussian type. However, the gaussian phase response is not as linear as the Bessel for the same number of poles, and the selectivity is not as sharp.

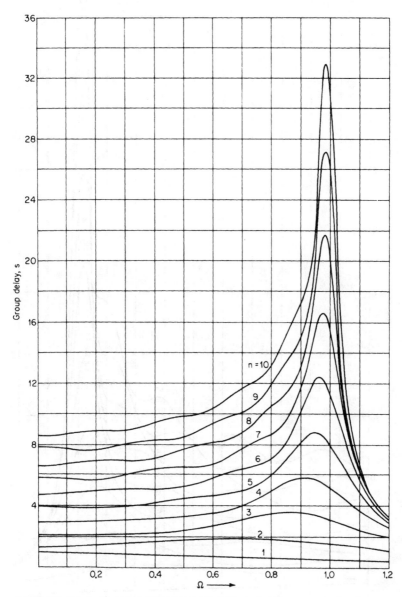

FIGURE 2-47 Group-delay characteristics for Chebyshev filters with 0.1-dB ripple. (*From Anatol I. Zverev,* Handbook of Filter Synthesis, *John Wiley and Sons, Inc., New York, 1967. By permission of the publishers.*)

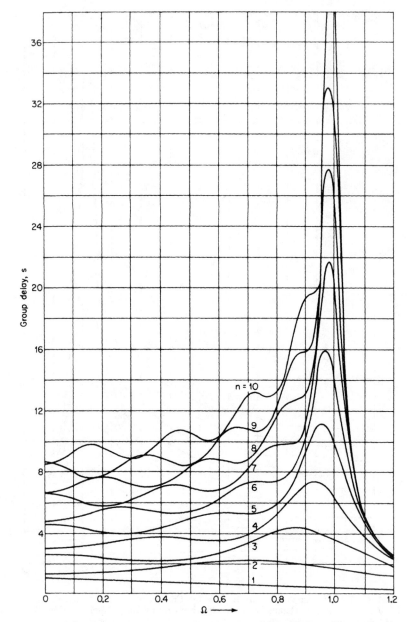

FIGURE 2-48 Group-delay characteristics for Chebyshev filters with 0.5-dB ripple. (*From Anatol I. Zverev,* Handbook of Filter Synthesis, *John Wiley and Sons, Inc., New York, 1967. By permission of the publishers.*)

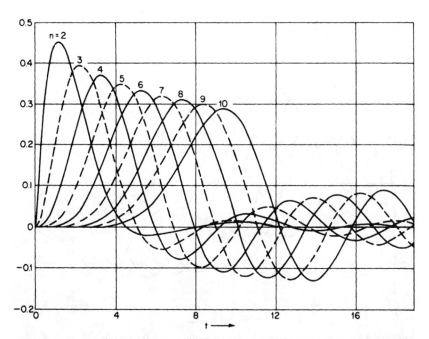

FIGURE 2-49 Impulse response for Chebyshev filters with 0.01-dB ripple. (*From Anatol I. Zverev,* Handbook of Filter Synthesis, *John Wiley and Sons, Inc., New York, 1967. By permission of the publishers.*)

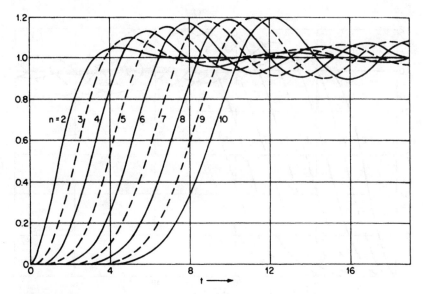

FIGURE 2-50 Step response for Chebyshev filters with 0.01-dB ripple. (*From Anatol I. Zverev,* Handbook of Filter Synthesis, *John Wiley and Sons, Inc., New York, 1967. By permission of the publishers.*)

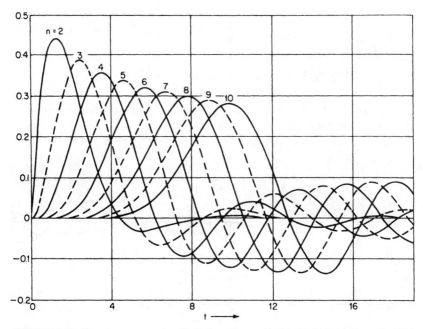

FIGURE 2-51 Impulse response for Chebyshev filters with 0.1-dB ripple. (*From Anatol I. Zverev,* Handbook of Filter Synthesis, *John Wiley and Sons, Inc., New York, 1967. By permission of the publishers.*)

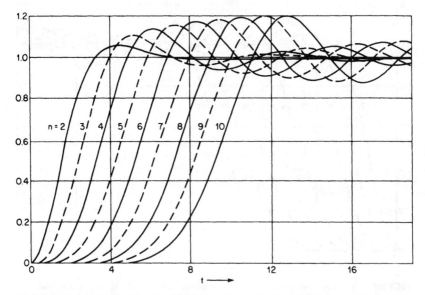

FIGURE 2-52 Step response for Chebyshev filters with 0.1-dB ripple. (*From Anatol I. Zverev,* Handbook of Filter Synthesis, *John Wiley and Sons, Inc., New York, 1967. By permission of the publishers.*)

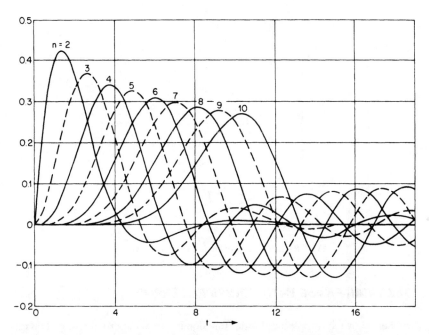

FIGURE 2-53 Impulse response for Chebyshev filters with 0.5-dB ripple. (*From Anatol I. Zverev,* Handbook of Filter Synthesis, *John Wiley and Sons, Inc., New York, 1967. By permission of the publishers.*)

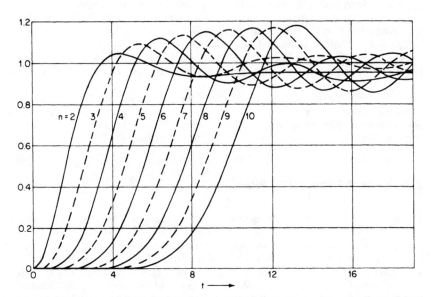

FIGURE 2-54 Step response for Chebyshev filters with 0.5-dB ripple. (*From Anatol I. Zverev,* Handbook of Filter Synthesis, *John Wiley and Sons, Inc., New York, 1967. By permission of the publishers.*)

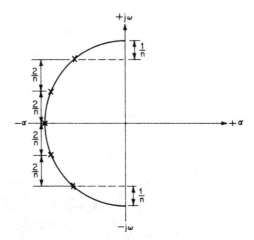

FIGURE 2-55   Approximate Bessel pole locations.

2.6   LINEAR PHASE WITH EQUIRIPPLE ERROR

The Chebyshev (equiripple amplitude) function is a better approximation of an ideal amplitude curve than the Butterworth. Therefore, it stands to reason that an equiripple approximation of a linear phase will be more efficient than the Bessel family of filters.

Figure 2-60 illustrates how a linear phase can be approximated to within a given ripple of ε degrees. For the same n, the equiripple-phase approximation results in a linear phase and, consequently, a constant delay over a larger interval than the Bessel approximation. Also the amplitude response is superior far from cutoff. In the transition region and below cutoff, both approximations have nearly identical responses.

As the phase ripple ε is increased, the region of constant delay is extended farther into the stopband. However, the delay develops ripples. The step response has slightly more overshoot than Bessel filters.

A closed-form method for computation of the pole positions is not available. The pole locations tabulated in chapter 11 were developed by iterative techniques. Values are provided for phase ripples of 0.05° and 0.5°, and the associated frequency and time-domain parameters are given in figures 2-61 through 2-68.

2.7   TRANSITIONAL FILTERS

The Bessel filters discussed in section 2.5 have excellent transient properties but poor selectivity. Chebyshev filters, on the other hand, have steep roll-off characteristics but poor time-domain behavior. A transitional filter offers a compromise between a gaussian filter, which is similar to the Bessel family, and Chebyshev filters.

Transitional filters have a near linear phase shift and smooth amplitude roll-off in the passband. Outside the passband, a sharp break in the amplitude characteristics occurs. Beyond this breakpoint the attenuation increases quite abruptly in comparison with Bessel filters, especially for the higher n's.

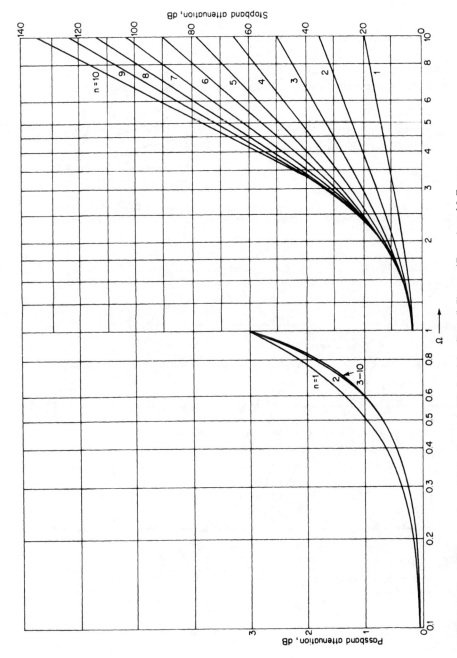

FIGURE 2-56 Attenuation characteristics for maximally flat delay (Bessel) filters. *(From Anatol I. Zverev, Handbook of Filter Synthesis, John Wiley and Sons, Inc., New York, 1967. By permission of the publishers.)*

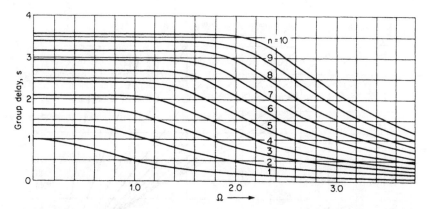

FIGURE 2-57 Group-delay characteristics for maximally flat delay (Bessel) filters. (*From Anatol I. Zverev,* Handbook of Filter Synthesis, *John Wiley and Sons, Inc., New York, 1967. By permission of the publishers.*)

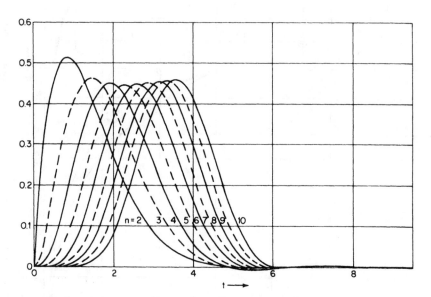

FIGURE 2-58 Impulse response for maximally flat delay (Bessel) filters. (*From Anatol I. Zverev,* Handbook of Filter Synthesis, *John Wiley and Sons, Inc., New York, 1967. By permission of the publishers.*)

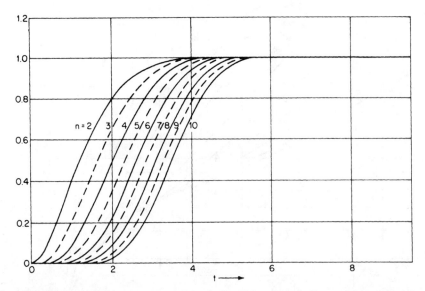

FIGURE 2-59 Step response for maximally flat delay (Bessel) filters. (*From Anatol I. Zverev,* Handbook of Filter Synthesis, *John Wiley and Sons, Inc., New York, 1967. By permission of the publishers.*)

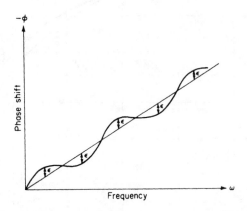

FIGURE 2-60 Equiripple linear-phase approximation.

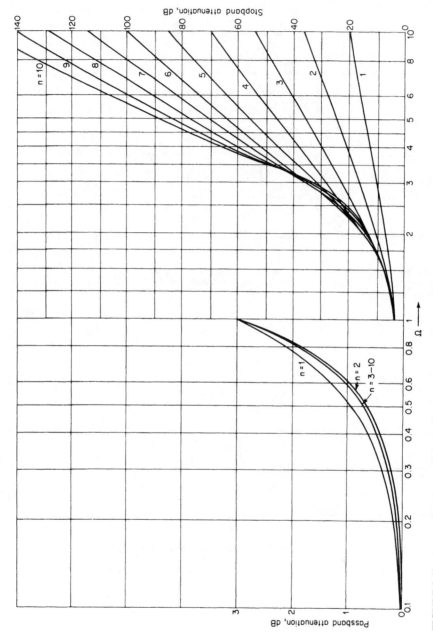

FIGURE 2-61 Attenuation characteristics for linear phase with equiripple error filters (phase error = 0.05°). (*From Anatol I. Zverev, Handbook of Filter Synthesis, John Wiley and Sons, Inc., New York, 1967. By permission of the publishers.*)

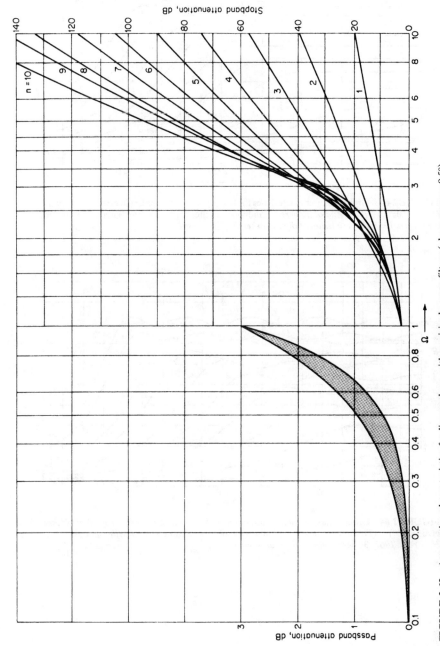

FIGURE 2-62 Attenuation characteristics for linear phase with equiripple error filters (phase error = 0.5°). *(From Anatol I. Zverev, Handbook of Filter Synthesis, John Wiley and Sons, Inc., New York, 1967. By permission of the publishers.)*

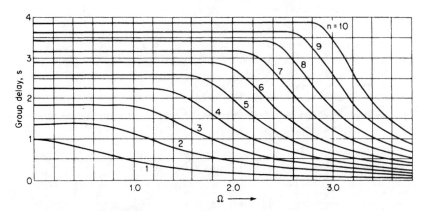

FIGURE 2-63   Group-delay characteristics for linear phase with equiripple error filters (phase error = 0.05°).   (*From Anatol I. Zverev,* Handbook of Filter Synthesis, *John Wiley and Sons, Inc., New York, 1967. By permission of the publishers.*)

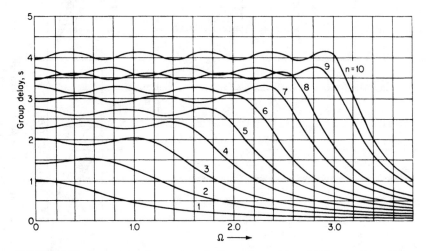

FIGURE 2-64   Group-delay characteristics for linear phase with equiripple error filters (phase error = 0.5°).   (*From Anatol I. Zverev,* Handbook of Filter Synthesis, *John Wiley and Sons, Inc., New York, 1967. By permission of the publishers.*)

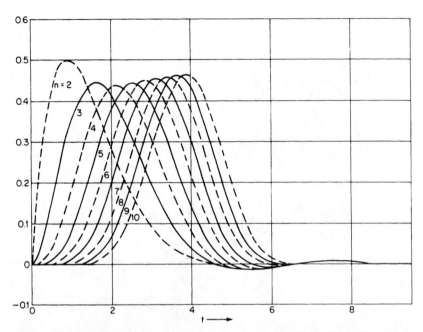

FIGURE 2-65 Impulse response for linear phase with equiripple error filters (phase error = 0.05°). (*From Anatol I. Zverev,* Handbook of Filter Synthesis, *John Wiley and Sons, Inc., New York, 1967. By permission of the publishers.*)

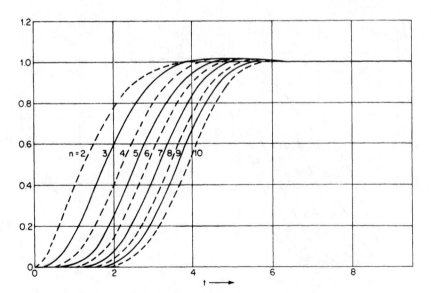

FIGURE 2-66 Step response for linear phase with equiripple error filters (phase error = 0.05°). (*From Anatol I. Zverev,* Handbook of Filter Synthesis, *John Wiley and Sons, Inc., New York, 1967. By permission of the publishers.*)

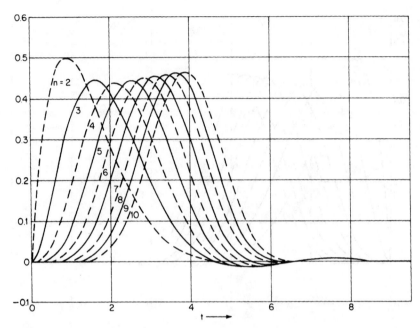

FIGURE 2-67 Impulse response for linear phase with equiripple error filters (phase error = 0.5°). (*From Anatol I. Zverev,* Handbook of Filter Synthesis, *John Wiley and Sons, Inc., New York, 1967. By permission of the publishers.*)

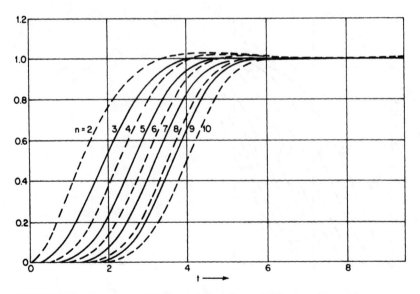

FIGURE 2-68 Step response for linear phase with equiripple error filters (phase error = 0.05°). (*From Anatol I. Zverev,* Handbook of Filter Synthesis, *John Wiley and Sons, Inc., New York, 1967. By permission of the publishers.*)

In the tables in chapter 11, transitional filters are listed which have gaussian characteristics to both 6 and 12 dB. The transient properties of the gaussian to 6-dB filters are somewhat superior to those of the Butterworth family. Beyond the 6-dB point, which occurs at approximately 1.5 rad/s, the attenuation characteristics are nearly comparable with Butterworth filters. The gaussian to 12-dB filters have time-domain parameters far superior to those of Butterworth filters. However, the 12-dB breakpoint occurs at 2 rad/s, and the attenuation characteristics beyond this point are inferior to those of Butterworth filters.

The transitional filters tabulated in chapter 11 were generated by mathematical techniques which involve interpolation of pole locations. Figures 2-69 through 2-76 indicate the frequency and time-domain properties of both the gaussian to 6-dB and gaussian to 12-dB transitional filters.

2.8 SYNCHRONOUSLY TUNED FILTERS

Synchronously tuned filters are the most basic filter type and are the easiest to construct and align. They consist of identical multiple poles. A typical application is in the case of a bandpass amplifier, where a number of stages are cascaded, with each stage having the same center frequency and Q.

The attenuation of a synchronously tuned filter can be expressed as

$$A_{dB} = 10n \log [1 + (2^{1/n} - 1)\Omega^2] \tag{2-47}$$

Equation (2-47) is normalized so that 3 dB of attenuation occurs at $\Omega = 1$.

The individual section Q can be defined in terms of the composite circuit Q requirement by the following relationship:

$$Q_{section} = Q_{overall}\sqrt{2^{1/n} - 1} \tag{2-48}$$

Alternately, we can state that the 3-dB bandwidth of the individual sections is reduced by the shrinkage factor $(2^{1/n} - 1)^{1/2}$. The individual section Q is less than the overall Q, whereas in the case of nonsynchronously tuned filters the section Qs may be required to be much higher than the composite Q.

EXAMPLE 2-21

REQUIRED: A three-section synchronously tuned bandpass filter is required to have a center frequency of 10 kHz and a 3-dB bandwidth of 100 Hz. Determine the attenuation corresponding to a bandwidth of 300 Hz, and calculate the Q of each section.

RESULT:

(a) The attenuation at the 300-Hz bandwidth can be computed as $\Omega = \frac{300}{100} = 3$

$$A_{dB} = 10n \log [1 + (2^{1/n} - 1)\Omega^2] = 15.7 \text{ dB} \tag{2-47}$$

where $n = 3$ and Ω, the bandwidth ratio, is 300 Hz/100 Hz, or 3. (Since the filter is a narrowband type, conversion to a geometrically symmetrical response requirement was not necessary.)

(b) The Q of each section is

$$Q_{section} = Q_{overall}\sqrt{2^{1/n} - 1} = 51 \tag{2-48}$$

where $Q_{overall}$ is 10 kHz/100 Hz, or 100.

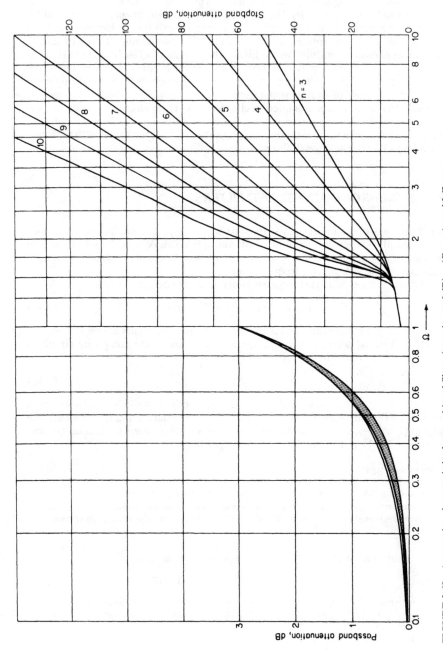

FIGURE 2-69 Attenuation characteristics for transitional filters (gaussian to 6 dB). (*From Anatol I. Zverev, Handbook of Filter Synthesis, John Wiley and Sons, Inc., New York, 1967. By permission of the publishers.*)

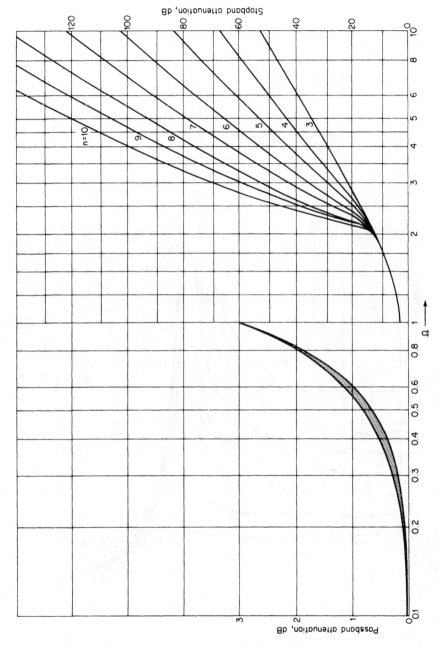

FIGURE 2-70 Attenuation characteristics for transitional filters (gaussian to 12 dB). (*From Anatol I. Zverev, Handbook of Filter Synthesis, John Wiley and Sons, Inc., New York, 1967. By permission of the publishers.*)

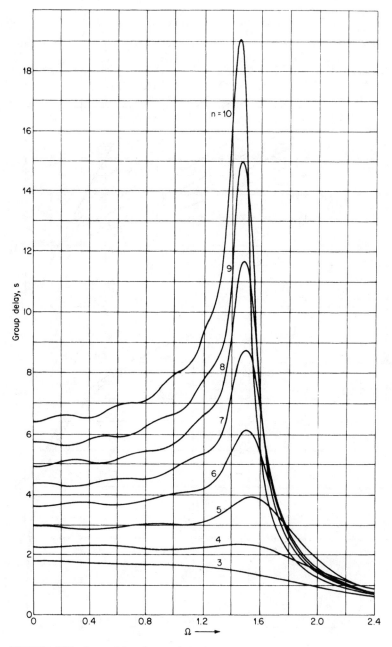

FIGURE 2-71 Group-delay characteristics for transitional filters (gaussian to 6 dB). (*From Anatol I. Zverev,* Handbook of Filter Synthesis, *John Wiley and Sons, Inc., New York, 1967. By permission of the publishers.*)

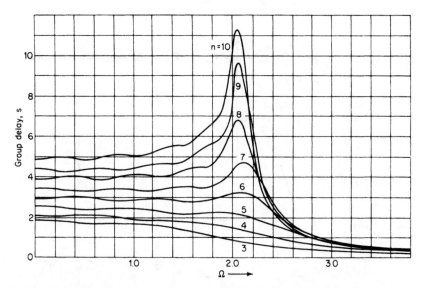

FIGURE 2-72 Group-delay characteristics for transitional filters (gaussian to 12 dB). (*From Anatol I. Zverev,* Handbook of Filter Synthesis, *John Wiley and Sons, Inc., New York, 1967. By permission of the publishers.*)

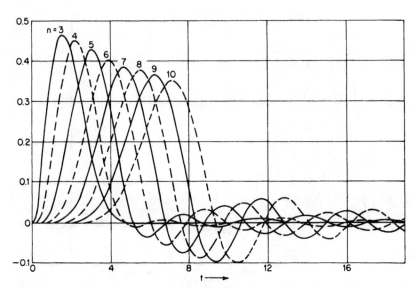

FIGURE 2-73 Impulse response for transitional filters (gaussian to 6 dB). (*From Anatol I. Zverev,* Handbook of Filter Synthesis, *John Wiley and Sons, Inc., New York, 1967. By permission of the publishers.*)

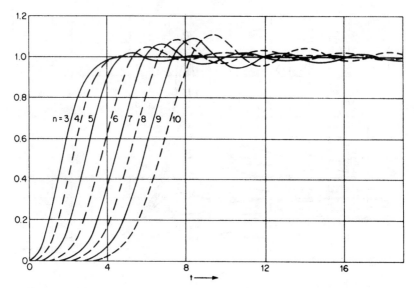

FIGURE 2-74 Step response for transitional filters (gaussian to 6 dB). (*From Anatol I. Zverev*, Handbook of Filter Synthesis, *John Wiley and Sons, Inc., New York, 1967. By permission of the publishers.*)

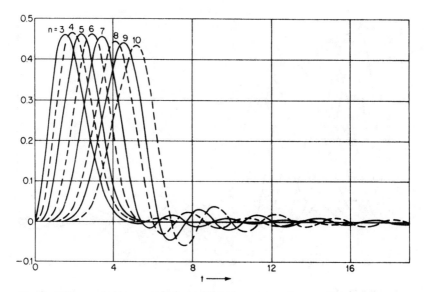

FIGURE 2-75 Impulse response for transitional filters (gaussian to 12 dB). (*From Anatol I. Zverev*, Handbook of Filter Synthesis, *John Wiley and Sons, Inc., New York, 1967. By permission of the publishers.*)

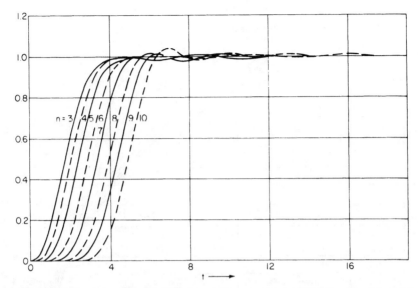

FIGURE 2-76 Step response for transitional filters (gaussian to 12 dB). (*From Anatol I. Zverev.* Handbook of Filter Synthesis, *John Wiley and Sons, Inc., New York, 1967. By permission of the publishers.*)

The synchronously tuned filter of example 2-21 has only 15.7 dB of attenuation at a normalized frequency ratio of 3 and for $n = 3$. Even the gradual roll-off characteristics of the Bessel family provide better selectivity than synchronously tuned filters for equivalent complexities.

The transient properties, however, are near optimum. The step response exhibits no overshoot at all and the impulse response lacks oscillatory behavior.

The poor selectivity of synchronously tuned filters limits their application to circuits requiring modest attenuation steepness and simplicity of alignment. The frequency and time-domain characteristics are illustrated in figures 2-77 through 2-80.

2.9 ELLIPTIC-FUNCTION FILTERS

All the filter types previously discussed are all-pole networks. They exhibit infinite rejection only at the extremes of the stopband. Elliptic-function filters have zeros as well as poles at finite frequencies. The location of the poles and zeros creates equiripple behavior in the passband similar to Chebyshev filters. Finite transmission zeros in the stopband reduce the transition region so that extremely sharp roll-off characteristics can be obtained. The introduction of these transmission zeros allows the steepest rate of descent theoretically possible for a given number of poles.

Figure 2-81 compares a five-pole Butterworth, a 0.1-dB Chebyshev, and a 0.1-dB elliptic-function filter having two transmission zeros. Clearly the elliptic-function filter has a much more rapid rate of descent in the transition region than the other filter types.

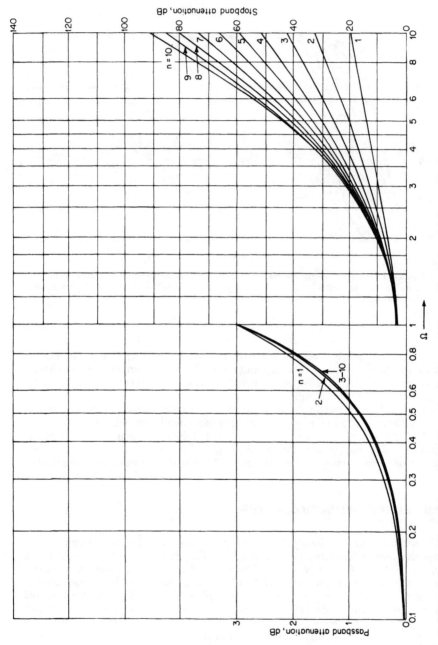

FIGURE 2-77 Attenuation characteristics for synchronously tuned filters. (*From Anatol I. Zverev, Handbook of Filter Synthesis, John Wiley and Sons, Inc., New York, 1967. By permission of the publishers.*)

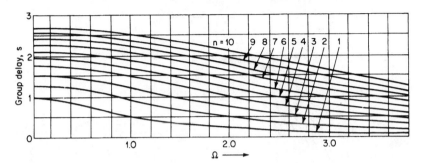

FIGURE 2-78   Group-delay characteristics for synchronously tuned filters.   (*From Anatol I. Zverev,* Handbook of Filter Synthesis, *John Wiley and Sons, Inc., New York, 1967. By permission of the publishers.*)

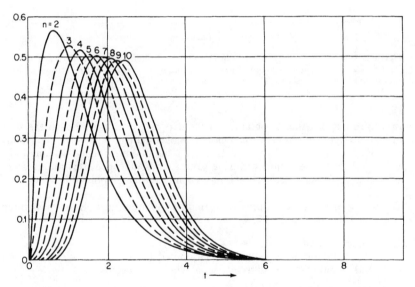

FIGURE 2-79   Impulse response for synchronously tuned filters.   (*From Anatol I. Zverev,* Handbook of Filter Synthesis, *John Wiley and Sons, Inc., New York, 1967. By permission of the publishers.*)

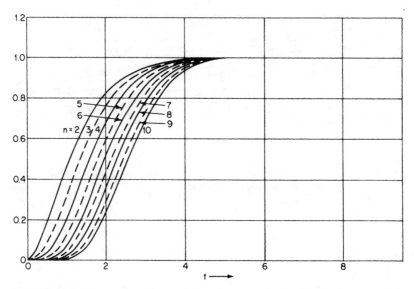

FIGURE 2-80 Step response for synchronously tuned filters. (*From Anatol I. Zverev, Handbook of Filter Synthesis, John Wiley and Sons, Inc., New York, 1967. By permission of the publishers.*)

Improved performance is obtained at the expense of return lobes in the stopband. Elliptic-function filters are also more complex than all-pole networks. Return lobes usually are acceptable to the user, since a minimum stopband attenuation is required and the chosen filter will have return lobes that meet this requirement. Also, even though each filter section is more complex than all-pole filters, fewer sections are required.

The following definitions apply to normalized elliptic-function low-pass filters and are illustrated in figure 2-82:

R_{dB} = passband ripple
A_{min} = minimum stopband attenuation in decibels
Ω_s = lowest stopband frequency at which A_{min} occurs

The response in the passband is similar to that of Chebyshev filters except that the attenuation at 1 rad/s is equal to the passband ripple instead of 3 dB. The stopband has transmission zeros, with the first zero occurring slightly beyond Ω_s. All returns (comebacks) in the stopband are equal to A_{min}.

The attenuation of elliptic filters can be expressed as

$$A_{dB} = 10 \log \left[1 + \varepsilon^2 Z_n^2 (\Omega)\right] \tag{2-49}$$

where ε is determined by the ripple [equation (2-37)] and $Z_n (\Omega)$ is an elliptic function of the nth order. Elliptic functions have both poles and zeros and can be expressed as

$$Z_n (\Omega) = \frac{\Omega(a_2^2 - \Omega^2)(a_4^2 - \Omega^2) \ldots (a_m^2 - \Omega^2)}{(1 - a_2^2\Omega^2)(1 - a_4^2\Omega^2) \ldots (1 - a_m^2\Omega^2)} \tag{2-50}$$

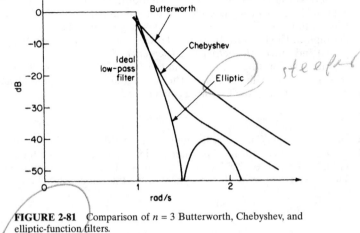

FIGURE 2-81   Comparison of $n = 3$ Butterworth, Chebyshev, and elliptic-function filters.

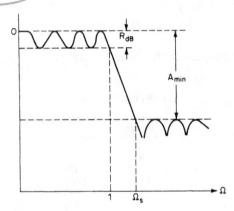

FIGURE 2-82   Normalized elliptic-function low-pass filter response.

where n is odd and $m = (n - 1)/2$, or

$$Z_n(\Omega) = \frac{(a_2^2 - \Omega)(a_4^2 - \Omega^2) \dots (a_m^2 - \Omega^2)}{(1 - a_2^2\Omega^2)(1 - a_4^2\Omega^2) \dots (1 - a_m^2\Omega^2)} \qquad (2\text{-}51)$$

where n is even and $m = n/2$.

The zeros of Z_n are $a_2, a_4, \dots, a_m$, whereas the poles are $1/a_2, 1/a_4, \dots, 1/a_m$. The reciprocal relationship between the poles and zeros of Z_n results in equiripple behavior in both the stopband and the passband.

The values for a_2 through a_m are derived from the elliptic integral, which is defined as

$$K_e = \int_0^{\pi/2} \frac{d\theta}{\sqrt{1 - k^2\sin^2\theta}} \qquad (2\text{-}52)$$

Numerical evaluation may be somewhat difficult. Glowatski (see bibliography) contains tables specifically intended for determining the poles and zeros of $Z_n(\Omega)$.

Elliptic-function filters have been extensively tabulated by Saal and Zverev (see bibliography). The basis for these tabulations was the order n and the parameters θ (degrees) and reflection coefficient ρ (percent).

Elliptic-function filters are sometimes called *Cauer filters* in honor of network theorist Professor Wilhelm Cauer. They are tabulated in chapter 11 and are commonly classified using the following convention:

$$C\, n\, \rho\, \theta$$

where C represents Cauer, n is the filter order, ρ is the reflection coefficient, and θ is the modular angle. A fifth-order filter having a ρ of 15% and a θ of 29° would be described as C05 15 $\theta = 29°$. This convention will be used throughout the handbook.

The angle θ determines the steepness of the filter and is defined as

$$\theta = \sin^{-1}\frac{1}{\Omega_s} \tag{2-53}$$

or alternately we can state

$$\Omega_s = \frac{1}{\sin\theta} \tag{2-54}$$

Table 2-2 gives some representative values of θ and Ω_s.

TABLE 2-2 Ω_s vs. θ

θ, degrees	Ω_s
0	∞
10	5.759
20	2.924
30	2.000
40	1.556
50	1.305
60	1.155
70	1.064
80	1.015
90	1.000

The parameter ρ, the reflection coefficient, can be derived from

$$\rho = \frac{\text{VSWR} - 1}{\text{VSWR} + 1} = \sqrt{\frac{\varepsilon^2}{1 + \varepsilon^2}} \tag{2-55}$$

where VSWR is the standing-wave ratio and ε is the ripple factor (see section 2.4 on the Chebyshev response). The passband ripple and reflection coefficient are related by

$$R_{dB} = -10 \log(1 - \rho^2) \tag{2-56}$$

Table 2-3 interrelates these parameters for some typical values of reflection coefficient, where ρ is expressed as a percentage.

TABLE 2-3 ρ vs. R_{dB}, VSWR, and ε

ρ, %	R_{dB}	VSWR	ε (ripple factor)
1	0.0004343	1.0202	0.0100
2	0.001738	1.0408	0.0200
3	0.003910	1.0619	0.0300
4	0.006954	1.0833	0.0400
5	0.01087	1.1053	0.0501
8	0.02788	1.1739	0.08026
10	0.04365	1.2222	0.1005
15	0.09883	1.3529	0.1517
20	0.1773	1.5000	0.2041
25	0.2803	1.6667	0.2582
50	1.249	3.0000	0.5774

As the parameter θ approaches 90°, the edge of the stopband Ω_s approaches unity. For θs near 90°, extremely sharp roll-offs are obtained. However, for a fixed n, the stopband attenuation A_{min} is reduced as the steepness increases. Figure 2-83 shows the frequency response of an $n = 3$ elliptic filter for a fixed ripple of 1 dB ($\rho \approx$ 50%) and different values of θ.

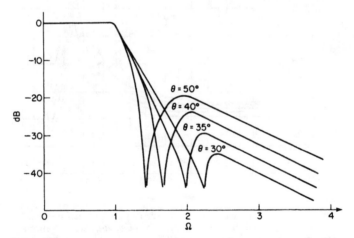

FIGURE 2-83   Elliptic-function low-pass filter response for $n = 3$ and $R_{dB} = 1$ dB.

For a given θ and order n, the stopband attenuation parameter A_{min} increases as the ripple is made larger. Since the poles of elliptic-function filters are approximately located on an ellipse, the delay curves behave in a similar manner to those of the Chebyshev family. Figure 2-84 compares the delay characteristics of $n = 3, 4,$ and 5 elliptic filters all having A_{min} of 60 dB. The delay variation tends to increase sharply with increasing ripple and filter order n.

The factor ρ determines the input impedance variation with frequency of LC elliptic filters as well as the passband ripple. As ρ is reduced, a better match is

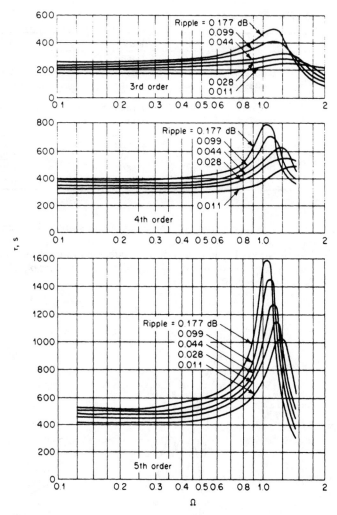

FIGURE 2-84 Delay characteristics of elliptic-function filters $n = 3, 4, 5$ and with A_{min} of 60 dB. (*From Claude S. Lindquist,* Active Network Design, *Steward and Sons, California, 1977.*)

achieved between the resistive terminations and the filter impedance. Figure 2-85 illustrates the input impedance variation with frequency of a normalized $n = 5$ elliptic-function low-pass filter. At DC, the input impedance is 1 Ω resistive. As the frequency increases, both positive and negative reactive components appear. All maximum values are within the diameter of a circle whose radius is proportional to the reflection coefficient ρ. As the complexity of the filter is increased, more gyrations occur within the circle.

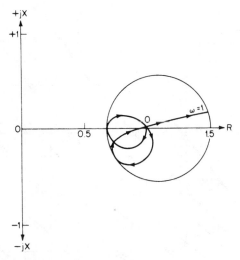

FIGURE 2-85 Impedance variation in the passband of a normalized $n = 5$ elliptic-function low-pass filter.

The relationship between ρ and filter input impedance is defined by

$$|\rho|^2 = \left| \frac{R - Z_{11}}{R + Z_{11}} \right|^2 \tag{2-57}$$

where R is the resistive termination and Z_{11} is the filter input impedance.

The closeness of matching between R and Z_{11} is frequently expressed in decibels as return loss, which is defined as

$$A_\rho = 20 \log \left| \frac{1}{\rho} \right| \tag{2-58}$$

ρ reflection coeff

Estimating the Required Order

A_{min} min stopband result

To estimate the required order of an elliptic-function filter, the curves of figure 2-86 are used. This diagram shows the relationship between Ω_s, filter order n, reflection coefficient ρ, and A_{min}, the minimum stopband rejection.

The abscissa is the stopband limit Ω_s. The ordinate consists of the terms $A_{min} + A_\rho$. To use these curves, first choose ρ. Convert ρ to A_ρ using the table provided. Determine the filter order n to meet or exceed the desired $A_{min} + A_\rho$ at the required Ω_s. A_{min} and A_ρ are given both in nepers (Np) and decibels (dB), where 1 Np = 8.69 dB.

The passband ripple behavior of elliptic-function filters is similar to that of the Chebyshev family, as shown in figure 2-39. Even-order filters are required to have a loss at DC equal to the passband ripple. This is accomplished by providing unequal terminations, and these filters are designated by b in figure 2-86. If the terminations are to be equal, a transformation is applied to the filter which results in the filters designated by c in the curves.

The following example demonstrates the selection of an elliptic-function filter.

b unequal Termination } even
c equal Termination }

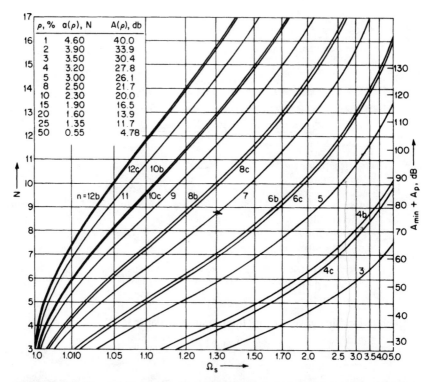

ρ, %	a(ρ), N	A(ρ), db
1	4.60	40.0
2	3.90	33.9
3	3.50	30.4
4	3.20	27.8
5	3.00	26.1
8	2.50	21.7
10	2.30	20.0
15	1.90	16.5
20	1.60	13.9
25	1.35	11.7
50	0.55	4.78

FIGURE 2-86 Curves for estimating the order of elliptic-function filters. (*From R. Saal, "Der Entwurf von Filtern mit Hilfe des Kataloges Normierter Tiefpasse," Telefunken GMBH, Backnang, West Germany, 1963. Reprinted by permission.*)

EXAMPLE 2-22

REQUIRED: Determine the order of an elliptic-function filter having a passband ripple less than 0.2 dB up to 1000 Hz and a minimum rejection of 60 dB at 1300 Hz and above.

RESULT:

(a) Compute the low-pass steepness factor A_s:

$$A_s = \frac{f_s}{f_c} = \frac{1300 \text{ Hz}}{1000 \text{ Hz}} = 1.3 \tag{2-11}$$

(b) Select a normalized low-pass filter having an A_{min} of at least 60 dB with a stopband limit Ω_s not exceeding 1.3. Let us choose a ρ of 20% which corresponds to a ripple of 0.18 dB from table 2-3. Using the table of figure 2-86, a ρ of 20% corresponds to an A_ρ of 13.9 dB. Therefore,

$$A_{min} + A_\rho = 60 \text{ dB} + 13.9 \text{ dB} = 73.9 \text{ dB}$$

The curve of figure 2-86 indicates that at an Ω_s of 1.3, a filter of $n = 7$ provides the required attenuation.

In comparison, a twenty-seventh-order Butterworth low-pass filter would have to meet the requirements of example 2-22; so the elliptic-function family is a *must* for steep filter requirements.

2.10 MAXIMALLY FLAT DELAY WITH CHEBYSHEV STOPBAND

The Bessel, linear phase with equiripple error, and transitional filter families all exhibit either a maximally flat or equiripple-delay characteristic over most of the passband and, except for the transitional type, even into the stopband. However, the amplitude versus frequency response is far from ideal. The passband region in the vicinity of cutoff is very rounded and the stopband attenuation in the first few octaves is poor.

Elliptic-function filters have an extremely steep rate of descent into the stopband because of transmission zeros. However, the delay variation in the passband is unacceptable when the transient behavior is of significance.

The maximally flat delay with Chebyshev stopband filters is derived by introducing transmission zeros into a Bessel-type transfer function. The constant delay properties in the passband are retained. However, the stopband rejection is significantly improved because of the effectiveness of the transmission zeros.

The step response exhibits no overshoot or ringing and the impulse response has essentially no oscillatory behavior. Constant delay properties extend well into the stopband for higher-order networks.

Normalized tables of element values for the maximally flat delay with the Chebyshev stopband family of filters are provided in table 11-57. These tables are normalized so that the 3-dB response occurs at 1 rad/s. The tables also provide the delay at DC and the normalized frequencies corresponding to a 1% and 10% deviation from the delay at DC. The amplitude response below the 3-dB point is identical to the attenuation characteristics of the Bessel filters shown in figure 2-56.

BIBLIOGRAPHY

Feistel, V. K., and R. Unbehauen, "Tiefpasse mit Tschebyscheff—Charakter der Betriebs-dampfung im Sperrbereich und Maximal geebneter Laufzeit," *Frequenz,* no. 8, West Germany, 1965.

Glowatski, E., "Sechsstellige Tafel der Cauer-Parameter," Verlag der Bayr, Akademie der Wissenchaften, Munich, Germany, 1955.

Lindquist, C. S., *Active Network Design,* Steward and Sons, California, 1977.

Saal, R., "Der Entwurf von Filtern mit Hilfe des Kataloges Normierter Tiefpasse," Telefunken GMBH, Backnang, West Germany, 1963.

White Electromagnetics, *A Handbook on Electrical Filters,* White Electromagnetics Inc., 1963.

Zverev, A. I., *Handbook of Filter Synthesis,* John Wiley and Sons, New York, 1967.

CHAPTER 3
LOW-PASS FILTER DESIGN

3.1 LC *LOW-PASS FILTERS*

All-Pole Filters

LC low-pass filters can be directly designed from the tables provided in chapter 11. A suitable filter must first be selected using the guidelines established in chapter 2. The chosen design is then frequency- and impedance-scaled to the desired cutoff and impedance level.

EXAMPLE 3-1

REQUIRED:

LC low-pass filter
3 dB at 1000 Hz
20 dB minimum at 2000 Hz
$R_s = R_L = 600\,\Omega$

RESULT:

(a) To normalize the low-pass requirement, compute A_s.

$$A_s = \frac{f_s}{f_c} = \frac{2000\,\text{Hz}}{1000\,\text{Hz}} = 2 \tag{2-11}$$

(b) Choose a normalized low-pass filter from the curves of chapter 2 having at least 20 dB of attenuation at 2 rad/s.

Examination of the curves indicates that an $n = 4$ Butterworth or third-order 0.1-dB Chebyshev satisfies this requirement. Let us select the latter, since fewer elements are required.

(c) Table 11-28 contains element values for normalized 0.1-dB Chebyshev *LC* filters ranging from $n = 2$ through $n = 10$. The circuit corresponding to $n = 3$ and equal source and load resistors ($R_s = 1\,\Omega$) is shown in figure 3-1a.

(d) Denormalize the filter using a Z of 600 and a frequency-scaling factor (FSF) of $2\pi f_c$ or 6280.

$$R'_s = R'_L = 600\,\Omega \tag{2-8}$$

$$L'_2 = \frac{L \times Z}{\text{FSF}} = \frac{1.5937 \times 600}{6280} = 0.152\,\text{H} \tag{2-9}$$

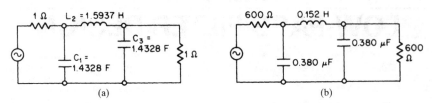

FIGURE 3-1   Results of example 3-1: (*a*) normalized filter from table 11-28; (*b*) frequency- and impedance-scaled filter.

$$C'_1 = C'_3 = \frac{C}{\text{FSF} \times Z} = \frac{1.4328}{6280 \times 600} = 0.380 \; \mu\text{F} \qquad (2\text{-}10)$$

The resulting filter is shown in figure 3-1*b*.

The normalized filter used in example 3-1 was shown in the table as having a current source input with a parallel resistor of 1 Ω. The reader will recall that Thévenin's theorems permit the replacement of this circuit with a voltage source having an equivalent series source resistance.

Elliptic-Function Filters

Normalized elliptic-function LC low-pass filters are presented in tabular form in table 11-56. They are classified using the convention outlined in section 2.9 and arranged in order of increasing n.

The following sample section of table 11-56 corresponds to C07 20:

Capacitors C_1 through C_7 and inductors L_2, L_4, and L_6 are defined by the table and are located directly above the branch numbers shown in the schematic. Branches 2, 4, and 6 consist of parallel resonant circuits comprising L_2C_2, L_4C_4, and L_6C_6. The branch resonant frequencies correspond to the transmission zeros and are respectively given in the tables as Ω_2, Ω_4, and Ω_6. All inductors are in henrys, capacitors are in farads, and resonant frequencies are in radians per second. The source and load terminations are both shown to be 1 Ω.

When an elliptic-function low-pass filter is frequency-scaled, the transmission zeros are scaled by the same factor; so the tabulated zeros can be used to determine the resulting branch resonances. Where very steep filters are required, precise adjustment of these resonances to compensate for component tolerances is a necessity; so these frequencies are very useful.

The following example illustrates the design of an elliptic-function low-pass filter using the normalized tables.

EXAMPLE 3-2

REQUIRED:

LC low-pass filter
0.25 dB maximum ripple DC to 100 Hz
60 dB minimum at 132 Hz
$R_s = R_L = 900 \; \Omega$

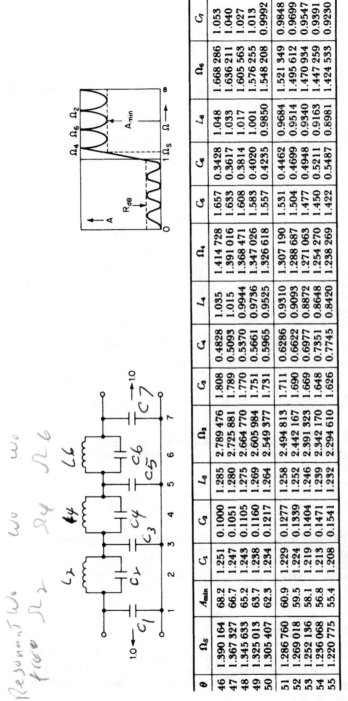

θ	Ω_s	A_{min}	C_1	C_2	L_2	Ω_2	C_3	C_4	L_4	Ω_4	C_5	C_6	L_6	Ω_6	C_7	θ
46	1.390 164	68.2	1.251	0.1000	1.285	2.789 476	1.808	0.4828	1.035	1.414 728	1.657	0.3428	1.048	1.668 286	1.053	46
47	1.367 327	66.7	1.247	0.1051	1.280	2.725 881	1.789	0.5093	1.015	1.391 016	1.633	0.3617	1.033	1.636 211	1.040	47
48	1.345 633	65.2	1.243	0.1105	1.275	2.664 770	1.770	0.5370	0.9944	1.368 471	1.608	0.3814	1.017	1.605 563	1.027	48
49	1.325 013	63.7	1.238	0.1160	1.269	2.605 984	1.751	0.5661	0.9736	1.347 026	1.583	0.4020	1.001	1.576 255	1.013	49
50	1.305 407	62.3	1.234	0.1217	1.264	2.549 377	1.731	0.5965	0.9525	1.326 618	1.557	0.4235	0.9850	1.548 208	0.9992	50
51	1.286 760	60.9	1.229	0.1277	1.258	2.494 813	1.711	0.6286	0.9310	1.307 190	1.531	0.4462	0.9684	1.521 349	0.9848	51
52	1.269 018	59.5	1.224	0.1339	1.252	2.442 167	1.690	0.6622	0.9093	1.288 687	1.504	0.4699	0.9514	1.495 612	0.9699	52
53	1.252 136	58.1	1.219	0.1404	1.246	2.391 323	1.669	0.6977	0.8872	1.271 063	1.477	0.4948	0.9340	1.470 934	0.9547	53
54	1.236 068	56.8	1.213	0.1471	1.239	2.342 170	1.648	0.7351	0.8648	1.254 270	1.450	0.5211	0.9163	1.447 259	0.9391	54
55	1.220 775	55.4	1.208	0.1541	1.232	2.294 610	1.626	0.7745	0.8420	1.238 269	1.422	0.5487	0.8981	1.424 533	0.9230	55

Example 3-2   A sample section of TABLE 11-56, Elliptic-Function LC Element Values, p. 11.68.

RESULT:

(a) To normalize the given requirement, compute the low-pass steepness factor A_s.

$$A_s = \frac{f_s}{f_c} = \frac{132}{100} = 1.32 \qquad (2\text{-}11)$$

(b) Figure 2-86 indicates that for a ρ of 20% (0.18-dB ripple) a filter of $n = 7$ is required. Using the table corresponding to C07 20, select a filter having an Ω_s not exceeding 1.32 and an A_{min} of 60 dB or more.

Let us choose the design which corresponds to θ = 50°, since Ω_s = 1.305 and A_{min} = 62.3 dB. The circuit of the C07 20 θ = 50° filter is shown in figure 3-2a and corresponds to the underlined values of the sample table.

(c) Denormalize the filter using a Z of 900 and a frequency-scaling factor (FSF) of $2\pi f_c$ or 628.

$$C_1' = \frac{C}{FSF \times Z} = \frac{1.234}{628 \times 900} = 2.1822 \ \mu F \qquad (2\text{-}10)$$

$$C_2' = 0.2152 \ \mu F$$

$$C_3' = 3.061 \ \mu F$$

$$C_4' = 1.055 \ \mu F$$

$$C_5' = 2.753 \ \mu F$$

$$C_6' = 0.7489 \ \mu F$$

$$C_7' = 1.767 \ \mu F$$

$$L_2 = \frac{L \times Z}{FSF} = \frac{1.264 \times 900}{628} = 1.811 \ H \qquad (2\text{-}9)$$

$$L_4' = 1.365 \ H$$

$$L_6' = 1.412 \ H$$

To compute the denormalized resonant frequencies of each parallel tuned circuit, multiply the design cutoff (f_c = 100 Hz) by $\Omega_2, \Omega_4,$ and Ω_6 to obtain

$$f_2 = 254.9 \ Hz$$

$$f_4 = 132.7 \ Hz$$

$$f_6 = 154.8 \ Hz$$

The resulting filter is given in figure 3-2b, having the frequency response shown in figure 3-2c.

The capacitor magnitudes in the tuned circuits can be reduced by using tapped inductors. This technique is explained in detail in the discussion in chapter 8.

Duality and Reciprocity

A network and its dual have identical response characteristics. Each LC filter tabulated in chapter 11 has an equivalent dual network. The circuit configuration shown at the bottom of each table and the bottom set of nomenclature corresponds to the dual of the upper filter.

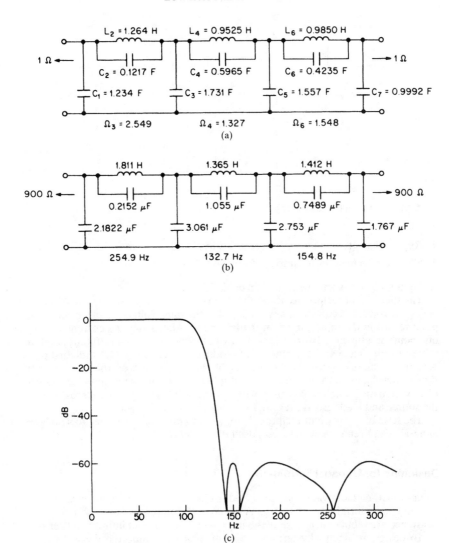

FIGURE 3-2 Filter of example 3-2: (*a*) normalized C07 20 θ = 50° low-pass filter; (*b*) frequency- and impedance-scaled network; (*c*) frequency response.

Any ladder-type network can be transformed into its dual by implementing the following rules:

1. Convert every series branch into a shunt branch and every shunt branch into a series branch.

2. Convert circuit branch elements in series to elements in parallel and vice versa.

3. Transform each inductor into a capacitor and vice versa. The values remain unchanged; i.e., 4 H becomes 4 F.

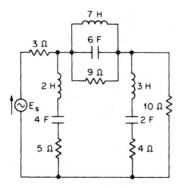 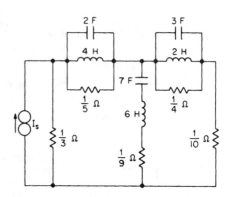

FIGURE 3-3   Example of dual networks.

4. Replace each resistance with a conductance; i.e., 3 Ω becomes 3 mhos or ⅓ Ω.

5. Change a voltage source into a current source and vice versa.

Figure 3-3 shows a network and its dual.

The theorem of reciprocity states that if a voltage located at one point of a linear network produces a current at any other point, the same voltage acting at the second point results in the same current at the first point. Alternately, if a current source at one point of a linear network results in a voltage measured at a different point, the same current source at the second point produces the same voltage at the first point. As a result, the response of an LC filter is the same regardless of which direction the signal flows in, except for a constant multiplier. It is perfectly permissible to turn a filter schematic completely around with regard to its driving source, provided that the source and load resistive terminations are also interchanged.

The laws of duality and reciprocity are used to manipulate a filter to satisfy termination requirements or to force a desired configuration.

Designing for Unequal Terminations

Tables of LC element values are provided in chapter 11 for both equally terminated and unequally terminated networks. A number of different ratios of source to load resistance are tabulated, including the impedance extremes of infinity and zero.

To design an unequally terminated filter, first determine the desired ratio of R_s/R_L. Select a normalized filter from the table that satisfies this ratio. The reciprocity theorem can be applied to turn a network around end for end and the source and load resistors can be interchanged. The tabulated impedance ratio is inverted if the dual network given by the lower schematic is used. The chosen filter is then frequency- and impedance-scaled.

EXAMPLE 3-3

REQUIRED:

LC low-pass filter
1 dB at 900 Hz
20 dB minimum at 2700 Hz
$R_s = 1\ \text{k}\Omega$
$R_L = 5\ \text{k}\Omega$

RESULT:

(a) Compute A_s.

$$A_s = \frac{f_s}{f_c} = \frac{2700 \text{ Hz}}{900 \text{ Hz}} = 3 \qquad (2\text{-}11)$$

(b) Normalized requirement:
1 dB at X rad/s
20 dB minimum at $3X$ rad/s
(where X is arbitrary)

(c) Select a normalized low-pass filter that makes the transition from 1 dB to at least 20 dB over a frequency ratio of 3:1. A Butterworth $n = 3$ design will satisfy these requirements, since figure 2-34 indicates that the 1-dB point occurs at 0.8 rad/s and that more than 20 dB of attenuation is obtained at 2.4 rad/s. Table 11-2 provides element values for normalized Butterworth low-pass filters for a variety of impedance ratios. Since the ratio of R_s/R_L is 1:5, we will select a design for $n = 3$ corresponding to $R_s = 0.2\ \Omega$ and use the upper schematic. (Alternately, we could have selected the lower schematic corresponding to $R_s = 5\ \Omega$ and turned the network end for end, but an additional inductor would have been required.)

(d) The normalized filter from table 11-2 is shown in figure 3-4a. Since the 1-dB point is required to be 900 Hz, the FSF is calculated by

$$\text{FSF} = \frac{\text{desired reference frequency}}{\text{existing reference frequency}}$$

$$= \frac{2\pi\,900 \text{ rad/s}}{0.8 \text{ rad/s}} = 7069 \qquad (2\text{-}1)$$

Using a Z of 5000 and an FSF of 7069, the denormalized component values are

$$R'_s = R \times Z = 1\ k\Omega \qquad (2\text{-}8)$$

$$R'_L = 5\ k\Omega$$

$$C'_1 = \frac{C}{\text{FSF} \times Z} = \frac{2.6687}{7069 \times 5000} = 0.0755\ \mu\text{F} \qquad (2\text{-}10)$$

$$C'_3 = 0.22\ \mu\text{F}$$

$$L_2 = \frac{L \times Z}{\text{FSF}} = \frac{0.2842 \times 5000}{7069} = 0.201\ \text{H} \qquad (2\text{-}9)$$

The scaled filter is shown in figure 3-4b.

If an infinite termination is required, a design having an R_s of infinity is selected. When the input is a current source, the configuration is used as given. For an infinite load impedance, the entire network is turned end for end.

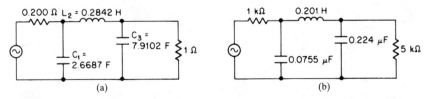

FIGURE 3-4 Low-pass filter with unequal terminations: *(a)* normalized low-pass filter; *(b)* frequency- and impedance-scaled filter.

If the design requires a source impedance of 0 Ω, the dual network is used corresponding to $1/R_s$ of infinity or $R_s = 0\ \Omega$.

In practice, impedance extremes of near zero or infinity are not always possible. However, for an impedance ratio of 20 or more, the load can be considered infinite in comparison with the source, and the design for an infinite termination is used. Alternately the source may be considered zero with respect to the load and the dual filter corresponding to $R_s = 0\ \Omega$ may be used. When n is odd, the configuration having the infinite termination has one less inductor than its dual.

An alternate method of designing filters to operate between unequal terminations involves partitioning the source or load resistor between the filter and the termination. For example, a filter designed for a 1-kΩ source impedance could operate from a 250-Ω source if a 750-Ω resistor were placed within the filter network in series with the source. However, this approach would result in higher insertion loss.

Bartlett's Bisection Theorem. A filter network designed to operate between equal terminations can be modified for unequal source and load resistors if the circuit is symmetrical. Bartlett's bisection theorem states that if a symmetrical network is bisected and one half is impedance-scaled including the termination, the response shape will not change. All tabulated odd-order Butterworth and Chebyshev filters having equal terminations satisfy the symmetry requirement.

EXAMPLE 3-4

REQUIRED:

LC low-pass filter
3 dB at 200 Hz
15 dB minimum at 400 Hz
$R_s = 1\ \text{k}\Omega$ $R_L = 1.5\ \text{k}\Omega$

RESULT:

(a) Compute A_s.

$$A_s = \frac{f_s}{f_c} = \frac{400}{200} = 2 \tag{2-11}$$

(b) Figure 2-34 indicates that an $n = 3$ Butterworth low-pass filter provides 18 dB rejection at 2 rad/s. Normalized *LC* values for Butterworth low-pass filters are given in table 11-2. The circuit corresponding to $n = 3$ and equal terminations is shown in figure 3-5a.

(c) Since the circuit of figure 3-5a is symmetrical, it can be bisected into two equal halves as shown in figure 3-5b. The requirement specifies a ratio of load to source resistance of 1.5 (1.5 kΩ/1 kΩ); so we must impedance-scale the right half of the circuit by a factor of 1.5. The circuit of figure 3-5c is obtained.

(d) The recombined filter of figure 3-5d can now be frequency- and impedance-scaled using an FSF of $2\pi200$ or 1256 and a Z of 1000.

$$R_s' = 1\ \text{k}\Omega$$

$$R_L' = 1.5\ \text{k}\Omega$$

$$C_1' = \frac{C}{\text{FSF} \times Z} = \frac{1}{1256 \times 1000} = 0.796\ \mu\text{F} \tag{2-10}$$

$$C_3' = 0.530\ \mu\text{F}$$

$$L_2' = \frac{L \times Z}{\text{FSF}} = \frac{2.5 \times 1000}{1256} = 1.99\ \text{H} \tag{2-9}$$

The final filter is shown in figure 3-5e.

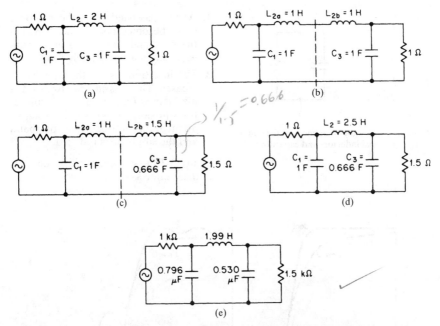

FIGURE 3-5 Example of Bartlett's bisection theorem: (*a*) normalized filter having equal termina-tions; (*b*) bisected filter; (*c*) impedance-scaled right half section; (*d*) recombined filter; (*e*) final scaled network.

Effects of Dissipation

Filters designed using the tables of *LC* element values in chapter 11 require lossless coils and capacitors to obtain the theoretical responses predicted in chapter 2. In the practical world, capacitors are usually obtainable that have low losses, but inductors are generally lossy, especially at low frequencies. Losses can be defined in terms of *Q*, the figure of merit or quality factor of a reactive component.

If a lossy coil or capacitor is resonated in parallel with a lossless reactance, the ratio of resonant frequency to 3-dB bandwidth of the resonant circuit's impedance, i.e., the band over which the magnitude of the impedance remains within 0.707 of the resonant value, is given by

$$Q = \frac{f_0}{BW_{3\,dB}} \tag{3-1}$$

Figure 3-6 gives the low-frequency equivalent circuits for practical inductors and capacitors. Their *Q*s can be calculated by

Inductors: $$Q = \frac{\omega L}{R_L} \tag{3-2}$$

Capacitors: $$Q = \omega C R_c \tag{3-3}$$

where ω is the frequency of interest, in radians per second.

Using elements having a finite *Q* in a design intended for lossless reactances has the following mostly undesirable effects:

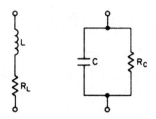

FIGURE 3-6 Low-frequency equivalent circuits of practical inductors and capacitors.

1. At the passband edge, the response shape becomes more rounded. Within the passband, the ripples are diminished and may completely vanish.

2. The insertion loss of the filter is increased. The loss in the stopband is maintained (except in the vicinity of transmission zeros); so the relative attenuation between the passband and the stopband is reduced.

Figure 3-7 shows some typical examples of these effects.

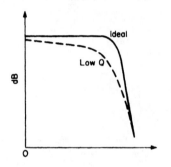
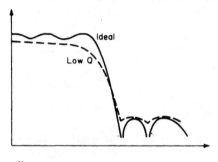

FIGURE 3-7 Effects of finite Q.

The most critical problem caused by finite element Q is the effect on the response shape near cutoff. Estimating the extent of this effect is somewhat difficult without extensive empirical data. The following variations in the filter design parameters will cause *increased* rounding of the frequency response near cutoff for a fixed Q:

1. Going to a larger passband ripple

2. Increasing the filter order n

3. Decreasing the transition region of elliptic-function filters

Changing these parameters in the opposite direction, of course, reduces the effects of dissipation.

Filters can be designed to have the responses predicted by modern network theory using finite element Qs. Figure 3-8 shows the minimum Qs required at cutoff for different low-pass responses. If elements are used having Qs slightly above the minimum values given in figure 3-8, the desired response can be obtained provided that certain predistorted element values are used. However, the insertion loss will be prohibitive. It is therefore highly desirable that element Qs be several times higher than the values indicated.

The effect of low Q on the response near cutoff can usually be compensated for by going to a higher-order network or a steeper filter and using a larger design bandwidth to allow for rounding. However, this design approach does not always result in satisfactory results, since the Q requirement may also increase. A method of compensating for low Q by using amplitude equalization is discussed in section 8.4.

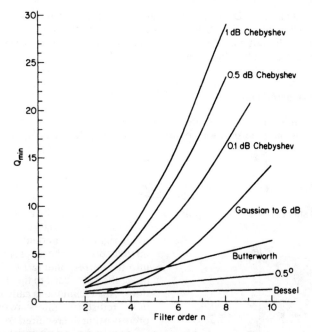

FIGURE 3-8 Minimum Q requirements for low-pass filters.

The insertion loss of low-pass filters can be computed by replacing the reactive elements with resistances corresponding to their Qs, since at DC, the inductors become short circuits and capacitors become open, which leaves the resistive elements only.

Figure 3-9a shows a normalized third-order 0.1-dB Chebyshev low-pass filter where each reactive element has a Q of 10 at the 1-rad/s cutoff. The series and shunt resistors for the coils and capacitors are calculated using equations (3-2) and (3-3), respectively. At 1 rad/s these equations can be simplified and reexpressed as

$$R_L = \frac{L}{Q} \tag{3-4}$$

$$R_c = \frac{Q}{C} \tag{3-5}$$

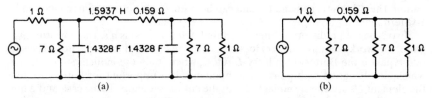

FIGURE 3-9 Calculation of insertion loss: (a) third-order 0.1-dB Chebyshev low-pass filter with $Q = 10$; (b) equivalent circuit at DC.

The equivalent circuit at DC is shown in figure 3-9b. The insertion loss is 1.9 dB. The actual loss calculated was 7.9 dB, but the 6-dB loss due to the source and load terminations is normally not considered part of the filter's insertion loss, since it would also occur in the event that the filter was completely lossless.

Using Predistorted Designs

The effect of finite element Q on an LC filter transfer function is to increase the real components of the pole positions by an amount equal to the dissipation factor d, where

$$d = \frac{1}{Q}$$

(3-6)

Figure 3-10 shows this effect. All poles are displaced to the left by an equal amount.

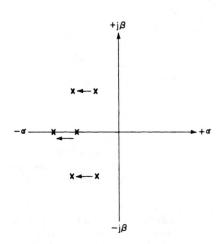

FIGURE 3-10 Effects of dissipation on pole pattern.

If the desired poles were first shifted to the right by an amount equal to d, the introduction of the appropriate losses into the corresponding LC filter would move the poles back to the desired locations. This technique is called *predistortion*. Predistorted filters are obtained by predistorting the required transfer function for a desired Q and then synthesizing an LC filter from the resulting transfer function. When the reactive elements of the filter have the required losses added, the response shape will correspond to the original transfer function.

The maximum amount that a group of poles can be displaced to the right in the process of predistortion is equal to the smallest real part among the poles, since further movement corresponds to locating a pole in the right half plane, which is an unstable condition. The minimum Q therefore is determined by the highest Q pole (i.e., the pole having the smallest real component). The Qs shown in figure 3-8 correspond to $1/d$, where d is the real component of the highest Q pole.

Tables are provided in chapter 11 for all-pole predistorted low-pass filters. These designs are all singly terminated with a source resistor of 1 Ω and an infinite termination. Their duals turned end for end can be used with a voltage source input and a 1-Ω termination.

Two types of predistorted filters are tabulated for various d's. The uniform dissipation networks require uniform losses in both the coils and the capacitors. The second type are the Butterworth lossy-L filters, where only the inductors have losses, which closely agrees with practical components. It is important for both types that the element Qs are closely equal to $1/d$ at the cutoff frequency. In the case of the uniform dissipation networks, losses must usually be added to the capacitors.

EXAMPLE 3-5

REQUIRED:

LC low-pass filter
3 dB at 500 Hz
24 dB minimum at 1200 Hz
$R_s = 600 \, \Omega$ $R_L = 100 \, k\Omega$ minimum
Inductor Qs of 5 at 500 Hz
Lossless capacitors

RESULT:

(a) Compute A_s.

$$A_s = \frac{1200}{500} = 2.4 \tag{2-11}$$

(b) The curves of figure 2-34 indicate that an $n = 4$ Butterworth low-pass filter has over 24 dB of rejection at 2.4 rad/s. Table 11-14 contains the element values for Butterworth lossy-L networks where $n = 4$. The circuit corresponding to $d = 0.2$ ($d = 1/Q$) is shown in figure 3-11a.

(c) The normalized filter can now be frequency- and impedance-scaled using an FSF of $2\pi500 = 3142$ and a Z of 600.

$$R'_s = 600 \, \Omega$$

$$L'_1 = \frac{L \times Z}{FSF} = \frac{0.4518 \times 600}{3142} = 86.3 \text{ mH} \tag{2-9}$$

$$L'_3 = 0.414 \text{ H}$$

$$C'_2 = \frac{C}{FSF \times Z} = \frac{1.098}{3142 \times 600} = 0.582 \, \mu F \tag{2-10}$$

$$C'_4 = 0.493 \, \mu F$$

(d) The resistive coil losses are

$$R_1 = \frac{\omega L}{Q} = 54.2 \, \Omega \tag{3-2}$$

and $R_3 = 260 \, \Omega$

where $\omega = 2\pi f_c = 3142$

The final filter is given in figure 3-11b.

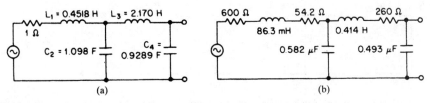

FIGURE 3-11   Lossy-L low-pass filter of example 3-5: (a) normalized filter; (b) scaled filter.

EXAMPLE 3-6

REQUIRED:

LC low-pass filter
3 dB at 100 Hz
58 dB minimum at 300 Hz
$R_s = 1\ k\Omega$ $R_L = 100\ k\Omega$ minimum
Inductor *Q*s of 11 at 100 Hz
Lossless capacitors

RESULT:

(*a*) Compute A_s.

$$A_s = \frac{300}{100} = 3 \tag{2-11}$$

(*b*) Figure 2-42 indicates that a fifth-order 0.1-dB Chebyshev has about 60 dB of rejection at 3 rad/s. Table 11-32 provides *LC* element values for 0.1-dB Chebyshev uniform dissipation networks. The available inductor *Q* of 11 corresponds to a *d* of 0.091 ($d = 1/Q$). Values are tabulated for an *n* = 5 network having a *d* of 0.0881, which is sufficiently close to the requirement. The corresponding circuit is shown in figure 3-12*a*.

(*c*) The normalized filter is frequency- and impedance-scaled using an FSF of $2\pi100 = 628$ and a *Z* of 1000.

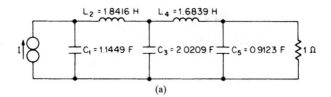

(a)

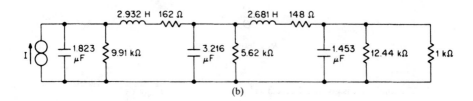

(b)

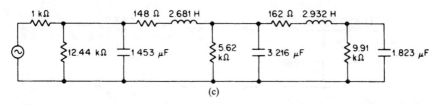

(c)

FIGURE 3-12 Design of uniform dissipation network of example 3-6: (*a*) normalized fifth-order 0.1-dB Chebyshev with *d* = 0.0881; (*b*) frequency- and impedance-scaled filter including losses; (*c*) final network.

$$C_1' = \frac{C}{\text{FSF} \times Z} = \frac{1.1449}{628 \times 1000} = 1.823 \ \mu\text{F} \tag{2-10}$$

$$C_3' = 3.216 \ \mu\text{F}$$

$$C_5' = 1.453 \ \mu\text{F}$$

$$L_2' = \frac{L \times Z}{\text{FSF}} = \frac{1.8416 \times 1000}{628} = 2.932 \ \text{H} \tag{2-9}$$

$$L_4' = 2.681 \ \text{H}$$

(d) The shunt resistive losses for capacitors C_1', C_3', and C_5' are

$$R_1' = \frac{Q}{\omega C} = 9.91 \ \text{k}\Omega \tag{3-3}$$

$$R_3' = 5.62 \ \text{k}\Omega$$

$$R_5' = 12.44 \ \text{k}\Omega$$

The series resistive inductor losses are

$$R_2' = \frac{\omega L}{Q} = 162 \ \Omega \tag{3-2}$$

$$R_4' = 148 \ \Omega$$

where

$$Q = \frac{1}{d} = \frac{1}{0.0881} = 11.35$$

and

$$\omega = 2\pi f_c = 2\pi 100 = 628$$

The resulting circuit, including all losses, is shown in figure 3-12*b*. This circuit can be turned end for end so that the requirement for a 1-kΩ source resistance is met. The final filter is given in figure 3-12*c*.

It is important to remember that uniform dissipation networks require the presence of losses in both the coils and the capacitors; so resistors must usually be added. Component Qs within 20% of $1/d$ are usually sufficient for satisfactory results.

Resistors can sometimes be combined to eliminate components. In the circuit of figure 3-12*c*, the 1-kΩ source and the 12.44-kΩ resistor can be combined, which results in a 926-Ω equivalent source resistance. The network can then be impedance-scaled to restore a 1-kΩ source.

3.2 ACTIVE LOW-PASS FILTERS

Active low-pass filters are designed using a sequence of operations similar to the design of *LC* filters. The specified low-pass requirement is first normalized and a particular filter type of the required complexity is selected using the response characteristics given in chapter 2. Normalized tables of active filter component values are provided in chapter 11 for each associated transfer function. The corresponding filter is denormalized by frequency and impedance scaling.

Active filters can also be designed directly from the poles and zeros. This approach sometimes offers some additional degrees of freedom and will also be covered.

All-Pole Filters

The transfer function of a passive RC network has poles that lie only on the negative real axis of the complex frequency plane. In order to obtain the complex poles required by the all-pole transfer functions of chapter 2, active elements must be introduced. Integrated circuit operational amplifiers are readily available that have nearly ideal properties, such as high gain. However, these properties are limited to frequencies below a few hundred kilohertz; so active filters beyond this range are difficult.

Unity-Gain Single-Feedback Realization.   Figure 3-13 shows two active low-pass filter configurations. The two-pole section provides a pair of complex conjugate poles, whereas the three-pole section produces a pair of complex conjugate poles and a single real-axis pole. The operational amplifier is configured in the voltage-follower configuration, which has a closed-loop gain of unity, very high input impedance, and nearly zero output impedance.

The two-pole section has the transfer function

$$T(s) = \frac{1}{C_1 C_2 s^2 + 2 C_2 s + 1} \tag{3-7}$$

A second-order low-pass transfer function can be expressed in terms of the pole locations as

$$T(s) = \frac{1}{\dfrac{1}{\alpha^2 + \beta^2} s^2 + \dfrac{2\alpha}{\alpha^2 + \beta^2} s + 1} \tag{3-8}$$

Equating coefficients and solving for the capacitors results in

$$C_1 = \frac{1}{\alpha} \tag{3-9}$$

$$C_2 = \frac{\alpha}{\alpha^2 + \beta^2} \tag{3-10}$$

where α and β are the real and imaginary coordinates of the pole pair.

The transfer function of the normalized three-pole section was discussed in section 1.2 and was given by

$$T(S) = \frac{1}{s^3 A + s^2 B + sC + 1} \tag{1-17}$$

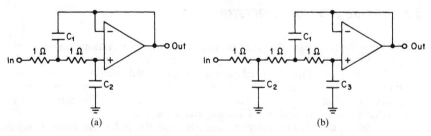

(a)   (b)

FIGURE 3-13   Unity-gain active low-pass configurations: (*a*) two-pole section; (*b*) three-pole section.

where $$A = C_1 C_2 C_3 \tag{1-18}$$

$$B = 2C_3(C_1 + C_2) \tag{1-19}$$

and $$C = C_2 + 3C_3 \tag{1-20}$$

Solution of these equations to find the values of C_1, C_2, and C_3 in terms of the poles is somewhat laborious and is best accomplished with a digital computer.

If the filter order n is an even order, $n/2$ two-pole filter sections are required. Where n is odd, $(n - 3)/2$ two-pole sections and a single three-pole section are necessary. This occurs because even-order filters have complex poles only, whereas an odd-order transfer function has a single real pole in addition to the complex poles.

At DC, the capacitors become open circuits; so the circuit gain becomes equal to that of the amplifier, which is unity. This can also be determined analytically from the transfer functions given by equations (3-7) and (1-17). At DC, $s = 0$ and $T(s)$ reduces to 1. Within the passband of a low-pass filter, the response of individual sections may have sharp peaks and some corresponding gain.

All resistors are 1 Ω in the two normalized filter circuits of figure 3-13. Capacitors C_1, C_2, and C_3 are tabulated in chapter 11. These values result in the normalized all-pole transfer functions of chapter 2 where the 3-dB cutoff occurs at 1 rad/s.

To design a low-pass filter, a filter type is first selected from chapter 2. The corresponding active low-pass filter values are then obtained from chapter 11. The normalized filter is denormalized by dividing all the capacitor values by FSF × Z, which is identical to the denormalization formula for LC filters, i.e.,

$$C' = \frac{C}{\text{FSF} \times Z} \tag{2-10}$$

where FSF is the frequency-scaling factor $2\pi f_c$ and Z is the impedance-scaling factor. The resistors are multiplied by Z, which results in equal resistors throughout of $Z\,\Omega$.

The factor Z does not have to be the same for each filter section, since the individual circuits are isolated by the operational amplifiers. The value of Z can be independently chosen for each section so that practical capacitor values occur, but the FSF must be the same for all sections. The sequence of the sections can be rearranged if desired.

The frequency response obtained from active filters is usually very close to theoretical predictions, provided that the component tolerances are small and that the amplifier has satisfactory properties. The effects of low Q which occur in LC filters do not apply, so the filters have no insertion loss and the passband ripples are well defined.

EXAMPLE 3-7

REQUIRED:

Active low-pass filter
3 dB at 100 Hz
70 dB minimum at 350 Hz

RESULT:

(a) Compute low-pass steepness factor A_s.

$$A_s = \frac{f_s}{f_c} = \frac{350}{100} = 3.5 \tag{2-11}$$

(b) The response curve of figure 2-44 indicates that a fifth-order 0.5-dB Chebyshev low-pass filter meets the 70-dB requirement at 3.5 rad/s.

(c) The normalized values can be found in table 11-39. The circuit consists of a three-pole section followed by a two-pole section and is shown in figure 3-14*a*.

(d) Let us arbitrarily select an impedance-scaling factor of 5×10^4. Using an FSF of $2\pi f_c$ or 628, the resulting new values are

Three-pole section:

$$C'_1 = \frac{C}{FSF \times Z} = \frac{6.842}{628 \times 5 \times 10^4} = 0.218 \ \mu F \tag{2-10}$$

$$C'_2 = 0.106 \ \mu F$$

$$C'_3 = 0.00966 \ \mu F$$

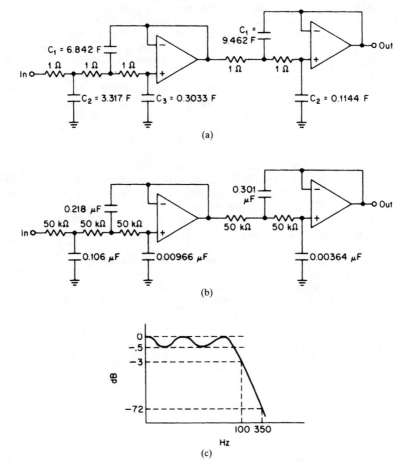

(a)

(b)

(c)

FIGURE 3-14 Low-pass filter of example 3-7: (*a*) normalized fifth-order 0.5-dB Chebyshev low-pass filter; (*b*) denormalized filter; (*c*) frequency response.

Two-pole section:

$$C_1' = \frac{C}{FSF \times Z} = \frac{9.462}{628 \times 5 \times 10^4} = 0.301 \ \mu F$$

$$C_2' = 0.00364 \ \mu F$$

The resistors in both sections are multiplied by Z, resulting in equal resistors throughout of 50 kΩ. The denormalized circuit is given in figure 3-14b having the frequency response of figure 3-14c.

The first section of the filter should be driven by a voltage source having a source impedance much less than the first resistor of the section. The input must have a DC return to ground if a blocking capacitor is present. Since the filter's output impedance is low, the frequency response is independent of the terminating load, provided that the operational amplifier has sufficient driving capability.

Real-Pole Configurations. All odd-order low-pass transfer functions have a single real-axis pole. This pole is realized as part of the $n = 3$ section of figure 3-13b when the tables of active low-pass values in chapter 11 are used. If an odd-order filter is designed directly from the tabulated poles, the normalized real-axis pole can be generated using one of the configurations given in figure 3-15.

The most basic form of a real pole is the circuit of figure 3-15a. The capacitor C is defined by

$$C = \frac{1}{\alpha_0} \tag{3-11}$$

where α_0 is the normalized real-axis pole. The circuit gain is unity with a high-impedance termination.

If gain is desirable, the circuit of figure 3-15a can be followed by a noninverting amplifier as in figure 3-15b, where A is the required gain. When the gain must be inverting, the circuit of figure 3-15c is used.

The chosen circuit is frequency- and impedance-scaled in a manner similar to the rest of the filter. The value R in figure 3-15b is arbitrary, since only the ratio of the two feedback resistors determines the gain of the amplifier.

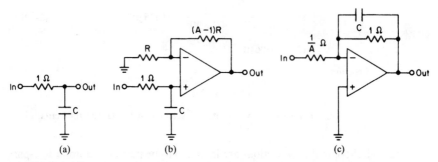

FIGURE 3-15 First-order pole configurations: (*a*) basic *RC* section; (*b*) noninverting gain configuration; (*c*) inverting gain circuit.

EXAMPLE 3-8

REQUIRED:

Active low-pass filter
3 dB at 75 Hz
15 dB minimum at 150 Hz
Gain of 40 dB ($A = 100$)

RESULT:

(a) Compute the steepness factor.

$$A_s = \frac{f_s}{f_c} = \frac{150}{75} = 2 \tag{2-11}$$

(b) Figure 2-34 indicates that an $n = 3$ Butterworth low-pass response satisfies the attenuation requirement. Since a gain of 100 is required, we will use the $n = 2$ section of
figure 3-13a followed by the $n = 1$ section of figure 3-15b, which provides the gain.
The circuit configuration is shown in figure 3-16a.

(c) The following pole locations of a normalized $n = 3$ Butterworth low-pass filter are
obtained from table 11-1:

Complex pole $\alpha = 0.5000$ $\beta = 0.8660$
Real pole $\alpha_0 = 1.0000$

The component values for the $n = 2$ section are

$$C_1 = \frac{1}{\alpha} = \frac{1}{0.5} = 2\,F \tag{3-9}$$

$$C_2 = \frac{\alpha}{\alpha^2 + \beta^2} = \frac{0.5}{0.5^2 + 0.866^2} = 0.5\,F \tag{3-10}$$

The capacitor in the $n = 1$ circuit is computed by

$$C = \frac{1}{\alpha_0} = \frac{1}{1.0} = 1\,F \tag{3-11}$$

Since $A = 100$, the feedback resistor is 99R in the normalized circuit shown in figure
3-16b.

(d) Using an FSF of $2\pi f_c$ or 471 and selecting an impedance-scaling factor of 10^5 the
denormalized capacitor values are
$n = 2$ section:

$$C_1' = \frac{C}{FSF \times Z} = \frac{2}{471 \times 10^5} = 0.0425\,\mu F \tag{2-10}$$

$$C_2' = 0.0106\,\mu F$$

$n = 1$ section:

$$C' = 0.0212\,\mu F$$

The value R for the $n = 1$ section is arbitrarily selected at 10 kΩ. The final circuit is
given in figure 3-16c.

Although these real-pole sections are intended to be part of odd-order low-pass
filters, they can be independently used as an $n = 1$ low-pass filter. They have the
transfer function

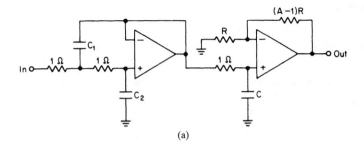

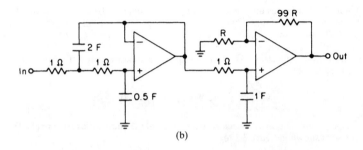

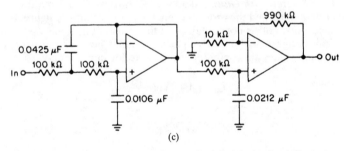

FIGURE 3-16 Low-pass filter of example 3-8: (a) circuit configuration; (b) normalized circuit; (c) scaled filter.

$$T(s) = K\frac{1}{sC + 1} \tag{3-12}$$

where $K = 1$ for figure 3-15a, $K = A$ for figure 3-15b, and $K = -A$ for figure 3-15c. If $C = 1$ F, the 3-dB cutoff occurs at 1 rad/s.

The attenuation of a first-order filter can be expressed as

$$A_{dB} = 10 \log \left[1 + \left(\frac{\omega_x}{\omega_c} \right)^2 \right] \tag{3-13}$$

where ω_x/ω_c is the ratio of a given frequency to the cutoff frequency. The normalized frequency response corresponds to the $n = 1$ curve of the Butterworth low-pass filter response curves of figure 2-34. The step response has no overshoot and the impulse response does not have any oscillatory behavior.

EXAMPLE 3-9

REQUIRED:

Active low-pass filter
3 dB at 60 Hz
12 dB minimum attenuation at 250 Hz
Gain of 20 dB with inversion

RESULT:

(a) Compute A_s.

$$A_s = \frac{f_s}{f_c} = \frac{250}{60} = 4.17 \tag{2-11}$$

(b) Figure 2-34 indicates that an $n = 1$ filter provides over 12 dB attenuation at 4.17 rad/s. Since an inverting gain of 20 dB is required, the configuration of figure 3-15c will be used. The normalized circuit is shown in figure 3-17a, where $C = 1$ F and $A = 10$ corresponding to a gain of 20 dB.

(c) Using an FSF of $2\pi60$ or 377 and an impedance-scaling factor of 10^6, the denormalized capacitor is

$$C' = \frac{C}{\text{FSF} \times Z} = \frac{1}{377 \times 10^6} = 0.00265 \ \mu\text{F} \tag{2-10}$$

The input and output feedback resistors are 100 kΩ and 1 MΩ, respectively. The final circuit is shown in figure 3-17b.

Second-Order Section with Gain.   If an active low-pass filter is required to have a gain higher than unity and the order is even, the $n = 1$ sections of figure 3-15 cannot be used, since a real pole is not contained in the transfer function.

The circuit of figure 3-18 realizes a pair of complex poles and provides a gain of $-A$. The element values are computed using the following formulas:

$$C_1 = (A + 1)\left(1 + \frac{\beta^2}{\alpha^2}\right) \tag{3-14}$$

$$R_1 = \frac{\alpha}{A(\alpha^2 + \beta^2)} \tag{3-15}$$

$$R_2 = \frac{AR_1}{A + 1} \tag{3-16}$$

$$R_3 = AR_1 \tag{3-17}$$

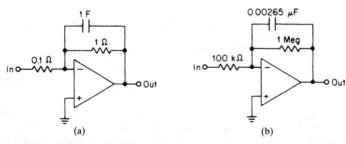

FIGURE 3-17 $n = 1$ low-pass filter of example 3-9: (a) normalized filter; (b) frequency- and impedance-scaled filter.

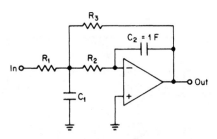

FIGURE 3-18 Second-order section with gain.

This section is used in conjunction with the $n = 2$ section of figure 3-13a to realize even-order low-pass filters with gain. This is shown in the following example:

EXAMPLE 3-10

REQUIRED:

Active low-pass filter
3 dB at 200 Hz
30 dB minimum at 800 Hz
No step-response overshoot
Gain of 6 dB with inversion ($A = 2$)

RESULT:

(a) Compute A_s.

$$A_s = \frac{f_s}{f_c} = \frac{800}{200} = 4 \tag{2-11}$$

(b) Since no overshoot is permitted, a Bessel filter type will be used. Figure 2-56 indicates that a fourth-order network provides over 30 dB of rejection at 4 rad/s. Since an inverting gain of 2 is required and $n = 4$, the circuit of figure 3-18 will be used, followed by the two-pole section of figure 3-13a. The basic circuit configuration is given in figure 3-19a.

(c) The following pole locations of a normalized $n = 4$ Bessel low-pass filter are obtained from table 11-41:

$$\alpha = 1.3596 \qquad \beta = 0.4071$$

and

$$\alpha = 0.9877 \qquad \beta = 1.2476$$

The normalized component values for the first section are determined by the following formulas, where $\alpha = 1.3596$, $\beta = 0.4071$, and $A = 2$:

$$C_1 = (A + 1)\left(1 + \frac{\beta^2}{\alpha^2}\right) = 3\left(1 + \frac{0.4071^2}{1.3596^2}\right) = 3.27 \text{ F} \tag{3-14}$$

$$R_1 = \frac{\alpha}{A(\alpha^2 + \beta^2)} = \frac{1.3596}{2(1.3596^2 + 0.4071^2)} = 0.3375 \text{ } \Omega \tag{3-15}$$

$$R_2 = \frac{AR_1}{A+1} = \frac{2 \times 0.3375}{3} = 0.225 \text{ } \Omega \tag{3-16}$$

$$R_3 = AR_1 = 2 \times 0.3375 = 0.675 \text{ } \Omega \tag{3-17}$$

The remaining pole pair of $\alpha = 0.9877$ and $\beta = 1.2476$ is used to compute the component values of the second section.

$$C_1 = \frac{1}{\alpha} = \frac{1}{0.9877} = 1.012 \text{ F} \tag{3-9}$$

$$C_2 = \frac{\alpha}{\alpha^2 + \beta^2} = \frac{0.9877}{0.9877^2 + 1.2476^2} = 0.39 \text{ F} \tag{3-10}$$

The normalized low-pass filter is shown in figure 3-19b.

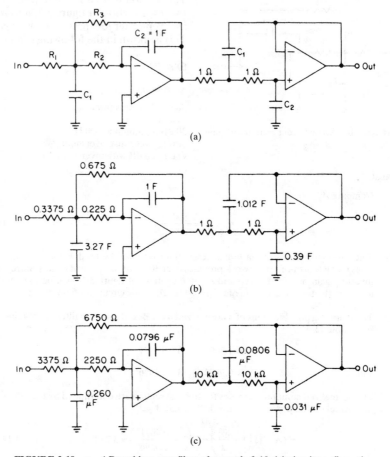

FIGURE 3-19 $n = 4$ Bessel low-pass filter of example 3-10: (a) circuit configuration; (b) normalized filter; (c) frequency- and impedance-scaled filter.

(d) Using an FSF of $2\pi f_c$ or 1256 and an impedance-scaling factor of 10^4 for both sections, the denormalized values are

$n = 2$ section with $A = 2$:

$$R_1' = R \times Z = 0.3375 \times 10^4 = 3375 \ \Omega \tag{2-8}$$

$$R_2' = 2250 \ \Omega$$

$$R_3' = 6750 \ \Omega$$

$$C_1' = \frac{C}{FSF \times Z} = \frac{3.27}{1256 \times 10^4} = 0.260 \ \mu F \tag{2-10}$$

$$C_2' = 0.0796 \ \mu F$$

$n = 2$ section having unity gain:

$$R' = 10 \text{ k}\Omega$$

$$C_1' = \frac{C}{FSF \times Z} = \frac{1.012}{1256 \times 10^4} = 0.0806 \, \mu F \qquad (2\text{-}10)$$

$$C_2' = 0.0310 \, \mu F$$

The final circuit is shown in figure 3-19c.

VCVS Uniform Capacitor Structure

The unity-gain n-2 all-pole configuration of figure 3-13a requires unequal capacitor values and noninteger capacitor ratios. This inconvenience usually results in either the use of nonstandard capacitor values or the paralleling of two or more standard values.

An alternate configuration is given in this section. This structure features equal capacitors. However, the circuit sensitivities are somewhat higher than the previously discussed configuration. Nevertheless the more convenient capacitor values may justify its use in many instances where higher sensitivities are tolerable.

The $n = 2$ low-pass circuit of figure 3-20 features equal capacitors and a gain of 2. The element values are computed as follows:

Select C.

Then
$$R_1 = \frac{1}{2\alpha' C} \qquad (3\text{-}18)$$

and
$$R_2 = \frac{2\alpha'}{C(\alpha'^2 + \beta'^2)} \qquad (3\text{-}19)$$

where α' and β' are the denormalized real and imaginary pole coordinates. R may be conveniently chosen.

EXAMPLE 3-11

REQUIRED: Design a fourth-order 0.1-dB Chebyshev active low-pass filter for a 3-dB cutoff of 100 Hz using 0.01-μF capacitors throughout.

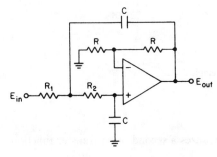

FIGURE 3-20 All-pole configuration.

RESULT:

(a) The pole locations for a normalized 0.1-dB Chebyshev low-pass filter are obtained from table 11-23 and are as follows:

$$\alpha = 0.2177 \qquad \beta = 0.9254$$

and
$$\alpha = 0.5257 \qquad \beta = 0.3833$$

(b) Two sections of the filter of figure 3-20 will be cascaded. The value of C is 0.01 μF, and R is chosen at 10 kΩ.

Section 1:

$$\alpha = 0.2177 \qquad \alpha' = \alpha \times \text{FSF} = 136.8$$

$$\beta = 0.9254 \qquad \alpha' = \beta \times \text{FSF} = 581.4$$

where $\text{FSF} = 2\pi f_c = 628.3$

$$R_1 = \frac{1}{2\alpha' C} = 365.5 \text{ k}\Omega \tag{3-18}$$

$$R_2 = \frac{2\alpha'}{C(\alpha'^2 + \beta'^2)} = 76.7 \text{ k}\Omega \tag{3-19}$$

Section 2:

$$\alpha = 0.5257 \qquad \alpha' = 330.3$$

$$\beta = 0.3833 \qquad \beta' = 240.8$$

$$R_1 = 151.4 \text{ k}\Omega \tag{3-18}$$

$$R_2 = 395.4 \text{ k}\Omega \tag{3-19}$$

The final filter is shown in figure 3-21. The gain is 2^2, or 4.

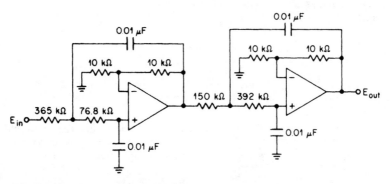

FIGURE 3-21   Equal capacitor circuit of example 3-11.

Low-Sensitivity Second-Order Section

The low-pass filter section of figure 3-22 realizes a second-order transfer function which can be expressed as

$$T(s) = \frac{1}{\tau_1 \tau_2 s^2 + \tau_2 s + 1} \tag{3-20}$$

where $\tau_1 = R_1 C_1$ and $\tau_2 = R_2 C_2$.

If we first equate equation 3-20 with equation 3-7, the general form for a second-order transfer function, and then solve for R_1 and R_2, we obtain

$$R_1 = \frac{1}{2\alpha C_1} \tag{3-21}$$

and
$$R_2 = \frac{2\alpha}{(\alpha^2 + \beta^2)C_2} \tag{3-22}$$

Two important observations can be made from figure 3-22 and the associated design equations. Since both operational amplifiers are configured as voltage followers, the circuit sensitivity to amplifier open-loop gain is not as severe as for the previous circuit which requires a gain of 2. Secondly, both the transfer function and design equations clearly indicate that the circuit operation is dictated by two time constants, R_1C_1 and R_2C_2. Thus C_1 and C_2 can be independently selected for convenient values or made equal, as desired.

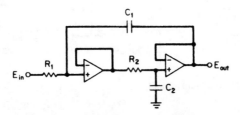

FIGURE 3-22   Low-sensitivity second-order section.

Example 3-12 illustrates the application of this configuration.

EXAMPLE 3-12

REQUIRED: Design a fourth-order 0.1-dB Chebyshev low-pass filter for a 3-dB cutoff frequency of 10 kHz using the low-sensitivity second-order section.

RESULT:

(*a*) The pole locations for a normalized 0.1-dB Chebyshev low-pass filter are given in the table 11-23 and are as follows:

$$\alpha = 0.2177 \qquad \beta = 0.9254$$
and
$$\alpha = 0.5257 \qquad \beta = 0.3833$$

(*b*) Denormalizing the pole locations (multiply α and β by the FSF):

$$\alpha' = 13{,}678 \qquad \beta' = 58{,}145$$
and
$$\alpha' = 33{,}031 \qquad \beta' = 24{,}083$$

(*c*) Compute the component values as follows:
Section 1:

$$\alpha' = 13{,}678 \qquad \beta' = 58{,}145$$

Let $C_1 = C_2 = 0.001 \; \mu F$

$$R_1 = \frac{1}{2\alpha C_1} = 36.56 \; k\Omega \tag{3-21}$$

$$R_2 = \frac{2\alpha}{(\alpha^2 + \beta^2)C_2} = 7.667 \; k\Omega \tag{3-22}$$

Section 2:

$$\alpha' = 33{,}031 \qquad \beta' = 24{,}083$$

$$R_1 = 15.14 \text{ k}\Omega \tag{3-21}$$

$$R_2 = 39.53 \text{ k}\Omega \tag{3-22}$$

The resulting circuit is shown in figure 3-23. The overall gain is unity.

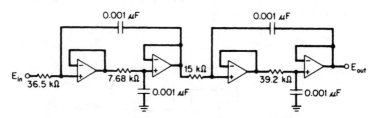

FIGURE 3-23   Circuit of example 3-12.

Elliptic-Function VCVS Filters

Elliptic-function filters were first discussed in section 2.9. They contain zeros as well as poles. The zeros begin just outside the passband and force the response to decrease rapidly as Ω_s is approached. (Refer to figure 2-82 for frequency-response definitions.)

Because of these finite zeros, the active filter circuit configurations of the previous section cannot be used, since they are restrained to the realization of poles only.

The schematic of an elliptic-function low-pass filter section is shown in figure 3-24*a*. This section provides a pair of complex conjugate poles and a pair of imaginary zeros as shown in figure 3-24*b*. The complex pole pair has a real component of α and an imaginary coordinate of β. The zeros are located at $\pm j\omega_\infty$. The RC section consisting of R_5 and C_5 introduces a real pole at α_0.

The configuration contains a voltage-controlled voltage source (VCVS) as the active element and is frequently referred to as a VCVS realization. Although this structure requires additional elements when compared with other VCVS configurations, it has been found to yield more reliable results and has lower sensitivity factors.

The normalized element values are determined by the following relations:
First calculate

$$a = \frac{2\alpha'}{\sqrt{\alpha'^2 + \beta'^2}} \tag{3-23}$$

$$b = \frac{\omega_\infty'^2}{\alpha'^2 + \beta'^2} \tag{3-24}$$

$$c = \sqrt{\alpha'^2 + \beta'^2} \tag{3-25}$$

where α', β', and ω_∞' are the denormalized pole-zero coordinates.

A controlled amplification of K is required between the noninverting amplifier input and the section output. Since the gain of a noninverting operational amplifier

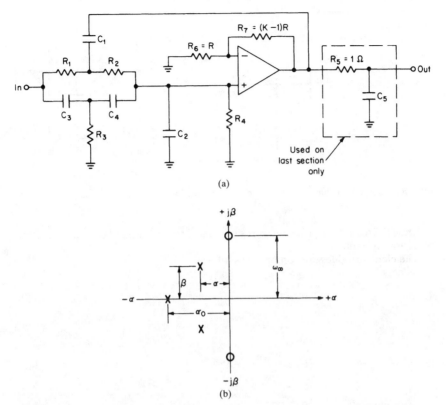

FIGURE 3-24 Elliptic-function low-pass filter section: (a) VCVS circuit configuration for $K > 1$; (b) pole-zero pattern.

is the ratio of the feedback resistors plus 1, R_6 and R_7 are R and $(K - 1) R$, respectively, where R can be any convenient value.

In the event that K is less than 1, the amplifier is reconfigured as a voltage follower and R_4 is split into two resistors R_{4a} and R_{4b} where

$$R_{4a} = (1 - K)R_4 \qquad (3\text{-}26)$$

$$R_{4b} = KR_4 \qquad (3\text{-}27)$$

The modified circuit is shown in figure 3-25.

The design of active elliptic-function filters proceeds in a manner similar to the design of the all-pole types. A low-pass requirement is first converted to a steepness factor A_s. A normalized low-pass filter is selected that meets the required passband to stopband transition steepness by having an Ω_s not in excess of A_s. The passband ripple as determined by the reflection coefficient ρ and the stopband attenuation A_{min} should also satisfy the specification. The filter complexity can first be estimated using the curves of figure 2-86 and a satisfactory design selected from the table. Alternatively, the tables can be approached directly and a filter can be chosen based on the tabulated design parameters.

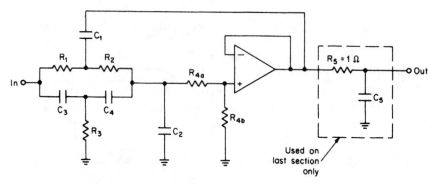

FIGURE 3-25   Elliptic-function VCVS low-pass filter section for $K < 1$.

The selected filter's poles and zeros are scaled to the required cutoff frequency f_c by denormalization.

The element values are computed as follows:

Select C.

Then
$$C_1 = C \tag{3-28}$$

$$C_3 = C_4 = \frac{C_1}{2} \tag{3-29}$$

let
$$C_2 \geq \frac{C_1(b-1)}{4} \tag{3-30}$$

$$R_3 = \frac{1}{cC_1\sqrt{b}} \tag{3-31}$$

$$R_1 = R_2 = 2R_3 \tag{3-32}$$

$$R_4 = \frac{4\sqrt{b}}{cC_1(1-b) + 4cC_2} \tag{3-33}$$

$$K = 2 + \frac{2C_2}{C_1} - \frac{a}{2\sqrt{b}} + \frac{2}{C_1\sqrt{b}}\left(\frac{1}{cR_4} - aC_2\right) \tag{3-34}$$

$$\text{Section gain} = \frac{bKC_1}{4C_2 + C_1} \tag{3-35}$$

Capacitor C_5 is determined from the denormalized real pole by

$$C_5 = \frac{1}{R_5\alpha_0'} \tag{3-36}$$

where both R and R_5 can be arbitrarily chosen and α_0' is $\alpha_0 \times$ FSF.

Zverev and Christian (see bibliography) have extensively tabulated design data for elliptic-function filters, including pole-zero locations. Some of Zverev's data is reproduced in table 11-56 and contain pole-zero parameters.

Odd-order elliptic-function filters are more efficient than even-order since maximum utilization is made of the number of component elements used. Since the circuit of figure 3-24 provides a single pole pair (along with a pair of zeros), the total number of sections required for an odd-order filter is determined by $(n-1)/2$, where n is the order of the filter. Because an odd-order transfer function has a single real pole, R_5 and C_5 appear on the output section only.

In the absence of a detailed analysis, it is a good rule of thumb to pair poles with their nearest zeros when allocating poles and zeros to each active section. This applies to high-pass, bandpass, and band-reject filters as well.

EXAMPLE 3-13

REQUIRED: Design an active elliptic-function low-pass filter corresponding to CO3 20 $\theta = 20°$ from table 11-56 for a cutoff of 100 Hz using the VCVS structure of figure 3-24.

RESULT:

(a) The following parameters are obtained from table 11-56:

$$n = 3$$

$$R_{dB} = 0.18 \text{ dB}$$

$$\Omega_s = 2.924$$

$$A_{min} = 37.44 \text{ dB}$$

The normalized poles and zeros are given as

$$\alpha = 0.3862 \quad \beta = 1.1390 \quad \omega_\infty = 3.350$$

$$\alpha_0 = 0.8867$$

(b) The poles and zeros are denormalized as follows:

$$\alpha' = \alpha \times FSF = 242.7$$

$$\beta' = \beta \times FSF = 715.7$$

$$\omega'_\infty = \omega_\infty \times FSF = 2105$$

$$\alpha'_0 = \alpha_0 \times FSF = 557.1$$

where $FSF = 2\pi f_c = 628.3$.

(c) The element values are computed as follows:

	$a = 0.6423$	(3-23)
	$b = 7.7584$	(3-24)
	$c = 755.7$	(3-25)
Select	$C_1 = C = 0.1 \ \mu F$	(3-28)
	$C_3 = C_4 = 0.05 \ \mu F$	(3-29)
	$C_2 \geq 0.169 \ \mu F$	(3-30)
Let	$C_2 = 0.22 \ \mu F$	
	$R_3 = 4751 \ \Omega$	(3-31)
	$R_1 = R_2 = 9502 \ \Omega$	(3-32)

$$R_4 = 72.2 \text{ k}\Omega \tag{3-33}$$

$$K = 5.402 \tag{3-34}$$

Let $\qquad R = R_5 = 10 \text{ k}\Omega$

then $\qquad C_5 = 0.180 \text{ }\mu\text{F} \tag{3-36}$

The resulting circuit is shown in figure 3-26.

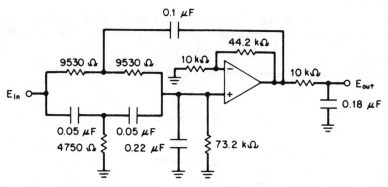

FIGURE 3-26   Circuit for active elliptic-function low-pass filter.

State-Variable Low-Pass Filters

The poles and zeros of the previously discussed active filter configurations cannot be easily adjusted because of the interaction of circuit elements. For most industrial requirements, sufficient accuracy is obtained by specifying 1% resistors and 1 or 2% capacitors. In the event that greater precision is required, the state-variable approach features independent adjustment of the pole and zero coordinates. Also, the state-variable configuration has a lower sensitivity to many of the inadequacies of operational amplifiers such as finite bandwidth and gain.

All-Pole Configuration.   The circuit of figure 3-27 realizes a single pair of complex poles. The low-pass transfer function is given by

$$T(s) = \frac{1}{R_2 R_4 C^2} \; \frac{1}{s^2 + \dfrac{1}{R_1 C} s + \dfrac{1}{R_2 R_3 C^2}} \tag{3-37}$$

If we equate equation (3-37) to the second-order low-pass transfer function expressed by equation (3-8) and solve for the element values, after some algebraic manipulation we obtain the following design equations:

$$R_1 = \frac{1}{2\alpha C} \tag{3-38}$$

$$R_2 = R_3 = R_4 = \frac{1}{C\sqrt{\alpha^2 + \beta^2}} \tag{3-39}$$

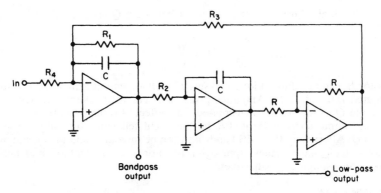

FIGURE 3-27 State-variable all-pole low-pass configuration.

where α and β are the real and imaginary components, respectively, of the pole locations and C is arbitrary. The value of R in figure 3-27 is also optional.

The element values computed by equations (3-38) and (3-39) result in a DC gain of unity. If a gain of A is desired, R_4 can instead be defined by

$$R_4 = \frac{1}{AC\sqrt{\alpha^2 + \beta^2}} \quad (3\text{-}40)$$

Sometimes it is desirable to design a filter directly at its cutoff frequency instead of calculating the normalized values and then frequency- and impedance-scaling the normalized network. Equations (3-38) and (3-39) result in the denormalized values if α and β are first denormalized by the frequency-scaling factor FSF as follows:

$$\alpha' = \alpha \times \text{FSF} \quad (3\text{-}41)$$

$$\beta' = \beta \times \text{FSF} \quad (3\text{-}42)$$

Direct design of the denormalized filter is especially advantageous when the design formulas permit the arbitrary selection of capacitors and all network capacitors are equal. A standard capacitance value can then be chosen.

Figure 3-27 indicates that a bandpass output is also provided. Although a discussion of bandpass filters will be deferred until chapter 5, this output is useful for tuning of the low-pass filter. To adjust the low-pass real and imaginary pole coordinates, first compute the bandpass resonant frequency:

$$f_0 = \frac{\sqrt{(\alpha')^2 + (\beta')^2}}{2\pi} \quad (3\text{-}43)$$

Trim the value of R_3 until resonant conditions occur at the bandpass output with f_0 applied. Resonance can be determined by exactly 180° of phase shift between input and output or by peak output amplitude. The 180° phase shift method normally results in more accuracy and resolution. By connecting the vertical channel of an oscilloscope to the section input and the horizontal channel to the bandpass output, a *Lissajous pattern* is obtained. This pattern is an ellipse that will collapse to a straight line (at a 135° angle) when the phase shift is 180°.

For the final adjustment, trim R_1 for a bandpass Q (i.e., f_0/3-dB bandwidth) equal to

$$Q = \frac{\pi f_0}{\alpha'} \qquad (3\text{-}44)$$

Resistor R_1 can be adjusted for a measured bandpass output gain at f_0 equal to the computed ratio of R_1/R_4. Amplifier phase shift creates a Q-enhancement effect where the Q of the section is increased. This effect also increases the gain at the bandpass output; so adjustment of R_1 for the calculated gain will usually restore the desired Q. Alternately, the 3-dB bandwidth can be measured and the Q computed. Although the Q measurement approach is the more accurate method, it certainly is slower than a simple gain adjustment.

EXAMPLE 3-14

REQUIRED:

Active low-pass filter
3 dB ± 0.25 dB at 500 Hz
40 dB minimum at 1375 Hz

RESULT:

(a) Compute A_s.

$$A_s = \frac{1375}{500} = 2.75 \qquad (2\text{-}11)$$

(b) Figure 2-42 indicates that a fourth-order 0.1-dB Chebyshev low-pass filter has over 40 dB of rejection at 2.75 rad/s. Since a precise cutoff is required, we will use the state-variable approach so that the filter parameters can be adjusted if necessary.
The pole locations for a normalized fourth-order 0.1-dB Chebyshev low-pass filter are obtained from table 11-23 and are as follows:

$$\alpha = 0.2183 \qquad \beta = 0.9262$$
and
$$\alpha = 0.5271 \qquad \beta = 0.3836$$

(c) Two sections of the circuit of figure 3-27 will be cascaded. The denormalized filter will be designed directly. The capacitor value C is chosen to be 0.01 μF, and R is arbitrarily selected to be 10 kΩ.
Section 1:

$$\alpha = 0.2183 \qquad \alpha' = \alpha \times FSF = 685.5 \qquad (3\text{-}41)$$

$$\beta = 0.9262 \qquad \beta' = \beta = FSF = 2908 \qquad (3\text{-}42)$$

where $FSF = 2\pi f_c = 2\pi500 = 3140$

$$R_1 = \frac{1}{2\,\alpha'\,C} = 72.94 \text{ k}\Omega \qquad (3\text{-}38)$$

$$R_2 = R_3 = R_4 = \frac{1}{C\sqrt{(\alpha')^2 + (\beta')^2}} = 33.47 \text{ k}\Omega \qquad (3\text{-}39)$$

Section 2:

$$\alpha = 0.5271 \qquad \alpha' = \alpha \times FSF = 1655 \qquad (3\text{-}41)$$

$$\beta = 0.3836 \qquad \beta' = \beta \times FSF = 1205 \qquad (3\text{-}42)$$

where FSF = 3140

$$R_1 = \frac{1}{2\,\alpha'\,C} = 30.21 \text{ k}\Omega \tag{3-38}$$

$$R_2 = R_3 = R_4 = \frac{1}{C\sqrt{(\alpha')^2 + (\beta')^2}} = 48.85 \text{ k}\Omega \tag{3-39}$$

(d) The resulting filter is shown in figure 3-28. The resistor values have been modified so that standard 1 percent resistors are used and adjustment capability is provided.
  The bandpass resonant frequency and Q are
  Section 1:

$$f_0 = \frac{\sqrt{(\alpha')^2 + (\beta')^2}}{2\pi} = 476 \text{ Hz} \tag{3-43}$$

$$Q = \frac{\pi f_0}{\alpha'} = 2.18 \tag{3-44}$$

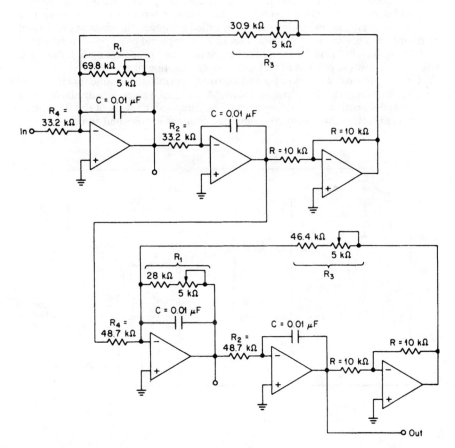

FIGURE 3-28   State-variable low-pass filter of example 3-14.

Section 2:

$$f_0 = 326 \text{ Hz} \tag{3-43}$$

$$Q = 0.619 \tag{3-44}$$

Elliptic-Function Configuration. When precise control of the parameters of elliptic-function filters is required, a state-variable elliptic-function approach is necessary. This is especially true in the case of very sharp filters where the location of the poles and zeros is highly critical.

The circuit of figure 3-29 has the transfer function

$$T(s) = -\frac{R_6}{R} \frac{s^2 + \dfrac{1}{R_2 R_3 C^2}\left(1 + \dfrac{R_3 R}{R_4 R_5}\right)}{s^2 + \dfrac{1}{R_1 C}s + \dfrac{1}{R_2 R_3 C^2}} \tag{3-45}$$

where $R_1 = R_4$ and $R_2 = R_3$. The numerator roots result in a pair of imaginary zeros, and the denominator roots determine a pair of complex poles. Since both the numerator and denominator are second-order, this transfer function form is frequently referred to as *biquadratic* and the circuit is called a *biquad*. The zeros are restricted to frequencies beyond the pole locations, i.e., the stopband of elliptic-function low-pass filters. If R_5 in figure 3-29 were connected to node 2 instead of node 1, the zeros will occur below the poles as in high-pass elliptic-function filters.

Table 11-56 provides the poles and zeros for normalized elliptic-function low-pass filters alongside the element values. Additional values are available from Zverev and Christian (see bibliography). The component values of the denormalized biquad section can be directly computed from these poles and zeros.

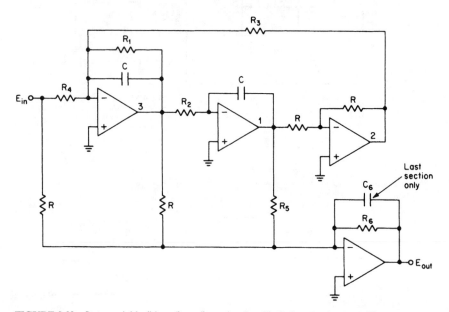

FIGURE 3-29 State-variable (biquad) configuration for elliptic-function low-pass filters.

First denormalize the tabulated pole coordinates α and β and the zero ω_∞ as follows:

$$\alpha' = \alpha \times \text{FSF} \tag{3-46}$$

$$\beta' = \beta \times \text{FSF} \tag{3-47}$$

$$\omega'_\infty = \omega_\infty \times \text{FSF} \tag{3-48}$$

where FSF is the desired frequency-scaling factor.

Compute the bandpass resonant frequency in radians per second:

$$\omega'_0 = \sqrt{(\alpha')^2 + (\beta')^2} \tag{3-49}$$

The component values are

$$R_1 = R_4 = \frac{1}{2\alpha' C} \tag{3-50}$$

$$R_2 = R_3 = \frac{1}{\omega'_0 C} \tag{3-51}$$

$$R_5 = \frac{2\alpha' \omega'_0 R}{(\omega'_\infty)^2 - (\omega'_0)^2} \tag{3-52}$$

$$R_6 = \left(\frac{\omega'_0}{\omega'_\infty}\right)^2 AR \tag{3-53}$$

where C and R are arbitrary and A is the desired low-pass gain at DC.

Since odd-order elliptic-function filters contain a real pole, the last section of a cascade of biquads should contain capacitor C_6 in parallel with R_6. To compute C_6, first denormalize the real pole α_0 as follows:

$$\alpha'_0 = \alpha_0 \times \text{FSF} \tag{3-54}$$

then
$$C_6 = \frac{1}{\alpha'_0 R_6} \tag{3-55}$$

The poles and zeros of the biquad configuration of figure 3-29 can be adjusted by implementing the following sequence of steps:

1. *Resonant frequency:*   The bandpass resonant frequency is defined by

$$f_0 = \frac{\omega'_0}{2\pi} \tag{3-56}$$

If R_3 is made adjustable, the section resonant frequency can be tuned to f_0 by monitoring the bandpass output at node 3. The 180° phase shift method is preferred for the determination of resonance.

2. *Q adjustment:*   The bandpass Q is given by

$$Q = \frac{\pi f_0}{\alpha'} \tag{3-57}$$

Adjustment of R_1 for unity gain at f_0 measured between the section input and the bandpass output at node 3 will usually compensate for any Q enhancement resulting from amplifier phase shift.

3. *Notch frequency:*   The notch frequency is given by

$$f_\infty = \omega_\infty \times f_c \qquad (3\text{-}58)$$

Adjustment of f_∞ usually is not required if the circuit is first tuned to f_0, since f_∞ will then fall in. However, if independent tuning of the notch frequency is desired, R_5 should be made variable. The notch frequency is measured by determining the input frequency where E_{out} is nulled.

EXAMPLE 3-15

REQUIRED:

Active low-pass filter
0.5-dB maximum ripple below 1000 Hz
18-dB minimum rejection above 1600 Hz

RESULT:

(a) Compute the steepness factor:

$$A_s = \frac{f_s}{f_c} = \frac{1600}{1000} = 1.6 \qquad (2\text{-}11)$$

(b) Select a normalized elliptic-function low-pass filter from table 11-56 that makes the transition from less than 0.5- to over 18-dB rejection within a frequency ratio of 1.6. A filter corresponding to C03 20 $\theta = 40°$ has the following parameters:

$$n = 3$$

$$R_{dB} = 0.28 \text{ dB}$$

$$\Omega_s = 1.556$$

$$A_{min} = 18.56 \text{ dB}$$

The normalized complex poles and zeros are

$$\alpha = 0.2849 \qquad \beta = 1.1484$$

$$\omega_\infty = 1.742$$

and the real pole is located at

$$\alpha_0 = 1.0577$$

(c) A state-variable approach will be used employing the biquad configuration of figure 3-29. The frequency-scaling factor is

$$FSF = 2\pi f_c = 2\pi 1000 = 6280$$

The poles and zeros are denormalized as follows:
   Complex Poles and Zeros:

$$\alpha = 0.2849 \qquad \alpha' = \alpha \times FSF = 1789 \qquad (3\text{-}46)$$

$$\beta = 1.1484 \qquad \beta' = \beta \times FSF = 7212 \qquad (3\text{-}47)$$

$$\omega_\infty = 1.742 \qquad \omega'_\infty = \omega_\infty \times FSF = 10{,}940 \qquad (3\text{-}48)$$

   Real Pole:

$$\alpha_0 = 1.0577 \qquad \alpha'_0 = \alpha_0 \times FSF = 6642 \qquad (3\text{-}54)$$

(d) A single section is required. Let $R = 100$ kΩ and $C = 0.1$ µF, and let the gain equal unity ($A = 1$). The values are computed as follows:

$$\omega'_0 = \sqrt{(\alpha')^2 + (\beta')^2} = 7431 \tag{3-49}$$

$$R_1 = R_4 = \frac{1}{2\alpha' C} = 2795 \ \Omega \tag{3-50}$$

$$R_2 = R_3 = \frac{1}{\omega'_0 C} = 1346 \ \Omega \tag{3-51}$$

$$R_5 = \frac{2\alpha'\omega'_0 R}{(\omega'_\infty)^2 - (\omega'_0)^2} = 41.24 \ \text{k}\Omega \tag{3-52}$$

$$R_6 = \left(\frac{\omega'_0}{\omega'_\infty}\right)^2 AR = 46.14 \ \text{k}\Omega \tag{3-53}$$

Since a real pole is also required, C_6 is introduced in parallel with R_6 and is calculated by

$$C_6 = \frac{1}{\alpha'_0 R_6} = 3260 \ \text{pF} \tag{3-55}$$

(e) The resulting filter is shown in figure 3-30. The resistor values are modified so that standard 1% values are used and the circuit is adjustable. The sections f_0 and Q are computed by

$$f_0 = \frac{\omega'_0}{2\pi} = 1183 \ \text{Hz} \tag{3-56}$$

$$Q = \frac{\pi f_0}{\alpha'} = 2.08 \tag{3-57}$$

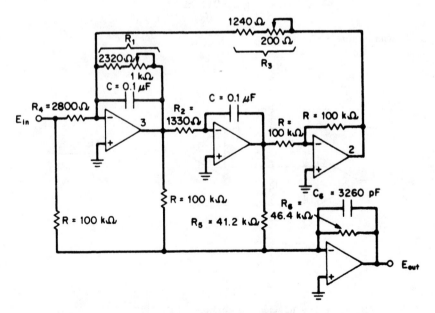

FIGURE 3-30 Elliptic-function low-pass filter of example 3-15.

The frequency of infinite attenuation is given by

$$f_\infty = \omega_\infty \times f_c = 1742 \text{ Hz} \qquad (3\text{-}58)$$

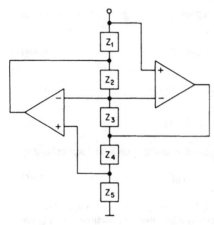

FIGURE 3-31 Generalized impedance converter (GIC).

Generalized Impedance Converters

The circuit of figure 3-31 is known as a generalized impedance converter (GIC). The driving-point impedance can be expressed as

$$Z_{11} = \frac{Z_1 Z_3 Z_5}{Z_2 Z_4} \qquad (3\text{-}59)$$

By substituting RC combinations of up to two capacitors for Z_1 through Z_5, a variety of impedances can be simulated. If, for instance, Z_4 consists of a capacitor having an impedance $1/sC$, where $s = j\omega$ and all other elements are resistors, the driving-point impedance is given by

$$Z_{11} = \frac{sCR_1 R_3 R_5}{R_2} \qquad (3\text{-}60)$$

The impedance is proportional to frequency and is therefore identical to an inductor having a value of

$$L = \frac{CR_1 R_3 R_5}{R_2} \qquad (3\text{-}61)$$

as shown in figure 3-32.

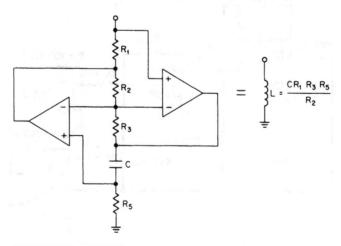

FIGURE 3-32   GIC inductor simulation.

If two capacitors are introduced for Z_1 and Z_3 and Z_2, Z_4, and Z_5 are resistors, the resulting driving-point impedance expression can be expressed in the form of

$$Z_{11} = \frac{R_5}{s^2 C^2 R_2 R_4} \qquad (3\text{-}62)$$

An impedance proportional to $1/s^2$ is called a D element, whose driving-point impedance is given by

$$Z_{11} = \frac{1}{s^2 D} \qquad (3\text{-}63)$$

Equation (3-62) therefore defines a D element having the value

$$D = \frac{C^2 R_2 R_4}{R_5} \qquad (3\text{-}64)$$

If we let $C = 1$ F, $R_2 = R_5 = 1\ \Omega$, and $R_4 = R$, equation (3-64) simplifies to $D = R$.

In order to gain some insight into the nature of this element, let us substitute $s = j\omega$ into equation (3-62). The resulting expression is

$$Z_{11} = -\frac{R_5}{\omega^2 C^2 R_2 R_4} \qquad (3\text{-}65)$$

Equation (3-65) corresponds to a frequency-dependent negative resistor (FDNR).

A GIC in the form of a normalized D element and its schematic designation are shown in figure 3-33. Bruton (see bibliography) has shown how the FDNR or D element can be used to generate active filters directly from the LC normalized low-pass prototype values. This technique will now be described.

The 1/s Transformation.   If all the impedances of an LC filter network are multiplied by $1/s$, the transfer function remains unchanged. This operation is equivalent to

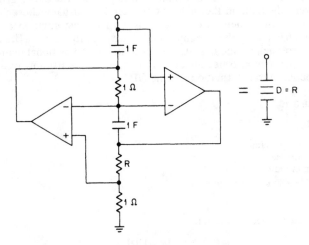

FIGURE 3-33   GIC realization of a normalized D element.

impedance-scaling a filter by the factor $1/s$ and should not be confused with the high-pass transformation which involves the substitution of $1/s$ for s. Section 2.1 under "Frequency and Impedance Scaling" demonstrated that the impedance scaling of a network by any factor Z does not change the frequency response, since the Zs cancel in the transfer function; so the validity of this transformation should be apparent.

When the elements of a network are impedance-scaled by $1/s$, they undergo a change in form. Inductors are transformed into resistors, resistors into capacitors, and capacitors into D elements as summarized in table 3-1. Clearly, this design technique is extremely powerful. It enables us to design active filters directly from the passive LC circuits, which are extensively tabulated. Knowledge of the pole and zero locations is unnecessary.

TABLE 3-1   The $1/s$ Impedance Transformation

Element	Impedance	Transformed Element	Transformed Impedance
L	sL	L	L
C	$\dfrac{1}{sC}$	C	$\dfrac{1}{s^2C}$
R	R	$\dfrac{1}{R}$	$\dfrac{R}{s}$

The design method proceeds by first selecting a normalized low-pass LC filter. All capacitors must be restricted to the shunt arms only, since they will be transformed into D elements which are connected to ground. The dual LC filter defined by the lower schematic in the tables of chapter 11 is usually chosen to be transformed. The circuit elements are modified by the $1/s$ transformation, and the D elements are realized using the normalized GIC circuit of figure 3-33. The transformed filter is then frequency- and impedance-scaled in the conventional manner. The following example demonstrates the design of an all-pole active low-pass filter using the $1/s$ impedance transformation and the GIC.

EXAMPLE 3-16

REQUIRED:

Active low-pass filter
3 dB to 400 Hz
20 dB minimum at 1200 Hz
Minimal ringing and overshoot

RESULT:

(a) Compute the steepness factor.

$$A_s = \frac{f_s}{f_c} = \frac{1200}{400} = 3 \tag{2-11}$$

(b) Since low transient distortion is desired, a linear phase filter with a phase error of 0.5° will be selected. The curves of figure 2-62 indicate that a filter complexity of $n = 3$ provides over 20 dB of attenuation at 3 rad/s.

The $1/s$ transformation and a GIC realization will be used.

(c) The normalized LC low-pass filter from table 11-47 corresponding to $n = 3$ is shown in figure 3-34a. The dual circuit has been selected so that only a single D element will be required.

(d) The normalized filter is transformed in accordance with table 3-1, resulting in the circuit of figure 3-34b. The D element is realized using the normalized GIC configuration of figure 3-33, as shown in figure 3-34c.

(e) Since all normalized capacitors are 1 F, it would be desirable if they were all denormalized to a standard value such as 0.01 μF. Using an FSF of $2\pi f_c$ or 2513 and a C' of 0.01 μF, the required impedance-scaling factor can be found by solving equation (2-10) for Z as follows:

$$Z = \frac{C}{FSF \times C'} = \frac{1}{2513 \times 0.01 \times 10^{-6}} = 39,800 \qquad (2\text{-}10)$$

Using an FSF of $2\pi f_c$ or 2513 and an impedance-scaling factor Z of 39.8×10^3, the normalized filter is scaled by dividing all capacitors by $Z \times FSF$ and multiplying all resistors by Z. The final circuit is given in figure 3-34d. The resistor values were modified for standard 1% values. The filter loss is 6 dB, corresponding to the loss due to the resistive source and load terminations of the LC filter.

The D elements are usually realized with dual operational amplifiers which are available as a matched pair in a single package. In order to provide a bias current for the noninverting input of the upper amplifier, a resistive termination to ground must

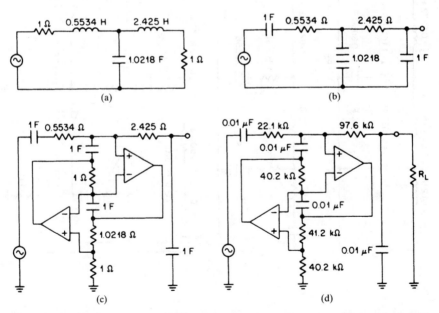

(a)

(b)

(c)

(d)

FIGURE 3-34 Network of example 3-16: (a) normalized low-pass prototype; (b) normalized circuit after $1/s$ transformation; (c) realization of D element; (d) final circuit.

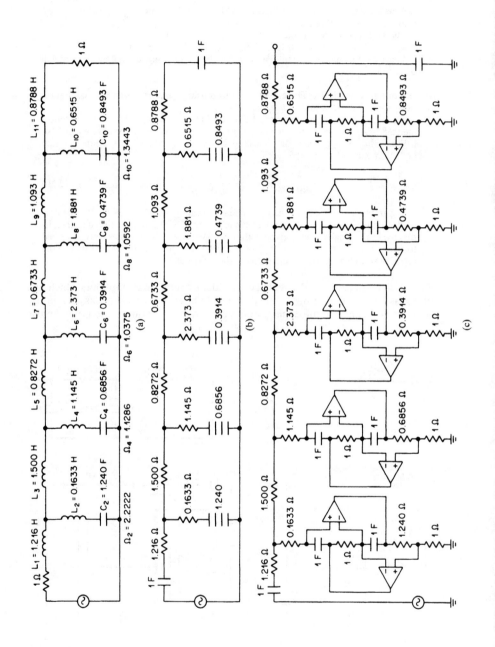

3.44

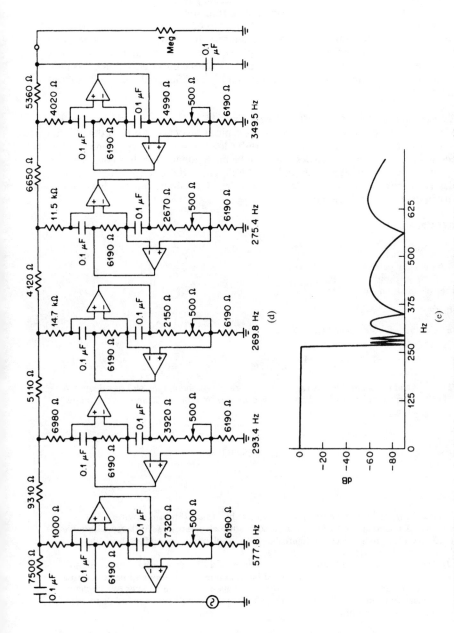

FIGURE 3-35 Filter of example 3-17: (a) normalized low-pass filter; (b) circuit after $1/s$ transformation; (c) normalized configuration using GICs for D elements; (d) denormalized filter; (e) frequency response.

be provided. This resistor will cause a low-frequency roll-off; so true DC-coupled operation will not be possible. However, if the termination is made much larger than the nominal resistor values of the circuit, the low-frequency roll-off can be made to occur well below the frequency range of interest. If a low output impedance is required, the filter can be followed by a voltage follower or an amplifier if gain is also desired. The filter input should be driven by a source impedance much less than the input resistor of the filter. A voltage follower or amplifier could be used for input isolation.

Elliptic-Function Low-Pass Filters Using the GIC.   The $1/s$ transformation and GIC realization are particularly suited for the realization of active high-order elliptic-function low-pass filters. These circuits exhibit low sensitivity to component tolerances and amplifier characteristics. They can be made tunable, are less complex than the state-variable configurations, and can be designed directly from the LC filter tables. The following example illustrates the design of an elliptic-function low-pass filter using the GIC as a D element.

EXAMPLE 3-17

REQUIRED:

Active low-pass filter
0.5 dB maximum at 260 Hz
60 dB minimum at 270 Hz

RESULT:

(a) Compute the steepness factor.

$$A_s = \frac{f_s}{f_c} = \frac{270}{260} = 1.0385 \tag{2-11}$$

(b) An extremely sharp filter is required; so an elliptic-function type will be selected. A filter corresponding to C11 20 $\theta = 75°$ is chosen from table 11-56 and has the following parameters:

$$n = 11$$

$$R_{dB} = 0.18 \text{ dB}$$

$$\Omega_s = 1.0353$$

$$A_{min} = 60.8 \text{ dB}$$

The normalized circuit corresponding to the dual filter is shown in figure 3-35a.

(c) The $1/s$ impedance transformation modifies the elements in accordance with table 3-1, resulting in the circuit of figure 3-35b. The D elements are realized using the GIC of figure 3-33, as shown in figure 3-35c.

(d) The normalized circuit can now be frequency- and impedance-scaled. Since all normalized capacitors are equal, it would be desirable if they could all be scaled to a standard value such as 0.1 μF. The required impedance-scaling factor can be determined from equation (2-10) by using an FSF of $2\pi f_c$ or 1634, corresponding to a cutoff of 260 Hz. Therefore,

$$Z = \frac{C}{\text{FSF} \times C'} = \frac{1}{1634 \times 0.1 \times 10^{-6}} = 6120 \tag{2-10}$$

Frequency and impedance scaling by dividing all capacitors by $Z \times$ FSF and multiplying all resistors by Z results in the final filter circuit of figure 3-35d having the frequency response of figure 3-35*e*. The resistor values have been modified so that 1% values are used and the transmission zeros can be adjusted. The frequency of each zero was computed by multiplying $\Omega_2, \Omega_4, \Omega_6, \Omega_8,$ and Ω_{10} by f_c. A termination is provided so that bias current can be supplied to the amplifiers.

The transmission zeros generated by the circuit of figure 3-35*d* occur because at specific frequencies the value of each FDNR is equal to the positive resistor in series, therefore creating cancellations or nulls in the shunt branches. By adjusting each *D* element, these nulls can be tuned to the required frequencies. These adjustments are usually sufficient to obtain satisfactory results. State-variable filters permit the adjustment of the poles and zeros directly for greater accuracy. However, the realization is more complex; for instance, the filter of example 3-17 would require twice as many amplifiers, resistors, and potentiometers if the state-variable approach were used.

BIBLIOGRAPHY

Bruton, L. T., "Active Filter Design Using Generalized Impedance Converters," *EDN*, February 1973.

Bruton, L. T., "Network Transfer Functions Using the Concept of Frequency-Dependent Negative Resistance," *IEEE Transactions on Circuit Theory*, vol. CT-16, pp. 406–408, August 1969.

Christian, E., and E. Eisenmann, *Filter Design Tables and Graphs*, John Wiley and Sons, New York, 1966.

Geffe, P., *Simplified Modern Filter Design*, John F. Rider, New York, 1963.

Huelsman, L. P., *Theory and Design of Active RC Circuits*, McGraw-Hill, 1968.

Saal, R., and E. Ulbrich, "On the Design of Filters by Synthesis," *IRE Transactions on Circuit Theory*, December 1958.

Saal, R., "Der Entwurf von Filtern mit Hilfe des Kataloges Normierter Tiefpasse," Telefunken GMBH, Backnang, West Germany, 1963.

Shepard, B. R., "Active Filters Part 12," *Electronics*, pp. 82–91, August 18, 1969.

Thomas, L. C., "The Biquad: Part I—Some Practical Design Considerations," *IEEE Transactions on Circuit Theory*, vol. CT-18, pp. 350–357, May 1971.

Tow, J., "A Step-by-Step Active Filter Design," *IEEE Spectrum*, vol. 6, pp. 64–68, December 1969.

Williams, A. B., "Design Active Elliptic Filters Easily from Tables," *Electronic Design*, vol. 19, no. 21, pp. 76–79, October 14, 1971.

Williams, A. B., *Active Filter Design*, Artech House, Dedham, Mass., 1975.

Zverev, A. I., *Handbook of Filter Synthesis*, John Wiley and Sons, New York, 1967.

CHAPTER 4
HIGH-PASS FILTER DESIGN

4.1 LC *HIGH-PASS FILTERS*

The Low-Pass to High-Pass Transformation

If $1/s$ is substituted for s in a normalized low-pass transfer function, a high-pass response is obtained. The low-pass attenuation values will now occur at high-pass frequencies which are the reciprocal of the corresponding low-pass frequencies. This was demonstrated in section 2.1.

A normalized LC low-pass filter can be transformed into the corresponding high-pass filter by simply replacing each coil with a capacitor and vice versa, using reciprocal element values. This can be expressed as

$$C_{hp} = \frac{1}{L_{Lp}} \tag{4-1}$$

and

$$L_{hp} = \frac{1}{C_{Lp}} \tag{4-2}$$

The source and load resistive terminations are unaffected.

The transmission zeros of a normalized elliptic-function low-pass filter are also reciprocated when the high-pass transformation occurs. Therefore,

$$\omega_{\infty}(hp) = \frac{1}{\omega_{\infty}(Lp)} \tag{4-3}$$

To minimize the number of inductors in the high-pass filter, the dual low-pass circuit defined by the lower schematic in the tables of chapter 11 is usually chosen to be transformed except for even-order all-pole filters, where either circuit may be used.

After the low-pass to high-pass transformation, the normalized high-pass filter is frequency- and impedance-scaled to the required cutoff frequency. The following two examples demonstrate the design of high-pass filters.

EXAMPLE 4-1

REQUIRED:

LC high-pass filter
3 dB at 1 MHz

28 dB minimum at 500 kHz
$R_s = R_L = 300 \ \Omega$

RESULT:

(a) To normalize the requirement, compute the high-pass steepness factor A_s.

$$A_s = \frac{f_c}{f_s} = \frac{1 \ \text{MHz}}{500 \ \text{kHz}} = 2 \tag{2-13}$$

(b) Select a normalized low-pass filter that offers over 28 dB of attenuation at 2 rad/s. Inspection of the curves of chapter 2 indicates that a normalized $n = 5$ Butterworth low-pass filter provides the required attenuation. Table 11-2 contains element values for the corresponding network. The normalized low-pass filter for $n = 5$ and equal

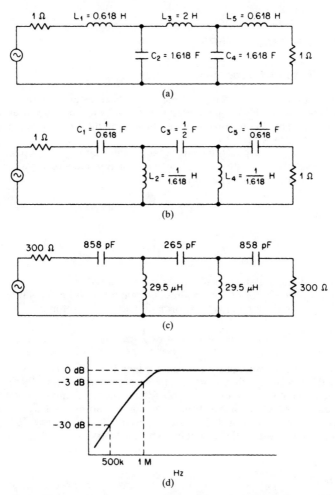

FIGURE 4-1 High-pass filter of example 4-1: (a) normalized low-pass filter; (b) high-pass transformation; (c) frequency- and impedance-scaled filter; (d) frequency response.

terminations is shown in figure 4-1a. The dual circuit as defined by the lower schematic of table 11-2 was chosen.

(c) To transform the normalized low-pass circuit to a high-pass configuration, replace each coil with a capacitor and vice versa, using reciprocal element values as shown in figure 4-1b.

(d) Denormalize the high-pass filter using a Z of 300 and a frequency-scaling factor (FSF) of $2\pi f_c$ or 6.28×10^6.

$$C_1' = \frac{C}{FSF \times Z} = \frac{\dfrac{1}{0.618}}{6.28 \times 10^6 \times 300} = 858 \text{ pF} \tag{2-10}$$

$$C_3' = 265 \text{ pF}$$

$$C_5' = 858 \text{ pF}$$

$$L_2' = \frac{L \times Z}{FSF} = \frac{\dfrac{1}{1.618} \times 300}{6.28 \times 10^6} = 29.5 \text{ μH} \tag{2-9}$$

$$L_4' = 29.5 \text{ μH}$$

The final filter is given in figure 4-1c, having the frequency response shown in figure 4-1d.

EXAMPLE 4-2

REQUIRED:

LC high-pass filter
2 dB maximum at 3220 Hz
52 dB minimum at 3020 Hz
$R_s = R_L = 300 \, \Omega$

RESULT:

(a) Compute the high-pass steepness factor A_s.

$$A_s = \frac{f_c}{f_s} = \frac{3220 \text{ Hz}}{3020 \text{ Hz}} = 1.0662 \tag{2-13}$$

(b) Since the filter requirement is very steep, an elliptic-function filter will be selected. The curves of figure 2-86 indicate that for a ρ of 20% (0.18-dB passband ripple), a filter of $n = 9$ is required. Using table 11-56, a ninth-order low-pass filter is selected that makes the transition from the passband to over 52 dB of attenuation in the stopband within a frequency ratio of 1.0662. The design corresponding to CO9 20 θ = 70° has the following parameters:

$$n = 9$$

$$R_{dB} = 0.18 \text{ dB}$$

$$\Omega_s = 1.0642$$

$$A_{min} = 53.6 \text{ dB}$$

The normalized low-pass filter corresponding to the lower schematic of the dual filter is shown in figure 4-2a.

(c) To transform the normalized low-pass circuit into a high-pass configuration, convert inductors into capacitors and vice versa, using reciprocal values. The transformed high-pass filter is illustrated in figure 4-2b. The transmission zeros occurring at Ω_2, Ω_4, Ω_6, and Ω_8 are also transformed by conversion to reciprocal values.

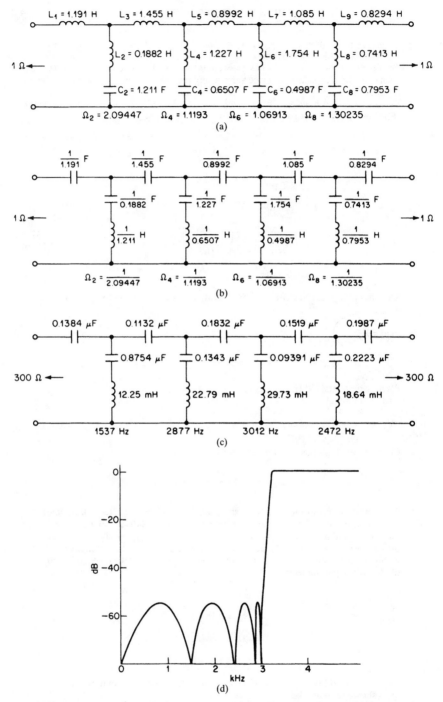

FIGURE 4-2 High-pass filter of example 4-2: (*a*) normalized CO9 20 θ = 70° low-pass filter; (*b*) transformed high-pass filter; (*c*) frequency- and impedance-scaled high-pass filter; (*d*) frequency response.

4.4

(*d*) Denormalize the high-pass filter using a *Z* of 300 and a frequency-scaling factor of $2\pi f_c$ or 20,232. The denormalized elements are computed by

$$L' = \frac{L \times Z}{\text{FSF}} \tag{2-9}$$

and

$$C' = \frac{C}{\text{FSF} \times Z} \tag{2-10}$$

The resulting denormalized high-pass filter is illustrated in figure 4-2*c*. The stopband peaks were obtained by multiplying Ω_2, Ω_4, Ω_6, and Ω_8 by the design cutoff frequency of $f_c = 3220$ Hz. The frequency response is given in figure 4-2*d*.

The T to Pi Capacitance Conversion

When the elliptic-function high-pass filters are designed for audio frequencies and at low impedance levels, the capacitor values tend to be large. The T to pi capacitance conversion will usually restore practical capacitor values.

The two circuits of figure 4-3 have identical terminal behavior and are therefore equivalent if

$$C_a = \frac{C_1 C_2}{\Sigma C} \tag{4-4}$$

$$C_b = \frac{C_1 C_3}{\Sigma C} \tag{4-5}$$

$$C_c = \frac{C_2 C_3}{\Sigma C} \tag{4-6}$$

where $\Sigma C = C_1 + C_2 + C_3$. The following example demonstrates the effectiveness of this transformation in reducing large capacitances.

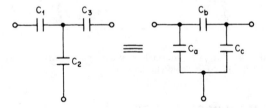

FIGURE 4-3 T to pi capacitance transformation.

EXAMPLE 4-3

REQUIRED: The high-pass filter of figure 4-2*c* contains a 0.8754-μF capacitor in the first shunt branch. Use the T to pi transformation to provide some relief.

RESULT: The circuit can be redrawn where the second series capacitor is split into two series capacitors, each having twice the original value. The modified circuit is shown in figure 4-4*a*. A T has been formed which includes the undesirable 0.8754-μF capacitor. The T to pi transformation results in

$$C_a = \frac{C_1 C_2}{\Sigma C} = 0.09769 \ \mu F \tag{4-4}$$

$$C_b = \frac{C_1 C_3}{\Sigma C} = 0.02527 \ \mu F \tag{4-5}$$

and
$$C_c = \frac{C_2 C_3}{\Sigma C} = 0.1598 \ \mu F \tag{4-6}$$

where $C_1 = 0.1384 \ \mu F$, $C_2 = 0.8754 \ \mu F$, and $C_3 = 0.2264 \ \mu F$. The transformed circuit is given in figure 4-4b, where the maximum capacitor value has undergone a 5:1 reduction.

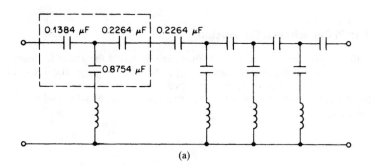

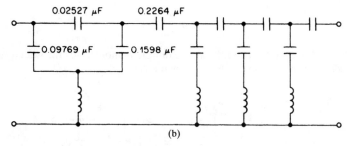

FIGURE 4-4   T to pi transformation of example 4-3: (a) high-pass filter of example 4-2; (b) modified configuration.

4.2 ACTIVE HIGH-PASS FILTERS

The Low-Pass to High-Pass Transformation

Active high-pass filters can be derived directly from the normalized low-pass configurations by a suitable transformation in a similar manner to LC high-pass filters. To make the conversion, replace each resistor by a capacitor having the reciprocal value and vice versa as follows:

$$C_{hp} = \frac{1}{R_{Lp}} \tag{4-7}$$

$$R_{hp} = \frac{1}{C_{Lp}} \tag{4-8}$$

It is important to recognize that only the resistors that are part of the low-pass RC networks are transformed into capacitors by equation (4-7). Feedback resistors that strictly determine operational amplifier gain, such as R_6 and R_7 in figure 3-20a, are omitted from the transformation.

After the normalized low-pass configuration is transformed into a high-pass filter, the circuit is frequency- and impedance-scaled in the same manner as in the design of low-pass filters. The capacitors are divided by $Z \times$ FSF and the resistors are multiplied by Z. A different Z can be used for each section, but the FSF must be uniform throughout the filter.

All-Pole High-Pass Filters. Active two-pole and three-pole low-pass filter sections were shown in figure 3-13 and correspond to the normalized active low-pass values tabulated in chapter 11. These circuits can be directly transformed into high-pass filters by replacing the resistors with capacitors and vice versa using reciprocal element values and then frequency- and impedance-scaling the filter network. The filter gain is unity at frequencies well into the passband corresponding to unity gain at DC for low-pass filters. The source impedance of the driving source should be much less than the reactance of the capacitors of the first filter section at the highest passband frequency of interest. The following example demonstrates the design of an all-pole high-pass filter.

EXAMPLE 4-4

REQUIRED:

Active high-pass filter
3 dB at 100 Hz
75 dB minimum at 25 Hz

RESULT:

(a) Compute the high-pass steepness factor.

$$A_s = \frac{f_c}{f_s} = \frac{100}{25} = 4 \tag{2-13}$$

(b) A normalized low-pass filter must first be selected that makes the transition from 3 to 75 dB within a frequency ratio of 4:1. The curves of figure 2-44 indicate that a fifth-order 0.5-dB Chebyshev filter is satisfactory. The corresponding active filter consists of a three-pole section and a two-pole section whose values are obtained from table 11-39 and is shown in figure 4-5a.

(c) To transform the normalized low-pass filter into a high-pass filter, replace each resistor with a capacitor and vice versa using reciprocal element values. The normalized high-pass filter is given in figure 4-5b.

(d) Since all normalized capacitors are equal, the impedance-scaling factor Z will be computed so that all capacitors become 0.015 μF after denormalization. Since the cutoff frequency is 100 Hz, the FSF is $2\pi f_c$ or 628, so that

$$Z = \frac{C}{\text{FSF} \times C'} = \frac{1}{628 \times 0.015 \times 10^{-6}} = 106.1 \times 10^3 \tag{2-10}$$

If we frequency- and impedance-scale the normalized high-pass filter by dividing all capacitors by $Z \times$ FSF and multiplying all resistors by Z, the circuit of figure 4-5c is obtained. The resistors were rounded off to standard 1% values.

Elliptic-Function High-Pass Filters. High-pass elliptic-function filters can be designed using the elliptic-function VCVS configuration discussed in section 3-2. This structure can introduce transmission zeros either above or below the pole locations and is, therefore, suitable for elliptic-function high-pass requirements.

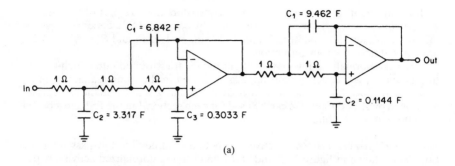

(a)

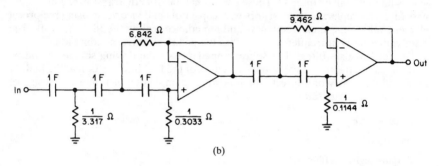

(b)

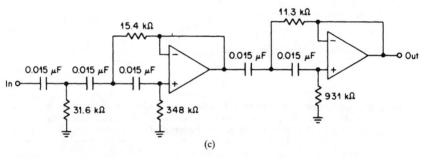

(c)

FIGURE 4-5   All-pole high-pass filter of example 4-4: (*a*) normalized low-pass filter; (*b*) high-pass transformation; (*c*) frequency- and impedance-scaled high-pass filter.

The normalized low-pass poles and zeros must first be transformed to the high-pass form. Each complex low-pass pole pair consisting of a real part α and imaginary part β is transformed into a normalized high-pass pole pair as follows:

$$\alpha_{hp} = \frac{\alpha}{\alpha^2 + \beta^2} \tag{4-9}$$

$$\beta_{hp} = \frac{\beta}{\alpha^2 + \beta^2} \tag{4-10}$$

The transformed high-pass pole pair can be denormalized by

$$\alpha'_{hp} = \alpha_{hp} \times \text{FSF} \tag{4-11}$$

$$\beta'_{hp} = \beta_{hp} \times \text{FSF} \tag{4-12}$$

where FSF is the frequency scaling factor $2\pi f_c$. If the pole is real, the normalized pole is transformed by

$$\alpha_{0,hp} = \frac{1}{\alpha_0} \tag{4-13}$$

The denormalized real pole is obtained from

$$\alpha'_{0,hp} = \alpha_{0,hp} \times \text{FSF} \tag{4-14}$$

To transform zeros, we first compute

$$\omega_\infty(hp) = \frac{1}{\omega_\infty(Lp)} \tag{4-3}$$

Denormalization occurs by

$$\omega'_\infty(hp) = \omega_\infty(hp) \times \text{FSF} \tag{4-15}$$

The elliptic-function VCVS circuit of section 3-2 is repeated in figure 4-6. The elements are computed as follows:
First calculate

$$a = \frac{2\alpha'_{hp}}{\sqrt{(\alpha'_{hp})^2 + (\beta'_{hp})^2}} \tag{4-16}$$

$$b = \frac{[\omega'_\infty(hp)]^2}{(\alpha'_{hp})^2 + (\beta'_{hp})^2} \tag{4-17}$$

$$c = \sqrt{(\alpha'_{hp})^2 + (\beta'_{hp})^2} \tag{4-18}$$

where α'_{hp}, β'_{hp}, and $\omega'_\infty(hp)$ are the denormalized high-pass pole-zero coordinates.
Select C.

$$C_1 = C \tag{4-19}$$

Then

$$C_3 = C_4 = \frac{C_1}{2} \tag{4-20}$$

Let

$$C_2 \geqq \frac{C_1(b-1)}{4} \tag{4-21}$$

$$R_3 = \frac{1}{cC_1 \sqrt{b}} \tag{4-22}$$

$$R_1 = R_2 = 2R_3 \tag{4-23}$$

$$R_4 = \frac{4\sqrt{b}}{cC_1(1-b) + 4cC_2} \tag{4-24}$$

$$K = 2 + \frac{2C_2}{C_1} - \frac{a}{2\sqrt{b}} + \frac{2}{C_1 \sqrt{b}} \left(\frac{1}{cR_4} - aC_2 \right) \tag{4-25}$$

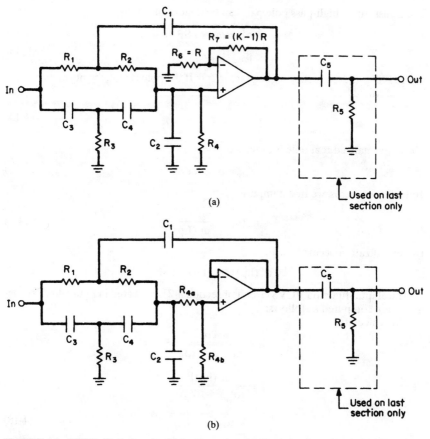

(a)

(b)

FIGURE 4-6   VCVS elliptic-function high-pass section: (*a*) circuit for $K > 1$; (*b*) circuit for $K < 1$.

$$R_6 = R \tag{4-26}$$

$$R_7 = (K - 1)R \tag{4-27}$$

where R can be arbitrarily chosen. If K is less than 1, the circuit of figure 4-6*b* is used. Then

$$R_{4a} = (1 - K)R_4 \tag{4-28}$$

$$R_{4b} = KR_4 \tag{4-29}$$

$$\text{Section gain} = \frac{bKC_1}{4C_2 + C_1} \tag{4-30}$$

R_5 is determined from the denormalized real pole by

$$R_5 = \frac{1}{C_5 \alpha'_{0,\text{hp}}} \tag{4-31}$$

where C_5 can be arbitrarily chosen and $\alpha'_{0,hp}$ is $\alpha_{0,hp} \times$ FSF. The design procedure is illustrated by example 4-5.

EXAMPLE 4-5

REQUIRED:

Active high-pass filter
0.5 dB maximum at 3000 Hz
35 dB minimum rejection at 1000 Hz

RESULT:

(a) Compute the high-pass steepness factor

$$A_s = \frac{f_c}{f_s} = \frac{3000}{1000} = 3 \qquad (2\text{-}13)$$

(b) Select a normalized low-pass filter which provides over 35 dB of rejection within a frequency ratio of 3 and has a passband ripple of less than 0.5 dB. An elliptic-function type will be used. The curves of figure 2-86 indicate that for a ρ of 20%, a third-order filter provides the required attenuation. The following parameters are found in table 11-56 for a filter corresponding to CO3 20 $\theta = 20°$

$$n = 3$$

$$\rho = 20\% \ (0.18 \text{ dB ripple})$$

$$\Omega_s = 2.924$$

$$A_{min} = 37.44 \text{ dB}$$

The corresponding normalized poles and zeros as given in the table are as follows:
Poles:

$$-0.3862 \pm j1.1396$$

$$-0.8867$$

Zero:

$$\pm j3.350$$

(c) To compute the element values, first transform the low-pass poles and zeros to the high-pass form.
Complex pole:

$$\alpha = 0.3862 \qquad \beta = 1.1396$$

$$\alpha_{hp} = 0.2667 \qquad (4\text{-}9)$$

$$\beta_{hp} = 0.7871 \qquad (4\text{-}10)$$

The pole-pair is denormalized by

$$\alpha'_{hp} = 5027 \qquad (4\text{-}11)$$

$$\beta'_{hp} = 14{,}836 \qquad (4\text{-}12)$$

where FSF $= 2\pi \times 3000$.
Real pole:

$$\alpha = 0.8867$$

$$\alpha_{0,hp} = 1.128 \qquad (4\text{-}13)$$

$$\alpha'_{0,hp} = 21{,}258 \qquad (4\text{-}14)$$

Zero:

$$\omega_\infty = 3.350$$

$$\omega_\infty(\text{hp}) = 0.2985 \tag{4-3}$$

$$\omega'_\infty(\text{hp}) = 5627 \tag{4-15}$$

(d) The results of (c) are summarized as follows:

$$\alpha'_{\text{hp}} = 5027$$

$$\beta'_{\text{hp}} = 14{,}836$$

$$\alpha'_{0,\text{hp}} = 21{,}258$$

$$\omega'_\infty(\text{hp}) = 5627$$

The element values can now be computed:

$$a = 0.6418 \tag{4-16}$$

$$b = 0.1290 \tag{4-17}$$

$$c = 15{,}665 \tag{4-18}$$

Let $\qquad\qquad\qquad C = 0.02 \ \mu\text{F}$

then $\qquad\qquad\qquad C_1 = 0.02 \ \mu\text{F} \tag{4-19}$

$$C_3 = C_4 = 0.01 \ \mu\text{F} \tag{4-20}$$

$$C_2 \geq -0.00436 \ \mu\text{F} \tag{4-21}$$

Let $\qquad\qquad\qquad C_2 = 0$

$$R_3 = 8.89 \ \text{k}\Omega \tag{4-22}$$

$$R_1 = R_2 = 17.8 \ \text{k}\Omega \tag{4-23}$$

$$R_4 = 5.26 \ \text{k}\Omega \tag{4-24}$$

$$K = 4.48 \tag{4-25}$$

Let $\qquad\qquad\qquad C_5 = 0.01 \ \mu\text{F}$

$$R_5 = 4.70 \ \text{k}\Omega \tag{4-31}$$

The resulting circuit is illustrated in figure 4-7.

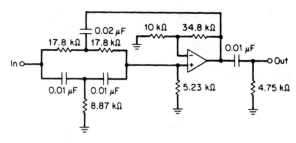

FIGURE 4-7   Circuit of example 4-5.

State-Variable High-Pass Filters

The all-pole and elliptic-function active high-pass filters previously discussed cannot be easily adjusted. If the required degree of accuracy results in unreasonable component tolerances, the state-variable or biquad approach will permit independent adjustment of the filter's pole and zero coordinates. Another feature of this circuit is the reduced sensitivity of the response to many of the amplifier limitations such as finite bandwidth and gain.

All-Pole Configuration.   In order to design a state-variable all-pole high-pass filter, the normalized low-pass poles must first undergo a low-pass to high-pass transformation. Each low-pass pole pair consisting of a real part α and imaginary part β is transformed into a normalized high-pass pole pair as follows:

$$\alpha_{hp} = \frac{\alpha}{\alpha^2 + \beta^2} \tag{4-9}$$

$$\beta_{hp} = \frac{\beta}{\alpha^2 + \beta^2} \tag{4-10}$$

The transformed high-pass pole pair can now be denormalized by

$$\alpha'_{hp} = \alpha_{hp} \times \text{FSF} \tag{4-11}$$

$$\beta'_{hp} = \beta_{hp} \times \text{FSF} \tag{4-12}$$

where FSF is the frequency-scaling factor $2\pi f_c$.
 The circuit of figure 4-8 realizes a high-pass second-order biquadratic transfer function. The element values for the all-pole case can be computed in terms of the high-pass pole coordinates as follows:
 First compute

$$\omega'_0 = \sqrt{(\alpha'_{hp})^2 + (\beta'_{hp})^2} \tag{4-32}$$

The component values are

$$R_1 = R_4 = \frac{1}{2\alpha'_{hp}C} \tag{4-33}$$

$$R_2 = R_3 = \frac{1}{\omega'_0 C} \tag{4-34}$$

$$R_5 = \frac{2\alpha'_{hp}}{\omega'_0} R \tag{4-35}$$

$$R_6 = AR \tag{4-36}$$

where C and R are arbitrary and A is the section gain.
 If the transfer function is of an odd order, a real pole must be realized. To transform the normalized low-pass real pole α_0, compute

$$\alpha_{0,hp} = \frac{1}{\alpha_0} \tag{4-13}$$

Then denormalize the high-pass real pole by

$$\alpha'_{0,hp} = \alpha_{0,hp} \times \text{FSF} \tag{4-14}$$

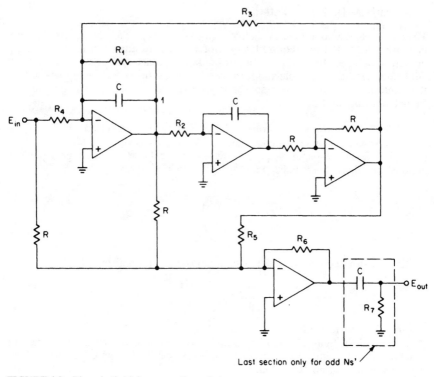

FIGURE 4-8   Biquadratic high-pass configuration.

The last section of the filter is followed by an RC network as shown in figure 4-8. The value of R_7 is computed by

$$R_7 = \frac{1}{\alpha'_{0,hp}C} \tag{4-37}$$

where C is arbitrary.

A bandpass output is provided at node 1 for tuning purposes. The bandpass resonant frequency is given by

$$f_0 = \frac{\omega'_0}{2\pi} \tag{4-38}$$

R_3 can be made adjustable and the circuit tuned to resonance by monitoring the phase shift between E_{in} and node 1 and adjusting R_3 for 180° of phase shift at f_0 using a Lissajous pattern.

The bandpass Q can then be monitored at node 1 and is given by

$$Q = \frac{\pi f_0}{\alpha'_{hp}} \tag{4-39}$$

R_1 controls the Q and can be adjusted until either the computed Q is obtained or, more conveniently, the gain is unity between E_{in} and node 1 with f_0 applied.

The following example demonstrates the design of an all-pole high-pass filter using the biquad configuration.

EXAMPLE 4-6

REQUIRED:

Active high-pass filter
3 ± 0.1 dB at 300 Hz
30 dB minimum at 120 Hz
Gain of 2

RESULT:

(a) Compute the high-pass steepness factor.

$$A_s = \frac{f_c}{f_s} = \frac{300}{120} = 2.5 \qquad (2\text{-}13)$$

(b) The curves of figure 2-45 indicate that a normalized third-order 1-dB Chebyshev low-pass filter has over 30 dB of attentuation at 2.5 rad/s. Since an accuracy of 0.1 dB is required at the cutoff frequency, a state-variable approach will be used so that adjustment capability is provided.

(c) The low-pass pole locations are found in table 11-26 and are as follows:

Complex pole $\alpha = 0.2257$ $\beta = 0.8822$

Real pole $\alpha_0 = 0.4513$

Complex pole-pair realization:
The complex low-pass pole pair is transformed to a high-pass pole pair as follows:

$$\alpha_{hp} = \frac{\alpha}{\alpha^2 + \beta^2} = \frac{0.2257}{0.2257^2 + 0.8822^2} = 0.2722 \qquad (4\text{-}9)$$

and

$$\beta_{hp} = \frac{\beta}{\alpha^2 + \beta^2} = \frac{0.8822}{0.2257^2 + 0.8822^2} = 1.0639 \qquad (4\text{-}10)$$

The transformed pole pair is then denormalized by

$$\alpha'_{hp} = \alpha_{hp} \times \text{FSF} = 513 \qquad (4\text{-}11)$$

$$\beta'_{hp} = \beta_{hp} \times \text{FSF} = 2005 \qquad (4\text{-}12)$$

where FSF is $2\,\pi f_c$ or 1885 since $f_c = 300$ Hz. If we choose $R = 10$ kΩ and $C = 0.01$ μF, the component values are calculated by

$$\omega'_0 = \sqrt{(\alpha'_{hp})^2 + (\beta'_{hp})^2} = 2070 \qquad (4\text{-}32)$$

then

$$R_1 = R_4 = \frac{1}{2\alpha'_{hp}C} = 97.47 \text{ k}\Omega \qquad (4\text{-}33)$$

$$R_2 = R_3 = \frac{1}{\omega'_0 C} = 48.31 \text{ k}\Omega \qquad (4\text{-}34)$$

$$R_5 = \frac{2\,\alpha'_{hp}}{\omega'_0} R = 4957 \text{ }\Omega \qquad (4\text{-}35)$$

$$R_6 = AR = 20 \text{ k}\Omega \qquad (4\text{-}36)$$

where $A = 2.$

The bandpass resonant frequency and Q are

$$f_0 = \frac{\omega_0'}{2\pi} = \frac{2070}{2\pi} = 329 \text{ Hz} \tag{4-38}$$

$$Q = \frac{\pi f_0}{\alpha_{hp}'} = \frac{\pi 329}{513} = 2.015 \tag{4-39}$$

Real-pole realization:
Transform the real pole:

$$\alpha_{0,hp} = \frac{1}{\alpha_0} = \frac{1}{0.4513} = 2.216 \tag{4-13}$$

To denormalize the transformed pole compute

$$\alpha_{0,hp}' = \alpha_{0,hp} \times \text{FSF} = 4177 \tag{4-14}$$

Using $C = 0.01$ μF the real pole section resistor is given by

$$R_7 = \frac{1}{\alpha_{0,hp}'} = 23.94 \text{ k}\Omega \tag{4-37}$$

The final filter configuration is shown in figure 4-9. The resistors were rounded off to standard 1% values, and R_1 and R_3 were made adjustable.

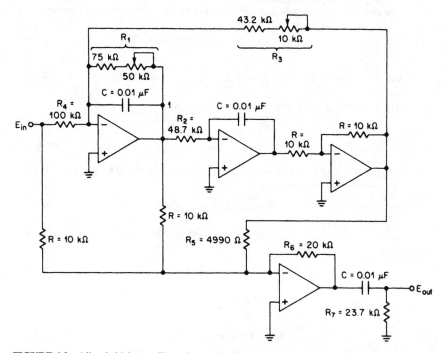

FIGURE 4-9   All-pole high-pass filter of example 4-6.

Elliptic-Function Configuration. The biquadratic configuration of figure 4-8 can also be applied to the design of elliptic-function high-pass filters. The component values are computed by using the same formulas as for the all-pole case except for R_5, which is given by

$$R_5 = \frac{2\,\alpha'_{hp}\,\omega'_0}{(\omega'_0)^2 - [\omega'_\infty(hp)]^2}\,R \tag{4-40}$$

where $\omega'_\infty(hp)$ is the denormalized high-pass transmission zero which is obtained from

$$\omega'_\infty(hp) = \omega_\infty(hp) \times FSF \tag{4-41}$$

As in the all-pole circuit, the bandpass resonant frequency f_0 is controlled by R_3 and the bandpass Q is determined by R_1. In addition, the section notch can be adjusted if R_5 is made variable. However, this adjustment is usually not required if the circuit is first tuned to f_0, since the notch will then usually fall in.

The following example illustrates the design of an elliptic-function high-pass filter using the biquad configuration of figure 4-8.

EXAMPLE 4-7

REQUIRED:

Active high-pass filter
0.3 dB maximum ripple above 1000 Hz
18 dB minimum at 635 Hz

RESULT:

(a) Compute the high-pass steepness factor.

$$A_s = \frac{f_c}{f_s} = \frac{1000}{635} = 1.575 \tag{2-13}$$

(b) An elliptic-function filter type will be used. A normalized low-pass filter corresponding to CO3 20 $\theta = 40°$ can be found in table 11-56 and has the following parameters:

$$n = 3$$

$$R_{dB} = 0.18\text{ dB}$$

$$\Omega_s = 1.556$$

$$A_{min} = 18.56\text{ dB}$$

The normalized complex poles and zeros are given as

$$\alpha = 0.2849 \qquad \beta = 1.148$$

$$\omega_\infty = 1.742$$

and a real pole is located at

$$\alpha_0 = 1.0577$$

The biquad configuration of figure 4-8 will be used.

(c) First transform the normalized complex low-pass poles and zeros to the high-pass values.

$$\alpha_{hp} = \frac{\alpha}{\alpha^2 + \beta^2} = 0.2036 \qquad (4\text{-}9)$$

$$\beta_{hp} = \frac{\beta}{\alpha^2 + \beta^2} = 0.8205 \qquad (4\text{-}10)$$

$$\omega_\infty(hp) = \frac{1}{\omega_\infty(Lp)} = \frac{1}{1.742} = 0.5741 \qquad (4\text{-}3)$$

The poles and zeros are denormalized as follows:

$$\alpha'_{hp} = \alpha_{hp} \times FSF = 1279 \qquad (4\text{-}11)$$

$$\beta'_{hp} = \beta_{hp} \times FSF = 5155 \qquad (4\text{-}12)$$

and
$$\omega'_\infty(hp) = \omega_\infty(hp) \times FSF = 3607 \qquad (4\text{-}41)$$

where $FSF = 2\pi f_c$ or 6283.

If we arbitrarily choose $C = 0.01\ \mu F$ and $R = 100\ k\Omega$, the component values can be obtained by

$$\omega'_0 = \sqrt{(\alpha'_{hp})^2 + (\beta'_{hp})^2} = 5311 \qquad (4\text{-}32)$$

then
$$R_1 = R_4 = \frac{1}{2\alpha'_{hp}C} = 39.1\ k\Omega \qquad (4\text{-}33)$$

$$R_2 = R_3 = \frac{1}{\omega'_0 C} = 18.8\ k\Omega \qquad (4\text{-}34)$$

$$R_5 = \frac{2\alpha'_{hp}\omega'_0}{(\omega'_0)^2 - [\omega'_\infty(hp)]^2} R = 89.4\ k\Omega \qquad (4\text{-}40)$$

and
$$R_6 = AR = 100\ k\Omega \qquad (4\text{-}36)$$

where the gain A is unity.

The bandpass resonant frequency and Q are determined from

$$f_0 = \frac{\omega'_0}{2\pi} = 845\ Hz \qquad (4\text{-}38)$$

and
$$Q = \frac{\pi f_0}{\alpha'_{hp}} = 2.08 \qquad (4\text{-}39)$$

The notch frequency occurs at $\omega_\infty(hp) \times f_c$ or 574 Hz.

(d) The normalized real low-pass pole is transformed to a high-pass pole:

$$\alpha_{0,hp} = \frac{1}{\alpha_0} = 0.9454 \qquad (4\text{-}13)$$

and is then denormalized by

$$\alpha'_{0,hp} = \alpha_{0,hp} \times FSF = 5940 \qquad (4\text{-}14)$$

Resistor R_7 is found by

$$R_7 = \frac{1}{\alpha'_{0,hp}C} = 16.8\ k\Omega \qquad (4\text{-}37)$$

where $C = 0.01\ \mu F$.

The final circuit is given in figure 4-10a using standard 1% values with R_1 and R_3 made adjustable. The frequency response is illustrated in figure 4-10b.

High-Pass Filters Using the GIC

The generalized impedance converter (GIC) was first introduced in section 3.2. This versatile device is capable of simulating a variety of different impedance functions. The circuit of figure 3-28 simulated an inductor whose magnitude was given by

$$L = \frac{CR_1R_3R_5}{R_2} \tag{3-61}$$

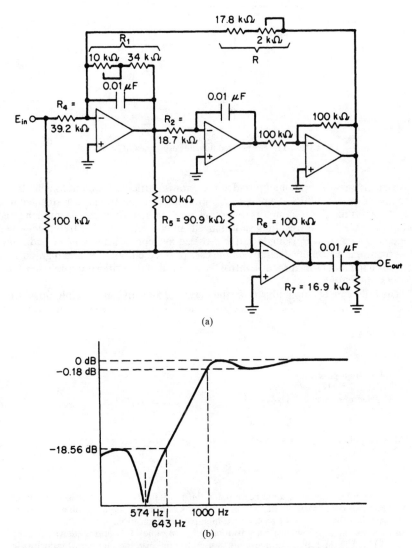

(a)

(b)

FIGURE 4-10 Elliptic-function high-pass filter of example 4-7: (*a*) filter using biquad configuration; (*b*) frequency response.

If we set R_1 through R_3 equal to 1 Ω and $C = 1$ F, a normalized inductor is obtained where $L = R_5$. This circuit is shown in figure 4-11.

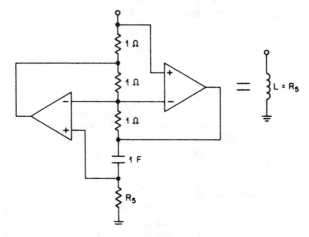

FIGURE 4-11   Normalized inductor using the GIC.

An active realization of a grounded inductor is particularly suited for the design of active high-pass filters. If a passive LC low-pass configuration is transformed into a high-pass filter, shunt inductors to ground are obtained which can be implemented using the GIC. The resulting normalized filter can then be frequency- and impedance-scaled. If R_5 is made variable, the equivalent inductance can be adjusted. This feature is especially desirable in the case of steep elliptic-function high-pass filters, since the inductors directly control the location of the critical transmission zeros in the stopband.

The following example illustrates the design of an active all-pole high-pass filter directly from the LC element values using the GIC as a simulated inductance.

EXAMPLE 4-8

REQUIRED:

Active high-pass filter
3 dB at 1200 Hz
35 dB minimum at 375 Hz

RESULT:

(a) Compute the high-pass steepness factor.

$$A_s = \frac{f_c}{f_s} = \frac{1200}{375} = 3.2 \tag{2-13}$$

The curves of figure 2-45 indicate that a third-order 1-dB Chebyshev low-pass filter provides over 35 dB of attenuation at 3.2 rad/s. For this example we will use a GIC to simulate the inductor of an $n = 3$ LC high-pass configuration.

(b) The normalized low-pass filter is obtained from table 11-31 and is shown in figure 4-12a. The dual filter configuration is used to minimize the number of inductors in the high-pass filter.

(c) To transform the normalized low-pass filter into a high-pass configuration, replace the inductors with capacitors and vice versa using reciprocal element values. The normalized high-pass filter is shown in figure 4-12b. The inductor can now be replaced by the GIC of figure 4-11, resulting in the high-pass filter of figure 4-12c.

(d) The filter is frequency- and impedance-scaled. Using an FSF of $2\pi f_c$ or 7540 and a Z of 10^4, divide all capacitors by $Z \times FSF$ and multiply all resistors by Z. The final configuration is shown in figure 4-12d using standard 1% resistor values.

Active elliptic-function high-pass filters can also be designed directly from the tables of LC element values using the GIC. This approach is much less complex than a high-pass configuration involving biquads and still permits adjustment of the transmission zeros. Design of an elliptic-function high-pass filter is demonstrated in the following example.

EXAMPLE 4-9

REQUIRED:

Active high-pass filter
0.5 dB maximum at 2500 Hz
60 dB minimum at 1500 Hz

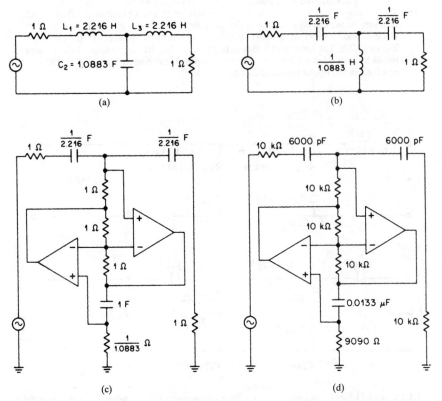

(a)

(b)

(c)

(d)

FIGURE 4-12 All-pole high-pass filter using the GIC: (a) normalized low-pass filter; (b) transformed high-pass filter; (c) active inductor realization; (d) final network after scaling.

RESULT:

(a) Compute the high-pass steepness factor.

$$A_s = \frac{f_c}{f_s} = \frac{2500}{1500} = 1.667 \qquad (2\text{-}13)$$

(b) Since the requirement is rather steep, we will choose an elliptic-function filter type. Using a ρ of 20% (0.18-dB ripple), the curves of figure 2-86 indicate that an $n = 6$ filter is required. A CO6 20c θ = 40° filter is selected from table 11-56 and has the following parameters:

$$n = 6$$

$$R_{dB} = 0.18 \text{ dB}$$

$$\Omega_s = 1.6406$$

$$A_{min} = 62.8 \text{ dB}$$

The normalized filter using the dual circuit configuration is shown in figure 4-13a.

(c) To transform the network into a normalized high-pass filter, replace each inductor with a capacitor having a reciprocal value and vice versa. The zeros are also reciprocated. The normalized high-pass filter is given in figure 4-13b.

(d) The inductors can be replaced using the GIC inductor simulation of figure 4-11, resulting in the circuit of figure 4-13c. To scale the network, divide all capacitors by $Z \times$ FSF and multiply all resistors by Z, where Z is arbitrarily chosen at 10^4 and FSF is $2\pi f_c$ or 15,708. The final filter is shown in figure 4-13d. The stopband peaks were computed by multiplying each normalized high-pass transmission zero by $f_c = 2500$ Hz, resulting in the frequencies indicated.

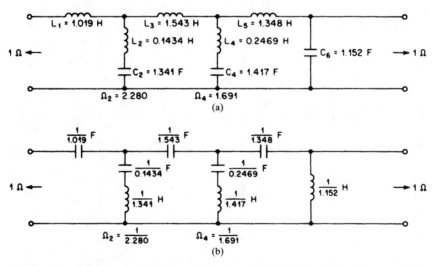

FIGURE 4-13 Elliptic-function high-pass filter of example 4-9: (a) normalized low-pass filter; (b) transformed high-pass filter.

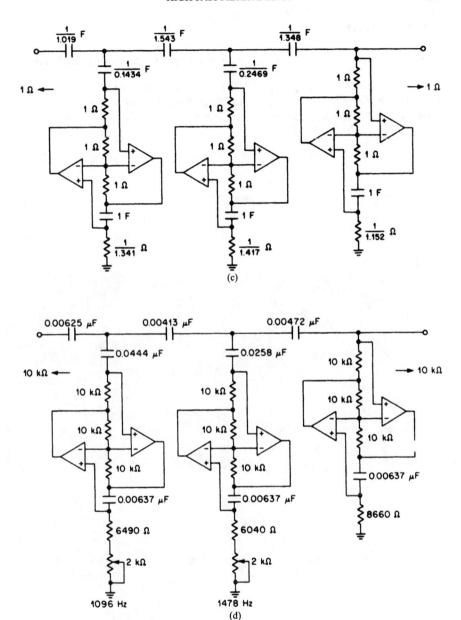

(c)

(d)

FIGURE 4-13 (*Continued*) Elliptic-function high-pass filter of example 4-9: (*c*) high-pass filter using GIC; (*d*) frequency- and impedance-scaled network.

BIBLIOGRAPHY

Bruton, L. T., "Active Filter Design Using Generalized Impedance Converters," *EDN,* February 1973.

Geffe, P., *Simplified Modern Filter Design,* John F. Rider, New York, 1963.

Williams, A. B., *Active Filter Design,* Artech House, Dedham, Mass., 1975.

Williams, A. B., "Design Active Elliptic Filters Easily from Tables," *Electronic Design,* vol. 19, no. 21, pp. 76–79, October 14, 1971.

CHAPTER 5
BANDPASS FILTERS

5.1 LC BANDPASS FILTERS

Bandpass filters were classified in section 2.1 as either narrowband or wideband. If the ratio of upper cutoff frequency to lower cutoff frequency is over an octave, the filter is considered a wideband type. The specification is separated into individual low-pass and high-pass requirements and is simply treated as a cascade of low-pass and high-pass filters.

The design of narrow-band filters becomes somewhat more difficult. The circuit configuration must be appropriately chosen and suitable transformations may have to be applied to avoid impractical element values. In addition, as the filter becomes narrower, the element Q requirements increase and component tolerances and stability become more critical.

Wideband Filters

Wideband bandpass filters are obtained by cascading a low-pass filter and a high-pass filter. The validity of this approach is based on the assumption that the filters maintain their individual responses even though they are cascaded.

The impedance observed at the input or output terminals of an LC low-pass or high-pass filter approaches the resistive termination at the other end at frequencies well in the passband. This is apparent from the equivalent circuit of the low-pass filter at DC and the high-pass filter at infinite frequency. At DC, the inductors become short circuits and capacitors become open circuits, and at infinite frequency the opposite conditions occur. If a low-pass and high-pass filter are cascaded and both filters are designed to have equal source and load terminations and identical impedances, the filters will each be properly terminated in their passbands if the cutoff frequencies are separated by at least one or two octaves.

If the separation between passbands is insufficient, the filters will interact because of impedance variations. This effect can be minimized by isolating the two filters through an attenuator. Usually 3 dB of loss is sufficient. Further attenuation provides increased isolation. Table 5-1 contains values for T and π attenuators ranging from 1 to 10 dB at an impedance level of 500 Ω. These networks can be impedance-scaled to the filter impedance level R if each resistor value is multiplied by $R/500$.

TABLE 5-1   T and π Attenuators

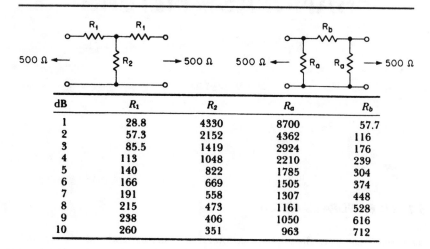

dB	R_1	R_2	R_a	R_b
1	28.8	4330	8700	57.7
2	57.3	2152	4362	116
3	85.5	1419	2924	176
4	113	1048	2210	239
5	140	822	1785	304
6	166	669	1505	374
7	191	558	1307	448
8	215	473	1161	528
9	238	406	1050	616
10	260	351	963	712

EXAMPLE 5-1

REQUIRED:

LC bandpass filter
3 dB at 500 and 2000 Hz
40 dB minimum at 100 and 4000 Hz
$R_s = R_L = 600 \, \Omega$

RESULT:

(a) Since the ratio of upper cutoff frequency to lower cutoff frequency is 4:1, a wideband approach will be used. The requirement is first separated into individual low-pass and high-pass specifications:

High-pass filter: **Low-pass filter:**
3 dB at 500 Hz   3 dB at 2000 Hz
40 dB minimum at 100 Hz   40 dB minimum at 4000 Hz

(b) The low-pass and high-pass filters are designed independently using the design methods outlined in sections 3.1 and 4.1 as follows:

Low-pass filter:
Compute the low-pass steepness factor.

$$A_s = \frac{f_s}{f_c} = \frac{4000 \text{ Hz}}{2000 \text{ Hz}} = 2 \qquad (2\text{-}11)$$

Figure 2-43 indicates that a fifth-order 0.25-dB Chebyshev normalized low-pass filter provides over 40 dB of attenuation at 2 rad/s. The normalized low-pass filter is obtained from table 11-29 and is shown in figure 5-1a. The filter is frequency- and impedance-scaled by multiplying all inductors by Z/FSF and dividing all capacitors by $Z \times FSF$, where Z is 600 and the frequency-scaling factor FSF is $2\pi f_c$ or 12,560. The denormalized low-pass filter is shown in figure 5-1b.

High-pass filter:
Compute the high-pass steepness factor:

$$A_s = \frac{f_c}{f_s} = \frac{500 \text{ Hz}}{100 \text{ Hz}} = 5 \qquad (2\text{-}13)$$

Using figure 2-34, an $n = 3$ Butterworth normalized low-pass filter is selected to meet the attenuation requirement. The normalized filter values are found in table 11-2 and shown in figure 5-1c. Since the low-pass filter is to be transformed into a high-pass filter, the dual configuration was selected. By reciprocating element values and replacing inductors with capacitors and vice versa, the normalized high-pass filter of figure 5-1d is obtained. The network is then denormalized by multiplying all inductors by Z/FSF and dividing all capacitors by $Z \times \text{FSF}$, where Z is 600 Ω and FSF is 3140. The denormalized high-pass filter is illustrated in figure 5-1e.

(c) The low-pass and high-pass filters can now be combined. A 3-dB T pad will be used to provide some isolation between filters, since the separation of cutoffs is only 2 octaves. The pad values are obtained by multiplying the resistances of table 5-1 corresponding to 3 dB by 600 Ω/500 Ω or 1.2 and rounding off to standard 1% values. The final circuit is shown in figure 5-1f.

Narrowband Filters

Narrowband bandpass filter terminology was introduced in section 2.1 using the concept of bandpass Q, which was defined by

$$Q_{\text{bp}} = \frac{f_0}{\text{BW}_{3\,\text{dB}}} \tag{2-16}$$

where f_0 is the geometric center frequency and BW is the 3-dB bandwidth. The geometric center frequency was given by

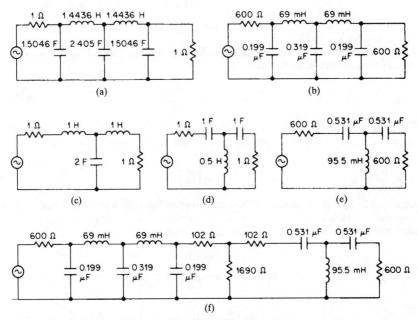

FIGURE 5-1 *LC* wideband bandpass filter of example 5-1: (*a*) normalized low-pass filter; (*b*) scaled low-pass filter; (*c*) normalized low-pass filter for high-pass requirement; (*d*) transformed high-pass filter; (*e*) scaled high-pass filter; (*f*) combined network.

$$f_0 = \sqrt{f_L f_u} \tag{2-14}$$

where f_L and f_u are the lower and upper 3-dB limits.

Bandpass filters obtained by transformation from a low-pass filter exhibit geometric symmetry, that is,

$$f_0 = \sqrt{f_1 f_2} \tag{2-15}$$

where f_1 and f_2 are any two frequencies having equal attenuation. Geometric symmetry must be considered when normalizing a bandpass specification. For each stopband frequency specified, the corresponding geometric frequency is calculated and a steepness factor is computed based on the more severe requirement.

For bandpass Qs of 10 or more, the passband response approaches arithmetic symmetry. The center frequency then becomes the average of the 3-dB points, i.e.,

$$f_0 = \frac{f_L + f_u}{2} \tag{2-17}$$

The stopband will also become arithmetically symmetrical as the Q increases even further.

The Low-Pass to Bandpass Transformation.   A bandpass transfer function can be obtained from a low-pass transfer function by replacing the frequency variable by a new variable, which is given by

$$f_{bp} = f_0 \left(\frac{f}{f_0} - \frac{f_0}{f} \right) \tag{5-1}$$

When f is equal to f_0, the bandpass center frequency, the response corresponds to that at DC for the low-pass filter.

If the low-pass filter has a 3-dB cutoff of f_c, the corresponding bandpass frequency f can be found by solving

$$\pm f_c = f_0 \left(\frac{f}{f_0} - \frac{f_0}{f} \right) \tag{5-2}$$

The $\pm$ signs occur because a low-pass filter has a mirrored response at negative frequencies in addition to the normal response. Solving equation (5-2) for f, we obtain

$$f = \pm \frac{f_c}{2} \pm \sqrt{\left(\frac{f_c}{2} \right)^2 + f_0^2} \tag{5-3}$$

Equation (5-3) implies that the bandpass response has two positive frequencies corresponding to the low-pass response at $\pm f_c$ as well as two negative frequencies with identical responses. These frequencies can be obtained from equation (5-3) and are given by

$$f_L = f_0 \left[\sqrt{1 + \left(\frac{f_c}{2f_0} \right)^2} - \frac{f_c}{2f_0} \right] \tag{5-4}$$

and

$$f_u = f_0 \left[\sqrt{1 + \left(\frac{f_c}{2f_0} \right)^2} + \frac{f_c}{2f_0} \right] \tag{5-5}$$

The bandpass 3-dB bandwidth is

$$BW_{3\,dB} = f_u - f_L = f_c \qquad (5\text{-}6)$$

The correspondence between a low-pass filter and the transformed bandpass filter is shown in figure 5-2. The response of a low-pass filter to positive frequencies is transformed into the response of the bandpass filter at an equivalent bandwidth. Therefore, a bandpass filter can be obtained by first designing a low-pass filter that has the required response corresponding to the desired bandwidth characteristics of the bandpass filter. The low-pass filter is then transformed into the bandpass filter.

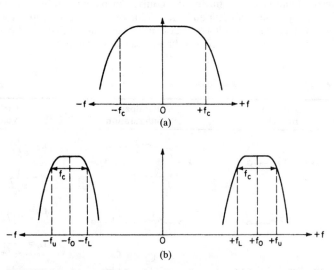

FIGURE 5-2 Low-pass to bandpass transformation: (a) low-pass filter; (b) transformed bandpass filter.

The reactance of a capacitor in the low-pass filter is given by

$$X_c = \frac{1}{j\,\omega\,C} \qquad (5\text{-}7)$$

where $\omega = 2\pi f$. If we replace the frequency variable f by the expression of equation (5-1), the impedance expression becomes

$$Z = \cfrac{1}{j\,\omega\,C + \cfrac{1}{j\,\dfrac{\omega}{\omega_0^2\,C}}} \qquad (5\text{-}8)$$

where $\omega_0 = 2\pi f_0$. This is the impedance of a parallel resonant LC circuit where the capacitance is still C and the inductance is $1/\omega_0^2 C$. The resonant frequency is ω_0.

The reactance of an inductor in the low-pass filter is

$$X_L = j\,\omega\,L \qquad (5\text{-}9)$$

If we again replace the frequency variable using equation (5-1), the resulting impedance expression becomes

$$Z = j\omega L + \dfrac{1}{j\dfrac{\omega}{\omega_0^2 L}} \tag{5-10}$$

This corresponds to a series resonant LC circuit where the inductance L is unchanged and C is $1/\omega_0^2 L$. The resonant frequency is ω_0.

We can summarize these results by stating that an LC low-pass filter can be transformed into a bandpass filter having the equivalent bandwidth by resonating each capacitor with a parallel inductor and each inductor with a series capacitor. The resonant frequency is f_0, the bandpass filter center frequency. Table 5-2 shows the circuits which result from the low-pass to bandpass transformation.

TABLE 5-2 The Low-Pass to Bandpass Transformation

	Low-Pass Branch	Bandpass Configuration	Circuit Values
Type I			$L = \dfrac{1}{\omega_0^2 C}$ (5-11) $C = \dfrac{1}{\omega_0^2 L}$ (5-12)
Type II			$C_a = \dfrac{1}{\omega_0^2 L_a}$ (5-13) $L_b = \dfrac{1}{\omega_0^2 C_b}$ (5-14)
Type III			$C_1 = \dfrac{1}{\omega_0^2 L_1}$ (5-15) $L_2 = \dfrac{1}{\omega_0^2 C_2}$ (5-16)
Type IV			

Transformation of All-Pole Low-Pass Filters. The LC bandpass filters discussed in this section are probably the most important type of filter. These networks are directly obtained by the bandpass transformation from the LC low-pass values tabulated in chapter 11. Each normalized low-pass filter defines an infinitely large family of bandpass filters having a geometrically symmetrical response predetermined by the low-pass characteristics.

A low-pass transfer function can be transformed to a bandpass type by substitution of the frequency variable using equation (5-1). This transformation can also be made directly to the circuit elements by first scaling the low-pass filter to the required bandwidth and impedance level. Each coil is then resonated with a series capacitor to the center frequency f_0 and an inductor is introduced across each capacitor to form a parallel tuned circuit also resonant at f_0. Every low-pass branch is replaced by the associated bandpass branch, as illustrated by table 5-2.

Some of the effects of dissipation in low-pass filters were discussed in section 3.1. These effects are even more severe in bandpass filters. The minimum Q requirement for the low-pass elements can be obtained from figure 3-8 for a variety of filter types. These minimum values are based on the assumption that the filter elements are predistorted so that the theoretical response is obtained. Since this is not always the case, the branch Qs should be several times higher than the values indicated. When the network undergoes a low-pass to bandpass transformation, the Q requirement is increased by the bandpass Q of the filter. This can be stated as

$$Q_{min} \text{ (bandpass)} = Q_{min} \text{ (low-pass)} \times Q_{bp} \qquad (5\text{-}17)$$

where $Q_{bp} = f_0/BW_{3\,dB}$. As in the low-pass case, the branch Qs should be several times higher than Q_{min}. Since capacitor losses are usually negligible, the branch Q is determined strictly by the inductor losses.

The spread of values in bandpass filters is usually wider than with low-pass filters. For some combinations of impedance and bandwidth, the element values may be impossible or impractical to realize because of their magnitude or the effects of parasitics. When this situation occurs, the designer can use a variety of circuit transformations to obtain a more practical circuit. These techniques are covered in chapter 8.

The design method can be summarized as follows:

1. Convert the response requirement into a geometrically symmetrical specification.
2. Compute the bandpass steepness factor A_s. Select a normalized low-pass filter from the frequency-response curves of chapter 2 that makes the passband to stopband transition within a frequency ratio of A_s.
3. Scale the corresponding normalized low-pass filter from the tables of chapter 11 to the required bandwidth and impedance level of the bandpass filter.
4. Resonate each L and C to f_0 in accordance with table 5-2.
5. The final design may require manipulation by various transformations so that the values are more practical. In addition, the branch Qs must be well in excess of Q_{min} (bandpass) as given by equation (5-17) to obtain near theoretical results.

EXAMPLE 5-2

REQUIRED:

Bandpass filter
Center frequency of 1000 Hz
3-dB points at 950 and 1050 Hz
25 dB minimum at 800 and 1150 Hz
$R_s = R_L = 600\ \Omega$
Available inductor Q of 100

RESULT:

(a) Convert to geometrically symmetrical bandpass requirement:
First calculate the geometric center frequency.

$$f_0 = \sqrt{f_L f_u} = \sqrt{950 \times 1050} = 998.8 \text{ Hz} \qquad (2\text{-}14)$$

Compute the corresponding geometric frequency for each stopband frequency given using equation (2-18).

$$f_1 f_2 = f_0^2 \tag{2-18}$$

f_1	f_2	$f_2 - f_1$
800 Hz	1247 Hz	447 Hz
867 Hz	1150 Hz	283 Hz

The second pair of frequencies will be retained, since they represent the more severe requirement. The resulting geometrically symmetrical requirement can be summarized as

$$f_0 = 998.8 \text{ Hz}$$

$$BW_{3\,dB} = 100 \text{ Hz}$$

$$BW_{25\,dB} = 283 \text{ Hz}$$

(b) Compute the bandpass steepness factor.

$$A_s = \frac{\text{stopband bandwidth}}{\text{passband bandwidth}} = \frac{283 \text{ Hz}}{100 \text{ Hz}} = 2.83 \tag{2-19}$$

(c) Select a normalized low-pass filter that makes the transition from 3 dB to more than 25 dB within a frequency ratio of 2.83:1. Figure 2-34 indicates that an $n = 3$ Butterworth type will satisfy the response requirement. The normalized low-pass filter is found in table 11-2 and is shown in figure 5-3a.

(d) Denormalize the low-pass filter using a Z of 600 and a frequency-scaling factor (FSF) of $2\pi f_c$ or 628 where $f_c = 100$ Hz.

$$C_1' = C_3' = \frac{C}{\text{FSF} \times Z} = \frac{1}{628 \times 600} = 2.653 \text{ μF} \tag{2-10}$$

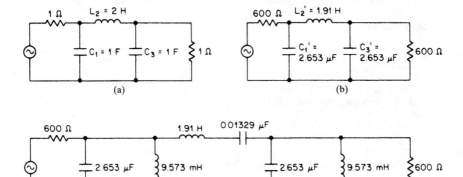

FIGURE 5-3 Bandpass filter of example 5-2: (a) normalized $n = 3$ Butterworth low-pass filter; (b) low-pass filter scaled to 600 Ω and f_c of 100 Hz; (c) transformed bandpass filter.

$$L_2' = \frac{L \times Z}{\text{FSF}} = \frac{2 \times 600}{628} = 1.91 \text{ H} \tag{2-9}$$

The denormalized low-pass filter is illustrated in figure 5-3b.
(e) To make the low-pass to bandpass transformation, resonate each capacitor with a parallel inductor and each inductor with a series capacitor using a resonate frequency of $f_0 = 998.8$ Hz.

$$L_1' = \frac{1}{\omega_0^2 C_1'} = \frac{1}{(6275)^2 \times 2.653 \times 10^{-6}} = 9.573 \text{ mH} \tag{5-11}$$

$$L_3' = L_1' = 9.573 \text{ mH}$$

$$C_2' = \frac{1}{\omega_0^2 L_2'} = \frac{1}{(6275)^2 \times 1.91} = 0.01329 \text{ } \mu\text{F} \tag{5-12}$$

where $\omega_0 = 2\pi f_0$. The resulting bandpass filter is given in figure 5-3c.
(f) Estimate if the available inductor Q of 100 is sufficient.

$$Q_{\min} \text{ (bandpass)} = Q_{\min} \text{ (low-pass)} \times Q_{bp} = 2 \times 10 = 20 \tag{5-17}$$

where $Q_{\min}$ (low-pass) was obtained from figure 3-8 and Q_{bp} is $f_0/\text{BW}_{3 \text{ dB}}$. Since the available Q is well in excess of $Q_{\min}$ (bandpass), the filter response will closely agree with the theoretical predictions.

The response requirement of example 5-2 was converted to a geometrically symmetrical specification by calculating the corresponding frequency for each stopband frequency specified at a particular attenuation level using the relationship $f_1 f_2 = f_0^2$. The pair of frequencies having the lesser separation was chosen, since this would represent the steeper filter requirement. This technique represents a general method for obtaining the geometrically related frequencies that determine the response requirements of the normalized low-pass filter.

Stopband requirements are frequently specified in an arithmetically symmetrical manner where the deviation on both sides of the center frequency is the same for a given attenuation. Because of the geometric symmetry of bandpass filters, the attenuation for a particular deviation below the center frequency will be greater than for the same deviation above the center frequency. The response curve would then appear compressed on the low side of the passband if plotted on a linear frequency axis. On a logarithmic scale the curve would be symmetrical.

When the specification is stated in arithmetic terms, the stopband bandwidth on a geometric basis can be computed directly by

$$\text{BW} = f_2 - \frac{f_0^2}{f_2} \tag{5-18}$$

where f_2 is the upper stopband frequency and f_0 is the geometric center frequency as determined from the passband limits. This approach is demonstrated in the following example.

EXAMPLE 5-3

REQUIRED:

Bandpass filter
Center frequency of 50 kHz
3-dB points at ±3 kHz (47 kHz, 53 kHz)

30 dB minimum at ±7.5 kHz (42.5 kHz, 57.5 kHz)
40 dB minimum at ±10.5 kHz (39.5 kHz, 60.5 kHz)
$R_s = 150\ \Omega$ $R_L = 300\ \Omega$

RESULT:

(a) Convert to the geometrically symmetrical bandpass requirement.

$$f_0 = \sqrt{f_L f_u} = \sqrt{47 \times 53 \times 10^6} = 49.91\ \text{kHz} \tag{2-14}$$

Since the stopband requirement is arithmetically symmetrical, compute the stopband bandwidth using equation (5-18).

$$BW_{30\ dB} = f_2 - \frac{f_0^2}{f_2} = 57.5 \times 10^3 - \frac{(49.91 \times 10^3)^2}{57.5 \times 10^3} = 14.18\ \text{kHz}$$

$$BW_{40\ dB} = 19.33\ \text{kHz}$$

Requirement:

$$f_0 = 49.91\ \text{kHz}$$

$$BW_{3\ dB} = 6\ \text{kHz}$$

$$BW_{30\ dB} = 14.18\ \text{kHz}$$

$$BW_{40\ dB} = 19.33\ \text{kHz}$$

(b) Since two stopband bandwidth requirements are given, they must both be converted into bandpass steepness factors.

$$A_s(30\ \text{dB}) = \frac{\text{stopband bandwidth}}{\text{passband bandwidth}} = \frac{14.18\ \text{kHz}}{6\ \text{kHz}} = 2.36 \tag{2-19}$$

$$A_s(40\ \text{dB}) = 3.22$$

(c) A normalized low-pass filter must be chosen that provides over 30 dB of rejection at 2.36 rad/s and more than 40 dB at 3.22 rad/s. Figure 2-41 indicates that a fourth-order 0.01-dB Chebyshev filter will meet this requirement. The corresponding low-pass filter can be found in table 11-27. Since a 2:1 ratio of R_L to R_s is required, the design for a normalized R_s of 2 Ω is chosen and is turned end for end. The circuit is shown in figure 5-4a.

(d) The circuit is now scaled to an impedance level Z of 150 and a cutoff of $f_c = 6$ kHz. All inductors are multiplied by Z/FSF, and the capacitors are divided by $Z \times$ FSF, where FSF is $2\pi f_c$. The 1-Ω source and 2-Ω load become 150 and 300 Ω, respectively. The denormalized network is illustrated in figure 5-4b.

(e) The scaled low-pass filter is transformed to a bandpass filter at $f_0 = 49.91$ kHz by resonating each capacitor with a parallel inductor and each inductor with a series capacitor using the general relationship $\omega_0^2 LC = 1$. The resulting bandpass filter is shown in figure 5-4c.

Design of Parallel Tuned Circuits.   The simple RC low-pass circuit of figure 5-5a has a 3-dB cutoff corresponding to

$$f_c = \frac{1}{2\pi RC} \tag{5-19}$$

If a bandpass transformation is performed, the circuit of figure 5-5b results, where

$$L = \frac{1}{\omega_0^2 C} \tag{5-11}$$

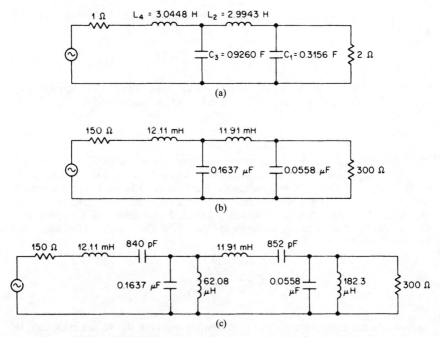

FIGURE 5-4 Bandpass filter of example 5-3: (*a*) normalized low-pass filter; (*b*) scaled low-pass filter; (*c*) transformed bandpass filter.

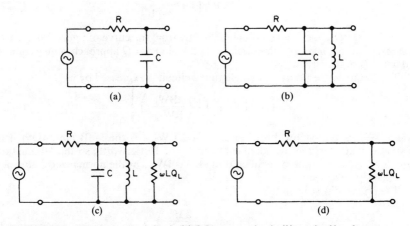

FIGURE 5-5 The single tuned circuit: (*a*) *RC* low-pass circuit; (*b*) result of bandpass transformation; (*c*) representation of coil losses; (*d*) equivalent circuit at resonance.

The center frequency is f_0 and the 3-dB bandwidth is equal to f_c. The bandpass Q is given by

$$Q_{bp} = \frac{f_0}{BW_{3\,dB}} = \frac{f_0}{f_c} = \omega_0 RC \tag{5-20}$$

Since the magnitudes of the capacitive and inductive susceptances are equal at resonance by definition, we can substitute $1/\omega_0 L$ for $\omega_0 C$ in equation (5-20) and obtain

$$Q_{bp} = \frac{R}{\omega_0 L} \tag{5-21}$$

The element R may be a single resistor as in figure 5-5b or the parallel combination of both the input and output terminations if an output load resistor is also present.

The circuit of figure 5-5b is somewhat ideal, since inductor losses are usually unavoidable. (The slight losses usually associated with the capacitor will be neglected.) If the inductor Q is given as Q_L, the inductor losses can be represented as a parallel resistor of $\omega L Q_L$ as shown in figure 5-5c. The effective Q of the circuit becomes

$$Q_{eff} = \frac{\dfrac{R}{\omega_0 L} Q_L}{\dfrac{R}{\omega_0 L} + Q_L} \tag{5-22}$$

As a result, the effective circuit Q is somewhat less than the values computed by equations (5-20) or (5-21). To compensate for the effect of finite inductor Q, the design Q should be somewhat higher. This value can be found from

$$Q_d = \frac{Q_{eff} Q_L}{Q_L - Q_{eff}} \tag{5-23}$$

At resonance, the equivalent circuit is represented by the resistive voltage divider of figure 5-5d, since the reactive elements cancel. The insertion loss at f_0 can be determined by the expression

$$IL_{dB} = 20 \log \left(1 + \frac{1}{k-1}\right) \tag{5-24}$$

where $k = Q_L/Q_{eff}$ and can be obtained directly from the curve of figure 5-6. Clearly the insertion loss increases dramatically as the inductor Q approaches the required effective Q of the circuit.

The frequency response of a single tuned circuit is expressed by

$$A_{dB} = 10 \log \left[1 + \left(\frac{BW_x}{BW_{3\,dB}}\right)^2\right] \tag{5-25}$$

where BW_x is the bandwidth of interest and $BW_{3\,dB}$ is the 3-dB bandwidth. The response characteristics are identical to an $n = 1$ Butterworth; so the attenuation curves of figure 2-34 can be applied using $BW_x/BW_{3\,dB}$ as the normalized frequency in radians per second.

The phase shift is given by

$$\theta = \tan^{-1} \left(\frac{2\Delta f}{BW_{3\,dB}}\right) \tag{5-26}$$

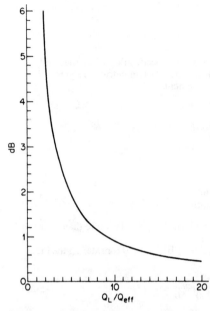

FIGURE 5-6 Insertion loss vs. Q_L/Q_{eff}.

where Δf is the frequency deviation from f_0. The output phase shift lags by 45° at the upper 3-dB frequency and leads by 45° at the lower 3-dB frequency. At DC and infinity, the phase shift reaches +90° and −90°, respectively. Equation (5-26) is plotted in figure 5-7.

The group delay can be estimated by the slope of the phase shift at f_0 and results in the approximation

$$T_{gd} \approx \frac{318}{BW_{3\,dB}} \qquad (5\text{-}27)$$

where $BW_{3\,dB}$ is the 3-dB bandwidth in hertz and T_{gd} is the resulting group delay in milliseconds.

EXAMPLE 5-4

REQUIRED:

LC bandpass filter
Center frequency of 10 kHz
3 dB at ±100 Hz (9.9 kHz, 10.1 kHz)
15 dB minimum at ±1 kHz (9 kHz, 11 kHz)

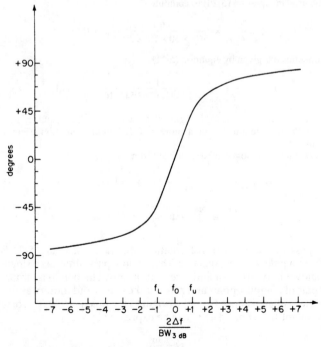

FIGURE 5-7 Phase shift vs. frequency.

Inductor $Q_L = 200$
$R_s = R_L = 6\ k\Omega$

RESULT:

(a) Convert to the geometrically symmetrical bandpass specification. Since the bandpass Q is much greater than 10, the specified arithmetically symmetrical frequencies are used to determine the following design requirements:

$$f_0 = 10\ kHz$$

$$BW_{3\ dB} = 200\ Hz$$

$$BW_{15\ dB} = 2000\ Hz$$

(b) Compute the bandpass steepness factor.

$$A_s = \frac{\text{stopband bandwidth}}{\text{passband bandwidth}} = \frac{2000}{200} = 10 \tag{2-19}$$

Figure 2-34 indicates that a single tuned circuit ($n = 1$) provides more than 15 dB of attenuation within a bandwidth ratio of 10:1.

(c) Calculate the design Q to obtain a Q_{eff} equal to $f_0/BW_{3\ dB} = 50$ considering the inductor Q_L of 200.

$$Q_d = \frac{Q_{eff}\ Q_L}{Q_L - Q_{eff}} = \frac{50 \times 200}{200 - 50} = 66.7 \tag{5-23}$$

(d) Since the source and load are both 6 kΩ, the total resistive loading on the tuned circuit is the parallel combination of both terminations; so $R = 3\ k\Omega$. The design Q can now be used in equation (5-20) to compute C.

$$C = \frac{Q_{bp}}{\omega_0 R} = \frac{66.7}{6.28 \times 10 \times 10^3 \times 3000} = 0.354\ \mu F \tag{5-20}$$

The inductance is given by equation (5-11).

$$L = \frac{1}{\omega_0^2 C} = \frac{1}{(2\pi \times 10\ kHz)^2 \times 3.54 \times 10^{-7}} = 716\ \mu H \tag{5-11}$$

The resulting circuit is shown in figure 5-8a, which has the frequency response of figure 5-8b. See section 8.1 for a more practical implementation using a tapped inductor.

(e) The circuit insertion loss can be calculated from

$$IL_{dB} = 20 \log \left(1 + \frac{1}{k-1}\right) = 20 \log 1.333 = 2.5\ dB \tag{5-24}$$

where $$k = \frac{Q_L}{Q_{eff}} = \frac{200}{50} = 4$$

The low-pass to bandpass transformation illustrated in figure 5-5 can also be examined from a pole-zero perspective. The RC low-pass filter has a single real pole at $1/RC$ as shown in figure 5-9a and a zero at infinity. The bandpass transformation results in a pair of complex poles and zeros at the origin and infinity as illustrated in figure 5-9b. The radial distance from the origin to the pole is $1/(LC)^{1/2}$ corresponding to ω_0, the resonant frequency. The Q can be expressed by

$$Q = \frac{\omega_0}{2\alpha} \tag{5-28}$$

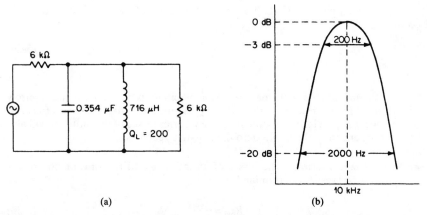

(a)   (b)

FIGURE 5-8 Tuned circuit of example 5-4: (*a*) circuit; (*b*) frequency response.

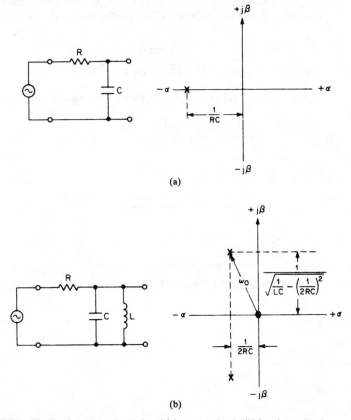

(a)

(b)

FIGURE 5-9 The bandpass transformation: (*a*) low-pass circuit; (*b*) bandpass circuit.

where α, the real part, is $1/2RC$. The transfer function of the circuit of figure 5-9*b* becomes

$$T(s) = \frac{s}{s^2 + \dfrac{\omega_0}{Q}s + \omega_0^2} \tag{5-29}$$

At ω_0, the impedance of the parallel resonant circuit is a maximum and is purely resistive, resulting in zero phase shift. If the Q is much less than 10, these effects do not both occur at precisely the same frequency. Series losses of the inductor will also displace the zero from the origin onto the negative real axis.

The Series Tuned Circuit.   The losses of an inductor can be conveniently represented by a series resistor determined by

$$R_{\text{coil}} = \frac{\omega L}{Q_L} \tag{5-30}$$

If we form a series resonant circuit and include the source and load resistors, we obtain the circuit of figure 5-10. Equations (5-24) through (5-27) for insertion loss, frequency response, phase shift, and group delay of the parallel tuned circuit apply, since the two circuits are duals of each other. The inductance is calculated from

$$L = \frac{R_s + R_L}{\omega_0\left(\dfrac{1}{Q_{\text{bp}}} - \dfrac{1}{Q_L}\right)} \tag{5-31}$$

where Q_{bp} is the required Q and Q_L is the inductor Q. The capacitance is given by

$$C = \frac{1}{\omega_0^2 L} \tag{5-12}$$

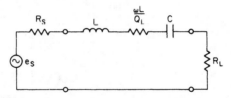

FIGURE 5-10   The series resonant circuit.

EXAMPLE 5-5

REQUIRED:

Series tuned circuit
Center frequency of 100 kHz
3-dB bandwidth of 2 kHz
$R_s = R_L = 100\ \Omega$
Inductor Q of 400

RESULT:

(a) Compute the bandpass Q.

$$Q_{bp} = \frac{f_0}{BW_{3\,dB}} = \frac{100\ kHz}{2\ kHz} = 50 \tag{2-16}$$

(b) Calculate the element values.

$$L = \frac{R_s + R_L}{\omega_0\left(\dfrac{1}{Q_{bp}} - \dfrac{1}{Q_L}\right)} = \frac{200}{2\pi \times 10^5\left(\dfrac{1}{50} - \dfrac{1}{400}\right)} - 18.2\ mH \tag{5-31}$$

$$C = \frac{1}{\omega_0^2 L} = 139\ pF \tag{5-12}$$

The circuit is shown in figure 5-11.

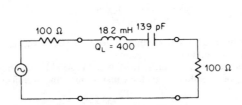

FIGURE 5-11   Series tuned circuit of example 5-5.

The reader may recall from AC circuit theory that one of the effects of series resonance is a buildup of voltage across both reactive elements. The voltage across either reactive element at resonance is equal to Q times the input voltage and may be excessively high, causing inductor saturation or capacitor breakdown. In addition, the L/C ratio becomes large as the bandwidth is reduced and will result in impractical element values where high Qs are required. As a result, series resonant circuits are less desirable than parallel tuned circuits.

Synchronously Tuned Filters.   Tuned circuits can be cascaded to obtain bandpass filters of a higher complexity. Each stage must be isolated from the previous section. If all circuits are tuned to the same frequency, a synchronously tuned filter is obtained. The characteristics of synchronously tuned bandpass filters are discussed in section 2.8, and the normalized frequency response is illustrated by the curves of figure 2-77. The design Q of each section was given by

$$Q_{section} = Q_{overall} \sqrt{2^{1/n} - 1} \tag{2-45}$$

where $Q_{overall}$ is defined by the ratio $f_0/BW_{3\,dB}$ of the composite filter. The individual circuits may be of either the series or the parallel resonant type.

Synchronously tuned filters are the simplest approximation to a bandpass response. Since all stages are identical and tuned to the same frequency, they are simple to construct and easy to align. The Q requirement of each individual section is less than the overall Q, whereas the opposite is true for conventional bandpass filters. The transient behavior exhibits no overshoot or ringing. On the other hand, the selectivity is extremely poor. To obtain a particular attenuation for a given steepness factor A_s, many more stages are required than for the other filter types. In addition, each section must be isolated from the previous section, so interstage amplifiers are required. The disadvantages generally outweigh the advantages, so synchronously tuned filters are usually restricted to special applications such as IF and RF amplifiers.

EXAMPLE 5-6

REQUIRED:

Synchronously tuned bandpass filter
Center frequency of 455 kHz
3 dB at ±5 kHz
30 dB minimum at ±35 kHz
Inductor Q of 400

RESULT:

(a) Compute the bandpass steepness factor.

$$A_s = \frac{\text{stopband bandwidth}}{\text{passband bandwidth}} = \frac{70\text{ kHz}}{10\text{ kHz}} = 7 \tag{2-19}$$

The curves of figure 2-77 indicate that a third-order ($n = 3$) synchronously tuned filter satisfies the attenuation requirement.

(b) Three sections are required which are all tuned to 455 kHz and have identical Q. To compute the Q of the individual sections, first calculate the overall Q, which is given by

$$Q_{bp} = \frac{f_0}{\text{BW}_{3\text{ dB}}} = \frac{455\text{ kHz}}{10\text{ kHz}} = 45.5 \tag{2-16}$$

The section Qs can be found from

$$Q_{\text{section}} = Q_{\text{overall}} \sqrt{2^{1/n} - 1} = 45.5 \sqrt{2^{1/3} - 1} = 23.2 \tag{2-45}$$

(c) The tuned circuits can now be designed using either a series or parallel realization. Let us choose a parallel tuned circuit configuration using a single-source resistor of 10 kΩ and a high-impedance termination. Since an effective circuit Q of 23.2 is desired and the inductor Q is 400, the design Q is calculated from

$$Q_d = \frac{Q_{\text{eff}} Q_L}{Q_L - Q_{\text{eff}}} = \frac{23.2 \times 400}{400 - 23.2} = 24.6 \tag{5-23}$$

The inductance is then given by

$$L = \frac{R}{\omega_0 Q_{bp}} = \frac{10 \times 10^3}{2\pi\,455 \times 10^3 \times 24.6} = 142\ \mu\text{H} \tag{5-21}$$

The resonating capacitor can be obtained from

$$C = \frac{1}{\omega_0^2 L} = 862\text{ pF} \tag{5-12}$$

The final circuit is shown in figure 5-12 utilizing buffer amplifiers to isolate the three sections.

Narrowband Coupled Resonators

Narrowband bandpass filters can be designed by using coupling techniques where parallel tuned circuits are interconnected by coupling elements such as inductors or capacitors. Figure 5-13 illustrates some typical configurations.

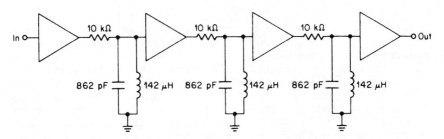

FIGURE 5-12 Synchronously tuned filter of example 5-6.

Coupled resonator configurations are desirable for narrowband filters having bandpass Qs of 10 or more. The values are generally more practical than the elements obtained by the low-pass to bandpass transformation, especially for very high Qs. The tuning is also simpler, since it turns out that all nodes are resonated to the same frequency. Of the three configurations shown in figure 5-13, the capacitive coupled configuration is the most desirable from the standpoint of economy and ease of manufacture.

The theoretical justification for the design method is based on the assumption that the coupling elements have a constant impedance with frequency. This assumption is approximately accurate over narrow bandwidths. At DC the coupling capaci-

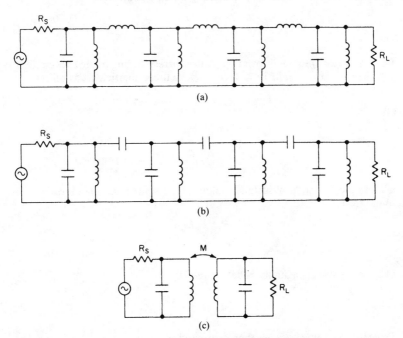

FIGURE 5-13 Coupled resonators: (*a*) inductive coupling; (*b*) capacitive coupling; (*c*) magnetic coupling.

tors will introduce additional response zeros. This causes the frequency response to be increasingly unsymmetrical both geometrically and arithmetically as we deviate from the center frequency. The response shape will be somewhat steeper on the low-frequency side of the passband.

The general form of a capacitive coupled resonator filter is shown in figure 5-14. An nth-order filter requires n parallel tuned circuits and contains n nodes. Tables 5-3 through 5-12 present in tabular form q and k parameters for all-pole filters. These parameters are used to generate the component values for filters having the form shown in figure 5-14. For each network a q_1 and q_n is given corresponding to the first and last resonant circuit. The k parameters are given in terms of k_{12}, k_{23}, etc., and are related to the coupling capacitors shown in figure 5-14. The design method proceeds as follows:

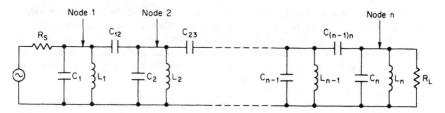

FIGURE 5-14   General form of capacitive coupled resonator filter.

1. Compute the desired filter's passband Q which was given by

$$Q_{bp} = \frac{f_0}{BW_{3\,dB}} \qquad (2\text{-}16)$$

2. Determine the q's and k's from the tables corresponding to the chosen filter type and the order of complexity n. Denormalize these coefficients as follows:

$$Q_1 = Q_{bp} \times q_1 \qquad (5\text{-}32)$$

$$Q_n = Q_{bp} \times q_n \qquad (5\text{-}33)$$

$$K_{xy} = \frac{k_{xy}}{Q_{bp}} \qquad (5\text{-}34)$$

3. Choose a convenient inductance value L. The source and load terminations are found from

$$R_s = \omega_0 L Q_1 \qquad (5\text{-}35)$$

and $$R_L = \omega_0 L Q_n \qquad (5\text{-}36)$$

4. The total nodal capacitance is determined by

$$C_{node} = \frac{1}{\omega_0^2 L} \qquad (5\text{-}37)$$

The coupling capacitors are then computed from

$$C_{xy} = K_{xy} C_{node} \qquad (5\text{-}38)$$

TABLE 5-3 Butterworth Capacitive Coupled Resonators

n	q_1	q_n	k_{12}	k_{23}	k_{34}	k_{45}	k_{56}	k_{67}	k_{78}
2	1.414	1.414	0.707						
3	1.000	1.000	0.707	0.707					
4	0.765	0.765	0.841	0.541	0.841				
5	0.618	0.618	1.000	0.556	0.556	1.000			
6	0.518	0.518	1.169	0.605	0.518	0.605	1.169		
7	0.445	0.445	1.342	0.667	0.527	0.527	0.667	1.342	
8	0.390	0.390	1.519	0.736	0.554	0.510	0.554	0.736	1.519

TABLE 5-4 0.01-dB Chebyshev Capacitive Coupled Resonators

n	q_1	q_n	k_{12}	k_{23}	k_{34}	k_{45}	k_{56}	k_{67}	k_{78}
2	1.483	1.483	0.708						
3	1.181	1.181	0.682	0.682					
4	1.046	1.046	0.737	0.541	0.737				
5	0.977	0.977	0.780	0.540	0.540	0.780			
6	0.937	0.937	0.809	0.550	0.518	0.550	0.809		
7	0.913	0.913	0.829	0.560	0.517	0.517	0.560	0.829	
8	0.897	0.897	0.843	0.567	0.520	0.510	0.520	0.567	0.843

TABLE 5-5 0.1-dB Chebyshev Capacitive Coupled Resonators

n	q_1	q_n	k_{12}	k_{23}	k_{34}	k_{45}	k_{56}	k_{67}	k_{78}
2	1.638	1.638	0.711						
3	1.433	1.433	0.662	0.662					
4	1.345	1.345	0.685	0.542	0.685				
5	1.301	1.301	0.703	0.536	0.536	0.703			
6	1.277	1.277	0.715	0.539	0.518	0.539	0.715		
7	1.262	1.262	0.722	0.542	0.516	0.516	0.542	0.722	
8	1.251	1.251	0.728	0.545	0.516	0.510	0.516	0.545	0.728

TABLE 5-6 0.5-dB Chebyshev Capacitive Coupled Resonators

n	q_1	q_n	k_{12}	k_{23}	k_{34}	k_{45}	k_{56}	k_{67}	k_{78}
2	1.950	1.950	0.723						
3	1.864	1.864	0.647	0.647					
4	1.826	1.826	0.648	0.545	0.648				
5	1.807	1.807	0.652	0.534	0.534	0.652			
6	1.796	1.796	0.655	0.533	0.519	0.533	0.655		
7	1.790	1.790	0.657	0.533	0.516	0.516	0.533	0.657	
8	1.785	1.785	0.658	0.533	0.515	0.511	0.515	0.533	0.658

TABLE 5-7 1-dB Chebyshev Capacitive Coupled Resonators

n	q_1	q_n	k_{12}	k_{23}	k_{34}	k_{45}	k_{56}	k_{67}
2	2.210	2.210	0.739					
3	2.210	2.210	0.645	0.645				
4	2.210	2.210	0.638	0.546	0.638			
5	2.210	2.210	0.633	0.535	0.538	0.633		
6	2.250	2.250	0.631	0.531	0.510	0.531	0.631	
7	2.250	2.250	0.631	0.530	0.517	0.517	0.530	0.631

TABLE 5-8 Bessel Capacitive Coupled Resonators

n	q_1	q_n	k_{12}	k_{23}	k_{34}	k_{45}	k_{56}	k_{67}	k_{78}
2	0.5755	2.148	0.900						
3	0.337	2.203	1.748	0.684					
4	0.233	2.240	2.530	1.175	0.644				
5	0.394	0.275	1.910	0.750	0.650	1.987			
6	0.415	0.187	2.000	0.811	0.601	1.253	3.038		
7	0.187	0.242	3.325	1.660	1.293	0.695	0.674	2.203	
8	0.139	0.242	4.284	2.079	1.484	1.246	0.678	0.697	2.286

TABLE 5-9 Linear Phase with Equiripple Error of 0.05° Capacitive Coupled Resonators

n	q_1	q_n	k_{12}	k_{23}	k_{34}	k_{45}	k_{56}	k_{67}	k_{78}
2	0.648	2.109	0.856						
3	0.433	2.254	1.489	0.652					
4	0.493	0.718	1.632	0.718	0.739				
5	0.547	0.446	1.800	0.848	0.584	1.372			
6	0.397	0.468	1.993	1.379	0.683	0.661	1.553		
7	0.316	0.484	2.490	1.442	1.446	0.927	0.579	1.260	
8	0.335	0.363	2.585	1.484	1.602	1.160	0.596	0.868	1.733

TABLE 5-10 Linear Phase with Equiripple Error of 0.5° Capacitive Coupled Resonators

n	q_1	q_n	k_{12}	k_{23}	k_{34}	k_{45}	k_{56}	k_{67}	k_{78}
2	0.825	1.980	0.783						
3	0.553	2.425	1.330	0.635					
4	0.581	1.026	1.575	0.797	0.656				
5	0.664	0.611	1.779	0.919	0.576	1.162			
6	0.552	0.586	1.874	1.355	0.641	0.721	1.429		
7	0.401	0.688	2.324	1.394	1.500	1.079	0.590	1.045	
8	0.415	0.563	2.410	1.470	1.527	1.409	0.659	0.755	1.335

TABLE 5-11 Transitional Gaussian to 6-dB Capacitive Coupled Resonators

n	q_1	q_n	k_{12}	k_{23}	k_{34}	k_{45}	k_{56}	k_{67}	k_{78}
3	0.404	2.338	1.662	0.691					
4	0.570	0.914	1.623	0.798	0.682				
5	0.891	0.670	1.418	0.864	0.553	1.046			
6	0.883	0.752	1.172	1.029	0.595	0.605	1.094		
7	0.736	0.930	1.130	0.955	0.884	0.534	0.633	1.104	
8	0.738	0.948	1.124	0.866	0.922	0.708	0.501	0.752	1.089

TABLE 5-12 Transitional Gaussian to 12-dB Capacitive Coupled Resonators

n	q_1	q_n	k_{12}	k_{23}	k_{34}	k_{45}	k_{56}	k_{67}	k_{78}
3	0.415	2.345	1.631	0.686					
4	0.419	0.766	1.989	0.833	0.740				
5	0.534	0.503	2.085	0.976	0.605	1.333			
6	0.543	0.558	1.839	1.442	0.686	0.707	1.468		
7	0.492	0.665	1.708	1.440	1.181	0.611	0.781	1.541	
8	0.549	0.640	1.586	1.262	1.296	0.808	0.569	1.023	1.504

5. The total capacity connected to each node must be equal to C_{node}. Therefore, the shunt capacitors of the parallel tuned circuits are equal to the total nodal capacitance C_{node} less the values of the coupling capacitors connected to that node. For example,

$$C_1 = C_{node} - C_{12}$$

$$C_2 = C_{node} - C_{12} - C_{23}$$

$$C_7 = C_{node} - C_{67} - C_{78}$$

Each node is tuned to f_0 with the adjacent nodes shorted to ground so that the coupling capacitors connected to that node are placed in parallel across the tuned circuit.

The completed filter may require impedance scaling so that the source and load terminating requirements are met. In addition, some of the impedance transformations discussed in chapter 8 may have to be applied.

The k and q values tabulated in tables 5-3 through 5-12 are based on infinite inductor Q. In reality, satisfactory results will be obtained for inductor Qs several times higher than Q_{min} (bandpass) determined by equation (5-17) in conjunction with figure 3-8 which shows the minimum theoretical low-pass Qs.

EXAMPLE 5-7

REQUIRED:

Bandpass filter
Center frequency of 100 kHz
3 dB at ±2.5 kHz
35 dB minimum at ±12.5 kHz
Constant delay over the passband

RESULT:

(a) Since a constant delay is required, a Bessel filter type will be chosen. The low-pass constant delay properties will undergo a minimum of distortion for the bandpass case since the bandwidth is relatively narrow, i.e., the bandpass Q is high. Because the bandwidth is narrow, we can treat the requirements on an arithmetically symmetrical basis.

The bandpass steepness factor is given by

$$A_s = \frac{\text{stopband bandwidth}}{\text{passband bandwidth}} = \frac{25\ \text{kHz}}{5\ \text{kHz}} = 5 \qquad (2\text{-}19)$$

The frequency-response curves of figure 2-56 indicate that an $n = 4$ Bessel filter provides over 35 dB of attenuation at 5 rad/s. A capacitive coupled resonator configuration will be used for the implementation.

(b) The q and k parameters for a Bessel filter corresponding to $n = 4$ are found in table 5-8 and are as follows:

$$q_1 = 0.233$$

$$q_4 = 2.240$$

$$k_{12} = 2.530$$

$$k_{23} = 1.175$$

$$k_{34} = 0.644$$

To denormalize these values, divide each k by the bandpass Q and multiply each q by the same factor as follows:

$$Q_{bp} = \frac{f_0}{BW_{3\,dB}} = \frac{100\ kHz}{5\ kHz} = 20 \tag{2-16}$$

The resulting values are

$$Q_1 = Q_{bp} \times q_1 = 20 \times 0.233 = 4.66 \tag{5-32}$$

$$Q_4 = 44.8$$

$$K_{12} = \frac{k_{12}}{Q_{bp}} = \frac{2.530}{20} = 0.1265 \tag{5-34}$$

$$K_{23} = 0.05875$$

$$K_{34} = 0.0322$$

(c) Let us choose an inductance of $L = 2.5$ mH. The source and load terminations are

$$R_s = \omega_0 L Q_1 = 6.28 \times 10^5 \times 2.5 \times 10^{-3} \times 4.66 = 7.32\ k\Omega \tag{5-35}$$

and

$$R_L = \omega_0 L Q_4 = 70.37\ k\Omega \tag{5-36}$$

where

$$\omega_0 = 2\pi f_0$$

(d) The total nodal capacitance is determined by

$$C_{node} = \frac{1}{\omega_0^2 L} = 1013\ pF \tag{5-37}$$

The coupling capacitors can now be calculated.

$$C_{12} = K_{12}\, C_{node} = 0.1265 \times 1.013 \times 10^{-9} = 128.1\ pF \tag{5-38}$$

$$C_{23} = K_{23}\, C_{node} = 59.5\ pF$$

$$C_{34} = K_{34}\, C_{node} = 32.6\ pF$$

The shunt capacitors are determined from

$$C_1 = C_{node} - C_{12} = 884.9\ pF$$

$$C_2 = C_{node} - C_{12} - C_{23} = 825.4\ pF$$

$$C_3 = C_{node} - C_{23} - C_{34} = 920.9\ pF$$

$$C_4 = C_{node} - C_{34} = 980.4\ pF$$

The final circuit is shown in figure 5-15.

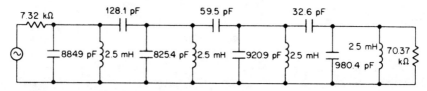

FIGURE 5-15   Capacitive coupled resonator filter of example 5-7.

Predistorted Bandpass Filters

The inductor Q requirements of bandpass filters are higher than those of low-pass filters, since the minimum theoretical branch Q is given by

$$Q_{\min} \text{ (bandpass)} = Q_{\min} \text{ (low-pass)} \times Q_{bp} \qquad (5\text{-}17)$$

where $Q_{bp} = f_0/\mathrm{BW_{3\,dB}}$. In the cases where the filter required is extremely narrow, a branch Q many times higher than the minimum theoretical Q may be difficult to obtain. Predistorted bandpass filters can then be used so that exact theoretical results can be obtained with reasonable branch Qs.

Predistorted bandpass filters can be obtained from the normalized predistorted low-pass filters given in chapter 11 by the conventional bandpass transformation. The low-pass filters must be of the uniform dissipation type, since the lossy-L networks would be transformed to a bandpass filter having losses in the series branches only.

The uniform dissipation networks are tabulated for different values of dissipation factor d. These values relate to the required inductor Q by the relationship

$$Q_L = \frac{Q_{bp}}{d} \qquad (5\text{-}39)$$

where $Q_{bp} = f_0/\mathrm{BW_{3\,dB}}$.

The losses of a predistorted low-pass filter having uniform dissipation are evenly distributed and occur as series losses in the inductors and shunt losses across the capacitors. The equivalent circuit of the filter is shown in figure 5-16a. The inductor losses were previously given by

$$R_L = \frac{\omega L}{Q} \qquad (3\text{-}2)$$

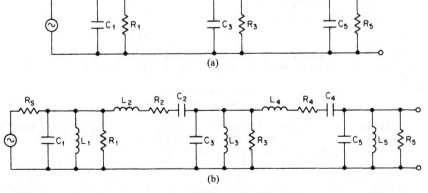

FIGURE 5-16 Location of losses in uniformly predistorted filters: (a) low-pass filter; (b) bandpass filter.

and the capacitor losses were defined by

$$R_c = \frac{Q}{\omega C} \tag{3-3}$$

When the circuit is transformed to a bandpass filter, the losses are still required to be distributed in series with the series branches and in parallel with the shunt branches, as shown in figure 5-16b. In reality, the capacitor losses are minimal and the inductor losses occur in series with the inductive elements in both the series and shunt branches. Therefore, as a narrowband approximation, the losses may be distributed between the capacitors and inductors in an arbitrary manner. The only restriction is that the combination of inductor and capacitor losses in each branch results in a total branch Q equal to the value computed by equation (5-39). The combined Q of a lossy inductor and a lossy capacitor in a resonant circuit is given by

$$Q_T = \frac{Q_L Q_C}{Q_L + Q_C} \tag{5-40}$$

where Q_T is the total branch Q, Q_L is the inductor Q, and Q_C is the Q of the capacitor.

The predistorted networks tabulated in chapter 11 require an infinite termination on one side. In practice, if the resistance used to approximate the infinite termination is large compared with the source termination, satisfactory results will be obtained. If the dual configuration is used, which ideally requires a zero impedance source, the source impedance should be much less than the load termination.

It is usually difficult to obtain inductor Qs precisely equal to the values computed from equation (5-39). A Q accuracy within 5 or 10% at f_0 is usually sufficient. If greater accuracy is required, an inductor Q higher than the calculated value is used. The Q is then degraded to the exact required value by adding resistors.

EXAMPLE 5-8

REQUIRED:

Bandpass filter
Center frequency of 10 kHz
3 dB at ±250 Hz
60 dB minimum at ±750 Hz
$R_s = 100 \, \Omega$ $R_L = 10 \, k\Omega$ minimum
Available inductor Q of 225

RESULT:

(a) Since the filter is narrow in bandwidth, the requirement is treated in its arithmetically symmetrical form. The bandpass-steepness factor is obtained from

$$A_s = \frac{\text{stopband bandwidth}}{\text{passband bandwidth}} = \frac{1500 \text{ Hz}}{500 \text{ Hz}} = 3 \tag{2-19}$$

The curves of figure 2-43 indicate that a fifth-order ($n = 5$) 0.25-dB Chebyshev filter will meet these requirements. A predistorted design will be used. The corresponding normalized low-pass filters are found in table 11-33.

(b) The specified inductor Q can be used to compute the required d of the low-pass filter as follows:

$$d = \frac{Q_{bp}}{Q_L} = \frac{20}{225} = 0.0889 \tag{5-39}$$

where $Q_{bp} = f_0/BW_{3\,dB}$. The circuit corresponding to $n = 5$ and $d = 0.0919$ will be selected, since this d is sufficiently close to the computed value. The schematic is shown in figure 5-17a.

(c) Denormalize the low-pass filter using a frequency-scaling factor (FSF) of $2\pi f_c$ or 3140 where $f_c = 500$ Hz, the required bandwidth of the bandpass filter, and an impedance-scaling factor Z of 100.

$$C_1' = \frac{C}{FSF \times Z} = \frac{1.0397}{3140 \times 100} = 3.309 \text{ }\mu\text{F} \tag{2-10}$$

$$C_3' = 7.014 \text{ }\mu\text{F}$$

$$C_5' = 3.660 \text{ }\mu\text{F}$$

and $$L_2' = \frac{L \times Z}{FSF} = \frac{1.8181 \times 100}{3140} = 57.87 \text{ mH} \tag{2-9}$$

$$L_4' = 55.79 \text{ mH}$$

The denormalized low-pass filter is shown in figure 5-17b, where the termination has been scaled to 100 Ω. The filter has also been turned end for end, since the high-impedance termination is required at the output and the 100-Ω source at the input.

(d) To transform the circuit into a bandpass filter, resonate each capacitor with an inductor in parallel and each inductor with a series capacitor using a resonant frequency of $f_0 = 10$ kHz. The parallel inductor is computed from

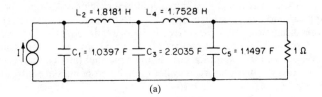

(a)

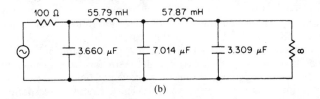

(b)

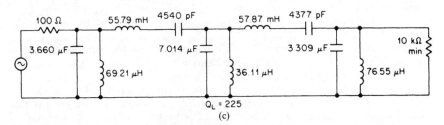

(c)

FIGURE 5-17 Predistorted bandpass filter of example 5-8: (*a*) normalized low-pass filter; (*b*) frequency- and impedance-scaled network; (*c*) resulting bandpass filter.

$$L = \frac{1}{\omega_0^2 C} \tag{5-11}$$

and the series capacitor is calculated by

$$C = \frac{1}{\omega_0^2 L} \tag{5-12}$$

where both formulas are forms of the general relationship for resonance $\omega_0^2 LC = 1$. The resulting bandpass filter is given in figure 5-17c. The large spread of values can be reduced by applying some of the techniques discussed in chapter 8.

Elliptic-Function Bandpass Filters

Elliptic-function low-pass filters were clearly shown to be far superior to the other filter types in terms of achieving a required attenuation within a given frequency ratio. This superiority is mainly the result of the presence of transmission zeros beginning just outside the passband.

Elliptic-function LC low-pass filters have been extensively tabulated by Saal and Ulbrich and by Zverev (see bibliography). Some of these tables are reproduced in chapter 11. These networks can be transformed into bandpass filters in the same manner as the all-pole filter types. The elliptic-function bandpass filters will then exhibit the same superiority over the all-pole types as their low-pass counterparts.

When an elliptic-function low-pass filter is transformed into a bandpass filter, each low-pass transmission zero is converted in a pair of zeros, one above and one below the passband and geometrically related to the center frequency. (For the purposes of this discussion, negative zeros will be disregarded.) The low-pass zeros are directly determined by the resonances of the parallel tuned circuits in the series branches. When each series branch containing a parallel tuned circuit is modified by the bandpass transformation, two parallel branch resonances are introduced corresponding to the upper and lower zeros.

A sixth-order elliptic-function low-pass filter structure is shown in figure 5-18a. After frequency- and impedance-scaling the low-pass values, we can make a bandpass transformation by resonating each inductor with a series capacitor and each capacitor with a parallel inductor, where the resonant frequency is f_0, the filter center frequency. The circuit of figure 5-18b results. The configuration obtained in branches 2 and 4 corresponds to a type III network from table 5-2.

The type III network realizes two parallel resonances corresponding to a geometrically related pair of transmission zeros above and below the passband. The circuit configuration itself is not very desirable. The elements corresponding to both parallel resonances are not distinctly isolated. Each resonance is determined by the interaction of a number of elements, so tuning is made difficult. Also, for very narrow filters, the values may become unreasonable. Fortunately an alternate circuit exists that provides a more practical relationship between the coils and capacitors. The two equivalent configurations are shown in figure 5-19. The alternate configuration utilizes two parallel tuned circuits where each condition of parallel resonance directly corresponds to a transmission zero.

The type III network of figure 5-19 is shown with reciprocal element values. These result when we normalize the bandpass filter to a center frequency of 1 rad/s. Since the general equation for resonance $\omega_0^2 LC = 1$ reduces to $LC = 1$ at $\omega_0 = 1$, the resonant elements become reciprocals of each other.

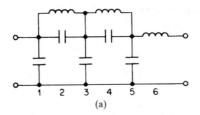

(a)

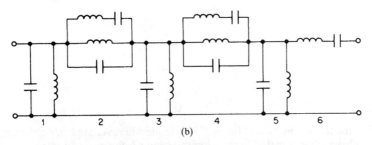

(b)

FIGURE 5-18 Low-pass to bandpass transformation of elliptic-function filter: (a) $n = 6$ low-pass filter; (b) transformed bandpass configuration.

The reason for this normalization is to greatly simplify the equations for the transformation of figure 5-19. Otherwise, the equations relating the two circuits would be extremely complex and unsuitable for computation by hand.

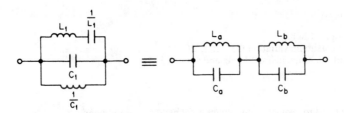

FIGURE 5-19 Equivalent circuit of type III network.

To obtain the normalized bandpass filter, first multiply all L and C values of the normalized low-pass filter by Q_{bp}, which is equal to f_0/BW, where BW is the passband bandwidth. The network can then be transformed directly into a normalized bandpass filter by resonating each inductor with a series capacitor and each capacitor with a parallel inductor. The resonant elements are merely reciprocals of each other, since $\omega_0 = 1$.

The transformation of figure 5-19 can now be performed. First calculate

$$\beta = 1 + \frac{1}{2L_1C_1} + \sqrt{\frac{1}{4L_1^2C_1^2} + \frac{1}{L_1C_1}} \qquad (5\text{-}41)$$

The values are then obtained from

$$L_a = \frac{1}{C_1(\beta + 1)} \tag{5-42}$$

$$L_b = \beta \, L_a \tag{5-43}$$

$$C_a = \frac{1}{L_b} \tag{5-44}$$

$$C_b = \frac{1}{L_a} \tag{5-45}$$

The resonant frequencies are given by

$$\Omega_{\infty,a} = \sqrt{\beta} \tag{5-46}$$

and

$$\Omega_{\infty,b} = \frac{1}{\Omega_{\infty,a}} \tag{5-47}$$

After the transformation of figure 5-19 is made wherever applicable, the normalized bandpass filter is scaled to the required center frequency and impedance level by multiplying all inductors by Z/FSF and dividing all capacitors by $Z \times FSF$. The frequency-scaling factor in this case is equal to ω_0 ($\omega_0 = 2\pi f_0$, where f_0 is the desired center frequency of the filter). The resonant frequencies in hertz can be found by multiplying all normalized radian resonant frequencies by f_0.

The design of an elliptic-function bandpass filter is demonstrated by the following example.

EXAMPLE 5-9

REQUIRED:

Bandpass filter
1 dB maximum variation from 15 to 20 kHz
50 dB minimum below 14 kHz and above 23 kHz
$R_s = R_L = 10 \text{ k}\Omega$

RESULT:

(a) Convert to geometrically symmetrical bandpass requirement:
First calculate the geometric center frequency.

$$f_0 = \sqrt{f_L f_u} = \sqrt{15 \times 20 \times 10^6} = 17.32 \text{ kHz} \tag{2-14}$$

Compute the corresponding geometric frequency for each stopband frequency given using the relationship

$$f_1 f_2 = f_0^2 \tag{2-18}$$

f_1	f_2	$f_2 - f_1$
14.00 kHz	21.43 kHz	7.43 kHz
13.04 kHz	23.00 kHz	9.96 kHz

The first pair of frequencies has the lesser separation and therefore represents the more severe requirement and will be retained. The geometrically symmetrical requirements can be summarized as

$$f_0 = 17.32 \text{ kHz}$$

$$BW_{1 \text{ dB}} = 5 \text{ kHz}$$

$$BW_{50 \text{ dB}} = 7.43 \text{ kHz}$$

(b) Compute the bandpass steepness factor.

$$A_s = \frac{\text{stopband bandwidth}}{\text{passband bandwidth}} = \frac{7.43 \text{ kHz}}{5 \text{ kHz}} = 1.486 \qquad (2\text{-}19)$$

(c) Select a normalized low-pass filter that makes the transition from less than 1 dB to more than 50 dB within a frequency ratio of 1.486. Since the requirement is rather steep, an elliptic-function type will be chosen.

Figure 2-86 indicates that for a ρ of 20% (0.18-dB ripple) a filter complexity of $n = 6$ is required. Using the tables of section 12-56, a design corresponding to C06 20C $\theta = 46°$ has the parameters $\Omega_s = 1.458$ and $A_{min} = 54.7$ dB, which meets these requirements. The normalized circuit is shown in figure 5-20a.

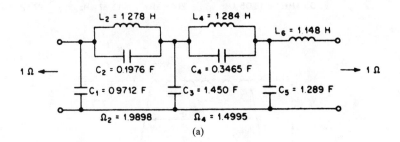

(a)

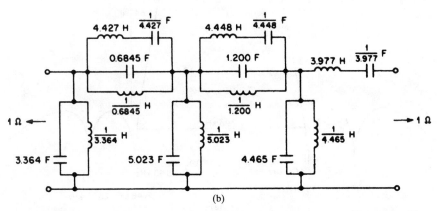

(b)

FIGURE 5-20 Elliptic-function bandpass filter: (a) normalized low-pass filter; (b) bandpass filter normalized to $\omega_0 = 1$.

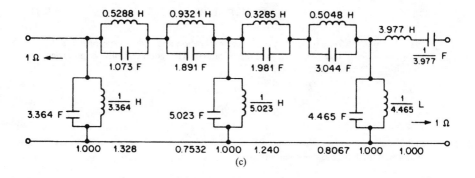

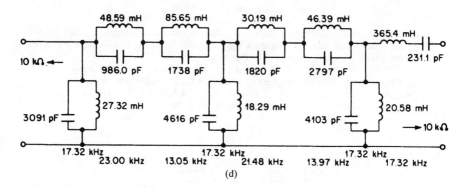

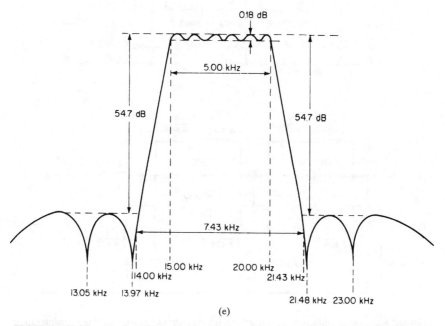

FIGURE 5-20 (*Continued*) Elliptic-function bandpass filter: (*c*) transformed type III branches; (*d*) final scaled circuit; (*e*) frequency response.

(d) The filter must now be converted to a normalized bandpass filter having a center frequency of $\omega_0 = 1$. The bandpass Q is first computed from

$$Q_{bp} = \frac{f_0}{BW} = \frac{17.32 \text{ kHz}}{5 \text{ kHz}} = 3.464$$

Multiply all inductance and capacitance values by Q_{bp}. Then transform the network into a bandpass filter centered at $\omega_0 = 1$ by resonating each capacitor with a parallel inductor and each inductor with a series capacitor. The resonating elements introduced are simply the reciprocal values as shown in figure 5-20b.

(e) The type III branches will now be transformed in accordance with figure 5-19.
For the first branch:

$$L_1 = 4.427 \text{ H} \qquad C_1 = 0.6845 \text{ F}$$

First compute

$$\beta = 1 + \frac{1}{2L_1C_1} + \sqrt{\frac{1}{4L_1^2C_1^2} + \frac{1}{L_1C_1}} = 1.763 \tag{5-41}$$

then

$$L_a = \frac{1}{C_1(\beta + 1)} = 0.5288 \text{ H} \tag{5-42}$$

$$L_b = \beta\, L_a = 0.9321 \text{ H} \tag{5-43}$$

$$C_a = \frac{1}{L_b} = 1.073 \text{ F} \tag{5-44}$$

$$C_b = \frac{1}{L_a} = 1.891 \text{ F} \tag{5-45}$$

The resonant frequencies are

$$\Omega_{\infty,a} = \sqrt{\beta} = 1.328 \tag{5-46}$$

$$\Omega_{\infty,b} = \frac{1}{\Omega_{\infty,a}} = 0.7532 \tag{5-47}$$

For the second branch:

$$L_1 = 4.448 \text{ H} \qquad C_1 = 1.200 \text{ F}$$

then

$$\beta = 1.5365$$

$$L_a = 0.3285 \text{ H}$$

$$L_b = 0.5048 \text{ H}$$

$$C_a = 1.981 \text{ F}$$

$$C_b = 3.044 \text{ F}$$

$$\Omega_{\infty,a} = 1.240$$

$$\Omega_{\infty,b} = 0.8067$$

The transformed filter is shown in figure 5-20c. The resonant frequencies in radians per second are indicated below the schematic.

(f) To complete the design, denormalize the filter to a center frequency (f_0) of 17.32 kHz and an impedance level of 10 kΩ. Multiply all inductors by Z/FSF and divide all capacitors by $Z \times$ FSF where $Z = 10^4$ and FSF $= 2\pi f_0$ or 1.0882×10^5. The final filter is shown in figure 5-20d. The resonant frequencies were obtained by direct multiplication of the normalized resonant frequencies of figure 5-20c by the geometric center frequency f_0. The frequency response is shown in figure 5-20e.

5.2 ACTIVE BANDPASS FILTERS

When the separation between the upper and lower cutoff frequencies exceeds a ratio of approximately 2, the bandpass filter is considered a wideband type. The specifications are then separated into individual low-pass and high-pass requirements and met by a cascade of active low-pass and high-pass filters.

Narrowband LC bandpass filters are usually designed by transforming a low-pass configuration directly into the bandpass circuit. Unfortunately, no such circuit transformation exists for active networks. The general approach involves transforming the low-pass transfer function into a bandpass type. The bandpass poles and zeros are then implemented by a cascade of bandpass filter sections.

Wideband Filters

When LC low-pass and high-pass filters were cascaded, care had to be taken to minimize terminal impedance variations so that each filter maintained its individual response in the cascaded form. Active filters can be interconnected with no interaction because of the inherent buffering of the operational amplifiers. The only exception occurs in the case of the elliptic-function VCVS filters of sections 3.2 and 4.2 where the last sections are followed by an RC network to provide the real poles. An amplifier must then be introduced for isolation.

Figure 5-21 shows two simple amplifier configurations which can be used after an active elliptic filter. The gain of the voltage follower is unity. The noninverting amplifier has a gain equal to $R_2/R_1 + 1$. The resistors R_1 and R_2 can have any convenient values, since only their ratio is of significance.

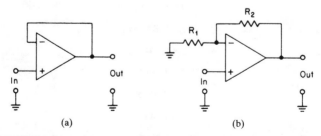

(a)   (b)

FIGURE 5-21   Isolation amplifiers: (a) voltage follower; (b) noninverting amplifier.

EXAMPLE 5-10

REQUIRED:

Active bandpass filter
1 dB maximum variation from 3000 to 9000 Hz
35 dB minimum below 1000 Hz and above 18,000 Hz
Gain of +20 dB

RESULT:

(a) Since the ratio of upper cutoff frequency to lower cutoff frequency is well in excess of an octave, the design will be treated as a cascade of low-pass and high-pass filters. The frequency-response requirement can be restated as the following set of individual low-pass and high-pass specifications:

High-pass filter:
1 dB maximum at 3000 Hz
35 dB minimum below 1000 Hz

Low-pass filter:
1 dB maximum at 9000 Hz
35 dB minimum above 18,000 Hz

(b) To design the high-pass filter, first compute the high-pass steepness factor.

$$A_s = \frac{f_c}{f_s} = \frac{3000 \text{ Hz}}{1000 \text{ Hz}} = 3 \qquad (2\text{-}13)$$

A normalized low-pass filter must now be chosen that makes the transition from less than 1 dB to more than 35 dB within a frequency ratio of 3:1. An elliptic-function type will be selected. The high-pass filter designed in example 4-5 illustrates this process and will meet this requirement. The circuit is shown in figure 5-22a.

(c) The low-pass filter is now designed. The low-pass steepness factor is computed by

$$A_s = \frac{f_s}{f_c} = \frac{18,000 \text{ Hz}}{9,000 \text{ Hz}} = 2 \qquad (2\text{-}11)$$

A low-pass filter must be selected that makes the transition from less than 1 dB to more than 35 dB within a frequency ratio of 2:1. The curves of figure 2-44 indicate that the attenuation of a normalized 0.5-dB Chebyshev filter of a complexity of $n = 5$ is less than 1 dB at 0.9 rad/s and more than 35 dB at 1.8 rad/s, which satisfies the requirements. The corresponding active filter is found in table 11-39 and is shown in figure 5-22b.

To denormalize the low-pass circuit, first compute the FSF, which is given by

$$FSF = \frac{\text{desired reference frequency}}{\text{existing reference frequency}}$$

$$= \frac{2\pi \times 9000 \text{ rad/s}}{0.9 \text{ rad/s}} = 62,830 \qquad (2\text{-}1)$$

The filter is then denormalized by dividing all capacitors by $Z \times FSF$ and multiplying all resistors by Z, where Z is arbitrarily chosen at 10^4. The denormalized circuit is shown in figure 5-22c.

(d) To complete the design, the low-pass and high-pass filters are cascaded. Since the real-pole RC network of the elliptic high-pass filter must be buffered and since a gain of +20 dB is required, the noninverting amplifier of figure 5-21b will be used.

The finalized design is shown in figure 5-22d, where the resistors have been rounded off to standard 1% values.

Bandpass Transformation of Low-Pass Poles and Zeros

Active bandpass filters are designed directly from a bandpass transfer function. To obtain the bandpass poles and zeros from the low-pass transfer function, a low-pass

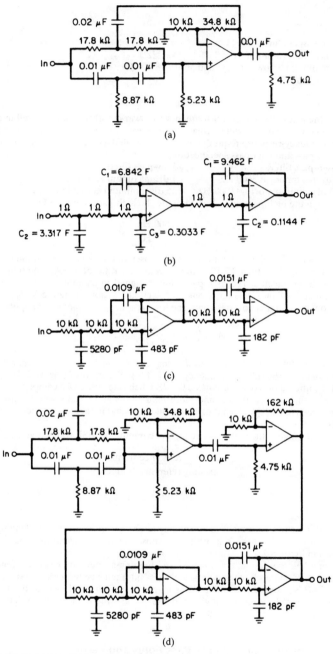

FIGURE 5-22 Wideband bandpass filter of example 5-10: (*a*) high-pass filter of example 4-5, (*b*) normalized low-pass filter, (*c*) denormalized low-pass filter, and (*d*) bandpass filter configuration.

to bandpass transformation must be performed. It was shown in section 5.1 how this transformation can be accomplished by replacing the frequency variable by a new variable which was given by

$$f_{bp} = f_0 \left(\frac{f}{f_0} - \frac{f_0}{f} \right) \tag{5-1}$$

This substitution maps the low-pass frequency response into a bandpass magnitude characteristic.

Two sets of bandpass poles are obtained from each low-pass complex pole pair. If the low-pass pole is real, a single pair of complex poles results for the bandpass case. Also, each pair of imaginary axis zeros is transformed into two pairs of conjugate zeros. This is shown in figure 5-23.

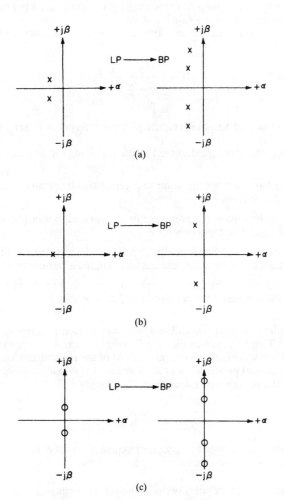

FIGURE 5-23 Low-pass to bandpass transformation: (*a*) low-pass complex pole pair; (*b*) low-pass real pole; (*c*) low-pass pair of imaginary zeros.

Clearly, the total number of poles and zeros is doubled when the bandpass transformation is performed. However, it is conventional to disregard the conjugate bandpass poles and zeros below the real axis. An n-pole low-pass filter is said to result in an nth-order bandpass filter even though the bandpass transfer function is of the order $2n$. An nth-order active bandpass filter will then consist of n bandpass sections.

Each all-pole bandpass section has a second-order transfer function given by

$$T(s) = \frac{Hs}{s^2 + \dfrac{\omega_r}{Q}s + \omega_r^2} \tag{5-48}$$

where ω_r is equal to $2\pi f_r$, the pole resonant frequency in radians per second, Q is the bandpass section Q, and H is a gain constant.

If transmission zeros are required, the section transfer function will then take the form

$$T(s) = \frac{H(s^2 + \omega_\infty^2)}{s^2 + \dfrac{\omega_r}{Q}s + \omega_r^2} \tag{5-49}$$

where ω_∞ is equal to $2\pi f_\infty$, the frequency of the transmission zero in radians per second.

Active bandpass filters are designed by the following sequence of operations:

1. Convert the bandpass specification to a geometrically symmetrical requirement as described in section 2.1.

2. Calculate the bandpass steepness factor A_s using equation (2-19) and select a normalized filter type from chapter 2.

3. Look up the corresponding normalized poles (and zeros) from the tables of chapter 11 and transform these coordinates into bandpass parameters.

4. Select the appropriate bandpass circuit configuration from the types presented in this chapter and cascade the required number of sections.

It is convenient to specify each bandpass filter section in terms of its center frequency and Q. Elliptic-function filters will require zeros. These parameters can be directly transformed from the poles (and zeros) of the normalized low-pass transfer function. A numerical procedure will be described for making this transformation.

First make the preliminary calculation

$$Q_{bp} = \frac{f_0}{BW} \tag{2-16}$$

where f_0 is the geometric bandpass center frequency and BW is the passband bandwidth. The bandpass transformation is made as follows:

Complex Poles.   Complex poles occur in the tables of chapter 11 having the form

$$-\alpha \pm j\beta$$

where α is the real coordinate and β is the imaginary part. Given α, β, Q_{bp}, and f_0, the following series of calculations results in two sets of values for Q and center frequency which define a pair of bandpass filter sections:

$$C = \alpha^2 + \beta^2 \qquad (5\text{-}50)$$

$$D = \frac{2\alpha}{Q_{bp}} \qquad (5\text{-}51)$$

$$E = \frac{C}{Q_{bp}^2} + 4 \qquad (5\text{-}52)$$

$$G = \sqrt{E^2 - 4D^2} \qquad (5\text{-}53)$$

$$Q = \sqrt{\frac{E+G}{2D^2}} \qquad (5\text{-}54)$$

$$M = \frac{\alpha Q}{Q_{bp}} \qquad (5\text{-}55)$$

$$W = M + \sqrt{M^2 - 1} \qquad (5\text{-}56)$$

$$f_{ra} = \frac{f_0}{W} \qquad (5\text{-}57)$$

$$f_{rb} = W f_0 \qquad (5\text{-}58)$$

The two bandpass sections have resonant frequencies of f_{ra} and f_{rb} (in hertz) and identical Qs as given by equation (5-54).

Real Poles. A normalized low-pass real pole having a real coordinate of magnitude α_0 is transformed into a single bandpass section having a Q defined by

$$Q = \frac{Q_{bp}}{\alpha_0} \qquad (5\text{-}59)$$

The section is tuned to f_0, the geometric center frequency of the filter.

Imaginary Zeros. Elliptic-function low-pass filters contain transmission zeros as well as poles. These zeros must be transformed along with the poles when a bandpass filter is required. Imaginary-axis zeros are tabulated alongside the low-pass normalized values in table 11-56 and are of the form $\pm j\omega_\infty$. The bandpass zeros can be obtained as follows:

$$H = \frac{\omega_\infty^2}{2\,Q_{bp}^2} + 1 \qquad (5\text{-}60)$$

$$Z = \sqrt{H + \sqrt{H^2 - 1}} \qquad (5\text{-}61)$$

$$f_{\infty,a} = \frac{f_0}{Z} \qquad (5\text{-}62)$$

$$f_{\infty,b} = Z \times f_0 \qquad (5\text{-}63)$$

A pair of imaginary bandpass zeros are obtained occurring at $f_{\infty,a}$ and $f_{\infty,b}$ (in hertz) from each low-pass zero.

Determining Section Gain.   The gain of a single bandpass section at the filter geometric center frequency f_0 is given by

$$A_0 = \frac{A_r}{\sqrt{1 + Q^2 \left(\dfrac{f_0}{f_r} - \dfrac{f_r}{f_0} \right)^2}} \tag{5-64}$$

where A_r is the section gain at its resonant frequency f_r. The section gain will always be less at f_0 than at f_r, since the circuit is peaked to f_r, except for transformed real poles where $f_r = f_0$. Equation (5-64) will then simplify to $A_0 = A_r$. The composite filter gain is determined by the product of the A_0 values of all the sections.

If the section Q is relatively high ($Q > 10$), equation (5-64) can be simplified to

$$A_0 = \frac{A_r}{\sqrt{1 + \left(\dfrac{2\,Q\Delta f}{f_r} \right)^2}} \tag{5-65}$$

where Δf is the frequency separation between f_0 and f_r.

EXAMPLE 5-11

REQUIRED: Determine the pole locations and section gains for a third-order Butterworth bandpass filter having a geometric center frequency of 1000 Hz, a 3-dB bandwidth of 100 Hz, and a midband gain of +30 dB.

RESULT:

(a) The normalized pole locations for an $n = 3$ Butterworth low-pass filter are obtained from table 11-1 and are
  $-0.500 \pm j0.8660$
  -1.000
To obtain the bandpass poles first compute

$$Q_{bp} = \frac{f_0}{BW_{3\,dB}} = \frac{1000\ \text{Hz}}{100\ \text{Hz}} = 10 \tag{2-16}$$

The low-pass to bandpass pole transformation is performed as follows:
  Complex pole:

$$\alpha = 0.5000 \qquad \beta = 0.8660$$

$$C = \alpha^2 + \beta^2 = 1.000000 \tag{5-50}$$

$$D = \frac{2\alpha}{Q_{bp}} = 0.100000 \tag{5-51}$$

$$E = \frac{C}{Q_{bp}^2} + 4 = 4.010000 \tag{5-52}$$

$$G = \sqrt{E^2 - 4D^2} = 4.005010 \tag{5-53}$$

$$Q = \sqrt{\frac{E + G}{2D^2}} = 20.018754 \tag{5-54}$$

$$M = \frac{\alpha Q}{Q_{bp}} = 1.000938 \tag{5-55}$$

$$W = M + \sqrt{M^2 - 1} = 1.044261 \tag{5-56}$$

$$f_{ra} = \frac{f_0}{W} = 957.6 \text{ Hz} \tag{5-57}$$

$$f_{rb} = Wf_0 = 1044.3 \text{ Hz} \tag{5-58}$$

Real pole:

$$\alpha_0 = 1.0000$$

$$Q = \frac{Q_{bp}}{\alpha_0} = 10 \tag{5-59}$$

$$f_r = f_0 = 1000 \text{ Hz}$$

(b) Since a composite midband gain of +30 dB is required, let us distribute the gain uniformly among the three sections. Therefore, $A_0 = 3.162$ for each section corresponding to +10 dB.

The gain at section resonant frequency f_r is obtained from the following form of equation (5-64):

$$A_r = A_0 \sqrt{1 + Q^2 \left(\frac{f_0}{f_r} - \frac{f_r}{f_0} \right)^2}$$

The resulting values are

Section 1: $f_r = 957.6 \text{ Hz}$

$Q = 20.02$

$A_r = 6.333$

Section 2: $f_r = 1044.3 \text{ Hz}$

$Q = 20.02$

$A_r = 6.335$

Section 3: $f_r = 1000.0 \text{ Hz}$

$Q = 10.00$

$A_r = 3.162$

The block diagram of the realization is shown in figure 5-24.

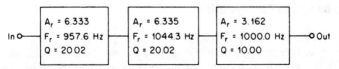

FIGURE 5-24 Block realization of example 5-11.

The calculations required for the bandpass pole transformation should be maintained to more than four significant figures after the decimal point to obtain accurate results, since differences of close numbers are involved. Equations (5-55) and (5-56) are especially critical, so the value of M should be computed to five or six places after the decimal point.

Sensitivity in Active Bandpass Circuits

Sensitivity defines the amount of change of a dependent variable resulting from the variation of an independent variable. Mathematically, the sensitivity of y with respect to x is expressed as

$$S_x^y = \frac{dy/y}{dx/x} \tag{5-66}$$

Sensitivity is used as a figure of merit to measure the change in a particular filter parameter such as Q or resonant frequency for a given change in a component value.

Deviations of components from their nominal values occur because of the effects of temperature, aging, humidity, and other environmental conditions in addition to the errors because of tolerances. These variations cause changes in parameters such as Q and center frequency from their design values.

As an example, let us assume we are given the parameter $S_{R_1}^Q = -3$ for a particular circuit. This means that for a 1% increment of R_1, the circuit Q will change 3% in the opposite direction.

In addition to component value sensitivity, the operation of a filter is dependent on the active elements as well. The Q and resonant frequency can be a function of amplifier open-loop gain and phase shift; so the sensitivity to these active parameters is useful in determining an amplifier's suitability for a particular design.

The Q sensitivity of a circuit is a good measure of its stability. With some circuits the Q can increase to infinity, which implies a self-oscillation. Low Q sensitivity of a circuit usually indicates that the configuration will be practical from a stability point of view.

Sometimes the sensitivity is expressed as an equation instead of a numerical value such as $S_A^Q = 2\,Q^2$. This expression implies that the sensitivity of Q with respect to amplifier gain A increases with Q^2, so the circuit is not suitable for high Q realizations.

The frequency-sensitivity parameters of a circuit are useful in determining whether the circuit will require resistive trimming and indicate which element should be made variable. It should be mentioned that, in general, only resonant frequency is made adjustable when the bandpass filter is sufficiently narrow. Q variations of 5 or 10% are usually tolerable, whereas a comparable frequency error would be disastrous in narrow filters. However, in the case of a state-variable realization, a Q-enhancement effect occurs caused by amplifier phase shift. The Q may increase very dramatically; so Q adjustment is usually required in addition to resonant frequency.

All-Pole Bandpass Configurations

Multiple-Feedback Bandpass (MFBP). The circuit of figure 5-25a realizes a bandpass pole pair and is commonly referred to as a multiple-feedback bandpass (MFBP) configuration. This circuit features a minimum number of components and low sensitivity to component tolerances. The transfer function is given by

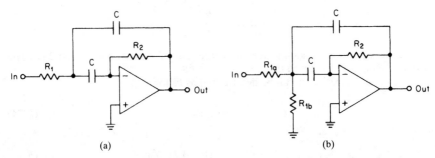

FIGURE 5-25 Multiple-feedback bandpass (MFBP) ($Q < 20$): (a) MFBP basic circuit; (b) modified configuration.

$$T(s) = -\frac{sC/R_1}{s^2C^2 + s2C/R_2 + 1/R_1R_2} \tag{5-67}$$

If we equate the coefficients of this transfer function with the general bandpass transfer function of equation (5-48), we can derive the following expressions for the element values:

$$R_2 = \frac{Q}{\pi f_r C} \tag{5-68}$$

and
$$R_1 = \frac{R_2}{4Q^2} \tag{5-69}$$

where C is arbitrary.

The circuit gain at resonant frequency f_r is given by

$$A_r = 2Q^2 \tag{5-70}$$

The open-loop gain of the operational amplifier at f_r should be well in excess of $2Q^2$, so that the circuit performance is controlled mainly by the passive elements. This requirement places a restriction on realizable Qs to values typically below 20, depending upon the amplifier type and frequency range.

Extremely high gains occur for moderate Q values because of the Q^2 gain proportionality; so there will be a tendency for clipping at the amplifier output for moderate input levels. Also the circuit gain is fixed by the Q, which limits flexibility.

An alternate and preferred form of the circuit is shown in figure 5-25b. The input resistor R_1 has been split into two resistors, R_{1a} and R_{1b}, to form a voltage divider so that the circuit gain can be controlled. The parallel combination of the two resistors is equal to R_1 to retain the resonant frequency. The transfer function of the modified circuit is given by

$$T(s) = -\frac{sR_2C}{s^2R_{1a}R_2C^2 + s2R_{1a}C + (1 + R_{1a}/R_{1b})} \tag{5-71}$$

The values of R_{1a} and R_{1b} are computed from

$$R_{1a} = \frac{R_2}{2A_r} \tag{5-72}$$

and
$$R_{1b} = \frac{R_2/2}{2\,Q^2 - A_r} \tag{5-73}$$

where A_r is the desired gain at resonant frequency f_r and cannot exceed $2\,Q^2$. The value of R_2 is still computed from equation (5-68).

The circuit sensitivities can be determined as follows:

$$S^Q_{R_{1a}} = S^{f_r}_{R_{1a}} = \frac{A_r}{4\,Q^2} \tag{5-74}$$

$$S^Q_{R_{1b}} = S^{f_r}_{R_{1b}} = \frac{1}{2}\,(1 + A_r/2\,Q^2) \tag{5-75}$$

$$S^{f_r}_{R_2} = S^{f_r}_C = -\frac{1}{2} \tag{5-76}$$

$$S^Q_{R_2} = \frac{1}{2} \tag{5-77}$$

For $Q^2/A_r \gg 1$, the resonant frequency can be directly controlled by R_{1b}, since $S^{f_r}_{R_{1b}}$ approaches ½. To use this result, let us assume that the capacitors have 2% tolerances and the resistors have a tolerance of 1%, which could result in a possible 3% frequency error. If frequency adjustment is desired, R_{1b} should be made variable over a minimum resistance range of ±6%. This would then permit a frequency adjustment of ±3%, since $S^{f_r}_{R_{1b}}$ is equal to ½. Resistor R_{1b} should be composed of a fixed resistor in series with a single-turn potentiometer to provide good resolution.

Adjustment of Q can be accomplished by making R_2 adjustable. However, this will affect resonant frequency and in any event is not necessary for most filters if 1 or 2% tolerance parts are used. The section gain can be varied by making R_{1a} adjustable, but again resonant frequency may be affected.

In conclusion, this circuit is highly recommended for low Q requirements. Although a large spread in resistance values can occur and the Q is limited by amplifier gain, the circuit simplicity, low element sensitivity, and ease of frequency adjustment make it highly desirable.

The following example demonstrates the design of a bandpass filter using the MFBP configuration.

EXAMPLE 5-12

REQUIRED: Design an active bandpass filter having the following specifications:

Center frequency of 300 Hz
3 dB at ±10 Hz
25 dB minimum at ±40 Hz
Essentially zero overshoot to a 300-Hz carrier pulse step
Gain of +12 dB at 300 Hz

RESULT:

(a) Since the bandwidth is narrow, the requirement can be treated on an arithmetically symmetrical basis. The bandpass steepness factor is given by

$$A_s = \frac{\text{stopband bandwidth}}{\text{passband bandwidth}} = \frac{80\text{ Hz}}{20\text{ Hz}} = 4 \tag{2-19}$$

The curves of figures 2-69 and 2-74 indicate that an $n = 3$ transitional gaussian to 6-dB filter will meet the frequency- and step-response requirements.
(b) The pole locations for the corresponding normalized low-pass filter are found in table 11-50 and are as follows:
$$-0.9622 \pm j1.2214$$
$$-0.9776$$
First compute the bandpass Q:

$$Q_{bp} = \frac{f_0}{BW_{3\,dB}} = \frac{300 \text{ Hz}}{20 \text{ Hz}} = 15 \qquad (2\text{-}16)$$

The low-pass poles are transformed to the bandpass form in the following manner:
Complex pole:

$$\alpha = 0.9622 \qquad \beta = 1.2214$$

$$C = 2.417647 \qquad (5\text{-}50)$$

$$D = 0.128293 \qquad (5\text{-}51)$$

$$E = 4.010745 \qquad (5\text{-}52)$$

$$G = 4.002529 \qquad (5\text{-}53)$$

$$Q = 15.602243 \qquad (5\text{-}54)$$

$$M = 1.000832 \qquad (5\text{-}55)$$

$$W = 1.041630 \qquad (5\text{-}56)$$

$$f_{ra} = 288.0 \text{ Hz} \qquad (5\text{-}57)$$

$$f_{rb} = 312.5 \text{ Hz} \qquad (5\text{-}58)$$

Real pole:

$$\alpha_0 = 0.9776$$

$$Q = 15.34 \qquad (5\text{-}59)$$

$$f_r = 300.0 \text{ Hz}$$

(c) A midband gain of +12 dB is required. Let us allocate a gain of +4 dB to each section corresponding to $A_0 = 1.585$. The value of A_r, the resonant frequency gain for each section, is obtained from equation (5-64) and is listed in the following table, which summarizes the design parameters of the filter sections:

	f_r	Q	A_r
Section 1	288.0 Hz	15.60	2.567
Section 2	312.5 Hz	15.60	2.567
Section 3	300.0 Hz	15.34	1.585

(d) Three MFBP bandpass sections will be connected in tandem. The following element values are computed where C is set equal to 0.1 µF:
Section 1:

$$R_2 = \frac{Q}{\pi f_r C} = \frac{15.6}{\pi \times 288 \times 10^{-7}} = 172.4 \text{ k}\Omega \qquad (5\text{-}68)$$

$$R_{1a} = \frac{R_2}{2A_r} = \frac{172.4 \times 10^3}{2 \times 2.567} = 33.6 \text{ k}\Omega \tag{5-72}$$

$$R_{1b} = \frac{R_2/2}{2Q^2 - A_r} = \frac{86.2 \times 10^3}{2 \times 15.6^2 - 2.567} = 178 \ \Omega \tag{5-73}$$

Section 2:   **Section 3:**

$R_2 = 158.9 \text{ k}\Omega$ $R_2 = 162.8 \text{ k}\Omega$

$R_{1a} = 30.9 \text{ k}\Omega$ $R_{1a} = 51.3 \text{ k}\Omega$

$R_{1b} = 164 \ \Omega$ $R_{1b} = 174 \ \Omega$

The final circuit is shown in figure 5-26. Resistor values have been rounded off to standard 1% values, and resistor R_{1b} has been made variable in each section for tuning purposes.

Each filter section can be adjusted by applying a sine wave at the section f_r to the filter input. The phase shift of the section being adjusted is monitored by connecting one channel of an oscilloscope to the section input and the other channel to the section output. A Lissajous pattern is obtained. Resistor R_{1b} is adjusted until the ellipse closes to a straight line.

Dual-Amplifier Bandpass (DABP) Structure.   The bandpass circuit of figure 5-27 was first introduced by Sedra and Espinoza (see bibliography). Truly remarkable performance in terms of available Q, low sensitivity, and flexibility can be obtained in comparison with alternate schemes involving two amplifiers.

The transfer function is given by

$$T(s) = \frac{s2/R_1C}{s^2 + s1/R_1C + 1/R_2R_3C^2} \tag{5-78}$$

If we compare this expression with the general bandpass transfer function of equation (5-48) and let $R_2R_3 = R^2$, the following design equations for the element values can be obtained.

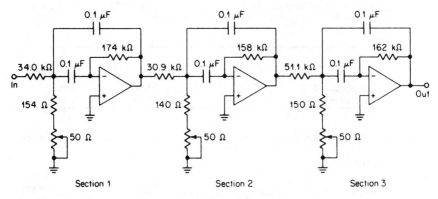

FIGURE 5-26 MFBP circuit of example 5-12.

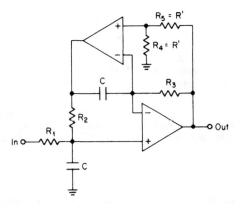

FIGURE 5-27 Dual-amplifier bandpass (DABP) configuration ($Q < 150$).

First compute

$$R = \frac{1}{2\pi f_r C} \tag{5-79}$$

then

$$R_1 = QR \tag{5-80}$$

$$R_2 = R_3 = R \tag{5-81}$$

where C is arbitrary. The value of R' in figure 5-27 can also be chosen at any convenient value. Circuit gain at f_r is equal to 2.

The following sensitivities can be derived:

$$S_{R_1}^{Q} = 1 \tag{5-82}$$

$$S_{R_2}^{f_r} = S_{R_3}^{f_r} = S_{R_4}^{f_r} = S_C^{f_r} = -\tfrac{1}{2} \tag{5-83}$$

$$S_{R_5}^{f_r} = \tfrac{1}{2} \tag{5-84}$$

An interesting result of sensitivity studies is that if the bandwidths of both amplifiers are nearly equivalent, extremely small deviations of Q from the design values will occur. This is especially advantageous at higher frequencies where the amplifier poles have to be taken into account. It is then suggested that a dual-type amplifier be used for each filter section, since both amplifier halves will be closely matched to each other.

A useful feature of this circuit is that resonant frequency and Q can be independently adjusted. Alignment can be accomplished by first adjusting R_2 for resonance at f_r. Resistor R_1 can then be adjusted for the desired Q without affecting the resonant frequency.

Since each section provides a fixed gain of 2 at f_r, a composite filter may require an additional amplification stage if higher gains are required. If a gain reduction is desired, resistor R_1 can be split into two resistors to form a voltage divider in the same manner as in figure 5-25b. The resulting values are

$$R_{1a} = \frac{2R_1}{A_r} \tag{5-85}$$

and
$$R_{1b} = \frac{R_{1a} A_r}{2 - A_r} \qquad (5\text{-}86)$$

where A_r is the desired gain at resonance.

The spread of element values of the MFBP section previously discussed is equal to $4Q^2$. In comparison this circuit has a ratio of resistances determined by Q; so the spread is much less.

The DABP configuration has been found very useful for designs covering a wide range of Qs and frequencies. Component sensitivity is small, resonant frequency and Q are easily adjustable, and the element spread is low. The following example illustrates the use of this circuit.

EXAMPLE 5-13

REQUIRED: Design an active bandpass filter to meet the following specifications:

Center frequency of 3000 Hz
3 dB at ±30 Hz
20 dB minimum at ±120 Hz

RESULT:

(*a*) If we consider the requirement as being arithmetically symmetrical, the bandpass steepness factor becomes

$$A_s = \frac{\text{stopband bandwidth}}{\text{passband bandwidth}} = \frac{240 \text{ Hz}}{60 \text{ Hz}} = 4 \qquad (2\text{-}19)$$

We can determine from the curve of figure 2-34 that a second-order Butterworth low-pass filter provides over 20 dB of rejection within a frequency ratio of 4:1. The corresponding poles of the normalized low-pass filter are found in table 11-1 and are as follows:

$$-0.7071 \pm j0.7071$$

(*b*) To convert these poles to the bandpass form, first compute:

$$Q_{bp} = \frac{f_0}{\text{BW}_{3\,\text{dB}}} = \frac{3000 \text{ Hz}}{60 \text{ Hz}} = 50 \qquad (2\text{-}16)$$

The bandpass pole transformation is performed in the following manner:

$$\alpha = 0.7071 \qquad \beta = 0.7071$$

$$C = 1.000000 \qquad (5\text{-}50)$$

$$D = 0.028284 \qquad (5\text{-}51)$$

$$E = 4.000400 \qquad (5\text{-}52)$$

$$G = 4.000000 \qquad (5\text{-}53)$$

$$Q = 70.713124 \qquad (5\text{-}54)$$

$$M = 1.000025 \qquad (5\text{-}55)$$

$$W = 1.007096 \qquad (5\text{-}56)$$

$$f_{ra} = 2978.9 \text{ Hz} \qquad (5\text{-}57)$$

$$f_{rb} = 3021.3 \text{ Hz} \qquad (5\text{-}58)$$

(c) Two DABP sections will be used. The element values are now computed, where C is set equal to 0.01 µF and R' is 10 kΩ.

Section 1:

$$f_r = 2978.9 \text{ Hz}$$

$$Q = 70.7$$

$$R = \frac{1}{2\pi f_r C} = \frac{1}{2\pi \times 2978.9 \times 10^{-8}} = 5343 \ \Omega \tag{5-79}$$

$$R_1 = QR = 70.7 \times 5343 = 377.7 \text{ k}\Omega \tag{5-80}$$

$$R_2 = R_3 = R = 5343 \ \Omega \tag{5-81}$$

Section 2:

$$f_r = 3021.3 \text{ Hz}$$

$$Q = 70.7$$

$$R = 5268 \ \Omega \tag{5-79}$$

$$R_1 = 372.4 \text{ k}\Omega \tag{5-80}$$

$$R_2 = R_3 = 5268 \ \Omega \tag{5-81}$$

The circuit is illustrated in figure 5-28, where resistors have been rounded off to standard 1% values and R_2 is made adjustable for tuning.

Low-Sensitivity Three-Amplifier Configuration. The dual-amplifier bandpass (DABP) circuit shown in figure 5-27 provides excellent performance and is useful for general-purpose bandpass filtering. A modified version utilizing a total of three amplifiers is shown in figure 5-29. This circuit will exhibit performance superior to the DABP configuration, especially at higher frequencies. Using this structure and

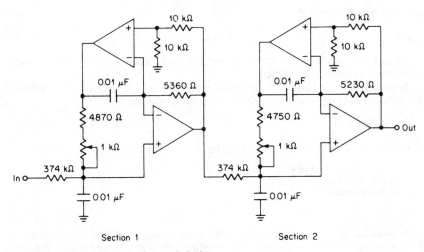

FIGURE 5-28 DABP filter of example 5-13.

off-the-shelf op amps, active bandpass filters having moderate percentage bandwidths can be designed to operate in the frequency range of a few hundred kilohertz.

The section within the dashed line in figure 5-29 realizes a shunt inductance to ground using a configuration called a *gyrator.** Both op amps within this block should be closely matched to obtain low op-amp sensitivity at high frequencies, so the use of a dual op amp for this location would be highly recommended. The third op amp serves as a voltage follower or buffer to obtain low output impedance.

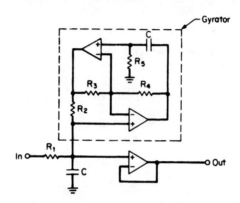

FIGURE 5-29 Low-sensitivity three-amplifier bandpass configuration.

As in the case of the DABP circuit, resonant frequency and Q can be adjusted independently. The design proceeds as follows:

First select a convenient value for C. Then compute:

$$R = \frac{1}{2\pi f_r C} \tag{5-87}$$

Let $R_2 = R_3 = R_4 = R_5 = R$

Then
$$R_1 = QR \tag{5-88}$$

Circuit gain at f_r is unity. For additional gain, the voltage follower can be configured as a noninverting amplifier.

For alignment, first adjust R_2 for resonance at f_r. Resistor R_1 can then be adjusted for the desired Q without affecting the resonant frequency.

EXAMPLE 5-14

REQUIRED: Design an active bandpass filter to meet the following specifications:

Center frequency of 30 kHz
3 dB at ±300 Hz
20 dB minimum at ±1200 Hz

---

* A gyrator is an impedance inverting device which converts an impedance Z into a reciprocal impedance $1/G^2Z$, where G is a constant. Therefore, a capacitor having an impedance $1/SC$ can be converted into an impedance SC/G^2, which corresponds to an inductance of C/G^2. For this circuit $G = 1/R$, so $L = R^2C$.

RESULT:

(a) Treating the requirement as being arithmetically symmetrical, the bandpass steepness factor is

$$A = \frac{\text{stopband bandwidth}}{\text{passband bandwidth}} = \frac{2400 \text{ Hz}}{600 \text{ Hz}} = 4 \qquad (2\text{-}19)$$

From figure 2-34 a second-order Butterworth low-pass filter meets the attenuation. The low-pass poles from table 11-1 are $-0.7071 \pm j0.7071$.

(b) These poles must now be converted to the bandpass form. The procedure is as follows:

$$Q = \frac{f_0}{BW_{3 \text{ dB}}} = \frac{30,000 \text{ Hz}}{600 \text{ Hz}} = 50 \qquad (2\text{-}16)$$

$$\alpha = 0.7071 \qquad \beta = 0.7071$$

$$C = 1 \qquad (5\text{-}50)$$

$$D = 0.028284 \qquad (5\text{-}51)$$

$$E = 4.000400 \qquad (5\text{-}52)$$

$$G = 4.000000 \qquad (5\text{-}53)$$

$$Q = 70.713124 \qquad (5\text{-}54)$$

$$M = 1.000025 \qquad (5\text{-}55)$$

$$W = 1.007096 \qquad (5\text{-}56)$$

$$f_{ra} = 29.789 \text{ kHz} \qquad (5\text{-}57)$$

$$f_{rb} = 30.213 \text{ kHz} \qquad (5\text{-}58)$$

(c) Compute the element values for the circuit of figure 5-29 using $C = 0.01$ µF.
Section 1:

$$f_r = 29.789 \text{ kHz}$$

$$Q = 70.71$$

$$R = \frac{1}{2\pi f_r C} = \frac{1}{2\pi \times 29.789 \times 10^{-5}}$$

$$= 534.3 \ \Omega \qquad (5\text{-}87)$$

$$R_1 = QR = 70.7 \times 534.3 = 37.8 \text{ k}\Omega \qquad (5\text{-}88)$$

Section 2:

$$f_r = 30.213 \text{ kHz}$$

$$Q = 70.71$$

$$R = 526.8 \ \Omega \qquad (5\text{-}87)$$

$$R_1 = 37.2 \text{K} \ \Omega \qquad (5\text{-}88)$$

The circuit of this example is illustrated in Figure 5-30 using standard 1% resistor values and a potentiometer for frequency adjustment.

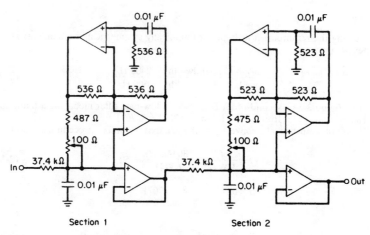

Section 1   **Section 2**

FIGURE 5-30   Bandpass filter of example 5-14.

State-Variable (Biquad) All-Pole Circuit.   The state-variable or biquad configuration was first introduced in section 3.2 for use as a low-pass filter section. A bandpass output is available as well. The biquad approach features excellent sensitivity properties and the capability to control resonant frequency and Q independently. It is especially suited for constructing precision-active filters in a standard form.

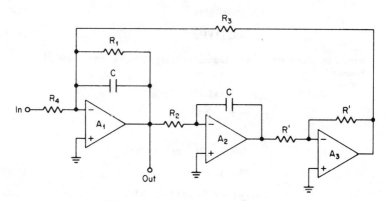

FIGURE 5-31   Biquad all-pole circuit ($Q < 200$).

The circuit of figure 5-31 is the all-pole bandpass form of the general biquadratic configuration. The transfer function is given by

$$T(s) = -\frac{s/CR_4}{s^2 + s/CR_1 + 1/R_2R_3C^2}$$ (5-89)

If we equate this expression to the general bandpass transfer function of equation (5-48), the circuit resonant frequency and 3-dB bandwidth can be expressed as

$$f_r = \frac{1}{2\pi\, C\sqrt{R_2 R_3}} \tag{5-90}$$

and
$$BW_{3\,dB} = \frac{1}{2\pi R_1 C} \tag{5-91}$$

where $BW_{3\,dB}$ is equal to f_r/Q.

Equations (5-90) and (5-91) indicate that the resonant frequency and 3-dB band-width can be independently controlled. This feature is highly desirable and can lead to many useful applications, such as variable filters.

If we substitute f_r/Q for $BW_{3\,dB}$ and set $R_2 = R_3$, the following design equations can be derived for the section:

$$R_1 = \frac{Q}{2\pi f_r C} \tag{5-92}$$

$$R_2 = R_3 = \frac{R_1}{Q} \tag{5-93}$$

and
$$R_4 = \frac{R_1}{A_r} \tag{5-94}$$

where A_r is the desired gain at resonant frequency f_r. The values of C and R' in fig-ure 5-31 can be conveniently selected. By making R_3 and R_1 adjustable, the resonant frequency and Q, respectively, can be adjusted.

The sensitivity factors are

$$S_{R_2}^{f_r} = S_{R_3}^{f_r} = S_C^{f_r} = -\tfrac{1}{2} \tag{5-95}$$

$$S_{R_1}^{Q} = 1 \tag{5-96}$$

and
$$S_{\mu}^{Q} = \frac{2Q}{\mu} \tag{5-97}$$

where μ is the open-loop gain of amplifiers A_1 and A_2. The section Q is then limited by the finite gain of the operational amplifier.

Another serious limitation occurs because of finite amplifier bandwidth. Thomas (see bibliography) has shown that, as the resonant frequency increases for a fixed design Q, the actual Q remains constant over a broad band and then begins to increase, eventually becoming infinite (oscillatory). This effect is called Q enhance-ment.

If we assume that the open-loop transfer function of the amplifier has a single pole, the effective Q can be approximated by

$$Q_{eff} = \frac{Q_{design}}{1 - \dfrac{2\,Q_{design}}{\mu_0 \omega_c}\,(2\omega_r - \omega_c)} \tag{5-98}$$

where ω_r is the resonant frequency, ω_c is the 3-dB breakpoint of the open-loop amplifier gain, and μ_0 is the open-loop gain at DC. As ω_r is increased, the denomina-tor approaches zero.

The Q-enhancement effect can be minimized by having a high gain-bandwidth product. If the amplifier requires external frequency compensation, the compensation can be made lighter than the recommended values. The state-variable circuit is well suited for light compensation, since the structure contains two integrators which have a stabilizing effect.

A solution suggested by Thomas is to introduce a leading phase component in the feedback loop which compensates for the lagging phase caused by finite amplifier bandwidth. This can be achieved by introducing a capacitor in parallel with resistor R_3 having the value

$$C_p = \frac{4}{\mu_0 \omega_c R_3} \tag{5-99}$$

Probably the most practical solution is to make resistor R_1 variable. The Q may be determined by measuring the 3-dB bandwidth. R_1 is adjusted until the ratio $f_r/\mathrm{BW}_{3\,\mathrm{dB}}$ is equal to the required Q.

As the Q is enhanced, the section gain is increased also. Empirically it has been found that correcting for the gain enhancement compensates for the Q enhancement as well. R_1 can be adjusted until the measured gain at f_r is equal to the design value of A_r used in equation (5-94). Although this technique is not as accurate as determining the actual Q from the 3-dB bandwidth, it certainly is much more convenient and will usually be sufficient.

The biquad is a low-sensitivity filter configuration suitable for precision applications. Circuit Qs of up to 200 are realizable over a broad frequency range. The following example demonstrates the use of this structure.

EXAMPLE 5-15

REQUIRED: Design an active bandpass filter satisfying the following specifications:

Center frequency of 2500 Hz
3 dB at ±15 Hz
15 dB minimum at ±45 Hz
Gain of +12 dB at 2500 Hz

RESULT:

(a) The bandpass steepness factor is determined from

$$A_s = \frac{\text{stopband bandwidth}}{\text{passband bandwidth}} = \frac{90\ \text{Hz}}{30\ \text{Hz}} = 3 \tag{2-19}$$

Using figure 2-42, we find that a second-order 0.1-dB Chebyshev normalized low-pass filter will meet the attenuation requirements. The corresponding poles are found in table 11-23 and are as follows:

$$-0.6125 \pm j0.7124$$

(b) To transform these low-pass poles to the bandpass form, first compute

$$Q_{bp} = \frac{f_0}{\text{BW}_{3\,\text{dB}}} = \frac{2500\ \text{Hz}}{30\ \text{Hz}} = 83.33 \tag{2-16}$$

The bandpass poles are determined from the following series of computations. Since the filter is very narrow, an extended number of significant figures will be used in equations (5-50) through (5-58) to maintain accuracy.

$$\alpha = 0.6125 \qquad \beta = 0.7124$$

$$C = 0.882670010 \tag{5-50}$$

$$D = 0.014700588 \tag{5-51}$$

$$E = 4.000127115 \tag{5-52}$$

$$G = 4.000019064 \tag{5-53}$$

$$Q = 136.0502228 \tag{5-54}$$

$$M = 1.000009138 \tag{5-55}$$

$$W = 1.004284182 \tag{5-56}$$

$$f_{ra} = 2489.3 \text{ Hz} \tag{5-57}$$

$$f_{rb} = 2510.7 \text{ Hz} \tag{5-58}$$

(c) Since a midband gain of +12 dB is required, each section will be allocated a midband gain of +6 dB corresponding to $A_0 = 2.000$. The gain A_r at the resonant frequency of each section is determined from equation (5-65) and is listed in the following table:

	f_r	Q	A_r
Section 1	2489.3 Hz	136	3.069
Section 2	2510.7 Hz	136	3.069

(d) Two biquad sections in tandem will be used. C is chosen to be 0.1 μF and R' is 10 kΩ. The element values are computed as follows:

Section 1:

$$R_1 = \frac{Q}{2\pi f_r C} = \frac{136}{2\pi \times 2489.3 \times 10^{-7}} = 86.9 \text{ k}\Omega \tag{5-92}$$

$$R_2 = R_3 = \frac{R_1}{Q} = \frac{86.9 \times 10^3}{136} = 639 \ \Omega \tag{5-93}$$

$$R_4 = \frac{R_1}{A_r} = \frac{86.9 \times 10^3}{3.069} = 28.3 \text{ k}\Omega \tag{5-94}$$

Section 2:

$$R_1 = 86.2 \text{ k}\Omega \tag{5-92}$$

$$R_2 = R_3 = 634 \ \Omega \tag{5-93}$$

$$R_4 = 28.1 \text{ k}\Omega \tag{5-94}$$

The final circuit is shown in figure 5-32. Resistors R_3 and R_1 are made variable so that resonant frequency and Q can be adjusted. Standard values of 1% resistors have been used.

The Q-Multiplier Approach. Certain active bandpass structures such as the MFBP configuration of section 5.2 are severely Q-limited because of insufficient amplifier gain or other inadequacies. The technique outlined in this section uses a low-Q-type bandpass circuit within a Q-multiplier structure which increases the circuit Q to the desired value.

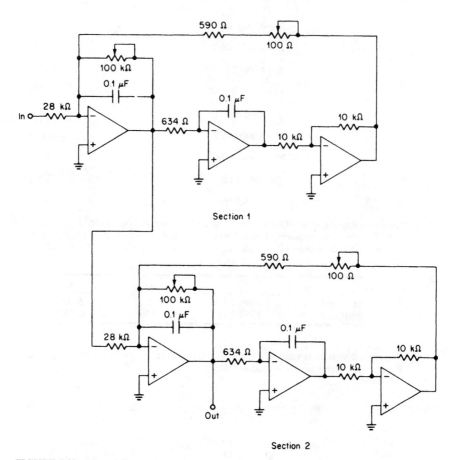

FIGURE 5-32 Biquad circuit of example 5-15.

A bandpass transfer function having unity gain at resonance can be expressed as

$$T(s) = \frac{\dfrac{\omega_r}{Q} s}{s^2 + \dfrac{\omega_r}{Q} s + \omega_r^2} \tag{5-100}$$

If the corresponding circuit is combined with a summing amplifier in the manner shown in figure 5-33a, where β is an attenuation factor, the following overall transfer function can be derived:

$$T(s) = \frac{\dfrac{\omega_r}{Q} s}{s^2 + \dfrac{\dfrac{\omega_r}{Q} s + \omega_r^2}{\dfrac{Q}{1-\beta}}} \tag{5-101}$$

The middle term of the denominator has been modified so that the circuit Q is given by $Q/(1 - \beta)$, where $0 < \beta < 1$. By selecting a β sufficiently close to unity, the Q can be increased by the factor $1/(1 - \beta)$. The circuit gain is also increased by the same factor.

If we use the MFBP section for the bandpass circuit, the Q-multiplier configuration will take the form of figure 5-33b. Since the MFBP circuit is inverting, an inverting amplifier can also be used for summing.

The value of β can be found from

$$\beta = 1 - \frac{Q_r}{Q_{\text{eff}}} \tag{5-102}$$

where Q_{eff} is the effective overall Q and Q_r is the design Q of the bandpass section. The component values are determined by the following equations:

$$R_3 = \frac{R}{\beta} \tag{5-103}$$

$$R_4 = R \tag{5-104}$$

and $$R_5 = \frac{R}{(1 - \beta)A_r} \tag{5-105}$$

where R can be conveniently chosen and A_r is the desired gain at resonance.

Design equations for the MFBP section were derived in section 5.2 and are repeated here corresponding to unity gain.

$$R_2 = \frac{Q_r}{\pi f_r C} \tag{5-68}$$

$$R_{1a} = \frac{R_2}{2} \tag{5-72}$$

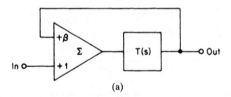

(a)

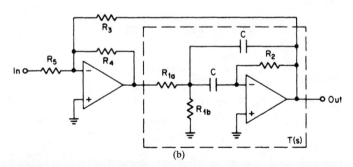

(b)

FIGURE 5-33 Q-multiplier circuit: (*a*) block diagram; (*b*) realization using MFBP section.

and
$$R_{1b} = \frac{R_{1a}}{2Q_r^2 - 1} \qquad (5\text{-}73)$$

The value of C can be freely chosen.

The configuration of figure 5-33b is not restricted to the MFBP section. The state-variable all-pole bandpass circuit may be used instead. The only requirements are that the filter section be of an inverting type and that the gain be unity at resonance. This last requirement is especially critical because of the positive feedback nature of the circuit. Small gain errors could result in large overall Q variations when β is close to 1. It may then be desirable to adjust section gain precisely to unity.

EXAMPLE 5-16

REQUIRED: Design a single bandpass filter section having the following characteristics:

Center frequency of 3600 Hz
3-dB bandwidth of 60 Hz
Gain of 3

RESULT:

(a) The bandpass Q is given by

$$Q = \frac{f_0}{\text{BW}_{3\,\text{dB}}} = \frac{3600\ \text{Hz}}{60\ \text{Hz}} = 60 \qquad (2\text{-}16)$$

A Q-multiplier implementation using the MFBP section will be employed.

(b) Let us use a Q_r of 10 for the MFBP circuit. The following component values are computed where C is set equal to 0.01 μF.

$$R_2 = \frac{Q_r}{\pi f_r C} = \frac{10}{\pi 3600 \times 10^{-8}} = 88.4\ \text{k}\Omega \qquad (5\text{-}68)$$

$$R_{1a} = \frac{R_2}{2} = \frac{88.4 \times 10^3}{2} = 44.2\ \text{k}\Omega \qquad (5\text{-}72)$$

$$R_{1b} = \frac{R_{1a}}{2\,Q_r^2 - 1} = \frac{44.2 \times 10^3}{2 \times 10^2 - 1} = 222\ \Omega \qquad (5\text{-}73)$$

The remaining values are given by the following design equations where R is chosen at 10 kΩ and gain A_r is equal to 3:

$$\beta = 1 - \frac{Q_r}{Q_{\text{eff}}} = 1 - \frac{10}{60} = 0.8333 \qquad (5\text{-}102)$$

$$R_3 = \frac{R}{\beta} = \frac{10^4}{0.8333} = 12.0\ \text{k}\Omega \qquad (5\text{-}103)$$

$$R_4 = R = 10\ \text{k}\Omega \qquad (5\text{-}104)$$

$$R_5 = \frac{R}{(1 - \beta)A_r} = \frac{10^4}{(1 - 0.8333)3} = 20\ \text{k}\Omega \qquad (5\text{-}105)$$

The resulting circuit is shown in figure 5-34 using standard resistor values. R_{1b} has been made adjustable for tuning.

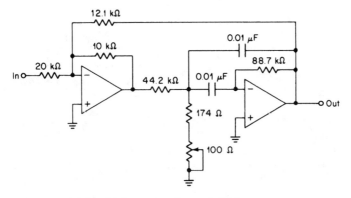

FIGURE 5-34 Q-multiplier section of example 5-16.

Elliptic-Function Bandpass Filters

An active elliptic-function bandpass filter is designed by first transforming the low-pass poles and zeros to the bandpass form using the formulas of section 5.2. The bandpass poles and zeros are then implemented using active structures.

Low-pass poles and zeros for elliptic-function low-pass filters have been extensively tabulated by Zverev (see bibliography) for complexities ranging from $n = 3$ through $n = 7$. Table 11-57 contains some of these values for odd-order n's alongside the active low-pass filter elements.

The general form of a bandpass transfer function containing zeros was given in section 5.2 as

$$T(s) = \frac{H(s^2 + \omega_\infty^2)}{s^2 + \dfrac{\omega_r}{Q}s + \omega_r^2} \tag{5-49}$$

Elliptic-function bandpass filters are composed of cascaded first-order bandpass sections. When n is odd, $n - 1$ zero-producing sections are required along with a single all-pole section. When n is even, $n - 2$ zero-producing sections are used along with two all-pole networks.

This section discusses the VCVS and biquad configurations which have a transfer function in the form of equation (5-49) and their use in the design of active elliptic-function bandpass filters.

VCVS Network. Section 3.2 discussed the design of active elliptic-function low-pass filters using an *RC* section containing a voltage-controlled voltage source (VCVS). The circuit is repeated in figure 5-35a. This structure is not restricted to the design of low-pass filters exclusively. Transmission zeros can be obtained at frequencies either above or below the pole locations as required by the bandpass transfer function.

First calculate:

$$a = \frac{1}{Q} \tag{5-106}$$

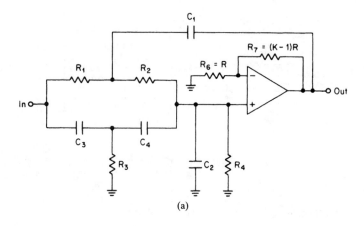

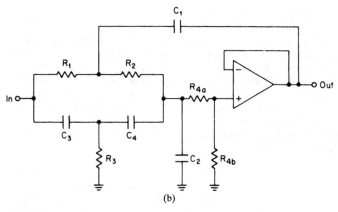

FIGURE 5-35 VCVS elliptic-function bandpass section: (a) circuit for $K > 1$ and (b) circuit for $K < 1$.

$$b = \left(\frac{f_\infty}{f_0} \right)^2 \tag{5-107}$$

$$C = 2\pi f_0 \tag{5-108}$$

The element values are computed as follows:
Select C.

Then
$$C_1 = C \tag{5-109}$$

$$C_3 = C_4 = \frac{C_1}{2} \tag{5-110}$$

and
$$C_2 \geq \frac{C_1(b-1)}{4} \tag{5-111}$$

$$R_3 = \frac{1}{cC_1\sqrt{b}} \tag{5-112}$$

$$R_1 = R_2 = 2R_3 \tag{5-113}$$

$$R_4 = \frac{4\sqrt{b}}{cC_1(1-b) + 4cC_2} \tag{5-114}$$

$$K = 2 + \frac{2C_2}{C_1} - \frac{a}{2\sqrt{b}} = \frac{2}{C_1\sqrt{b}} \left(\frac{1}{cR_4} - aC_2 \right) \tag{5-115}$$

$$R_6 = R \tag{5-116}$$

$$R_7 = (K-1)R \tag{5-117}$$

where R can be arbitrarily chosen.

In the event that K is less than 1, the circuit of figure 5-35b is used. Resistor R_4 is split into two resistors, R_{4a} and R_{4b}, which are given by

$$R_{4a} = (1-K)R_4 \tag{5-118}$$

and $$R_{4b} = KR_4 \tag{5-119}$$

The section Q can be controlled independently of resonant frequency by making R_6 or R_7 adjustable when $K > 1$. The resonant frequency, however, is not easily adjusted. Experience has shown that with 1% resistors and capacitors, section Qs of up to 10 can be realized with little degradation of overall filter response due to component tolerances.

The actual circuit Q cannot be measured directly, since the section's 3-dB bandwidth is determined not only by the design Q but by the transmission zero as well. Nevertheless, the VCVS configuration uses a minimum number of amplifiers and is widely used for low-Q elliptic-function realizations. The design technique is demonstrated in the following example.

EXAMPLE 5-17

REQUIRED:

Active bandpass filter
Center frequency of 500 Hz
1 dB maximum at ±100 Hz (400 Hz, 600 Hz)
35 dB minimum at ±375 Hz (125 Hz, 875 Hz)

RESULT:

(a) Convert to geometrically symmetrical bandpass requirement:
First calculate geometric center frequency

$$f_0 = \sqrt{f_L f_u} = \sqrt{400 \times 600} = 490.0 \text{ Hz} \tag{2-14}$$

Since the stopband requirement is arithmetically symmetrical, compute stopband bandwidth using equation (5-18).

$$BW_{35 \text{ dB}} = f_2 - \frac{f_0^2}{f_2} = 875 - \frac{490^2}{875} = 600.6 \text{ Hz}$$

The bandpass steepness factor is given by

$$A_s = \frac{\text{stopband bandwidth}}{\text{passband bandwidth}} = \frac{600.6 \text{ Hz}}{200 \text{ Hz}} = 3.003 \qquad (2\text{-}19)$$

(b) An elliptic-function filter type will be used. A normalized low-pass filter is required that makes a transition from less than 1 dB to more than 35 dB within a frequency ratio of 3.003:1. A satisfactory filter can be found in table 11-56 corresponding to CO3 20 $\theta = 20°$; it has the following parameters:

$$n = 3$$

$$\rho = 20\% \text{ (0.18-dB ripple)}$$

$$\Omega_s = 2.924$$

$$A_{\min} = 37.44 \text{ dB}$$

The pole-zero coordinates are as follows:
Poles:

$$-0.3862 \pm j1.1396$$

$$-0.8867$$

Zero:

$$\pm j3.350$$

(c) To determine the bandpass parameters, first compute

$$Q_{bp} = \frac{f_0}{BW_{1\,dB}} = \frac{490 \text{ Hz}}{200 \text{ Hz}} = 2.45 \qquad (2\text{-}16)$$

The poles and zeros are transformed as follows:
Complex pole:

$$\alpha = 0.3862 \qquad \beta = 1.1396$$

$$C = 1.447839 \qquad (5\text{-}50)$$

$$D = 0.315265 \qquad (5\text{-}51)$$

$$E = 4.241206 \qquad (5\text{-}52)$$

$$G = 4.194074 \qquad (5\text{-}53)$$

$$Q = 6.514169 \qquad (5\text{-}54)$$

$$M = 1.026846 \qquad (5\text{-}55)$$

$$W = 1.260110 \qquad (5\text{-}56)$$

$$f_{ra} = 389 \text{ Hz} \qquad (5\text{-}57)$$

$$f_{rb} = 617 \text{ Hz} \qquad (5\text{-}58)$$

Real pole:

$$\alpha_0 = 0.8867$$

$$Q = 2.76 \qquad (5\text{-}59)$$

$$f_r = 490 \text{ Hz}$$

Zero:

$$\omega_\infty = 3.350$$

$$H = 1.934819 \tag{5-60}$$

$$Z = 1.895040 \tag{5-61}$$

$$f_{\infty,a} = 259 \text{ Hz} \tag{5-62}$$

$$f_{\infty,b} = 929 \text{ Hz} \tag{5-63}$$

The bandpass parameters are summarized in the following table, where the zeros are arbitrarily assigned to the first two sections:

Section	f_r	Q	f_∞
1	389 Hz	6.51	259 Hz
2	617 Hz	6.51	929 Hz
3	490 Hz	2.76	

(d) Sections 1 and 2 are realized using the VCVS configuration of figure 5-35. The element values are computed as follows, where R' and R are both 10 kΩ.

Section 1:

$$f_r = 389 \text{ Hz}$$

$$Q = 6.51$$

$$f_\infty = 259 \text{ Hz}$$

$$a = 0.15361 \tag{5-106}$$

$$b = 0.44330 \tag{5-107}$$

$$c = 2444 \tag{5-108}$$

Let

$$C = 0.02 \text{ }\mu\text{F}$$

then

$$C_1 = 0.02 \text{ }\mu\text{F} \tag{5-109}$$

$$C_3 = C_4 = 0.01 \text{ }\mu\text{F} \tag{5-110}$$

$$C_2 \geq -0.00278 \text{ }\mu\text{F} \tag{5-111}$$

Let

$$C_2 = 0$$

$$R_3 = 30.73 \text{ k}\Omega \tag{5-112}$$

$$R_1 = R_2 = 61.45 \text{ k}\Omega \tag{5-113}$$

$$R_4 = 97.87 \text{ k}\Omega \tag{5-114}$$

$$K = 2.5126 \tag{5-115}$$

Section 2:

$$f_r = 617 \text{ Hz}$$

$$Q = 6.51$$

$$f_\infty = 929 \text{ Hz}$$

$$a = 0.15361 \tag{5-106}$$

$$b = 2.26705 \tag{5-107}$$

$$c = 3877 \tag{5-108}$$

Let
$$C = 0.02 \text{ μF}$$

then
$$C = 0.02 \text{ μF} \tag{5-109}$$

$$C_3 = C_4 = 0.01 \text{ μF} \tag{5-110}$$

$$C_2 \geq 0.00634 \text{ μF} \tag{5-111}$$

Let
$$C = 0.01 \text{ μF}$$

$$R_3 = 8565 \text{ Ω} \tag{5-112}$$

$$R_1 = R_2 = 17.13 \text{ kΩ} \tag{5-113}$$

$$R_4 = 106 \text{ kΩ} \tag{5-114}$$

$$K = 3.0086 \tag{5-115}$$

(e) Section 3 is required to be of the all-pole type; so the MFBP configuration of figure 5-25b will be used, where C is chosen at 0.01 μF and section gain A_r is set to unity:
Section 3:

$$f_r = 490 \text{ Hz}$$

$$Q = 2.76$$

$$R_2 = 179 \text{ kΩ} \tag{5-68}$$

$$R_{1a} = 89.6 \text{ kΩ} \tag{5-72}$$

$$R_{1b} = 6.3 \text{ kΩ} \tag{5-73}$$

The complete circuit is shown in figure 5-36 using standard 1% resistor values.

State-Variable (Biquad) Circuit. The all-pole bandpass form of the state-variable or biquad section was discussed in section 5.2. With the addition of an operational amplifier, the circuit can be used to realize transmission zeros as well as poles. The configuration is shown in figure 5-37. This circuit is identical to the elliptic-function low-pass and high-pass filter configurations of sections 3.2 and 4.2. By connecting R_5 either to node 1 or to node 2, the zero can be located above or below the resonant frequency.

On the basis of sensitivity and flexibility, the biquad configuration has been found to be the optimum method of constructing precision active elliptic-function bandpass filters. Section Qs of up to 200 can be obtained, whereas the VCVS section is limited to Qs below 10. Resonant frequency f_r, Q and notch frequency f_∞ can be independently monitored and adjusted.

For the case where $f_\infty < f_r$, the transfer function is given by

$$T(s) = -\frac{R_6}{R} \frac{s^2 + \dfrac{1}{R_2 R_3 C^2}\left(1 - \dfrac{R_3 R}{R_4 R_5}\right)}{s^2 + \dfrac{1}{R_1 C} s + \dfrac{1}{R_2 R_3 C^2}} \tag{5-120}$$

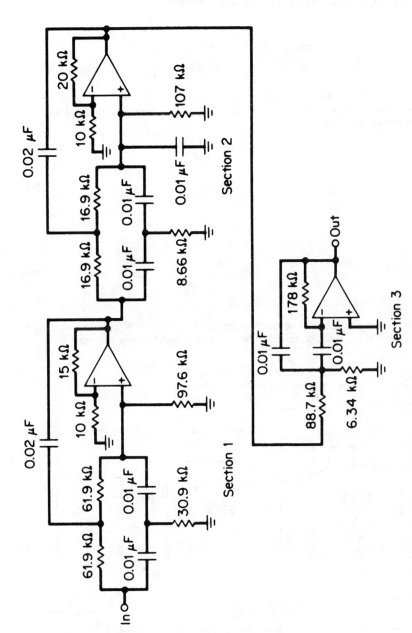

FIGURE 5-36 Circuit of elliptic-function bandpass filter in example 5-17.

5.65

and when $f_\infty > f_r$, the corresponding transfer function is

$$T(s) = -\frac{R_6}{R}\frac{s^2 + \dfrac{1}{R_2 R_3 C^2}\left(1 + \dfrac{R_3 R}{R_4 R_5}\right)}{s^2 + \dfrac{1}{R_1 C}s + \dfrac{1}{R_2 R_3 C^2}} \tag{5-121}$$

If we equate the transfer-function coefficients to those of the general bandpass transfer function (with zeros) of equation (5-49), the following series of design equations can be derived:

$$R_1 = R_4 = \frac{Q}{2\pi f_r C} \tag{5-122}$$

$$R_2 = R_3 = \frac{R_1}{Q} \tag{5-123}$$

$$R_5 = \frac{f_r^2 R}{Q|f_r^2 - f_\infty^2|} \tag{5-124}$$

for $f_\infty > f_r$:
$$R_6 = \frac{f_r^2 R}{f_\infty^2} \tag{5-125}$$

and when $f_\infty < f_r$:
$$R_6 = R \tag{5-126}$$

where C and R can be conveniently selected. The value of R_6 is based on unity section gain. The gain can be raised or lowered by proportionally changing R_6.

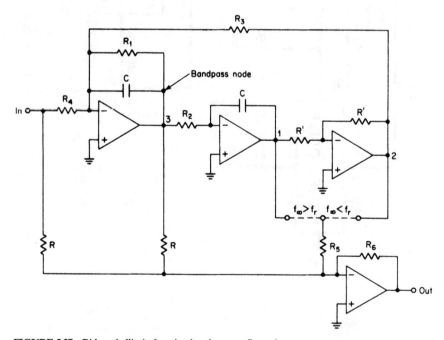

FIGURE 5.37 Bidquad elliptic-function bandpass configuration.

The section can be tuned by implementing the following steps in the indicated sequence. Both resonant frequency and Q are monitored at the bandpass output occurring at node 3, whereas the notch frequency f_∞ is observed at the section output.

1. *Resonant frequency f_r:* If R_3 is made variable, the section resonant frequency can be adjusted. Resonance is monitored at node 3 (see figure 5-37) and can be determined by the 180° phase shift method.

2. *Q adjustment:* The section Q is controlled by R_1 and can be directly measured at node 3. The configuration is subject to the Q-enhancement effect discussed in section 5.2 under "All-Pole Bandpass Configurations"; so a Q adjustment is normally required. The Q can be monitored in terms of the 3-dB bandwidth at node 3 or R_1 can be adjusted until unity gain occurs between the section input and node 3 with f_r applied.

3. *Notch frequency f_∞:* Adjustment of the notch frequency (transmission zero) usually is not required if the circuit is previously tuned to f_r, since f_∞ will usually then fall in. If an adjustment is desired, the notch frequency can be controlled by making R_5 variable.

The biquad approach is a highly stable and flexible implementation for precision active elliptic-function filters. Independent adjustment capability for resonant frequency, Q, and notch frequency preclude its use when Qs in excess of 10 are required. Stable Qs of up to 200 are obtainable.

EXAMPLE 5-18

REQUIRED:

Active bandpass filter
Center frequency 500 Hz
0.2 dB maximum at ±50 Hz (450 Hz, 550 Hz)
30 dB minimum at ±150 Hz (350 Hz, 650 Hz)

RESULT:

(a) Convert to geometrically symmetrical requirement

$$f_0 = \sqrt{f_L f_u} = \sqrt{450 \times 550} = 497.5 \text{ Hz} \tag{2-14}$$

$$BW_{30 \text{ dB}} = f_2 - \frac{f_0^2}{f_2} = 650 - \frac{497.5^2}{650} = 269 \text{ Hz} \tag{5-18}$$

$$A_s = \frac{\text{stopband bandwidth}}{\text{passband bandwidth}} = \frac{269}{100} = 2.69 \tag{2-19}$$

(b) A normalized low-pass filter must be chosen that makes the transition from less than 0.2 dB to more than 30 dB within a frequency ratio of 2.69:1. An elliptic-function filter will be chosen from table 11-56. The design corresponding to C03 20 $\theta = 25°$ has the following characteristics:

$$n = 3$$

$$\rho = 20\% \text{ (0.18-dB ripple)}$$

$$\Omega_s = 2.366$$

$$A_{min} = 31.47 \text{ dB}$$

The pole-zero coordinates are tabulated alongside the low-pass element values and are as follows:

Poles:

$$-0.3670 \pm j1.1423$$

$$-0.91469$$

Zero:

$$\pm j2.700$$

(c) The bandpass pole-zero transformation is now performed. First compute

$$Q_{bp} = \frac{f_0}{BW_{0.2\,dB}} = \frac{497.5\ Hz}{100\ Hz} = 4.975 \qquad (2\text{-}16)$$

The transformation proceeds as follows:
Complex pole:

$$\alpha = 0.3670 \qquad \beta = 1.1423$$

$$C = 1.439538 \qquad\qquad (5\text{-}50)$$

$$D = 0.147538 \qquad\qquad (5\text{-}51)$$

$$E = 4.058162 \qquad\qquad (5\text{-}52)$$

$$G = 4.047420 \qquad\qquad (5\text{-}53)$$

$$Q = 13.645000 \qquad\qquad (5\text{-}54)$$

$$M = 1.006576 \qquad\qquad (5\text{-}55)$$

$$W = 1.121445 \qquad\qquad (5\text{-}56)$$

$$f_{ra} = 443.6\ Hz \qquad\qquad (5\text{-}57)$$

$$f_{rb} = 557.9\ Hz \qquad\qquad (5\text{-}58)$$

Real Pole:

$$\alpha = 0.91469$$

$$Q = 5.439 \qquad\qquad (5\text{-}59)$$

$$f_r = 497.5\ Hz$$

Zero:

$$\omega_\infty = 2.700$$

$$H = 1.147269 \qquad\qquad (5\text{-}60)$$

$$Z = 1.307520 \qquad\qquad (5\text{-}61)$$

$$f_{\infty,a} = 380.49\ Hz \qquad\qquad (5\text{-}62)$$

$$f_{\infty,b} = 650.49\ Hz \qquad\qquad (5\text{-}63)$$

The computed bandpass parameters are summarized in the following table. The zeros are assigned to the first two sections.

Section	f_r	Q	f_∞
1	443.6 Hz	13.6	380.5 Hz
2	557.6 Hz	13.6	650.5 Hz
3	497.5 Hz	5.44	

(d) Sections 1 and 2 will be realized in the form of the biquad configuration of figure 5-37 where R' and R are both 10 kΩ and $C = 0.047$ μF.

Section 1:

$$f_r = 443.6 \text{ Hz}$$

$$Q = 13.6$$

$$f_\infty = 380.5 \text{ Hz}$$

$$R_1 = R_4 = \frac{Q}{2\pi f_r C} = 103.8 \text{ k}\Omega \tag{5-122}$$

$$R_2 = R_3 = \frac{R_1}{Q} = 7.63 \text{ k}\Omega \tag{5-123}$$

$$R_5 = \frac{f_r^2 R}{Q|f_r^2 - f_\infty^2|} = 2.78 \text{ k}\Omega \tag{5-124}$$

$$R_6 = R = 10 \text{ k}\Omega \tag{5-126}$$

Section 2:

$$f_r = 557.9 \text{ Hz}$$

$$Q = 13.6$$

$$f_\infty = 650.5 \text{ Hz}$$

$$R_1 = R_4 = 82.5 \text{ k}\Omega \tag{5-122}$$

$$R_2 = R_3 = 6.07 \text{ k}\Omega \tag{5-123}$$

$$R_5 = 2.05 \text{ k}\Omega \tag{5-124}$$

$$R_6 = 7.36 \text{ k}\Omega \tag{5-125}$$

(e) The MFBP configuration of figure 5-25b will be used for the all-pole circuit of section 3. The value of C is 0.047 μF, and A_r is unity.

Section 3:

$$f_r = 497.5 \text{ Hz}$$

$$Q = 5.44$$

$$R_2 = 74.1 \text{ k}\Omega \tag{5-68}$$

$$R_{1a} = 37.0 \text{ k}\Omega \tag{5-72}$$

$$R_{1b} = 636 \text{ }\Omega \tag{5-73}$$

The resulting filter is shown in figure 5-38, where standard 1% resistors are used. The resonant frequency and Q of each section have been made adjustable.

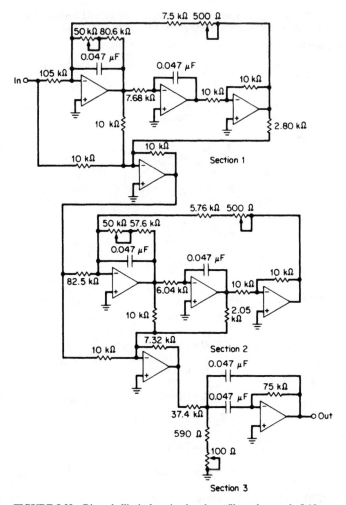

FIGURE 5-38 Biquad elliptic-function bandpass filter of example 5-18.

BIBLIOGRAPHY

Huelsman, L. P., *Theory and Design of Active RC Circuits,* McGraw-Hill, New York, 1968.

Sedra, A. S., and J. L. Espinoza, "Sensitivity and Frequency Limitations of Biquadratic Active Filters," *IEEE Transactions on Circuits and Systems,* vol. CAS-22, no. 2, February 1975.

Thomas, L. C., "The Biquad: Part I—Some Practical Design Considerations," *IEEE Transactions on Circuit Theory,* vol. CT–18, May 1971.

Tow, J., "A Step-by-Step Active Filter Design," *IEEE Spectrum,* vol. 6, December 1969.

Williams, A. B., *Active Filter Design,* Artech House, Dedham, Mass., 1975.

Williams, A. B., "Q-Multiplier Techniques Increase Filter Selectivity," *EDN,* October 5, 1975, pp. 74–76.

Zverev, A. I., *Handbook of Filter Synthesis,* John Wiley and Sons, New York, 1967.

CHAPTER 6
BAND-REJECT FILTERS

6.1 LC *BAND-REJECT FILTERS*

Normalization of a band-reject requirement and the definitions of the response shape parameters were discussed in section 2.1. Like bandpass filters, band-reject networks can also be derived from a normalized low-pass filter by a suitable transformation.

In section 5.1 we discussed the design of wideband bandpass filters by cascading a low-pass filter and a high-pass filter. In a similar manner, wideband band-reject filters could also be obtained by combining low-pass and high-pass filters. Both the input and output terminals are paralleled, and each filter must have a high input and output impedance in the band of the other filter to prevent interaction. Therefore, the order n must be odd and the first and last branches should consist of series elements. These restrictions make the design of band-reject filters by combining low-pass and high-pass filters undesirable. The impedance interaction between filters is a serious problem unless the separation between cutoffs is many octaves; so the design of band-reject filters is best approached by transformation techniques.

The Band-Reject Circuit Transformation

Bandpass filters were obtained by first designing a low-pass filter having a cutoff frequency equivalent to the required bandwidth and then resonating each element to the desired center frequency. The response of the low-pass filter at DC will correspond to the response of the bandpass filter at center frequency.

Band-reject filters are designed by initially transforming the normalized low-pass filter into a high-pass network having a cutoff frequency equal to the required bandwidth and at the desired impedance level. Every high-pass element is then resonated to the center frequency in the same manner as bandpass filters.

This corresponds to replacing the frequency variable in the high-pass transfer function by a new variable which is given by

$$f_{\text{br}} = f_0 \left(\frac{f}{f_0} - \frac{f_0}{f} \right) \tag{6-1}$$

As a result, the response of the high-pass filter at DC is transformed to the band-reject network at the center frequency. The bandwidth response of the band-reject filter is identical to the frequency response of the high-pass filter. The high-pass to band-reject transformation is shown in figure 6-1. Negative frequencies, of course, are strictly of theoretical interest, so only the response shape corresponding to positive frequencies is applicable. As in the case of bandpass filters, the response curve exhibits geometric symmetry.

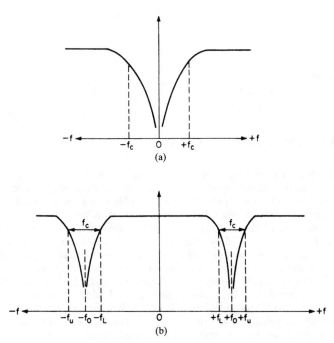

FIGURE 6-1   The band-reject transformation: (*a*) high-pass filter response; (*b*) transformed band-reject filter response.

The design procedure can be summarized as follows:

1. Normalize the band-reject filter specification and select a normalized low-pass filter that provides the required attenuation within the computed steepness factor.
2. Transform the normalized low-pass filter to a normalized high-pass filter. Then scale the high-pass filter to a cutoff frequency equal to the desired bandwidth and to the preferred impedance level.
3. Resonate each element to the center frequency by introducing a capacitor in series with each inductor and an inductor in parallel with each capacitor to complete the design. The transformed circuit branches are summarized in table 6-1.

All-Pole Band-Reject Filters

Band-reject filters can be derived from any all-pole or elliptic-function LC low-pass network. Although not as efficient as elliptic-function filters, the all-pole approach

TABLE 6-1 The High-Pass to Band-Reject Transformation

	High-Pass Branch	Band-Reject Configuration	Circuit Values
Type I			$L = \dfrac{1}{\omega_0^2 C}$ (6-2)
Type II			$C = \dfrac{1}{\omega_0^2 L}$ (6-3)
Type III			$C_a = \dfrac{1}{\omega_0^2 L_a}$ (6-4)
			$L_b = \dfrac{1}{\omega_0^2 C_b}$ (6-5)
			$C_1 = \dfrac{1}{\omega_0^2 L_1}$ (6-6)
Type IV			$L_2 = \dfrac{1}{\omega_0^2 C_2}$ (6-7)

results in a simpler band-reject structure where all sections are tuned to the center frequency.

The following example demonstrates the design of an all-pole band-reject filter.

EXAMPLE 6-1

REQUIRED:

Band-reject filter
Center frequency of 10 kHz
3 dB at ± 250 Hz (9.75 kHz, 10.25 kHz)
30 dB minimum at ±100 Hz (9.9 kHz, 10.1 kHz)
Source and load impedance of 600 Ω

RESULT:

(a) Convert to geometrically symmetrical requirement. Since the bandwidth is relatively narrow, the specified arithmetically symmetrical frequencies will determine the following design parameters:

$$f_0 = 10 \text{ kHz}$$

$$\text{BW}_{3 \text{ dB}} = 500 \text{ Hz}$$

$$\text{BW}_{30 \text{ dB}} = 200 \text{ Hz}$$

(b) Compute the band-reject steepness factor.

$$A_s = \frac{\text{passband bandwidth}}{\text{stopband bandwidth}} = \frac{500 \text{ Hz}}{200 \text{ Hz}} = 2.5 \qquad (2\text{-}20)$$

The response curves of figure 2-45 indicate that an $n = 3$ Chebyshev normalized low-pass filter having a 1-dB ripple provides over 30 dB of attenuation within a frequency ratio of 2.5:1. The corresponding circuit is found in table 11-31 and is shown in figure 6-2a.

(c) To transform the normalized low-pass circuit into a normalized high-pass filter, replace inductors with capacitors and vice versa using reciprocal element values. The transformed structure is shown in figure 6-2b.

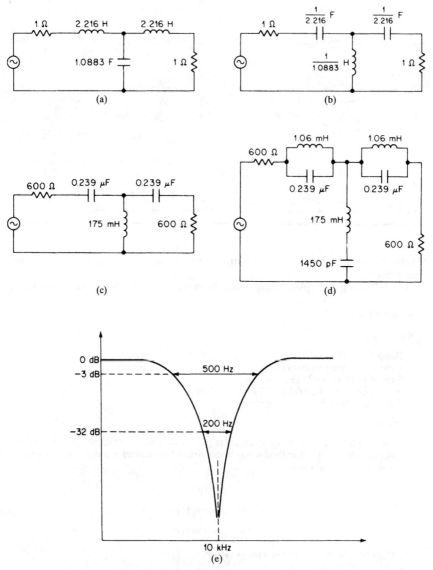

(a)

(b)

(c)

(d)

(e)

FIGURE 6-2 Band-reject filter of example 6-1: (a) normalized low-pass filter; (b) transformed normalized high-pass filter; (c) frequency- and impedance-scaled high-pass filter; (d) transformed band-reject filter; (e) frequency response.

(d) The normalized high-pass filter is scaled to a cutoff frequency of 500 Hz corresponding to the desired bandwidth and to an impedance level of 600 Ω. The capacitors are divided by $Z \times$ FSF and the inductors are multiplied by Z/FSF, where Z is 600 and the FSF (frequency-scaling factor) is given by $2\pi f_c$, where f_c is 500 Hz. The scaled high-pass filter is illustrated in figure 6-2c.

(e) To make the high-pass to band-reject transformation, resonate each capacitor with a parallel inductor and each inductor with a series capacitor. The resonating inductors for the series branches are both given by

$$L = \frac{1}{\omega_0^2 C} = \frac{1}{(2\pi 10 \times 10^3)^2 \times 0.239 \times 10^{-6}} = 1.06 \text{ mH} \tag{6-2}$$

The tuning capacitor for the shunt inductor is determined from

$$C = \frac{1}{\omega_0^2 L} = \frac{1}{(2\pi 10 \times 10^3)^2 \times 0.175} = 1450 \text{ pF} \tag{6-3}$$

The final filter is shown in figure 6-2d, where all peaks are tuned to the center frequency of 10 kHz. The theoretical frequency response is illustrated in figure 6-2e.

When a low-pass filter undergoes a high-pass transformation followed by a band-reject transformation, the minimum Q requirement is increased by a factor equal to the Q of the band-reject filter. This can be expressed as

$$Q_{\min} \text{ (band-reject)} = Q_{\min} \text{ (low-pass)} \times Q_{br} \tag{6-8}$$

where values for $Q_{\min}$ (low-pass) are given in figure 3-8 and $Q_{br} = f_0/\text{BW}_{3 \text{ dB}}$. The branch Q should be several times larger than $Q_{\min}$ (band-reject) to obtain near theoretical results.

The equivalent circuit of a band-reject filter at center frequency can be determined by replacing each parallel tuned circuit by a resistor of $\omega_0 L Q_L$ and each series tuned circuit by a resistor of $\omega_0 L/Q_L$. These resistors correspond to the branch impedances at resonance, where ω_0 is $2\pi f_0$, L is the branch inductance, and Q_L is the branch Q which is normally determined only by the inductor losses.

It is then apparent that at center frequency, the circuit can be replaced by a resistive voltage divider. The amount of attenuation that can be obtained is then directly controlled by the branch Qs. Let us determine the attenuation of the circuit of example 6-1 for a finite value of inductor Q.

EXAMPLE 6-2

REQUIRED: Estimate the amount of rejection obtainable at the center frequency of 10 kHz for the band-reject filter of example 6-1. An inductor Q of 100 is available and the capacitors are assumed to be lossless. Also determine if the Q is sufficient to retain the theoretical passband characteristics.

RESULT:

(a) Compute the equivalent resistances at resonance for all tuned circuits.
   Parallel tuned circuits:

$$R = \omega_0 L Q_L = 2\pi \times 10^4 \times 1.06 \times 10^{-3} \times 100 = 6660 \ \Omega \tag{5-21}$$

   Series tuned circuit:

$$R = \frac{\omega_0 L}{Q_L} = \frac{2\pi \times 10^4 \times 0.175}{100} = 110 \ \Omega \tag{5-30}$$

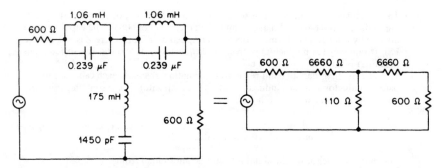

FIGURE 6-3 Equivalent circuit at center frequency for filter of figure 6-2.

(b) The equivalent circuit at 10 kHz is shown in figure 6-3. Using conventional circuit analysis methods such as mesh equations or approximation techniques, the overall loss is found to be 58 dB. Since the flat loss due to the 600-Ω terminations is 6 dB, the relative attenuation at 10 kHz will be 52 dB.

(c) The curves of figure 3-8 indicate that an $n = 3$ Chebyshev filter with a 1-dB ripple has a minimum theoretical Q requirement of 4.5. The minimum Q of the band-reject filter is given by

$$Q_{min} \text{ (band-reject)} = Q_{min} \text{ (low-pass)} \times Q_{br} = 4.5 \times \frac{10{,}000}{500} = 90 \qquad (6\text{-}8)$$

Therefore, the available Q of 100 is barely adequate and some passband rounding will occur in addition to the reduced stopband attenuation. The resulting effect on frequency response is shown in figure 6-4.

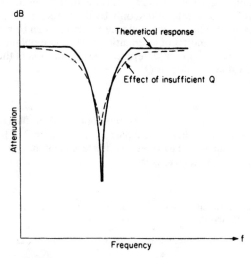

FIGURE 6-4 Effects of insufficient Q upon a band-reject filter.

Elliptic-Function Band-Reject Filters

The superior properties of the elliptic-function family of filters can also be applied to band-reject requirements. Extremely steep characteristics in the transition region between passband and stopband can be achieved much more efficiently than with all-pole filters.

Saal and Ulbrich as well as Zverev (see bibliography) have extensively tabulated the LC values for normalized elliptic-function low-pass networks. These circuits can be transformed to high-pass filters and subsequently to a band-reject filter in the same manner as the all-pole filters.

Since each tabulated low-pass filter can be realized in dual forms as defined by the upper and lower schematics shown in the tables, the resulting band-reject filters can also take on two different configurations, as illustrated in figure 6-5.

Branch 2 of the standard band-reject filter circuit corresponds to the type III network shown in table 6-1. This branch provides a pair of geometrically related zeros, one above and one below the center frequency. These zeros result from two conditions of parallel resonance. However, the circuit configuration itself is not very desirable. The elements corresponding to the individual parallel resonances are not

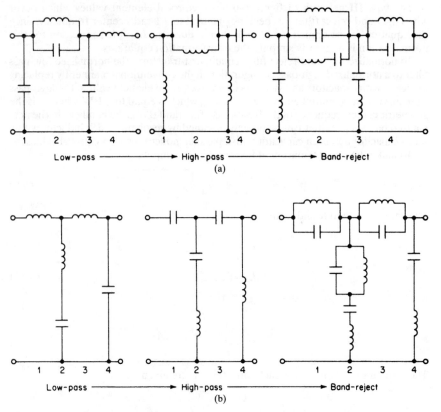

FIGURE 6-5 The band-reject transformation of elliptic-function filters: (*a*) standard configuration; (*b*) dual configuration.

distinctly isolated, since each resonance is determined by the interaction of a number of elements. This makes tuning somewhat difficult. For very narrow filters, the element values also become somewhat unreasonable.

An identical situation occurred during the bandpass transformation of an elliptic-function low-pass filter discussed in section 5.1. An equivalent configuration was presented as an alternate and is repeated in figure 6-6.

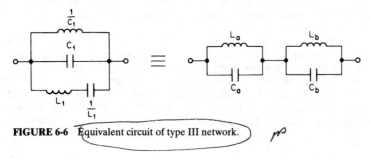

FIGURE 6-6 Equivalent circuit of type III network.

The type III network of figure 6-6 has reciprocal element values which occur when the band-reject filter has been normalized to a 1-rad/s center frequency, since the equation for resonance, $\omega_0^2 LC = 1$, then reduces to $LC = 1$. The reason for this normalization is to greatly simplify the transformation equations.

To normalize the band-reject filter circuit, first transform the normalized low-pass filter to a normalized high-pass configuration in the conventional manner by replacing inductors with capacitors and vice versa using reciprocal element values. The high-pass elements are then multiplied by the factor Q_{br}, which is equal to f_0/BW, where f_0 is the geometric center frequency of the band-reject filter and BW is the bandwidth. The normalized band-reject filter can be directly obtained by resonating each inductor with a series capacitor and each capacitor with a parallel inductor using reciprocal values.

To make the transformation of figure 6-6 first compute

$$\beta = 1 + \frac{1}{2L_1C_1} + \sqrt{\frac{1}{4L_1^2C_1^2} + \frac{1}{L_1C_1}} \tag{6-9}$$

The values are then found from

$$L_a = \frac{1}{C_1(\beta + 1)} \tag{6-10}$$

$$L_b = \beta L_a \tag{6-11}$$

$$C_a = \frac{1}{L_b} \tag{6-12}$$

$$C_b = \frac{1}{L_a} \tag{6-13}$$

The resonant frequencies for each tuned circuit are given by

$$\Omega_{\infty,a} = \sqrt{\beta} \tag{6-14}$$

and

$$\Omega_{\infty,b} = \frac{1}{\Omega_{\infty,a}} \tag{6-15}$$

After the normalized band-reject filter has undergone the transformation of figure 6-6 wherever applicable, the circuit can be scaled to the desired impedance level and frequency. The inductors are multiplied by Z/FSF and capacitors are divided by $Z \times \text{FSF}$. The value of Z is the desired impedance level, and the frequency-scaling factor (FSF) in this case is equal to ω_0 ($\omega_0 = 2\pi f_0$). The resulting resonant frequencies in hertz are determined by multiplying the normalized radian resonant frequencies by f_0.

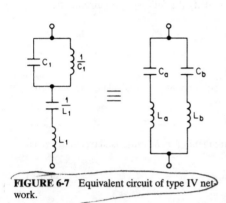

FIGURE 6-7 Equivalent circuit of type IV network.

Branch 2 of the band-reject filter derived from the dual low-pass structure of figure 6-5b corresponds to the type IV network of table 6-1. This configuration realizes a pair of finite zeros resulting from two conditions of series resonance. However, as in the case of the type III network, the individual resonances are determined by the interaction of all the elements, which makes tuning difficult and can result in unreasonable values for narrow filters. An alternate configuration is shown in figure 6-7 consisting of two series resonant circuits in parallel.

To simplify the transformation equations, the type IV network requires reciprocal values, so the band-reject filter must be normalized to a 1-rad/s center frequency. This is accomplished as previously described, and the filter is subsequently denormalized after the transformations have been made.

The transformation is accomplished as follows:
First compute

$$\beta = 1 + \frac{1}{2L_1C_1} + \sqrt{\frac{1}{4L_1^2C_1^2} + \frac{1}{L_1C_1}} \qquad (6\text{-}16)$$

then

$$L_a = \frac{(\beta + 1)L_1}{\beta} \qquad (6\text{-}17)$$

$$C_a = \frac{1}{(\beta + 1)L_1} \qquad (6\text{-}18)$$

$$L_b = \frac{1}{C_a} \qquad (6\text{-}19)$$

$$C_b = \frac{1}{L_a} \qquad (6\text{-}20)$$

$$\Omega_{\infty,a} = \sqrt{\beta} \qquad (6\text{-}21)$$

$$\Omega_{\infty,b} = \frac{1}{\Omega_{\infty,a}} \qquad (6\text{-}22)$$

The standard configuration of the elliptic-function filter is usually preferred over the dual circuit so that the transformed low-pass zeros can be realized using the structure of figure 6-6. Parallel tuned circuits are generally more desirable than series tuned circuits since they can be transformed to alternate L/C ratios to optimize Q and reduce capacitor values (see section 8.2 on tapped inductors).

EXAMPLE 6-3

REQUIRED: Design a band-reject filter to satisfy the following requirements:

1 dB maximum at 2200 and 2800 Hz
50 dB minimum at 2300 and 2700 Hz
Source and load impedance of 600 Ω

RESULT:

(a) Convert to geometrically symmetrical requirement. First calculate the geometric center frequency.

$$f_0 = \sqrt{f_l f_u} = \sqrt{2200 \times 2800} = 2482 \text{ Hz} \qquad (2\text{-}14)$$

Compute the corresponding geometric frequency for each stopband frequency given using equation (2-18).

$$f_1 f_2 = f_0^2 \qquad (2\text{-}18)$$

$(2482)^2 = 2300 \times f_2 \qquad f_2 = 2678$

$(2482)^2 = f_1 (2700) \qquad$

$f_1 = 2282$

f_1	f_2	$f_2 - f_1$
2300 Hz	2678 Hz	378 Hz
2282 Hz	2700 Hz	418 Hz

The second pair of frequencies is retained, since they represent the steeper requirement. The complete geometrically symmetrical specification can be stated as

$$f_0 = 2482 \text{ Hz}$$

$$BW_{1 \text{ dB}} = 600 \text{ Hz}$$

$$BW_{50 \text{ dB}} = 418 \text{ Hz}$$

(b) Compute the band-reject steepness factor.

$$A_s = \frac{\text{passband bandwidth}}{\text{stopband bandwidth}} = \frac{600 \text{ Hz}}{418 \text{ Hz}} = 1.435 \qquad (2\text{-}20)$$

A normalized low-pass filter must be chosen that makes the transition from less than 1 dB to more than 50 dB within a frequency ratio of 1.435. An elliptic-function filter will be selected.

Figure 2-86 indicates that with $\rho = 20\%$ (0.18-dB ripple) a complexity of $n = 6$ is required. Examination of table 11-56 results in the selection of a design corresponding to C06 20C $\theta = 47°$ which has the parameters $\Omega_s = 1.433$ and $A_{min} = 53.4$ dB. This filter can then provide over 50 dB of attenuation within a frequency ratio of 1.435 as required by the specification. The normalized circuit is shown in figure 6-8a.

(c) The normalized low-pass filter is now transformed into a normalized high-pass structure by replacing all inductors with capacitors and vice versa using reciprocal values. The resulting filter is given in figure 6-8b.

(d) To obtain a normalized band-reject filter so that the transformation of figure 6-6 can be performed, first multiply all the high-pass elements by Q_{br}, which is given by

$$Q_{br} = \frac{f_0}{BW_{1\,dB}} = \frac{2482\ Hz}{600\ Hz} = 4.137$$

The modified high-pass filter is shown in figure 6-8c.

(e) Each high-pass inductor is resonated with a series capacitor and each capacitor is resonated with a parallel inductor to obtain the normalized band-reject filter. Since the center frequency is 1 rad/s, the resonant elements are simply the reciprocals of each other as illustrated in figure 6-8d.

(f) The type III networks of the second and fourth branches are now transformed to the equivalent circuit of figure 6-6 as follows:

Type III network of second branch:

$$L_1 = 19.90\ H \qquad C_1 = 3.268\ F$$

$$\beta = 1 + \frac{1}{2L_1C_1} + \sqrt{\frac{1}{4L_1^2C_1^2} + \frac{1}{L_1C_1}} = 1.1319 \qquad (6\text{-}9)$$

$$L_a = \frac{1}{C_1(\beta + 1)} = 0.1435\ H \qquad (6\text{-}10)$$

$$L_b = \beta L_a = 0.1625\ H \qquad (6\text{-}11)$$

$$C_a = \frac{1}{L_b} = 6.155\ F \qquad (6\text{-}12)$$

$$C_b = \frac{1}{L_a} = 6.969\ F \qquad (6\text{-}13)$$

$$\Omega_{\infty,a} = \sqrt{\beta} = 1.0639 \qquad (6\text{-}14)$$

$$\Omega_{\infty,b} = \frac{1}{\Omega_{\infty,a}} = 0.9399 \qquad (6\text{-}15)$$

Type III network of fourth branch:

$$L_1 = 11.31\ H \qquad C_1 = 3.283\ F$$

$$\beta = 1.1781$$

$$L_a = 0.1398\ H$$

$$L_b = 0.1648\ H$$

$$C_a = 6.068\ F$$

$$C_b = 7.153\ F$$

$$\Omega_{\infty,a} = 1.0854$$

$$\omega_{\infty,b} = 0.9213$$

The resulting normalized band-reject filter is shown in figure 6-8e.

(g) The final filter can now be obtained by frequency- and impedance-scaling the normalized band-reject filter to a center frequency of 2482 Hz and 600 Ω. The inductors are multiplied by Z/FSF, and the capacitors are divided by Z × FSF, where Z is 600 and the FSF is $2\pi f_0$, where f_0 is 2482 Hz. The circuit is given in figure 6-8f, where the resonant frequencies of each section were obtained by multiplying the normalized frequencies by f_0. The frequency response is illustrated in figure 6-8g.

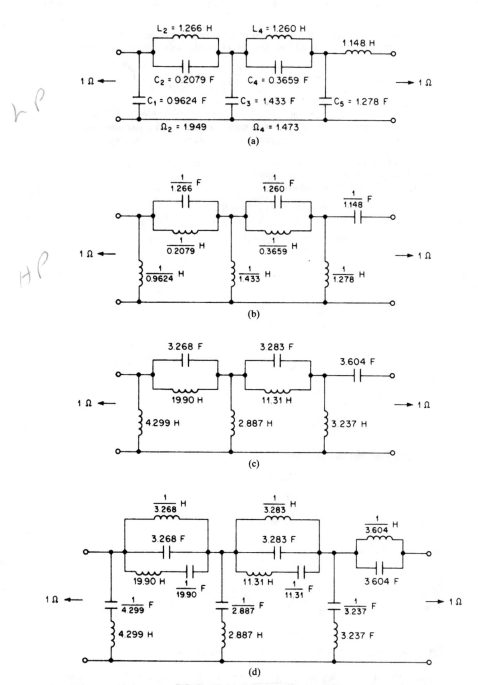

FIGURE 6-8 Elliptic-function band-reject filter: (a) normalized low-pass filter; (b) transformed high-pass filter; (c) high-pass filter with elements multiplied by Q_{br}; (d) normalized band-reject filter.

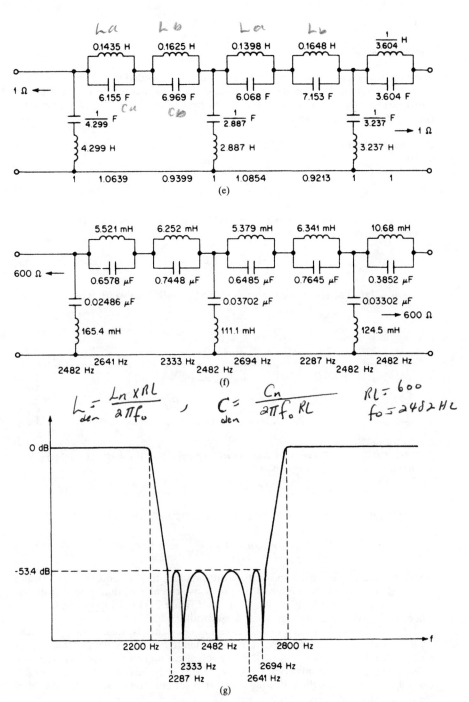

FIGURE 6-8 (*Continued*)   Elliptic-function band-reject filter: (*e*) transformed type III networks; (*f*) frequency- and impedance-scaled circuit; (*g*) frequency response.

Null Networks

A null network can be loosely defined as a circuit intended to reject a single frequency or a very narrow band of frequencies and is frequently referred to as a trap. Notch depth rather than rate of roll-off is the prime consideration, and the circuit is restricted to a single section.

Parallel Resonant Trap.   The RC high-pass circuit of figure 6-9a has a 3-dB cutoff given by

$$f_c = \frac{1}{2\pi RC} \qquad (6\text{-}23)$$

A band-reject transformation will result in the circuit of figure 6-9b. The value of L is computed from

$$L = \frac{1}{\omega_0^2 C} \qquad (6\text{-}24)$$

where $\omega_0 = 2\pi f_0$. The center frequency is f_0 and the 3-dB bandwidth is f_c.

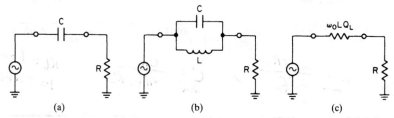

FIGURE 6-9   Parallel resonant trap: (a) RC high-pass filter; (b) results of band-reject transformation; (c) equivalent circuit at f_0.

The frequency response of a first-order band-reject filter can be expressed as

$$A_{\text{dB}} = 10 \log \left[1 + \left(\frac{\text{BW}_{3\,\text{dB}}}{\text{BW}_{x\,\text{dB}}} \right)^2 \right] \qquad (6\text{-}25)$$

where $\text{BW}_{3\,\text{dB}}$ is the 3-dB bandwidth corresponding to f_c in equation (6-23) and $\text{BW}_{x\,\text{dB}}$ is the bandwidth of interest. The response can also be determined from the normalized Butterworth attenuation curves of figure 2-34 corresponding to $n = 1$, where $\text{BW}_{3\,\text{dB}}/\text{BW}_{x\,\text{dB}}$ is the normalized bandwidth.

The impedance of a parallel tuned circuit at resonance is equal to $\omega_0 L Q_L$, where Q_L is the inductor Q and the capacitor is assumed to be lossless. We can then represent the band-reject filter at f_0 by the equivalent circuit of figure 6-9c. After some algebraic manipulation involving equations (6-23) and (6-24) and the circuit of figure 6-9c, we can derive the following expression for the attenuation at resonance of the $n = 1$ band-reject filter of figure 6-9:

$$A_{\text{dB}} = 20 \log \left(\frac{Q_L}{Q_{\text{br}}} + 1 \right) \qquad (6\text{-}26)$$

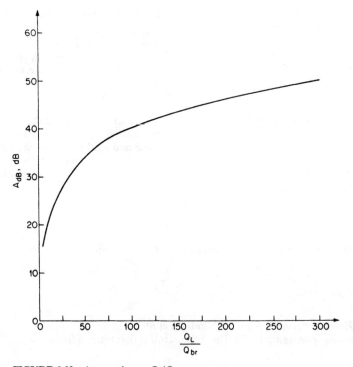

FIGURE 6-10 Attenuation vs. Q_L/Q_{br}.

where $Q_{br} = f_0 / BW_{3\,dB}$. Equation (6-26) is plotted in figure 6-10. When Q_{br} is high, the required inductor Q may become prohibitively large in order to attain sufficient attenuation at f_0.

The effect of insufficient inductor Q will not only reduce relative attenuation but will also cause some rounding of the response near the cutoff frequencies. Therefore, the ratio Q_L/Q_{br} should be as high as possible.

EXAMPLE 6-4

REQUIRED: Design a parallel resonant circuit which has a 3-dB bandwidth of 500 Hz and a center frequency of 7500 Hz. The source resistance is zero and the load is 1 kΩ. Also determine the minimum inductor Q for a relative attenuation of at least 30 dB at 7500 Hz.

RESULT:

(a) Compute the value of the capacitor from

$$C = \frac{1}{2\pi f_c R} = \frac{1}{2\pi 500 \times 1000} = 0.3183 \ \mu F \qquad (6\text{-}23)$$

The inductance is given by

$$L = \frac{1}{\omega_0^2 C} = \frac{1}{(2\pi 7500)^2 \times 3.183 \times 10^{-7}} = 1.415 \ mH \qquad (6\text{-}24)$$

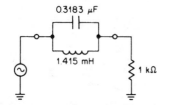

0.3183 µF
1.415 mH
1 kΩ

FIGURE 6-11 Parallel resonant trap of example 6-4.

The resulting circuit is shown in figure 6-11.

(b) The required ratio of Q_L/Q_{br} for 30-dB attenuation at f_0 can be determined from figure 6-10 or equation (6-26) and is approximately 30. Therefore, the inductor Q should exceed 30 Q_{br} or 450 where $Q_{br} = f_0/\text{BW}_{3\,\text{dB}}$.

Frequently it is desirable to operate the band-reject network between equal source and load terminations instead of a voltage source as in figure 6-9. If a source and load resistor are specified where both are equal to R, equation (6-23) is modified to

$$f_c = \frac{1}{4\pi RC} \tag{6-27}$$

When the source and load are unequal, the cutoff frequency is given by

$$f_c = \frac{1}{2\pi(R_s + R_L)C} \tag{6-28}$$

Series Resonant Trap. An $n = 1$ band-reject filter can also be derived from the RL high-pass filter of figure 6-12a. The 3-dB cutoff is determined from

$$f_c = \frac{R}{2\pi L} \tag{6-29}$$

The band-reject filter of figure 6-12b is obtained by resonating the coil with a series capacitor where

$$C = \frac{1}{\omega_0^2 L} \tag{6-24}$$

The center frequency is f_0 and the 3-dB bandwidth is equal to f_c. The series losses of an inductor can be represented by a resistor of $\omega_0 L/Q_L$. The equivalent circuit of the

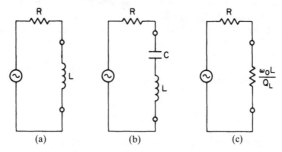

R   R   R
               C
L   L $\frac{\omega_0 L}{Q_L}$

(a)   (b)   (c)

FIGURE 6-12 Series resonant trap: (a) RL high-pass filter; (b) result of band-reject transformation; (c) equivalent circuit at f_0.

band-reject network at resonance is given by the circuit of figure 6-12c and the attenuation computed from equation (6-26) or figure 6-10.

EXAMPLE 6-5

REQUIRED: Design a series resonant circuit having a 3-dB bandwidth of 500 Hz and a center frequency of 7500 Hz as in the previous example. The source impedance is 1 kΩ and the load is assumed infinite.

RESULT: Compute the element values from the following relationships:

$$L = \frac{R}{2\pi f_c} = \frac{1000}{2\pi 500} = 0.318 \text{ H} \tag{6-29}$$

and

$$C = \frac{1}{\omega_0^2 L} = \frac{1}{(2\pi 7500)^2 0.318} = 1420 \text{ pF} \tag{6-24}$$

The circuit is given in figure 6-13.

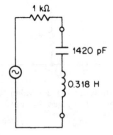

When a series resonant trap is to be terminated with a load resistance equal to the source, the high-pass 3-dB cutoff and resulting 3-dB bandwidth of the band-reject filter are given by

$$f_c = \frac{R}{4\pi L} \tag{6-30}$$

FIGURE 6-13 Series resonant trap of example 6-5.

For the more general case where source and load are unequal, the cutoff frequency is determined from

$$f_c = \frac{R_{eq}}{2\pi L} \tag{6-31}$$

where R_{eq} is the equivalent value of the source and load resistors in parallel.

The Bridged-T Configuration. The resonant traps previously discussed suffer severe degradation of notch depth unless the inductor Q is many magnitudes greater than Q_{br}. The bridged-T band-reject structure can easily provide rejection of 60 dB or more with practical values of inductor Q. The configuration is shown in figure 6-14a.

To understand the operation of the circuit, let us first consider the equivalent circuit of a center-tapped inductor having a coefficient of magnetic coupling equal to unity which is shown in figure 6-14b. The inductance between terminals A and C corresponds to L of figure 6-14a. The inductance between A and B or B and C is equal to $L/4$ since, as the reader may recall, the impedance across one-half of a center-tapped autotransformer is one-fourth the overall impedance. This occurs because the impedance is proportional to the turns ratio squared.

The impedance of a parallel tuned circuit at resonance was previously determined to be equivalent to a resistor of $\omega_0 L Q_L$. Since the circuit of figure 6-14a is center-tapped, the equivalent three-terminal network is shown in figure 6-14c. The impedance between A and C is still $\omega_0 L Q_L$. A negative resistor must then exist in the middle shunt branch so that the impedance across one-half the tuned circuit is one-fourth the overall impedance, or $\omega_0 L Q_L/4$. Of course, negative resistors or inductors

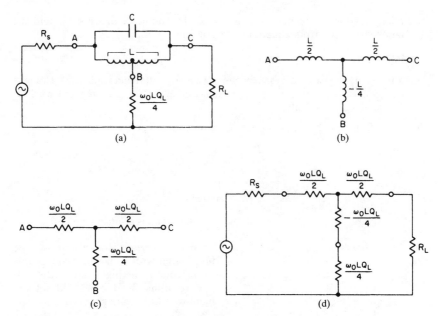

FIGURE 6-14 Bridged-T null network: (*a*) circuit configuration; (*b*) equivalent circuit of center-tapped inductor; (*c*) tuned circuit equivalent at resonance; (*d*) bridged-T equivalent circuit at resonance.

are physically impossible as individual passive two-terminal elements but can be embedded within an equivalent circuit.

If we combine the equivalent circuit of figure 6-14*c* with the bridged-T network of figure 6-14*a*, we obtain the circuit of figure 6-14*d*. The positive and negative resistors in the center branch will cancel, resulting in infinite rejection at center frequency. The degree of rejection actually obtained is dependent upon a variety of factors such as center-tap accuracy, coefficient of coupling, and magnitude of Q_L. When the bridged-T configuration is implemented by modifying a parallel trap design of figure 6-9*b* by adding a center tap and a resistor of $\omega_0 L Q_L / 4$, a dramatic improvement in notch depth will usually occur.

A center-tapped inductor is not always available or practical. An alternate form of a bridged-T is given in figure 6-15. The parallel resonant trap design of figure 6-9 is modified by splitting the capacitor into two capacitors of twice the value, and a resistor of $\omega_0 L Q_L / 4$ is introduced. The two capacitors should be closely matched.

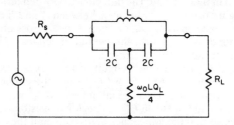

FIGURE 6-15 Alternate form of bridged-T.

In conclusion, the bridged-T structure is an economical and effective means of increasing the available notch rejection of a parallel resonant trap without increasing the inductor Q. However, as a final general comment, a single null section can provide high rejection only at a single frequency or relatively narrow band of frequencies for a given 3-dB bandwidth, since $n = 1$. The stability of the circuit then becomes a significant factor. A higher-order band-reject filter design can have a wider stopband and yet maintain the same 3-dB bandwidth.

6.2 ACTIVE BAND-REJECT FILTERS

This section considers the design of active band-reject filters for both wideband and narrowband applications. Active null networks are covered, and the popular twin-T circuit is discussed in detail.

Wideband Active Band-Reject Filters

Wideband filters can be designed by first separating the specification into individual low-pass and high-pass requirements. Low-pass and high-pass filters are then independently designed and combined by paralleling the inputs and summing both outputs to form the band-reject filter.

A wideband approach is valid when the separation between cutoffs is an octave or more for all-pole filters so that minimum interaction occurs in the stopband when the outputs are summed (see section 2.1 and figure 2-13). Elliptic-function networks will require less separation, since their characteristics are steeper.

An inverting amplifier is used for summing and can also provide gain. Filters can be combined using the configuration of figure 6-16a, where R is arbitrary and A is the desired gain. The individual filters should have a low output impedance to avoid loading by the summing resistors.

The VCVS elliptic-function low-pass and high-pass filters of sections 3.2 and 4.2 each require an RC termination on the last stage to provide the real pole. These elements can be combined with the summing resistors, resulting in the circuit of figure 6-16b. R_a and C_a correspond to the denormalized values of R_5 and C_5 for the low-pass filter of figure 3-20. The denormalized high-pass filter real-pole values are R_b and C_b. If only one filter is of the VCVS type, the summing network of the filter having the low output impedance can be replaced by a single resistor having a value of R.

When one or both filters are of the elliptic-function type, the ultimate attenuation obtainable is determined by the filter having the lesser value of A_{min}, since the stopband output is the summation of the contributions of both filters.

EXAMPLE 6-6

REQUIRED: Design an active band-reject filter having 3-dB points at 100 and 400 Hz and greater than 35 dB of attenuation between 175 and 225 Hz.

RESULT:

(a) Since the ratio of upper cutoff to lower cutoff is well in excess of an octave, a wideband approach can be used. First, separate the specification into individual low-pass and high-pass requirements.

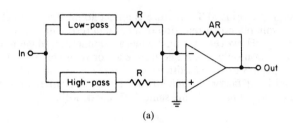

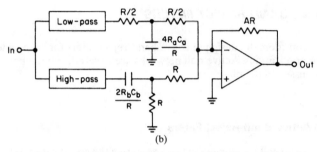

FIGURE 6-16 Wideband band-reject filters: (a) combining of filters having low output impedance; (b) combined filters requiring RC real poles.

Low-pass:	**High-pass:**
3 dB at 100 Hz	3 dB at 400 Hz
35 dB minimum at 175 Hz	35 dB minimum at 225 Hz

(b) The low-pass and high-pass filters can now be independently designed as follows:

Low-pass filter:

Compute the steepness factor.

$$A_s = \frac{f_s}{f_c} = \frac{175 \text{ Hz}}{100 \text{ Hz}} = 1.75 \qquad (2\text{-}11)$$

An $n = 5$ Chebyshev filter having a 0.5-dB ripple is chosen using figure 2-44. The normalized active low-pass filter values are given in table 11-39 and the circuit is shown in figure 6-17a.

To denormalize the filter, multiply all resistors by Z and divide all capacitors by $Z \times$ FSF, where Z is conveniently selected at 10^5 and the FSF is $2\pi f_c$, where f_c is 100 Hz. The denormalized low-pass filter is given in figure 6-17b.

High-pass filter:

Compute the steepness factor.

$$A_s = \frac{f_c}{f_s} = \frac{400 \text{ Hz}}{225 \text{ Hz}} = 1.78 \qquad (2\text{-}13)$$

An $n = 5$ Chebyshev filter with a 0.5-dB ripple will also satisfy the high-pass requirement. A high-pass transformation can be performed on the normalized low-pass filter of figure 6-17a to obtain the circuit of figure 6-17c. All resistors have been replaced with capacitors and vice versa using reciprocal element values.

The normalized high-pass filter is then frequency- and impedance-scaled by multiplying all resistors by Z and dividing all capacitors by $Z \times$ FSF, where Z is chosen at 10^5 and FSF is $2\pi f_c$, using an f_c of 400 Hz. The denormalized high-pass filter is shown in figure 6-17d using standard 1% resistor values.

(c) The individual low-pass and high-pass filters can now be combined using the configuration of figure 6-16a. Since no gain is required, A is set equal to unity. The value of R is conveniently selected at 10 kΩ, resulting in the circuit of figure 6-17e.

Band-Reject Transformation of Low-Pass Poles

The wideband approach to the design of band-reject filters using combined low-pass and high-pass networks is applicable to bandwidths of typically an octave or more. If the separation between cutoffs is insufficient, interaction in the stopband will occur, resulting in inadequate stopband rejection (see figure 2-13).

A more general approach involves normalizing the band-reject requirement and selecting a normalized low-pass filter type that meets these specifications. The corresponding normalized low-pass poles are then directly transformed to the band-reject form and realized using active sections.

A band-reject transfer function can be derived from a low-pass transfer function by substituting the frequency variable f by a new variable given by

$$f_{br} = \frac{1}{f_0\left(\dfrac{f}{f_0} - \dfrac{f_0}{f}\right)} \qquad (6\text{-}32)$$

This transformation combines the low-pass to high-pass and subsequent band-reject transformation discussed in section 6.1 so that a band-reject filter can be obtained directly from the low-pass transfer function.

The band-reject transformation results in two pairs of complex poles and a pair of second-order imaginary zeros from each low-pass complex pole pair. A single low-pass real pole is transformed into a complex pole pair and a pair of first-order imaginary zeros. These relationships are illustrated in figure 6-18. The zeros occur at center frequency and result from the transformed low-pass zeros at infinity.

The band-reject pole-zero pattern of figure 6-18a corresponds to two band-reject sections where each section provides a zero at center frequency and provides one of the pole pairs. The pattern of figure 6-18b is realized by a single band-reject section where the zero also occurs at center frequency.

To make the low-pass to band-reject transformation, first compute

$$Q_{br} = \frac{f_0}{\text{BW}} \qquad (6\text{-}33)$$

where f_0 is the geometric center frequency and BW is the passband bandwidth. The transformation then proceeds as follows:

Complex Poles. The tables of chapter 11 contain tabulated poles corresponding to the all-pole low-pass filter families discussed in chapter 2. Complex poles are given in the form: $-\alpha \pm j\beta$ where α is the real coordinate and β is the imaginary part. Given α, β, Q_{br}, and f_0, the following computations result in two sets of values for Q and frequency which defines two band-reject filter sections. Each section also has a zero at f_0.

$$C = \alpha^2 + \beta^2 \qquad (6\text{-}34)$$

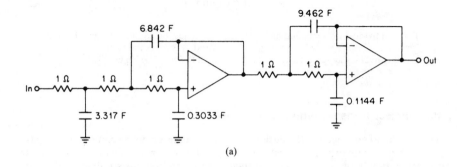

(a)

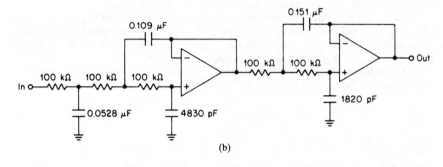

(b)

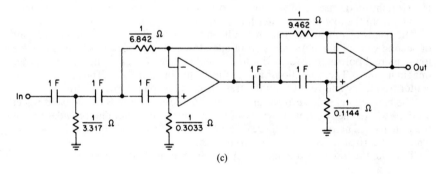

(c)

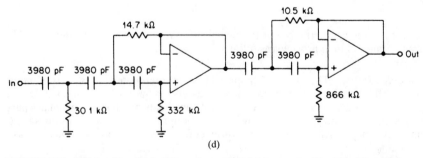

(d)

FIGURE 6-17 Wideband band-reject filter of example 6-6: (a) normalized low-pass filter; (b) denormalized low-pass filter; (c) transformed normalized high-pass filter; (d) denormalized high-pass filter.

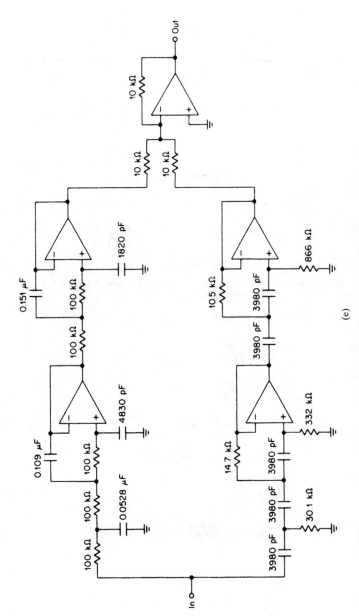

FIGURE 6-17 (*Continued*) Wideband band-reject filter of example 6-6: (*e*) combining filters to obtain band-reject response.

6.23

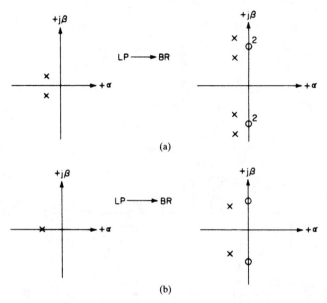

FIGURE 6-18 Band-reject transformation of low-pass poles: (a) low-pass complex pole pair; (b) low-pass real pole.

$$D = \frac{\alpha}{Q_{br}C}$$ (6-35)

$$E = \frac{\beta}{Q_{br}C}$$ (6-36)

$$F = E^2 - D^2 + 4$$ (6-37)

$$G = \sqrt{\frac{F}{2} + \sqrt{\frac{F^2}{4} + D^2E^2}}$$ (6-38)

$$H = \frac{DE}{G}$$ (6-39)

$$K = \frac{1}{2}\sqrt{(D+H)^2 + (E+G)^2}$$ (6-40)

$$Q = \frac{K}{D+H}$$ (6-41)

$$f_{ra} = \frac{f_0}{K}$$ (6-42)

$$f_{rb} = Kf_0$$ (6-43)

$$f_\infty = f_0$$ (6-44)

The two band-reject sections have resonant frequencies of f_{ra} and f_{rb} (in hertz) and identical Qs given by equation (6-41). In addition, each section has a zero at f_0, the filter geometric center frequency.

Real Poles. A normalized low-pass real pole having a real coordinate of α_0 is transformed into a single band-reject section having a Q given by

$$Q = Q_{br}\alpha_0 \qquad (6\text{-}45)$$

The section resonant frequency is equal to f_0, and the section must also have a transmission zero at f_0.

EXAMPLE 6-7

REQUIRED: Determine the pole and zero locations for a band-reject filter having the following specifications:

Center frequency of 3600 Hz
3 dB at ±150 Hz
40 dB minimum at ±30 Hz

RESULT:

(a) Since the filter is narrow, the requirement can be treated directly in its arithmetically symmetrical form:

$$f_0 = 3600 \text{ Hz}$$

$$BW_{3\,dB} = 300 \text{ Hz}$$

$$BW_{40\,dB} = 60 \text{ Hz}$$

The band-reject steepness factor is given by

$$A_s = \frac{\text{passband bandwidth}}{\text{stopband bandwidth}} = \frac{300 \text{ Hz}}{60 \text{ Hz}} = 5 \qquad (2\text{-}20)$$

(b) An $n = 3$ Chebyshev normalized low-pass filter having a 0.1-dB ripple is selected using figure 2-42. The corresponding pole locations are found in table 11-23 and are

$$-0.3500 \pm j0.8695$$

$$-0.6999$$

First make the preliminary computation:

$$Q_{br} = \frac{f_0}{BW_{3\,dB}} = \frac{3600 \text{ Hz}}{300 \text{ Hz}} = 12 \qquad (6\text{-}33)$$

The low-pass to band-reject pole transformation is performed as follows:
Complex-pole transformation:

$$\alpha = 0.3500 \qquad \beta = 0.8695$$

$$C = \alpha^2 + \beta^2 = 0.878530 \qquad (6\text{-}34)$$

$$D = \frac{\alpha}{Q_{br}C} = 0.033199 \qquad (6\text{-}35)$$

$$E = \frac{\beta}{Q_{br}C} = 0.082477 \tag{6-36}$$

$$F = E^2 - D^2 + 4 = 4.005700 \tag{6-37}$$

$$G = \sqrt{\frac{F}{2} + \sqrt{\frac{F^2}{4} + D^2 E^2}} = 2.001425 \tag{6-38}$$

$$H = \frac{DE}{G} = 0.001368 \tag{6-39}$$

$$K = \frac{1}{2} \sqrt{(D+H)^2 + (E+G)^2} = 1.042094 \tag{6-40}$$

$$Q = \frac{K}{D+H} = 30.15 \tag{6-41}$$

$$f_{ra} = \frac{f_0}{K} = 3455 \text{ Hz} \tag{6-42}$$

$$f_{rb} = K f_0 = 3752 \text{ Hz} \tag{6-43}$$

$$f_\infty = f_0 = 3600 \text{ Hz} \tag{6-44}$$

Real-pole transformation:

$$\alpha_0 = 0.6999$$

$$Q = Q_{br}\alpha_0 = 8.40 \tag{6-45}$$

$$f_r = f_\infty = f_0 = 3600 \text{ Hz}$$

The block diagram is shown in figure 6-19.

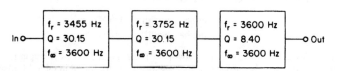

In o—
f_r = 3455 Hz	f_r = 3752 Hz	f_r = 3600 Hz
Q = 30.15	Q = 30.15	Q = 8.40
f_∞ = 3600 Hz	f_∞ = 3600 Hz	f_∞ = 3600 Hz
—o Out

FIGURE 6-19   Block diagram of example 6-7.

Narrowband Active Band-Reject Filters

Narrowband active band-reject filters are designed by first transforming a set of normalized low-pass poles to the band-reject form. The band-reject poles are computed in terms of resonant frequency f_r, Q, and f_∞ using the results of section 6.2 and are then realized with active band-reject sections.

The VCVS Band-Reject Section.   Complex low-pass poles result in a set of band-reject parameters where f_r and f_∞ do not occur at the same frequency. Band-reject sections are then required that permit independent selection of f_r and f_∞ in their design procedure. Both the VCVS and biquad circuits covered in section 5.2 under "Elliptic-Function Bandpass Filters" have this degree of freedom.

The VCVS realization is shown in figure 6-20. The design equations were given in section 5.2 under "Elliptic-Function Bandpass Filters" and are repeated here for convenience, where f_r, Q, and f_∞ are obtained by the band-reject transformation procedure of section 6.2. The values are computed from

$$R_1 = \frac{f_\infty^2 + f_r^2}{3f_\infty^2} \, R' \tag{6-46}$$

$$R_2 = 2R_1 \tag{6-47}$$

$$R_3 = \frac{f_\infty^2 + f_r^2}{4.5f_r^2} \, R' \tag{6-48}$$

$$R_4 = 4.5R_3 \tag{6-49}$$

$$C_1 = \frac{1.5}{2\pi f_r R_1} \tag{6-50}$$

$$C_2 = \frac{C_1}{4.5} \tag{6-51}$$

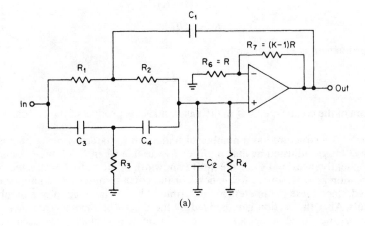

(a)

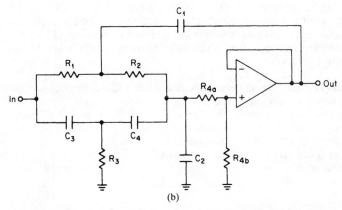

(b)

FIGURE 6-20   VCVS realization for band-reject filters: (*a*) circuit for $K > 1$; (*b*) circuit for $K < 1$.

$$C_3 = \frac{f_r}{2\pi R_1 f_\infty^2} \tag{6-52}$$

$$C_4 = \frac{C_3}{2} \tag{6-53}$$

$$K = \frac{\left(2.5 - \dfrac{1}{Q}\right)\left(\dfrac{f_r^2}{f_\infty^2} + 1\right)}{1.5} \tag{6-54}$$

$$R_6 = R \tag{6-55}$$

$$R_7 = (K - 1)R \tag{6-56}$$

where R' and R can be arbitrarily chosen.

The circuit of figure 6-20a is used when $K > 1$. In the cases where $K < 1$, the configuration of figure 6-20b is utilized, where

$$R_{4a} = (1 - K)R_4 \tag{6-57}$$

and

$$R_{4b} = KR_4 \tag{6-58}$$

The section gain at DC is given by

$$A_{dc} = \frac{f_\infty^2}{f_r^2 + f_\infty^2} \tag{6-59}$$

The gain of the composite filter in the passband is the product of the DC gains of all the sections.

The VCVS structure has a number of undesirable characteristics. Although the circuit Q can be adjusted by making R_6 or R_7 variable when $K > 1$, the Q cannot be independently measured since the 3-dB bandwidth at the output is affected by the transmission zero. Resonant frequency f_r or the notch frequency f_∞ cannot be easily adjusted, since these parameters are determined by the interaction of a number of elements. Also, the section gain is fixed by the design parameters. Another disadvantage of the circuit is that a large spread in capacitor values* may occur so that standard values cannot be easily used. Nevertheless, the VCVS realization makes effective use of a minimum number of operational amplifiers in comparison with other implementations and is widely used. However, because of its lack of adjustment capability, its application is generally restricted to Qs below 10 and with 1% component tolerances.

The State-Variable Band-Reject Section. The biquad or state-variable elliptic-function bandpass filter section discussed in section 5.2 is highly suitable for implementing band-reject transfer functions. The circuit is given in figure 6-21. By connecting resistor R_5 to either node 1 or to node 2, the notch frequency f_∞ will be located above or below the pole resonant frequency f_r.

Section Qs of up to 200 can be obtained. The design parameters f_r, Q, and f_∞, as well as the section gain, can be independently chosen, monitored, and adjusted.

---

* The elliptic-function configuration of the VCVS uniform capacitor structure given in section 3.2 can be used at the expense of additional sensitivity.

From the point of view of low sensitivity and maximum flexibility, the biquad approach is the most desirable method of realization.

The design equations were stated in section 5.2 under "Elliptic-Function Bandpass Filters" and are repeated here for convenience, where f_r, Q, and f_∞ are given and the values of C, R, and R' can be arbitrarily chosen.

$$R_1 = R_4 = \frac{Q}{2\pi f_r C} \tag{6-60}$$

$$R_2 = R_3 = \frac{R_1}{Q} \tag{6-61}$$

$$R_5 = \frac{f_r^2 R}{Q|f_r^2 - f_\infty^2|} \tag{6-62}$$

for $f_\infty > f_r$:
$$R_6 = \frac{f_r^2 R}{f_\infty^2} \tag{6-63}$$

and when $f_\infty < f_r$:
$$R_6 = R \tag{6-64}$$

The value of R_6 is based on unity section gain at DC. The gain can be raised or lowered by proportionally increasing or decreasing R_6.

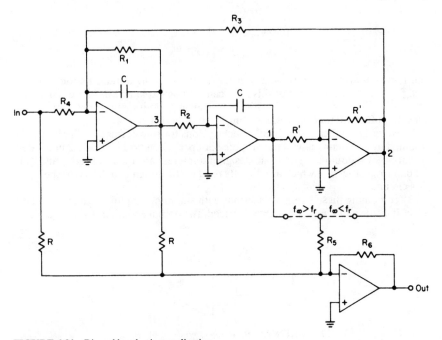

FIGURE 6-21 Biquad band-reject realization.

Resonance is adjusted by monitoring the phase shift between the section input and node 3 using a Lissajous pattern and adjusting R_3 for 180° phase shift with an input frequency of f_r.

The Q is controlled by R_1 and can be measured at node 3 in terms of section 3-dB bandwidth, or R_1 can be adjusted until unity gain occurs between the input and node 3 with f_r applied. Because of the Q-enhancement effect discussed in section 5.2 under "All-Pole Bandpass Configurations," a Q adjustment is usually necessary.

The notch frequency is then determined by monitoring the section output for a null. Adjustment is normally not required, since tuning of f_r will usually bring in f_∞ with acceptable accuracy. If an adjustment is desired, R_5 can be made variable.

Sections for Transformed Real Poles. When a real pole undergoes a band-reject transformation, the result is a single pole pair and a single set of imaginary zeros. Complex poles resulted in two sets of pole pairs and two sets of zeros. The resonant frequency f_r of the transformed real pole is exactly equal to the notch frequency f_∞; so the design flexibility of the VCVS and biquad structures is not required.

A general second-order bandpass transfer function can be expressed as

$$T(s) = \frac{\dfrac{\omega_r}{Q}\,s}{s^2 + \dfrac{\omega_r}{Q}\,s + \omega_r^2} \tag{6-65}$$

where the gain is unity at ω_r. If we realize the circuit of figure 6-22 where $T(s)$ corresponds to the above transfer function, the composite transfer function at the output is given by

$$T(s) = \frac{s^2 + \omega_r^2}{s^2 + \dfrac{\omega_r}{Q}\,s + \omega_r^2} \tag{6-66}$$

This corresponds to a band-reject transfer function having a transmission zero at f_r (i.e., $f_\infty = f_r$). The occurrence of this zero can also be explained intuitively from the structure of figure 6-22. Since $T(s)$ is unity only at f_r, both input signals to the summing amplifier will then cancel, resulting in no output signal.

These results indicate that band-reject sections for transformed real poles can be obtained by combining any of the all-pole bandpass circuits of section 5.2 in the configuration of figure 6-22. The basic design parameters are the required f_r and Q of the band-reject section which are directly used in the design equations for the bandpass circuits.

By combining these bandpass sections with summing amplifiers, the three band-reject structures of figure 6-23 can be derived. The design equations for the bandpass

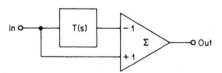

FIGURE 6-22 Band-reject configuration for $f_r = f_\infty$.

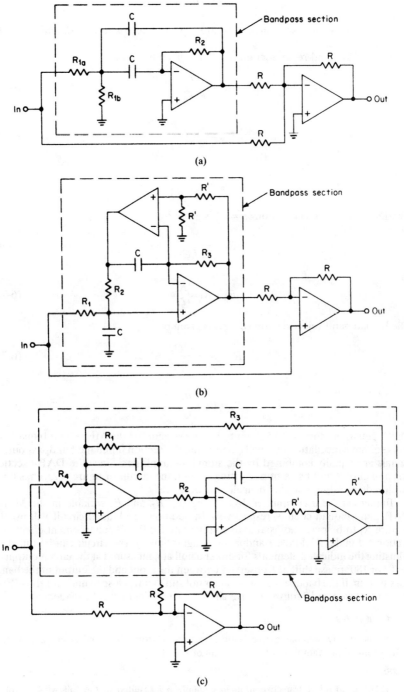

FIGURE 6-23 Band-reject circuits for $f_r = f_\infty$: (a) MFBP band-reject section ($Q < 20$); (b) DABP band-reject section ($Q < 150$); (c) biquad band-reject section ($Q < 200$).

6.31

sections were given in section 5.2 and are repeated here where C, R, and R' can be arbitrarily chosen.

The MFBP band-reject section ($f_r = f_\infty$) is given by

$$R_2 = \frac{Q}{\pi f_r C} \tag{6-67}$$

$$R_{1a} = \frac{R_2}{2} \tag{6-68}$$

$$R_{1b} = \frac{R_{1a}}{2Q^2 - 1} \tag{6-69}$$

The DABP band-reject section ($f_r = f_\infty$) is given by

$$R_1 = \frac{Q}{2\pi f_r C} \tag{6-70}$$

$$R_2 = R_3 = \frac{R_1}{Q} \tag{6-71}$$

The biquad band-reject section ($f_r = f_\infty$) is given by

$$R_1 = R_4 = \frac{Q}{2\pi f_r C} \tag{6-72}$$

$$R_2 = R_3 = \frac{R_1}{Q} \tag{6-73}$$

These equations correspond to unity bandpass gain for the MFBP and biquad circuits so that cancellation at f_r will occur when the section input and bandpass output signals are equally combined by the summing amplifiers. Since the DABP section has a gain of 2 and has a noninverting output, the circuit of figure 6-23*b* has been modified accordingly so that cancellation occurs.

Tuning can be accomplished by making R_{1b}, R_2, and R_3 variable in the MFBP, DABP, and biquad circuits, respectively. In addition, the biquad circuit will usually require R_1 to be made adjustable to compensate for the Q-enhancement effect (see section 5.2 under "All-Pole Bandpass Configurations"). The circuit can be tuned by adjusting the indicated elements for either a null at f_r measured at the circuit output or for 0° or 180° phase shift at f_r observed between the input and the output of the band-pass section. If the bandpass section gain is not sufficiently close to unity for the MFBP and biquad case and 2 for the DABP circuit, the null depth may be inadequate.

EXAMPLE 6-8

REQUIRED: Design an active band-reject filter from the band-reject parameters determined in example 6-7 having a gain of +6 dB.

RESULT:

(a) The band-reject transformation in example 6-7 resulted in the following set of requirements for a three-section filter:

Section	f_r	Q	f_∞
1	3455 Hz	30.15	3600 Hz
2	3752 Hz	30.15	3600 Hz
3	3600 Hz	8.40	3600 Hz

(b) Two biquad circuits in tandem will be used for sections 1 and 2 followed by a DABP band-reject circuit for section 3. The value of C is chosen at 0.01 μF and R as well as R' at 10 kΩ. Since the DABP section has a gain of 2 at DC, which satisfies the 6-dB gain requirement, both biquad sections should then have unity gain. The element values are determined as follows:

Section 1 (biquad of figure 6-21):

$$f_r = 3455 \text{ Hz} \qquad Q = 30.15 \qquad f_\infty = 3600 \text{ Hz}$$

$$R_1 = R_4 = \frac{Q}{2\pi f_r C} = \frac{30.15}{2\pi \times 3455 \times 10^{-8}} = 138.9 \text{ k}\Omega \tag{6-60}$$

$$R_2 = R_3 = \frac{R_1}{Q} = \frac{138.9 \times 10^3}{30.15} = 4610 \ \Omega \tag{6-61}$$

$$R_5 = \frac{f_r^2 R}{Q|f_r^2 - f_\infty^2|} = \frac{3455^2 \times 10^4}{30.15/|3455^2 - 3600^2|} = 3870 \ \Omega \tag{6-62}$$

$$R_6 = \frac{f_r^2 R}{f_\infty^2} = \frac{3455^2 \times 10^4}{3600^2} = 9210 \ \Omega \tag{6-63}$$

Section 2 (biquad of figure 6-21):

$$f_r = 3752 \text{ Hz} \qquad Q = 30.15 \qquad f_\infty = 3600 \text{ Hz}$$

$$R_1 = R_4 = 127.9 \text{ k}\Omega \tag{6-60}$$

$$R_2 = R_3 = 4240 \ \Omega \tag{6-61}$$

$$R_5 = 4180 \ \Omega \tag{6-62}$$

$$R_6 = 10 \text{ k}\Omega \tag{6-64}$$

Section 3 (DABP of figure 6-23):

$$f_r = f_\infty = 3600 \text{ Hz} \qquad Q = 8.40$$

$$R_1 = \frac{Q}{2\pi f_r C} = \frac{8.40}{2\pi \times 3600 \times 10^{-8}} = 37.1 \text{ k}\Omega \tag{6-70}$$

$$R_2 = R_3 = \frac{R_1}{Q} = \frac{37.1 \times 10^3}{8.40} = 4420 \ \Omega \tag{6-71}$$

The final circuit is shown in figure 6-24 with standard 1% resistor values. The required resistors have been made variable so that the resonant frequencies can be adjusted for all sections and, in addition, the Q is variable for the biquad circuits.

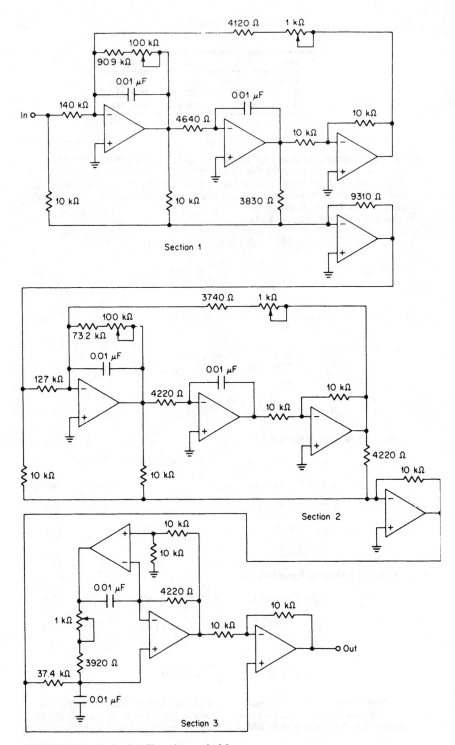

FIGURE 6-24 Band-reject filter of example 6-8.

6.34

Active Null Networks

Active null networks are single sections used to provide attenuation at a single frequency or over a narrow band of frequencies. The most popular sections are of the twin-T form, so this circuit will be discussed in detail along with some other structures.

The Twin-T. The twin-T was first discovered by H. W. Augustadt in 1934. Although this circuit is passive by nature, it is also used in many active configurations to obtain a variety of different characteristics.

The circuit of figure 6-25a is an RC bridge structure where balance or an output null occurs at 1 rad/s when all arms have an equal impedance ($0.5 - j0.5 \, \Omega$). The circuit is redrawn in the form of a symmetrical lattice in figure 6-25b (refer to Guillemin and Stewart in bibliography for detailed discussions of the lattice). The lattice of figure 6-25b can be redrawn again in the form of two parallel lattices as shown in figure 6-25c.

If identical series elements are present in both the series and shunt branches of a lattice, the element may be extracted and symmetrically placed outside the lattice structure. A 1-Ω resistor satisfies this requirement for the upper lattice and a 1-F capacitor for the lower lattice. Removal of these components to outside the lattice results in the twin-T of figure 6-25d.

The general form of a twin-T is shown in figure 6-25e. The value of R_1 is computed from

$$R_1 = \frac{1}{2\pi f_0 C} \tag{6-74}$$

where C is arbitrary. This denormalizes the circuit of figure 6-25d so that the null now occurs at f_0 instead of at 1 rad/s.

When a twin-T is driven from a voltage source and terminated in an infinite load,* the transfer function is given by

$$T(s) = \frac{s^2 + \omega_0^2}{s^2 + 4\omega_0 s + \omega_0^2} \tag{6-75}$$

If we compare this expression with the general transfer function of a second-order pole-zero section as given by equation (6-66), we can determine that a twin-T provides a notch at f_0 with a Q of ¼. The attenuation at any bandwidth can be computed by

$$A_{dB} = 10 \log \left[1 + \left(\frac{4f_0}{BW_{x \, dB}} \right)^2 \right] \tag{6-76}$$

The frequency response is shown in figure 6-26. The requirement for geometric symmetry applies.

Twin-T with Positive Feedback. The twin-T has gained widespread usage as a general-purpose null network. However, a major shortcoming is a fixed Q of ¼. This limitation can be overcome by introducing positive feedback.

The transfer function of the circuit of figure 6-27a can be derived as

$$T(s) = \frac{\beta}{1 + K(\beta - 1)} \tag{6-77}$$

---

* Since the source and load are always finite, the value of R_1 should be in the vicinity of $\sqrt{R_s R_L}$, provided that the ratio R_L/R_s is in excess of 10.

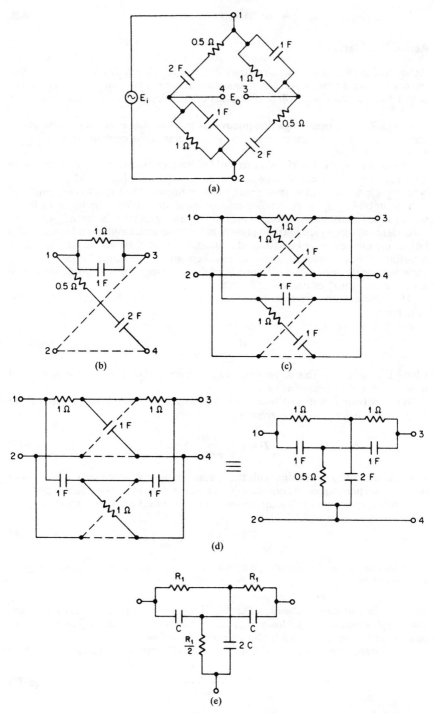

FIGURE 6-25 Derivation of the twin-T: (a) RC bridge; (b) lattice circuit; (c) parallel lattice; (d) twin-T equivalent; (e) general form of twin-T.

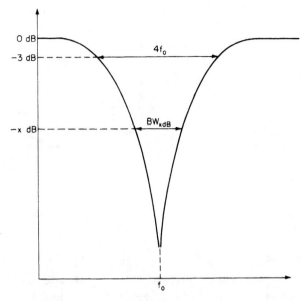

FIGURE 6-26 Frequency response of twin-T.

If β is replaced by equation (6-75), the transfer function of a twin-T, the resulting circuit transfer function expression becomes

$$T(s) = \frac{s^2 + \omega_0^2}{s^2 + 4\omega_0 (1 - K)s + \omega_0^2} \qquad (6\text{-}78)$$

The corresponding Q is

$$Q = \frac{1}{4(1 - K)} \qquad (6\text{-}79)$$

By selecting a positive K of < 1 and sufficiently close to unity, the circuit Q can be dramatically increased. The required value of K can be determined by

$$K = 1 - \frac{1}{4Q} \qquad (6\text{-}80)$$

The block diagram of figure 6-27a can be implemented using the circuit of figure 6-27b, where R is arbitrary. By choosing C and R so that $R_1 \gg (1 - K)R$, the circuit may be simplified to the configuration of figure 6-27c, which uses only one amplifier.

The attenuation at any bandwidth is given by

$$A_{dB} = 10 \log \left[1 + \left(\frac{f_0}{Q \times BW_{x\,dB}} \right)^2 \right] \qquad (6\text{-}81)$$

Equation (6-81) is the general expression for the attenuation of a single band-reject section where the resonant frequency and notch frequency are identical (i.e., $f_r = f_\infty$). The attenuation formula can be expressed in terms of the 3-dB bandwidth as follows:

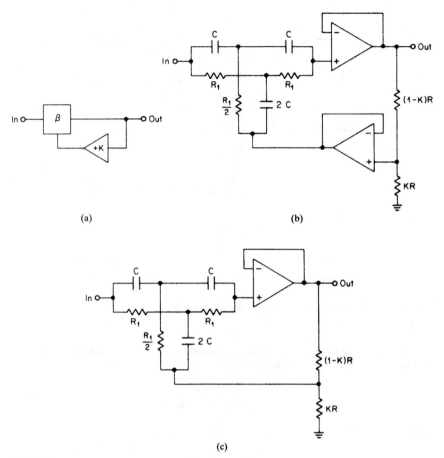

FIGURE 6-27   Twin-T with positive feedback: (*a*) block diagram; (*b*) circuit realization; (*c*) simplified configuration $R_1 \gg (1 - K) R$.

$$A_{dB} = 10 \log \left[1 + \left(\frac{BW_{3\ dB}}{BW_{x\ dB}} \right)^2 \right] \tag{6-82}$$

The attenuation characteristics can also be determined from the frequency-response curve of a normalized $n = 1$ Butterworth low-pass filter (see figure 2-34) by using the ratio $BW_{3\ dB}/BW_{x\ dB}$ for the normalized frequency.

The twin-T in its basic form or in the positive-feedback configuration is widely used for single-section band-reject sections. However, it suffers from the fact that tuning cannot be easily accomplished. Tight component tolerances may then be required to ensure sufficient accuracy of tuning and adequate notch depth. About 40- to 60-dB rejection at the notch could be expected using 1% components.

EXAMPLE 6-9

REQUIRED: Design a single null network having a center frequency of 1000 Hz and a 3-dB bandwidth of 100 Hz. Also determine the attenuation at the 30-Hz bandwidth.

RESULT:

(a) A twin-T structure with positive feedback will be used. To design the twin-T, first choose a capacitance C of 0.01 μF. The value of R_1 is given by

$$R_1 = \frac{1}{2\pi f_0 C} = \frac{1}{2\pi \times 10^3 \times 10^{-8}} = 15.9 \text{ k}\Omega \qquad (6\text{-}74)$$

(b) The required value of K for the feedback network is calculated from

$$K = 1 - \frac{1}{4Q} = 1 - \frac{1}{4 \times 10} = 0.975 \qquad (6\text{-}80)$$

where $Q = f_0/\text{BW}_{3\text{ dB}}$.

(c) The single amplifier circuit of figure 6-27c will be used. If R is chosen at 1 kΩ, the circuit requirement for $R_1 \gg (1 - K)R$ is satisfied. The resulting section is shown in figure 6-28.

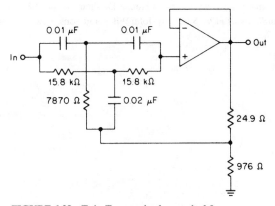

FIGURE 6-28   Twin-T network of example 6-9.

(d) To determine the attenuation at a bandwidth of 30 Hz, calculate

$$A_{\text{dB}} = 10 \log \left[1 + \left(\frac{\text{BW}_{3\text{ dB}}}{\text{BW}_{x\text{ dB}}} \right)^2 \right] = 10 \log \left[1 + \left(\frac{100 \text{ Hz}}{30 \text{ Hz}} \right)^2 \right]$$

$$= 10.8 \text{ dB} \qquad (6\text{-}82)$$

Bandpass Structure Null Networks.   Section 6.2 under "Narrowband Active Band-Reject Filters" showed how a first-order bandpass section can be combined with a summing amplifier to obtain a band-reject circuit for transformed real poles where $f_r = f_\infty$. Three types of sections were illustrated in figure 6-23 corresponding to different Q ranges of operation. These same sections can be used as null networks. They offer more flexibility than the twin-T, since the null frequency can be adjusted to compensate for component tolerances. In addition, the DABP and biquad circuits permit Q adjustment as well.

The design formulas were given by equations (6-67) through (6-73). The values of f_r and Q in the equations correspond to the section center frequency and Q, respectively.

Frequently, a bandpass and band-reject output are simultaneously required. A typical application might involve separation of signals for comparison of in-band and out-of-band spectral energy. The band-reject sections of figure 6-23 can each provide a bandpass output from the bandpass section along with the null output signal. An additional feature of this technique is that the bandpass and band-reject outputs will track.

BIBLIOGRAPHY

Guillemin, E. A., *Communication Networks,* vol. 2, John Wiley and Sons, New York, 1935.

Saal, R., and E. Ulbrich, "On the Design of Filters by Synthesis," *IRE Transactions on Circuit Theory,* December 1958.

Stewart, J. L., *Circuit Theory and Design,* John Wiley and Sons, New York, 1956.

Tow, J., "A Step-by-Step Active Filter Design," *IEEE Spectrum,* vol. 6, December 1969, pp. 64–68.

Williams, A. B., *Active Filter Design,* Artech House, Dedham, Mass., 1975.

Zverev, A. I., *Handbook of Filter Synthesis,* John Wiley and Sons, New York, 1967.

CHAPTER 7

NETWORKS FOR THE TIME DOMAIN

7.1 ALL-PASS TRANSFER FUNCTIONS

Up until now, the networks we discussed were used to obtain a desired amplitude versus frequency characteristic. No less important is the all-pass family of filters. This class of networks exhibits a flat frequency response but introduces a pre-scribed phase shift versus frequency. All-pass filters are frequently called *delay equalizers*.

If a network is to be of an all-pass type, the absolute magnitudes of the numera-tor and denominator of the transfer function must be related by a fixed constant at all frequencies. This condition will be satisfied if the zeros are the images of the poles. Since poles are restricted to the left half quadrants of the complex frequency plane to maintain stability, the zeros must occur in the right half plane as the mirror image of the poles about the $j\omega$ axis. Figure 7-1 illustrates the all-pass pole-zero rep-resentations in the complex frequency plane for first-order and second-order all-pass transfer functions.

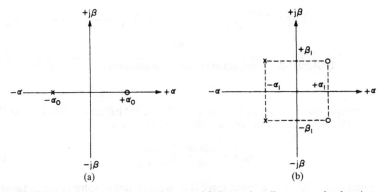

FIGURE 7-1 All-pass pole-zero patterns: (*a*) first-order all-pass transfer function; (*b*) second-order all-pass transfer function.

First-Order All-Pass Transfer Functions

The real pole-zero pair of figure 7-1a has a separation of $2\alpha_0$ between the pole and zero and corresponds to the following first-order all-pass transfer function:

$$T(s) = \frac{s - \alpha_0}{s + \alpha_0} \tag{7-1}$$

To determine the absolute magnitude of $T(s)$, compute

$$|T(s)| = \frac{|s - \alpha_0|}{|s + \alpha_0|} = \frac{\sqrt{\alpha_0^2 + \omega^2}}{\sqrt{\alpha_0^2 + \omega^2}} = 1 \tag{7-2}$$

where $s = j\omega$. For any value of frequency the numerator and denominator of equation (7-2) are equal; so the transfer function is clearly all-pass and has an absolute magnitude of unity at all frequencies.

The phase shift is given by

$$\beta(\omega) = -2 \tan^{-1} \frac{\omega}{\alpha_0} \tag{7-3}$$

where $\beta(\omega)$ is in radians.

The phase shift versus the ratio ω/α_0 as defined by equation (7-3) is plotted in figure 7-2. The phase angle is 0° at DC and −90° at $\omega = \alpha_0$. The phase shift asymptotically approaches −180° with increasing frequency.

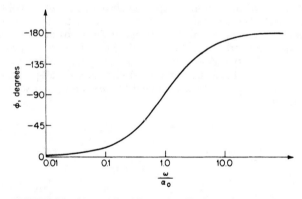

FIGURE 7-2   Phase shift of first-order all-pass section.

The group delay was defined in section 2.2, under "Effect of Nonuniform Time Delay," as the derivative of the phase shift which results in

$$T_{gd} = -\frac{d\beta(\omega)}{d\omega} = \frac{2\alpha_0}{\alpha_0^2 + \omega^2} \tag{7-4}$$

If equation (7-4) is plotted with respect to ω for different values of α_0, a family of curves are obtained as shown in figure 7-3. First-order all-pass sections exhibit maximum delay at DC and decreasing delay with increasing frequency. For small values of α_0 the delay becomes large at low frequencies and decreases quite rapidly above this range. The delay at DC is found by setting ω equal to zero in equation (7-4), which results in

$$T_{gd}(DC) = \frac{2}{\alpha_0} \tag{7-5}$$

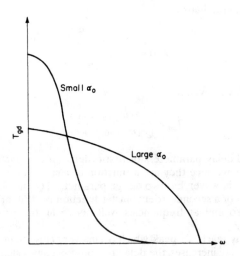

FIGURE 7-3 Group delay of first-order all-pass transfer functions.

Second-Order All-Pass Transfer Functions

The second-order all-pass transfer function represented by the pole-zero pattern of figure 7-1*b* is given by

$$T(s) = \frac{s^2 - \dfrac{\omega_r}{Q}\,s + \omega_r^2}{s^2 + \dfrac{\omega_r}{Q}\,s + \omega_r^2} \tag{7-6}$$

where ω_r and Q are the pole resonant frequency (in radians per second) and the pole Q. These terms may also be computed from the real and imaginary pole-zero coordinates of figure 7-1*b* by

$$\omega_r = \sqrt{\alpha_1^2 + \beta_1^2} \tag{7-7}$$

and
$$Q = \frac{\omega_r}{2\alpha_1} \tag{7-8}$$

The absolute magnitude of $T(s)$ is found to be

$$|T(s)| = \frac{\sqrt{(\omega_r^2 - \omega^2)^2 + \dfrac{\omega^2 \omega_r^2}{Q^2}}}{\sqrt{(\omega_r^2 - \omega^2)^2 + \dfrac{\omega^2 \omega_r^2}{Q^2}}} = 1 \tag{7-9}$$

which is all-pass.

The phase shift in radians is

$$\beta(\omega) = -2 \tan^{-1} \frac{\dfrac{\omega \omega_r}{Q}}{\omega_r^2 - \omega^2} \tag{7-10}$$

and the group delay is given by

$$T_{gd} = \frac{2Q\omega_r(\omega^2 + \omega_r^2)}{Q^2(\omega^2 - \omega_r^2)^2 + \omega^2 \omega_r^2} \tag{7-11}$$

The phase and delay parameters of first-order transfer functions are relatively simple to manipulate, since they are a function of a single design parameter α_0. A second-order type, however, has two design parameters, Q and ω_r.

The phase shift of a second-order transfer function is $-180°$ at $\omega = \omega_r$. At DC the phase shift is zero and at frequencies well above ω_r the phase asymptotically approaches $-360°$.

The group delay reaches a peak which occurs very close to ω_r. As the Q is made larger, the peak delay increases, the delay response becomes sharper, and the delay at DC decreases as shown in figure 7-4.

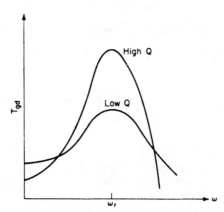

FIGURE 7-4 Group delay of second-order all-pass transfer functions.

The frequency of maximum delay is slightly below ω_r and is expressed in radians per second by

$$\omega(T_{gd,\max}) = \omega_r \sqrt{\sqrt{4 - \frac{1}{Q^2}} - 1} \qquad (7\text{-}12)$$

For all practical purposes, the maximum delay occurs at ω_r for Qs in excess of 2. By setting $\omega = \omega_r$ in equation (7-11), the delay at ω_r is given by

$$T_{gd,\max} = \frac{4Q}{\omega_r} = \frac{2Q}{\pi f_r} \qquad (7\text{-}13)$$

If we set $\omega = 0$, the delay at DC is found from

$$T_{gd}(\text{DC}) = \frac{2}{Q\omega_r} = \frac{1}{Q\pi f_r} \qquad (7\text{-}14)$$

7.2 DELAY EQUALIZER SECTIONS

Passive or active networks that realize first- or second-order all-pass transfer functions are called *delay equalizers*, since they are normally used to provide a required delay characteristic without disturbing the amplitude response. All-pass networks can be realized in a variety of configurations both passive and active. Equalizers with adjustable characteristics can also be designed and are discussed in section 7.6.

LC All-Pass Structures

First-Order Constant-Resistance Circuit.   The lattice of figure 7-5a realizes a first-order all-pass transfer function. The network is also a constant-resistance type, which means that the input impedance has a constant value of R over the entire frequency range. Constant-resistance networks can be cascaded with no interaction so that composite delay curves can be built up by accumulating the individual delay contributions. The lattice has an equivalent unbalanced form shown in figure 7-5b. The design formulas are given by

$$L = \frac{2R}{\alpha_0} \qquad (7\text{-}15)$$

$$C = \frac{2}{\alpha_0 R} \qquad (7\text{-}16)$$

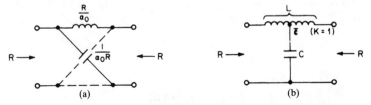

FIGURE 7-5   First-order LC equalizer section: (*a*) lattice form; (*b*) unbalanced form.

where R is the desired impedance level and α_0 is the real pole–zero coordinate. The phase shift and delay properties were defined by equations (7-3) through (7-5).

The circuit of figure 7-5b requires a center-tapped inductor having a coefficient of magnetic coupling K equal to unity.

Second-Order Constant-Resistance Sections.   A second-order all-pass lattice with constant-resistance properties is shown in figure 7-6a. The circuit may be transformed into the unbalanced bridged-T form of figure 7-6b. The elements are given by

$$L_a = \frac{2R}{\omega_r Q} \tag{7-17}$$

$$C_a = \frac{Q}{\omega_r R} \tag{7-18}$$

$$L_b = \frac{QR}{2\omega_r} \tag{7-19}$$

$$C_b = \frac{2Q}{\omega_r(Q^2 - 1)R} \tag{7-20}$$

For tuning and test purposes the section can be split into parallel and series resonant branches by opening the shunt branch and shorting the bridging or series branch as shown in figure 7-6c. Both circuits will resonate at ω_r.

The T to pi transformation was first introduced in section 4.1. This transformation may be applied to the T of capacitors that are embedded in the section of figure 7-6b to reduce capacitor values if desired. The resulting circuit is given in figure 7-6d. Capacitors C_1 and C_2 are computed as follows:

$$C_1 = \frac{C_a^2}{2C_a + C_b} \tag{7-21}$$

$$C_2 = \frac{C_a C_b}{2C_a + C_b} \tag{7-22}$$

The branch resonances are obtained by opening the shunt branch and then shorting the bridging branch, which results in the parallel and series resonant circuits of figure 7-6e. Both resonances occur at ω_r.

Close examination of equation (7-20) indicates that C_b will be negative if the Q is less than 1. (If $Q = 1$, C_b can be replaced by a short.) This restricts the circuits of figure 7-6 to those cases where the Q is in excess of unity. Fortunately, this is true in most instances.

In those cases where the Q is below 1, the configurations of figure 7-7 are used. The circuit of figure 7-7a uses a single inductor with a controlled coefficient of coupling given by

$$K_3 = \frac{1 - Q^2}{1 + Q^2} \tag{7-23}$$

The element values are given by

$$L_{3a} = \frac{(Q^2 + 1)R}{2\,Q\,\omega_r} \tag{7-24}$$

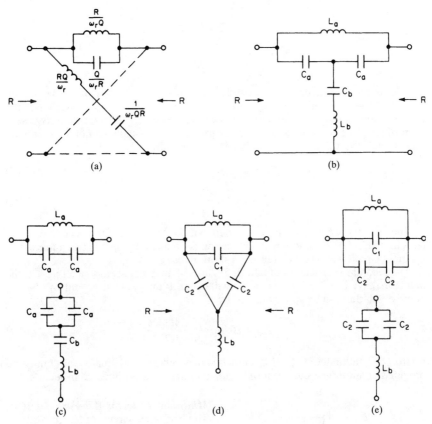

FIGURE 7-6 Second-order section $Q > 1$: (a) lattice form; (b) unbalanced form; (c) circuit for measuring branch resonances; (d) circuit modified by T to pi transformation; (e) resonant branches of modified circuit.

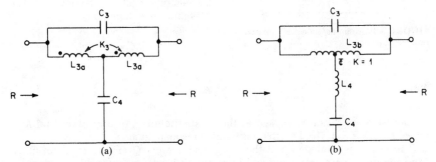

FIGURE 7-7 Second-order section $Q < 1$: (a) circuit with controlled coefficient of coupling; (b) circuit with unity coefficient of coupling.

$$C_3 = \frac{Q}{2\omega_r R} \tag{7-25}$$

$$C_4 = \frac{2}{Q\omega_r R} \tag{7-26}$$

It is not always convenient to control the coefficient of coupling of a coil to obtain the specific value required by equation (7-23). A more practical approach uses the circuit of figure 7-7b. The inductor L_{3b} is center-tapped and requires a unity coefficient of coupling (typical values of 0.95 or greater can usually be obtained and are acceptable). The values of L_{3b} and L_4 are computed from

$$L_{3b} = 2(1 + K_3)L_{3a} \tag{7-27}$$

$$L_4 = \frac{(1 - K_3)L_{3a}}{2} \tag{7-28}$$

The sections of figure 7-7 may be tuned to ω_r in the same manner as in the equalizers in figure 7-6. A parallel resonant circuit is obtained by opening C_4 and a series resonant circuit will result by placing a short across C_3.

The second-order section of figures 7-6 and 7-7 may not always be all-pass. If the inductors have insufficient Q, a notch will occur at the resonances and will have a notch depth that can be approximated by

$$A_{dB} = 20 \log \frac{Q_L + 4Q}{Q_L - 4Q} \tag{7-29}$$

where Q_L is the inductor Q. If the notch is unacceptable, adequate coil Q must be provided or amplitude-equalization techniques are used as discussed in section 8.4.

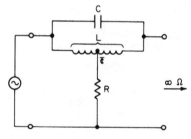

FIGURE 7-8 Minimum inductor type, second-order section.

Minimum Inductor All-Pass Sections.
The bridged-T circuit of figure 7-8 realizes a second-order all-pass transfer function with a single inductor. The section is not a constant-resistance type and operates between a zero impedance source and an infinite load. If the ratio of load to source is well in excess of 10, satisfactory results will be obtained. The elements are computed by

$$C = \frac{Q}{4\omega_r R} \tag{7-30}$$

and

$$L = \frac{1}{\omega_r^2 C} \tag{7-31}$$

The value of R can be chosen as the geometric mean of the source and load impedance ($\sqrt{R_s R_L}$). The LC circuit is parallel resonant at ω_r.

The reader is reminded that the design parameters Q and ω_r are determined from the delay parameters defined in section 7.1, which covers all-pass transfer functions.

A notch will occur at resonance due to finite inductor Q and can be calculated from

$$A_{dB} = 20 \log \frac{4R + \omega_r L Q_L}{4R - \omega_r L Q_L} \tag{7-32}$$

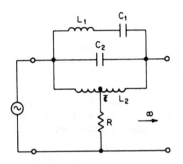

FIGURE 7-9 Fourth-order minimum inductance, all-pass structure.

If R is set equal to $\omega_r L Q_L/4$, the notch attenuation becomes infinite and the circuit is then identical to the bridged-T null network of section 6.1.

Two sets of all-pass poles and zeros corresponding to a fourth-order transfer function can also be obtained by using a minimum-inductance-type structure. The circuit configuration is shown in figure 7-9.

Upon being given two sets of equalizer parameters Q_1, ω_{r1} and Q_2, ω_{r2} as defined in section 7.1, the following equations are used to determine the element values:

First compute

$$A = \omega_1^2 \omega_{r2}^2 \tag{7-33}$$

$$B = A\left(\frac{1}{\omega_{r2} Q_2} + \frac{1}{\omega_{r1} Q_1} \right) \tag{7-34}$$

$$C = \frac{Q_1 Q_2}{A(Q_2 \omega_{r1} + Q_1 \omega_{r2})} \tag{7-35}$$

$$D = \frac{Q_1 Q_2 (\omega_{r1}^2 + \omega_{r2}^2) + \omega_{r1} \omega_{r2}}{ABQ_1 Q_2} - C - \frac{1}{AB^2 C} \tag{7-36}$$

$$E = \frac{1}{ABCD} \tag{7-37}$$

The element values are then given by

$$L_1 = \frac{4ER}{A} \tag{7-38}$$

$$C_1 = \frac{AD}{4R} \tag{7-39}$$

$$L_2 = \frac{4BR}{A} \tag{7-40}$$

$$C_2 = \frac{AC}{4R} \tag{7-41}$$

The value of R is generally chosen as the geometric mean of the source and load terminations as with the second-order minimum-inductance section. The series and parallel branch resonant frequencies are found from

$$\omega_{L1C1} = \frac{1}{\sqrt{ED}} \tag{7-42}$$

and

$$\omega_{L2C2} = \frac{1}{\sqrt{BC}} \tag{7-43}$$

Active All-Pass Structures

First- and second-order all-pass transfer functions can be obtained by using an active approach. The general form of the active all-pass section is represented by the block diagram of figure 7-10, where $T(s)$ is a first- or second-order transfer function having a gain of unity.

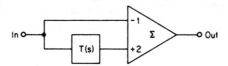

FIGURE 7-10   General form of active all-pass section.

First-Order Sections.   The transfer function of the circuit of figure 7-10 is given by

$$\frac{E_{\text{out}}}{E_{\text{in}}} = 2T(s) - 1 \tag{7-44}$$

If $T(s)$ is a first-order RC high-pass network having the transfer function $sCR/(sCR + 1)$, the composite transfer function becomes

$$\frac{E_{\text{out}}}{E_{\text{in}}} = \frac{s - 1/RC}{s + 1/RC} \tag{7-45}$$

This expression corresponds to the first-order all-pass transfer function of equation (7-1), where

$$\alpha_0 = \frac{1}{RC} \tag{7-46}$$

The circuit can be directly implemented by the configuration of figure 7-11a, where R' is arbitrary. The phase shift is then given by

$$\beta(\omega) = -2 \tan^{-1}\omega RC \tag{7-47}$$

and the delay is found from

$$T_{gd} = \frac{2RC}{(\omega RC)^2 + 1} \tag{7-48}$$

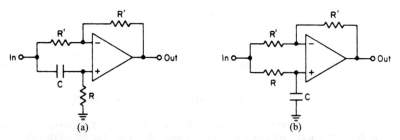

FIGURE 7-11   First-order all-pass sections: (*a*) circuit with lagging phase shift; (*b*) circuit with leading phase shift.

At DC the delay is a maximum and is computed from

$$T_{gd}(DC) = 2RC \qquad (7\text{-}49)$$

The corresponding phase shift is shown in figure 7-2. A phase shift of −90° occurs at $\omega = 1/RC$ and approaches −180° and 0° at DC and infinity, respectively. By making the element R variable, an all-pass network can be obtained having a phase shift adjustable between 0 and −180°.

A sign inversion of the phase will occur if the circuit of figure 7-11*b* is used. The circuit will remain all-pass and first-order, and the group delay is still defined by equations (7-48) and (7-49).

Second-Order Sections.   If $T(s)$ in figure 7-10 is a second-order bandpass network having the general bandpass transfer function

$$T(s) = \frac{\dfrac{\omega_r}{Q}\,s}{s^2 + \dfrac{\omega_r}{Q}\,s + \omega_r^2} \qquad (7\text{-}50)$$

the composite transfer function then becomes

$$\frac{E_{out}}{E_{in}} = 2T(s) - 1 = -\frac{s^2 - \dfrac{\omega_r}{Q}\,s + \omega_r^2}{s^2 + \dfrac{\omega_r}{Q}\,s + \omega_r^2} \qquad (7\text{-}51)$$

which corresponds to the second-order all-pass expression given by equation (7-6) (except for a simple sign inversion). Therefore, a second-order all-pass equalizer can be obtained by implementing the structure of figure 7-10 using a single active bandpass section for $T(s)$.

Section 5-2 discussed the MFBP, DABP, and biquad all-pole bandpass sections. Each circuit can be combined with a summing amplifier to generate a delay equalizer.

The MFBP equalizer section is shown in figure 7-12*a*. The element values are given by

$$R_2 = \frac{2Q}{\omega_r C} = \frac{Q}{\pi f_r C} \qquad (7\text{-}52)$$

$$R_{1a} = \frac{R_2}{2} \tag{7-53}$$

$$R_{1b} = \frac{R_{1a}}{2Q^2 - 1} \tag{7-54}$$

The values of C and R can be arbitrarily chosen, and A in figure 7-12a corresponds to the desired gain.

The maximum delay which occurs at f_r was given by equation (7-13). This expression can be combined with equations (7-52) and (7-54); so the element values can alternately be expressed in terms of $T_{gd,\text{max}}$ as follows for $Q > 2$:

$$R_2 = \frac{T_{gd,\text{max}}}{2C} \tag{7-55}$$

$$R_{1b} = \frac{R_2}{(\pi f_r T_{gd,\text{max}})^2 - 2} \tag{7-56}$$

where R_{1a} remains $R_2/2$.

The MFBP section can be tuned by making R_{1b} variable. R_{1b} can then be adjusted until 180° of phase shift occurs between the input and output of the bandpass section at f_r. In order for the response to be all-pass, the bandpass section gain must be

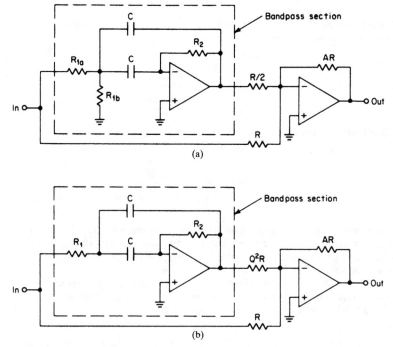

(a)

(b)

FIGURE 7-12   MFBP delay equalizer $Q < 20$: (a) circuit for $0.707 < Q < 20$; (b) circuit for $Q < 0.707$.

exactly unity at resonance. Otherwise an amplitude ripple will occur in the frequency-response characteristic in the vicinity of f_r.

The section Q is limited to values below 20 or is expressed in terms of delay

$$T_{gd,\max} < \frac{40}{\pi f_r} \tag{7-57}$$

Experience has indicated that required Qs are usually well under 20, so this circuit will suffice in most cases. However, if the Q is below 0.707, the value of R_{1b} as given by equation (7-54) is negative, so the circuit of figure 7-12b is used. The value of R_1 is given by

$$R_1 = \frac{R_2}{4Q^2} \tag{7-58}$$

In the event that higher Qs are required, the DABP section can be applied to the block diagram of figure 7-10. Since the DABP circuit has a gain of 2 and is noninverting, the implementation shown in figure 7-13 is used. The element values are given by

$$R_1 = \frac{Q}{\omega_r C} = \frac{Q}{2\pi f_r C} \tag{7-59}$$

and

$$R_2 = R_3 = \frac{R_1}{Q} \tag{7-60}$$

where C, R, and R' can be conveniently chosen. Resistor R_2 may be made variable if tuning is desired. The Q and therefore the delay can also be trimmed by making R_1 adjustable.

The biquad structure can be configured in the form of a delay equalizer. The circuit is shown in figure 7-14. The element values are computed from

$$R_1 = R_4 = \frac{Q}{\omega_r C} = \frac{Q}{2\pi f_r C} \tag{7-61}$$

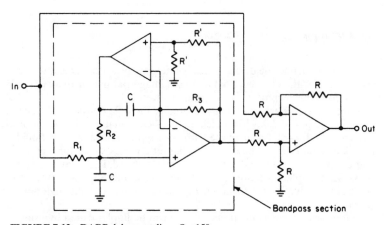

FIGURE 7-13 DABP delay equalizer $Q < 150$.

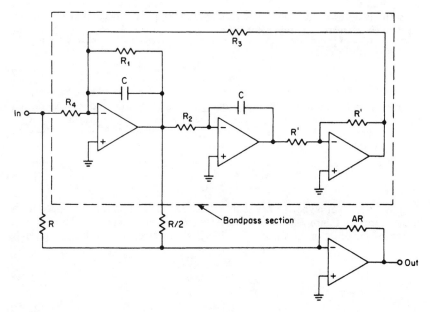

FIGURE 7-14 Biquad delay equalizer $Q < 200$.

and
$$R_2 = R_3 = \frac{R_1}{Q} \qquad (7\text{-}62)$$

where C, R, and R' are arbitrary.

Resistor R_3 can be made variable for tuning. The Q is adjusted for the nominal value by making R_1 variable and monitoring the 3-dB bandwidth at the output of the bandpass section or adjusting for unity bandpass gain at f_r. The biquad is subject to the Q-enhancement effect discussed in section 5.2, under All-Pole Bandpass Configurations, so a Q adjustment is usually required.

7.3 DESIGN OF DELAY LINES

The classical approach to the design of delay lines involves a cascade of identical LC sections (except for the end sections) and uses image-parameter theory (see Wallis in bibliography). This technique is an approximation at best.

Modern network theory permits us to predict the delay of networks accurately and to obtain a required delay in a much more efficient manner than with the classical approach. The Bessel, linear phase with equiripple error and transitional filters all feature a constant delay. The curves in chapter 2 indicate that for n greater than 3, the flat delay region is extended well into the stopband. If a delay line is desired, a low-pass filter implementation is not a very desirable approach from a delay-bandwidth perspective. A significant portion of the constant delay region would be attenuated.

All the low-pass transfer functions covered can be implemented by using an all-pass realization to overcome the bandwidth limitations. This results in a very precise and efficient means of designing delay lines.

The Low-Pass to All-Pass Transformation

A low-pass transfer function can be transformed to an all-pass transfer function simply by introducing zeros in the right half plane of the $j\omega$ axis corresponding to each pole. If the real and complex poles tabulated in chapter 11 are realized using the first- and second-order all-pass structures of section 7.2, complementary zeros will also occur. When a low-pass to all-pass transformation is made, the low-pass delay is increased by a factor of exactly 2 because of the additional phase-shift contributions of the zeros.

An all-pass delay-bandwidth factor can be derived from the delay curves of chapter 2 which is given by

$$TU = \omega_u T_{gd} \,(\text{DC}) \tag{7-63}$$

The value of T_{gd} (DC) is the delay at DC, which is twice the delay shown in the curves because of the all-pass transformation, and ω_u is the upper limit radian frequency where the delay deviates a specified amount from the DC value.

Table 7-1 lists the delay at DC, ω_u, and the delay-bandwidth product TU for an all-pass realization of the Bessel maximally flat delay family. Values are provided for both 1 and 10% deviations of delay at ω_u.

TABLE 7-1 All-Pass Bessel Delay Characteristics

N	T_{gd} (DC)	1% Deviation		10% Deviation	
		ω_u	TU	ω_u	TU
2	2.72	0.412	1.121	0.801	2.179
3	3.50	0.691	2.419	1.109	3.882
4	4.26	0.906	3.860	1.333	5.679
5	4.84	1.120	5.421	1.554	7.521
6	5.40	1.304	7.042	1.737	9.380
7	5.90	1.478	8.720	1.912	11.280
8	6.34	1.647	10.440	2.079	13.180
9	6.78	1.794	12.160	2.227	15.100

To choose a transfer-function type and determine the complexity required, first compute

$$TU_{\text{req}} = 2\pi f_{gd} T_{gd} \tag{7-64}$$

where f_{gd} is the maximum desired frequency of operation and T_{gd} is the nominal delay needed. A network is then selected that has a delay-bandwidth factor TU that exceeds TU_{req}.

Compute the delay-scaling factor (DSF), which is the ratio of the normalized delay at DC to the required nominal delay, i.e.,

$$DSF = \frac{T_{gd}(\text{DC})}{T_{gd}} \tag{7-65}$$

The corresponding poles of the filter selected are denormalized by the DSF and can then be realized by the all-pass circuits of section 7.2.

A real pole α_0 is denormalized by the formula

$$\alpha_0' = \alpha_0 \times DSF \tag{7-66}$$

Complex poles tabulated in the form $\alpha + j\beta$ are denormalized and transformed into the all-pass section design parameters ω_r and Q by the relationships

$$\omega_r = \text{DSF}\sqrt{\alpha^2 + \beta^2} \tag{7-67}$$

$$Q = \frac{\omega_r}{2\alpha\,\text{DSF}} \tag{7-68}$$

The parameters α_0', ω_r, and Q are then directly used in the design equations for the circuits of section 7.2.

Sometimes the required delay-bandwidth factor TU_{req} as computed by equation (7-64) is in excess of the TU factors available from the standard filter families tabulated. The total delay required can then be subdivided into N smaller increments and realized by N delay lines in cascade, since the delays will add algebraically.

LC Delay Lines

LC delay lines are designed by first selecting a normalized filter type and then denormalizing the corresponding real and complex poles, all in accordance with section 7.3, under "The Low-Pass to All-Pass Transformation."

The resulting poles and associated zeros are then realized using the *LC* all-pass circuits of section 7.2. This procedure is best illustrated by the following design example.

EXAMPLE 7-1

REQUIRED: Design a passive delay line to provide 1 ms of delay constant within 10% from DC to 3200 Hz. The source and load impedances are both 10 kΩ.

RESULT:

(a) Compute the required delay-bandwidth factor.

$$TU_{\text{req}} = 2\pi f_{gd} T_{gd} = 2\pi 3200 \times 0.001 = 20.1 \tag{7-64}$$

A linear phase design with an equiripple error of 0.5° will be chosen. The delay characteristics for the corresponding low-pass filters are shown in figure 2-64. The delay at DC of a normalized all-pass network for $n = 9$ is equal to 7.5 s, which is twice the value obtained from the curves. Since the delay remains relatively flat to 3 rad/s, the delay-bandwidth factor is given by

$$TU = \omega_u T_{gd}\,(\text{DC}) = 3 \times 7.5 = 22.5 \tag{7-63}$$

Since TU is in excess of TU_{req}, the $n = 9$ design will be satisfactory.
(b) The low-pass poles are found in table 11-45 and are as follows:

$$-0.5688 \pm j0.7595$$

$$-0.5545 \pm j1.5089$$

$$-0.5179 \pm j2.2329$$

$$-0.4080 \pm j2.9028$$

$$-0.5728$$

Four second-order all-pass sections and a single first-order section will be required. The delay-scaling factor is given by

$$DSF = \frac{T_{gd}(DC)}{T_{gd}} = \frac{7.5}{10^{-3}} = 7500 \qquad (7\text{-}65)$$

The denormalized design parameters ω_r and Q for the second-order sections are computed by equations (7-67) and (7-68), respectively, and are tabulated as follows:

Section	α	β	ω_r	Q
1	0.5688	0.7595	7117	0.8341
2	0.5545	1.5089	12057	1.450
3	0.5179	2.2329	17191	2.213
4	0.4080	2.9028	21985	3.592

The design parameter α_0' for section 5 corresponding to the real pole is found from

$$\alpha_0' = \alpha_0 \times DSF = 4296 \qquad (7\text{-}66)$$

where α_0 is 0.5728.

(c) The element values can now be computed as follows:

Section 1:

Since the Q is less than unity, the circuit of figure 7-7b will be used. The element values are found from

$$K_3 = \frac{1-Q^2}{1+Q^2} = \frac{1-0.8341^2}{1+0.8341^2} = 0.1794 \qquad (7\text{-}23)$$

$$L_{3a} = \frac{(Q^2+1)R}{2Q\omega_r} = \frac{(0.8341^2+1)10^4}{2 \times 0.8341 \times 7117} = 1.428 \text{ H} \qquad (7\text{-}24)$$

$$C_3 = \frac{Q}{2\omega_r R} = \frac{0.8341}{2 \times 7117 \times 10^4} = 5860 \text{ pF} \qquad (7\text{-}25)$$

$$C_4 = \frac{2}{Q\omega_r R} = \frac{2}{0.8341 \times 7117 \times 10^4} = 0.0337 \text{ }\mu\text{F} \qquad (7\text{-}26)$$

$$L_{3b} = 2(1+K_3)L_{3a} = 3.368 \text{ H} \qquad (7\text{-}27)$$

$$L_4 = \frac{(1-K_3)L_{3a}}{2} = 0.586 \text{ H} \qquad (7\text{-}28)$$

Sections 2 through 4:

Since the Qs are in excess of unity, the circuit of figure 7-6b will be used. The values for section 2 are found from

$$L_a = \frac{2R}{\omega_r Q} = \frac{2 \times 10^4}{12,057 \times 1.450} = 1.144 \text{ H} \qquad (7\text{-}17)$$

$$C_a = \frac{Q}{\omega_r R} = \frac{1.450}{12,057 \times 10^4} = 0.012 \text{ }\mu\text{F} \qquad (7\text{-}18)$$

$$L_b = \frac{QR}{2\omega_r} = \frac{1.450 \times 10^4}{2 \times 12,057} = 0.601 \text{ H} \qquad (7\text{-}19)$$

$$C_b = \frac{2Q}{\omega_r(Q^2-1)R} = \frac{2 \times 1.450}{12,057(1.45^2-1)10^4} = 0.0218 \ \mu F \tag{7-20}$$

In the same manner, the remaining element values can be computed, which results in:
Section 3:

$$L_a = 0.526 \text{ H}$$

$$C_a = 0.0129 \ \mu F$$

$$L_b = 0.644 \text{ H}$$

$$C_b = 6606 \text{ pF}$$

Section 4:

$$L_a = 0.253 \text{ H}$$

$$C_a = 0.0163 \ \mu F$$

$$L_b = 0.817 \text{ H}$$

$$C_b = 2745 \text{ pF}$$

Section 5:

The remaining first-order all-pass section is realized using the circuit of figure 7-5b.
The element values are given by

$$L = \frac{2R}{\alpha_0'} = \frac{2 \times 10^4}{4296} = 4.655 \text{ H} \tag{7-15}$$

$$C = \frac{2}{\alpha_0' R} = \frac{2}{4296 \times 10^4} = 0.0466 \ \mu F \tag{7-16}$$

(d) The resulting delay line is illustrated in figure 7-15a. The resonant frequencies shown
are in hertz corresponding to $\omega_r/2\pi$ for each section. The center-tapped inductors
require a unity coefficient of coupling. The delay characteristics as a function of frequency are also shown in figure 7-15b.

The delay line of example 7-1 requires a total of nine inductors. If the classical
design approach (see Wallis in bibliography), which is based on image-parameter
theory, were used, the resulting delay line would use about twice as many coils.
Although the inductors would all be uniform in value (except for the end sections),
this feature is certainly not justified by the added cost and complexity.

Active Delay Lines

An active delay line is designed by initially choosing a normalized filter and then
denormalizing the associated poles in the same manner as in the case of LC delay
lines. The resulting all-pass design parameters are implemented using the first- and
second-order active structures of section 7.2.

Active delay lines do not suffer from the Q limitations of LC delay lines and are
especially suited for low-frequency applications where inductor values may become
impractical. The following example illustrates the design of an active delay line.

EXAMPLE 7-2

REQUIRED: Design an active delay line having a delay of 100 μs constant within 3%
to 3 kHz. A gain of 10 is also required.

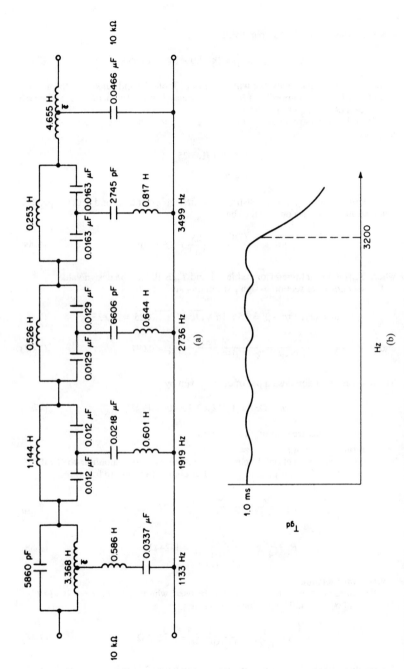

FIGURE 7-15 1-ms delay line of example 7-1: (*a*) delay-line circuit; (*b*) frequency response.

7.19

RESULT:

(a) Compute the required delay-bandwidth factor.

$$TU_{req} = 2\pi f_{gd} T_{gd} = 2\pi 3000 \times 10^{-4} = 1.885 \tag{7-64}$$

A Bessel-type all-pass network will be chosen. Table 7-1 indicates that for a delay deviation of 1%, a complexity of $n = 3$ has a delay-bandwidth factor of 2.419, which is in excess of the required value.

(b) The Bessel low-pass poles are given in table 12-41 and the corresponding values for $n = 3$ are

$$-1.0509 \pm j1.0025$$

$$-1.3270$$

Two sections are required consisting of a first-order and second-order type. The delay-scaling factor is computed to be

$$DSF = \frac{T_{gd}(DC)}{T_{gd}} = \frac{3.5}{10^{-4}} = 3.5 \times 10^4 \tag{7-65}$$

where $T_{gd}(DC)$ is obtained from table 7-1 and T_{gd} is 100 µs, the design value. The second-order section design parameters are

$$\omega_r = DSF \sqrt{\alpha^2 + \beta^2} = 3.5 \times 10^4 \sqrt{1.0509^2 + 1.0025^2} = 50,833 \tag{7-67}$$

and

$$Q = \frac{\omega_r}{2\,\alpha\,DSF} = \frac{50,833}{2 \times 1.0509 \times 3.5 \times 10^4} = 0.691 \tag{7-68}$$

The first-order section design parameter is given by

$$\alpha_0' = \alpha_0 \times DSF = 1.327 \times 3.5 \times 10^4 = 46,450 \tag{7-66}$$

(c) The element values are computed as follows:

Second-order section:
The MFBP equalizer section of figure 7-12b will be used corresponding to $Q < 0.707$, where $R = 10$ kΩ, $C = 0.01$ µF, and $A = 10$. The element values are found from

$$R_2 = \frac{2Q}{\omega_r C} = \frac{2 \times 0.691}{50,833 \times 10^{-8}} = 2719\ \Omega \tag{7-52}$$

$$R_1 = \frac{R_2}{4\,Q^2} = \frac{2719}{4 \times 0.691^2} = 1424\ \Omega \tag{7-58}$$

First-order section:
The first-order section of figure 7-11a will be used, where R' is chosen at 10 kΩ, C at 0.01 µF, and α_0' is 46,450. The value of R is given by

$$R = \frac{1}{\alpha_0' C} = \frac{1}{46,450 \times 10^{-8}} = 2153\ \Omega \tag{7-46}$$

(d) The resulting 100-µs active delay line is shown in figure 7-16 using standard 1% resistor values.

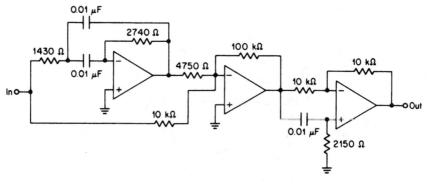

FIGURE 7-16   100-μs delay line of example 7-2.

7.4   *DELAY EQUALIZATION OF FILTERS*

The primary emphasis in previous chapters has been the attenuation characteristics of filters. However, if the signal consists of a modulated waveform, the delay characteristics are also of importance. To minimize distortion of the input signal, a constant delay over the frequency range of interest is desirable.

The Bessel, linear phase with equiripple error, and transitional filter families all exhibit a flat delay. However, the amplitude response is less selective than that of other families. Frequently the only solution to an attenuation requirement is a Butterworth, Chebyshev, or elliptic-function filter type. To also maintain the delay constant, delay equalizers are required.

Delay equalizer networks are frequently at least as complex as the filter being equalized. The number of sections required is dependent on the initial delay curve, the portion of the curve to be equalized, and the degree of equalization necessary. A very crude approximation to the number of equalizer sections required is given by

$$n = 2\Delta_{BW}\Delta_T + 1 \qquad (7\text{-}69)$$

where Δ_{BW} is the bandwidth of interest in hertz and Δ_T is the delay distortion over Δ_{BW} in seconds.

The approach to delay equalization discussed in this section is graphical rather than analytical. A closed-form solution to the delay equalization of filters is not available. However, computer programs can be obtained that achieve a least-squares approximation to the required delay specifications and are preferred to trial-and-error techniques.

Simply stated, delay equalization of a filter involves designing a network that has a delay shape which complements the delay curve of the filter being equalized. The composite delay will then exhibit the required flatness. Although the absolute delay increases as well, this result is usually of little significance, since it is the delay variation over the band of interest that disperses the spectral components of the signal. Typical delay curves of a bandpass filter, the delay equalizer network, and the composite characteristics are shown in figure 7-17.

To equalize the delay of a low-pass filter graphically, the highest frequency of interest and corresponding delay should be scaled to 1 rad/s so that the lower portion of the curve falls within the frequency region between DC and $\omega = 1$. This is

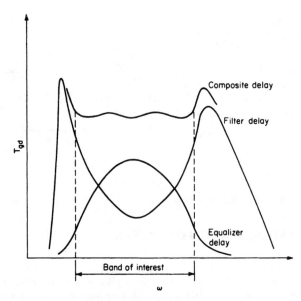

FIGURE 7-17 Delay equalization of a bandpass filter.

accomplished by multiplying the delay axis by $2\pi f_h$, where f_h is the highest frequency to be equalized. The frequency axis is also divided by f_h and interpreted in radians per second so that f_h is transformed to 1 rad/s and all other frequencies are normalized to this point.

The normalized low-pass filter delay curves shown in section 2 for the various filter families may also be used directly. In either case the required equalizer delay characteristic is obtained by subtracting the delay curve from a constant equal to the maximum delay that occurs over the band. The resulting curve is then approximated by adding the delay contributions of equalizer sections. A sufficient number of sections is used to obtain the required composite delay flatness.

When a suitable match to the required curve is found, the equalizer parameters may be directly used to design the equalizer, and the circuit is then denormalized to the required frequency range and impedance level. Alternately, the equalizer parameters can first be denormalized and the equalizer designed directly.

Bandpass filters are equalized in a manner similar to low-pass filters. The delay curve is first normalized by multiplying the delay axis by $2\pi f_0$, where f_0 is the filter center frequency. The frequency axis is divided by f_0 and interpreted in radians per second so that the center frequency is 1 rad/s and all other frequencies are normalized to the center frequency. A complementary curve is found and appropriate equalizer sections are used until a suitable fit occurs. The equalizer is then denormalized.

First-Order Equalizers

First-order all-pass transfer functions were first introduced in section 7.1. The delay of a first-order all-pass section is characterized by a maximum delay at low frequencies and decreasing delay with increasing frequency. As the value of α_0 is reduced, the delay tends to peak at DC and will roll off more rapidly with increasing frequencies.

The delay of a first-order all-pass section was given in section 7.1 by

$$T_{gd} = \frac{2\alpha_0}{\alpha_0^2 + \omega^2} \qquad (7\text{-}4)$$

Working directly with equation (7-4) is somewhat tedious, so a table of delay values for α_0 ranging between 0.05 and 2.00 at frequencies from $\omega = 0$ to $\omega = 1$ is provided in table 7-2. This table can be directly used to determine the approximate α_0 necessary to equalize the normalized filter delay. A more exact value of α_0 can then be determined from equation (7-4) if desired.

TABLE 7-2 First-Order Equalizer Delay, Seconds

α_0	ω, rad/s										
	0	0.1	0.2	0.3	0.4	0.5	0.6	0.7	0.8	0.9	1.0
0.05	40.00	8.00	2.35	1.08	0.62	0.40	0.28	0.20	0.16	0.12	0.10
0.10	20.00	10.00	4.00	2.00	1.18	0.77	0.54	0.40	0.31	0.24	0.20
0.15	13.33	9.23	4.80	2.67	1.64	1.10	0.78	0.59	0.45	0.36	0.29
0.20	10.00	8.00	5.00	3.08	2.00	1.38	1.00	0.75	0.59	0.47	0.38
0.25	8.00	6.90	4.88	3.28	2.25	1.60	1.18	0.91	0.71	0.57	0.47
0.30	6.67	6.00	4.62	3.33	2.40	1.76	1.33	1.03	0.82	0.67	0.55
0.35	5.71	5.28	4.31	3.29	2.48	1.88	1.45	1.14	0.92	0.75	0.62
0.40	5.00	4.71	4.00	3.20	2.50	1.95	1.54	1.23	1.00	0.82	0.69
0.45	4.44	4.24	3.71	3.08	2.48	1.99	1.60	1.30	1.07	0.89	0.75
0.50	4.00	3.85	3.45	2.94	2.44	2.00	1.64	1.35	1.12	0.94	0.80
0.55	3.64	3.52	3.21	2.80	2.38	1.99	1.66	1.39	1.17	0.99	0.84
0.60	3.33	3.24	3.00	2.67	2.31	1.97	1.67	1.41	1.20	1.03	0.88
0.65	3.08	3.01	2.81	2.54	2.23	1.93	1.66	1.42	1.22	1.05	0.91
0.70	2.86	2.80	2.64	2.41	2.15	1.89	1.65	1.43	1.24	1.08	0.94
0.75	2.67	2.62	2.49	2.30	2.08	1.85	1.63	1.43	1.25	1.09	0.96
0.80	2.50	2.46	2.35	2.19	2.00	1.80	1.60	1.42	1.25	1.10	0.98
0.85	2.35	2.32	2.23	2.09	1.93	1.75	1.57	1.40	1.25	1.11	0.99
0.90	2.22	2.20	2.12	2.00	1.86	1.70	1.54	1.38	1.24	1.11	0.99
0.95	2.11	2.08	2.02	1.91	1.79	1.65	1.50	1.36	1.23	1.11	1.00
1.00	2.00	1.98	1.92	1.83	1.72	1.60	1.47	1.34	1.22	1.10	1.00
1.25	1.60	1.59	1.56	1.51	1.45	1.38	1.30	1.22	1.14	1.05	0.98
1.50	1.33	1.33	1.31	1.28	1.24	1.20	1.15	1.09	1.04	0.98	0.92
1.75	1.14	1.14	1.13	1.11	1.09	1.06	1.02	0.99	0.95	0.90	0.86
2.00	1.00	1.00	0.99	0.98	0.97	0.94	0.92	0.89	0.86	0.83	0.80

Use of table 7-2 is best illustrated by an example as follows.

EXAMPLE 7-3

REQUIRED: Design a delay equalizer for an $n = 5$ Butterworth low-pass filter having a 3-dB cutoff of 1600 Hz. The delay variation should not exceed 75 μs from DC to 1600 Hz.

RESULT:

(a) The Butterworth normalized delay curves of figure 2-35 can be used directly, since the region between DC and 1 rad/s corresponds to the frequency range of interest.

The curve for $n = 5$ indicates that the peak delay occurs near 0.9 rad/s and is approximately 1.9 s greater than the value at DC. This corresponds to a denormalized variation of $1.9/2\pi f_h$ or 190 µs where f_h is 1600 Hz; so an equalizer is required.

(b) Examination of table 7-2 indicates that a first-order equalizer with an α_0 of 0.7 has a delay at DC that is approximately 1.8 s greater than the delay at 0.9 rad/s; so a reasonable fit to the required shape should occur.

The delay of the normalized filter and the first-order equalizer for $\alpha_0 = 0.7$ is shown in figure 7.18a. The combined delay is given in figure 7-18b. The peak-to-peak delay variation is about 0.7 s, which corresponds to a denormalized delay variation of $0.7/2\pi f_h$ or 70 µs.

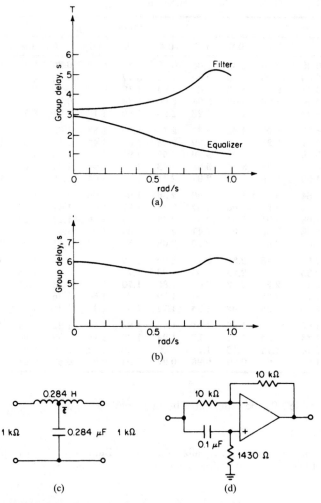

FIGURE 7-18 Delay equalization of example 7-3: (a) filter and equalizer delay curves; (b) composite delay curve; (c) LC equalizer; (d) active equalizer.

(c) The first-order equalizer parameter $\alpha_0 = 0.7$ is denormalized by the factor $2\pi f_h$, resulting in $\alpha_0' = 7037$. The corresponding passive equalizer is designed as follows, where the impedance level R is chosen to be 1 kΩ:

$$L = \frac{2R}{\alpha_0'} = \frac{2 \times 10^3}{7037} = 0.284 \text{ H} \tag{7-15}$$

$$C = \frac{2}{\alpha_0' R} = \frac{2}{7037 \times 10^3} = 0.284 \text{ }\mu\text{F} \tag{7-16}$$

The first-order LC equalizer section is shown in figure 7-18c.

(d) An active first-order equalizer section can also be designed using the circuit of figure 7-11a. If we select a C of 0.1 μF and $R' = 10$ kΩ, the value of R is given by

$$R = \frac{1}{\alpha_0' C} = \frac{1}{7037 \times 10^{-7}} = 1421 \text{ }\Omega \tag{7-46}$$

The active equalizer circuit is illustrated in figure 7-18d.

Highly selective low-pass filters such as the elliptic-function type have a corresponding delay characteristic that increases very dramatically near cutoff. First-order all-pass sections cannot then provide a complementary delay shape; so they are limited to applications involving low-pass filters of moderate selectivity.

Second-Order Equalizers

First-order equalizers have a maximum delay at DC and a single design parameter α_0 which limits their use. Second-order sections have two design parameters, ω_r and Q. The delay shape is bandpass in nature and can be made broad or sharp by changing the Q. The peak delay frequency is determined by the design parameter ω_r. As a result of this flexibility, second-order sections can be used to equalize virtually any type of delay curve. The only limitation is in the number of sections the designer is willing to use and the effort required to achieve a given degree of equalization.

The group delay of a second-order all-pass section was given by

$$T_{gd} = \frac{2\,Q\omega_r(\omega^2 + \omega_r^2)}{Q^2(\omega^2 - \omega_r^2)^2 + \omega^2\omega_r^2} \tag{7-11}$$

If we normalize this expression by setting ω_r equal to 1, we obtain

$$T_{gd} = \frac{2\,Q(\omega^2 + 1)}{Q^2(\omega^2 - 1)^2 + \omega^2} \tag{7-70}$$

To determine the delay at DC, we can set ω equal to zero, which results in

$$T_{gd}(\text{DC}) = \frac{2}{Q} \tag{7-71}$$

For Qs below 0.577, the maximum delay occurs at DC. As the Q is increased, the frequency of maximum delay approaches 1 rad/s and is given by

$$\omega(T_{gd,\text{max}}) = \sqrt{\sqrt{4 - \frac{1}{Q^2}} - 1} \tag{7-72}$$

For Qs of 2 or more, the maximum delay can be assumed to occur at 1 rad/s and may be determined from

$$T_{gd,\max} = 4\,Q \tag{7-73}$$

Equations (7-70) through (7-72) are evaluated in table 7-3 for Qs ranging from 0.25 to 10.

To use table 7-3 directly, first normalize the curve to be equalized so that the minimum delay occurs at 1 rad/s. Then select an equalizer from the table that provides the best fit for a complementary curve.

A composite curve is then plotted. If the delay ripple is excessive, additional equalizer sections are required to fill in the delay gaps. The data of table 7-3 can again be used by scaling the region to be equalized to a 1-rad/s center and selecting a complementary equalizer shape from the table. The equalizer parameters can then be shifted to the region of interest by scaling.

The procedure described is an oversimplification of the design process. The equalizer responses will interact with each other, so each delay region to be filled in cannot be treated independently. Every time a section is added, the previous sections may require an adjustment of their design parameters.

Delay equalization generally requires considerably more skill than the actual design of filters. Standard pole-zero patterns are defined for the different filter families, whereas the design of equalizers involves the approximation problem where a pole-zero pattern must be determined for a suitable fit to a curve. The following example illustrates the use of second-order equalizer sections to equalize delay.

EXAMPLE 7-4

REQUIRED: A bandpass filter with the delay measurements of table I must be equalized to within 700 μs.

TABLE I   Specified Delay

Frequency, Hz	Delay, μs
500	1600
600	960
700	640
800	320
900	50
1000	0
1100	160
1200	480
1300	800
1400	1120
1500	1500

The corresponding delay curve is plotted in figure 7-19*a*.

RESULT:

(a) Since the minimum delay occurs at 1000 Hz, normalize the curve by dividing the frequency axis by 1000 Hz and multiplying the delay axis by $2\pi\,1000$. The results are tabulated as follows and plotted in figure 7-19*b*.

TABLE II   Normalized Delay

Frequency, rad/s	Delay, s
0.5	10.1
0.6	6.03
0.7	4.02
0.8	2.01
0.9	0.31
1.0	0
1.1	1.01
1.2	3.02
1.3	5.03
1.4	7.04
1.5	9.42

(b) An equalizer is required that has a nominal delay peak of 10 s at 1 rad/s relative to the delay at 0.5 and 1.5 rad/s. Examination of table 7-3 indicates that the delay corresponding to a Q of 2.75 will meet this requirement.

   If we add this delay, point by point, to the normalized delay of table II, the following table of values is obtained.

TABLE III   Equalized Delay

Frequency, rad/s	Delay, s
0.5	11.6
0.6	8.19
0.7	7.36
0.8	7.58
0.9	9.50
1.0	11.0
1.1	8.89
1.2	7.64
1.3	7.83
1.4	8.86
1.5	10.7

The corresponding curve is plotted in figure 7-19c. This curve can be denormalized by dividing the delay by $2\pi\ 1000$ and multiplying the frequency axis by 1000, resulting in the final curve of figure 7-19d. The differential delay variation over the band is about 675 μs.

The equalizer of example 7-4 provides over a 2:1 reduction in the differential delay. Further equalization can be obtained with two additional equalizers to fill in the concave regions around 750 and 1250 Hz.

7.5   WIDEBAND 90° PHASE-SHIFT NETWORKS

Wideband 90° phase-shift networks have a single input and two output ports. Both outputs maintain a constant phase difference of 90° within a prescribed error over a

TABLE 7-3 Delay of Normalized Second-Order Section ($\omega_r = 1$ rad/s)

Q	T_{gd}(DC)	$\omega(T_{gd,max})$	$T_{gd,max}$	0.1	0.2	0.3	0.4	0.5	0.6	0.7	0.8	0.9
0.25	8.00	DC	8.00	7.09	5.33	3.85	2.84	2.19	1.76	1.42	1.27	1.11
0.50	4.00	DC	4.00	3.96	3.85	3.67	3.45	3.20	2.94	2.69	2.44	2.21
0.75	2.67	0.700	3.51	2.70	2.79	2.94	3.12	3.31	3.46	3.51	3.45	3.27
1.00	2.00	0.856	4.31	2.04	2.16	2.37	2.68	3.08	3.53	3.97	4.26	4.28
1.25	1.60	0.913	5.23	1.64	1.76	1.97	2.30	2.77	3.40	4.16	4.87	5.22
1.50	1.33	0.941	6.18	1.37	1.47	1.67	1.99	2.47	3.18	4.16	5.28	6.09
1.75	1.14	0.957	7.15	1.17	1.27	1.45	1.75	2.22	2.95	4.05	5.54	6.88
2.00	1.00	0.968	8.13	1.03	1.12	1.28	1.56	2.00	2.72	3.89	5.66	7.59
2.25	0.89	0.975	9.12	0.91	0.99	1.15	1.40	1.82	2.52	3.71	5.69	8.20
2.50	0.80	0.980	10.1	0.82	0.90	1.04	1.27	1.66	2.33	3.52	5.66	8.74
2.75	0.73	0.983	11.1	0.75	0.82	0.94	1.16	1.53	2.16	3.34	5.57	9.19
3.00	0.67	0.986	12.1	0.69	0.75	0.87	1.07	1.41	2.02	3.16	5.45	9.57
3.25	0.61	0.988	13.1	0.63	0.69	0.80	0.99	1.31	1.89	2.99	5.31	9.88
3.50	0.57	0.990	14.1	0.59	0.64	0.75	0.92	1.23	1.77	2.84	5.15	10.1
3.75	0.53	0.991	15.1	0.55	0.60	0.70	0.86	1.15	1.67	2.69	5.00	10.3
4.00	0.50	0.992	16.1	0.51	0.56	0.65	0.81	1.08	1.57	2.56	4.84	10.4
4.25	0.47	0.993	17.1	0.48	0.53	0.62	0.76	1.02	1.49	2.44	4.68	10.5
4.50	0.44	0.994	18.1	0.46	0.50	0.58	0.72	0.97	1.41	2.33	4.52	10.6
4.75	0.42	0.994	19.1	0.43	0.47	0.55	0.69	0.92	1.35	2.22	4.37	10.6
5.00	0.40	0.995	20.1	0.41	0.45	0.52	0.65	0.87	1.28	2.13	4.23	10.6
6.00	0.33	0.997	24.0	0.34	0.38	0.44	0.54	0.73	1.08	1.82	3.71	10.3
7.00	0.29	0.997	28.0	0.29	0.32	0.38	0.47	0.63	0.93	1.58	3.28	9.83
8.00	0.25	0.998	32.0	0.26	0.28	0.33	0.41	0.55	0.82	1.39	2.94	9.28
9.00	0.22	0.999	36.0	0.23	0.25	0.29	0.36	0.49	0.73	1.24	2.65	8.73
10.00	0.20	0.999	40.0	0.21	0.23	0.26	0.33	0.44	0.66	1.13	2.41	8.19

wide range of frequencies. The overall transfer function is all-pass. These networks are widely used in the design of single-sideband systems and in other applications requiring 90° phase splitting.

Bedrosian (see bibliography) solved the approximation problem for this family of networks on a computer. The general structure is shown in figure 7-20a and consists of N and P networks. Each network provides real-axis pole-zero pairs and is all-pass. The transfer function is of the form

$$T(s) = \frac{(s - \alpha_1)(s - \alpha_2) \cdots (s - \alpha_{n/2})}{(s + \alpha_1)(s + \alpha_2) \cdots (s + \alpha_{n/2})} \tag{7-74}$$

where $n/2$ is the order of the numerator and denominator polynomials. The total complexity of both networks is then n.

Real-axis all-pass transfer functions can be realized using a cascade of passive or active first-order sections. Both versions are shown in figure 7-20b and c.

The transfer functions tabulated in table 7-4 approximate a 90° phase difference in an equiripple manner. This approximation occurs within the bandwidth limits ω_L and ω_u as shown in figure 7-21. These frequencies are normalized so that $\sqrt{\omega_L\omega_u} = 1$. For a specified bandwidth ratio ω_u/ω_L, the individual band limits can be found from

TABLE 7-3 Delay of Normalized Second-Order Section ($\omega_r = 1$ rad/s) (*Continued*)

ω, rad/s

1.0	1.1	1.2	1.3	1.4	1.5	1.6	1.7	1.8	1.9	2.0	3.0	4.0	5.0
1.00	0.91	0.84	0.78	0.73	0.69	0.66	0.62	0.60	0.57	0.55	0.38	0.28	0.21
2.00	1.81	1.64	1.49	1.35	1.23	1.12	1.03	0.94	0.87	0.80	0.40	0.24	0.15
3.00	2.69	2.36	2.06	1.79	1.56	1.36	1.19	1.05	0.93	0.83	0.33	0.18	0.11
4.00	3.52	2.99	2.48	2.05	1.71	1.43	1.20	1.03	0.88	0.77	0.27	0.14	0.09
5.00	4.32	3.50	2.76	2.18	1.73	1.40	1.15	0.96	0.81	0.69	0.23	0.11	0.07
6.00	5.06	3.90	2.92	2.20	1.69	1.33	1.07	0.88	0.73	0.62	0.20	0.10	0.06
7.00	5.75	4.20	2.99	2.17	1.62	1.24	0.98	0.80	0.66	0.55	0.17	0.08	0.05
8.00	6.38	4.41	2.99	1.10	1.53	1.16	0.91	0.73	0.60	0.50	0.15	0.07	0.04
9.00	6.94	4.54	2.95	2.01	1.44	1.08	0.83	0.66	0.54	0.45	0.14	0.06	0.04
10.0	7.44	4.60	2.88	1.92	1.35	1.00	0.77	0.61	0.50	0.41	0.12	0.06	0.04
11.0	7.88	4.62	2.80	1.82	1.27	0.93	0.72	0.57	0.46	0.38	0.11	0.05	0.03
12.0	8.25	4.60	2.70	1.73	1.20	0.87	0.67	0.53	0.43	0.35	0.10	0.05	0.03
13.0	8.57	4.55	2.60	1.65	1.13	0.82	0.62	0.49	0.40	0.33	0.09	0.05	0.03
14.0	8.84	4.48	2.50	1.56	1.06	0.77	0.58	0.46	0.37	0.31	0.09	0.04	0.03
15.0	9.06	4.40	2.41	1.49	1.01	0.73	0.55	0.43	0.35	0.29	0.08	0.04	0.02
16.0	9.23	4.30	2.31	1.42	0.95	0.69	0.52	0.41	0.33	0.27	0.08	0.04	0.02
17.0	9.36	4.20	2.22	1.35	0.91	0.65	0.49	0.38	0.31	0.26	0.07	0.04	0.02
18.0	9.46	4.10	2.14	1.29	0.86	0.62	0.47	0.36	0.29	0.24	0.07	0.03	0.02
19.0	9.52	3.99	2.06	1.24	0.82	0.59	0.44	0.35	0.29	0.23	0.07	0.03	0.02
20.0	9.56	3.89	1.98	1.18	0.79	0.56	0.42	0.33	0.27	0.22	0.06	0.03	0.02
24.0	9.48	3.48	1.71	1.01	0.67	0.47	0.36	0.28	0.22	0.18	0.05	0.03	0.02
28.0	9.18	3.13	1.51	0.88	0.58	0.41	0.31	0.24	0.19	0.16	0.04	0.02	0.01
32.0	8.77	2.82	1.34	0.78	0.51	0.36	0.27	0.21	0.17	0.14	0.04	0.02	0.01
36.0	8.32	2.57	1.20	0.70	0.45	0.32	0.24	0.19	0.15	0.12	0.03	0.02	0.01
40.0	7.87	2.35	1.09	0.69	0.41	0.30	0.22	0.17	0.13	0.11	0.03	0.02	0.01

$$\omega_L = \sqrt{\frac{\omega_L}{\omega_u}} \qquad (7\text{-}75)$$

and

$$\omega_u = \sqrt{\frac{\omega_u}{\omega_L}} \qquad (7\text{-}76)$$

As the total complexity n is made larger, the phase error decreases for a fixed bandwidth ratio or, for a fixed phase error, the bandwidth ratio will increase.

To use table 7-4, first determine the required bandwidth ratio from the frequencies given. A network is then selected that has a bandwidth ratio ω_u/ω_L that exceeds the requirement and a phase error $\pm\Delta\phi$ that is acceptable.

A frequency-scaling factor (FSF) is determined from

$$\text{FSF} = 2\pi f_0 \qquad (7\text{-}77)$$

where f_0 is the geometric mean of the specified band limits or $\sqrt{f_L f_u}$. The tabulated α's are then multiplied by the FSF for denormalization. The resulting pole-zero pairs can be realized by a cascade of active or passive first-order sections for each network.

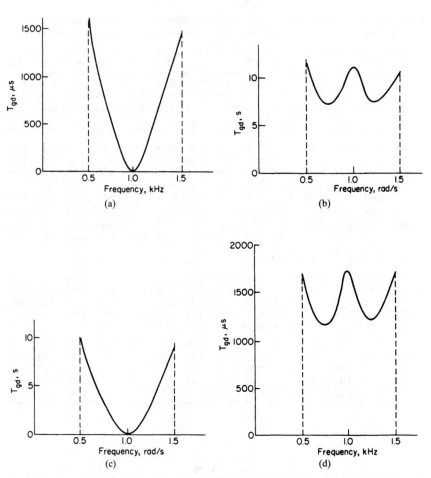

FIGURE 7-19 Delay equalization of example 7-4: (*a*) unequalized delay; (*b*) normalized delay; (*c*) normalized equalized delay; (*d*) denormalized equalized delay.

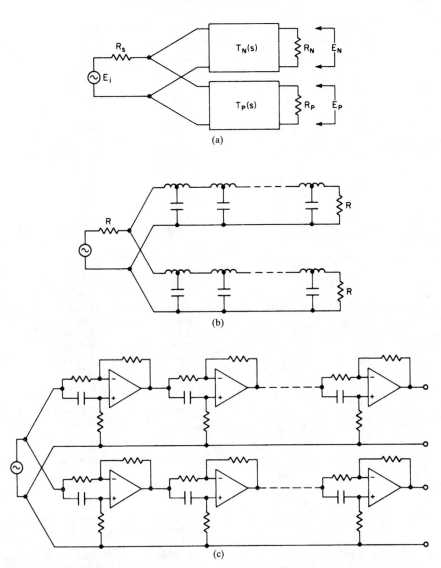

FIGURE 7-20 Wideband 90° phase-shift networks: (*a*) general structure; (*b*) passive realization; (*c*) active realization.

TABLE 7-4 Pole-Zero Locations for 90° Phase-Shift Networks*

n	$\Delta\phi$	α_N	α_P
		$\omega_u/\omega_L = 1146$	
6	6.84°	43.3862	8.3350
		2.0264	0.4935
		0.1200	0.0231
8	2.12°	59.7833	14.4159
		4.8947	1.6986
		0.5887	0.2043
		0.0694	0.0167
10	0.66°	75.8845	20.4679
		8.3350	3.5631
		1.5279	0.6545
		0.2807	0.1200
		0.0489	0.0132
		$\omega_u/\omega_L = 573.0$	
6	4.99°	34.3132	7.0607
		1.9111	0.5233
		0.1416	0.0291
8	1.39°	47.0857	11.8249
		4.3052	1.6253
		0.6153	0.2323
		0.0846	0.0212
10	0.39°	59.6517	16.5238
		7.0607	3.2112
		1.4749	0.6780
		0.3114	0.1416
		0.0605	0.0168
		$\omega_u/\omega_L = 286.5$	
4	13.9°	16.8937	2.4258
		0.4122	0.0592
6	3.43°	27.1337	5.9933
		1.8043	0.5542
		0.1669	0.0369
8	0.84°	37.0697	9.7136
		3.7944	1.5566
		0.6424	0.2636
		0.1030	0.0270
10	0.21°	46.8657	13.3518
		5.9933	2.8993
		1.4247	0.7019
		0.3449	0.1669
		0.0749	0.0213
		$\omega_u/\omega_L = 143.2$	
4	10.2°	13.5875	2.2308
		0.4483	0.0736

* Numerical values for table 7-4 obtained from S. D. Bedrosian, "Normalized Design of 90° Phase-Difference Networks," *IRE Transactions on Circuit Theory,* June 1960.

TABLE 7-4 Pole-Zero Locations for 90° Phase-Shift Networks
(*Continued*)

	$\omega_u/\omega_L = 143.2$	*Continued*	
8	0.46°	29.3327	8.0126
		3.3531	1.4921
		0.6702	0.2982
		0.1248	0.0341
10	0.10°	37.0091	10.8375
		5.1050	2.6233
		1.3772	0.7261
		0.3812	0.1959
		0.0923	0.0270

	$\omega_u/\omega_L = 81.85$		
4	7.58°	11.4648	2.0883
		0.4789	0.0918
6	1.38°	18.0294	4.5017
		1.6316	0.6129
		0.2221	0.0555
8	0.25°	24.4451	6.8929
		3.0427	1.4432
		0.6929	0.3287
		0.1451	0.0409
10	0.046°	30.7953	9.2085
		4.5017	2.4248
		1.3409	0.7458
		0.4124	0.2221
		0.1086	0.0325

	$\omega_u/\omega_L = 57.30$		
4	6.06°	10.3270	2.0044
		0.4989	0.0968
6	0.99°	16.1516	4.1648
		1.5873	0.6300
		0.2401	0.0619
8	0.16°	21.8562	6.2817
		2.8648	1.4136
		0.7074	0.3491
		0.1592	0.0458
10	0.026°	27.5087	8.3296
		4.1648	2.3092
		1.3189	0.7582
		0.4331	0.2401
		0.1201	0.0364

	$\omega_u/\omega_L = 28.65$		
4	3.57°	8.5203	1.6157
		0.5387	0.1177
6	0.44°	13.1967	3.6059
		1.5077	0.6633
		0.2773	0.0758
8	0.056°	17.7957	5.2924
		2.5614	1.3599
		0.7354	0.3904
		0.1890	0.0562

TABLE 7-4 Pole-Zero Locations for 90° Phase-Shift Networks
(*Continued*)

$\omega_u/\omega_L = 28.65$	*Continued*		
10	0.0069°	22.3618	6.9242
		3.6059	2.1085
		1.2786	0.7821
		0.4743	0.2773
		0.1444	0.0447

$\omega_u/\omega_L = 11.47$			
4	1.31°	5.9339	1.5027
		0.5055	0.1280
6	0.10°	10.4285	3.0425
		1.4180	0.7052
		0.3287	0.0959
8	0.0075°	14.0087	4.3286
		2.2432	1.2985
		0.7701	0.4458
		0.2310	0.0714

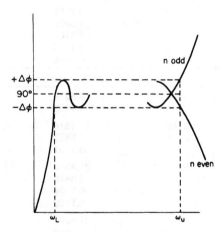

FIGURE 7-21 Wideband 90° phase-shift approximation.

The following example illustrates the design of a 90° phase-shift network.

EXAMPLE 7-5

REQUIRED: Design a network having dual outputs which maintain a phase difference of 90° within ±0.2° over the frequency range of 300 to 3000 Hz. The circuit should be all-pass and active.

RESULT:

(*a*) Since a 10:1 bandwidth ratio is required (3000 Hz/300 Hz), the design corresponding to $n = 6$ and $\omega_u/\omega_L = 11.47$ is chosen. The phase-shift error will be ±0.1°.

(b) The normalized real pole-zero coordinates for both networks are given as follows:

P Network	N Network
$a_1 = 10.4285$	$a_4 = 3.0425$
$a_2 = 1.4180$	$a_5 = 0.7052$
$a_3 = 0.3287$	$a_6 = 0.0959$

The frequency-scaling factor is

$$\text{FSF} = 2\pi f_0 = 2\pi \times 948.7 = 5961 \qquad (7\text{-}77)$$

where f_0 is $\sqrt{300 \times 3000}$. The pole-zero coordinates are multiplied by the FSF, resulting in the following set of denormalized values for α:

P Network	N Network
$a_1' = 62164$	$a_4' = 18136$
$a_2' = 8453$	$a_5' = 4204$
$a_3' = 1959$	$a_6' = 571.7$

(c) The P and N networks can now be realized using the active first-order all-pass circuit of section 7.2 and figure 7-11a.
   If we let $R' = 10\text{ k}\Omega$ and $C = 1000\text{ pF}$, the value of R is given by

$$R = \frac{1}{\alpha_0 C} \qquad (7\text{-}46)$$

Using the denormalized α's for the P and N networks, the following values are obtained:

Section	P Network	N Network
1	$R = 16.09\text{ k}\Omega$	$R = 55.14\text{ k}\Omega$
2	$R = 118.3\text{ k}\Omega$	$R = 237.9\text{ k}\Omega$
3	$R = 510.5\text{ k}\Omega$	$R = 1.749\text{ M}\Omega$

The final circuit is shown in figure 7-22 using standard 1% resistor values.

7.6 ADJUSTABLE DELAY AND AMPLITUDE EQUALIZERS

Delay equalizers were discussed in section 7.2 and applied to the delay equalization of filters in section 7.4. Frequently a telephone channel must be equalized to reduce the delay and amplitude variation. This process is called *line conditioning*. Since the initial parameters of lines vary and the line characteristics may change from time to time, the equalizer will consist of multiple sections where each stage is required to be adjustable.

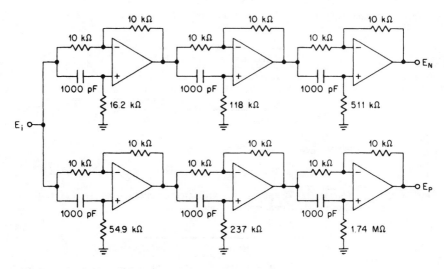

FIGURE 7-22   Wideband 90° phase-shift network of example 7-5.

LC Delay Equalizers

The circuit of figure 7-23a illustrates a simplified adjustable LC delay equalizer section. The emitter and collector load resistors R_e and R_c are equal; so Q_1 serves as a phase splitter. Transistor Q_2 is an emitter follower output stage.

The equivalent circuit is shown in figure 7-23b. The transfer function can be determined by superposition as

$$T(s) = \frac{s^2 - \dfrac{1}{RC} s + \dfrac{1}{LC}}{s^2 + \dfrac{1}{RC} s + \dfrac{1}{LC}} \qquad (7\text{-}78)$$

This expression is of the same form as the general second-order all-pass transfer function of equation (7-6). By equating coefficients we obtain

$$\omega_r = \frac{1}{\sqrt{LC}} \qquad (7\text{-}79)$$

and $$Q = \omega_r RC \qquad (7\text{-}80)$$

Equation (7-80) can be substituted in equation (7-13) for the maximum delay of a second-order section resulting in

$$T_{gd,\max} = 4RC \qquad (7\text{-}81)$$

By making R variable, the delay can be directly controlled while retaining the all-pass properties. The peak delay will occur at or near the LC resonant frequency.

The all-pass transfer function of equation (7-78) can also be implemented using an operational amplifier. This configuration is shown in figure 7-23c, where R' is arbitrary. Design equations (7-79) through (7-81) still apply.

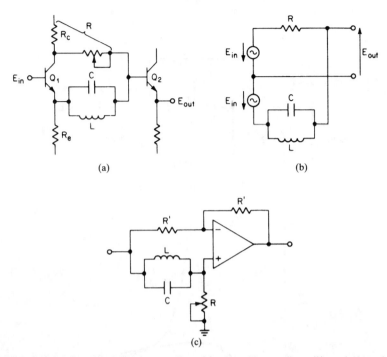

FIGURE 7-23 Adjustable LC delay equalizer: (*a*) adjustable equalizer; (*b*) equivalent circuit; (*c*) operational-amplifier realization.

EXAMPLE 7-6

REQUIRED: Design an adjustable LC delay equalizer using the two-transistor circuit of figure 7-23*a*. The delay should be variable from 0.5 to 2.5 ms with a center frequency of 1700 Hz.

RESULT: Using a capacitor C of 0.05 μF, the range of resistance R is given by

$$R_{\min} = \frac{T_{gd,\max}}{4C} = \frac{0.5 \times 10^{-3}}{4 \times 0.05 \times 10^{-6}} = 2500 \ \Omega \tag{7-81}$$

$$R_{\max} = \frac{2.5 \times 10^{-3}}{4 \times 0.05 \times 10^{-6}} = 12.5 \ \text{k}\Omega$$

The inductor is computed by the general formula for resonance $\omega^2 LC = 1$, resulting in an inductance of 175 mH. The circuit is shown in figure 7-24*a*. The emitter resistor R_e is composed of two resistors for proper biasing of phase splitter Q_1, and electrolytic capacitors are used for DC blocking. The delay extremes are shown in the curves of figure 7-24*b*.

LC Delay and Amplitude Equalizers

Frequently the magnitude response of a transmission channel must be equalized along with the delay. An equalizer circuit featuring both adjustable amplitude and

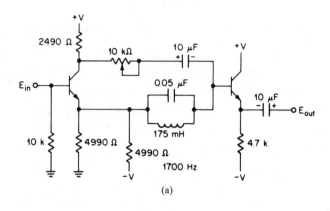

(a)

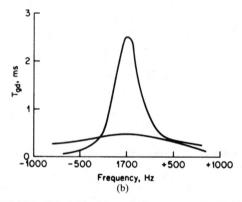

(b)

FIGURE 7-24   Adjustable delay equalizer of example 7-6: (*a*) equalizer circuit; (*b*) delay adjustment range.

delay is shown in figure 7-25*a*. Transistor Q_1 serves as a phase splitter where the signal applied to emitter follower Q_2 is K times the input signal. The equivalent circuit is illustrated in figure 7-25*b*. The transfer function can be determined by superposition as

$$T(s) = \frac{s^2 - \dfrac{K}{RC}s + \dfrac{1}{LC}}{s^2 + \dfrac{K}{RC}s + \dfrac{1}{LC}} \tag{7-82}$$

If K is set equal to unity, this expression is then equivalent to equation (7-78) corresponding to a second-order all-pass transfer function. As K increases or decreases from unity, a boost or null occurs at midfrequency with an asymptotic return to unity gain at DC and infinity.

The amount of amplitude equalization at midfrequency in decibels is given by

$$A_{\text{dB}} = 20 \log K \tag{7-83}$$

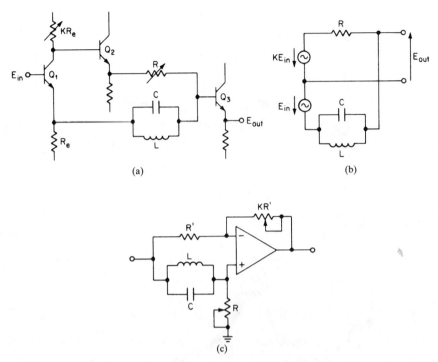

FIGURE 7-25 Adjustable LC delay and amplitude equalizer: (a) adjustable delay and amplitude equalizer; (b) equivalent circuit; (c) operational-amplifier realization.

The maximum delay occurs at the LC resonant frequency and can be derived as

$$T_{gd,\max} = \frac{2\,RC}{K} + 2\,RC \tag{7-84}$$

If K is unity, equation (7-84) reduces to $4\,RC$, which is equivalent to equation (7-81) for the all-pass circuit of figure 7-23.

An operational-amplifier implementation is also shown in figure 7-25c. The value of R' is arbitrary, and equations (7-83) and (7-84) are still applicable.

The following conclusions may be reached based on evaluation of equations (7-82) through (7-84):

1. The maximum delay is equal to $4\,RC$ for $K = 1$; so R is a delay magnitude control.

2. The maximum delay will be minimally affected by a nonunity K, as is evident from equation (7-84).

3. The amount of amplitude equalization at the LC resonant frequency is independent of the delay setting and is strictly a function of K. However, the selectivity of the amplitude response is a function of the delay setting and becomes more selective with increased delay.

The curves of figure 7-26 show some typical delay and amplitude characteristics. The interaction between delay and amplitude is not restricted to LC equalizers and will

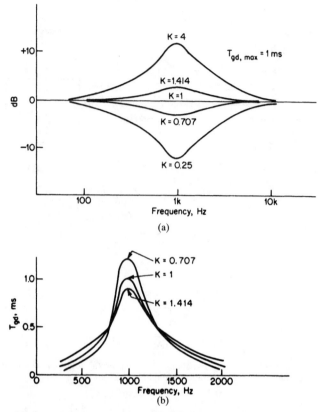

FIGURE 7-26 Typical delay and amplitude response for LC delay and amplitude equalizer: (*a*) amplitude characteristics for a fixed delay; (*b*) delay variation for ± 3 dB of amplitude equalization.

occur whenever the same resonant element, either passive or active, is used to provide both the amplitude and delay equalization. However, for small amounts of amplitude correction such as ± 3 dB, the effect on the delay is minimal.

Active Delay and Amplitude Equalizers

The dual-amplifier bandpass (DABP) delay equalizer structure of section 7.2, under "Active All-Pass Structures," and figure 7-13 has a fixed gain and remains all-pass regardless of the design Q. If resistor R_1 is made variable, the Q, and therefore the delay, can be directly adjusted with no effect on resonant frequency or the all-pass behavior. The adjustable delay equalizer is shown in figure 7-27a. The design equations are

$$T_{gd,\max} = 4\,R_1 C \tag{7-85}$$

and
$$R_2 = R_3 = \frac{1}{\omega_r C} \tag{7-86}$$

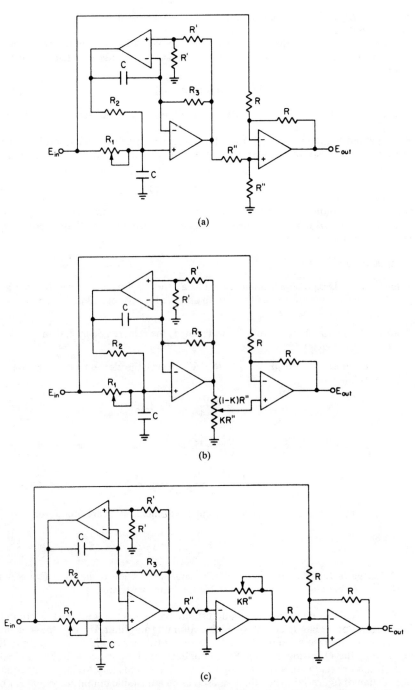

FIGURE 7-27 DABP delay and amplitude equalizer: (*a*) adjustable delay equalizer; (*b*) adjustable delay and amplitude equalizer; (*c*) adjustable delay and amplitude equalizer with extended amplitude range.

where C, R, R', and R'' can be conveniently chosen. Resistor R_2 can be made variable for frequency trimming.

If amplitude equalization capability is also desired, a potentiometer can be introduced, resulting in the circuit of figure 7-27b. The amplitude equalization at ω_r is given by

$$A_{dB} = 20 \log (4K - 1) \qquad (7-87)$$

where a K variation of 0.25 to 1 covers an amplitude equalization range of $-\infty$ to $+9.5$ dB.

To extend the equalization range above $+9.5$ dB, an additional amplifier can be introduced, as illustrated in figure 7-27c. The amplitude equalization at ω_r is then obtained from

$$A_{dB} = 20 \log (2K - 1) \qquad (7-88)$$

where a K variation of 0.5 to ∞ results in an infinite range of equalization capability. In reality, a ± 15 dB maximum range has been found to be more than adequate for most equalization requirements.

EXAMPLE 7-7

REQUIRED: Design an adjustable active delay and amplitude equalizer that has a delay adjustment range of 0.5 to 3 ms, an amplitude range of ± 12 dB, and a center frequency of 1000 Hz.

RESULT: The circuit of figure 7-27c will provide the required delay and amplitude adjustment capability.

If we choose $C = 0.01$ μF and $R = R' = R'' = 10$ kΩ, the element values are computed as follows:

$$R_{1,\min} = \frac{T_{gd,\max}}{4C} = \frac{0.5 \times 10^{-3}}{4 \times 10^{-8}} = 12.5 \text{ k}\Omega \qquad (7-85)$$

$$R_{1,\max} = \frac{3 \times 10^{-3}}{4 \times 10^{-8}} = 75 \text{ k}\Omega$$

$$R_2 = R_3 = \frac{1}{\omega_r C} = \frac{1}{2\pi \times 1000 \times 10^{-8}} = 15.9 \text{ k}\Omega \qquad (7-86)$$

The extreme values of K for ± 12 dB of amplitude equalization are found from

$$K = \frac{1}{2} \left[\log^{-1}\left(\frac{A_{dB}}{20} \right) + 1 \right] \qquad (7-88)$$

The range of K is then 0.626 to 2.49. The equalizer section is shown in figure 7-28. Resistor R_2 has also been made adjustable for frequency trimming.

An active delay equalizer having adjustable delay was implemented by combining a second-order bandpass section with a summing amplifier. The bandpass section was required to have a fixed gain and a resonant frequency which were both independent of the Q setting. If amplitude equalization alone is needed, the bandpass section can operate with a fixed design Q. The low-complexity MFBP delay equalizer section of figure 7-12a can then be used as an adjustable amplitude equalizer by making one of the summing resistors variable.

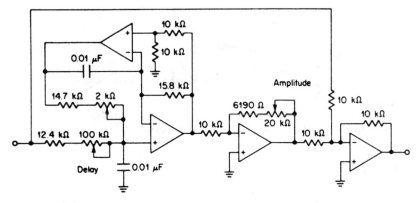

FIGURE 7-28   Adjustable delay and amplitude equalizer of example 7-7.

This circuit is shown in figure 7-29*a*. The design equations are given by

$$R_2 = \frac{2Q}{\omega_r C} \qquad (7\text{-}89)$$

$$R_{1a} = \frac{R_2}{2} \qquad (7\text{-}90)$$

$$R_{1b} = \frac{R_{1a}}{2Q^2 - 1} \qquad (7\text{-}91)$$

The amount of amplitude equalization at ω_r is computed from

$$A_{dB} = 20 \log \left(\frac{1}{K} - 1 \right) \qquad (7\text{-}92)$$

where K will range from 0 to 1 for an infinite range of amplitude equalization.

If the Q is below 0.707, the value of R_{1b} becomes negative, so the circuit of figure 7-29*b* is used. R_2 is given by equation (7-89) and R_1 is found from

$$R_1 = \frac{R_2}{4Q^2} \qquad (7\text{-}93)$$

The attenuation or boost at resonance is computed from

$$A_{dB} = 20 \log \left(\frac{2Q^2}{K} - 1 \right) \qquad (7\text{-}94)$$

The magnitude of Q determines the selectivity of the response in the region of resonance and is limited to values typically below 20 because of amplifier limitations.

If higher Qs are required or if a circuit featuring independently adjustable Q and amplitude equalization is desired, the DABP circuits of figure 7-27 may be used, where R_1 becomes the Q adjustment and is given by

$$R_1 = QR_2 \qquad (7\text{-}95)$$

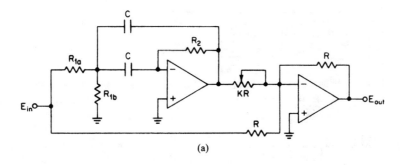

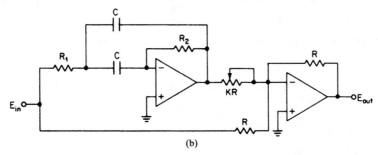

FIGURE 7-29   MFBP amplitude equalizer: (*a*) amplitude equalizer $0.707 < Q < 20$; (*b*) amplitude equalizer $0 < Q < 20$.

To compute the required Q of an amplitude equalizer, first define f_b, which is the frequency corresponding to one-half the pad loss (in decibels). The Q is then given by

$$Q = \frac{f_b b^2 \sqrt{K_r}}{f_r(b^2 - 1)} \tag{7-96}$$

where

$$K_r = \log^{-1}\left(\frac{A_{dB}}{20}\right) - 10^{A_{dB}/20} \tag{7-97}$$

and

$$b = \frac{f_b}{f_r} \tag{7-98}$$

or

$$b = \frac{f_r}{f_b} \tag{7-99}$$

whichever b is greater than unity.

EXAMPLE 7-8

REQUIRED: Design a fixed active amplitude equalizer that provides a +12-dB boost at 3200 Hz and has a boost of +6 dB at 2500 Hz.

RESULT:

(*a*) First compute

$$K_r = 10^{A_{dB}/20} = 10^{12/20} = 3.98 \tag{7-97}$$

and
$$b = \frac{f_r}{f_b} = \frac{3200 \text{ Hz}}{2500 \text{ Hz}} = 1.28 \qquad (7\text{-}99)$$

The Q is then found from

$$Q = \frac{f_b b^2 \sqrt{K_r}}{f_r(b^2 - 1)} = \frac{2500 \times 1.28^2 \sqrt{3.98}}{3200 (1.28^2 - 1)} = 4.00 \qquad (7\text{-}96)$$

(b) The MFBP amplitude equalizer circuit of figure 7-29a will be used. Using a C of 0.0047 μF and an R of 10 kΩ, the element values are given by

$$R_2 = \frac{2Q}{\omega_r C} = \frac{2 \times 4}{2\pi 3200 \times 4.7 \times 10^{-9}} = 84.6 \text{ k}\Omega \qquad (7\text{-}89)$$

$$R_{1a} = \frac{R_2}{2} = 42.3 \text{ k}\Omega \qquad (7\text{-}90)$$

$$R_{1b} = \frac{R_{1a}}{2Q^2 - 1} = \frac{42.3 \times 10^3}{2 \times 4^2 - 1} = 1365 \text{ }\Omega \qquad (7\text{-}91)$$

$$K = \frac{1}{1 + 10^{A_{\text{dB}}/20}} = \frac{1}{1 + 10^{12/20}} = 0.200 \qquad (7\text{-}92)$$

The equalizer circuit and corresponding frequency response are shown in figure 7-30.

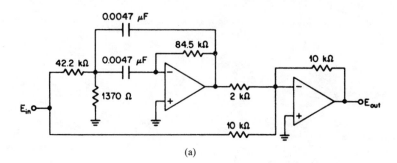

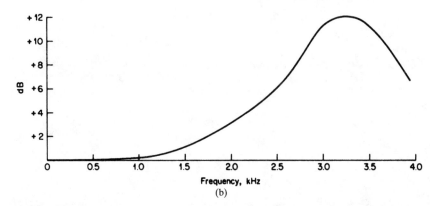

FIGURE 7-30 Amplitude equalizer of example 7-8: (a) amplitude equalizer circuit; (b) frequency response.

BIBLIOGRAPHY

Bedrosian, S. D., "Normalized Design of 90° Phase-Difference Networks," *IRE Transactions on Circuit Theory,* vol. CT-7, June 1960.

Geffe, P. R., *Simplified Modern Filter Design,* John F. Rider, New York, 1963.

Lindquist, C. S., *Active Network Design,* Steward and Sons, Long Beach, Calif., 1977.

Wallis, C. M., "Design of Low-Frequency Constant Time Delay Lines," *AIEE Proceedings,* vol. 71, 1952.

Williams, A. B., "An Active Equalizer with Adjustable Amplitude and Delay," *IEEE Transactions on Circuit Theory,* vol. CT-16, November 1969.

Williams, A. B., *Active Filter Design,* Artech House, Dedham, Mass., 1975.

CHAPTER 8

REFINEMENTS IN *LC* FILTER DESIGN

8.1 INTRODUCTION

The straightforward application of the design techniques outlined for LC filters will not always result in practical element values or desirable circuit configurations. Extreme cases of impedance or bandwidth can produce designs which may be extremely difficult or even impossible to realize. This chapter is concerned mainly with circuit transformations so that impractical designs can be transformed into alternate configurations having the identical response and using more practical elements.

8.2 TAPPED INDUCTORS

An extremely useful tool for eliminating impractical element values is the transformer. As the reader may recall from introductory AC circuit analysis, a transformer having a turns ratio N will transform an impedance by a factor of N^2. A parallel element can be shifted between the primary and secondary at will, provided that its impedance is modified by N^2.

Figure 8-1 illustrates how a tapped inductor is used to reduce the value of a resonating capacitor. The tuned circuit of figure 8-1a is first modified by introducing an impedance step-up transformer as shown in figure 8-1b so that capacitor C can be moved to the secondary and reduced by a factor of N^2. This can be carried a step fur-

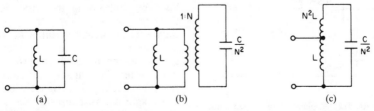

FIGURE 8-1 The tapped inductor: (a) basic tuned circuit; (b) introduction of transformer; (c) absorbed transformer.

8.1

ther, resulting in the circuit of figure 8-1c. The transformer has been absorbed as a continuation of the inductor, resulting in an autotransformer. The ratio of the overall inductance to the tap inductance becomes N^2.

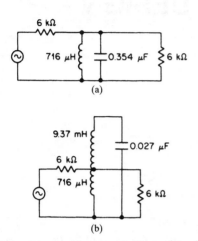

(a)

(b)

FIGURE 8-2 Reducing resonant capacitor value: (a) tuned circuit; (b) modified circuit.

As an example, let us modify the tuned circuit of example 5-4 shown in figure 8-2a. To reduce the capacitor from 0.354 to 0.027 µF, the overall inductance is increased by the impedance ratio 0.354 µF/0.027 µF, resulting in the circuit of figure 8-2b. The resonant frequency remains unchanged, since the overall LC product is still the same.

As a further example, let us consider LC elliptic-function low-pass filters. The parallel resonant circuits may also contain high capacity values which can be reduced by this method. Figure 8-3 shows a section of the low-pass filter of example 3-2. To reduce the resonating capacitor to 0.1 µF, the overall inductance is increased by the factor 1.055 µF/0.1 µF and a tap is provided at the original inductance value.

The tapped coil is useful not only for reducing resonating capacitors but also for transforming entire sections of a filter including terminations. The usefulness of the tapped inductor is limited only by the ingenuity and resourcefulness of the designer. Figure 8-4 illustrates some applications of this technique using designs from previous examples. In the case of figure 8-4a, where a tapped coil enables operation from unequal terminations, the same result could have been achieved using Bartlett's bisection theorem or other methods (see section 3.1). However, the transformer approach results in maximum power transfer (minimum insertion loss). The circuits of figure 8-4b and c demonstrate how element values can be manipulated by taps. The tapped inductance values shown are all measured from the grounded end of the shunt inductors. Series branches can be manipulated up or down in impedance level by multiplying the shunt inductance taps on both sides of the branch by the desired impedance-scaling factor.

Transformers or autotransformers are by no means ideal. Imperfect coupling within the magnetic structure will result in a leakage inductance which can cause spurious responses at higher frequencies, as shown in figure 8-5. These effects can be minimized by using near-

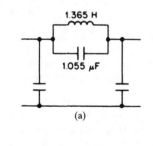

(a)

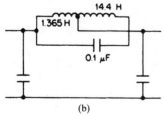

(b)

FIGURE 8-3 Application of tapped inductor in elliptic-function low-pass filters: (a) filter section; (b) tapped inductor.

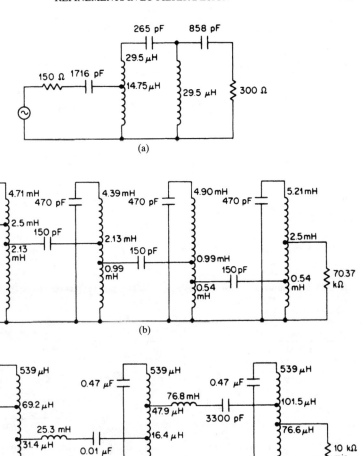

FIGURE 8-4 Applications of tapped inductors: (*a*) high-pass filter of example 4-1 modified for unequal terminations; (*b*) filter of example 5-7 modified for standard capacitor values; (*c*) filter of example 5-8 modified for standard capacitor values.

unity turns ratios. Another solution is to leave a portion of the original capacity at the tap for high-frequency bypassing. This method is shown in figure 8-6.

8.3 CIRCUIT TRANSFORMATIONS

Circuit transformations fall into two categories, equivalent circuits or narrowband approximations. The impedance of a circuit branch can be expressed as a ratio of two polynomials in *s*, similar to a transfer function. If two branches are equivalent, their impedance expressions are identical. A narrowband approximation to a particular

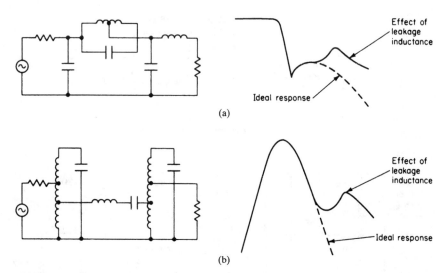

FIGURE 8-5 Spurious responses from leakage inductance: (*a*) low-pass filter; (*b*) bandpass filter.

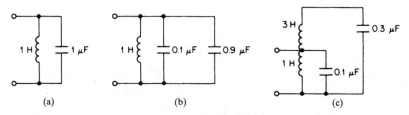

FIGURE 8-6 Preventing spurious response from leakage inductance: (*a*) initial circuit; (*b*) split capacity; (*c*) transformed circuit.

filter branch is valid only over a small frequency range. Outside of this region, the impedances depart considerably; so the filter response is affected. As a result, narrowband approximations are essentially limited to small percentage bandwidth bandpass filters.

Norton's Capacitance Transformer

Let us consider the circuit of figure 8-7*a* consisting of impedance Z interconnected between impedances Z_1 and Z_2. If it is desired to raise impedance Z_2 by a factor of N^2 without disturbing an overall transfer function (except for possibly a constant multiplier), a transformer can be introduced as shown in figure 8-7*b*.

Determinant manipulation can provide us with an alternate approach. The nodal determinant of a two-port network is given by

$$\begin{vmatrix} Y_{11} & -Y_{12} \\ -Y_{21} & Y_{22} \end{vmatrix}$$

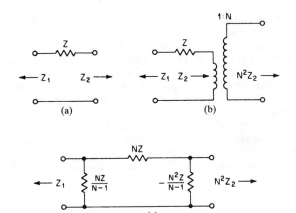

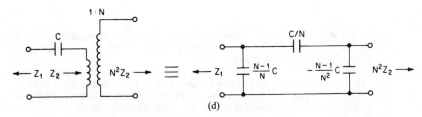

FIGURE 8-7 Norton's capacitance transformer: (*a*) general two-port network; (*b*) transformer step-up of output impedance; (*c*) Norton impedance transformation; (*d*) Norton capacitance transformation.

where Y_{11} and Y_{22} are the input and output nodal admittances, respectively, and Y_{12} and Y_{21} are the transfer admittances, which are normally equal to each other.

If we consider the two-port network of figure 8-7*a*, the nodal determinant becomes

$$\begin{vmatrix} \dfrac{1}{Z_1} + \dfrac{1}{Z} & -\dfrac{1}{Z} \\ -\dfrac{1}{Z} & \dfrac{1}{Z_2} + \dfrac{1}{Z} \end{vmatrix}$$

To raise the impedance of the output or Y_{22} node by N^2, the second row and second column are multiplied by $1/N$, resulting in

$$\begin{vmatrix} \dfrac{1}{Z_1} + \dfrac{1}{Z} & -\dfrac{1}{NZ} \\ -\dfrac{1}{NZ} & \dfrac{1}{N^2 Z_2} + \dfrac{1}{N^2 Z} \end{vmatrix}$$

This determinant corresponds to the circuit of figure 8-7*c*. The Y_{11} total nodal admittance is unchanged and the Y_{22} total nodal admittance has been reduced by N^2 or the impedance has been increased by N^2. This result was originated by Norton and is called *Norton's transformation*.

If the element Z is a capacitor C, this transformation can be applied to obtain the equivalent circuit of figure 8-7d. This transformation is important, since it can be used to modify the impedance on one side of a capacitor by a factor of N^2 without a transformer. However, the output shunt capacitor introduced is negative. A positive capacitor must then be present external to the network so that the negative capacitance can be absorbed.

If an N^2 of less than unity is used, the impedance at the output node will be reduced. The shunt capacitor at the input node will then become negative and must be absorbed by an external positive capacitor across the input.

The following example illustrates the use of the capacitance transformer.

EXAMPLE 8-1

REQUIRED: Using the capacitance transformation, modify the bandpass filter circuit of figure 5-3c so that the 1.91-H inductor is reduced to 100 mH. The source and load impedances should remain 600 Ω.

RESULT:

(a) The circuit to be transformed is shown in figure 8-8a. To facilitate the capacitance transformation, the 0.01329-μF series capacitor is split into two equal capacitors of twice the value and redrawn in figure 8-8b.

   To reduce the 1.91-H inductor to 100 mH, let us first lower the impedance of the network to the right of the dashed line in figure 8-8b by factor of 100 mH/1.91 H or 0.05236. Using the capacitance transformation of figure 8-7d, where $N^2 = 0.05236$, the circuit of figure 8-8c is obtained where the input negative capacitor has been absorbed.

(b) To complete the transformation, the output node must be transformed back up in impedance to restore the 600-Ω termination. Again using the capacitance transformation with an N^2 of 600 Ω/31.42 Ω or 19.1, the final circuit of figure 8-8d is obtained. Because of the symmetrical nature of the circuit of figure 8-8b, both capacitor transformations are also symmetrical.

(c) Each parallel resonant circuit is tuned by opening the inductors of the adjacent series resonant circuits, and each series resonant circuit is resonated by shorting the inductors of the adjacent parallel tuned circuits as shown in figure 8-8e.

Narrowband Approximations

A narrowband approximation to a circuit branch consists of an alternate network which is theoretically equivalent only at a single frequency. Nevertheless, good results can be obtained with bandpass filters having small percentage bandwidths typically up to 20%.

The series and parallel RL and RC circuits of table 8-1 are narrowband approximations which are equivalent at ω_0. This frequency is generally set equal to the bandpass center frequency in equations (8-1) through (8-8). These equations were derived simply by determining the expressions for the network impedances and equating the real parts and the imaginary parts to solve for the resistive and reactive components, respectively.

Narrowband approximations can be used to manipulate the source and load terminations of bandpass filters. If a parallel RC network is converted to a series RC circuit, it is apparent from equation (8-8) that the resistor value decreases. When we

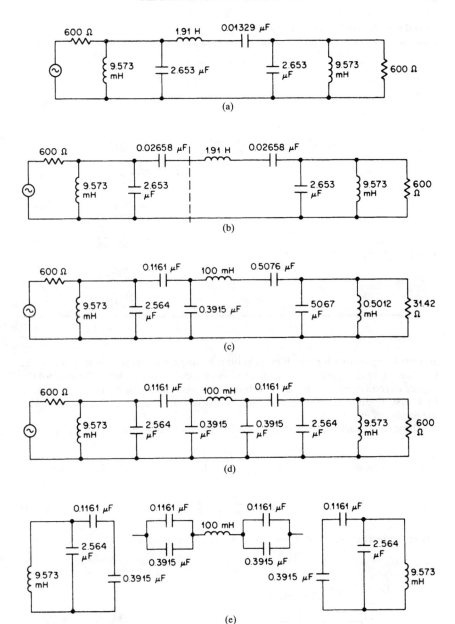

FIGURE 8-8 Capacitance transformation applied to filter of example 5-2: (*a*) bandpass filter of example 5-2; (*b*) split series capacitors; (*c*) reduction of 1.91-H inductor using capacitance transformation; (*d*) restoration of 600-Ω output impedance using capacitance transformation; (*e*) equivalent circuits for tuning.

TABLE 8-1 Narrowband Approximations

Circuit	Design Equations
	$L_1 = L_a + \dfrac{R_a^2}{\omega_0^2 L_a}$ (8-1)
	$R_1 = R_a + \dfrac{\omega_0^2 L_a^2}{R_a}$ (8-2)
	$L_a = \dfrac{L_1 R_1^2}{R_1^2 + \omega_0^2 L_1^2}$ (8-3)
	$R_a = \dfrac{\omega_0^2 L_1^2 R_1}{R_1^2 + \omega_0^2 L_1^2}$ (8-4)
	$C_2 = \dfrac{C_b}{1 + \omega_0^2 C_b^2 R_b^2}$ (8-5)
	$R_2 = R_b + \dfrac{1}{\omega_0^2 C_b^2 R_b}$ (8-6)
	$C_b = C_2 + \dfrac{1}{\omega_0^2 R_2^2 C_2}$ (8-7)
	$R_b = \dfrac{R_2}{1 + \omega_0^2 C_2^2 R_2^2}$ (8-8)

apply this approximation to a bandpass filter having a parallel resonant circuit as the terminating branch, the source or load resistor can be made smaller. To control the degree of reduction so that a desired termination can be obtained, the shunt capacitor is first subdivided into two capacitors where only one capacitor is associated with the termination.

These results are illustrated in figure 8-9. The element values are given by

$$C_2 = \frac{1}{\omega_0 \sqrt{R_1 R_2 - R_2^2}} \tag{8-9}$$

and

$$C_1 = C_T - \frac{1}{\omega_0} \sqrt{\frac{R_1 - R_2}{R_1^2 R_2}} \tag{8-10}$$

where the restrictions $R_2 < R_1$ and $(R_1 - R_2)/(R_1^2 R_2) < \omega_0^2 C_T^2$ apply.

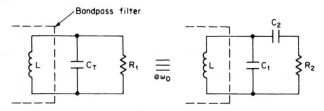

FIGURE 8-9 Narrowband transformation of terminations.

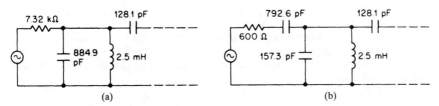

FIGURE 8-10 Narrowband source transformation of example 8-2: (*a*) source input to filter of example 5-7; (*b*) transformed source.

EXAMPLE 8-2

REQUIRED: Modify the 100-kHz bandpass filter of example 5-7 for a source impedance of 600 Ω.

RESULT: The filter is shown in figure 8-10*a*. If we use the narrowband source transformation of figure 8-9, the values are given by

$$C_2 = \frac{1}{\omega_0 \sqrt{R_1 R_2 - R_2^2}} = \frac{1}{2\pi \times 10^5 \sqrt{7.32 \times 6 \times 10^5 - 600^2}}$$

$$= 792.6 \text{ pF} \tag{8-9}$$

$$C_1 = C_T - \frac{1}{\omega_0} \sqrt{\frac{R_1 - R_2}{R_1^2 R_2}} = 884.9 \times 10^{-12}$$

$$- \frac{1}{2\pi \times 10^5} \sqrt{\frac{7.32 \times 10^3 - 600}{7320^2 \times 600}} = 157.3 \text{ pF} \tag{8-10}$$

The resulting filter is illustrated in figure 8-10*b*.

8.4 DESIGNING WITH PARASITIC CAPACITANCE

As a first approximation, inductors and capacitors are considered pure lumped reactive elements. Most physical capacitors are nearly perfect reactances. Inductors, on the other hand, have impurities which can be detrimental in many cases. In addition to the highly critical resistive losses, distributed capacity across the coil will occur because of interturn capacitance of the coil winding and other stray capacities involving the core, etc. The equivalent circuit of an inductor is shown in figure 8-11.

The result of this distributed capacitance is to create the effect of a parallel resonant circuit instead of an inductor. If the coil is to be located in shunt with an external capacitance, the external capacitor value can be decreased accordingly, thus absorbing the distributed capacitance.

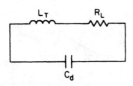

FIGURE 8-11 Equivalent circuit of inductor.

The distributed capacity across the inductor in a series resonant circuit causes parallel resonances resulting in nulls in the frequency response. If the self-resonant frequency is too low, the null may even occur in the passband, thus severely distorting the expected response.

To determine the effective inductance of a practical inductor, the coil is resonated to the frequency of interest with an external capacitor and the effective inductance is calculated using the standard formula for resonance. The effective inductance can also be found from

$$L_{\text{eff}} = \frac{L_T}{1 - \left(\dfrac{f}{f_r}\right)^2} \tag{8-11}$$

where L_T is the true (low-frequency) inductance, f is the frequency of interest, and f_r is the inductor's self-resonant frequency. As f approaches f_r, the value of L_{eff} will increase quite dramatically and will become infinite at self-resonance. Equation (8-11) is plotted in figure 8-12.

To compensate for the effect of distributed capacity in a series resonant circuit, the true inductance L_T can be appropriately decreased so that the effective inductance given by equation (8-11) is the required value. However, the Q of a practical series resonant circuit is given by

$$Q_{\text{eff}} = Q_L \left[1 - \left(\frac{f}{f_r}\right)^2\right] \tag{8-12}$$

where Q_L is the Q of the inductor as determined by the series losses (i.e., $\omega L_T/R_L$). The effective Q is therefore reduced by the distributed capacity.

Distributed capacity is determined by the mechanical parameters of the core and winding and, as a result, is subject to change due to mechanical stresses, etc. There-

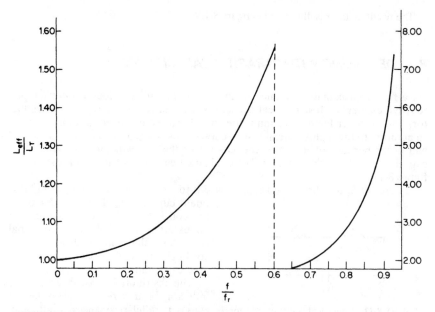

FIGURE 8-12 Effective inductance with frequency.

fore, for maximum stability, the distributed capacity should be kept as small as possible. Techniques for minimizing inductor capacity are discussed in chapter 9.

Another form of parasitic capacity is stray capacitance between the circuit nodes and ground. These strays may be especially harmful at high frequencies and with high-impedance nodes. In the case of low-pass filters where the circuit nodes already have shunt capacitors to ground, these strays can usually be neglected, especially when the impedance levels are low.

A portion of an elliptic-function bandpass filter is shown in figure 8-13. The stray capacity at nodes not connected to ground by a design capacitor may cause problems, since these nodes have high impedances.

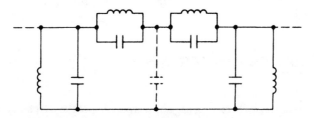

FIGURE 8-13   Elliptic-function bandpass filter.

Geffe (see bibliography) has derived a transformation to introduce a design capacitor from the junction of the parallel tuned circuits to ground. The stray capacity can then be absorbed. The design of elliptic-function bandpass filters was discussed in section 5.1. This transformation is performed upon the filter while it is normalized to a 1-rad/s center frequency and a 1-Ω impedance level. A section of the normalized network is shown in figure 8-14a. The transformation proceeds as follows:

Choose an arbitrary value of $m < 1$. Then

$$n = 1 - \frac{L_b}{L_c}\frac{1-m}{m^2} \tag{8-13}$$

$$C_0 = \frac{1-n}{n^2 L_c} - \frac{1-m}{mn^2 L_b} \tag{8-14}$$

$$C_1 = \frac{1}{L_a} - \frac{1-n}{nL_c} \tag{8-15}$$

$$C_2 = \frac{1}{nL_c} \tag{8-16}$$

$$C_3 = \frac{1}{mn^2 L_b} \tag{8-17}$$

$$C_4 = \frac{1-m}{m^2 n^2 L_b} + \frac{1}{n^2 L_d} \tag{8-18}$$

$$L_1 = \frac{L_a}{1 - \frac{L_a}{L_b}\frac{1-n}{n}} \tag{8-19}$$

$$L_2 = nL_b \tag{8-20}$$

$$L_3 = mn^2 L_c \tag{8-21}$$

$$L_4 = \frac{m^2 n^2 L_c}{1 + \dfrac{L_c}{L_d}\dfrac{m^2}{1-m}} \tag{8-22}$$

The resulting network is given in figure 8-14*b*. The output node has been transformed to an impedance level of $m^2 n^2$ Ω. Therefore, all the circuitry to the right of this node up to and including the termination must be impedance-scaled by this same factor. The filter is subsequently denormalized by scaling to the desired center frequency and impedance level.

8.5 AMPLITUDE EQUALIZATION FOR INADEQUATE Q

Insufficient element Q will cause a sagging or rounding of the frequency response in the region of cutoff. Some typical cases are shown in figure 8-15, where the solid curve represents the theoretical response. Finite Q will also result in less rejection in the vicinity of any stopband zeros and increased filter insertion loss.

    Amplitude-equalization techniques can be applied to compensate for the sagging response near cutoff. A passive amplitude equalizer will not actually "boost" the corner response, since a gain cannot be achieved as with active equalizer circuits. However, the equalizer will introduce attenuation except in the region of interest, therefore resulting in a boost in terms of the relative response.

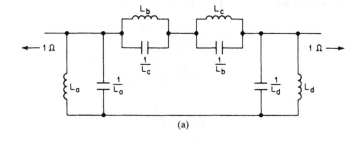

(a)

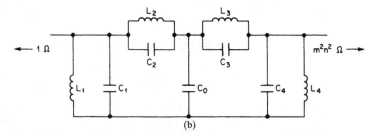

(b)

FIGURE 8-14 Transformation to absorb stray capacitance: (*a*) normalized filter section; (*b*) transformed circuit.

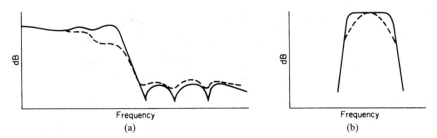

FIGURE 8-15   Effects of insufficient Q: (a) low-pass response; (b) bandpass response.

Amplitude equalizers used for low Q compensation are of the bandpass type. They have either constant-impedance or nonconstant-impedance characteristics. The constant-impedance types can be cascaded with each other and the filter with no interaction. The nonconstant-impedance equalizer sections are less complex but will result in some interaction when cascaded with other networks. However, for a boost of 1 or 2 dB, these effects are usually minimal and can be neglected.

Both types of equalizers are shown in figure 8-16. The nonconstant-impedance type can be used in either the series or shunt form. In general, the shunt form is preferred, since the resonating capacitor may be reduced by tapping the inductor.

To design a bandpass equalizer, the following characteristics must be determined from the curve to be equalized:

A_{dB} = total amount of equalization required in decibels
f_r = frequency corresponding to A_{dB}
f_b = frequency corresponding to $A_{dB}/2$

These parameters are illustrated in figure 8-17, where the corner response and corresponding equalizer are shown for both upper and lower cutoff frequencies.

To design the equalizer, first compute K from

$$A_{dB} = 20 \log K \qquad (8\text{-}23)$$

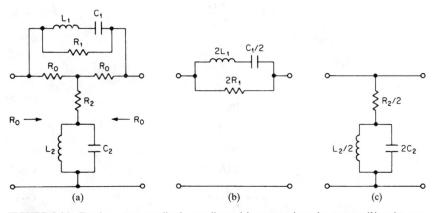

FIGURE 8-16   Bandpass-type amplitude equalizers: (a) constant-impedance type; (b) series nonconstant-impedance type; (c) shunt nonconstant-impedance type.

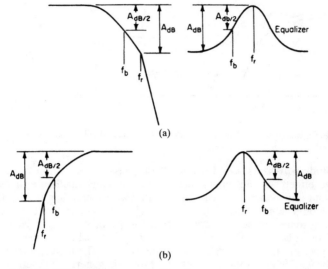

FIGURE 8-17   Bandpass equalization of corner response: (*a*) equalization of upper cutoff; (*b*) equalization of lower cutoff.

Then calculate *b* where

$$b = \frac{f_r}{f_b} \tag{8-24}$$

or
$$b = \frac{f_b}{f_r} \tag{8-25}$$

selecting whichever *b* is greater than unity.

The element values corresponding to the sections of figure 8-16 are found as follows:

$$L_1 = \frac{R_0(K-1)}{2\pi f_b(b^2-1)\sqrt{K}} \tag{8-26}$$

$$C_1 = \frac{1}{(2\pi f_r)^2 L_1} \tag{8-27}$$

$$L_2 = \frac{R_0(b^2-1)\sqrt{K}}{2\pi f_b b^2(K-1)} \tag{8-28}$$

$$C_2 = \frac{1}{(2\pi f_r)^2 L_2} \tag{8-29}$$

$$R_1 = R_0(K-1) \tag{8-30}$$

$$R_2 = \frac{R_0}{K-1} \tag{8-31}$$

where R_0 is the terminating impedance of the filter.

To equalize a low-pass or high-pass filter, a single equalizer is required at the cutoff. For bandpass or band-reject filters, a pair of equalizer sections is needed for the upper and lower cutoff frequencies.

The following example illustrates the design of an equalizer to compensate for low *Q*.

EXAMPLE 8-3

REQUIRED: A low-pass filter should have a theoretical roll-off of 0.1 dB at 2975 Hz but has instead the following response in the vicinity of cutoff due to insufficient *Q*:

2850 Hz   −0.5 dB
2975 Hz   −1.0 dB

Design a shunt nonconstant-impedance equalizer to restore the sagging response. The filter impedance level is 1000 Ω.

RESULT: First make the following preliminary computations:

$$K = 10^{A_{dB}/20} = 10^{1/20} = 1.122 \tag{8-23}$$

$$b = \frac{f_r}{f_b} = \frac{2975 \text{ Hz}}{2850 \text{ Hz}} = 1.0439 \tag{8-24}$$

then

$$L_2 = \frac{R_0(b^2 - 1)\sqrt{K}}{2\pi f_b b^2 (K-1)} = \frac{10^3(1.0439^2 - 1)\sqrt{1.122}}{2\pi 2850 \times 1.0439^2 (1.122 - 1)}$$

$$= 40.0 \text{ mH} \tag{8-28}$$

$$C_2 = \frac{1}{(2\pi f_r)^2 L_2} = \frac{1}{(2\pi 2975)^2 \times 0.04} = 0.0715 \text{ μF} \tag{8-29}$$

$$R_2 = \frac{R_0}{K-1} = \frac{1000}{1.122 - 1} = 8197 \text{ Ω} \tag{8-31}$$

The resulting equalizer is shown in figure 8-18 using the circuit of figure 8-16c.

8.6 COIL-SAVING ELLIPTIC-FUNCTION BANDPASS FILTERS

If an even-order elliptic-function low-pass filter as shown in figure 8-19a is transformed into a bandpass filter using the methods of section 5.1, the bandpass circuit of figure 8-19b is obtained.

A method has been developed to transform the low-pass filter into the configuration of figure 8-19c. The transfer function is unchanged except for a constant multiplier, and 1/2 (*n* − 2) coils are saved in comparison with the conventional transformation. These structures are called minimum-inductance or zigzag bandpass filters. However, this transformation requires a very large number of calculations (see Saal and Ulbrich in bibliography) and is therefore considered impractical without a computer.

Geffe (see bibliography) has presented a series of formulas so that this transformation can be performed on an *n* = 4 low-pass network. A tabulation of low-pass element values for *n* = 4 can be found in either Zverev's *Handbook of Filter Synthesis* or Saal's "Der Entwurf von Filtern mit Hilfe des Kataloges Normierter Tiefpasse" (see bibliography) as well as in table 11-56.

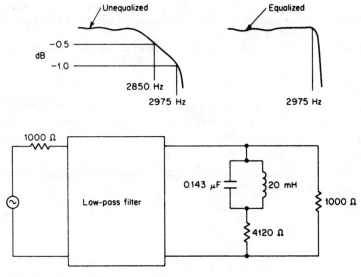

FIGURE 8-18 Equalizer of example 8-3.

The low-pass filter and corresponding bandpass network are shown in figure 8-20. The following preliminary computations are required:

$$Q_{bp} = \frac{f_0}{BW} \tag{8-32}$$

$$a = \frac{\omega_\infty}{2\,Q_{bp}} \tag{8-33}$$

$$x = 1 + \sqrt{a^2 + 1} \tag{8-34}$$

$$t_1 = 1 + \frac{c_3}{c_2} \tag{8-35}$$

$$T = \frac{1 + t_1 x^2}{t_1 + x^2} \tag{8-36}$$

$$k = \frac{Q_{bp}T}{t_1} \tag{8-37}$$

$$t_2 = \frac{x^2}{x^2 + t_1} \tag{8-38}$$

$$t_3 = \frac{t_1 t_2}{T} \tag{8-39}$$

$$\alpha = 1 - \frac{1}{x^2} \tag{8-40}$$

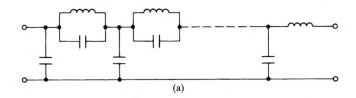

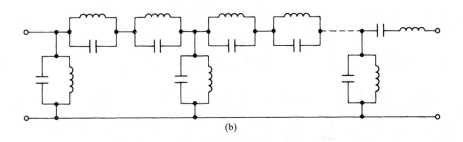

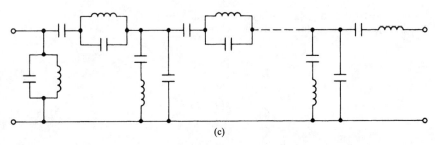

FIGURE 8-19 Coil-saving bandpass transformation: (*a*) elliptic-function low-pass filter; (*b*) conventional bandpass transformation; (*c*) minimum-inductance bandpass transformation.

$$\beta = x^2 - 1 \tag{8-41}$$

$$A = \frac{C_3 k\alpha}{T} \tag{8-42}$$

$$B = \frac{t_2 t_3}{C_3 k\beta} \tag{8-43}$$

The bandpass element values can now be computed as follows:

$$R_L = t_3^2 R \tag{8-44}$$

$$C_{11} = \frac{C_3 k\beta}{t_1 t_2} \tag{8-45}$$

$$C_{12} = \frac{C_3 k\alpha}{T - 1} \tag{8-46}$$

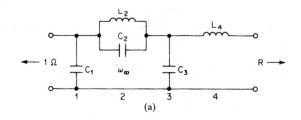

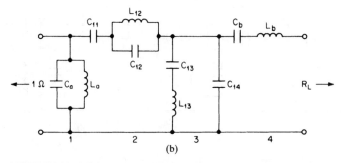

FIGURE 8-20 Minimum-inductance transformation for $n = 4$: (a) $n = 4$ low-pass filter; (b) transformed bandpass filter.

$$L_{12} = \frac{1}{x^2 C_{12}} \tag{8-47}$$

$$C_{13} = \frac{C_{11}(T-1)}{t_2} \tag{8-48}$$

$$L_{13} = \frac{x^2}{C_{13}} \tag{8-49}$$

$$C_{14} = \frac{C_3 k \alpha}{t_2} \tag{8-50}$$

$$L_a = \frac{1}{Q_{bp}\left(C_1 + \dfrac{C_3}{t_1}\right)} \tag{8-51}$$

$$C_a = \frac{1}{L_a} - A \tag{8-52}$$

$$L_b = t_3^2 Q_{bp} L_4 \tag{8-53}$$

$$C_b = \frac{1}{L_b - B} \tag{8-54}$$

The bandpass filter of figure 8-20b must be denormalized to the required impedance level and center frequency f_0. Since the source and load impedance levels are unequal, either the tapped inductor or the capacitance transformation can be used to obtain equal terminations if required.

The transmission zero above the passband is provided by the parallel resonance of $L_{12}C_{12}$ in branch 2 and the lower zero corresponds to the series resonance of $L_{13}C_{13}$ in branch 3. The circuits of branches 2 and 3 each have conditions of both series and parallel resonance and can be transformed from one form to the other. The following equations relate the type 1 and 2 networks shown in figure 8-21:

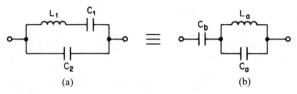

FIGURE 8-21   Equivalent branches: (*a*) type 1 network; (*b*) type 2 network.

For a type 1 network:

$$L_1 = L_a\left(1 + \frac{C_a}{C_b}\right)^2 \tag{8-55}$$

$$C_1 = C_b\frac{1}{1 + \dfrac{C_a}{C_b}} \tag{8-56}$$

$$C_2 = C_a\frac{1}{1 + \dfrac{C_a}{C_b}} \tag{8-57}$$

$$f_{\text{series}} = \frac{1}{2\pi\sqrt{L_1 C_1}} \tag{8-58}$$

$$f_{\text{par}} = \frac{1}{2\pi\sqrt{\dfrac{L_1 C_1 C_2}{C_1 + C_2}}} \tag{8-59}$$

For a type 2 network:

$$L_a = L_1\frac{1}{\left(1 + \dfrac{C_2}{C_1}\right)^2} \tag{8-60}$$

$$C_a = C_2\left(1 + \frac{C_2}{C_1}\right) \tag{8-61}$$

$$C_b = C_1 + C_2 \tag{8-62}$$

$$f_{\text{series}} = \frac{1}{2\pi\sqrt{L_a(C_a + C_b)}} \tag{8-63}$$

$$f_{\text{par}} = \frac{1}{2\pi\sqrt{L_a C_a}} \tag{8-64}$$

In general, the bandpass series arms are of the type 2 form and the shunt branches are of the type 1 form as in figure 8-19c. The tuning usually consists of adjusting the parallel resonances of the series branches and the series resonances of the shunt branches, i.e., the transmission zeros.

8.7 FILTER TUNING METHODS

LC filters are typically assembled using elements with 1 or 2% tolerances. For many applications, the deviation in the desired response caused by component variations may be unacceptable, so adjustment of elements will be required. It has been found that wherever resonances occur, the LC product of the resonant circuit is significantly more critical than the L/C ratio. As a result, filter adjustment normally involves adjusting each tuned circuit for resonance at the specified frequency.

Adjustment techniques are based on the impedance extremes that occur at resonance. In the circuit of figure 8-22a, an output null will occur at parallel resonance because of voltage-divider action. Series LC circuits are tuned using the circuit of figure 8-22b, where an output null will also occur at resonance.

The adjustment method in both cases involves setting the oscillator for the required frequency and adjusting the variable element, usually the inductor, for an output null. Resistors R_L and R_s are chosen so that an approximately 20- to 30-dB drop occurs between the oscillator and the output at resonance. These values can be estimated from

$$R_L \approx \frac{2\pi f_r L_p Q_L}{20} \tag{8-65}$$

and

$$R_s \approx \frac{40\pi f_r L_s}{Q_L} \tag{8-66}$$

where Q_L is the inductor Q. A feature of this technique is that no tuning errors result from stray capacity across the VTVM. Care should be taken that the oscillator does not have excessive distortion, since a sharp null may then be difficult to obtain. Also, excessive levels should be avoided, as detuning can occur from inductor saturation effects.

When inductor Qs are below 10, sharp nulls cannot be obtained. A more desirable tuning method is to adjust for the condition of zero phase shift at resonance,

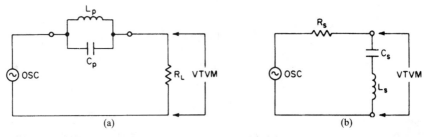

FIGURE 8-22 Test circuits for adjusting resonant frequencies: (a) adjusting parallel resonance; (b) adjusting series resonance.

which will be more distinct than the null. The circuits of figure 8-22 can still be used in conjunction with an oscilloscope having both vertical and horizontal inputs. One channel monitors the oscillator and the other channel is connected to the output instead of using the VTVM. A Lissajous pattern is obtained, and the tuned circuit is then adjusted for a closed ellipse.

Certain construction practices must be used so that the assembled filter can be tuned. There must be provision for access to each tuned circuit on an individual basis. This is usually accomplished by leaving all the grounds disconnected until after tuning so that each branch can be individually inserted into the tuning configurations of figure 8-22 with all the other branches present.

8.8 MEASUREMENT METHODS

This section discusses some major filter parameters and describes techniques for their measurement. Also, some misconceptions associated with these characteristics are clarified. All measurements should be made using rated operating levels so that the results are meaningful. After fabrication, filters should be subjected to insertion-loss and frequency-response measurements as a minimum production test.

Insertion Loss and Frequency Response

The frequency response of filters is always considered as relative to the attenuation occurring at a particular reference frequency. The actual attenuation at this reference is called *insertion loss*.

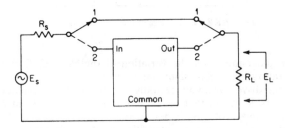

FIGURE 8-23   Test circuit for insertion loss.

The classical definition of insertion loss is the decrease in power delivered to the load when a filter is inserted between the source and the load. Using figure 8-23, the insertion loss is given by

$$IL_{dB} = 10 \log \frac{P_{L1}}{P_{L2}} \tag{8-67}$$

where P_{L1} is the power delivered to the load with both switches in position 1 (filter bypassed) and P_{L2} is the output power with both switches in position 2. Equation (8-67) can also be expressed in terms of a voltage ratio as

$$IL_{dB} = 10 \log \frac{E_{L1}^2/R_L}{E_{L2}^2/R_L} = 20 \log \frac{E_{L1}}{E_{L2}} \tag{8-68}$$

so a decibel meter can be used at the output to measure insertion loss directly in terms of output voltage.

The classical definition of insertion loss may be somewhat inapplicable when the source and load terminations are unequal. In reality, if the filter were not used, the source and load would probably be connected through an impedance-matching transformer instead of a direct connection. Therefore, the comparison of figure 8-23 would be invalid.

An alternate definition is *transducer loss,* which is defined as the decrease in power delivered to the load when an ideal impedance-matching transformer is replaced by the filter. The test circuit of figure 8-23 can still be used if a correction factor is added to equation (8-68). The resulting expression becomes

$$IL_{dB} = 20 \log \frac{E_{L1}}{E_{L2}} + 20 \log \frac{R_s + R_L}{2 \sqrt{R_s R_L}} \tag{8-69}$$

Frequency response or relative attenuation is measured using the test circuit of figure 8-24. The input source E_s is set to the reference frequency and the level is arbitrarily set for a 0-dB reference at the output. As the input frequency is changed, the variation in output level is the relative attenuation.

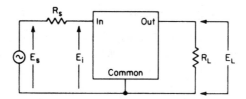

FIGURE 8-24 Test circuit for frequency response.

It must be understood that the variation of the ratio E_L/E_s is the frequency response. The ratio E_L/E_i is of no significance, since it reflects the frequency response of the filter when driven by a voltage source. As the source frequency is varied, the voltage E_s must be kept constant. Any attempt to keep E_i constant will distort the response shape, since voltage-divider action between R_s and the filter input impedance must normally occur to satisfy the transfer function.

The oscillator source itself, E_s, may contain some internal impedance. Nevertheless, the value of R_s should correspond to the design source impedance, since the internal impedance of E_s is allowed for by maintaining the terminal voltage of E_s constant.

Input Impedance of Filter Networks

The input or output impedance of filters must frequently be determined to ensure compatibility with external circuitry. The input impedance of a filter is the impedance measured at the input terminals with the output appropriately terminated. Conversely, the output impedance can be measured by terminating the input.

Let us first consider the test circuit of figure 8-25a. A common fallacy is to adjust the value of R until $|E_2|$ is equal to $\frac{1}{2} |E_1|$, i.e., a 6-dB drop.

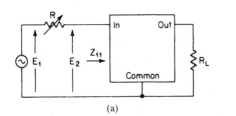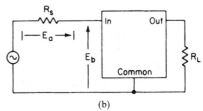

FIGURE 8-25   Measurement of input impedance: (*a*) indirect method; (*b*) direct method.

The input impedance Z_{11} is then said to be equal to R. However, this will be true only if Z_{11} is purely resistive. As an example, if Z_{11} is purely reactive and its absolute magnitude is equal to R, the value of E_2 will be 0.707 or 3 dB below E_1 and not 6 dB.

Using the circuit of figure 8-25*a*, an alternate approach will result in greater accuracy. If R is adjusted until a 20-dB drop occurs between $|E_2|$ and $|E_1|$, then $|Z_{11}|$ is determined by $R/10$. The accuracy will be within 10%. For even more accurate results, the 40-dB method can be used where R is adjusted for a 40-dB drop. The magnitude of Z_{11} is then given by $R/100$.

If a more precise measurement is required, a floating meter can be used in the configuration of figure 8-25*b*. The input impedance is then directly given by

$$|Z_{11}| = \frac{|E_b|}{|E_a|}\, R_s \tag{8-70}$$

Return Loss.   Return loss is a figure of merit which indicates how closely a measured impedance matches a standard impedance, both in magnitude and in phase angle. Return loss is expressed as

$$A_\rho = 20\log\left|\frac{Z_s + Z_x}{Z_s - Z_x}\right| \tag{8-71}$$

where Z_s is the standard impedance and Z_x is the measured impedance. For a perfect match, the return loss would be infinite.

Return loss can be directly measured using the bridge arrangement of figure 8-26. The return loss is given by

$$A_p = 20\log\left|\frac{V_{01}}{V_{02}}\right| \tag{8-72}$$

where V_{01} is the output voltage with the switch closed and V_{02} is the output voltage with the switch open. The return loss can then be read directly using a decibel meter. The value of R is arbitrary, but both resistors must be closely matched to each other.

The family of curves in figure 8-27 represents the return loss using a standard impedance of 600 Ω with phase angle of impedance as a parameter. Clearly the return loss is very sensitive

FIGURE 8-26   Measurement of return loss.

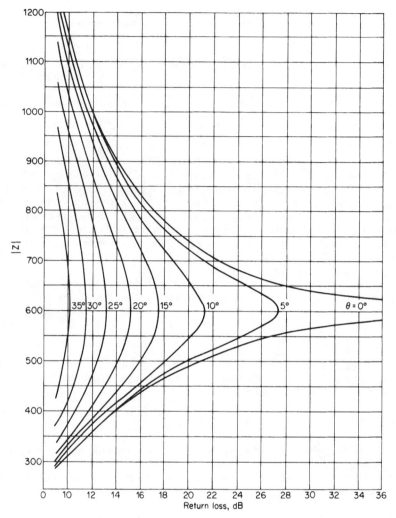

FIGURE 8-27   Return loss vs. |Z|.

to phase angle. If the impedance were 600 Ω at an angle of only 10°, the return loss would be 21 dB. If there was no phase shift, an impedance error of as much as 100 Ω would correspond to 21 dB of return loss.

Time-Domain Characteristics

Step Response.   The step response of a filter network is a useful criterion since low transient distortion is a necessary requirement for good transmission of modulated signals. To determine the step response of a low-pass filter, an input DC step is applied. For bandpass filters a carrier step is used where the carrier frequency is equal to the filter center frequency f_0. Since it is difficult to view a single transient on an oscilloscope unless it is of the storage type, a square-wave generator is used instead of the DC step and a tone-burst generator is substituted for the carrier step. However, the repetition rate must be chosen that is slow enough that the transient behavior has stabilized prior to the next pulse to obtain meaningful results.

The test configuration is shown in figure 8-28a. The output waveforms are depicted in figures 8-28b and c for a DC step and tone burst, respectively. The following definitions are applicable:

Percent overshoot P_T: The difference between the peak response and the final steady-state value expressed as a percentage

Rise time T_r: The interval between 10 and 90% of the final value

Settling time T_s: Time required for the response to settle within a specified percent of its final value

The waveform definitions shown in figure 8-28b also apply to figure 8-28c if we consider the envelope of the carrier waveform instead of the instantaneous values.

Group Delay.   The phase shift of a filter can be measured by using the Lissajous pattern method. By connecting the vertical channel of an oscilloscope to the input source and the horizontal channel to the load, an ellipse is obtained, as shown in figure 8-29. The phase angle in degrees is given by

$$\phi = \sin^{-1} \frac{Y_{int}}{Y_{max}} \qquad (8\text{-}73)$$

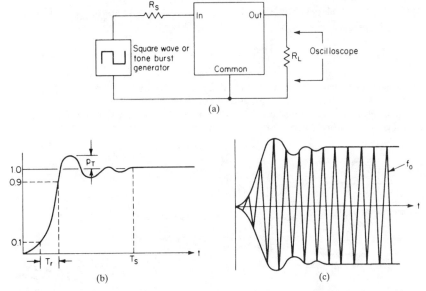

FIGURE 8-28   Step response of networks: (*a*) test circuit; (*b*) step response to DC step; (*c*) step response to tone burst.

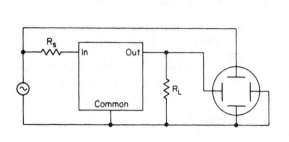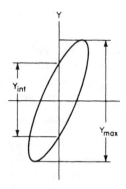

FIGURE 8-29   Measurement of phase shift.

Since group delay is the derivative with respect to frequency of the phase shift, we can measure the phase shift at two closely spaced frequencies and approximate the delay as follows:

$$T_{gd} \approx \frac{\Delta\phi}{360\Delta f} \qquad (8\text{-}74)$$

where $\Delta\phi$ is $\phi_2 - \phi_1$ in degrees, Δf is $f_2 - f_1$ in hertz, and T_{gd} is the group delay at the midfrequency, i.e., $(f_1 + f_2)/2$.

A less accurate method involves determining the 180° phase-shift points. As the frequency is varied throughout the passband of a high-order filter, the phase shift will go through many integer multiples of 180° where the Lissajous pattern adopts a straight line at either 45° or 225°. If we record the separation between adjacent 180° points, the nominal group delay at the midfrequency can be approximated by

$$T_{gd} \approx \frac{1}{2\Delta f} \qquad (8\text{-}75)$$

The classical approach for the measurement of group delay directly is shown in figure 8-30. A sine-wave source, typically 25 Hz, is applied to an amplitude modulator along with a carrier signal. The output consists of an amplitude-modulated signal comprising the carrier and two sidebands at ±25 Hz on either side of the carrier. The signal is then applied to the network under test.

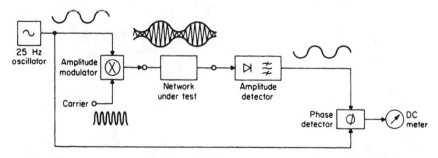

FIGURE 8-30   Direct measurement of group delay.

The output signal from the network is of the same form as the input, but the 25-Hz envelope has been shifted in time by an amount equal to the group delay at the carrier frequency. The output envelope is recovered by an AM detector and applied to a phase detector along with a reference 25-Hz signal.

The phase detector output is a DC signal proportional to the phase shift between the 25-Hz reference and the demodulated 25-Hz carrier envelope. As the carrier is varied in frequency, the DC signal will vary in accordance with the change in group delay (differential delay distortion) and the delay can be displayed on a DC meter having the proper calibration. If an adjustable phase-shift network is interposed between the AM detector and phase detector, the meter indication can be adjusted to establish a reference level at a desired reference frequency.

The theoretical justification for this scheme is based on the fact that the delay of the envelope is determined by the slope of a line segment interconnecting the phase shift of the two sidebands at ±25 Hz about the carrier, i.e., $(\phi_2 - \phi_1)/(\omega_2 - \omega_1)$. This definition is sometimes called the *envelope delay,* for obvious reasons. As the separation between sidebands is decreased, the envelope delay approaches the theoretical group delay at the carrier frequency, since group delay is defined as the derivative of the phase shift. For most measurements, a modulation rate of 25 Hz is adequate.

Measuring the *Q* of Inductors

A device called a *Q meter* is frequently used to measure the *Q* of inductors at a specified frequency. The principle of the *Q* meter is based on the fact that in a series resonant circuit, the voltage across each reactive element is *Q* times the voltage applied to the resonant circuit. The *Q* can then be directly determined by the ratio of two voltages.

A test circuit is shown in figure 8-31*a*. Care should be taken that the applied voltage does not result in an excessive voltage developed across the inductor during the measurement. Also, the resonating capacitor should have a much higher *Q* than the inductor, and the meter used for the voltage measurements should be a high-impedance type to avoid loading errors.

An alternate approach involves measuring the impedance of a parallel resonant circuit consisting of the inductor and the required resonating capacitor for the frequency of interest. Using the voltage divider of figure 8-31*b*, the *Q* at resonance is found from

$$Q = \frac{R}{2\pi f_r L} \left(\frac{V_1}{V_2} - 1 \right) \tag{8-76}$$

A null will occur in V_2 at resonance.

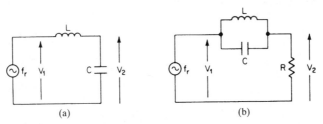

FIGURE 8-31 Measurement of coil *Q*: (*a*) *Q* meter method; (*b*) parallel resonant circuit method.

For meaningful Q measurements, it is important that the measurement frequency corresponds to the frequency of interest of the filter, since coil Q can decrease quite dramatically outside a particular range. In low-pass and high-pass filters, the Q should be measured at the cutoff, and for bandpass and band-reject filters, the center frequency is the frequency of interest.

BIBLIOGRAPHY

Geffe, P. R., *Simplified Modern Filter Design,* John F. Rider, New York, 1963.

Saal, R., "Der Entwurf von Filtern mit Hilfe des Kataloges Normierter Tiefpasse," Telefunken GMBH, Backnang, West Germany, 1963.

Saal, R., and E. Ulbrich, "On the Design of Filters by Synthesis," *IRE Transactions on Circuit Theory,* vol. CT-5, December 1958.

Zverev, A. I., *Handbook of Filter Synthesis,* John Wiley and Sons, New York, 1967.

frequency separator

CHAPTER 9

DESIGN OF MAGNETIC COMPONENTS

9.1 BASIC PRINCIPLES OF MAGNETIC-CIRCUIT DESIGN

Units of Measurement

Magnetic permeability is represented by the symbol μ and is defined by

$$\mu = \frac{B}{H} \tag{9-1}$$

B is the magnetic flux density in lines per square centimeter and is measured in gauss, and H is the magnetizing force in oersteds that produced the flux. Permeability is dimensionless and can be considered a figure of merit of a particular magnetic material, since it represents the ease of producing a magnetic flux for a given input. The permeability of air or that of a vacuum is 1.

Magnetizing force is caused by current flowing through turns of wire; so H can be determined from ampere-turns by

$$H = \frac{4\pi NI}{10 \text{ mL}} \qquad \frac{0.4\pi NI}{\ell e} \tag{9-2}$$

where N is the number of turns, I is the current in amperes, and mL is the mean length of the magnetic path in centimeters.

The inductance of a coil is directly proportional to the number of flux linkages per unit current. The total flux is found from

$$\phi = BA = \mu HA = \frac{4\pi NI\mu A}{10 \text{ mL}} \tag{9-3}$$

where A is the cross-sectional area in square centimeters.

The inductance proportionality may then be expressed as

$$L \propto \frac{4\pi NI\mu A}{10 \text{ mL}} \frac{N}{I} \tag{9-4}$$

9.1

or directly in henrys by

$$L = \frac{4\pi N^2 \mu A}{mL} \, 10^{-9} \tag{9-5}$$

A number of things should be apparent from equation (9-5). First of all, the inductance of a coil is directly proportional to the permeability of the core material. If an iron core is inserted into an air-core inductor, the inductance will increase in direct proportion to the iron core's permeability. The inductance is also proportional to N^2.

All the previous design equations make the assumption that the magnetic path is uniform and closed with negligible leakage flux in the surrounding air such as would occur with a single-layer toroidal coil structure. However, this assumption is really never completely valid, so some deviations from the theory can be expected.

The induced voltage of an inductor can be related to the flux density by

$$E_{rms} = 4.44 BNfA \times 10^{-8} \tag{9-6}$$

where B is the maximum flux density in gauss, N is the number of turns, f is the frequency in hertz, and A is the cross-sectional area of the core in square centimeters. This important equation is derived from Faraday's law.

Saturation and DC Polarization

A plot of B vs. H is shown in figure 9-1. Let us start at point A and increase the magnetizing force to point B. A decrease in magnetizing force will pass through point C and then D and E as the magnetizing force is made negative. An increasing magnetizing force, again in the positive direction, will travel to B through point F. The enclosed area formed by the curve is called a *hysteresis loop* and results from the energy required to reverse the magnetic molecules of the core. The magnitude of H between points D and A is called *coercive force* and is the amount of H necessary to reduce the residual magnetism in the core to zero.

Permeability was defined as the ratio B/H and can be obtained from the slope of the BH curve. Since we normally deal with low-level AC signals, the region of interest is restricted to a relatively narrow range. We can then assume that the permeability is determined by the derivative of the curve at the origin. The derivative of a B/H curve is sometimes called *incremental permeability*.

If a DC bias is introduced, the quiescent point will move from the origin to a point farther out on the curve. Since the curve tends to flatten out with higher values of H, the incremental permeability will decrease, which reduces the inductance. This effect is known as *saturation* and can also occur without a DC

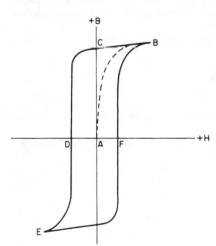

FIGURE 9-1 Hysteresis loop.

bias for large AC signals. Severe waveform distortion usually accompanies saturation. The B/H curve for an air core is a straight line at a 45° angle through the origin. The permeability is unity, and no saturation can occur.

Inductor Losses

The Q of a coil can be found from

$$Q = \frac{\omega L}{R_{dc} + R_{ac} + R_d} \tag{9-7}$$

where R_{dc} is the copper loss, R_{ac} is the core loss, and R_d is the dielectric loss. Copper loss consists strictly of the DC winding resistance and is determined by the wire size and total length of wire required. The core loss is composed mostly of losses due to eddy currents and hysteresis. Eddy currents are induced in the core material by changing magnetic fields. These circulating currents produce losses that are proportional to the square of the inducing frequency.

When a core is subjected to an AC or pulsating DC magnetic field, the B vs. H characteristics can be represented by the curve of figure 9-1. The enclosed area was called a hysteresis loop and resulted from the energy required to reverse the magnetic molecules of the core. These core losses increase in direct proportion to frequency, since each cycle traverses the hysteresis loop.

The dielectric losses are important at higher frequencies and are determined by the power factor of the distributed capacity. Keeping the distributed capacity small as well as using wire insulation with good dielectric properties will minimize dielectric losses.

Above approximately 50 kHz the current will tend to travel on the surface of a conductor rather than through the cross section. This phenomenon is called *skin effect*. To reduce this effect, litz wire is commonly used. This wire consists of many braided strands of insulated conductors so that a larger surface area is available in comparison with a single solid conductor of the equivalent cross section. Above 1 or 2 MHz, solid wire can again be used.

A figure of merit of the efficiency of a coil at low frequencies is the ratio of ohms per henry (Ω/H), where the ohms correspond to R_{dc}, i.e., the copper losses. For a given coil structure and permeability, the ratio Ω/H is a constant independent of the total number of turns, provided that the winding cross-sectional area is kept constant.

Effect of an Air Gap

If an ideal toroidal core has a narrow air gap introduced, the flux will decrease and the permeability is reduced. The resulting effective permeability can be found from

$$\mu_e = \frac{\mu_i}{1 + \mu_i \left(\dfrac{g}{mL} \right)} \tag{9-8}$$

where μ_i is the initial permeability of the core and g/mL is the ratio of gap to length of the magnetic path. Equation (9-8) applies to closed magnetic structures of any shape if the initial permeability is high and the gap ratio small.

The effect of an air gap is to reduce the permeability and make the coil's characteristics less dependent upon the initial permeability of the core material. However, lower permeability requires more turns and the associated copper losses, so a suitable compromise is required.

Design of Coil Windings

Inductors are normally wound using insulated copper wire. The general method used to express wire size is the American Wire Gauge (AWG) system. As the wire

TABLE 9-1   Wire Chart—Round Heavy Film Insulated Solid Copper*

AWG	Diameter over Bare, in			Insulation Additions		Diameter over Insulation		Pounds per 1000 Feet
	Minimum	Nominal	Maximum	Minimum	Maximum	Minimum	Maximum	
4	0.2023	0.2043	0.2053	0.0037	0.0045	0.2060	0.2098	127.20
5	0.1801	0.1819	0.1828	0.0036	0.0044	0.1837	0.1872	100.84
6	0.1604	0.1620	0.1628	0.0035	0.0043	0.1639	0.1671	80.00
7	0.1429	0.1443	0.1450	0.0034	0.0041	0.1463	0.1491	63.51
8	0.1272	0.1285	0.1292	0.0033	0.0040	0.1305	0.1332	50.39
9	0.1133	0.1144	0.1150	0.0032	0.0039	0.1165	0.1189	39.98
10	0.1009	0.1019	0.1024	0.0031	0.0037	0.1040	0.1061	31.74
11	0.0898	0.0907	0.0912	0.0030	0.0036	0.0928	0.0948	25.16
12	0.0800	0.0808	0.0812	0.0029	0.0035	0.0829	0.0847	20.03
13	0.0713	0.0720	0.0724	0.0028	0.0033	0.0741	0.0757	15.89
14	0.0635	0.0641	0.0644	0.0032	0.0038	0.0667	0.0682	12.60
15	0.0565	0.0571	0.0574	0.0030	0.0035	0.0595	0.0609	10.04
16	0.0503	0.0508	0.0511	0.0029	0.0034	0.0532	0.0545	7.95
17	0.0448	0.0453	0.0455	0.0028	0.0033	0.0476	0.0488	6.33
18	0.0399	0.0403	0.0405	0.0026	0.0032	0.0425	0.0437	5.03
19	0.0355	0.0359	0.0361	0.0025	0.0030	0.0380	0.0391	3.99
20	0.0317	0.0320	0.0322	0.0023	0.0029	0.0340	0.0351	3.18
21	0.0282	0.0285	0.0286	0.0022	0.0028	0.0302	0.0314	2.53
22	0.0250	0.0253	0.0254	0.0021	0.0027	0.0271	0.0281	2.00
23	0.0224	0.0226	0.0227	0.0020	0.0026	0.0244	0.0253	1.60
24	0.0199	0.0201	0.0202	0.0019	0.0025	0.0218	0.0227	1.26
25	0.0177	0.0179	0.0180	0.0018	0.0023	0.0195	0.0203	1.00
26	0.0157	0.0159	0.0160	0.0017	0.0022	0.0174	0.0182	0.794
27	0.0141	0.0142	0.0143	0.0016	0.0021	0.0157	0.0164	0.634
28	0.0125	0.0126	0.0127	0.0016	0.0020	0.0141	0.0147	0.502
29	0.0112	0.0113	0.0114	0.0015	0.0019	0.0127	0.0133	0.405
30	0.0099	0.0100	0.0101	0.0014	0.0018	0.0113	0.0119	0.318
31	0.0088	0.0089	0.0090	0.0013	0.0018	0.0101	0.0108	0.253
32	0.0079	0.0080	0.0081	0.0012	0.0017	0.0091	0.0098	0.205
33	0.0070	0.0071	0.0072	0.0011	0.0016	0.0081	0.0088	0.162
34	0.0062	0.0063	0.0064	0.0010	0.0014	0.0072	0.0078	0.127
35	0.0055	0.0056	0.0057	0.0009	0.0013	0.0064	0.0070	0.101
36	0.0049	0.0050	0.0051	0.0008	0.0012	0.0057	0.0063	0.0805
37	0.0044	0.0045	0.0046	0.0008	0.0011	0.0052	0.0057	0.0655
38	0.0039	0.0040	0.0041	0.0007	0.0010	0.0046	0.0051	0.0518
39	0.0034	0.0035	0.0036	0.0006	0.0009	0.0040	0.0045	0.0397
40	0.0030	0.0031	0.0032	0.0006	0.0008	0.0036	0.0040	0.0312
41	0.0027	0.0028	0.0029	0.0005	0.0007	0.0032	0.0036	0.0254
42	0.0024	0.0025	0.0026	0.0004	0.0006	0.0028	0.0032	0.0203

* Courtesy Belden Corp.

size numerically decreases, the diameter increases, where the ratio of diameters of one size to the next larger size is 1.1229. The ratio of cross-sectional areas of adjacent wire sizes corresponds to the square of the diameter, or 1.261. Therefore, for an available cross-sectional winding area, reducing the wire by one size permits 1.261 times as many turns. Two wire sizes correspond to a factor of 1.261^2, or 1.59, and three wire sizes permit twice as many turns.

Physical and electrical properties of a range of wire sizes are given in the wire chart of table 9-1. These data are based on using a standard heavy film for the insulation. In the past, enamel insulations were used which required acid or abrasives for stripping the insulation from the wire ends to make electrical connections. Solder-

TABLE 9-1　Wire Chart—Round Heavy Film Insulated Solid Copper (*Continued*)

Weight		Resistance at 20°C (68°F)			Turns		
Feet per Pound	Pounds per Cubic Inch	Ohms per 1000 Feet	Ohms per Pound	Ohms per Cubic Inch	Per Linear Inch	Per Square Inch	AWG
7.86	0.244	0.2485	0.001954	0.0004768	4.80	24.0	4
9.92	0.243	0.3134	0.003108	0.0007552	5.38	28.9	5
12.50	0.242	0.3952	0.004940	0.001195	6.03	36.4	6
15.75	0.241	0.4981	0.007843	0.001890	6.75	45.6	7
19.85	0.240	0.6281	0.01246	0.002791	7.57	57.3	8
25.0	0.239	0.7925	0.01982	0.004737	8.48	71.9	9
31.5	0.238	0.9988	0.03147	0.007490	9.50	90.3	10
39.8	0.237	1.26	0.0501	0.0119	10.6	112	11
49.9	0.236	1.59	0.0794	0.0187	11.9	142	12
62.9	0.235	2.00	0.126	0.0296	13.3	177	13
82.9	0.230	2.52	0.200	0.0460	14.8	219	14
99.6	0.229	3.18	0.317	0.0726	16.6	276	15
126	0.228	4.02	0.506	0.115	18.5	342	16
158	0.226	5.05	0.798	0.180	20.7	428	17
199	0.224	6.39	1.27	0.284	23.1	534	18
251	0.223	8.05	2.02	0.450	25.9	671	19
314	0.221	10.1	3.18	0.703	28.9	835	20
395	0.219	12.8	5.06	1.11	32.3	1,043	21
500	0.217	16.2	8.10	1.76	36.1	1,303	22
625	0.215	20.3	12.7	2.73	40.2	1,616	23
794	0.211	25.7	20.4	4.30	44.8	2,007	24
1,000	0.210	32.4	32.4	6.80	50.1	2,510	25
1,259	0.208	41.0	51.6	10.7	56.0	3,136	26
1,577	0.205	51.4	81.1	16.6	62.3	3,831	27
1,992	0.202	65.3	130	26.3	69.4	4,816	28
2,469	0.200	81.2	200	40.0	76.9	5,914	29
3,145	0.197	104	327	64.4	86.2	7,430	30
4,000	0.193	131	520	100	96	9,200	31
4,900	0.191	162	790	151	106	11,200	32
6,200	0.189	206	1,270	240	118	13,900	33
7,900	0.189	261	2,060	388	133	17,700	34
9,900	0.187	331	3,280	613	149	22,200	35
12,400	0.186	415	5,150	959	167	27,900	36
15,300	0.184	512	7,800	1,438	183	33,500	37
19,300	0.183	648	12,500	2,289	206	42,400	38
25,200	0.183	847	21,300	3,904	235	55,200	39
32,100	0.183	1,080	34,600	6,335	263	69,200	40
39,400	0.183	1,320	52,000	9,510	294	86,400	41
49,300	0.182	1,660	81,800	14,883	328	107,600	42

able insulations have been available for the last 20 years, so that the wire ends can be easily tinned. In the event that litz wire is required, a cross reference between litz wire sizes and the solid equivalent is given in table 9-2. The convention for specifying litz wire is number of strands/wire size. For example, using the chart, a litz equivalent to No. 31 solid is 20 strands of No. 44, or 20/44. In general a large number of strands is desirable for more effective surface area.

The temperature coefficient of resistance for copper is 0.393% per degree Celsius. The DC resistance of a winding at a particular temperature is given by

$$R_{t_1} = R_t[1 + 0.00393\,(t_1 - t)] \tag{9-9}$$

where t is the initial temperature and t_1 is the final temperature, both in degrees Celsius. The maximum permitted temperature of most wire insulations is about 130°C.

To compute the number of turns for a required inductance, the inductance factor for the coil structure must be used. This factor is generally called A_L and is the nominal inductance per 1000 turns. Since inductance is proportional to the number of turns squared, the required number of turns N for an inductance L is given by

$$N = 10^3 \sqrt{\frac{L}{A_L}} \tag{9-10}$$

where L and A_L must be in identical units.

After the required number of turns is computed, a wire size must be chosen. For each winding structure an associated chart can be tabulated which indicates the

TABLE 9-2   Stranded Wire Equivalent Chart

Solid Equivalent	Size per Strand										
	34	35	36	37	38	39	40	41	42	43	44
15	80	100									
16	64	80	100								
17	50	64	80	100							
18	40	50	64	80	100						
19	32	40	50	64	80	100					
20	25	32	40	50	64	80	100				
21	20	25	32	40	50	64	80	100			
22	16	20	25	32	40	50	64	80	100		
23	12	16	20	25	32	40	50	64	80	100	
24	10	12	16	20	25	32	40	50	64	80	100
25	8	10	12	16	20	25	32	40	50	64	80
26	6	8	10	12	16	20	25	32	40	50	64
27	5	6	8	10	12	16	20	25	32	40	50
28	4	5	6	8	10	12	16	20	25	32	40
29		4	5	6	8	10	12	16	20	25	32
30			4	5	6	8	10	12	16	20	25
31				4	5	6	8	10	12	16	20
32					4	5	6	8	10	12	16
33						4	5	6	8	10	12
34							4	5	6	8	10
35								4	5	6	8
36									4	5	6
37										4	5
38											4

maximum number of turns for each wire size. A wire size can then be chosen which results in the maximum utilization of the available winding cross-sectional area.

Coil winding methods are very diverse since the winding techniques depend upon the actual coil structure, the operating frequency range, etc. Coil winding techniques are discussed in the remainder of this chapter on an individual basis for each coil structure type.

9.2 TOROIDAL COILS

Toroidal cores are manufactured by pulverizing a magnetic alloy consisting of approximately 2% molybdenum, 81% nickel, and 17% iron into a fine powder, insulating the powder with a ceramic binder to form a uniformly distributed air gap, and then compressing it into a toroidal core at extremely high pressures. Finally, the cores are coated with an insulating finish.

Molypermalloy powder cores (MPP cores) result in extremely stable inductive components for use below a few hundred kilohertz. Core losses are low over a wide range of available permeabilities. Inductance remains stable with large changes in flux density, frequency, temperature, and DC magnetization due to high resistivity, low hysteresis, and low eddy-current losses.

Characteristics of Cores

MPP cores are categorized according to size, permeability, and temperature stability. Generally, the largest core size that physical and economical considerations permit should be chosen. Larger cores offer higher Qs, since flux density is lower due to the larger cross-sectional area, resulting in lower core losses, and the larger window area reduces the copper losses.

Cores range in size from an OD of 0.155 to 2.250 in. Table 9-3 contains physical data for some selected core sizes as well as the approximate overall dimensions for the wound coil.

Available core permeabilities range from 14 to 550. The lower permeabilities are more suitable for use at the higher frequencies, since the core losses are lower. Table 9-4 lists the A_L (inductance per 1000 turns) and ohms per henry for cores with a permeability of 125. For other permeabilities, the A_L is directly proportional to μ and the ohms per henry is inversely proportional to μ. The ohms per henry corresponds to the DC resistance factor when the core window is approximately 50% utilized. Full window utilization is not possible, since a hole must be provided for a shuttle in the coil winding machine which applies the turns. The corresponding wire chart for each size core is given in table 9-5.

DC Bias and AC Flux Density.   Under conditions of DC bias current, MPP cores may exhibit a reduction in permeability because of the effects of saturation. Figure 9-2 illustrates this effect, which is more pronounced for higher permeabilities. To use these curves, the magnetizing force for the design is computed using equation (9-2). If the reduction in permeability and resulting inductance decrease is no more than about 30%, the turns can be increased to compensate for the effect of the bias. If the decrease in permeability is more than 30%, the permeability will further decrease faster than N^2 if turns are added. A larger core is then required.

The core permeability will also change as a function of AC flux density. This effect is shown in figure 9-3. The flux density can be computed using equation (9-6). As the

TABLE 9-3 Toroidal Core Dimensions

OD, in	ID, in	HT, in	Cross Section, cm²	Path Length, cm	Window Area, circular mils	Wound OD, in	Coil HT, in
0.310	0.156	0.125	0.0615	1.787	18,200	11/32	3/16
0.500	0.300	0.187	0.114	3.12	75,600	19/32	9/32
0.650	0.400	0.250	0.192	4.11	140,600	25/32	3/8
0.800	0.500	0.250	0.226	5.09	225,600	1	3/8
0.900	0.550	0.300	0.331	5.67	277,700	1 3/32	1/2
1.060	0.580	0.440	0.654	6.35	308,000	1 1/4	5/8
1.350	0.920	0.350	0.454	8.95	788,500	1 5/8	5/8
1.570	0.950	0.570	1.072	9.84	842,700	1 7/8	7/8
2.000	1.250	0.530	1.250	12.73	1,484,000	2 3/8	1 1/8

NOTE: Core dimensions are before finish.

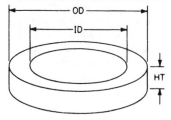

AC flux density is increased, the permeability will rise initially and then fall beyond approximately 2000 G. Flux density can be reduced by going to a larger core size.

The core losses can be assumed to be relatively constant for flux densities below 200 G. For higher excitations, the Q may be adversely affected.

Temperature Stability.   MPP cores are available in three categories of temperature stabilities: unstabilized, stabilized, and linear. Stabilizing techniques are based on the addition of a small amount of special compensating alloys having curie points within the temperature range of operation. (The curie point is the temperature where the material becomes nonmagnetic.) As each curie point is passed, the particles act as distributed air gaps which can be used to compensate for permeability changes of the basic alloy so as to maintain the inductance nearly constant.

TABLE 9-4   Electrical Properties for $\mu = 125$

OD, in	A_L, mH	Ω/H
0.310	52	900
0.500	56	480
0.650	72	160
0.800	68	220
0.900	90	150
1.060	157	110
1.350	79	80
1.570	168	45
2.000	152	30

TABLE 9-5 Wire Capacities of Standard Toroidal Cores

					Core OD, in				
Wire Size	0.310	0.500	0.650	0.800	0.900	1.060	1.350	1.570	2.000
25		75	148	189	257	284	750	930	1,735
26		95	186	238	323	357	946	1,172	2,180
27		119	235	300	406	450	1,190	1,470	2,750
28		150	295	377	513	567	1,500	1,860	3,470
29		190	375	475	646	714	1,890	2,350	4,365
30	59	238	472	605	814	925	2,390	2,960	5,550
31	74	300	595	765	1,025	1,180	3,000	3,720	7,090
32	94	376	750	985	1,290	1,510	3,780	4,700	9,000
33	118	475	945	1,250	1,625	1,970	4,763	5,920	11,450
34	150	600	1,190	1,580	2,050	2,520	6,000	7,440	14,550
35	188	753	1,500	2,000	2,585	3,170	7,560	9,400	18,500
36	237	950	1,890	2,520	3,245	4,000	9,510	11,840	23,500
37	300	1,220	2,380	3,170	4,100	5,050	12,000	14,880	30,000
38	378	1,550	3,000	4,000	5,175	6,300	15,150	18,800	38,000
39	476	1,970	3,780	5,050	6,510	8,000	19,050	23,680	48,500
40	600	2,500	4,750	6,300	8,200	10,100	24,000	30,000	61,300
41	755								
42	950								
43	1,200								
44	1,510								
45	1,900								

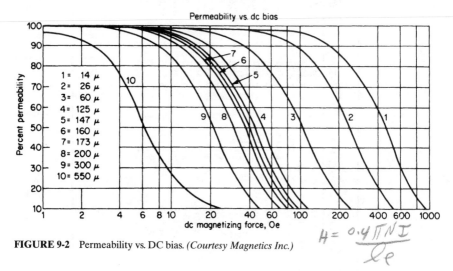

FIGURE 9-2   Permeability vs. DC bias. *(Courtesy Magnetics Inc.)*

$$H = \frac{0.4 \pi N I}{\ell_e}$$

Unstabilized cores, also called "A" stabilization, have no guaranteed limits for permeability variations with temperature. Typically the temperature coefficient of permeability is positive and ranges from 25 to 100 ppm/°C, but these limits are not guaranteed. Stabilized cores, on the other hand, have guaranteed limits over wide temperature ranges. These cores are available in three degrees of stabilization, M, W, and D. The limits are as given in table 9-6.

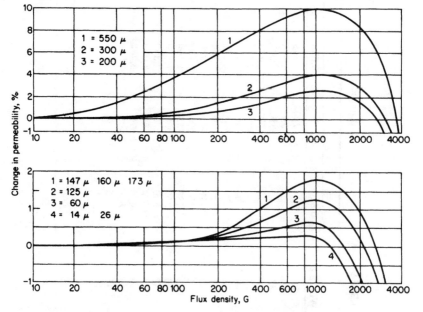

FIGURE 9-3   Permeability vs. AC flux density. *(Courtesy Magnetics Inc.)*

TABLE 9-6 Stabilized Cores

Stabilization	Temperature Range, °C	Inductance Stability, %
M	−65 to +125	±0.25
W	−55 to +85	±0.25
D	0 to +55	±0.1

Because of the nature of the compensation technique, the slope of inductance change with temperature can be either positive or negative within the temperature range of operation but will not exceed the guaranteed limits.

Polystyrene capacitors maintain a precise temperature coefficient of −120 ppm/°C from −55 to +85°C. Cores are available which provide a matching positive temperature coefficient so that a constant LC product can be maintained over the temperature range of operation. These cores are said to have linear temperature characteristics. Two types of linear temperature characteristics can be obtained. The L6 degree of stabilization has a positive temperature coefficient ranging between +25 and +90 ppm/°C from −55°C to +25°C and between +65 and +150 ppm/°C over the temperature range of +25 to +85°C.

In general, the temperature stability of MPP cores is affected by factors such as winding stresses and moisture. To minimize these factors, suitable precautions can be taken. Before adjustment, the coils should be temperature-cycled from −55 to +100°C at least once. After cooling to room temperature, the coils are adjusted and should be kept dry until encapsulated. Encapsulation compounds should be chosen carefully to minimize mechanical stresses. A common technique involves dipping the coils in a silicon rubber compound for a cushioning and sealing effect prior to encapsulation.

Winding Methods for Q Optimization

At low frequencies, the dominant losses are caused by the DC resistance of the winding. The major consideration then is to utilize the maximum possible winding area. Distributed capacity is of little consequence unless the inductance is extremely high, causing self-resonance to occur near the operating frequency range.

The most efficient method of packing the most turns on a toroidal core is to rotate the core continuously in the same direction in the winding machine until maximum capacity is obtained. This technique is called the *360° method.*

At medium frequencies, special winding techniques are required to minimize distributed capacity. By winding half the turns over a 180° sector of the core in a back-and-forth manner and then applying the remaining turns over the second half in the same fashion, the capacity will be reduced. This technique is called the *two-section method.* If after winding half the turns the coil is removed from the machine, turned over, reinserted, and completed, the two starts can be tied together, and the resulting coil using the two finishes as terminals has even less capacity. This modified two-section winding structure is commonly referred to as *two-section reversed.*

If the core is divided into four 90° quadrants and each sector is completed in a back-and-forth winding fashion using one-fourth the total turns, a four-section coil will be obtained. A four-section winding structure has lower distributed capacity than the two-section method. However, whereas the two-section and 360° methods correspond to the wire chart of table 9-5, the wire must be reduced one size for a four-section coil, resulting in more copper losses.

At frequencies near 50 kHz or higher, the distributed capacity becomes a serious limiting factor of the obtainable Q from both self-resonance and dielectric losses of the winding insulation. The optimum winding method for minimizing distributed capacity is *back-to-back progressive*. Half the total number of turns are applied over a 180° sector of the core by gradually filling up a 30° sector at a time. The core is then removed from the machine, turned over, reinserted in the machine, and completed in the same manner. The two starts are joined and the two finish leads are used for the coil terminals. A barrier is frequently used to separate the two finish leads for further capacity reduction. Litz wire can be combined with the back-to-back progressive winding method to reduce skin-effect losses. As with a four-section winding, the wire must be reduced one size from the wire chart of table 9-5. If the core is not removed from the winding machine after completion of a 180° sector but instead is continued for approximately 360°, a *straight-progressive* type of winding is obtained. Although slightly inferior to the back-to-back progressive, the reduction in winding time will frequently warrant its use.

When a coil includes a tap, a coefficient of magnetic coupling near unity is desirable to avoid leakage inductance. The 360° winding method will have a typical coefficient of coupling of about 0.99 for permeabilities of 125 and higher. A two-section winding has a coefficient of coupling near 0.8. The four-section and progressive winding methods result in coupling coefficients of approximately 0.3, which is usually unacceptable. A compromise between the 360° and the progressive method to improve coupling for tapped inductors involves applying the turns up to the tap in a straight-progressive fashion over the total core. The remaining turns are then distributed completely over the initial winding, also using the straight-progressive method.

In general, to obtain good coupling, the portion of the winding up to the tap should be in close proximity to the remainder of the winding. However, this results in higher distributed capacity, so a compromise may be desirable. Higher core permeability will increase the coupling but can sometimes result in excessive core loss. The higher the ratio of overall to tap inductance, the lower the corresponding coefficient of coupling. Inductance ratios of 10 or more should be avoided if possible.

Designing MPP Toroids from Q Curves

The Q curves given in figure 9-4 are based on empirical data using the 360° winding method. The range of distributed capacity is typically between 10 and 25 pF for cores under 0.500 in OD, 25 to 50 pF for cores between 0.500 and 1.500 in OD, and 50 to 80 pF for cores over 1.500 in OD.

Curves are presented for permeabilities of 60 and 125 and for a range of core sizes. For a given size and permeability, the Q curves converge on the low-frequency portion of the curve, where the losses are determined almost exclusively by the DC resistance of the winding. The Q in this region can be approximated by

$$Q = \frac{2\pi f}{\Omega/H} \qquad (9\text{-}11)$$

where f is the frequency of interest and Ω/H is the rated ohms per henry of the core as given by table 9-4 and modified for permeability if other than 125.

As the frequency is increased, the curves start to diverge and reach a maximum at a frequency where the copper and core losses are equal. Beyond this region the core losses begin to dominate along with increased dielectric losses and self-

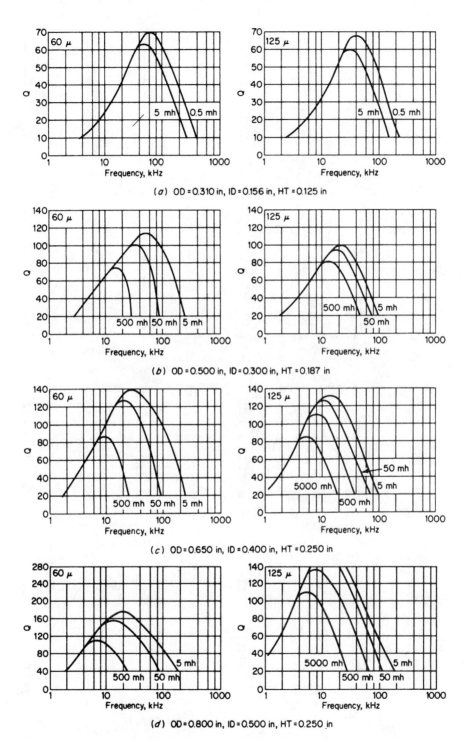

FIGURE 9-4 *Q* curves of toroidal cores. *(Courtesy Magnetics Inc.)*

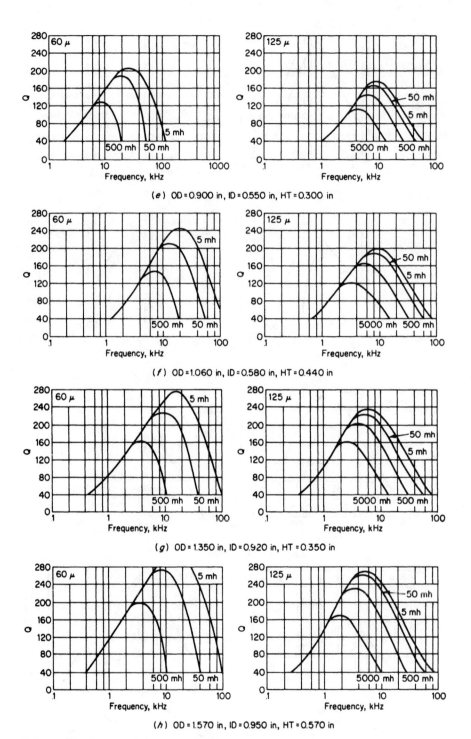

(e) OD = 0.900 in, ID = 0.550 in, HT = 0.300 in

(f) OD = 1.060 in, ID = 0.580 in, HT = 0.440 in

(g) OD = 1.350 in, ID = 0.920 in, HT = 0.350 in

(h) OD = 1.570 in, ID = 0.950 in, HT = 0.570 in

FIGURE 9-4 (*Continued*) *Q* curves of toroidal cores.

9.14

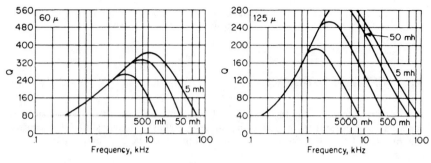

(*i*) OD = 2.000 in, ID = 1.250 in, HT = 0.530 in

FIGURE 9-4 (*Continued*) *Q* curves of toroidal cores.

resonance is approached; so the *Q* will roll off dramatically. It is always preferable to operate on the rising portion of *Q* curves, since the losses can be tightly controlled and the effective inductance remains relatively constant with frequency.

EXAMPLE 9-1

REQUIRED: Design a toroidal inductor having an inductance of 1.5 H and a minimum *Q* of 55 at 1 kHz. The coil must pass a DC current of up to 10 mA and operate with AC signals as high as 10 V_{rms} with negligible effect.

RESULT:

(*a*) Using the *Q* curves of figure 9-4, a 1.060-in-diameter core having a μ of 125 will have a *Q* of approximately 60 at 1 kHz. The required number of turns is found from

$$N = 10^3 \sqrt{\frac{L}{A_L}} = 10^3 \sqrt{\frac{1.5}{0.157}} = 3090 \qquad (9\text{-}10)$$

where the value of A_L was given in table 9-4. The corresponding wire size is determined from table 9-5 as No. 35 AWG.

(*b*) To estimate the effect of the DC current, compute the magnetizing force from

$$H = \frac{4\pi NI}{10\,mL} = \frac{4\pi \times 3090 \times 0.01}{10 \times 6.35} = 6.1\ \text{Oe} \qquad (9\text{-}2)$$

where mL, the magnetic path length, is obtained from table 9-3. According to figure 9-2 the permeability will remain essentially constant.

(*c*) An excitation level of 10 V_{rms} at 1000 Hz results in a flux density of

$$B = \frac{E_{rms}}{4.44 NfA \times 10^{-8}}$$

$$= \frac{10}{4.44 \times 3090 \times 1000 \times 0.654 \times 10^{-8}}$$

$$= 111\ \text{G} \qquad (9\text{-}6)$$

where A, the core's cross-sectional area, is also found in table 9-3. Figure 9-3 indicates that at the calculated flux density the permeability change will be of little consequence.

9.3   FERRITE POTCORES

Ferrites are ceramic structures created by combining iron oxide with oxides or carbonates of other metals such as manganese, nickel, or magnesium. The mixtures are pressed, fired in a kiln at very high temperatures, and machined into the required shapes.

The major advantage of ferrites over laminations and MPP cores is their high resistivity so that core losses are extremely low even at higher frequencies where eddy-current losses become critical. Additional properties such as high permeability and good stability with time and temperature have made ferrites the optimum core-material choice for frequencies from 10 kHz to well in the megahertz region.

The Potcore Structure

A typical potcore assembly is shown in figure 9-5. A winding supported on a bobbin is mounted in a set of symmetrical ferrite potcore halves. The assembly is held rigid by a metal clamp. An air gap is introduced in the center post of each half, since only the outside surfaces of the potcore halves mate with each other. By introducing an adjustment slug containing a ferrite sleeve, the effect of the gap can be partially neutralized as the slug is inserted into the gap region.

A ferrite potcore has a number of distinct advantages over other approaches. Since the wound coil is contained within the ferrite core, the structure is self-shielding, since stray magnetic fields are prevented from entering or leaving the structure.

Very high Qs and good temperature stability can be obtained by appropriate selection of materials and by controlling the effective permeability μ_e through the air gap. Fine adjustment of the effective permeability is accomplished using the adjustment slug.

Compared with other structures, ferrite potcores are more economical. Bobbins can be rapidly wound using multiple-bobbin winding machines in contrast to toroids, which must be individually wound. Assembly and mounting

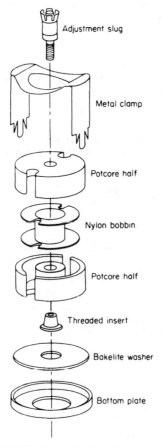

FIGURE 9-5   Typical ferrite potcore assembly.

Labels in figure:
- Adjustment slug
- Metal clamp
- Potcore half
- Nylon bobbin
- Potcore half
- Threaded insert
- Bakelite washer
- Bottom plate

TABLE 9-7 Standard Potcore Sizes

Manufacturer Core Size Designation	Diameter (max)		Height (max)		Cross Section, cm²	Path Length, cm
	in	mm	in	mm		
905	0.366	9.3	0.212	5.4	0.101	1.25
1107	0.445	11.3	0.264	6.7	0.167	1.55
1408	0.559	14.2	0.334	8.5	0.251	1.98
1811	0.727	18.5	0.426	10.8	0.433	2.58
2213	0.858	21.8	0.536	13.6	0.635	3.15
2616	1.024	26.0	0.638	16.2	0.948	3.76
3019	1.201	30.5	0.748	19.0	1.38	4.52
3622	1.418	36.0	0.864	22.0	2.02	5.32
4229	1.697	43.1	1.162	29.5	2.66	6.81

is easily accomplished using a variety of hardware available from the ferrite manufacturer. Printed circuit-type brackets and bobbins facilitate the use of potcores on printed circuit boards.

Potcores have been standardized into nine international sizes ranging from 9 by 5 to 42 by 29 mm, where these dimensions represent the diameter and height, respectively, of a potcore pair. These sizes are summarized in table 9-7.

Electrical Properties of Ferrite Potcores

Ferrite materials are available having a wide range of electrical properties. Let us first consider initial permeability as a function of frequency and temperature. Typical curves for a selection of materials from a particular manufacturer, Ferroxcube Corporation, are shown in figure 9-6.

A material must be chosen that provides uniform permeability over the frequency range of interest. It is evident from figure 9-6a that the lower-permeability materials are more suitable for higher-frequency ranges.

The temperature coefficient of permeability is also an important factor in LC-tuned circuits and filters. The 3D3 and 4C4 permeabilities remain relatively flat over a wide temperature range, as indicated in figure 9-6b. However, the permeability magnitude is lower than that of the other types. The 3B7 material has a higher permeability but a more restricted temperature range. By proper selection of size and gap in conjunction with 3B9-type material, a positive linear temperature coefficient can be obtained to match the negative temperature coefficient of polystyrene capacitors to maintain a constant LC product.

The initial permeability, saturation flux density, and temperature factor for selected ferrite materials are given in table 9-8. The temperature factor is the temperature coefficient of permeability. This factor must be multiplied by the rated effective permeability of the core to obtain the core's temperature coefficient.

For a given core size, a wide range of A_L factors are available. This parameter is determined by the effective permeability of the core, which in turn is controlled by the initial permeability of the ferrite material, the core dimensions, and the size of the air gap introduced in the center post. Table 9-9 lists the effective permeability and the ohms per henry rating for all the standard core sizes where the A_L is maintained constant at 250 mH. For other values, the effective permeability is proportional to the rated A_L and the ohms per henry is inversely proportional to this same factor.

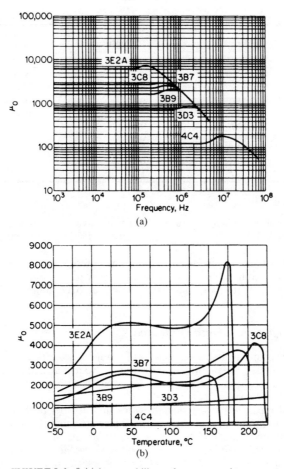

FIGURE 9-6 Initial permeability vs. frequency and temperature: (*a*) initial permeability vs. frequency; (*b*) initial permeability vs. temperature. *(Courtesy Ferroxcube Corp.)*

Potcores are also available having no gap. However, since the resulting electrical characteristics are essentially equivalent to the initial properties of the ferrite material, these cores should be restricted to applications where high permeability is the major requirement, such as for wideband transformers.

Most ferrite materials saturate with AC flux densities in the region of 3000 to 4000 G. AC excitation levels should be kept below a few hundred gauss to avoid nonlinear saturation effects and to minimize core losses. Superimposing a DC bias will also cause saturation when the ampere-turns exceed a critical value dependent upon the core size, material, and gap. DC saturation curves are shown in figure 9-7 for the 1811, 2213, and 2616 sizes. For a given size and material, the cores corresponding to the lower A_L values have greater immunity to saturation, since the air gaps are larger.

TABLE 9-8 Basic Electrical Properties of Standard Ferrite Materials

	3B7	3B9	3D3	4C4
Initial permeability at 25°C	2300 ± 20%	1800 ± 20%	750 ± 20%	125 ± 20%
Saturation flux density at 25°C	3800 G	3200 G	3800 G	3000 G
Temperature factor	-0.6×10^{-6} min $+0.6 \times 10^{-6}$ max ($+20$ to $+70°C$)	$+0.9 \times 10^{-6}$ min $+1.9 \times 10^{-6}$ max (-30 to $+70°C$)	$+1.0 \times 10^{-6}$ min $+3.0 \times 10^{-6}$ max (-30 to $+70°C$)	-6.0×10^{-6} min $+6.0 \times 10^{-6}$ max ($+5$ to $+55°C$)

TABLE 9-9 Electrical Properties of Standard Core
Sizes for $A_L = 250$ mH

Size Designation	μ_e	Ω/H
905	230	700
1107	184	570
1408	156	380
1811	119	260
2213	98	190
2616	78	170
3019	64	140
3622	52	130
4229	51	80

For a specific potcore size and rated A_L, a variety of different adjusters is available featuring ranges of adjustment from a few percent to over 25%. For most applications, an adjustment range of about 10 or 15% will be satisfactory, since this should cover both the capacitor and core tolerances. The larger-range slugs should be avoided for precision requirements, since the adjustment may be too coarse.

To compensate for the effect of an adjuster, the nominal A_L rating of the core should be increased by a percentage equal to one-half the adjustment range for the actual turns computation. This is because the resulting A_L will be higher by one-half the range with the slug set for the midrange position.

Winding of Bobbins

Bobbins are normally wound by guiding the wire feed back and forth as the bobbin is rotated. In the event that the inductor's self-resonant frequency becomes a problem, a multisection bobbin can be used to reduce distributed capacitance. One section at a time is filled to capacity. Most bobbin sizes are available with up to three sections.

A wire capacity chart for standard single-section bobbins is shown in table 9-10. Multisection bobbins have slightly less winding area than single-section bobbins, so the wire gauge may require reduction by one size in some cases.

Because of the air gap, the permeability is not uniform throughout the interior of the potcore. If the bobbin is only partially filled, the A_L will be reduced as a function of the relative winding height. The decrease in A_L for a 2616 size core can be approximated from the graph of figure 9-8. This effect becomes more pronounced as the gap is made larger.

To maximize Q over the frequency range of 50 kHz to 1 or 2 MHz, litz wire should be used. The litz wire equivalents to solid wire gauges can be determined from table 9-2.

Design of Potcores from Q Curves

Various methods are used by designers to determine the optimum core size, material, and gap for a particular application. Depending upon the requirements, some parameters are more significant than others. Generally, Q and temperature coefficient are of prime importance.

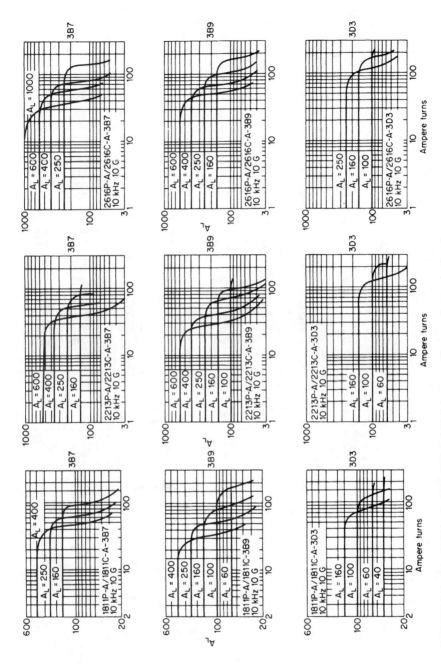

FIGURE 9-7 A_L vs. DC bias for 1811, 2213, and 2616 size cores. (*Courtesy Ferroxcube Corp.*)

9.21

TABLE 9-10 Wire Capacities of Standard Bobbins

Wire Size	905	1107	1408	1811	2213	2616	3019	3622	4229
20							63	100	160
21						50	79	125	200
22						63	100	160	250
23					50	79	125	200	315
24					63	100	160	250	400
25				50	79	125	200	315	500
26		17		63	100	160	250	400	630
27		21	50	79	125	200	315	500	794
28		27	63	100	160	250	400	630	1,000
29		34	79	125	200	315	500	794	1,260
30		43	100	160	250	400	630	1,000	1,588
31	50	54	125	200	315	500	794	1,260	2,000
32	63	68	160	250	400	630	1,000	1,588	2,520
33	79	86	200	315	500	794	1,260	2,000	3,176
34	100	108	250	400	630	1,000	1,588	2,520	4,000
35	125	136	315	500	794	1,260	2,000	3,176	5,042
36	160	171	400	630	1,000	1,588	2,520	4,000	6,353
37	200	216	500	794	1,260	2,000	3,176	5,042	8,000
38	250	272	630	1,000	1,588	2,520	4,000	6,353	10,086
39	315	343	794	1,260	2,000	3,176	5,042	8,000	
40	400	432	1,000	1,588	2,520	4,000	6,353	10,086	
41	500	544	1,260	2,000	3,176	5,042	8,000		
42	630	686	1,588	2,520	4,000	6,353	10,086		
43	794	864	2,000	3,176	5,042	8,000			
44	1,000	1089	2,520	4,000	6,353	10,086			
45	1,260	1372	3,176	5,042	8,000				

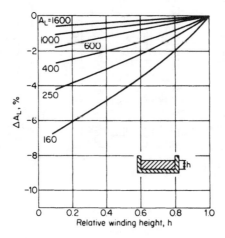

FIGURE 9-8 Change in A_L vs. relative winding height for 2616 size potcore.

A set of standard Q curves facilitates the rapid selection of the optimum core for a given Q requirement. In general, larger cores provide higher Q, lower temperature coefficient, and better immunity from saturation. For a given core size, the lowest A_L which provides sufficient Q should be chosen to minimize temperature coefficient and saturation effects. Operation should be restricted to the rising portion of the curves to avoid the effects of core and dielectric losses as well as those of self-resonance.

Selected Q curves are illustrated in figure 9-9. These curves represent measured Qs for specific turns using both solid and litz wire and single-section bobbins. In the event that the actual design requirement involves excessive inductance values, multisection bobbins can be used to reduce distributed capacity.

EXAMPLE 9-2

REQUIRED: Design a coil having an inductance of 1 mH with a minimum Q of 400 at 100 kHz. The inductor should be capable of supporting 50 mA of DC current.

RESULT:

(a) Using the curves of figure 9-9, a 2616 size potcore having an A_L of 160 and 3B9 material (Ferroxcube 2616C-A160-3B9) will meet the Q requirements. The turns are found from

$$N = 10^3 \sqrt{\frac{L}{A_L}} = 10^3 \sqrt{\frac{1}{160}} = 79 \text{ turns} \tag{9-10}$$

Using table 9-10, the required wire size is No. 23. For optimum Q, litz wire should be used. The litz equivalent is determined from table 9-2 as 100/43.

(b) The DC excitation results in an NI of 79×0.05, or 4. Using the curves of figure 9-7 the operating point is well below the saturation region.

9.4   HIGH-FREQUENCY COIL DESIGN

Powdered-Iron Toroids

Above 1 or 2 MHz, the core losses of most ferrite materials become prohibitive. Toroidal cores composed of compressed iron powder then become desirable for use up to the VHF range.

These cores consist of finely divided iron particles which are insulated and then compressed at very high pressures into a toroidal form in a manner similar to MPP cores. A variety of iron powders is available which are suitable for use over different frequency bands. The more commonly used materials are listed in table 9-11 along with the nominal permeability, temperature coefficient, and maximum frequency of operation above which the core losses can become excessive. In general, a material should be selected that has the highest permeability at the frequency of operation.

For optimum Q, the distributed and stray capacities should be minimized. By maximizing permeability, the number of turns can be kept small. In addition, the turns should be applied as a single-layer winding using the largest wire size that the core will accommodate. However, there is usually a point of diminishing return with increasing wire gauge, so unwieldy wire sizes should be avoided. The turns should be spread evenly around the core except that the start and finish should be separated by a small unwound sector. Litz wire can be used up to about 2 MHz. To approxi-

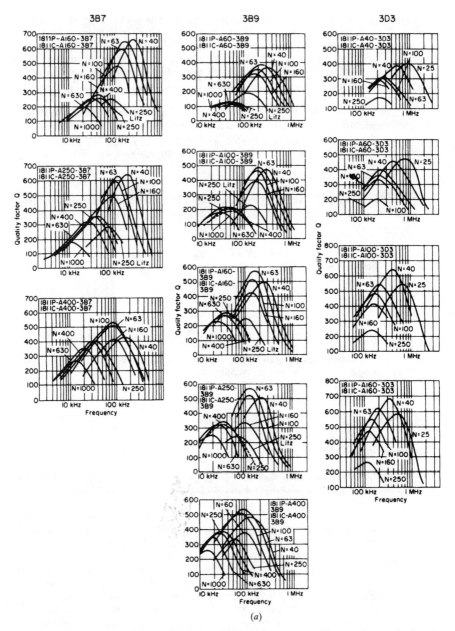

(a)

FIGURE 9-9 *Q* curves for (*a*) 1811, (*b*) 2213, and (*c*) 2616 size potcores. *(Courtesy Ferroxcube Corp.)*

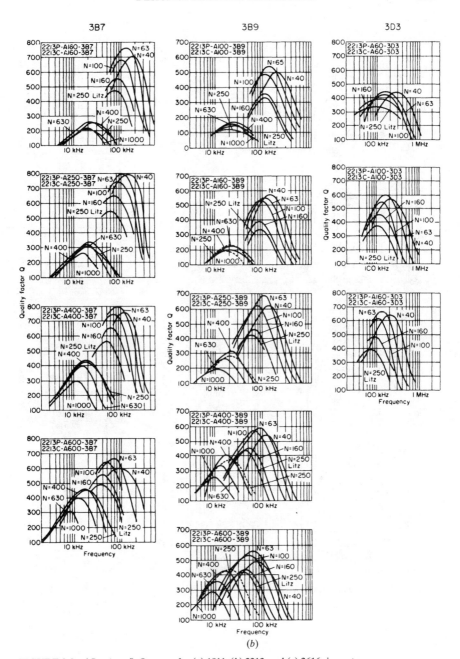

FIGURE 9-9 (*Continued*) *Q* curves for (*a*) 1811, (*b*) 2213, and (*c*) 2616 size potcores.

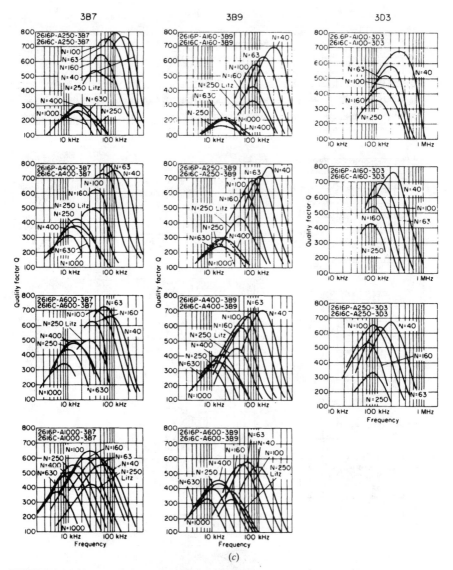

FIGURE 9-9 (*Continued*) *Q* curves for (*a*) 1811, (*b*) 2213, and (*c*) 2616 size potcores.

TABLE 9-11 Iron-Powder Core Materials

Material Designation	Nominal Permeability	Temperature Coefficient, ppm/°C	Maximum Frequency, MHz
GAF carbonyl HP	25	+140	2
GAF carbonyl C	25	+110	10
GAF carbonyl E	10	+40	40
GAF carbonyl TH	8.5	+20	40
GAF carbonyl SF	8	+30	150
GAF carbonyl W	7.5	+140	250

mate the required wire size, the inside circumference of the core can be computed and then divided by the number of turns to yield an approximate wire diameter. A gauge can then be chosen using table 9-1. Generally, it should be about two sizes smaller than computed.

To minimize dielectric losses, teflon-coated wire is occasionally used, since this material has an extremely small power factor in comparison with the more commonly used polyurethane insulation. Also, wrapping the core with teflon tape prior to applying the winding helps to keep stray capacity low. If potting compounds are used, they should be very carefully chosen, since inductor Qs can be easily degraded upon impregnation by lossy materials.

Table 9-12 lists some physical properties of selected standard-size powdered-iron toroidal cores. For convenience, the A_L is specified in terms of $\mu H/100$ turns. The required number of turns can then be computed from

$$N = 10^2 \sqrt{\frac{L}{A_L}} \tag{9-12}$$

where both L and A_L are in microhenrys. Some selected Q curves are illustrated in figure 9-10.

Air-Core Inductors

Coils containing no magnetic materials are said to be air-cored. Inductors of this form are useful above 10 MHz. Air has a μ of 1, will not saturate, and has no core losses, so the Q is strictly dependent upon the winding.

For a single-layer solenoid wound on a nonmagnetic material such as ceramic or phenolic, the inductance in henrys can be approximated within a reasonable accuracy by

$$L = N^2 \frac{r^2}{9r + 10l} \times 10^{-6} \tag{9-13}$$

where N is the number of turns, r is the radius (diameter/2), and l is the coil length, with r and l both in inches.

Air-core solenoid inductors have high leakage inductance, so they are easily affected by nearby metallic surfaces. A toroidal shape will have less leakage, since the magnetic field will be better contained. The expression for the inductance of an air-core toroid with a single-layer winding was given by equation (9-5) with $\mu = 1$.

TABLE 9-12 Powdered-Iron Toroidal Cores

OD, in	ID, in	HT, in	Cross Section, cm²	Path Length, cm	Material	A_L, µH/100 turns
0.120	0.062	0.035	0.0065	0.73	HP	28
					C	28
					E	11
					TH	10
					SF	9
					W	8
0.197	0.092	0.082	0.0278	1.57	HP	76
					C	76
					E	30
					TH	26
					SF	24
					W	23
0.309	0.156	0.125	0.0615	1.86	HP	105
					C	105
					E	42
					TH	36
					SF	33
					W	31
0.500	0.300	0.187	0.114	3.19	HP	118
					C	118
					E	47
					TH	40
					SF	38
					W	35
0.800	0.500	0.250	0.226	5.19	HP	146
					C	146
					E	58
					TH	50
					SF	47
					W	42
1.060	0.580	0.440	0.654	6.54	HP	327
					C	327
					E	130
					TH	111
					SF	104
					W	92
1.570	0.965	0.570	1.072	10.11	HP	345
					C	345
					E	138
					TH	117
					SF	110
					W	98

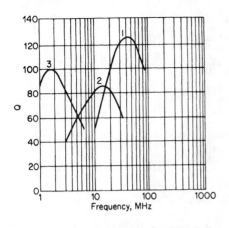

Curve	Material	Winding	L
1	W	11T#30	0.1 μH
2	TH	25T#36	0.6 μH
3	C	50T#40	7 μH

OD = 0.120 in, ID = 0.062 in, HT = 0.035 in

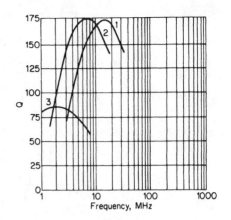

Curve	Material	Winding	L
1	SF	17T#26	1 μH
2	E	29T#28	5 μH
3	C	50T#32	26 μH

OD = 0.309 in, ID = 0.156 in, HT = 0.125 in

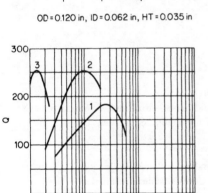

Curve	Material	Winding	L
1	W	10T#20	0.35 μH
2	SF	19T#20	1.4 μH
3	E	125T#15/44	73 μH

OD = 0.500 in, ID = 0.300 in, HT = 0.187 in

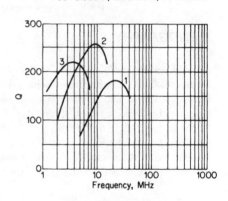

Curve	Material	Winding	L
1	W	10T#20	0.4 μH
2	SF	25T#22	3 μH
3	E	45T#26	12 μH

OD = 0.800 in, ID = 0.500 in, HT = 0.250 in

FIGURE 9-10 Q curves of powdered-iron toroidal cores.

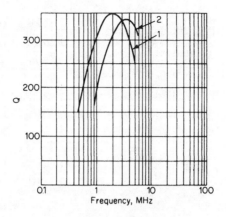

Curve	Material	Winding	L
1	E	40T#20	21 μH
2	E	20T#16	5 μH

OD = 1.06 in, ID = 0.58 in, HT = 0.44 in

FIGURE 9-10 (*Continued*) *Q* curves of powdered-iron toroidal cores.

BIBLIOGRAPHY

Arnold Engineering Co., "Arnold Iron Powder Cores," Marengo, Ill.

Ferroxcube Corp., "Linear Ferrite Magnetic Design Manual—Bulletin 550," Saugerties, N.Y.

Ferroxcube Corp., "Linear Ferrite Materials and Components," Saugerties, N.Y.

Magnetics Inc., "Ferrite Cores," Butler, Pa.

Magnetics Inc., "Magnetic Laminations," Catalog ML-303T, Butler, Pa.

Magnetics Inc., "Molypermalloy Power Cores," Catalog MPP-303S, Butler, Pa.

Micrometals, "Q Curves for Iron Powder Toroidal Cores," Anaheim, Calif.

Welsby, V. G., *The Theory and Design of Inductance Coils,* Macdonald and Sons, London, 1950.

CHAPTER 10

COMPONENT SELECTION FOR
LC AND ACTIVE FILTERS

10.1 CAPACITOR SELECTION

An extensive selection of capacitor types is available for the designer to choose from. They differ in terms of construction and electrical characteristics. The abundance of different capacitors often results in a dilemma in choosing the appropriate type for a specific application. Some of the factors to consider are stability, size, losses, voltage rating, tolerances, cost, and construction.

The initial step in the selection process is to determine the capacitor dielectric. These substances include air, glass, ceramic, mica, plastic films, aluminum, and tantalum. The type of mechanical construction must also be chosen. Since miniaturization is usually a prime consideration, the smallest possible capacitors will require thin dielectrics and efficient packaging without degrading performance.

Properties of Dielectrics

Capacitors in their most fundamental form consist of a pair of metallic plates or electrodes separated by an insulating substance called the dielectric. The capacitance in farads is given by

$$C = \frac{kA}{D}\, 8.85 \times 10^{-12} \tag{10-1}$$

where k is the dielectric constant, A is the plate area in square meters, and D is the separation between plates in meters. The dielectric constant of air is 1. Since capacity is proportional to the dielectric constant, the choice of dielectric highly influences the physical size of the capacitor.

A practical capacitor can be represented by the equivalent circuit of figure 10-1a, where L_s is the series inductance, R_s is the series resistance, and R_p is the parallel resistance. $L_s, R_s,$ and R_p are all parasitic elements. If we assume L_s negligible and R_p infinite, the equivalent impedance can be found by the vector addition of R_s and the capacitive reactance X_c, as shown in figure 10-1b.

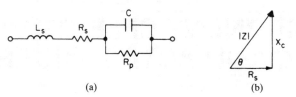

FIGURE 10-1   Equivalent representation of a capacitor: (*a*) equivalent circuit; (*b*) simplified vector diagram.

An important characteristic of capacitors is dissipation factor. This parameter is the reciprocal of capacitor Q and is given by

$$d = \frac{1}{Q} = 2\pi f C R_s = \cot \theta \tag{10-2}$$

where f is the frequency of operation. Dissipation factor is an important figure of merit and should be as low as possible. This is especially true for selective LC filters where branch Qs should be high. Capacitor Q must be sufficiently higher than inductor Q so that the effective Q is not degraded.

Power factor is another figure of merit similar to dissipation factor. Referring to figure 10-1, the power factor is defined as

$$\text{PF} = \frac{R_s}{|Z|} = \cos \theta \tag{10-3}$$

For capacitor Q in excess of 10, we can state $d = \text{PF} = 1/Q$. Dissipation factor or power factor is sometimes expressed as a percentage.

The shunt resistive element R_p in figure 10-1 is often referred to as insulation resistance and results from dielectric leakage currents. A commonly used figure of merit is the $R_p C$ time constant, normally given in $\text{M}\Omega \times \mu\text{F}$. It is frequently convenient to combine all the losses in terms of a single resistor in parallel with C, which is given by

$$R = \frac{1}{2\pi f C d} \tag{10-4}$$

Temperature coefficient (TC) is the rate of change of capacity with temperature and is usually given in parts per million per degree Celsius (ppm/°C). This parameter is extremely important when filter stability is critical. TC should either be minimized or of a specific nominal value so that cancellation will occur with an inductor or resistor's TC of the opposite sign. A dielectric material will also have an operating temperature range beyond which the material can undergo permanent molecular changes.

Another important parameter is *retrace,* which is defined as the capacity deviation from the initial value after temperature cycling. To maintain long-term stability in critical filters that are subjected to temperature variation, retrace should be small.

Table 10-1 summarizes some of the properties of the more commonly used dielectric materials when applied to capacitors.

Capacitor Construction

Capacitors are composed of interleaved layers of electrode and dielectric (except for the diffused types). With film-type capacitors such as polycarbonate, mylar,

TABLE 10-1 Properties of Capacitor Dielectrics

Capacitor Type	Dielectric Constant	TC, ppm/°C	Dissipation Factor, %	Insulation Resistance, MΩ-μF	Temperature Range, °C
Aluminum	8	+2500	10	100	−40 to +85
Ceramic (NPO)	30	±30	0.02	5×10^3	−55 to +125
Glass	5	+140	0.001	10^6	−55 to +125
Mica	6	±50	0.001	2.5×10^4	−55 to +150
Paper	3	±800	1.0	5×10^3	−55 to +125
Polycarbonate	3	±50	0.2	5×10^5	−55 to +125
Polyester (mylar)	3.2	+400	0.75	10^5	−55 to +125
Polypropylene	2.3	−200	0.2	10^5	−55 to +105
Polystyrene	2.5	−120	0.01	3.5×10^7	−55 to +85
Polysulfone	3.1	+80	0.3	10^5	−55 to +150
Porcelain	5	+120	0.1	5×10^5	−55 to +125
Tantalum	28	+800	4.0	20	−55 to +85
Teflon	2.1	−200	0.04	2.5×10^5	−70 to +250

polypropylene, and polystyrene, the electrodes are either a conductive foil such as aluminum or a layer of metallization directly on the dielectric film. The electrode and dielectric combination is tightly rolled onto a core. The alternate layers of foil or metallization are slightly offset so that leads can be attached.

The assembly is heat-shrunk to form a tight package. It can then be sealed by coating with epoxy or by encapsulating in a molded package. A more economical form of sealing is to wrap the capacitor in a plastic film and fill the ends with epoxy. This method is called *wrap-and-fill construction.*

The most economical form of construction involves inserting the wound capacitor in a polystyrene sleeve and heat shrinking the entire assembly to obtain a rigid package. However, the capacitor is not truly sealed and can be affected by humidity and cleaning solvents entering through the porous end seals. Increased protection against humidity or chemical effects is obtained by sealing the ends with epoxy in a manner similar to the wrap-and-fill construction. If a true hermetic seal is required for extremely harsh environments, the capacitor can be encased in a metal can having glass-to-metal end seals. A cutaway view of a film capacitor is illustrated in figure 10-2a.

Capacitors such as ceramic, mica, and porcelain contain a more rigid dielectric substance and cannot be rolled like the film capacitors. They are constructed in stacks or layers, as shown in figure 10-2b. Leads are attached to the end electrodes and the entire assembly is molded or dipped in epoxy. Ceramic-chip capacitors for use in hybrid circuits are constructed as in figure 10-2b and then directly bonded onto the metal substrate of the hybrid.

Capacitors having the highest possible capacitance per unit volume are the electrolytics made of either aluminum or tantalum. Basically, these capacitors consist of two electrodes immersed in a liquid electrolyte (figure 10-3). One or both electrodes are coated with an extremely thin oxide layer of aluminum or tantalum, forming a film having a high dielectric constant and good electrical characteristics. The electrolyte liquid makes contact between the film and the electrodes. The entire unit is housed in a leakproof metal can. The dielectric film is "formed" by applying a DC voltage between cathode and anode, resulting in a permanent polarization of the electrodes. If both plates are "formed," a nonpolar unit will result having half the capacitance of the equivalent polarized type.

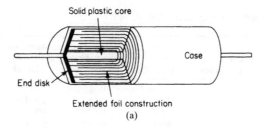

Solid plastic core

Case

End disk

Extended foil construction

(a)

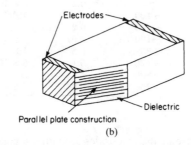

Electrodes

Dielectric

Parallel plate construction

(b)

FIGURE 10-2 Capacitor construction: (*a*) cutaway view or film capacitor; (*b*) stacked construction.

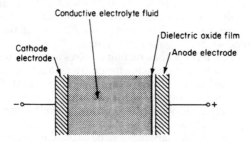

Conductive electrolyte fluid

Dielectric oxide film

Cathode electrode

Anode electrode

FIGURE 10-3 Electrolytic capacitor.

A solid-anode tantalum capacitor is composed of a sintered anode pellet on which is a tantalum oxide layer. The pellet is coated with a solid electrolyte of manganese dioxide which also becomes the cathode. This construction is superior electrically to the other forms of electrolytic construction.

Selecting Capacitors for Filter Applications

Film Capacitors. Polyester (mylar) capacitors are the smallest and most economical of the film types. They should be considered first for general-purpose filters operating below a few hundred kilohertz and at temperatures up to 125°C. They are available with either foil construction for normal applications or in metallized form, where size is restricted to values ranging from 1000 pF to a few microfarads.

Polycarbonate capacitors are slightly larger than mylar but have superior electrical properties, especially at higher temperatures. The dissipation factor remains low over a wide temperature range, and retrace characteristics are better than mylar. Polysufone is similar to polycarbonate but can be used up to 150°C.

Polystyrene capacitors have the best electrical properties of all film capacitors. Temperature coefficient is precisely controlled, almost perfectly linear, and has a nominal value of –120 ppm/°C. Because of the predictable temperature characteristics, these capacitors are highly suited for *LC* resonant circuits, where the inductors have a corresponding positive temperature coefficient. Capacity retrace is typically 0.1%. Losses are extremely small, resulting in a dissipation factor of approximately 0.01%. The maximum temperature, however, is limited to 85°C. Polypropylene capacitors are comparable in performance to polystyrene, although they have a slightly higher dissipation factor and temperature coefficient. Their maximum temperature rating, however, is 105°C. They are more economical than polystyrene and priced to be nearly competitive with mylar.

Figure 10-4 compares the capacitance and dissipation factor versus temperature for mylar, polycarbonate, and polystyrene capacitors. Clearly, polystyrene is superior, although polycarbonate exhibits slightly less capacity variation with temperature over a limited temperature range.

Film capacitors are available with standard tolerances of 1, 2½, 5, 10, and 20%. For most applications the 2½ or 5% tolerances will be adequate. This is especially true when resonant frequency is adjustable by tuning the inductor or with a potentiometer in active filters. Precision capacitors tend to become more expensive with decreasing tolerance.

The first two significant figures for standard values are given in table 10-2. Frequently a design may require nonstandard values. It is nearly always far more economical to parallel a few off-the-shelf capacitors of standard values when possible than to order a custom-manufactured component unless the quantities involved are substantial.

If the differential voltage across a capacitor becomes excessive, the dielectric will break down and may become permanently damaged. Most film capacitors are avail-

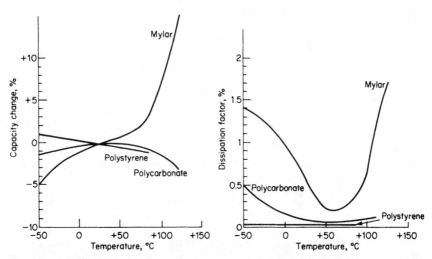

FIGURE 10-4   Capacity and dissipation factor vs. temperature of film capacitors.

TABLE 10-2 Standard Capacitor Values

10	18	33	56
11	20	36	62
12	22	39	68
13	24	43	75
15	27	47	82
16	30	51	91

able with DC voltage ratings ranging from 33 to 600 V or more. Since most filters process signals of a few volts, voltage rating is normally not a critical requirement. Since capacitor volume increases with voltage rating, unnecessarily high ratings should be avoided. However, polystyrene capacitors below 0.01 µF having a low voltage rating will have a tendency to change value from the printed circuit-board soldering process because of distortion of the dielectric film from heat conducted through the leads. Capacitors rated at 100 V or more will generally be immune, since the dielectric film will be sufficiently thick.

In addition to resistive losses, the equivalent circuit of figure 10-1a contains a parasitic inductance I_s. As the frequency of operation is increased, series resonance of L_s and C is approached, resulting in a dramatic drop in impedance as shown in figure 10-5. Above self-resonance, the reactance becomes inductive. The self-resonant frequency is highly dependent upon construction and value, but in general, film capacitors are limited to operation below a megahertz.

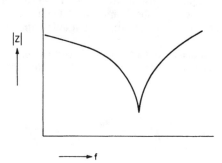

FIGURE 10-5 Self-resonant effect in capacitors.

Mica Capacitors. Mica capacitors, although more costly than the film types, have unequaled electrical properties. Temperature coefficients as low as a few parts per million can be obtained. Retrace is better than 0.1% and the dissipation factor is typically 0.001%. Mica capacitors can operate to 150°C. Values above 10,000 pF become prohibitively expensive and should be avoided.

Mica plates are silvered on both sides to form electrodes, stacked, and thermally bonded together. This results in a mechanically stable assembly with characteristics indicative of the mica itself. A coating of epoxy resin is then applied by dipping or other means. An alternate form of construction involves using eyelets to join together the mica plates. This form of construction has poor stability of capacity, since it may permit relative movement between plates. Silvered mica capacitors are also available in a molded package. These capacitors are comparable electrically with the epoxy-dipped variety. However, they are normally designed to operate at higher DC voltages ranging from 1000 to 2500 V and are not needed for most filter requirements.

The stacked construction of mica capacitors results in excellent performance well into the VHF region. The dissipation factor remains low at higher frequencies, and parasitic inductance is small.

A comprehensive MIL-type designation system is frequently used to specify mica capacitors. This nomenclature is illustrated below:

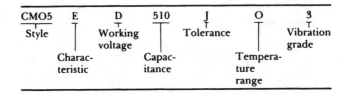

Style:
The style is defined by the two-letter symbol CM followed by two digits to designate case size and lead configurations as follows:

Capacity Range, pF	Straight Leads	Crimped Leads
1–390	CM04	CM09
1–390	CM05	CM10
430–4,700	CM06	CM11
5,100–20,000	CM07	CM12
22,000–91,000	CM08	CM13

Characteristic:
The characteristic letter symbol defines the stability of capacity with temperature and retrace limits.

Letter	Temperature Coefficient, ppm/°C	Retrace
B	Not specified	Not specified
C	±200	±(0.5% + 0.1 pF)
D	±100	±(0.3% + 0.1 pF)
E	−20 to +100	±(0.1% + 0.1 pF)
F	0 to +70	±(0.05% + 0.1 pF)

Working voltage:
The DC working voltage is specified in terms of a letter.

Letter	DC Voltage
Y	50
A	100
C	300
D	500

Capacitance:

The capacitance in picofarads is identified by a three-digit number, where the first two digits represent the two significant figures corresponding to table 10-2 and the third digit is the number of zeros to follow.

Tolerance:

Tolerances are indicated by a letter.

Letter	Tolerance
A	±1 pF
D	±0.5 pF
M	±20%
K	±10%
J	±5%
G	±2%
F	±1%
E	±0.5%

Temperature range:

A letter indicates the temperature range.

Letter	Temperature Range, °C
M	−55 to +70
N	−55 to +85
O	−55 to +125
P	−55 to +150

Vibration range:

The vibration range is identified as follows:

Number	Vibration Frequency, Hz
1	10–55
3	10–2000

Ceramic Capacitors.   Ceramic capacitors are formed in stacks or layers using the construction illustrated in figure 10-2b. The ceramic plates are formed by first casting a film slurry of barium titanate and binders, which is then coated with a metallic ink to form electrodes. The plates are stacked into layers, fired in ovens, and separated into individual capacitors.

Ceramic capacitors are manufactured in a variety of shapes including monolithic chips which can be directly bonded to a metallized substrate.

The basic dielectric material barium titanate has a dielectric constant k as high as 3000 at room temperature which can become as high as 10,000 at 125°C. The temperature at which the maximum k occurs is called the *curie point*. By introducing additives, the curie point can be lowered, the temperature variation reduced, and negative temperature coefficients can be obtained.

Ceramic capacitors in disk form are available in specific temperature coefficients. Some typical values are shown in figure 10-6, where the P100 has a positive temperature coefficient of 100 ppm/°C and the negative types range from NPO (approximately zero temperature coefficient) through N4700 (4700 ppm/°C). These capacitors become very useful for temperature compensation of passive and active filter networks.

Capacities range from 0.5 pF to values as high as 2.2 µF. The DC working voltages may be as high as a few kilovolts or as little as 3 V for the larger capacitance values. Dissipation factor in most cases is less than 1%. Tolerances are normally 10 or 20%, which restricts this family of capacitors to very general applications.

Ceramic capacitors exhibit minimum parasitic inductance and little variation in dissipation factor from low audio to high radio frequencies. These properties make them particularly suited for RF decoupling and bypass applications in addition to temperature compensation. Using the feed-through type of construction to further minimize parasitic inductance, they can be used up to 10 GHz.

Electrolytic Capacitors. Aluminum electrolytic capacitors are intended for low-frequency bypassing or nonprecision timing and are generally unsuitable for active or passive filters. They have unsymmetrical and broad tolerances such as +80%/–20% and require a DC polarization. They also have poor stability and a shelf-life limitation. Large parasitic inductances and series resistances preclude usage at high frequencies.

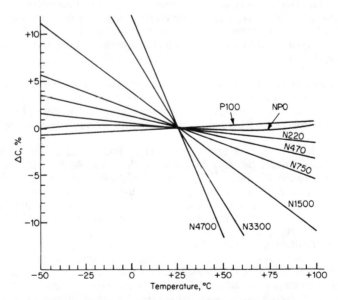

FIGURE 10-6   Temperature characteristics of ceramic capacitors.

Tantalum capacitors, on the other hand, can be used in low-frequency passive or active filters which require very large capacity values in a small volume. They have fairly high temperature coefficients (approximately +800 ppm/°C) and dissipation factors (approximately 4%). However, these limitations may not be serious when applied to low-selectivity filters. The high-frequency characteristics are superior to those of aluminum electrolytics. Tolerances of 10 or 20% are standard.

Tantalum capacitors are formed in a similar manner to aluminum electrolytics and are polarized. However, they have no shelf-life restrictions and can even operate indefinitely without DC polarization. A momentary reverse polarity usually will not damage the capacitor, which is not true in the case of the aluminum electrolytics.

A polarization voltage may not always be present. Nonpolar tantalums can be obtained but are somewhat more expensive and not always available off the shelf. If two identical tantalum capacitors are series-connected back to back as shown in figure 10-7, a nonpolar type will result. The total value will be $C/2$ corresponding to capacitors in series.

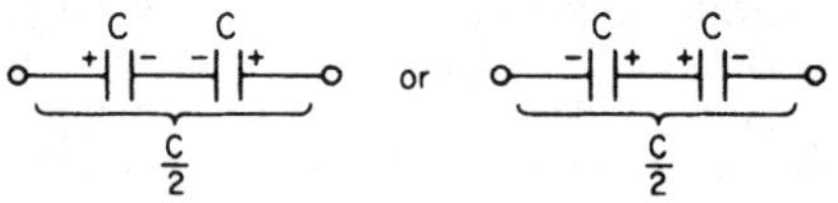

FIGURE 10-7   Nonpolar tantalum capacitors.

Tantalum capacitors are available in three forms: dry foil, wet, and solid. The dry form consists of foil anodes and cathodes which are stacked or rolled using a paper spacer and impregnated with electrolyte. The wet forms are constructed using a porous slug of tantalum for the anode electrode and the silver-plated case as the cathode. The unit is filled with sulfuric acid for the electrolyte. Solid tantalums consist of a slab of compressed tantalum powder for the anode with a lead attached. A layer of tantalum pentoxide is formed on the surface for the dielectric, which is then connected to a lead to form the cathode, and the entire assembly is encapsulated in epoxy.

Trimmer Capacitors.   In LC filters, particularly those for RF use, it is sometimes found to be more convenient to resonate a tuned circuit by adjusting capacity rather than inductance. A smaller trimmer is then placed in parallel with a fixed resonating capacitor. These trimmers usually consist of air, ceramic, mica, or glass as the dielectric.

Air capacitors consist of two sets of plates, one called the *rotor,* which is mounted on a shaft, and the other the *stator,* which is fixed. As the rotor is revolved, the plates intermesh without making contact, resulting in increasing capacity. For high-capacity values the plate size and number must increase dramatically, since the dielectric constant of air is only 1. This becomes a serious limitation when the available room is restricted. Air trimmers range from maximum values of a few picofarads up to 500 pF.

Ceramic trimmers are smaller than air for comparable values due to increased dielectric constant. They are usually composed of a single pair of ceramic disks joined at the center in a manner which permits rotation of one of the disks. A silvered region covers part of each disk, forming the plates of the capacitor. As the disk is rotated, the silvered areas begin to overlap, resulting in increasing capacity.

Ceramic trimmers are available with maximum capacity values up to 50 or 100 pF. Good performance is obtained well into the VHF frequency range.

Piston trimmers are composed of a glass or quartz tube with an outside conductive coating corresponding to one electrode. The other plate or electrode is a piston which by rotation is inserted deeper into the outside tube, resulting in increased capacitance. Multiturn construction results in excellent resolution. Piston trimmers have the best electrical properties of all trimmer types but are the most costly. They are suitable for use even at microwave frequencies.

10.2 RESISTORS

A fundamental component of active filters are resistors. Sensitivity studies show that resistors are usually at least as important as capacitors, so their proper selection is crucial to the success of a particular design.

Resistors are formed by connecting leads across a resistive element. The resistance in ohms is determined by

$$R = \frac{\rho L}{A} \tag{10-5}$$

where ρ is the resistivity of the element in ohm-centimeters, L is the length of the element in centimeters, and A is the cross-sectional area in square centimeters. By using materials of particular resistivities and special geometries, resistors can be manufactured having the desired properties. Resistors fall into one of two general categories: fixed or variable.

Fixed Resistors

Fixed resistors are normally classified as either carbon composition, carbon film, cermet film, metal film, or wirewound, according to the resistive element. They are also grouped in terms of tolerance and wattage rating. Table 10-3 summarizes some typical properties of fixed resistors.

Carbon Composition. Probably the most widely used fixed resistor is the carbon composition type shown in figure 10-8. It consists of a solid cylinder composed mainly of carbon with wire leads which is molded under high pressure and temperature in an insulated jacket. By changing the proportion of carbon powder and filler,

TABLE 10-3 Typical Properties of Fixed Resistors

Type	Range, Ω	Standard Tolerances, %	Wattage Rating	Temperature Coefficient, ppm/°C
Carbon composition	1–100 M	5, 10, 20	⅛, ¼, ½, 1, 2	±1000
Carbon film	1–10 M	2, 5	⅛, ¼, ½	±200
Cermet film	10–22 M	0.5, 1	¼, ½	±100
Metal film	0.1–1 M	0.1, 0.25, 0.5, 1	⅛, ¼, ½, 1, 2	±25
Wirewound	1–100 k	5, 10, 20	3, 5, 10, 20	±50

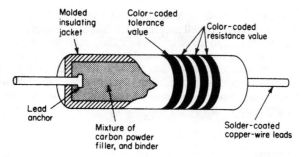

FIGURE 10-8   Carbon composition resistor construction.

different resistance values can be obtained. Standard wattage ratings are 1/8, 1/4, 1/2, 1, and 2 W. Resistance values are maintained to about ±10% by the manufacturing process. Values within a ±5% tolerance band are obtained using automatic sorting equipment.

A series of standard values has been adopted by RETMA based on $10^{1/12}$ and $10^{1/24}$ and is widely used for 10 and 5% resistors. These preferred values are rounded to two significant figures which are given in table 10-4. All 10% values are also available in 5% tolerances but not conversely.

TABLE 10-4   Preferred 5 and 10% Resistor Values

±10%	±5%	±10%	±5%
10	10	33	33
	11		36
12	12	39	39
	13		43
15	15	47	47
	16		51
18	18	56	56
	20		62
22	22	68	68
	24		75
27	27	82	82
	30		91

The value and tolerance of carbon composition resistors are indicated by a series of color-coded bands beginning on one end of the resistor body. The first and second bands determine the two significant figures, the third band the multiplier, and the fourth band the tolerance. Sometimes a fifth band is present to establish a reliability rating, as shown in table 10-5.

The power rating of resistors corresponds to the maximum power that can be continually dissipated with no permanent damage. This rating is normally applicable up to ambient temperatures of 70°C, above which derating is required. In general, a safety margin corresponding to a factor of 2 is desirable to obtain a high level of reliability.

TABLE 10-5 Standard Color Code for Carbon Composition Resistors

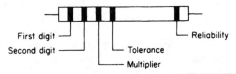

First digit
Second digit
Reliability
Tolerance
Multiplier

Color	Digit	Multiplier	Tolerance, %	Reliability Level (Failures per 1000 h), %
Black	0	1		
Brown	1	10		1
Red	2	100		0.1
Orange	3	1000		0.01
Yellow	4	10,000		0.001
Green	5	100,000		
Blue	6	1,000,000		
Violet	7	10,000,000		
Gray	8			
White	9			
Gold		0.1	5	
Silver			10	

Carbon composition resistors have a high temperature coefficient, typically 1000 ppm/°C. In addition, permanent resistance changes of a few percent will occur to poor retrace and aging. Generally, the lower resistance values exhibit better stability. Carbon composition resistors exhibit few parasitic effects and then only above 10 MHz.

Carbon composition resistors are also the most economical of the various resistor types. They are often used in general-purpose active filters, where stability is not a critical requirement.

Carbon Film. Film resistors are manufactured by depositing a thin layer of a resistance element on a nonconductive substrate. This form of construction is illustrated in figure 10-9. The resistive element is usually spiral in form to increase the net resistance.

Carbon film resistors use this form of construction. They are manufactured by heating carbon-bearing gases so that a deposit of carbon film forms on the ceramic substrate. Temperature coefficients are in the region of 200 ppm/°C, which is a sig-

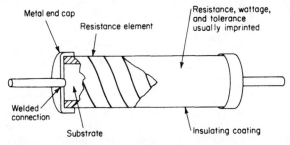

Metal end cap
Resistance element
Resistance, wattage, and tolerance usually imprinted
Welded connection
Substrate
Insulating coating

FIGURE 10-9 Construction of film resistors.

nificant improvement over carbon composition. Resistance changes from aging and temperature cycling are typically specified at 1% or less. Normal tolerances are ±5%, although ±1% tolerance units can be obtained. The values are in accordance with table 10-4.

Carbon film resistors are especially suited for general-purpose applications requiring better performance than can be obtained using the carbon composition type at competitive pricing.

Metal Film.   Metal film resistors are without any doubt the most widely used type for precision requirements. They are manufactured by depositing nichrome alloys on a rod substrate. Exceptional characteristics can be obtained. Normal tolerances are ±1%, but tolerances of ±0.1%, ±0.25%, and ±0.5% are available. Temperature coefficients are typically 25 ppm/°C. Retrace and aging result in changes usually not exceeding 0.25%.

Metal film resistors are normally specified using a military numbering system as follows:

RN60	D	1023	F
Power	Characteristic	Value	Tolerance

Power:

Designation	Power Rating (70°C), W
RN50	$\frac{1}{10}$
RN55	$\frac{1}{8}$
RN60	$\frac{1}{4}$
RN65	$\frac{1}{2}$
RN70	$\frac{3}{4}$
RN75	1
RN80	2

Characteristic:

Letter	Temperature Coefficient, ppm/°C
B	±500
C	±50
D	±100
E	±25
F	±50

Value:

The value is given by four digits, where the first three digits are significant and are selected from the following table and the fourth digit is the number of zeros. The bold values in this table specifically correspond to standard 1% values, and all listed numbers are standard for 0.1, 0.25, and 0.5% tolerances.

10.0	**12.1**	**14.7**	**17.8**	**21.5**	**26.1**	**31.6**	**38.3**	**46.4**	**56.2**	**68.1**	**82.5**
10.1	12.3	14.9	18.0	21.8	26.4	32.0	38.8	47.0	56.9	69.0	83.5
10.2	**12.4**	**15.0**	**18.2**	**22.1**	**26.7**	**32.4**	**39.2**	**47.5**	**57.6**	**69.8**	**84.5**
10.4	12.6	15.2	18.4	22.3	27.1	32.8	39.7	48.1	58.3	70.6	85.6
10.5	**12.7**	**15.4**	**18.7**	**22.6**	**27.4**	**33.2**	**40.2**	**48.7**	**59.0**	**71.5**	**86.6**
10.6	12.9	15.6	18.9	22.9	27.7	33.6	40.7	49.3	59.7	72.3	87.6
10.7	**13.0**	**15.8**	**19.1**	**23.2**	**28.0**	**34.0**	**41.2**	**49.9**	**60.4**	**73.2**	**88.7**
10.9	13.2	16.0	19.3	23.4	28.4	34.4	41.7	50.5	61.2	74.1	89.8
11.0	**13.3**	**16.2**	**19.6**	**23.7**	**28.7**	**34.8**	**42.2**	**51.1**	**61.9**	**75.0**	**90.9**
11.1	13.5	16.4	19.8	24.0	29.1	35.2	42.7	51.7	62.6	75.9	92.0
11.3	**13.7**	**16.5**	**20.0**	**24.3**	**29.4**	**35.7**	**43.2**	**52.3**	**63.4**	**76.8**	**93.1**
11.4	13.8	16.7	20.3	24.6	29.8	36.1	43.7	53.0	64.2	77.7	94.2
11.5	**14.0**	**16.9**	**20.5**	**24.9**	**30.1**	**36.5**	**44.2**	**53.6**	**64.9**	**78.7**	**95.3**
11.7	14.2	17.2	20.8	25.2	30.5	37.0	44.8	54.2	65.7	79.6	96.5
11.8	**14.3**	**17.4**	**21.0**	**25.5**	**30.9**	**37.4**	**45.3**	**54.9**	**66.5**	**80.6**	**97.6**
12.0	14.5	17.6	21.3	25.8	31.2	37.9	45.9	55.6	67.3	81.6	98.8

Tolerance:

Letter	Tolerance
B	±0.1%
C	±0.25%
D	±0.5%
F	±1%

Metal film resistors have many highly desirable features. In addition to low temperature coefficients and good long-term stability, they exhibit the lowest noise attainable in resistors. Parasitic effects are minimal and have no significant effect below 10 MHz. Metal film resistors are rugged in design, have excellent immunity to environmental stress, and have high reliability. Although tolerances to 0.1% are available, 1% values are used almost exclusively because of their lower cost.

Cermet film resistors are manufactured by screening a layer of combined metal and ceramic or glass particles on a ceramic core and firing it at high temperatures. They can provide higher resistance values for a particular size than most other types, up to a few hundred megohms. However, they are somewhat inferior electrically to the metal film type. Their temperature coefficients are higher (typically 200 ppm/°C). Retrace and long-term stability are typically 0.5%. Tolerances of 1% are standard.

Precision resistors are also available in wirewound form. They consist essentially of resistance wire such as nichrome, wound on an insulated core. They are costlier than the metal film type and comparable in performance except for higher parasitics. Wirewound resistors are best suited for applications with higher power requirements.

In addition to the discrete resistors discussed, thin-film and thick-film resistive elements can be formed on chips for LSI and hybrid circuits. Thin-film resistors are obtained by evaporating, sputtering, or silk screening resistive elements on an insulating substrate. Thick-film resistors are produced by depositing resistive elements in ink form on the substrate using photographic techniques.

TABLE 10-6 Typical Properties of Potentiometers

Type	Range, Ω	Standard Tolerances, %	Wattage Rating	Temperature Coefficient, ppm/°C
Carbon composition	100–10 M	10, 20	0.5, 1, 2	±1000
Cermet	100–1 M	5, 10, 20	0.5, 1	±100
Wirewound	10–100 M	5, 10	0.5, 1, 5, 10	±100

Variable Resistors

Variable resistors are commonly referred to as potentiometers or trimmers. They are classified by the type of resistance element such as carbon, cermet, or wirewound and also by whether they are single- or multiple-turn. The electrical properties of the three basic element types are given in table 10-6.

Potentiometers are always three-terminal devices as depicted in figure 10-10a. (CW indicates direction of travel of the wiper for clockwise rotation.) Since most applications require a two-terminal variable resistor or rheostat rather than a voltage divider, the wiper is normally externally joined to one of the end terminals, as shown in figure 10-10b.

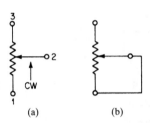

(a)   (b)

FIGURE 10-10 Potentiometer connections: (a) potentiometer; (b) rheostat configuration.

Construction. The basic types of construction are the single-turn and multiturn forms. Single-turn potentiometers are rotary devices having a centrally located adjustment hub which contains the movable contact for the wiper. The movable contact rests upon the circular resistive element. The entire assembly may be exposed or enclosed in a plastic case containing PC pins or wire leads for the external connections. The adjustable hub is usually slotted for screwdriver access. Some types have a toothed thumbwheel for manual adjustment.

Single-turn trimpots require 270° of rotation to fully traverse the entire resistance element. Increasing the number of turns will improve the operator's ability to make very fine adjustments. Multiturn trimmers contain a threaded shaft. A threaded collar travels along this shaft, making contact with the resistive element. The collar functions as the wiper. This general construction is shown in figure 10-11.

Trimmer controls, especially the single-turn variety, are subject to movement of the wiper adjustment due to vibration. To assure stability, it is desirable to prevent movement by placing a small amount of a rigid sealer such as Glyptal on the adjuster after circuit alignment.

Types of Resistance Elements. Carbon composition potentiometers are formed by molding a carbon mixture on a nonconductive disk or base containing previously embedded leads. The wiper mechanism is then attached to complete the assembly.

Carbon composition potentiometers are available in both the single- and multiple-turn configurations. They are the most economical of all types and also have the poorest characteristics. TC is about 1000 ppm/°C. Retrace and long-term stability

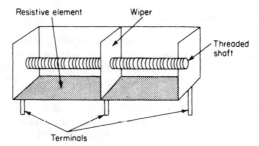

FIGURE 10-11 Multiturn potentiometer construction.

are poor. Therefore, carbon composition potentiometers find limited usage in filter circuits.

Cermet film potentiometers are the most commonly used type for filter networks. They are moderate in cost, have a wide range of available values, and have good temperature characteristics and stability. Parasitic effects are minimal. They are manufactured by depositing cermet film on a nonconductive disk or base in thicknesses varying from 0.0005 to 0.005 in.

Wirewound potentiometers are formed by winding resistance wire (usually nichrome) on an insulated base. They have comparable temperature characteristics to cermet and are higher in cost. Their major attribute is high power capability. However, for most filter requirements this feature is of little importance.

Wirewound potentiometers have quite different adjustment characteristics than the other types. As the other type wipers are rotated, the resistance varies linearly with degrees of rotation, providing nearly infinite resolution. (Nonlinear tapers are also available, such as logarithmic.) The resistance of wirewound potentiometers, however, changes in discrete steps as the wiper moves from turn to turn. The resolution (or settability) therefore is not as good as the cermet or carbon composition types.

Ratings. Since potentiometers are almost always used as variable elements, the overall tolerances are not critical and are generally 10 or 20%. For the same reason, many different standard values are not required. Standard values are given by one significant figure, which is either 1, 2, or 5 and range from 10 Ω to 10 MΩ.

10.3 OPERATIONAL AMPLIFIERS

The versatility and low cost of integrated-circuit (IC) operational amplifiers have made them one of the most popular building blocks in the industry. The op amp is capable of performing many mathematical processes upon signals. For active filters, op amps are specifically used to provide gain and isolation.

IC op amps have evolved from the Fairchild µA 709 in the mid-sixties to the many different types available today having a variety of special features. This section reviews some of the essential characteristics, discusses some important considerations, and provides a survey of the most popular IC amplifier types. An extensive formal analysis is covered by many standard texts and will not be repeated here.

Review of Basic Operational-Amplifier Theory

A simplified equivalent circuit of an operational amplifier is shown in figure 10-12. The output voltage e_0 is the difference of the input voltages at the two input terminals amplified by amplifier gain A. A positive changing signal applied to the positive (+) input terminal results in a positive change at the output, whereas a positive changing signal applied to the negative input terminal (–) results in a negative change at the output. Hence, the positive input terminal is called the *noninverting* input and the negative input terminal is referred to as the *inverting* input. If we consider the amplifier ideal, the input impedance R_i is infinite, the output impedance R_0 is zero, and the voltage gain A_0 is infinite.

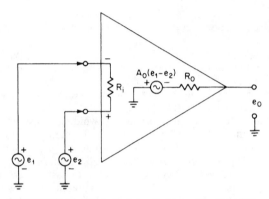

FIGURE 10-12   Equivalent circuit of operational amplifier.

Negative feedback applied from the output to the inverting input results in zero differential input voltage if A_0 is infinite, and is called the *virtual ground effect*. This property permits a wide variety of different amplifier configurations and simplifies circuit analysis.

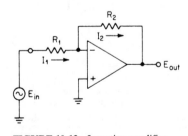

FIGURE 10-13   Inverting amplifier.

Let us first consider the basic inverting amplifier circuit of figure 10-13. If we consider the amplifier ideal, the differential input voltage becomes zero because of the negative feedback path through R_2. Therefore, the inverting input terminal is at ground potential. The currents through resistors R_1 and R_2 are

$$I_1 = \frac{E_{in}}{R_1} \qquad (10\text{-}6)$$

and

$$I_2 = -\frac{E_{out}}{R_2} \qquad (10\text{-}7)$$

If the amplifier input impedance is infinite, no current can flow into the inverting terminal, so $I_1 = I_2$. If we equate expressions (10-6) and (10-7) and solve for the overall transfer function, we obtain

$$\frac{E_{out}}{E_{in}} = -\frac{R_2}{R_1} \tag{10-8}$$

The circuit amplification is determined directly from the ratio of two resistors and is independent of the amplifier itself. Also, the input impedance is R_1 and the output impedance is zero.

Multiple inputs can be summed at the inverting input terminal as a direct result of the virtual ground effect. The triple-input summing amplifier of figure 10-14 has the following output based on superposition:

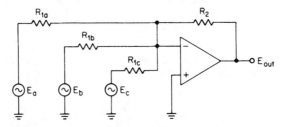

FIGURE 10-14   Summing amplifier.

$$E_{out} = -\frac{R_2}{R_{1a}} E_a - \frac{R_2}{R_{1b}} E_b - \frac{R_2}{R_{1c}} E_c \tag{10-9}$$

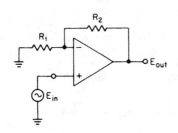

FIGURE 10-15   Noninverting amplifier.

A noninverting amplifier can be configured using the circuit of figure 10-15. Since the differential voltage between the amplifier input terminal is zero, the voltage across R_1 is E_{in}. Since R_1 and R_2 form a voltage divider, we can state

$$\frac{E_{out}}{E_{in}} = \frac{R_1 + R_2}{R_1} \tag{10-10}$$

or the more popular form

$$\frac{E_{out}}{E_{in}} = 1 + \frac{R_2}{R_1} \tag{10-11}$$

where the input impedance is infinite and the output impedance is zero.

If we set R_1 to infinity and R_2 to zero, the gain becomes unity, which corresponds to the voltage follower configuration of figure 10-16.

The applications of operational amplifiers are by no means restricted to summing and amplification. If R_2 in figure 10-13, for example, were replaced by a capacitor, the circuit would serve as an integrator. Alternately, a capacitor for R_1 would result in a differentiator. Nonlinear functions can be performed by introducing nonlinear elements in the feedback paths.

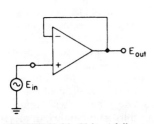

FIGURE 10-16   Voltage follower.

Analysis of Nonideal Amplifiers

The fundamental equation for the closed-loop gain of the noninverting amplifier of figure 10-15 is given by

$$A_c = \frac{A_0}{1 + A_0\beta} \qquad (10\text{-}12)$$

where A_0 is the amplifier's open-loop gain and β is the feedback factor. This expression should be familiar to those who have studied feedback systems or servo theory. The closed-loop gain of the inverting amplifier structure of figure 10-13 is expressed as

$$A_c = \frac{A_0\,(\beta - 1)}{1 + A_0\beta} \qquad (10\text{-}13)$$

In both cases, the feedback factor, which corresponds to the portion of the output that is fed back to the input, is determined by

$$\beta = \frac{R_1}{R_1 + R_2} \qquad (10\text{-}14)$$

Let us examine the term $1 + A_0\beta$ corresponding to the denominator of the closed-loop gain expressions. The open-loop gain of practical amplifiers is neither infinite nor real (zero phase shift). The magnitude and phase of A_0 will be a function of frequency. If at some frequency $A_0\beta$ were equal to -1, the denominator of equations (10-12) and (10-13) would vanish. The closed-loop gain then becomes infinite, which implies an oscillatory condition.

To prevent oscillations, the amplifier open-loop gain must be band-limited so that the product $A_0\beta$ is less than 1 below the frequency where the amplifier phase shift reaches 180°. This is achieved by introducing a gain roll-off beginning at low frequencies and continuing at a 6-dB per octave rate. This technique of ensuring stability is called *frequency compensation*. It is evident from the closed-loop gain equations that for high closed-loop gains, β is diminished so that less frequency compensation will be required. Conversely, the voltage follower will need the most compensation.

Effects of Finite Amplifier Gain. The most critical factor in most op amp applications is the open-loop gain. In order to maintain stability, the open-loop gain must be band-limited. This is usually accomplished by introducing a real pole at a low frequency so that the gain rolls off at 6 dB per octave.

A typical open-loop gain plot is shown in figure 10-17a. The gain has two break-points. The low-frequency breakpoint is caused by a real pole resulting from the frequency compensation. The output phase lag increases to 45° at the breakpoint and asymptotically approaches 90° as the frequency is increased. The amplitude response rolls off at a rate of 6 dB per octave.

Another amplifier breakpoint occurs near 100 kHz. Above this second pole, the gain rolls off at 12 dB per octave, an additional 45° of phase shift occurs, and the asymptotic phase limit becomes 180°. The corresponding phase curve is shown in figure 10-17b.

Most operational amplifiers have a built-in frequency compensation network. These values correspond to the worst case for guaranteed stability, which is the voltage follower configuration. The penalty paid for this convenience is that, in the case of high closed-loop gain ($\beta \ll 1$), the open-loop gain is less than it really could be and yet retain stability; so some unnecessary closed-loop gain degradation will occur.

Amplifiers are frequently specified in terms of their unity gain-bandwidth product, i.e., the frequency at which the open-loop gain is unity.

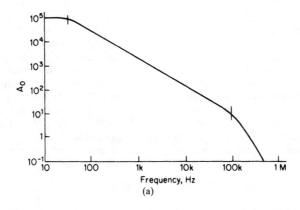

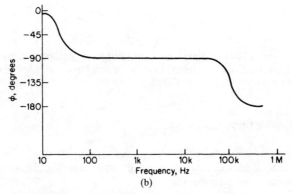

FIGURE 10-17 Typical open-loop gain and phase shift vs. frequency: (*a*) open-loop gain vs. frequency; (*b*) open-loop phase shift vs. frequency.

To determine the effects of open-loop gain on closed-loop gain, let us substitute equation (10-14) into equations (10-12) and (10-13) for the noninverting and inverting amplifiers. The resulting gain expressions are

Noninverting amplifier:
$$A_c = \frac{1 + \dfrac{R_2}{R_1}}{\dfrac{1}{A_0}\left(1 + \dfrac{R_2}{R_1}\right) + 1} \tag{10-15}$$

and

Inverting amplifier:
$$A_c = \frac{\dfrac{R_2}{R_1}}{\dfrac{1}{A_0}\left(1 + \dfrac{R_2}{R_1}\right) + 1} \tag{10-16}$$

If A_0 were infinite, both denominators would reduce to unity. Equations (10-15) and (10-16) would then be equal to equations (10-11) and (10-8), the fundamental expressions for the gain of a noninverting and inverting amplifier.

To reduce the degrading effect of open-loop gain upon closed-loop gain, A_0 should be much higher than the desired A_c. Since the open-loop phase shift is usually 90° over most of the band of interest, the error term in the denominator of equations (10-15) and (10-16) is in quadrature with unity. This relationship minimizes the effect of open-loop gain upon closed-loop gain when the feedback network is purely resistive. An open-loop to closed-loop gain ratio of 10:1 will result in an error of only 0.5%, which is more than adequate for most requirements.

Finite open-loop gain also affects circuit input and output impedance. The input impedance of the noninverting amplifier can be derived as

$$R_{in} = (1 + A_0\beta)\, R_i \tag{10-17}$$

and the output impedance is given by

$$R_{out} = \frac{R_0}{A_0\beta} \tag{10-18}$$

where R_i and R_0 are the amplifiers' input and output impedance, respectively. Usually the closed-loop input and output impedance will have a negligible effect on circuit operation with moderate values of $A_0\beta$.

Practical Amplifier Considerations

DC Offsets. An inverting amplifier is shown in figure 10-18 with the addition of two bias currents I_a and I_b and an input offset voltage V_{dc}. These effects occur because of amplifier imperfections.

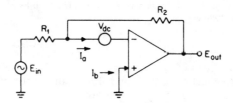

FIGURE 10-18   Inverting amplifier with offsets.

The input offset voltage results in an offset voltage at the output equal to V_{dc} times the closed-loop gain. The polarity of V_{dc} is random and is typically less than 10 mV.

The two bias currents are nearly equal except for a small difference or offset current I_0. In the circuit of figure 10-18, I_a produces an additional error voltage at the input given by $I_a R_{eq}$ where

$$R_{eq} = \frac{R_1 R_2}{R_1 + R_2} \tag{10-19}$$

The noninverting input bias current I_b has no effect. To minimize the effect of I_a, high values of R_{eq} should be avoided.

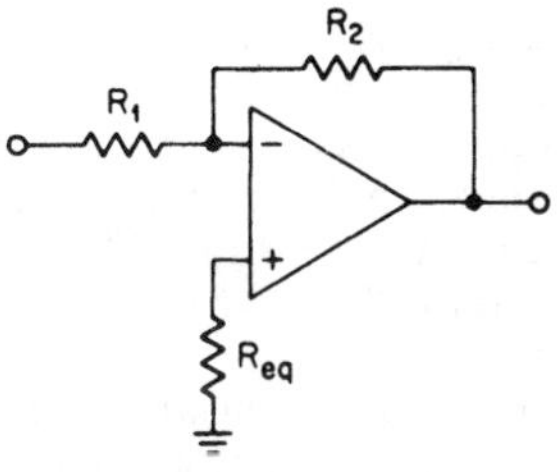

FIGURE 10-19 Minimization of DC offsets due to bias currents.

A more commonly used approach involves introducing a resistor having the value R_{eq} between the noninverting input and ground as shown in figure 10-19. This has no effect on the overall gain. However, a DC offset voltage of $I_b R_{eq}$ is introduced at the noninverting input. Since the amplifier is a differential device, the net error voltage due to the offset currents is $(I_a - I_b) R_{eq}$ or $I_0 R_{eq}$. Since I_a and I_b are each typically 80 nA and the offset current I_0 is in the range of 20 nA, a 4:1 reduction is obtained.

In the case of the noninverting amplifier configuration of figure 10-15, the ratio R_2/R_1 is determined by gain equation (10-11). However, the actual values of R_1 and R_2 are nearly arbitrary and can be chosen so that their parallel combination (R_{eq}) is approximately equal to the DC loading on the noninverting input, i.e., the parallel combination of all resistances connected between the noninverting input and AC ground.

In general, for moderate closed-loop gains or AC-coupled circuits, the effects of DC offsets are of little consequence. For critical applications such as precision active low-pass filters for the recovery of low-level DC components, the methods discussed can be implemented. Some amplifiers will provide an input terminal for nulling of output DC offsets.

Slew-Rate Limiting. When an operational amplifier is used to provide a high-level sine wave at a high frequency, the output will tend to approach a triangular waveform. This effect is called *slew-rate limiting,* and the slope of the triangular waveform in volts/μs is referred to as the *slew rate.* Typical values range from 1 to 100 V/μs, depending upon the amplifier type. If the peak-to-peak output voltage is small, the effects of slew rate will be minimized. Bandwidth can also be extended by using the minimum frequency compensation required for the given closed-loop gain.

Power-Supply Considerations. Most IC op amps require dual supply voltages, typically ranging from ±5 to ±18 V. The actual voltage magnitude is not critical, provided that the output swing from the amplifier is a few volts less than the supply voltages to avoid clipping. Maximum supply-voltage ratings should not be exceeded, of course.

To ensure stability, both the positive and negative power-supply voltages should be adequately bypassed to ground for high frequencies. Bypass capacitors can be 0.1 μF ceramic or 10 μF tantalum in most cases. Regulated supplies are desirable but not required. Most amplifiers have a typical supply-voltage sensitivity of 30 μV/V; i.e., a 1-V power-supply variation will result in only a 30-μV change reflected at the amplifier input.

In many cases, only a single positive supply voltage is available. Dual-voltage-type op amps can still be used by generating a reference voltage V_r which replaces the circuit's ground connections. The amplifier's negative power terminal is returned to ground and the positive power terminal is connected to the positive supply voltage.

The reference voltage should be midway between the positive supply voltage and ground and should be provided from a low-impedance source. A convenient means of generating V_r directly from the positive supply is shown in figure 10-20 using the voltage follower configuration.

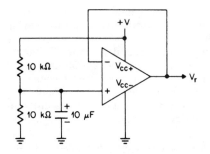

FIGURE 10-20 Generation of a reference voltage.

Input signals referenced to ground must be AC-coupled and then superimposed upon V_r. The signals are decoupled at the output to restore the ground reference. A low-pass filter design using this method will not pass low-frequency components near DC.

This technique is illustrated in figure 10-21 as applied to some previous design examples. The circuit of figure 10-20 is used to generate V_r and all amplifiers are powered using single-ended power supplies.

Operational Amplifier Selection

Bipolar Input. There is a variety of families of operational amplifiers. Some are differentiated by the type of input stage used within the monolithic integrated circuit. The most common form is a bipolar input device.

Bipolar inputs are the most commonly used type where the entire device, including the input stage, consists of bipolar transistors. Input bias and offset currents are a few hundred nanoamperes and offset voltages are typically under 10 mV. The open-loop input impedance is a few hundred K-ohms.

JFET Input. JFET input types have rapidly been replacing the bipolar input devices. The input stage consists of a pair of JFET transistors which results in much lower offset and bias currents than the bipolar type. Typically, the input offset and bias currents are less than a nanoampere. Input offset voltages for JFET-input amplifiers are comparable to that of the bipolar input devices. Open-loop input impedance is extremely high and in the range of 10^{12} ohms.

LinCMOS Low Voltage. The LinCMOS technology was developed for use in low-voltage, single supply applications such as battery-operated equipment or intermixed digital and linear systems operating off a single +5-V supply. Amplifiers can be used down to supply voltages as low as +2 V. Input offset and bias currents are in the range of a picoampere at room ambient. Input offset voltages are under 10 mV and have a very low temperature coefficient of about 1 μV/°C. Typical input impedance is in the range of 10^{12} ohms.*

Survey of Popular Amplifier Types

IC operational amplifiers range from economical general-purpose devices to the more costly high-performance units. Although many different types are available to choose from, certain units are more popular than others. These devices are listed in table 10-7 along with their typical characteristics.

Note: LinCMOS is a trademark of Texas Instruments Incorporated.

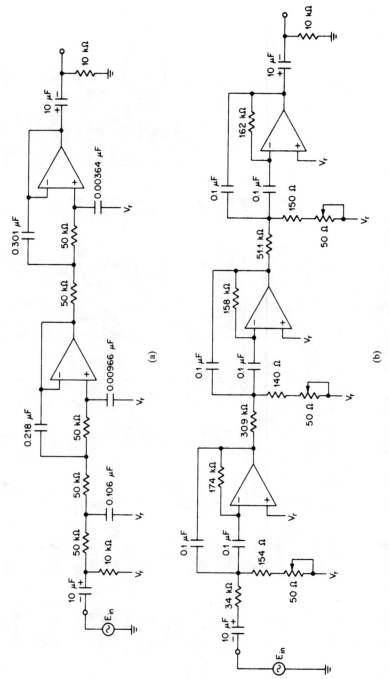

FIGURE 10-21 Designing filters for single supply operation: (a) low-pass filter of example 3-7; (b) bandpass filter of example 5-12.

TABLE 10-7 Operational Amplifier Selection Guide

Type	Bias Current, nA max	Offset Current, nA max	Offset Voltage, mV Max	Unity Gain, BW MHz Typ	Slew Rate, V/µS Typ	Min Supply Voltage	Max Supply Voltage	Comments
Single								
LF351	200 pA	100 pA	10	4	13	±5	±18	JFET input
LF355	200 pA	50 pA	10	1	5	±5	±18	JFET input
LF356	200 pA	50 pA	10	2	15	±5	±18	JFET input
LF357	200 pA	50 pA	10	3	75	±5	±18	JFET input, wideband
LM301A	250	50	7.5	1	0.5	±3	±18	General-purpose, uncompensated
LM307	250	50	7.5	1	0.5	±5	±18	General-purpose
LM308A	7 µA	1	0.5	1	0.3	±3	±18	Precision, uncompensated
LM318	250	50	10	15	70	±5	±20	High-performance
µA741	500	200	6	1	0.5	±5	±18	General-purpose
NE5534	1500	500	4	10	13	±3	±22	Low noise, wideband
TL060C	400 pA	200 pA	15	1	3.5	±3.5	±18	JFET input, low power, uncompensated
TL061C	200 pA	200 pA	15	1	3.5	±3.5	±18	JFET input, low power
TL070C	200 pA	100 pA	10	3	13	±3.5	±18	JFET input, low noise, uncompensated
TL071AC	200 pA	50 pA	6	4	13	±5	±18	JFET input, low noise
TL071C	200 pA	100 pA	10	3	13	±3.5	±18	JFET input, low noise
TL080C	400 pA	100 pA	15	3	13	±3.5	±18	JFET input, uncompensated
TL081AC	200 pA	100 pA	6	4	13	±5	±18	JFET input

Dual	TL081C	400 pA	100 pA	15	3	13	±3.5	±18	JFET input
	µA709	300 µA	100	2	10	0.3	±9	±18	General-purpose, uncompensated
	LF353	200 pA	100 pA	10	4	13	±5	±18	JFET input
	LF422C	100 pA	50 pA	5	2	6	±5	±18	JFET input, low power
	LM358	250	50	6	1	0.6	±1.5	±18	Single-supply, low power
	MC1458C	700	300	10	1.1	0.8	±3	±18	General-purpose
	MC4558C	500	200	6	2.8	1.6	±3	±18	Wide bandwidth
	NE5532	800	500	4	10	9	±3	±20	Low noise, wideband
	TL062C	200 pA	200 pA	15	2	13	±5	±18	JFET input, low noise
	TL072C	200 pA	50 pA	6	4	13	±5	±18	JFET input, low noise
	TL082C	400 pA	200 pA	15	4	13	±5	±18	JFET input
	TLV2322I	0.6 pA	0.1 pA	9	27 kHz	0.03	2	8	LinCMOS low-power 3 V
	TLV2332I	0.6 pA	0.1 pA	9	300 kHz	0.43	2	8	LinCMOS medium-power 3-V
	TLV2342I	0.6	0.1 pA	9	790 kHz	2.1	2	8	LinCMOS high-speed 3-V
Quad	LF347	200 pA	100 pA	10	4	13	±5	±18	JFET input
	LM324	250	50	6	1	0.6	±3	±16	Low power
	LM348	200	50	6	1	0.5	±3	±18	Quad 741
	TL044C	250	200	5	0.5	0.5	±2	±18	General-purpose
	TL054C	200 pA	1	4	2.7	16	±3.5	±18	JFET input
	TL064C	200 pA	200 pA	15	2	6	±2.5	±18	JFET input, low power
	TL074C	200 pA	50 pA	10	4	13	±5	±18	JFET input, low noise
	TL084C	400 pA	200 pA	15	4	13	±5	±18	JFET input
	TLV2324I	0.6 pA	0.1 pA	8	27 kHz	0.03	2	8	LinCMOS low-power 3-V
	TLV2334I	0.6 pA	0.1 pA	8	300 kHz	0.43	2	8	LinCMOS medium-power 3-V
	TLV2344I	0.6 pA	0.1 pA	8	790 kHz	2.1	2	8	LinCMOS high-speed 3-V

The parameters of this table are intended as a general guideline and correspond to commercial-grade op amps at a 25°C ambient temperature. The manufacturers' data sheets will provide more detailed and specific information.

Single Op Amps. The first general-purpose IC op amp was the μA709 which required external frequency compensation. The μA741 is a second-generation improvement with external compensation, offset voltage null capability, short-circuit protection, and a wider common-mode and differential voltage range than the μA709. The built-in frequency compensation results in a unity-gain bandwidth of 1 MHz. The LM301A and LM308A are similar to the μA741, except frequency compensation is externally provided.

The LF and TLO series have a JFET input circuit which dramatically reduces bias and offset currents. The NE5534 is a wideband low-noise device.

Dual Op Amps. Dual unit packages have evolved to save space and cost. Another useful feature is that both amplifiers in the same package are virtually identical electrically.

The MC1458C consists of a pair of μA741-type amplifiers and is very popular for use in active filters in the audio range. Channel separation between sections is typically 120 dB. The NE5532 has wider bandwidth and low noise.

The LF and TLO series have a JFET input circuit for lower bias and offset currents. The NE5532 is a wideband low-noise device and is a dual version of the NE5534. The TLV series uses LinCMOS technology and is capable of operation from supply voltages as low as 2 V. Bias and offset currents are extremely low, input impedance is in the range of 10^{12}, but bandwidth is somewhat limited compared to the other types.

Quad Op Amps. The TLO and LF series are popular and feature a JFET input circuit for reduced bias and offset currents. The TLV series is best suited for low-voltage operation typically in battery-operated devices and also features extremely low bias and offset currents and very high input impedance.

10.4 SURFACE-MOUNT TECHNOLOGY

Surface-mount technology provides circuit densities previously unattainable using through-hole methods. This technology allows the placement of subminiature passive and active components on both sides of a circuit board. As a result, densities can be nearly quadrupled in practice since the components are much smaller than their through-hole counterparts and the available board area for their placement is essentially doubled.

Surface-Mount Ceramic Capacitors

Monolithic ceramic chip capacitors intended for surface mount are constructed of interleaved layers of ceramic having a high dielectric constant k with metallic electrodes printed on the surface. These layers are sintered at extremely high temperatures to bond into a monolithic device. Alternate electrodes are bonded to end terminations so as to form a capacitor. This is illustrated in figure 10-22.

Two parameters mainly determine the operating characteristics of the capacitor, the temperature coefficient of the ceramic material, and the dissipation factor d.

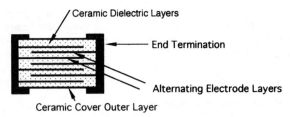

FIGURE 10-22   Construction of surface-mount ceramic capacitors.

Table 10-8 provides the three most readily available temperature characteristics and their associated dissipation factors.

TABLE 10-8   Properties of Surface-Mount Ceramic Capacitors

Material	Temperature Characteristic	Dissipation Factor
NPO	0 ± 30 ppm/°C –55 to +125°C	0.1% max
X7R	±15% from –55 to +125°C	2.5% max
Z5U	+22 to –56% +10 to +85°C	4% max

Table 10-8 indicates that NPO-type material is best suited for precision filter requirements. Tolerances as tight as ±1% are available in this material, but a cost premium occurs for tolerances closer than ±5%.

Surface-Mount Chip Resistors

Surface-mount chip resistors are manufactured by screening a layer of thick-film resistive paste onto an alumina ceramic substrate. By controlling the properties of the paste and the thickness of the resistive layer, the ohmic value and temperature coefficient of resistivity can be determined. Figure 10-23 shows the construction details of thick-film surface-mount resistors.

Surface-mount thick-film resistors are most commonly found in the 1206-size package and are rated for 1/8-watt dissipation. Although 5% tolerances are avail-

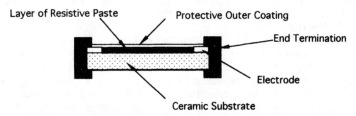

FIGURE 10-23   Surface-mount thick-film resistors.

able, the cost differential between 1 and 5% is insignificant and, given the precision requirements of active filters, 1% tolerance parts are suggested. Temperature coefficients as low as ±50PPM/°C can be obtained, but the most readily available temperature coefficient is ±200PPM/°C.

Surface-Mount Operational Amplifiers

The vast majority of IC operational amplifiers are available in surface-mount packages. In most cases, it is the same die or chip as used in a through-hole part except it is repackaged. Figure 10-24 shows the most popular package which is called *small outline* (SO). These packages consist of a circuit attached to a lead frame and encapsulated with a plastic compound. This compound can withstand the high temperatures resulting from soldering without deforming and provides a hermetic seal.

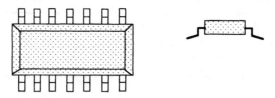

FIGURE 10-24   Plastic small outline (SO) package.

Manufacturing Considerations

Specific mechanical considerations determine the robustness of the connections to the circuit board for surface-mount parts. In most cases, the coefficient of expansion of the components differs from that of the board itself. For example, the expansion coefficient of the ceramic dielectric of a chip capacitor is different than that of an epoxy glass printed circuit board. Since the part is held in place only by placing it on top of pads and applying solder, the absence of a further mechanical connection could cause the part to break free with time.

Pad design is dependent on which of two soldering processes is used, *reflow* or *wave*. In the reflow process, the pad is coated by a dried solder paste. The chip is placed on these pads and the board is gradually heated until this solder melts and reflows, joining the part to the pad. With the wave solder method, the parts are first held in place with a glue and then the board is covered by a wave of solder. Each method imposes unique requirements on the pad design to ensure reliability and longevity of the connections.

Although use of surface-mount technology results in high circuit densities, there is a penalty to be paid. Through-hole parts allow the use of the component leads to convey signals from the surface of the board to the inner layers as well as to the other outside surface of the board. Since the leads of surface-mount components lie flat on the board surface attached to pads, extra feed-throughs (referred to as *vias*) are required on the board to interconnect layers, and sometimes this results in extra layers as well. The end result is a costlier PC board.

BIBLIOGRAPHY

Fairchild Semiconductor, *Linear Integrated Circuits Data Book,* Mountain View, Calif.

Lindquist, C. S., *Active Network Design,* Steward and Sons, Long Beach, Calif., 1977.

Motorola Inc., *Motorola Master Selection Guide,* Phoenix, Ariz., 1992.

Stout, D. F., and Kaufman, M., *Handbook of Operational Amplifier Circuit Design,* McGraw-Hill, New York, 1976.

Texas Instruments, "Linear Circuits Operational Amplifiers," Texas Instruments, Dallas, Tex., 1992.

CHAPTER 11

NORMALIZED FILTER DESIGN TABLES

TABLE 11-1 Butterworth Pole Locations

Order n	Real Part $-\alpha$	Imaginary Part $\pm j\beta$
2	0.7071	0.7071
3	0.5000	0.8660
	1.0000	
4	0.9239	0.3827
	0.3827	0.9239
5	0.8090	0.5878
	0.3090	0.9511
	1.0000	
6	0.9659	0.2588
	0.7071	0.7071
	0.2588	0.9659
7	0.9010	0.4339
	0.6235	0.7818
	0.2225	0.9749
	1.0000	
8	0.9808	0.1951
	0.8315	0.5556
	0.5556	0.8315
	0.1951	0.9808
9	0.9397	0.3420
	0.7660	0.6428
	0.5000	0.8660
	0.1737	0.9848
	1.0000	
10	0.9877	0.1564
	0.8910	0.4540
	0.7071	0.7071
	0.4540	0.8910
	0.1564	0.9877

TABLE 11-2   Butterworth LC Element Values*

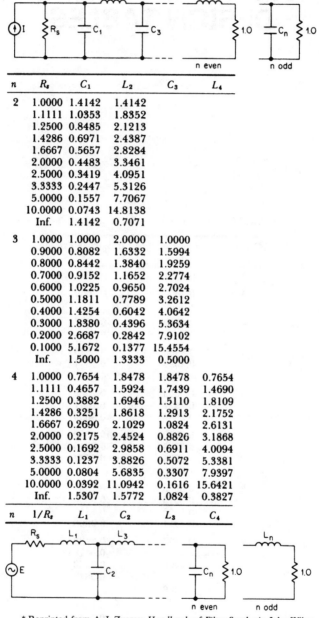

n	R_s	C_1	L_2	C_3	L_4
2	1.0000	1.4142	1.4142		
	1.1111	1.0353	1.8352		
	1.2500	0.8485	2.1213		
	1.4286	0.6971	2.4387		
	1.6667	0.5657	2.8284		
	2.0000	0.4483	3.3461		
	2.5000	0.3419	4.0951		
	3.3333	0.2447	5.3126		
	5.0000	0.1557	7.7067		
	10.0000	0.0743	14.8138		
	Inf.	1.4142	0.7071		
3	1.0000	1.0000	2.0000	1.0000	
	0.9000	0.8082	1.6332	1.5994	
	0.8000	0.8442	1.3840	1.9259	
	0.7000	0.9152	1.1652	2.2774	
	0.6000	1.0225	0.9650	2.7024	
	0.5000	1.1811	0.7789	3.2612	
	0.4000	1.4254	0.6042	4.0642	
	0.3000	1.8380	0.4396	5.3634	
	0.2000	2.6687	0.2842	7.9102	
	0.1000	5.1672	0.1377	15.4554	
	Inf.	1.5000	1.3333	0.5000	
4	1.0000	0.7654	1.8478	1.8478	0.7654
	1.1111	0.4657	1.5924	1.7439	1.4690
	1.2500	0.3882	1.6946	1.5110	1.8109
	1.4286	0.3251	1.8618	1.2913	2.1752
	1.6667	0.2690	2.1029	1.0824	2.6131
	2.0000	0.2175	2.4524	0.8826	3.1868
	2.5000	0.1692	2.9858	0.6911	4.0094
	3.3333	0.1237	3.8826	0.5072	5.3381
	5.0000	0.0804	5.6835	0.3307	7.9397
	10.0000	0.0392	11.0942	0.1616	15.6421
	Inf.	1.5307	1.5772	1.0824	0.3827
n	$1/R_s$	L_1	C_2	L_3	C_4

* Reprinted from A. I. Zverev, *Handbook of Filter Synthesis,* John Wiley and Sons, New York, 1967.

TABLE 11-2 Butterworth *LC* Element Values (*Continued*)

n	R_s	C_1	L_2	C_3	L_4	C_5	L_6	C_7
5	1.0000	0.6180	1.6180	2.0000	1.6180	0.6180		
	0.9000	0.4416	1.0265	1.9095	1.7562	1.3887		
	0.8000	0.4698	0.8660	2.0605	1.5443	1.7380		
	0.7000	0.5173	0.7313	2.2849	1.3326	2.1083		
	0.6000	0.5860	0.6094	2.5998	1.1255	2.5524		
	0.5000	0.6857	0.4955	3.0510	0.9237	3.1331		
	0.4000	0.8378	0.3877	3.7357	0.7274	3.9648		
	0.3000	1.0937	0.2848	4.8835	0.5367	5.3073		
	0.2000	1.6077	0.1861	7.1849	0.3518	7.9345		
	0.1000	3.1522	0.0912	14.0945	0.1727	15.7103		
	Inf.	1.5451	1.6944	1.3820	0.8944	0.3090		
6	1.0000	0.5176	1.4142	1.9319	1.9319	1.4142	0.5176	
	1.1111	0.2890	1.0403	1.3217	2.0539	1.7443	1.3347	
	1.2500	0.2445	1.1163	1.1257	2.2389	1.5498	1.6881	
	1.4286	0.2072	1.2363	0.9567	2.4991	1.3464	2.0618	
	1.6667	0.1732	1.4071	0.8011	2.8580	1.1431	2.5092	
	2.0000	0.1412	1.6531	0.6542	3.3687	0.9423	3.0938	
	2.5000	0.1108	2.0275	0.5139	4.1408	0.7450	3.9305	
	3.3333	0.0816	2.6559	0.3788	5.4325	0.5517	5.2804	
	5.0000	0.0535	3.9170	0.2484	8.0201	0.3628	7.9216	
	10.0000	0.0263	7.7053	0.1222	15.7855	0.1788	15.7375	
	Inf.	1.5529	1.7593	1.5529	1.2016	0.7579	0.2588	
7	1.0000	0.4450	1.2470	1.8019	2.0000	1.8019	1.2470	0.4450
	0.9000	0.2985	0.7111	1.4043	1.4891	2.1249	1.7268	1.2961
	0.8000	0.3215	0.6057	1.5174	1.2777	2.3338	1.5461	1.6520
	0.7000	0.3571	0.5154	1.6883	1.0910	2.6177	1.3498	2.0277
	0.6000	0.4075	0.4322	1.9284	0.9170	3.0050	1.1503	2.4771
	0.5000	0.4799	0.3536	2.2726	0.7512	3.5532	0.9513	3.0640
	0.4000	0.5899	0.2782	2.7950	0.5917	4.3799	0.7542	3.9037
	0.3000	0.7745	0.2055	3.6706	0.4373	5.7612	0.5600	5.2583
	0.2000	1.1448	0.1350	5.4267	0.2874	8.5263	0.3692	7.9079
	0.1000	2.2571	0.0665	10.7004	0.1417	16.8222	0.1823	15.7480
	Inf.	1.5576	1.7988	1.6588	1.3972	1.0550	0.6560	0.2225
n	$1/R_s$	L_1	C_2	L_3	C_4	L_5	C_6	L_7

TABLE 11-2 Butterworth LC Element Values (*Continued*)

n	R_s	C_1	L_2	C_3	L_4	C_5	L_6	C_7	L_8	C_9	L_{10}
8	1.0000	0.3902	1.1111	1.6629	1.9616	1.9616	1.6629	1.1111	0.3902		
	1.1111	0.2075	0.7575	0.9925	1.6362	1.5900	2.1612	1.7092	1.2671		
	1.2500	0.1774	0.8199	0.8499	1.7779	1.3721	2.3874	1.5393	1.6246		
	1.4286	0.1513	0.9138	0.7257	1.9852	1.1760	2.6879	1.3490	2.0017		
	1.6667	0.1272	1.0455	0.6102	2.2740	0.9912	3.0945	1.1530	2.4524		
	2.0000	0.1042	1.2341	0.5003	2.6863	0.8139	3.6678	0.9558	3.0408		
	2.5000	0.0822	1.5201	0.3945	3.3106	0.6424	4.5308	0.7594	3.8825		
	3.3333	0.0608	1.9995	0.2919	4.3563	0.4757	5.9714	0.5650	5.2400		
	5.0000	0.0400	2.9608	0.1921	6.4523	0.3133	8.8538	0.3732	7.8952		
	10.0000	0.0198	5.8479	0.0949	12.7455	0.1547	17.4999	0.1846	15.7510		
	Inf.	1.5607	1.8246	1.7287	1.5283	1.2588	0.9371	0.5776	0.1951		
9	1.0000	0.3473	1.0000	1.5321	1.8794	2.0000	1.8794	1.5321	1.0000	0.3473	
	0.9000	0.2242	0.5388	1.0835	1.1859	1.7905	1.6538	2.1796	1.6930	1.2447	
	0.8000	0.2434	0.4623	1.1777	1.0200	1.9542	1.4336	2.4189	1.5318	1.6033	
	0.7000	0.2719	0.3954	1.3162	0.8734	2.1885	1.2323	2.7314	1.3464	1.9812	
	0.6000	0.3117	0.3330	1.5092	0.7361	2.5124	1.0410	3.1516	1.1533	2.4328	
	0.5000	0.3685	0.2735	1.7846	0.6046	2.9734	0.8565	3.7426	0.9579	3.0223	
	0.4000	0.4545	0.2159	2.2019	0.4775	3.6706	0.6771	4.6310	0.7624	3.8654	
	0.3000	0.5987	0.1600	2.9006	0.3539	4.8373	0.5022	6.1128	0.5680	5.2249	
	0.2000	0.8878	0.1054	4.3014	0.2333	7.1750	0.3312	9.0766	0.3757	7.8838	
	0.1000	1.7558	0.0521	8.5074	0.1153	14.1930	0.1638	17.9654	0.1862	15.7504	
	Inf.	1.5628	1.8424	1.7772	1.6202	1.4037	1.1408	0.8414	0.5155	0.1736	
10	1.0000	0.3129	0.9080	1.4142	1.7820	1.9754	1.9754	1.7820	1.4142	0.9080	0.3129
	1.1111	0.1614	0.5924	0.7853	1.3202	1.3230	1.8968	1.6956	2.1883	1.6785	1.2267
	1.2500	0.1388	0.6452	0.6762	1.4400	1.1420	2.0779	1.4754	2.4377	1.5245	1.5861
	1.4286	0.1190	0.7222	0.5797	1.6130	0.9802	2.3324	1.2712	2.7592	1.3431	1.9646
	1.6667	0.1004	0.8292	0.4891	1.8528	0.8275	2.6825	1.0758	3.1895	1.1526	2.4169
	2.0000	0.0825	0.9818	0.4021	2.1943	0.6808	3.1795	0.8864	3.7934	0.9588	3.0072
	2.5000	0.0652	1.2127	0.3179	2.7108	0.5384	3.9302	0.7018	4.7002	0.7641	3.8512
	3.3333	0.0484	1.5992	0.2358	3.5754	0.3995	5.1858	0.5211	6.2118	0.5700	5.2122
	5.0000	0.0319	2.3740	0.1556	5.3082	0.2636	7.7010	0.3440	9.2343	0.3775	7.8738
	10.0000	0.0158	4.7005	0.0770	10.5104	0.1305	15.2505	0.1704	18.2981	0.1872	15.7481
	Inf.	1.5643	1.8552	1.8121	1.6869	1.5100	1.2921	1.0406	0.7626	0.4654	0.1564
n	$1/R_s$	L_1	C_2	L_3	C_4	L_5	C_6	L_7	C_8	L_9	C_{10}

TABLE 11-3 Butterworth Uniform Dissipation Network*

$n = 2$

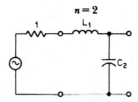

d	L_1	C_2	$\alpha_0,$ dB
0	0.7071	1.414	0
0.05	0.7609	1.410	0.614
0.10	0.8236	1.398	1.22
0.15	0.8974	1.374	1.83
0.20	0.9860	1.340	2.42
0.25	1.094	1.290	2.99
0.30	1.228	1.223	3.53
0.35	1.400	1.138	4.05
0.40	1.628	1.034	4.52
0.45	1.944	0.9083	4.94
0.50	2.414	0.7630	5.30
0.55	3.183	0.5989	5.59
0.60	4.669	0.4188	5.82
0.65	8.756	0.2267	5.96

d	C_2	L_1	$\alpha_0,$ dB

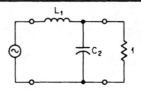

* By permission of P. R. Geffe.

TABLE 11-4   Butterworth Uniform Dissipation Network*

$$n = 3$$

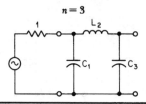

d	C_1	L_2	C_3	$\alpha_0,$ dB
0	0.5000	1.333	1.500	0
0.05	0.5405	1.403	1.457	0.868
0.10	0.5882	1.481	1.402	1.73
0.15	0.6452	1.567	1.334	2.60
0.20	0.7143	1.667	1.250	3.45
0.25	0.8000	1.786	1.149	4.30
0.30	0.9091	1.939	1.026	5.15
0.35	1.053	2.164	0.8743	5.98
0.40	1.250	2.581	0.6798	6.82
0.45	1.538	3.806	0.4126	7.66
d	L_3	C_2	L_1	$\alpha_0,$ dB

* By permission of P. R. Geffe.

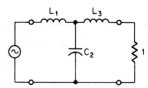

TABLE 11-5 Butterworth Uniform Dissipation Network*

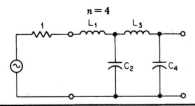

$n = 4$

d	L_1	C_2	L_3	C_4	α_0, dB
0	0.3827	1.082	1.577	1.531	0
0.05	0.4144	1.156	1.636	1.454	1.13
0.10	0.4518	1.240	1.701	1.362	2.27
0.15	0.4967	1.339	1.777	1.250	3.39
0.20	0.5515	1.459	1.879	1.113	4.51
0.25	0.6199	1.609	2.039	0.9400	5.63
0.30	0.7077	1.812	2.384	0.7099	6.73
0.35	0.8243	2.124	3.848	0.3651	7.82
d	C_4	L_3	C_2	L_1	α_0, dB

* By permission of P. R. Geffe.

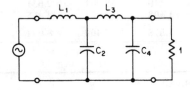

TABLE 11-6 Butterworth Uniform Dissipation Network*

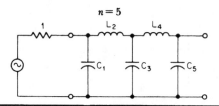

$n = 5$

d	C_1	L_2	C_3	L_4	C_5	$\alpha_0,$ dB
0	0.3090	0.8944	1.382	1.694	1.545	0
0.02	0.3189	0.9199	1.412	1.712	1.504	0.562
0.04	0.3294	0.9468	1.443	1.730	1.461	1.12
0.06	0.3406	0.9754	1.476	1.750	1.414	1.69
0.08	0.3526	1.006	1.512	1.771	1.364	2.25
0.10	0.3654	1.038	1.549	1.794	1.309	2.81
0.12	0.3794	1.073	1.589	1.822	1.250	3.37
0.14	0.3943	1.111	1.633	1.854	1.184	3.93
0.16	0.4104	1.151	1.681	1.894	1.113	4.48
0.18	0.4281	1.195	1.734	1.946	1.034	5.04
0.20	0.4472	1.243	1.796	2.018	0.9452	5.59
0.22	0.4681	1.296	1.867	2.124	0.8434	6.15
0.24	0.4911	1.354	1.953	2.300	0.7242	6.70
0.26	0.5165	1.419	2.061	2.631	0.5798	7.25
0.28	0.5446	1.493	2.204	3.453	0.3965	7.79
0.30	0.5760	1.578	2.409	8.084	0.1476	8.34
d	L_5	C_4	L_3	C_2	L_1	$\alpha_0,$ dB

* By permission of P. R. Geffe.

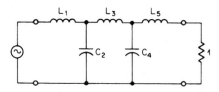

TABLE 11-7 Butterworth Uniform Dissipation Network*

$n = 6$

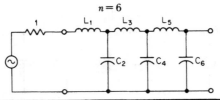

d	L_1	C_2	L_3	C_4	L_5	C_6	α_0, dB
0	0.2588	0.7579	1.202	1.553	1.759	1.533	0
0.02	0.2671	0.7804	1.232	1.581	1.727	1.502	0.671
0.04	0.2760	0.8043	1.264	1.611	1.786	1.446	1.34
0.06	0.2854	0.8297	1.297	1.643	1.802	1.386	2.01
0.08	0.2955	0.8569	1.333	1.679	1.821	1.321	2.68
0.10	0.3064	0.8860	1.372	1.714	1.844	1.250	3.35
0.12	0.3181	0.9172	1.413	1.755	1.874	1.171	4.02
0.14	0.3307	0.9508	1.458	1.802	1.917	1.083	4.69
0.16	0.3443	0.9871	1.508	1.860	1.979	0.9839	5.30
0.18	0.3594	1.027	1.558	1.923	2.080	0.8690	6.00
0.20	0.3754	1.070	1.621	2.008	2.258	0.7313	6.68
0.22	0.3931	1.117	1.690	2.122	2.646	0.5586	7.34
d	C_6	L_5	C_4	L_3	C_2	L_1	α_0, dB

* By permission of P. R. Geffe.

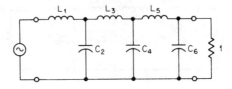

TABLE 11-8   Butterworth Uniform Dissipation Network*

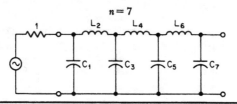

$n = 7$

d	C_1	L_2	C_3	L_4	C_5	L_6	C_7	$\alpha_0,$ dB
0	0.2225	0.6560	1.054	1.397	1.659	1.799	1.588	0
0.02	0.2297	0.6759	1.084	1.428	1.684	1.808	1.496	0.781
0.04	0.2373	0.6972	1.114	1.461	1.712	1.818	1.428	1.56
0.06	0.2454	0.7198	1.146	1.496	1.742	1.832	1.354	2.34
0.08	0.2542	0.7440	1.180	1.533	1.775	1.851	1.274	3.12
0.10	0.2636	0.7699	1.217	1.573	1.813	1.878	1.184	3.90
0.12	0.2739	0.7980	1.254	1.614	1.860	1.923	1.085	4.68
0.14	0.2846	0.8281	1.294	1.659	1.910	1.992	0.9701	5.45
0.16	0.2966	0.8608	1.344	1.715	1.979	2.111	0.8350	6.23
0.18	0.3091	0.8960	1.394	1.778	2.073	2.356	0.6679	7.00
0.20	0.3232	0.9243	1.453	1.862	2.233	3.177	0.4220	7.77
d	L_7	C_6	L_5	C_4	L_3	C_2	L_1	$\alpha_0,$ dB

* By permission of P. R. Geffe.

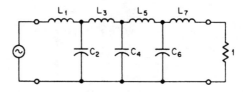

TABLE 11-9 Butterworth Uniform Dissipation Network*

$n = 8$

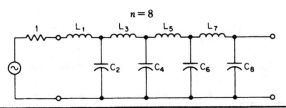

d	L_1	C_2	L_3	C_4	L_5	C_6	L_7	C_8	a_0, dB
0	0.1951	0.5776	0.9371	1.259	1.528	1.729	1.824	1.561	0
0.02	0.2014	0.5954	0.9636	1.290	1.558	1.752	1.830	1.488	0.890
0.04	0.2081	0.6144	0.9918	1.323	1.590	1.777	1.838	1.409	1.78
0.06	0.2152	0.6347	1.022	1.357	1.624	1.806	1.851	1.321	2.67
0.08	0.2229	0.6564	1.054	1.394	1.622	1.839	1.872	1.224	3.56
0.10	0.2312	0.6796	1.088	1.434	1.703	1.880	1.908	1.114	4.45
0.12	0.2400	0.7046	1.124	1.478	1.750	1.932	1.972	0.9856	5.33
0.14	0.2496	0.7316	1.164	1.526	1.804	2.003	2.101	0.8305	6.22
0.16	0.2600	0.7608	1.208	1.579	1.869	2.110	2.414	0.6307	7.10
0.18	0.2713	0.7926	1.255	1.639	1.951	2.294	3.683	0.3439	7.98
d	C_8	L_7	C_6	L_5	C_4	L_3	C_2	L_1	a_0, dB

* By permission of P. R. Geffe.

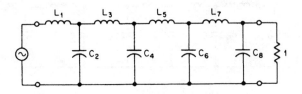

TABLE 11-10   Butterworth Uniform Dissipation Network*

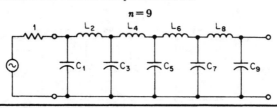

$n = 9$

d	C_1	L_2	C_3	L_4	C_5	L_6	C_7	L_8	C_9	α_0, dB
0	0.1736	0.5155	0.8414	1.141	1.404	1.620	1.777	1.842	1.563	0
0.02	0.1793	0.5316	0.8659	1.171	1.435	1.649	1.798	1.845	1.480	1.00
0.04	0.1852	0.5488	0.8921	1.202	1.469	1.680	1.822	1.851	1.388	2.00
0.06	0.1916	0.5671	0.9199	1.236	1.504	1.713	1.850	1.864	1.286	3.00
0.08	0.1984	0.5867	0.9496	1.272	1.543	1.751	1.884	1.891	1.171	4.00
0.10	0.2058	0.6077	0.9814	1.311	1.584	1.794	1.931	1.942	1.036	5.00
0.12	0.2137	0.6303	1.016	1.353	1.630	1.844	1.997	2.054	0.8735	5.99
0.14	0.2223	0.6547	1.053	1.398	1.682	1.907	2.101	2.340	0.6614	6.99
0.16	0.2315	0.6812	1.093	1.448	1.742	1.991	2.293	3.620	0.3486	7.98
d	L_9	C_8	L_7	C_6	L_5	C_4	L_3	C_2	L_1	α_0, dB

* By permission of P. R. Geffe.

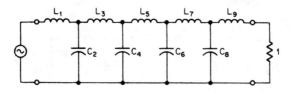

TABLE 11-11 Butterworth Uniform Dissipation Network*

$n = 10$

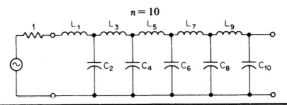

d	L_1	C_2	L_3	C_4	L_5	C_6	L_7	C_8	L_9	C_{10}	α_0, dB
0	0.1564	0.4654	0.7626	1.041	1.292	1.510	1.687	1.812	1.855	1.564	0
0.02	0.1614	0.4800	0.7854	1.069	1.324	1.541	1.714	1.831	1.855	1.471	1.11
0.04	0.1669	0.4956	0.8096	1.099	1.357	1.574	1.744	1.853	1.860	1.367	2.22
0.06	0.1726	0.5123	0.8353	1.132	1.392	1.610	1.777	1.882	1.875	1.249	3.33
0.08	0.1788	0.5301	0.8629	1.166	1.430	1.648	1.814	1.920	1.910	1.114	4.44
0.10	0.1854	0.5493	0.8924	1.203	1.471	1.692	1.860	1.976	1.991	0.9508	5.55
0.12	0.1926	0.5698	0.9242	1.243	1.516	1.741	1.918	2.067	2.201	0.7409	6.65
0.14	0.2003	0.5921	0.9584	1.286	1.566	1.798	1.997	2.239	3.051	0.4349	7.76

d	C_{10}	L_9	C_8	L_7	C_6	L_5	C_4	L_3	C_2	L_1	α_0, dB

* By permission of P. R. Geffe.

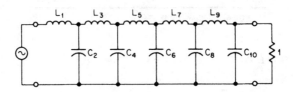

TABLE 11-12   Butterworth Lossy-L Network*

$n = 2$

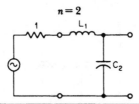

d	L_1	C_2
0	0.7071	1.414
0.05	0.7330	1.364
0.10	0.7609	1.314
0.15	0.7910	1.264
0.20	0.8236	1.214
0.25	0.8589	1.164
0.30	0.8975	1.114
0.35	0.9397	1.064
0.40	0.9860	1.014
0.45	1.037	0.9642
0.50	1.094	0.9142
0.55	1.157	0.8642
0.60	1.228	0.8142
0.65	1.309	0.7642

     * By permission of P. R. Geffe.

TABLE 11-13   Butterworth Lossy-L Network*

$n = 3$

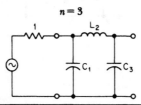

d	C_1	L_2	C_3
0	0.5000	1.333	1.500
0.05	0.5128	1.403	1.390
0.10	0.5263	1.480	1.284
0.15	0.5405	1.565	1.182
0.20	0.5556	1.660	1.084
0.25	0.5714	1.766	0.9911
0.30	0.5882	1.885	0.9018
0.35	0.6061	2.021	0.8164
0.40	0.6250	2.177	0.7350
0.45	0.6452	2.358	0.6573

     * By permission of P. R. Geffe.

TABLE 11-14 Butterworth Lossy-L Network*

$n = 4$

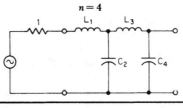

d	L_1	C_2	L_3	C_4
0	0.3827	1.082	1.577	1.531
0.05	0.3979	1.087	1.698	1.362
0.10	0.4144	1.091	1.834	1.205
0.15	0.4323	1.095	1.990	1.061
0.20	0.4518	1.098	2.170	0.9289
0.25	0.4732	1.100	2.380	0.8072
0.30	0.4967	1.102	2.628	0.6955
0.35	0.5227	1.102	2.926	0.5933

* By permission of P. R. Geffe.

TABLE 11-15 Butterworth Lossy-L Network*

$n = 5$

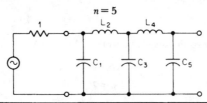

d	C_1	L_2	C_3	L_4	C_5
0	0.3090	0.8944	1.382	1.694	1.545
0.02	0.3129	0.9127	1.369	1.762	1.452
0.04	0.3168	0.9316	1.355	1.834	1.363
0.06	0.3209	0.9514	1.342	1.911	1.278
0.08	0.3251	0.9719	1.327	1.993	1.197
0.10	0.3294	0.9934	1.313	2.080	1.119
0.12	0.3338	1.016	1.298	2.173	1.046
0.14	0.3383	1.039	1.283	2.273	0.9754
0.16	0.3429	1.063	1.268	2.380	0.9086
0.18	0.3477	1.089	1.253	2.494	0.8450
0.20	0.3526	1.116	1.237	2.620	0.7844
0.22	0.3576	1.144	1.221	2.754	0.7269
0.24	0.3628	1.173	1.204	2.901	0.6721
0.26	0.3682	1.204	1.188	3.061	0.6201
0.28	0.3737	1.237	1.171	3.237	0.5076
0.30	0.3794	1.271	1.154	3.431	0.5236

* By permission of P. R. Geffe.

TABLE 11-16   Butterworth Lossy-L Network*

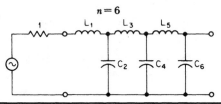

$n = 6$

d	L_1	C_2	L_3	C_4	L_5	C_6
0	0.2588	0.7579	1.202	1.553	1.759	1.553
0.02	0.2629	0.7631	1.235	1.519	1.850	1.436
0.04	0.2671	0.7683	1.271	1.485	1.947	1.326
0.06	0.2714	0.7736	1.308	1.451	2.052	1.223
0.08	0.2760	0.7789	1.347	1.417	2.165	1.125
0.10	0.2806	0.7843	1.388	1.383	2.228	1.034
0.12	0.2854	0.7897	1.432	1.349	2.421	0.9487
0.14	0.2904	0.7952	1.478	1.315	2.565	0.8684
0.16	0.2955	0.8007	1.527	1.281	2.723	0.7932
0.18	0.3009	0.8063	1.579	1.248	2.896	0.7227
0.20	0.3064	0.8118	1.634	1.214	3.807	0.6567
0.22	0.3121	0.8174	1.692	1.181	3.298	0.5949

* By permission of P. R. Geffe.

TABLE 11-17   Butterworth Lossy-L Network*

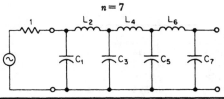

$n = 7$

d	C_1	L_2	C_3	L_4	C_5	L_6	C_7
0	0.2225	0.6560	1.054	1.397	1.659	1.799	1.588
0.02	0.2255	0.6688	1.053	1.449	1.602	1.913	1.417
0.04	0.2286	0.6822	1.051	1.504	1.546	2.038	1.288
0.06	0.2318	0.6960	1.048	1.564	1.490	2.173	1.167
0.08	0.2351	0.7104	1.045	1.627	1.436	2.322	1.056
0.10	0.2384	0.7255	1.043	1.694	1.382	2.484	0.9532
0.12	0.2419	0.7412	1.039	1.766	1.330	2.664	0.8581
0.14	0.2454	0.7575	1.036	1.842	1.278	2.862	0.7703
0.16	0.2491	0.7746	1.032	1.924	1.228	3.083	0.6892
0.18	0.2529	0.7924	1.028	2.013	1.178	3.330	0.6144
0.20	0.2568	0.8110	1.024	2.108	1.130	3.609	0.5454

* By permission of P. R. Geffe.

TABLE 11-18 Butterworth Lossy-L Network*

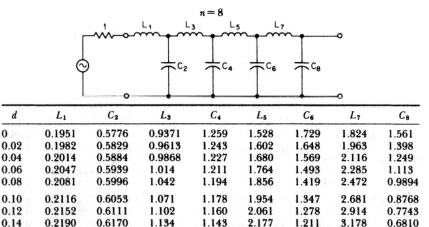

$n = 8$

d	L_1	C_2	L_3	C_4	L_5	C_6	L_7	C_8
0	0.1951	0.5776	0.9371	1.259	1.528	1.729	1.824	1.561
0.02	0.1982	0.5829	0.9613	1.243	1.602	1.648	1.963	1.398
0.04	0.2014	0.5884	0.9868	1.227	1.680	1.569	2.116	1.249
0.06	0.2047	0.5939	1.014	1.211	1.764	1.493	2.285	1.113
0.08	0.2081	0.5996	1.042	1.194	1.856	1.419	2.472	0.9894
0.10	0.2116	0.6053	1.071	1.178	1.954	1.347	2.681	0.8768
0.12	0.2152	0.6111	1.102	1.160	2.061	1.278	2.914	0.7743
0.14	0.2190	0.6170	1.134	1.143	2.177	1.211	3.178	0.6810
0.16	0.2229	0.6231	1.169	1.124	2.302	1.147	3.477	0.5962
0.18	0.2270	0.6292	1.206	1.107	2.440	1.084	3.819	0.5191

* By permission of P. R. Geffe.

TABLE 11-19 Butterworth Lossy-L Network*

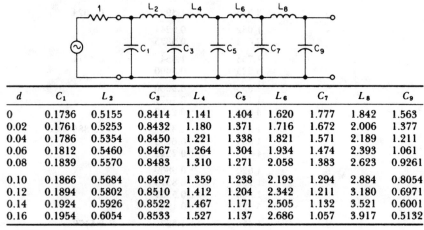

$n = 9$

d	C_1	L_2	C_3	L_4	C_5	L_6	C_7	L_8	C_9
0	0.1736	0.5155	0.8414	1.141	1.404	1.620	1.777	1.842	1.563
0.02	0.1761	0.5253	0.8432	1.180	1.371	1.716	1.672	2.006	1.377
0.04	0.1786	0.5354	0.8450	1.221	1.338	1.821	1.571	2.189	1.211
0.06	0.1812	0.5460	0.8467	1.264	1.304	1.934	1.474	2.393	1.061
0.08	0.1839	0.5570	0.8483	1.310	1.271	2.058	1.383	2.623	0.9261
0.10	0.1866	0.5684	0.8497	1.359	1.238	2.193	1.294	2.884	0.8054
0.12	0.1894	0.5802	0.8510	1.412	1.204	2.342	1.211	3.180	0.6971
0.14	0.1924	0.5926	0.8522	1.467	1.171	2.505	1.132	3.521	0.6001
0.16	0.1954	0.6054	0.8533	1.527	1.137	2.686	1.057	3.917	0.5132

* By permission of P. R. Geffe.

TABLE 11-20   Butterworth Lossy-L Network*

$$n = 10$$

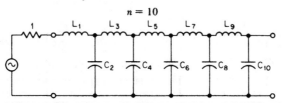

d	L_1	C_2	L_3	C_4	L_5	C_6	L_7	C_8	L_9	C_{10}
0	0.1564	0.4654	0.7626	1.041	1.292	1.510	1.687	1.812	1.855	1.564
0.02	0.1589	0.4704	0.7812	1.034	1.348	1.457	1.807	1.682	2.044	1.357
0.04	0.1614	0.4754	0.8006	1.027	1.408	1.404	1.939	1.560	2.258	1.173
0.06	0.1641	0.4806	0.8209	1.019	1.472	1.353	2.084	1.444	2.501	1.010
0.08	0.1669	0.4859	0.8422	1.011	1.541	1.302	2.245	1.336	2.778	0.8660
0.10	0.1697	0.4913	0.8603	1.003	1.614	1.251	2.423	1.234	3.096	0.7387
0.12	0.1726	0.4969	0.8880	0.9949	1.694	1.201	2.621	1.139	3.466	0.6263
0.14	0.1757	0.5024	0.9127	0.9861	1.780	1.152	2.842	1.050	3.901	0.5270

* By permission of P. R. Geffe.

TABLE 11-21   Butterworth Active Low-Pass Values*

Order n	C_1	C_2	C_3
2	1.414	0.7071	
3	3.546	1.392	0.2024
4	1.082	0.9241	
	2.613	0.3825	
5	1.753	1.354	0.4214
	3.235	0.3090	
6	1.035	0.9660	
	1.414	0.7071	
	3.863	0.2588	
7	1.531	1.336	0.4885
	1.604	0.6235	
	4.493	0.2225	
8	1.020	0.9809	
	1.202	0.8313	
	1.800	0.5557	
	5.125	0.1950	
9	1.455	1.327	0.5170
	1.305	0.7661	
	2.000	0.5000	
	5.758	0.1736	
10	1.012	0.9874	
	1.122	0.8908	
	1.414	0.7071	
	2.202	0.4540	
	6.390	0.1563	

* Reprinted from *Electronics*, McGraw-Hill, Inc., August 18, 1969.

TABLE 11-22 0.01-dB Chebyshev Pole Locations

Order n	Real Part $-\alpha$	Imaginary Part $\pm j\beta$
2	0.6743	0.7075
3	0.4233 0.8467	0.8663
4	0.6762 0.2801	0.3828 0.9241
5	0.5120 0.1956 0.6328	0.5879 0.9512
6	0.5335 0.3906 0.1430	0.2588 0.7072 0.9660
7	0.4393 0.3040 0.1085 0.4876	0.4339 0.7819 0.9750
8	0.4268 0.3618 0.2418 0.08490	0.1951 0.5556 0.8315 0.9808
9	0.3686 0.3005 0.1961 0.06812 0.3923	0.3420 0.6428 0.8661 0.9848

TABLE 11-23   0.1-dB Chebyshev Pole Locations

Order n	Real Part $-\alpha$	Imaginary Part $\pm j\beta$
2	0.6104	0.7106
3	0.3490	0.8684
	0.6979	
4	0.2177	0.9254
	0.5257	0.3833
5	0.3842	0.5884
	0.1468	0.9521
	0.4749	
6	0.3916	0.2590
	0.2867	0.7077
	0.1049	0.9667
7	0.3178	0.4341
	0.2200	0.7823
	0.0785	0.9755
	0.3528	
8	0.3058	0.1952
	0.2592	0.5558
	0.1732	0.8319
	0.06082	0.9812
9	0.2622	0.3421
	0.2137	0.6430
	0.1395	0.8663
	0.04845	0.9852
	0.2790	

TABLE 11-24   0.25-dB Chebyshev Pole Locations

Order n	Real Part $-\alpha$	Imaginary Part $\pm j\beta$
2	0.5621	0.7154
3	0.3062	0.8712
	0.6124	
4	0.4501	0.3840
	0.1865	0.9272
5	0.3247	0.5892
	0.1240	0.9533
	0.4013	
6	0.3284	0.2593
	0.2404	0.7083
	0.08799	0.9675
7	0.2652	0.4344
	0.1835	0.7828
	0.06550	0.9761
	0.2944	
8	0.2543	0.1953
	0.2156	0.5561
	0.1441	0.8323
	0.05058	0.9817
9	0.2176	0.3423
	0.1774	0.6433
	0.1158	0.8667
	0.04021	0.9856
	0.2315	

TABLE 11-25 0.5-dB Chebyshev Pole Locations

Order n	Real Part $-\alpha$	Imaginary Part $\pm j\beta$
2	0.5129	0.7225
3	0.2683	0.8753
	0.5366	
4	0.3872	0.3850
	0.1605	0.9297
5	0.2767	0.5902
	0.1057	0.9550
	0.3420	
6	0.2784	0.2596
	0.2037	0.7091
	0.07459	0.9687
7	0.2241	0.4349
	0.1550	0.7836
	0.05534	0.9771
	0.2487	
8	0.2144	0.1955
	0.1817	0.5565
	0.1214	0.8328
	0.04264	0.9824
9	0.1831	0.3425
	0.1493	0.6436
	0.09743	0.8671
	0.03383	0.9861
	0.1949	

TABLE 11-26 1-dB Chebyshev Pole Locations

Order n	Real Part $-\alpha$	Imaginary Part $\pm j\beta$
2	0.4508	0.7351
3	0.2257	0.8822
	0.4513	
4	0.3199	0.3868
	0.1325	0.9339
5	0.2265	0.5918
	0.08652	0.9575
	0.2800	
6	0.2268	0.2601
	0.1660	0.7106
	0.06076	0.9707
7	0.1819	0.4354
	0.1259	0.7846
	0.04494	0.9785
	0.2019	
8	0.1737	0.1956
	0.1473	0.5571
	0.09840	0.8337
	0.03456	0.9836
9	0.1482	0.3427
	0.1208	0.6442
	0.07884	0.8679
	0.02739	0.9869
	0.1577	

TABLE 11-27   0.01-dB Chebyshev *LC* Element Values*

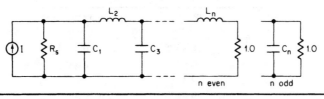

n	R_s	C_1	L_2	C_3	L_4
2	1.1007	1.3472	1.4829		
	1.1111	1.2472	1.5947		
	1.2500	0.9434	1.9974		
	1.4286	0.7591	2.3442		
	1.6667	0.6091	2.7496		
	2.0000	0.4791	3.2772		
	2.5000	0.3634	4.0328		
	3.3333	0.2590	5.2546		
	5.0000	0.1642	7.6498		
	10.0000	0.0781	14.7492		
	Inf.	1.4118	0.7415		
3	1.0000	1.1811	1.8214	1.1811	
	0.9000	1.0917	1.6597	1.4802	
	0.8000	1.0969	1.4431	1.8057	
	0.7000	1.1600	1.2283	2.1653	
	0.6000	1.2737	1.0236	2.5984	
	0.5000	1.4521	0.8294	3.1644	
	0.4000	1.7340	0.6452	3.9742	
	0.3000	2.2164	0.4704	5.2800	
	0.2000	3.1934	0.3047	7.8338	
	0.1000	6.1411	0.1479	15.3899	
	Inf.	1.5012	1.4330	0.5905	
4	1.1000	0.9500	1.9382	1.7608	1.0457
	1.1111	0.8539	1.9460	1.7439	1.1647
	1.2500	0.6182	2.0749	1.5417	1.6170
	1.4286	0.4948	2.2787	1.3336	2.0083
	1.6667	0.3983	2.5709	1.1277	2.4611
	2.0000	0.3156	2.9943	0.9260	3.0448
	2.5000	0.2418	3.6406	0.7293	3.8746
	3.3333	0.1744	4.7274	0.5379	5.2085
	5.0000	0.1121	6.9102	0.3523	7.8126
	10.0000	0.0541	13.4690	0.1729	15.5100
	Inf.	1.5287	1.6939	1.3122	0.5229
n	$1/R_s$	L_1	C_2	L_3	C_4

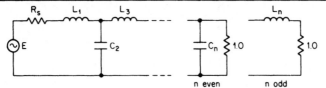

* Reprinted from A. I. Zverev, *Handbook of Filter Synthesis,* John Wiley and Sons, New York, 1967.

TABLE 11-27 0.01-dB Chebyshev *LC* Element Values (*Continued*)

n	R_s	C_1	L_2	C_3	L_4	C_5	L_6	C_7
5	1.0000	0.9766	1.6849	2.0366	1.6849	0.9766		
	0.9000	0.8798	1.4558	2.1738	1.6412	1.2739		
	0.8000	0.8769	1.2350	2.3785	1.4991	1.6066		
	0.7000	0.9263	1.0398	2.6582	1.3228	1.9772		
	0.6000	1.0191	0.8626	3.0408	1.1345	2.4244		
	0.5000	1.1658	0.6985	3.5835	0.9421	3.0092		
	0.4000	1.3983	0.5442	4.4027	0.7491	3.8453		
	0.3000	1.7966	0.3982	5.7721	0.5573	5.1925		
	0.2000	2.6039	0.2592	8.5140	0.3679	7.8257		
	0.1000	5.0406	0.1266	16.7406	0.1819	15.6126		
	Inf.	1.5466	1.7950	1.6449	1.2365	0.4883		
6	1.1007	0.8514	1.7956	1.8411	2.0266	1.6312	0.9372	
	1.1111	0.7597	1.7817	1.7752	2.0941	1.6380	1.0533	
	1.2500	0.5445	1.8637	1.4886	2.4025	1.5067	1.5041	
	1.4286	0.4355	2.0383	1.2655	2.7346	1.3318	1.8987	
	1.6667	0.3509	2.2978	1.0607	3.1671	1.1451	2.3568	
	2.0000	0.2786	2.6781	0.8671	3.7683	0.9536	2.9483	
	2.5000	0.2139	3.2614	0.6816	4.6673	0.7606	3.7899	
	3.3333	0.1547	4.2448	0.5028	6.1631	0.5676	5.1430	
	5.0000	0.0997	6.2227	0.3299	9.1507	0.3760	7.7852	
	10.0000	0.0483	12.1707	0.1623	18.1048	0.1865	15.5950	
	Inf.	1.5510	1.8471	1.7897	1.5976	1.1904	0.4686	
7	1.0000	0.9127	1.5947	2.0021	1.8704	2.0021	1.5947	0.9127
	0.9000	0.8157	1.3619	2.0886	1.7217	2.2017	1.5805	1.2060
	0.8000	0.8111	1.1504	2.2618	1.5252	2.4647	1.4644	1.5380
	0.7000	0.8567	0.9673	2.5158	1.3234	2.8018	1.3066	1.9096
	0.6000	0.9430	0.8025	2.8720	1.1237	3.2496	1.1310	2.3592
	0.5000	1.0799	0.6502	3.3822	0.9276	3.8750	0.9468	2.9478
	0.4000	1.2971	0.5072	4.1563	0.7350	4.8115	0.7584	3.7900
	0.3000	1.6692	0.3716	5.4540	0.5459	6.3703	0.5682	5.1476
	0.2000	2.4235	0.2423	8.0565	0.3604	9.4844	0.3776	7.8019
	0.1000	4.7006	0.1186	15.8718	0.1784	18.8179	0.1879	15.6523
	Inf.	1.5593	1.8671	1.8657	1.7651	1.5633	1.1610	0.4564
n	$1/R_s$	L_1	C_2	L_3	C_4	L_5	C_6	L_7

TABLE 11-27 0.01-dB Chebyshev LC Element Values (Continued)

n	R_s	C_1	L_2	C_3	L_4	C_5	L_6	C_7	L_8	C_9	L_{10}
8	1.1007	0.8145	1.7275	1.7984	2.0579	1.8695	1.9796	1.5694	0.8966		
	1.1111	0.7248	1.7081	1.7239	2.1019	1.8259	2.0595	1.5827	1.0111		
	1.2500	0.5176	1.7772	1.4315	2.3601	1.5855	2.4101	1.4754	1.4597		
	1.4286	0.4138	1.9422	1.2141	2.6686	1.3723	2.7734	1.3142	1.8544		
	1.6667	0.3336	2.1896	1.0169	3.0808	1.1660	3.2393	1.1369	2.3136		
	2.0000	0.2650	2.5533	0.8313	3.6598	0.9639	3.8820	0.9518	2.9073		
	2.5000	0.2036	3.1118	0.6537	4.5303	0.7653	4.8393	0.7627	3.7524		
	3.3333	0.1474	4.0539	0.4826	5.9828	0.5697	6.4287	0.5718	5.1118		
	5.0000	0.0951	5.9495	0.3170	8.8889	0.3770	9.6002	0.3804	7.7668		
	10.0000	0.0462	11.6509	0.1562	17.6067	0.1870	19.1009	0.1895	15.6158		
	Inf.	1.5588	1.8848	1.8988	1.8556	1.7433	1.5391	1.1412	0.4483		
9	1.0000	0.8854	1.5513	1.9614	1.8616	2.0717	1.8616	1.9614	1.5513	0.8854	
	0.9000	0.7886	1.3192	2.0330	1.6941	2.2249	1.7402	2.1774	1.5478	1.1764	
	0.8000	0.7834	1.1127	2.1959	1.4930	2.4614	1.5603	2.4565	1.4423	1.5076	
	0.7000	0.8273	0.9353	2.4404	1.2924	2.7808	1.3 62	2.8093	1.2927	1.8793	
	0.6000	0.9109	0.7761	2.7852	1.0962	3.2140	1.1688	3.2747	1.1233	2.3295	
	0.5000	1.0436	0.6290	3.2805	0.9045	3.8249	0.9710	3.9223	0.9436	2.9193	
	0.4000	1.2542	0.4910	4.0329	0.7167	4.7444	0.7739	4.8900	0.7582	3.7637	
	0.3000	1.6151	0.3599	5.2951	0.5325	6.2792	0.5780	6.4989	0.5697	5.1254	
	0.2000	2.3468	0.2349	7.8274	0.3518	9.3504	0.3835	9.7114	0.3797	7.7882	
	0.1000	4.5556	0.1150	15.4334	0.1743	18.5641	0.1908	19.3382	0.1895	15.6645	
	Inf.	1.5646	1.8884	1.9242	1.8977	1.8425	1.7261	1.5217	1.1273	0.4427	
10	1.1007	0.7970	1.6930	1.7690	2.0395	1.8827	2.0724	1.8529	1.9472	1.5380	0.8773
	1.1111	0.7083	1.6714	1.6921	2.0763	1.8281	2.1308	1.8167	2.0310	1.5541	0.9910
	1.2500	0.5049	1.7353	1.4005	2.3184	1.5706	2.4371	1.5953	2.3952	1.4574	1.4381
	1.4286	0.4037	1.8958	1.1871	2.6178	1.3552	2.7830	1.3895	2.7685	1.3027	1.8327
	1.6667	0.3255	2.1375	0.9942	3.0205	1.1497	3.2370	1.1863	3.2448	1.1300	2.2923
	2.0000	0.2586	2.4932	0.8128	3.5878	0.9497	3.8698	0.9849	3.9004	0.9484	2.8867
	2.5000	0.1988	3.0398	0.6394	4.4418	0.7538	4.8173	0.7849	4.8757	0.7617	3.7333
	3.3333	0.1440	3.9619	0.4723	5.8678	0.5612	6.3951	0.5863	6.4939	0.5722	5.0955
	5.0000	0.0930	5.8175	0.3103	8.7220	0.3715	9.5486	0.3893	9.7217	0.3814	7.7563
	10.0000	0.0451	11.3993	0.1530	17.2866	0.1844	19.0046	0.1938	19.3905	0.1904	15.6234
	Inf.	1.5625	1.8978	1.9323	1.9288	1.8907	1.8309	1.7128	1.5088	1.1173	0.4386
n	$1/R_s$	L_1	C_2	L_3	C_4	L_5	C_6	L_7	C_8	L_9	C_{10}

10

TABLE 11-28   0.1-dB Chebyshev *LC* Element Values*

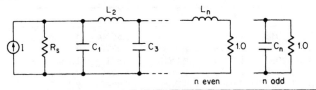

n	R_s	C_1	L_2	C_3	L_4
2	1.3554	1.2087	1.6382		
	1.4286	0.9771	1.9824		
	1.6667	0.7326	2.4885		
	2.0000	0.5597	3.0538		
	2.5000	0.4169	3.8265		
	3.3333	0.2933	5.0502		
	5.0000	0.1841	7.4257		
	10.0000	0.0868	14.4332		
	Inf.	1.3911	0.8191		
3	1.0000	1.4328	1.5937	1.4328	
	0.9000	1.4258	1.4935	1.6219	
	0.8000	1.4511	1.3557	1.8711	
	0.7000	1.5210	1.1927	2.1901	
	0.6000	1.6475	1.0174	2.6026	
	0.5000	1.8530	0.8383	3.1594	
	0.4000	2.1857	0.6603	3.9675	
	0.3000	2.7630	0.4860	5.2788	
	0.2000	3.9418	0.3172	7.8503	
	0.1000	7.5121	0.1549	15.4656	
	Inf.	1.5133	1.5090	0.7164	
4	1.3554	0.9924	2.1476	1.5845	1.3451
	1.4286	0.7789	2.3480	1.4292	1.7001
	1.6667	0.5764	2.7304	1.1851	2.2425
	2.0000	0.4398	3.2269	0.9672	2.8563
	2.5000	0.3288	3.9605	0.7599	3.6976
	3.3333	0.2329	5.1777	0.5602	5.0301
	5.0000	0.1475	7.6072	0.3670	7.6143
	10.0000	0.0704	14.8873	0.1802	15.2297
	Inf.	1.5107	1.7682	1.4550	0.6725

n	$1/R_s$	L_1	C_2	L_3	C_4

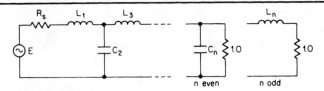

* Reprinted from A. I. Zverev, *Handbook of Filter Synthesis,* John Wiley and Sons, New York, 1967.

TABLE 11-28   0.1-dB Chebyshev *LC* Element Values (*Continued*)

n	R_s	C_1	L_2	C_3	L_4	C_5	L_6	C_7
5	1.0000	1.3013	1.5559	2.2411	1.5559	1.3013		
	0.9000	1.2845	1.4329	2.3794	1.4878	1.4883		
	0.8000	1.2998	1.2824	2.5819	1.3815	1.7384		
	0.7000	1.3580	1.1170	2.8679	1.2437	2.0621		
	0.6000	1.4694	0.9469	3.2688	1.0846	2.4835		
	0.5000	1.6535	0.7777	3.8446	0.9126	3.0548		
	0.4000	1.9538	0.6119	4.7193	0.7333	3.8861		
	0.3000	2.4765	0.4509	6.1861	0.5503	5.2373		
	0.2000	3.5457	0.2950	9.1272	0.3659	7.8890		
	0.1000	6.7870	0.1447	17.9569	0.1820	15.7447		
	Inf.	1.5613	1.8069	1.7659	1.4173	0.6507		
6	1.3554	0.9419	2.0797	1.6581	2.2473	1.5344	1.2767	
	1.4286	0.7347	2.2492	1.4537	2.5437	1.4051	1.6293	
	1.6667	0.5422	2.6003	1.1830	3.0641	1.1850	2.1739	
	2.0000	0.4137	3.0679	0.9575	3.7119	0.9794	2.7936	
	2.5000	0.3095	3.7652	0.7492	4.6512	0.7781	3.6453	
	3.3333	0.2195	4.9266	0.5514	6.1947	0.5795	4.9962	
	5.0000	0.1393	7.2500	0.3613	9.2605	0.3835	7.6184	
	10.0000	0.0666	14.2200	0.1777	18.4267	0.1901	15.3495	
	Inf.	1.5339	1.8838	1.8306	1.7485	1.3937	0.6383	
7	1.0000	1.2615	1.5196	2.2392	1.6804	2.2392	1.5196	1.2615
	0.9000	1.2422	1.3946	2.3613	1.5784	2.3966	1.4593	1.4472
	0.8000	1.2550	1.2449	2.5481	1.4430	2.6242	1.3619	1.6967
	0.7000	1.3100	1.0826	2.8192	1.2833	2.9422	1.2326	2.0207
	0.6000	1.4170	0.9169	3.2052	1.1092	3.3841	1.0807	2.4437
	0.5000	1.5948	0.7529	3.7642	0.9276	4.0150	0.9142	3.0182
	0.4000	1.8853	0.5926	4.6179	0.7423	4.9702	0.7384	3.8552
	0.3000	2.3917	0.4369	6.0535	0.5557	6.5685	0.5569	5.2167
	0.2000	3.4278	0.2862	8.9371	0.3692	9.7697	0.3723	7.8901
	0.1000	6.5695	0.1405	17.6031	0.1838	19.3760	0.1862	15.8127
	Inf.	1.5748	1.8577	1.9210	1.8270	1.7340	1.3786	0.6307
n	$1/R_s$	L_1	C_2	L_3	C_4	L_5	C_6	L_7

TABLE 11-28 0.1-dB Chebyshev *LC* Element Values (*Continued*)

n	R_g	C_1	L_2	C_3	L_4	C_5	L_6	C_7	L_8	C_9	L_{10}
8	1.3554	0.9234	2.0454	1.6453	2.2826	1.6841	2.2300	1.5091	1.2515		
	1.4286	0.7186	2.2054	1.4350	2.5554	1.4974	2.5422	1.3882	1.6029		
	1.6667	0.5298	2.5459	1.1644	3.0567	1.2367	3.0869	1.1769	2.1477		
	2.0000	0.4042	3.0029	0.9415	3.6917	1.0118	3.7619	0.9767	2.7690		
	2.5000	0.3025	3.6859	0.7365	4.6191	0.7990	4.7388	0.7787	3.6240		
	3.3333	0.2147	4.8250	0.5421	6.1483	0.5930	6.3423	0.5820	4.9811		
	5.0000	0.1364	7.1050	0.3554	9.1917	0.3917	9.5260	0.3863	7.6164		
	10.0000	0.0652	13.9469	0.1749	18.3007	0.1942	19.0437	0.1922	15.3880		
	Inf.	1.5422	1.9106	1.9008	1.9252	1.8200	1.7231	1.3683	0.6258		
9	1.0000	1.2446	1.5017	2.2220	1.6829	2.2957	1.6829	2.2220	1.5017	1.2446	
	0.9000	1.2244	1.3765	2.3388	1.5756	2.4400	1.5870	2.3835	1.4444	1.4297	
	0.8000	1.2361	1.2276	2.5201	1.4365	2.6561	1.4572	2.6168	1.3505	1.6788	
	0.7000	1.2898	1.0670	2.7856	1.2751	2.9647	1.3019	2.9422	1.2248	2.0029	
	0.6000	1.3950	0.9035	3.1653	1.1008	3.3992	1.1304	3.3937	1.0761	2.4264	
	0.5000	1.5701	0.7419	3.7166	0.9198	4.0244	0.9494	4.0377	0.9121	3.0020	
	0.4000	1.8566	0.5840	4.5594	0.7359	4.9750	0.7630	5.0118	0.7382	3.8412	
	0.3000	2.3560	0.4307	5.9781	0.5509	6.5700	0.5736	6.6413	0.5579	5.2068	
	0.2000	3.3781	0.2822	8.8291	0.3661	9.7699	0.3827	9.9047	0.3737	7.8891	
	0.1000	6.4777	0.1386	17.3994	0.1823	19.3816	0.1912	19.6976	0.1873	15.8393	
	Inf.	1.5804	1.8727	1.9584	1.9094	1.9229	1.8136	1.7150	1.3611	0.6223	
10	1.3554	0.9146	2.0279	1.6346	2.2777	1.6963	2.2991	1.6805	2.2155	1.4962	1.2397
	1.4286	0.7110	2.1837	1.4231	2.5425	1.5002	2.5915	1.5000	2.5322	1.3789	1.5903
	1.6667	0.5240	2.5194	1.1536	3.0362	1.2349	3.1229	1.2444	3.0839	1.1717	2.1351
	2.0000	0.3998	2.9713	0.9326	3.6647	1.0089	3.7923	1.0214	3.7669	0.9741	2.7572
	2.5000	0.2993	3.6476	0.7295	4.5843	0.7962	4.7673	0.8090	4.7547	0.7779	3.6136
	3.3333	0.2124	4.7758	0.5370	6.1022	0.5907	6.3734	0.6020	6.3758	0.5822	4.9735
	5.0000	0.1350	7.0347	0.3522	9.1248	0.3902	9.5681	0.3987	9.5942	0.3871	7.6148
	10.0000	0.0646	13.8141	0.1734	18.1739	0.1935	19.1282	0.1981	19.2158	0.1929	15.4052
	Inf.	1.5460	1.9201	1.9216	1.9700	1.9102	1.9194	1.8083	1.7090	1.3559	0.6198
n	$1/R_g$	L_1	C_2	L_3	C_4	L_5	C_6	L_7	C_8	L_9	C_{10}

TABLE 11-29   0.25-dB Chebyshev *LC* Element Values

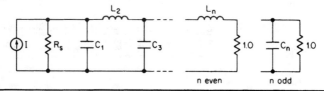

n	R_s	C_1	L_2	C_3	L_4
2	2	0.6552	2.7632		
	3	0.3740	4.3118		
	4	0.2637	5.7389		
	8	0.1215	11.2589		
	Inf.	1.3584	0.8902		
3	1	1.6325	1.4360	1.6325	
	0.5	3.2663	1.0775	1.6325	
	0.333	4.8988	0.9572	1.6325	
	0.25	6.5326	0.8971	1.6325	
	0.125	13.0639	0.8081	1.6325	
	Inf.	1.5348	1.5285	0.8169	
4	2	0.6747	3.6860	1.0247	1.8806
	3	0.4149	6.2744	0.7682	2.1302
	4	0.3020	8.8161	0.6667	2.2533
	8	0.1448	19.0204	0.5334	2.4516
	Inf.	1.4817	1.8213	1.5068	0.7853
n	$1/R_s$	L_1	C_2	L_3	C_4

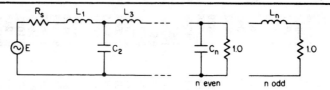

TABLE 11-29 0.25-dB Chebyshev LC Element Values (*Continued*)

n	R_s	C_1	L_2	C_3	L_4	C_5	L_6	C_7
5	1	1.5046	1.4436	2.4050	1.4436	1.5046		
	0.5	3.0103	0.7218	3.6080	1.4436	1.5046		
	0.333	4.5149	0.4812	4.8100	1.4436	1.5046		
	0.25	6.0196	0.3615	6.0130	1.4436	1.5046		
	0.125	12.0402	0.1807	10.8230	1.4436	1.5046		
	Inf.	1.5765	1.7822	1.8225	1.4741	0.7523		
6	2	0.6867	3.2074	0.9308	3.8102	1.2163	1.7088	
	3	0.4330	5.0976	0.5392	6.0963	1.0804	1.8393	
	4	0.3173	6.9486	0.3821	8.2530	1.0221	1.8987	
	8	0.1539	14.3100	0.1762	16.7193	0.9393	1.9868	
	Inf.	1.5060	1.9221	1.8191	1.8329	1.4721	0.7610	
7	1	1.5120	1.4169	2.4535	1.5350	2.4535	1.4169	1.5120
	0.5	3.024	0.7085	4.9069	1.1515	2.4535	1.4169	1.5120
	0.333	4.5361	0.4723	7.3596	1.0230	2.4535	1.4169	1.5120
	0.25	6.0471	0.3542	9.8120	0.9593	2.4535	1.4169	1.5120
	0.125	12.0952	0.1776	19.6251	0.8631	2.4535	1.4169	1.5120
	Inf.	1.6009	1.8287	1.9666	1.8234	1.8266	1.4629	0.7555
n	$1/R_s$	L_1	C_2	L_3	C_4	L_5	C_6	L_7

TABLE 11-30   0.5-dB Chebyshev *LC* Element Values*

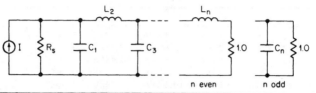

n	R_s	C_1	L_2	C_3	L_4	C_5	L_6
2	1.9841	0.9827	1.9497				
	2.0000	0.9086	2.1030				
	2.5000	0.5635	3.1647				
	3.3333	0.3754	4.4111				
	5.0000	0.2282	6.6995				
	10.0000	0.1052	13.3221				
	Inf.	1.3067	0.9748				
3	1.0000	1.8636	1.2804	1.8636			
	0.9000	1.9175	1.2086	2.0255			
	0.8000	1.9965	1.1203	2.2368			
	0.7000	2.1135	1.0149	2.5172			
	0.6000	2.2889	0.8937	2.8984			
	0.5000	2.5571	0.7592	3.4360			
	0.4000	2.9854	0.6146	4.2416			
	0.3000	3.7292	0.4633	5.5762			
	0.2000	5.2543	0.3087	8.2251			
	0.1000	9.8899	0.1534	16.1177			
	Inf.	1.5720	1.5179	0.9318			
4	1.9841	0.9202	2.5864	1.3036	1.8258		
	2.0000	0.8452	2.7198	1.2383	1.9849		
	2.5000	0.5162	3.7659	0.8693	3.1205		
	3.3333	0.3440	5.1196	0.6208	4.4790		
	5.0000	0.2100	7.7076	0.3996	6.9874		
	10.0000	0.0975	15.3520	0.1940	14.2616		
	Inf.	1.4361	1.8888	1.5211	0.9129		

TABLE 11-30   0.5-dB Chebyshev LC Element Values* (*Continued*)

n	R_s	C_1	L_2	C_3	L_4	C_5	L_6
5	1.0000	1.8068	1.3025	2.6914	1.3025	1.8068	
	0.9000	1.8540	1.2220	2.8478	1.2379	1.9701	
	0.8000	1.9257	1.1261	3.0599	1.1569	2.1845	
	0.7000	2.0347	1.0150	3.3525	1.0582	2.4704	
	0.6000	2.2006	0.8901	3.7651	0.9420	2.8609	
	0.5000	2.4571	0.7537	4.3672	0.8098	3.4137	
	0.4000	2.8692	0.6091	5.2960	0.6640	4.2447	
	0.3000	3.5877	0.4590	6.8714	0.5075	5.6245	
	0.2000	5.0639	0.3060	10.0537	0.3430	8.3674	
	0.1000	9.5560	0.1525	19.6465	0.1731	16.5474	
	Inf.	1.6299	1.7400	1.9217	1.5138	0.9034	
6	1.9841	0.9053	2.5774	1.3675	2.7133	1.2991	1.7961
	2.0000	0.8303	2.7042	1.2912	2.8721	1.2372	1.9557
	2.5000	0.5056	3.7219	0.8900	4.1092	0.8808	3.1025
	3.3333	0.3370	5.0554	0.6323	5.6994	0.6348	4.4810
	5.0000	0.2059	7.6145	0.4063	8.7319	0.4121	7.0310
	10.0000	0.0958	15.1862	0.1974	17.6806	0.2017	14.4328
	Inf.	1.4618	1.9799	1.7803	1.9253	1.5077	0.8981
n	$1/R_s$	L_1	C_2	L_3	C_4	L_5	C_6

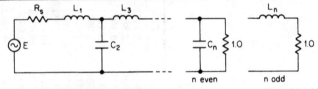

* Reprinted from A. I. Zverev, *Handbook of Filter Synthesis,* John Wiley and Sons, New York, 1967.

TABLE 11-30 0.5-dB Chebyshev LC Element Values (*Continued*)

n	R_s	C_1	L_2	C_3	L_4	C_5	L_6	C_7	L_8	C_9	L_{10}
7	1.0000	1.7896	1.2961	2.7177	1.3848	2.7177	1.2961	1.7896			
	0.9000	1.8348	1.2146	2.8691	1.3080	2.8829	1.2335	1.9531			
	0.8000	1.9045	1.1182	3.0761	1.2149	3.1071	1.1546	2.1681			
	0.7000	2.0112	1.0070	3.3638	1.1050	3.4163	1.0582	2.4554			
	0.6000	2.1744	0.8824	3.7717	0.9786	3.8524	0.9441	2.8481			
	0.5000	2.4275	0.7470	4.3695	0.8377	4.4886	0.8137	3.4050			
	0.4000	2.8348	0.6035	5.2947	0.6846	5.4698	0.6090	4.2428			
	0.3000	3.5456	0.4548	6.8674	0.5221	7.1341	0.5129	5.6350			
	0.2000	5.0070	0.3034	10.0491	0.3524	10.4959	0.3478	8.4041			
	0.1000	9.4555	0.1513	19.6486	0.1778	20.6314	0.1761	16.6654			
	Inf.	1.6464	1.7772	2.0306	1.7892	1.9239	1.5034	0.8948			
8	1.9841	0.8998	2.5670	1.3697	2.7585	1.3903	2.7175	1.2938	1.7852		
	2.0000	0.8249	2.6916	1.2919	2.9134	1.3160	2.8800	1.2331	1.9449		
	2.5000	0.5017	3.6988	0.8878	4.1404	0.9184	4.1470	0.8815	3.0953		
	3.3333	0.3344	5.0234	0.6304	5.7323	0.6577	5.7761	0.6370	4.4807		
	5.0000	0.2044	7.5682	0.4052	8.7771	0.4257	8.8833	0.4146	7.0453		
	10.0000	0.0951	15.1014	0.1969	17.7747	0.2081	18.0544	0.2035	14.4924		
	Inf.	1.4710	2.0022	1.8248	2.0440	1.7911	1.9218	1.5003	0.8926		

n	$1/R_s$	L_1	C_2	L_3	C_4	L_5	C_6	L_7	C_8	L_9	C_{10}
9	1.0000	1.7822	1.2921	2.7162	1.3922	2.7734	1.3922	2.7162	1.2921	1.7822	
	0.9000	1.8267	1.2103	2.8658	1.3135	2.9353	1.3165	2.8834	1.2302	1.9458	
	0.8000	1.8955	1.1139	3.0709	1.2189	3.1565	1.2246	3.1102	1.1523	2.1611	
	0.7000	2.0013	1.0028	3.3565	1.1075	3.4635	1.1157	3.4232	1.0568	2.4489	
	0.6000	2.1634	0.8786	3.7621	0.9801	3.8985	0.9900	3.8647	0.9436	2.8426	
	0.5000	2.4150	0.7436	4.3573	0.8385	4.5355	0.8493	4.5087	0.8140	3.4010	
	0.4000	2.8203	0.6008	5.2792	0.6850	5.5207	0.6957	5.5023	0.6700	4.2416	
	0.3000	3.5279	0.4528	6.8474	0.5223	7.1951	0.5318	7.1876	0.5142	5.6390	
	0.2000	4.9830	0.3021	10.0212	0.3526	10.5818	0.3600	10.5925	0.3491	8.4189	
	0.1000	9.4131	0.1507	19.5995	0.1779	20.8006	0.1822	20.8588	0.1770	16.7140	
	Inf.	1.6533	1.7890	2.0570	1.8383	2.0481	1.7910	1.9199	1.4981	0.8911	
10	1.9841	0.8972	2.5610	1.3683	2.7631	1.4009	2.7795	1.3927	2.7148	1.2908	1.7801
	2.0000	0.8223	2.6845	1.2901	2.9166	1.3246	2.9390	1.3191	2.8783	1.2306	1.9398
	2.5000	0.4999	3.6868	0.8858	4.1383	0.9216	4.2020	0.9238	4.1540	0.8812	3.0919
	3.3333	0.3332	5.0071	0.6289	5.7274	0.6594	5.8399	0.6631	5.7948	0.6376	4.4804
	5.0000	0.2037	7.5446	0.4042	8.7695	0.4266	8.9727	0.4300	8.9249	0.4154	7.0518
	10.0000	0.0948	15.0578	0.1965	17.7624	0.2086	18.2313	0.2107	18.1644	0.2041	14.5199
	Inf.	1.4753	2.0107	1.8386	2.0733	1.8432	2.0494	1.7904	1.9183	1.4965	0.8900
n	$1/R_s$	L_1	C_2	L_3	C_4	L_5	C_6	L_7	C_8	L_9	C_{10}

TABLE 11-31 1-dB Chebyshev LC Element Values

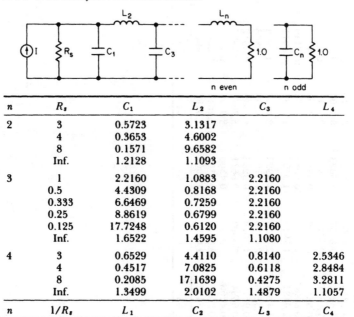

n	R_s	C_1	L_2	C_3	L_4
2	3	0.5723	3.1317		
	4	0.3653	4.6002		
	8	0.1571	9.6582		
	Inf.	1.2128	1.1093		
3	1	2.2160	1.0883	2.2160	
	0.5	4.4309	0.8168	2.2160	
	0.333	6.6469	0.7259	2.2160	
	0.25	8.8619	0.6799	2.2160	
	0.125	17.7248	0.6120	2.2160	
	Inf.	1.6522	1.4595	1.1080	
4	3	0.6529	4.4110	0.8140	2.5346
	4	0.4517	7.0825	0.6118	2.8484
	8	0.2085	17.1639	0.4275	3.2811
	Inf.	1.3499	2.0102	1.4879	1.1057
n	$1/R_s$	L_1	C_2	L_3	C_4

n	R_s	C_1	L_2	C_3	L_4	C_5	L_6	C_7
5	1	2.2072	1.1279	3.1025	1.1279	2.2072		
	0.5	4.4144	0.5645	4.6532	1.1279	2.2072		
	0.333	6.6216	0.3763	6.2050	1.1279	2.2072		
	0.25	8.8288	0.2822	7.7557	1.1279	2.2072		
	0.125	17.6565	0.1406	13.9606	1.1279	2.2072		
	Inf.	1.7213	1.6448	2.0614	1.4928	1.1031		
6	3	0.6785	3.8725	0.7706	4.7107	0.9692	2.4060	
	4	0.4810	5.6441	0.4759	7.3511	0.8494	2.5820	
	8	0.2272	12.3095	0.1975	16.740	0.7256	2.7990	
	Inf.	1.3775	2.0969	1.6896	2.0744	1.4942	1.1022	
7	1	2.2043	1.1311	3.1472	1.1942	3.1472	1.1311	2.2043
	0.5	4.4075	0.5656	6.2934	0.8951	3.1472	1.1311	2.2043
	0.333	6.6118	0.3774	9.4406	0.7955	3.1472	1.1311	2.2043
	0.25	8.8151	0.2828	12.5879	0.7466	3.1472	1.1311	2.2043
	0.125	17.6311	0.1414	25.175	0.6714	3.1472	1.1311	2.2043
	Inf.	1.7414	1.6774	2.1554	1.7028	2.0792	1.4943	1.1016
n	$1/R_s$	L_1	C_2	L_3	C_4	L_5	C_6	L_7

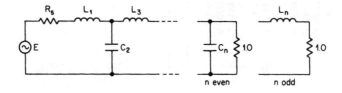

RL=1

TABLE 11-32   0.1-dB Chebyshev Uniform Dissipation Network

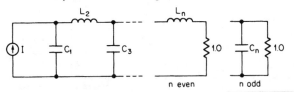

n	d	C_1	L_2	C_3	L_4	C_5	L_6	C_7
2	0.0172	1.3855	0.8433					
	0.0257	1.3816	0.8550					
	0.0515	1.3680	0.8939					
3	0.024	1.4848	1.5390	0.7556				
	0.036	1.4696	1.5543	0.7765				
	0.072	1.4168	1.6015	0.8473				
4	0.0275	1.4375	1.7978	1.5103	0.7266			
	0.0412	1.3975	1.8148	1.5394	0.7570			
	0.0824	1.2556	1.8767	1.6353	0.8637			
5	0.0294	1.4558	1.8064	1.8280	1.4933	0.7194		
	0.0441	1.3945	1.8076	1.8643	1.5352	0.7591		
	0.0881	1.1449	1.8416	2.0209	1.6839	0.9123		
6	0.0305	1.3672	1.8874	1.8612	1.8361	1.4907	0.7224	
	0.0457	1.2645	1.8973	1.8842	1.8907	1.5454	0.7738	
	0.0915	0.6579	2.3639	2.1574	2.1803	1.7574	0.9825	
7	0.0312	1.3628	1.8252	1.9694	1.8797	1.8455	1.4963	0.7316
	0.0468	1.2079	1.8220	2.0207	1.9213	1.9192	1.5646	0.7957

n	d	L_1	C_2	L_3	C_4	L_5	C_6	L_7

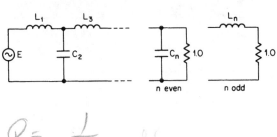

$$Q = \frac{1}{d}$$

$$Q_{max} = \frac{1}{0.017\,8} = 58$$

TABLE 11-33 0.25-dB Chebyshev Uniform Dissipation Network

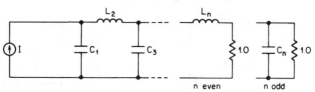

n	d	C_1	L_2	C_3	L_4	C_5	L_6	C_7
2	0.0209	1.3504	0.9157					
	0.0313	1.3376	0.9413					
	0.0626	1.3120	1.0004					
3	0.0266	1.5022	1.5548	0.8733				
	0.0399	1.4834	1.5674	0.9046				
	0.0798	1.4220	1.6062	1.0149				
4	0.0292	1.3894	1.8590	1.5593	0.8651			
	0.0439	1.3370	1.8818	1.5866	0.9107			
	0.0877	1.1444	1.9764	1.6823	1.0839			
5	0.0306	1.4599	1.7670	1.8976	1.5503	0.8503		
	0.0459	1.3881	1.7604	1.9455	1.5917	0.9102		
	0.0919	1.0397	1.8181	2.2035	1.7528	1.1497		
6	0.0314	1.3054	1.9347	1.8339	1.9443	1.5697	0.8883	
	0.0471	1.1696	1.9560	1.8541	2.0218	1.6259	0.9700	
7	0.0319	1.3584	1.7680	2.0376	1.8610	1.9707	1.5820	0.9091
	0.0479	1.1264	1.7722	2.1452	1.9132	2.0814	1.6541	1.0125
n	d	L_1	C_2	L_3	C_4	L_5	C_6	L_7

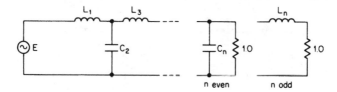

TABLE 11-34   0.5-dB Chebyshev Uniform Dissipation Network

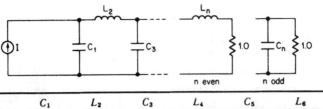

n	d	C_1	L_2	C_3	L_4	C_5	L_6	C_7
2	0.0240	1.2855	1.0228					
	0.0360	1.2730	1.0478					
	0.0720	1.2313	1.1340					
3	0.0286	1.5376	1.5341	1.0122				
	0.0428	1.5189	1.5423	1.0589				
	0.0856	1.4489	1.5621	1.2247				
4	0.0305	1.3205	1.9413	1.5631	1.0275			
	0.0457	1.2549	1.9741	1.5850	1.0964			
	0.0915	0.9991	2.1359	1.6692	1.3707			
5	0.0315	1.5031	1.6980	2.0264	1.5773	1.0529		
	0.0472	1.4162	1.6768	2.0995	1.6133	1.1482		
	0.0944	0.7139	2.0994	2.7297	1.8007	1.5751		
6	0.0320	1.2200	2.0123	1.7707	2.0758	1.5927	1.0858	
	0.0480	1.0389	2.0612	1.7895	2.1976	1.6448	1.2117	
7	0.0324	1.3659	1.6801	2.1488	1.8047	2.1230	1.6090	1.1228
	0.0485	0.9024	1.8171	2.4475	1.8985	2.3126	1.6811	1.2856
n	d	L_1	C_2	L_3	C_4	L_5	C_6	L_7

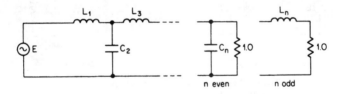

TABLE 11-35   1-dB Chebyshev Uniform Dissipation Network

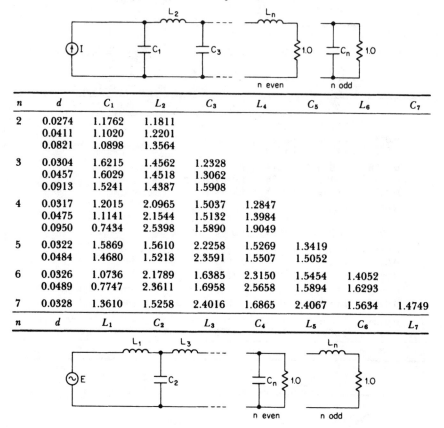

n	d	C_1	L_2	C_3	L_4	C_5	L_6	C_7
2	0.0274	1.1762	1.1811					
	0.0411	1.1020	1.2201					
	0.0821	1.0898	1.3564					
3	0.0304	1.6215	1.4562	1.2328				
	0.0457	1.6029	1.4518	1.3062				
	0.0913	1.5241	1.4387	1.5908				
4	0.0317	1.2015	2.0965	1.5037	1.2847			
	0.0475	1.1141	2.1544	1.5132	1.3984			
	0.0950	0.7434	2.5398	1.5890	1.9049			
5	0.0322	1.5869	1.5610	2.2258	1.5269	1.3419		
	0.0484	1.4680	1.5218	2.3591	1.5507	1.5052		
6	0.0326	1.0736	2.1789	1.6385	2.3150	1.5454	1.4052	
	0.0489	0.7747	2.3611	1.6958	2.5658	1.5894	1.6293	
7	0.0328	1.3610	1.5258	2.4016	1.6865	2.4067	1.5634	1.4749
n	d	L_1	C_2	L_3	C_4	L_5	C_6	L_7

TABLE 11-36   0.01-dB Chebyshev Active
Low-Pass Values

Order n	C_1	C_2
2	1.4826	0.7042
4	1.4874	1.1228
	3.5920	0.2985
6	1.8900	1.5249
	2.5820	0.5953
	7.0522	0.1486
8	2.3652	1.9493
	2.7894	0.8196
	4.1754	0.3197
	11.8920	0.08672

TABLE 11-37 0.1-dB Chebyshev Active Low-Pass Values*

Order n	C_1	C_2	C_3
2	1.638	0.6955	
3	6.653	1.825	0.1345
4	1.900	1.241	
	4.592	0.2410	
5	4.446	2.520	0.3804
	6.810	0.1580	
6	2.553	1.776	
	3.487	0.4917	
	9.531	0.1110	
7	5.175	3.322	0.5693
	4.546	0.3331	
	12.73	0.08194	
8	3.270	2.323	
	3.857	0.6890	
	5.773	0.2398	
	16.44	0.06292	
9	6.194	4.161	0.7483
	4.678	0.4655	
	7.170	0.1812	
	20.64	0.04980	
10	4.011	2.877	
	4.447	0.8756	
	5.603	0.3353	
	8.727	0.1419	
	25.32	0.04037	

* Reprinted from *Electronics*, McGraw-Hill, Inc., August 18, 1969.

TABLE 11-38   0.25-dB Chebyshev Active Low-Pass Values*

Order n	C_1	C_2	C_3
2	1.778	0.6789	
3	8.551	2.018	0.1109
4	2.221	1.285	
	5.363	0.2084	
5	5.543	2.898	0.3425
	8.061	0.1341	
6	3.044	1.875	
	4.159	0.4296	
	11.36	0.09323	
7	6.471	3.876	0.5223
	5.448	0.2839	
	15.26	0.06844	
8	3.932	2.474	
	4.638	0.6062	
	6.942	0.2019	
	19.76	0.05234	
9	7.766	4.891	0.6919
	5.637	0.3983	
	8.639	0.1514	
	24.87	0.04131	
10	4.843	3.075	
	5.368	0.7725	
	6.766	0.2830	
	10.53	0.1181	
	30.57	0.03344	

* Reprinted from *Electronics,* McGraw-Hill, Inc., August 18, 1969.

TABLE 11-39   0.5-dB Chebyshev Active Low-Pass Values*

Order n	C_1	C_2	C_3
2	1.950	0.6533	
3	11.23	2.250	0.0895
4	2.582	1.300	
	6.233	0.1802	
5	6.842	3.317	0.3033
	9.462	0.1144	
6	3.592	1.921	
	4.907	0.3743	
	13.40	0.07902	
7	7.973	4.483	0.4700
	6.446	0.2429	
	18.07	0.05778	
8	4.665	2.547	
	5.502	0.5303	
	8.237	0.1714	
	23.45	0.04409	
9	9.563	5.680	0.6260
	6.697	0.3419	
	10.26	0.1279	
	29.54	0.03475	
10	5.760	3.175	
	6.383	0.6773	
	8.048	0.2406	
	12.53	0.09952	
	36.36	0.02810	

* Reprinted from *Electronics*, McGraw-Hill, Inc., August 18, 1969.

TABLE 11-40 1-dB Chebyshev Active Low-Pass Values*

Order n	C_1	C_2	C_3
2	2.218	0.6061	
3	16.18	2.567	0.06428
4	3.125	1.269	
	7.546	0.1489	
5	8.884	3.935	0.2540
	11.55	0.09355	
6	4.410	1.904	
	6.024	0.3117	
	16.46	0.06425	
7	10.29	5.382	0.4012
	7.941	0.1993	
	22.25	0.04684	
8	5.756	2.538	
	6.792	0.4435	
	10.15	0.1395	
	28.94	0.03568	
9	12.33	6.853	0.5382
	8.281	0.2813	
	12.68	0.1038	
	36.51	0.02808	
10	7.125	3.170	
	7.897	0.5630	
	9.952	0.1962	
	15.50	0.08054	
	44.98	0.02269	

* Reprinted from *Electronics*, McGraw-Hill, Inc., August 18, 1969.

TABLE 11-41   Bessel Pole Locations

Order n	Real Part $-\alpha$	Imaginary Part $\pm j\beta$
2	1.1030	0.6368
3	1.0509	1.0025
	1.3270	
4	1.3596	0.4071
	0.9877	1.2476
5	1.3851	0.7201
	0.9606	1.4756
	1.5069	
6	1.5735	0.3213
	1.3836	0.9727
	0.9318	1.6640
7	1.6130	0.5896
	1.3797	1.1923
	0.9104	1.8375
	1.6853	
8	1.7627	0.2737
	0.8955	2.0044
	1.3780	1.3926
	1.6419	0.8253
9	1.8081	0.5126
	1.6532	1.0319
	1.3683	1.5685
	0.8788	2.1509
	1.8575	

TABLE 11-42   Bessel LC Element Values*

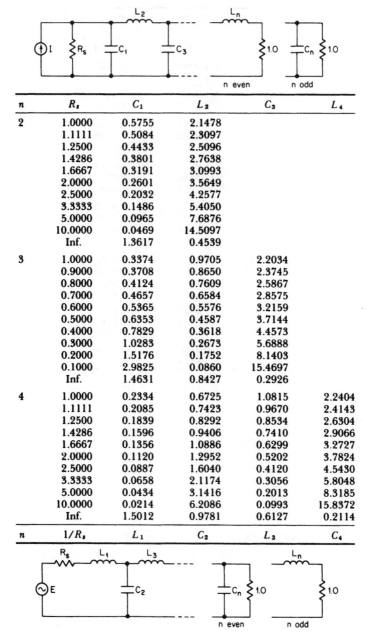

n	R_s	C_1	L_2	C_3	L_4
2	1.0000	0.5755	2.1478		
	1.1111	0.5084	2.3097		
	1.2500	0.4433	2.5096		
	1.4286	0.3801	2.7638		
	1.6667	0.3191	3.0993		
	2.0000	0.2601	3.5649		
	2.5000	0.2032	4.2577		
	3.3333	0.1486	5.4050		
	5.0000	0.0965	7.6876		
	10.0000	0.0469	14.5097		
	Inf.	1.3617	0.4539		
3	1.0000	0.3374	0.9705	2.2034	
	0.9000	0.3708	0.8650	2.3745	
	0.8000	0.4124	0.7609	2.5867	
	0.7000	0.4657	0.6584	2.8575	
	0.6000	0.5365	0.5576	3.2159	
	0.5000	0.6353	0.4587	3.7144	
	0.4000	0.7829	0.3618	4.4573	
	0.3000	1.0283	0.2673	5.6888	
	0.2000	1.5176	0.1752	8.1403	
	0.1000	2.9825	0.0860	15.4697	
	Inf.	1.4631	0.8427	0.2926	
4	1.0000	0.2334	0.6725	1.0815	2.2404
	1.1111	0.2085	0.7423	0.9670	2.4143
	1.2500	0.1839	0.8292	0.8534	2.6304
	1.4286	0.1596	0.9406	0.7410	2.9066
	1.6667	0.1356	1.0886	0.6299	3.2727
	2.0000	0.1120	1.2952	0.5202	3.7824
	2.5000	0.0887	1.6040	0.4120	4.5430
	3.3333	0.0658	2.1174	0.3056	5.8048
	5.0000	0.0434	3.1416	0.2013	8.3185
	10.0000	0.0214	6.2086	0.0993	15.8372
	Inf.	1.5012	0.9781	0.6127	0.2114
n	$1/R_s$	L_1	C_2	L_3	C_4

* Reprinted from A. I. Zverev, *Handbook of Filter Synthesis,* John Wiley and Sons, New York, 1967.

TABLE 11-42 Bessel LC Element Values (*Continued*)

n	R_s	C_1	L_2	C_3	L_4	C_5	L_6	C_7
5	1.0000	0.1743	0.5072	0.8040	1.1110	2.2582		
	0.9000	0.1926	0.4542	0.8894	0.9945	2.4328		
	0.8000	0.2154	0.4016	0.9959	0.8789	2.6497		
	0.7000	0.2447	0.3494	1.1323	0.7642	2.9272		
	0.6000	0.2836	0.2977	1.3138	0.6506	3.2952		
	0.5000	0.3380	0.2465	1.5672	0.5382	3.8077		
	0.4000	0.4194	0.1958	1.9464	0.4270	4.5731		
	0.3000	0.5548	0.1457	2.5768	0.3174	5.8433		
	0.2000	0.8251	0.0964	3.8352	0.2095	8.3747		
	0.1000	1.6349	0.0478	7.6043	0.1036	15.9487		
	Inf.	1.5125	1.0232	0.7531	0.4729	0.1618		
6	1.0000	0.1365	0.4002	0.6392	0.8538	1.1126	2.2645	
	1.1111	0.1223	0.4429	0.5732	0.9456	0.9964	2.4388	
	1.2500	0.1082	0.4961	0.5076	1.0600	0.8810	2.6554	
	1.4286	0.0943	0.5644	0.4424	1.2069	0.7665	2.9325	
	1.6667	0.0804	0.6553	0.3775	1.4022	0.6530	3.3001	
	2.0000	0.0666	0.7824	0.3131	1.6752	0.5405	3.8122	
	2.5000	0.0530	0.9725	0.2492	2.0837	0.4292	4.5770	
	3.3333	0.0395	1.2890	0.1859	2.7633	0.3193	5.8467	
	5.0000	0.0261	1.9209	0.1232	4.1204	0.2110	8.3775	
	10.0000	0.0130	3.8146	0.0612	8.1860	0.1045	15.9506	
	Inf.	1.5124	1.0329	0.8125	0.6072	0.3785	0.1287	
7	1.0000	0.1106	0.3259	0.5249	0.7020	0.8690	1.1052	2.2659
	0.9000	0.1224	0.2923	0.5815	0.6302	0.9630	0.9899	2.4396
	0.8000	0.1372	0.2589	0.6521	0.5586	1.0803	0.8754	2.6556
	0.7000	0.1562	0.2257	0.7428	0.4873	1.2308	0.7618	2.9319
	0.6000	0.1815	0.1927	0.8634	0.4163	1.4312	0.6491	3.2984
	0.5000	0.2168	0.1599	1.0321	0.3457	1.7111	0.5374	3.8090
	0.4000	0.2698	0.1274	1.2847	0.2755	2.1304	0.4269	4.5718
	0.3000	0.3579	0.0951	1.7051	0.2058	2.8280	0.3177	5.8380
	0.2000	0.5338	0.0630	2.5448	0.1365	4.2214	0.2100	8.3623
	0.1000	1.0612	0.0313	5.0616	0.0679	8.3967	0.1040	15.9166
	Inf.	1.5087	1.0293	0.8345	0.6752	0.5031	0.3113	0.1054
n	$1/R_s$	L_1	C_2	L_3	C_4	L_5	C_6	L_7

TABLE 11-42 Bessel *LC* Element Values (*Continued*)

n	R_s	C_1	L_2	C_3	L_4	C_5	L_6	C_7	L_8	C_9	L_{10}
8	1.0000	0.0919	0.2719	0.4409	0.5936	0.7303	0.8695	1.0956	2.2656		
	1.1111	0.0825	0.3013	0.3958	0.6580	0.6559	0.9639	0.9813	2.4388		
	1.2500	0.0731	0.3380	0.3509	0.7385	0.5817	1.0816	0.8678	2.6541		
	1.4286	0.0637	0.3850	0.3061	0.8418	0.5078	1.2328	0.7552	2.9295		
	1.6667	0.0545	0.4477	0.2616	0.9794	0.4342	1.4340	0.6435	3.2949		
	2.0000	0.0452	0.5354	0.2173	1.1718	0.3608	1.7153	0.5329	3.8041		
	2.5000	0.0360	0.6667	0.1732	1.4599	0.2878	2.1367	0.4233	4.5645		
	3.3333	0.0269	0.8852	0.1294	1.9396	0.2151	2.8380	0.3151	5.8271		
	5.0000	0.0179	1.3218	0.0859	2.8981	0.1429	4.2389	0.2083	8.3441		
	10.0000	0.0089	2.6307	0.0427	5.7710	0.0711	8.4376	0.1032	15.8768		
	Inf.	1.5044	1.0214	0.8392	0.7081	0.5743	0.4253	0.2616	0.0883		
9	1.0000	0.0780	0.2313	0.3770	0.5108	0.6306	0.7407	0.8639	1.0863	2.2649	
	0.9000	0.0864	0.2077	0.4180	0.4588	0.6994	0.6655	0.9578	0.9730	2.4376	
	0.8000	0.0970	0.1841	0.4691	0.4069	0.7854	0.5905	1.0750	0.8604	2.6524	
	0.7000	0.1105	0.1607	0.5348	0.3553	0.8957	0.5157	1.2255	0.7488	2.9271	
	0.6000	0.1286	0.1373	0.6222	0.3038	1.0427	0.4411	1.4258	0.6380	3.2915	
	0.5000	0.1538	0.1141	0.7445	0.2525	1.2483	0.3667	1.7059	0.5283	3.7993	
	0.4000	0.1916	0.0910	0.9278	0.2014	1.5563	0.2926	2.1256	0.4197	4.5578	
	0.3000	0.2545	0.0680	1.2329	0.1506	2.0692	0.2189	2.8241	0.3124	5.8171	
	0.2000	0.3803	0.0452	1.8426	0.1000	3.0941	0.1455	4.2196	0.2065	8.3276	
	0.1000	0.7573	0.0225	3.6704	0.0498	6.1666	0.0725	8.4023	0.1023	15.8408	
	Inf.	1.5006	1.0127	0.8361	0.7220	0.6142	0.4963	0.3654	0.2238	0.0754	
10	1.0000	0.0672	0.1998	0.3270	0.4454	0.5528	0.6493	0.7420	0.8561	1.0781	2.2641
	1.1111	0.0604	0.2216	0.2937	0.4941	0.4967	0.7205	0.6668	0.9492	0.9656	2.4365
	1.2500	0.0536	0.2488	0.2606	0.5548	0.4408	0.8093	0.5918	1.0654	0.8539	2.6508
	1.4286	0.0467	0.2836	0.2275	0.6327	0.3850	0.9233	0.5170	1.2147	0.7430	2.9249
	1.6667	0.0400	0.3301	0.1945	0.7366	0.3294	1.0753	0.4423	1.4134	0.6331	3.2885
	2.0000	0.0332	0.3951	0.1617	0.8818	0.2739	1.2879	0.3678	1.6913	0.5242	3.7953
	2.5000	0.0265	0.4924	0.1290	1.0995	0.2186	1.6064	0.2936	2.1076	0.4164	4.5521
	3.3333	0.0198	0.6546	0.0965	1.4620	0.1635	2.1369	0.2197	2.8007	0.3099	5.8087
	5.0000	0.0132	0.9786	0.0641	2.1864	0.1087	3.1971	0.1461	4.1854	0.2049	8.3137
	10.0000	0.0066	1.9499	0.0319	4.3583	0.0542	6.3759	0.0728	8.3359	0.1015	15.8108
	Inf.	1.4973	1.0045	0.8297	0.7258	0.6355	0.5401	0.4342	0.3182	0.1942	0.0653
n	$1/R_s$	L_1	C_2	L_3	C_4	L_5	C_6	L_7	C_8	L_9	C_{10}

TABLE 11-43 Bessel Active Low-Pass Values

Order n	C_1	C_2	C_3
2	0.9066	0.6800	
3	1.423	0.9880	0.2538
4	0.7351	0.6746	
	1.012	0.3900	
5	1.010	0.8712	0.3095
	1.041	0.3100	
6	0.6352	0.6100	
	0.7225	0.4835	
	1.073	0.2561	
7	0.8532	0.7792	0.3027
	0.7250	0.4151	
	1.100	0.2164	
8	0.5673	0.5540	
	0.6090	0.4861	
	0.7257	0.3590	
	1.116	0.1857	
9	0.7564	0.7070	0.2851
	0.6048	0.4352	
	0.7307	0.3157	
	1.137	0.1628	
10	0.5172	0.5092	
	0.5412	0.4682	
	0.6000	0.3896	
	0.7326	0.2792	
	1.151	0.1437	

TABLE 11-44   Linear Phase with Equiripple Error of 0.05° Pole Locations

Order n	Real Part −α	Imaginary Part ±jβ
2	1.0087	0.6680
3	0.8541	1.0725
	1.0459	
4	0.9648	0.4748
	0.7448	1.4008
5	0.8915	0.8733
	0.6731	1.7085
	0.9430	
6	0.8904	0.4111
	0.8233	1.2179
	0.6152	1.9810
7	0.8425	0.7791
	0.7708	1.5351
	0.5727	2.2456
	0.8615	
8	0.8195	0.3711
	0.7930	1.1054
	0.7213	1.8134
	0.5341	2.4761
9	0.7853	0.7125
	0.7555	1.4127
	0.6849	2.0854
	0.5060	2.7133
	0.7938	
10	0.7592	0.3413
	0.7467	1.0195
	0.7159	1.6836
	0.6475	2.3198
	0.4777	2.9128

TABLE 11-45 Linear Phase with Equiripple Error of 0.5° Pole Locations

Order n	Real Part $-\alpha$	Imaginary Part $\pm j\beta$
2	0.8590	0.6981
3	0.6969	1.1318
	0.8257	
4	0.7448	0.5133
	0.6037	1.4983
5	0.6775	0.9401
	0.5412	1.8256
	0.7056	
6	0.6519	0.4374
	0.6167	1.2963
	0.4893	2.0982
7	0.6190	0.8338
	0.5816	1.6453
	0.4598	2.3994
	0.6283	
8	0.5791	0.3857
	0.5665	1.1505
	0.5303	1.8914
	0.4184	2.5780
9	0.5688	0.7595
	0.5545	1.5089
	0.5179	2.2329
	0.4080	2.9028
	0.5728	
10	0.5249	0.3487
	0.5193	1.0429
	0.5051	1.7261
	0.4711	2.3850
	0.3708	2.9940

TABLE 11-46   Linear Phase with Equiripple Error of 0.05° *LC* Element Values*

n	R_s	C_1	L_2	C_3	L_4
2	1.0000	0.6480	2.1085		
	1.1111	0.5703	2.2760		
	1.2500	0.4955	2.4817		
	1.4286	0.4235	2.7422		
	1.6667	0.3544	3.0848		
	2.0000	0.2880	3.5589		
	2.5000	0.2244	4.2630		
	3.3333	0.1637	5.4270		
	5.0000	0.1059	7.7400		
	10.0000	0.0513	14.6480		
	Inf.	1.3783	0.4957		
3	1.0000	0.4328	1.0427	2.2542	
	0.9000	0.4745	0.9330	2.4258	
	0.8000	0.5262	0.8238	2.6400	
	0.7000	0.5925	0.7153	2.9146	
	0.6000	0.6805	0.6078	3.2795	
	0.5000	0.8032	0.5015	3.7884	
	0.4000	0.9865	0.3967	4.5487	
	0.3000	1.2910	0.2938	5.8106	
	0.2000	1.8983	0.1931	8.3253	
	0.1000	3.7161	0.0950	15.8472	
	Inf.	1.5018	0.9328	0.3631	
4	1.0000	0.3363	0.7963	1.1428	2.2459
	1.1111	0.2993	0.8810	1.0212	2.4241
	1.2500	0.2631	0.9865	0.9012	2.6445
	1.4286	0.2275	1.1216	0.7826	2.9254
	1.6667	0.1926	1.3009	0.6657	3.2970
	2.0000	0.1584	1.5509	0.5502	3.8138
	2.5000	0.1250	1.9244	0.4364	4.5844
	3.3333	0.0923	2.5448	0.3242	5.8626
	5.0000	0.0606	3.7818	0.2139	8.4091
	10.0000	0.0298	7.4845	0.1058	16.0266
	Inf.	1.5211	1.0444	0.7395	0.2925
n	$1/R_s$	L_1	C_2	L_3	C_4

* Reprinted from A. I. Zverev, *Handbook of Filter Synthesis,* John Wiley and Sons, New York, 1967.

TABLE 11-46 Linear Phase with Equiripple Error of 0.05° LC Element Values (*Continued*)

n	R_s	C_1	L_2	C_3	L_4	C_5	L_6	C_7
5	1.0000	0.2751	0.6541	0.8892	1.1034	2.2873		
	0.9000	0.3031	0.5868	0.9841	0.9904	2.4589		
	0.8000	0.3380	0.5197	1.1026	0.8774	2.6733		
	0.7000	0.3827	0.4529	1.2548	0.7648	2.9484		
	0.6000	0.4420	0.3865	1.4575	0.6526	3.3144		
	0.5000	0.5248	0.3204	1.7408	0.5410	3.8254		
	0.4000	0.6486	0.2549	2.1651	0.4302	4.5896		
	0.3000	0.8544	0.1899	2.8713	0.3205	5.8595		
	0.2000	1.2649	0.1257	4.2817	0.2120	8.3922		
	0.1000	2.4940	0.0624	8.5082	0.1051	15.9739		
	Inf.	1.5144	1.0407	0.8447	0.6177	0.2456		
6	1.0000	0.2374	0.5662	0.7578	0.8760	1.1163	2.2448	
	1.1111	0.2120	0.6272	0.6799	0.9726	0.9977	2.4214	
	1.2500	0.1870	0.7032	0.6023	1.0931	0.8807	2.6396	
	1.4286	0.1622	0.8008	0.5253	1.2475	0.7652	2.9174	
	1.6667	0.1378	0.9306	0.4487	1.4530	0.6512	3.2849	
	2.0000	0.1138	1.1118	0.3725	1.7401	0.5387	3.7958	
	2.5000	0.0901	1.3830	0.2969	2.1698	0.4277	4.5579	
	3.3333	0.0669	1.8340	0.2217	2.8849	0.3182	5.8220	
	5.0000	0.0441	2.7343	0.1472	4.3129	0.2103	8.3408	
	10.0000	0.0218	5.4312	0.0732	8.5924	0.1041	15.8769	
	Inf.	1.5050	1.0306	0.8554	0.7283	0.5389	0.2147	
7	1.0000	0.2085	0.4999	0.6653	0.7521	0.8749	1.0671	2.2845
	0.9000	0.2302	0.4488	0.7374	0.6768	0.9687	0.9580	2.4538
	0.8000	0.2573	0.3978	0.8274	0.6013	1.0861	0.8489	2.6655
	0.7000	0.2919	0.3470	0.9431	0.5258	1.2369	0.7400	2.9375
	0.6000	0.3380	0.2964	1.0972	0.4503	1.4381	0.6314	3.2996
	0.5000	0.4023	0.2461	1.3127	0.3749	1.7196	0.5235	3.8051
	0.4000	0.4986	0.1960	1.6356	0.2995	2.1416	0.4163	4.5613
	0.3000	0.6585	0.1463	2.1734	0.2242	2.8445	0.3101	5.8180
	0.2000	0.9778	0.0970	3.2480	0.1492	4.2496	0.2052	8.3246
	0.1000	1.9340	0.0482	6.4698	0.0744	8.4623	0.1017	15.8281
	Inf.	1.4988	1.0071	0.8422	0.7421	0.6441	0.4791	0.1911
n	$1/R_s$	L_1	C_2	L_3	C_4	L_5	C_6	L_7

TABLE 11-46 Linear Phase with Equiripple Error of 0.05° LC Element Values (*Continued*)

n	R_s	C_1	L_2	C_3	L_4	C_5	L_6	C_7	L_8	C_9	L_{10}
8	1.0000	0.1891	0.4543	0.6031	0.6750	0.7590	0.8427	1.0901	2.2415		
	1.1111	0.1691	0.5035	0.5415	0.7500	0.6813	0.9362	0.9735	2.4176		
	1.2500	0.1494	0.5650	0.4802	0.8435	0.6041	1.0527	0.8588	2.6349		
	1.4286	0.1298	0.6438	0.4191	0.9637	0.5272	1.2019	0.7459	2.9113		
	1.6667	0.1105	0.7487	0.3583	1.1237	0.4508	1.4004	0.6345	3.2767		
	2.0000	0.0914	0.8953	0.2978	1.3475	0.3748	1.6776	0.5247	3.7846		
	2.5000	0.0725	1.1148	0.2376	1.6827	0.2991	2.0927	0.4164	4.5418		
	3.3333	0.0539	1.4801	0.1776	2.2411	0.2237	2.7833	0.3096	5.7978		
	5.0000	0.0356	2.2095	0.1180	3.3568	0.1488	4.1627	0.2046	8.3004		
	10.0000	0.0176	4.3954	0.0588	6.7021	0.0742	8.2969	0.1013	15.7878		
	Inf.	1.4953	1.0018	0.8264	0.7396	0.6688	0.5858	0.4369	0.1743		
9	1.0000	0.1718	0.4146	0.5498	0.6132	0.6774	0.7252	0.8450	1.0447	2.2834	
	0.9000	0.1900	0.3724	0.6097	0.5519	0.7513	0.6529	0.9352	0.9382	2.4512	
	0.8000	0.2125	0.3302	0.6846	0.4905	0.8436	0.5805	1.0481	0.8314	2.6613	
	0.7000	0.2415	0.2882	0.7807	0.4291	0.9624	0.5079	1.1933	0.7247	2.9315	
	0.6000	0.2800	0.2463	0.9088	0.3676	1.1207	0.4352	1.3870	0.6184	3.2914	
	0.5000	0.3337	0.2046	1.0880	0.3062	1.3424	0.3624	1.6581	0.5125	3.7941	
	0.4000	0.4141	0.1631	1.3565	0.2448	1.6749	0.2897	2.0647	0.4075	4.5462	
	0.3000	0.5478	0.1219	1.8038	0.1834	2.2289	0.2170	2.7420	0.3035	5.7960	
	0.2000	0.8148	0.0809	2.6977	0.1222	3.3369	0.1445	4.0960	0.2007	8.2890	
	0.1000	1.6146	0.0403	5.3782	0.0610	6.6602	0.0721	8.1556	0.0995	15.7520	
	Inf.	1.4907	0.9845	0.8116	0.7197	0.6646	0.6089	0.5359	0.4003	0.1598	
10	1.0000	0.1601	0.3867	0.5125	0.5702	0.6243	0.6557	0.7319	0.8178	1.0767	2.2387
	1.1111	0.1433	0.4288	0.4604	0.6336	0.5609	0.7290	0.6567	0.9089	0.9608	2.4151
	1.2500	0.1267	0.4812	0.4084	0.7127	0.4977	0.8205	0.5820	1.0221	0.8471	2.6323
	1.4286	0.1102	0.5486	0.3567	0.8143	0.4348	0.9380	0.5079	1.1672	0.7354	2.9082
	1.6667	0.0939	0.6383	0.3051	0.9498	0.3721	1.0944	0.4342	1.3600	0.6254	3.2727
	2.0000	0.0778	0.7637	0.2537	1.1392	0.3096	1.3131	0.3609	1.6291	0.5170	3.7791
	2.5000	0.0618	0.9515	0.2024	1.4232	0.2473	1.6408	0.2880	2.0320	0.4102	4.5340
	3.3333	0.0460	1.2641	0.1515	1.8961	0.1852	2.1866	0.2154	2.7022	0.3049	5.7860
	5.0000	0.0304	1.8885	0.1007	2.8416	0.1232	3.2775	0.1433	4.0406	0.2014	8.2806
	10.0000	0.0151	3.7600	0.0502	5.6766	0.0615	6.5485	0.0714	8.0520	0.0997	15.7441
	Inf.	1.4905	0.9858	0.8018	0.7123	0.6540	0.6141	0.5669	0.5003	0.3741	0.1494
n	$1/R_s$	L_1	C_2	L_3	C_4	L_5	C_6	L_7	C_8	L_9	C_{10}

TABLE 11-47 Linear Phase with Equiripple Error of 0.5° LC Element Values*

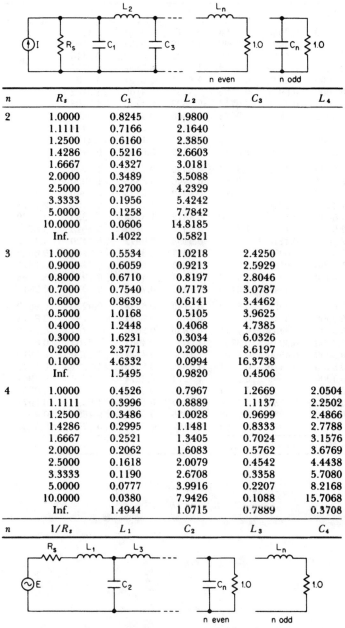

n	R_s	C_1	L_2	C_3	L_4
2	1.0000	0.8245	1.9800		
	1.1111	0.7166	2.1640		
	1.2500	0.6160	2.3850		
	1.4286	0.5216	2.6603		
	1.6667	0.4327	3.0181		
	2.0000	0.3489	3.5088		
	2.5000	0.2700	4.2329		
	3.3333	0.1956	5.4242		
	5.0000	0.1258	7.7842		
	10.0000	0.0606	14.8185		
	Inf.	1.4022	0.5821		
3	1.0000	0.5534	1.0218	2.4250	
	0.9000	0.6059	0.9213	2.5929	
	0.8000	0.6710	0.8197	2.8046	
	0.7000	0.7540	0.7173	3.0787	
	0.6000	0.8639	0.6141	3.4462	
	0.5000	1.0168	0.5105	3.9625	
	0.4000	1.2448	0.4068	4.7385	
	0.3000	1.6231	0.3034	6.0326	
	0.2000	2.3771	0.2008	8.6197	
	0.1000	4.6332	0.0994	16.3738	
	Inf.	1.5495	0.9820	0.4506	
4	1.0000	0.4526	0.7967	1.2669	2.0504
	1.1111	0.3996	0.8889	1.1137	2.2502
	1.2500	0.3486	1.0028	0.9699	2.4866
	1.4286	0.2995	1.1481	0.8333	2.7788
	1.6667	0.2521	1.3405	0.7024	3.1576
	2.0000	0.2062	1.6083	0.5762	3.6769
	2.5000	0.1618	2.0079	0.4542	4.4438
	3.3333	0.1190	2.6708	0.3358	5.7080
	5.0000	0.0777	3.9916	0.2207	8.2168
	10.0000	0.0380	7.9426	0.1088	15.7068
	Inf.	1.4944	1.0715	0.7889	0.3708

n	$1/R_s$	L_1	C_2	L_3	C_4

* Reprinted from A. I. Zverev, *Handbook of Filter Synthesis*, John Wiley and Sons, New York, 1967.

TABLE 11-47   Linear Phase with Equiripple Error of 0.5° LC Element Values (*Continued*)

n	R_s	C_1	L_2	C_3	L_4	C_5	L_6	C_7
5	1.0000	0.3658	0.6768	0.9513	1.0113	2.4446		
	0.9000	0.4027	0.6099	1.0486	0.9157	2.6062		
	0.8000	0.4485	0.5427	1.1700	0.8182	2.8114		
	0.7000	0.5069	0.4752	1.3260	0.7189	3.0787		
	0.6000	0.5843	0.4074	1.5341	0.6181	3.4387		
	0.5000	0.6921	0.3395	1.8253	0.5160	3.9462		
	0.4000	0.8530	0.2714	2.2623	0.4130	4.7108		
	0.3000	1.1201	0.2033	2.9908	0.3094	5.9881		
	0.2000	1.6524	0.1352	4.4478	0.2057	8.5444		
	0.1000	3.2454	0.0674	8.8185	0.1024	16.2117		
	Inf.	1.5327	1.0180	0.8740	0.6709	0.3182		
6	1.0000	0.3313	0.5984	0.8390	0.7964	1.2734	2.0111	
	1.1111	0.2934	0.6667	0.7446	0.8985	1.1050	2.2282	
	1.2500	0.2571	0.7515	0.6542	1.0223	0.9549	2.4742	
	1.4286	0.2219	0.8600	0.5666	1.1787	0.8164	2.7718	
	1.6667	0.1876	1.0040	0.4812	1.3848	0.6859	3.1529	
	2.0000	0.1541	1.2051	0.3976	1.6709	0.5615	3.6720	
	2.5000	0.1216	1.5058	0.3155	2.0972	0.4420	4.4362	
	3.3333	0.0898	2.0058	0.2347	2.8044	0.3266	5.6935	
	5.0000	0.0589	3.0038	0.1553	4.2137	0.2146	8.1871	
	10.0000	0.0290	5.9928	0.0771	8.4320	0.1058	15.6296	
	Inf.	1.4849	1.0430	0.8427	0.7651	0.5972	0.2844	
7	1.0000	0.2826	0.5332	0.7142	0.6988	0.9219	0.9600	2.4404
	0.9000	0.3118	0.4802	0.7896	0.6322	1.0137	0.8718	2.5953
	0.8000	0.3481	0.4271	0.8836	0.5649	1.1287	0.7809	2.7936
	0.7000	0.3945	0.3739	1.0043	0.4967	1.2768	0.6875	3.0535
	0.6000	0.4560	0.3206	1.1650	0.4277	1.4750	0.5919	3.4051
	0.5000	0.5416	0.2671	1.3899	0.3580	1.7531	0.4947	3.9025
	0.4000	0.6695	0.2136	1.7271	0.2874	2.1714	0.3961	4.6534
	0.3000	0.8819	0.1601	2.2890	0.2163	2.8700	0.2969	5.9091
	0.2000	1.3054	0.1066	3.4127	0.1445	4.2690	0.1974	8.4236
	0.1000	2.5731	0.0532	6.7835	0.0724	8.4691	0.0983	15.9666
	Inf.	1.5079	0.9763	0.8402	0.7248	0.6741	0.5305	0.2532
n	$1/R_s$	L_1	C_2	L_3	C_4	L_5	C_6	L_7

TABLE 11-47 Linear Phase with Equiripple Error of 0.5° *LC* Element Values (*Continued*)

n	R_s	C_1	L_2	C_3	L_4	C_5	L_6	C_7	L_8	C_9	L_{10}
8	1.0000	0.2718	0.4999	0.6800	0.6312	0.8498	0.7447	1.3174	1.9626		
	1.1111	0.2408	0.5567	0.6045	0.7116	0.7452	0.8529	1.1169	2.2146		
	1.2500	0.2114	0.6271	0.5324	0.8086	0.6506	0.9780	0.9551	2.4766		
	1.4286	0.1828	0.7173	0.4622	0.9315	0.5612	1.1331	0.8117	2.7837		
	1.6667	0.1549	0.8373	0.3934	1.0939	0.4753	1.3355	0.6795	3.1715		
	2.0000	0.1276	1.0049	0.3256	1.3201	0.3920	1.6148	0.5550	3.6960		
	2.5000	0.1009	1.2559	0.2589	1.6580	0.3107	2.0297	0.4362	4.4654		
	3.3333	0.0747	1.6734	0.1930	2.2194	0.2311	2.7164	0.3220	5.7294		
	5.0000	0.0492	2.5074	0.1279	3.3400	0.1530	4.0835	0.2114	8.2345		
	10.0000	0.0242	5.0066	0.0636	6.6971	0.0760	8.1733	0.1042	15.7101		
	Inf.	1.4915	1.0265	0.8169	0.7548	0.6709	0.6318	0.4995	0.2387		
9	1.0000	0.2347	0.4493	0.5914	0.5747	0.7027	0.6552	0.8944	0.9255	2.4332	
	0.9000	0.2594	0.4045	0.6547	0.5193	0.7754	0.5943	0.9809	0.8427	2.5822	
	0.8000	0.2900	0.3597	0.7336	0.4635	0.8662	0.5322	1.0895	0.7566	2.7745	
	0.7000	0.3291	0.3148	0.8348	0.4073	0.9829	0.4690	1.2299	0.6673	3.0283	
	0.6000	0.3810	0.2699	0.9695	0.3505	1.1388	0.4046	1.4183	0.5753	3.3734	
	0.5000	0.4533	0.2249	1.1580	0.2932	1.3572	0.3392	1.6834	0.4812	3.8629	
	0.4000	0.5613	0.1799	1.4405	0.2355	1.6854	0.2727	2.0828	0.3855	4.6032	
	0.3000	0.7407	0.1348	1.9111	0.1772	2.2331	0.2054	2.7508	0.2889	5.8424	
	0.2000	1.0986	0.0898	2.8522	0.1185	3.3299	0.1373	4.0895	0.1921	8.3246	
	0.1000	2.1702	0.0448	5.6744	0.0594	6.6230	0.0688	8.1099	0.0956	15.7718	
	Inf.	1.4888	0.9495	0.8044	0.6892	0.6589	0.5952	0.5645	0.4475	0.2141	
10	1.0000	0.2359	0.4369	0.5887	0.5428	0.7034	0.5827	0.8720	0.6869	1.4317	1.8431
	1.1111	0.2081	0.4866	0.5218	0.6141	0.6141	0.6729	0.7394	0.8187	1.1397	2.1907
	1.2500	0.1827	0.5480	0.4601	0.6972	0.5376	0.7708	0.6394	0.9483	0.9616	2.4734
	1.4286	0.1582	0.6267	0.3999	0.8024	0.4651	0.8922	0.5487	1.1042	0.8122	2.7907
	1.6667	0.1343	0.7314	0.3407	0.9416	0.3948	1.0514	0.4631	1.3052	0.6777	3.1847
	2.0000	0.1108	0.8777	0.2823	1.1356	0.3263	1.2719	0.3811	1.5809	0.5525	3.7138
	2.5000	0.0877	1.0969	0.2247	1.4258	0.2591	1.6003	0.3017	1.9888	0.4338	4.4876
	3.3333	0.0651	1.4619	0.1676	1.9085	0.1931	2.1451	0.2242	2.6628	0.3200	5.7573
	5.0000	0.0429	2.1910	0.1112	2.8724	0.1280	3.2311	0.1483	4.0033	0.2100	8.2726
	10.0000	0.0212	4.3764	0.0553	5.7612	0.0636	6.4830	0.0736	8.0118	0.1035	15.7776
	Inf.	1.4973	1.0192	0.8005	0.7312	0.6498	0.6331	0.5775	0.5501	0.4369	0.2091
n	$1/R_s$	L_1	C_2	L_3	C_4	L_5	C_6	L_7	C_8	L_9	C_{10}

TABLE 11-48   Linear Phase with Equiripple
Error of 0.05° Active Low-Pass Values

Order n	C_1	C_2
2	0.9914	0.6891
4	1.0365	0.8344
	1.3426	0.2959
6	1.1231	0.9257
	1.2146	0.3810
	1.6255	0.1430
8	1.2203	1.0126
	1.2610	0.4285
	1.3864	0.1894
	1.8723	0.08324
10	1.3172	1.0957
	1.3392	0.4676
	1.3968	0.2139
	1.5444	0.1116
	2.0934	0.05483

TABLE 11-49   Linear Phase with Equiripple
Error of 0.5° Active Low-Pass Values

Order n	C_1	C_2
2	1.1641	0.7011
4	1.3426	0.9103
	1.6565	0.2314
6	1.5340	1.0578
	1.6215	0.2993
	2.0437	0.1054
8	1.7268	1.1962
	1.7652	0.3445
	1.8857	0.1374
	2.3901	0.06134
10	1.9051	1.3218
	1.9257	0.3826
	1.9798	0.1562
	2.1227	0.07971
	2.6969	0.04074

TABLE 11-50 Transitional Gaussian to 6-dB Pole
Locations

Order n	Real Part $-\alpha$	Imaginary Part $\pm j\beta$
3	0.9622	1.2214
	0.9776	
4	0.7940	0.5029
	0.6304	1.5407
5	0.6190	0.8254
	0.3559	1.5688
	0.6650	
6	0.5433	0.3431
	0.4672	0.9991
	0.2204	1.5067
7	0.4580	0.5932
	0.3649	1.1286
	0.1522	1.4938
	0.4828	
8	0.4222	0.2640
	0.3833	0.7716
	0.2878	1.2066
	0.1122	1.4798
9	0.3700	0.4704
	0.3230	0.9068
	0.2309	1.2634
	0.08604	1.4740
	0.3842	
10	0.3384	0.2101
	0.3164	0.6180
	0.2677	0.9852
	0.1849	1.2745
	0.06706	1.4389

TABLE 11-51 Transitional Gaussian to 12-dB Pole Locations

Order n	Real Part $-\alpha$	Imaginary Part $\pm j\beta$
3	0.9360	1.2168
	0.9630	
4	0.9278	1.6995
	0.9192	0.5560
5	0.8075	0.9973
	0.7153	2.0532
	0.8131	
6	0.7019	0.4322
	0.6667	1.2931
	0.4479	2.1363
7	0.6155	0.7703
	0.5486	1.5154
	0.2905	2.1486
	0.6291	
8	0.5441	0.3358
	0.5175	0.9962
	0.4328	1.6100
	0.1978	2.0703
9	0.4961	0.6192
	0.4568	1.2145
	0.3592	1.7429
	0.1489	2.1003
	0.5065	
10	0.4535	0.2794
	0.4352	0.8289
	0.3886	1.3448
	0.2908	1.7837
	0.1136	2.0599

TABLE 11-52 Transitional Gaussian to 6-dB LC Element Values*

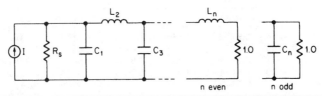

n	R_s	C_1	L_2	C_3	L_4	C_5	L_6	C_7
3	1.0000	0.4042	0.8955	2.3380				
	0.9000	0.4440	0.8038	2.5027				
	0.8000	0.4935	0.7121	2.7088				
	0.7000	0.5568	0.6205	2.9739				
	0.6000	0.6407	0.5292	3.3275				
	0.5000	0.7575	0.4384	3.8223				
	0.4000	0.9319	0.3482	4.5635				
	0.3000	1.2213	0.2590	5.7972				
	0.2000	1.7980	0.1709	8.2605				
	0.1000	3.5236	0.0845	15.6391				
	Inf.	1.4742	0.8328	0.3446				
4	1.0000	0.4198	0.7832	1.1598	2.1427			
	1.1111	0.3720	0.8717	1.0279	2.3286			
	1.2500	0.3256	0.9816	0.9010	2.5539			
	1.4286	0.2804	1.1220	0.7781	2.8367			
	1.6667	0.2365	1.3083	0.6587	3.2069			
	2.0000	0.1938	1.5678	0.5424	3.7179			
	2.5000	0.1524	1.9552	0.4289	4.4761			
	3.3333	0.1122	2.5982	0.3180	5.7296			
	5.0000	0.0733	3.8797	0.2095	8.2221			
	10.0000	0.0359	7.7138	0.1035	15.6717			
	Inf.	1.4871	1.0222	0.7656	0.3510			
5	1.0000	0.4544	0.8457	1.0924	1.0774	2.4138		
	0.9000	0.4991	0.7622	1.2046	0.9769	2.5746		
	0.8000	0.5543	0.6781	1.3452	0.8739	2.7797		
	0.7000	0.6247	0.5936	1.5263	0.7687	3.0475		
	0.6000	0.7179	0.5086	1.7683	0.6615	3.4087		
	0.5000	0.8476	0.4233	2.1077	0.5527	3.9183		
	0.4000	1.0411	0.3379	2.6176	0.4428	4.6863		
	0.3000	1.3621	0.2526	3.4680	0.3321	5.9690		
	0.2000	2.0019	0.1677	5.1693	0.2212	8.5360		
	0.1000	3.9166	0.0833	10.2723	0.1103	16.2354		
	Inf.	1.5392	1.0993	1.0203	0.8269	0.3824		
6	1.0000	0.5041	0.9032	1.2159	1.0433	1.4212	2.0917	
	1.1111	0.4427	1.0079	1.0739	1.1892	1.2274	2.3324	
	1.2500	0.3853	1.1364	0.9415	1.3611	1.0620	2.5935	
	1.4286	0.3306	1.2999	0.8145	1.5753	0.9111	2.9053	
	1.6667	0.2779	1.5162	0.6914	1.8557	0.7692	3.3032	
	2.0000	0.2271	1.8169	0.5713	2.2433	0.6333	3.8456	
	2.5000	0.1780	2.2654	0.4534	2.8200	0.5016	4.6459	
	3.3333	0.1308	3.0091	0.3376	3.7758	0.3730	5.9662	
	5.0000	0.0853	4.4902	0.2235	5.6803	0.2468	8.5904	
	10.0000	0.0416	8.9199	0.1109	11.3810	0.1225	16.4352	
	Inf.	1.5664	1.2166	1.1389	1.1010	0.8844	0.4062	

TABLE 11-52   Transitional Gaussian to 6-dB LC Element Values* (*Continued*)

n	R_s	C_1	L_2	C_3	L_4	C_5	L_6	C_7
7	1.0000	0.4918	0.9232	1.2146	1.1224	1.3154	1.1407	2.5039
	0.9000	0.5403	0.8318	1.3393	1.0196	1.4426	1.0434	2.6575
	0.8000	0.6001	0.7399	1.4950	0.9141	1.6040	0.9401	2.8593
	0.7000	0.6760	0.6474	1.6952	0.8061	1.8144	0.8317	3.1285
	0.6000	0.7763	0.5545	1.9626	0.6956	2.0986	0.7190	3.4967
	0.5000	0.9157	0.4613	2.3373	0.5829	2.5004	0.6029	4.0203
	0.4000	1.1236	0.3681	2.9002	0.4684	3.1072	0.4844	4.8129
	0.3000	1.4685	0.2750	3.8389	0.3524	4.1232	0.3644	6.1397
	0.2000	2.1560	0.1823	5.7166	0.2354	6.1604	0.2433	8.7977
	0.1000	4.2137	0.0905	11.3483	0.1178	12.2787	0.1217	16.7743
	Inf.	1.5950	1.2166	1.2240	1.1784	1.1260	0.8975	0.4110
n	$1/R_s$	L_1	C_2	L_3	C_4	L_5	C_6	L_7

* Reprinted from A. I. Zverev, *Handbook of Filter Synthesis*, John Wiley and Sons, New York, 1967.

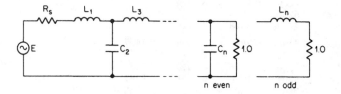

TABLE 11-52 Transitional Gaussian to 6-dB LC Element Values (*Continued*)

n	R_s	C_1	L_2	C_3	L_4	C_5	L_6	C_7	L_8	C_9	L_{10}
8	1.0502	0.5031	0.9699	1.2319	1.1324	1.4262	1.0449	1.6000	1.9285		
	1.1111	0.4586	1.0338	1.1286	1.2497	1.2635	1.2099	1.3372	2.2286		
	1.2500	0.3964	1.1670	0.9831	1.4404	1.0842	1.4259	1.1197	2.5453		
	1.4286	0.3392	1.3351	0.8487	1.6698	0.9299	1.6706	0.9502	2.8771		
	1.6667	0.2848	1.5571	0.7195	1.9674	0.7863	1.9808	0.7989	3.2846		
	2.0000	0.2325	1.8656	0.5939	2.3776	0.6487	2.4039	0.6569	3.8326		
	2.5000	0.1822	2.3255	0.4710	2.9870	0.5151	3.0295	0.5204	4.6374		
	3.3333	0.1337	3.0879	0.3504	3.9962	0.3840	4.0640	0.3874	5.9636		
	5.0000	0.0872	4.6062	0.2318	6.0063	0.2547	6.1243	0.2566	8.5995		
	10.0000	0.0425	9.1467	0.1150	12.0217	0.1268	12.2919	0.1276	16.4808		
	Inf.	1.5739	1.2698	1.2325	1.2633	1.2017	1.1404	0.9066	0.4148		
9	1.0000	0.4979	0.9367	1.2371	1.1589	1.3845	1.1670	1.3983	1.1422	2.5277	
	0.9000	0.5475	0.8439	1.3648	1.0517	1.5194	1.0673	1.5233	1.0527	2.6698	
	0.8000	0.6083	0.7505	1.5238	0.9424	1.6894	0.9625	1.6850	0.9540	2.8635	
	0.7000	0.6854	0.6567	1.7278	0.8306	1.9103	0.8527	1.8996	0.8472	3.1279	
	0.6000	0.7870	0.5624	1.9998	0.7165	2.2081	0.7383	2.1929	0.7342	3.4938	
	0.5000	0.9280	0.4679	2.3811	0.6002	2.6288	0.6202	2.6105	0.6166	4.0174	
	0.4000	1.1383	0.3732	2.9537	0.4820	3.2641	0.4993	3.2438	0.4960	4.8118	
	0.3000	1.4873	0.2788	3.9087	0.3625	4.3274	0.3763	4.3062	0.3734	6.1429	
	0.2000	2.1829	0.1848	5.8191	0.2421	6.4590	0.2518	6.4381	0.2496	8.8109	
	0.1000	4.2652	0.0918	11.5490	0.1211	12.8601	0.1262	12.8438	0.1250	16.8186	
	Inf.	1.6014	1.2508	1.2817	1.2644	1.2805	1.2103	1.1456	0.9096	0.4160	
10	1.1372	0.4682	1.0839	1.1516	1.2991	1.3293	1.2748	1.4216	1.1730	1.5040	2.1225
	1.1372	0.4682	1.0839	1.1516	1.2991	1.3293	1.2748	1.4216	1.1730	1.5040	2.1225
	1.2500	0.4087	1.1987	1.0148	1.4855	1.1389	1.5155	1.1705	1.4593	1.1798	2.5537
	1.4286	0.3489	1.3718	0.8744	1.7253	0.9733	1.7813	0.9908	1.7344	0.9878	2.9155
	1.6667	0.2928	1.6000	0.7409	2.0334	0.8219	2.1124	0.8338	2.0664	0.8275	3.3380
	2.0000	0.2389	1.9169	0.6114	2.4574	0.6776	2.5622	0.6868	2.5129	0.6799	3.8995
	2.5000	0.1872	2.3893	0.4848	3.0868	0.5377	3.2264	0.5451	3.1699	0.5387	4.7218
	3.3333	0.1373	3.1723	0.3606	4.1290	0.4007	4.3241	0.4065	4.2549	0.4011	6.0762
	5.0000	0.0895	4.7317	0.2385	6.2048	0.2657	6.5094	0.2698	6.4154	0.2659	8.7681
	10.0000	0.0437	9.3953	0.1183	12.4165	0.1322	13.0503	0.1345	12.8837	0.1323	16.8178
	Inf.	1.6077	1.3178	1.2927	1.3406	1.3070	1.3160	1.2409	1.1733	0.9311	0.4257
n	$1/R_s$	L_1	C_2	L_3	C_4	L_5	C_6	L_7	C_8	L_9	C_{10}

TABLE 11-53 Transitional Gaussian to 12-dB LC Element Values*

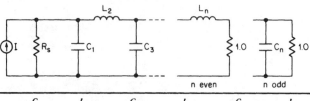

n even   n odd

n	R_s	C_1	L_2	C_3	L_4	C_5	L_6	C_7
3	1.0000	0.4152	0.9050	2.3452				
	0.9000	0.4560	0.8126	2.5101				
	0.8000	0.5067	0.7202	2.7166				
	0.7000	0.5715	0.6278	2.9825				
	0.6000	0.6573	0.5356	3.3372				
	0.5000	0.7769	0.4438	3.8336				
	0.4000	0.9554	0.3526	4.5775				
	0.3000	1.2517	0.2623	5.8157				
	0.2000	1.8420	0.1732	8.2884				
	0.1000	3.6083	0.0856	15.6955				
	Inf.	1.4800	0.8440	0.3527				
4	1.0000	0.3097	0.6545	1.0598	2.1518			
	1.1111	0.2757	0.7262	0.9418	2.3289			
	1.2500	0.2423	0.8156	0.8268	2.5459			
	1.4286	0.2096	0.9300	0.7146	2.8203			
	1.6667	0.1775	1.0821	0.6050	3.1814			
	2.0000	0.1461	1.2944	0.4980	3.6812			
	2.5000	0.1153	1.6118	0.3934	4.4241			
	3.3333	0.0853	2.1393	0.2913	5.6532			
	5.0000	0.0560	3.1917	0.1916	8.0979			
	10.0000	0.0276	6.3425	0.0944	15.4048			
	Inf.	1.4585	0.9300	0.6294	0.2707			
5	1.0000	0.2909	0.5837	0.8112	0.9660	2.3745		
	0.9000	0.3207	0.5253	0.8961	0.8707	2.5377		
	0.8000	0.3577	0.4667	1.0019	0.7746	2.7433		
	0.7000	0.4051	0.4081	1.1379	0.6777	3.0092		
	0.6000	0.4680	0.3495	1.3192	0.5804	3.3650		
	0.5000	0.5556	0.2908	1.5727	0.4827	3.8642		
	0.4000	0.6865	0.2322	1.9528	0.3850	4.6138		
	0.3000	0.9038	0.1738	2.5859	0.2875	5.8631		
	0.2000	1.3372	0.1155	3.8515	0.1907	8.3597		
	0.1000	2.6347	0.0575	7.6464	0.0947	15.8420		
	Inf.	1.4953	0.9388	0.7587	0.5724	0.2592		

TABLE 11-53   Transitional Gaussian to 12-dB LC Element Values* (*Continued*)

n	R_s	C_1	L_2	C_3	L_4	C_5	L_6	C_7
6	1.0000	0.3164	0.6070	0.7962	0.7880	1.1448	2.1154	
	1.1111	0.2813	0.6750	0.7108	0.8826	1.0087	2.3076	
	1.2500	0.2470	0.7597	0.6273	0.9994	0.8804	2.5365	
	1.4286	0.2135	0.8681	0.5452	1.1481	0.7580	2.8209	
	1.6667	0.1807	1.0123	0.4644	1.3451	0.6402	3.1908	
	2.0000	0.1487	1.2136	0.3847	1.6194	0.5263	3.6993	
	2.5000	0.1174	1.5148	0.3060	2.0292	0.4157	4.4522	
	3.3333	0.0868	2.0154	0.2282	2.7098	0.3080	5.6952	
	5.0000	0.0570	3.0146	0.1513	4.0679	0.2028	8.1654	
	10.0000	0.0280	6.0071	0.0753	8.1355	0.1002	15.5460	
	Inf.	1.4732	0.9894	0.8129	0.7484	0.5979	0.2752	
7	1.0000	0.3207	0.6267	0.8091	0.7753	0.9241	0.9649	2.3829
	0.9000	0.3534	0.5641	0.8946	0.7016	1.0176	0.8750	2.5374
	0.8000	0.3940	0.5015	1.0015	0.6270	1.1350	0.7824	2.7351
	0.7000	0.4458	0.4387	1.1388	0.5513	1.2867	0.6876	2.9937
	0.6000	0.5146	0.3758	1.3218	0.4747	1.4899	0.5910	3.3428
	0.5000	0.6102	0.3128	1.5781	0.3972	1.7755	0.4931	3.8355
	0.4000	0.7531	0.2498	1.9626	0.3189	2.2054	0.3943	4.5779
	0.3000	0.9902	0.1869	2.6034	0.2399	2.9236	0.2951	5.8175
	0.2000	1.4630	0.1243	3.8851	0.1603	4.3624	0.1961	8.2974
	0.1000	2.8780	0.0619	7.7299	0.0803	8.6825	0.0976	15.7326
	Inf.	1.4861	0.9693	0.8643	0.8040	0.7689	0.6157	0.2826
n	$1/R_s$	L_1	C_2	L_3	C_4	L_5	C_6	L_7

* Reprinted from A. I. Zverev, *Handbook of Filter Synthesis*, John Wiley and Sons, New York, 1967.

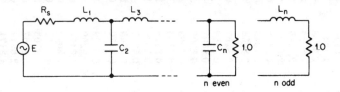

TABLE 11-53 Transitional Gaussian to 12-dB LC Element Values (*Continued*)

n	R_s	C_1	L_2	C_3	L_4	C_5	L_6	C_7	L_8	C_9	L_{10}
8	1.0000	0.3449	0.6565	0.8686	0.8028	0.9701	0.8182	1.2503	2.0612		
	1.1111	0.3053	0.7304	0.7729	0.9044	0.8550	0.9339	1.0753	2.2930		
	1.2500	0.2674	0.8221	0.6810	1.0276	0.7489	1.0694	0.9272	2.5445		
	1.4286	0.2308	0.9394	0.5913	1.1837	0.6480	1.2378	0.7929	2.8444		
	1.6667	0.1952	1.0953	0.5034	1.3898	0.5504	1.4579	0.6673	3.2267		
	2.0000	0.1604	1.3128	0.4168	1.6764	0.4553	1.7620	0.5476	3.7473		
	2.5000	0.1265	1.6381	0.3314	2.1045	0.3621	2.2143	0.4323	4.5145		
	3.3333	0.0934	2.1788	0.2471	2.8155	0.2702	2.9640	0.3203	5.7789		
	5.0000	0.0613	3.2575	0.1638	4.2343	0.1794	4.4583	0.2111	8.2899		
	10.0000	0.0301	6.4874	0.0814	8.4843	0.0894	8.9330	0.1044	15.7917		
	Inf.	1.4974	1.0324	0.8943	0.8908	0.8494	0.8098	0.6452	0.2955		
9	1.0000	0.3318	0.6500	0.8467	0.8167	0.9426	0.8239	0.9857	0.9630	2.4140	
	0.9000	0.3657	0.5852	0.9363	0.7389	1.0390	0.7492	1.0803	0.8785	2.5608	
	0.8000	0.4078	0.5201	1.0480	0.6602	1.1599	0.6725	1.2003	0.7894	2.7524	
	0.7000	0.4614	0.4550	1.1914	0.5806	1.3160	0.5936	1.3568	0.6963	3.0070	
	0.6000	0.5324	0.3897	1.3825	0.4999	1.5251	0.5127	1.5681	0.6001	3.3538	
	0.5000	0.6312	0.3243	1.6500	0.4183	1.8192	0.4301	1.8667	0.5015	3.8460	
	0.4000	0.7787	0.2590	2.0512	0.3358	2.2620	0.3460	2.3177	0.4016	4.5897	
	0.3000	1.0234	0.1938	2.7200	0.2526	3.0021	0.2607	3.0729	0.3009	5.8332	
	0.2000	1.5113	0.1288	4.0574	0.1687	4.4850	0.1744	4.5875	0.2000	8.3219	
	0.1000	2.9716	0.0641	8.0692	0.0845	8.9384	0.0875	9.1379	0.0996	15.7849	
	Inf.	1.4917	0.9908	0.9105	0.8770	0.8910	0.8457	0.8022	0.6376	0.2917	
10	1.0139	0.3500	0.6698	0.8817	0.8148	1.0183	0.7949	1.0929	0.7508	1.4303	1.8322
	1.1111	0.3092	0.7364	0.7856	0.9200	0.8864	0.9293	0.9147	0.9187	1.1138	2.2110
	1.2500	0.2701	0.8290	0.6907	1.0477	0.7734	1.0708	0.7890	1.0712	0.9404	2.4914
	1.4286	0.2328	0.9474	0.5992	1.2075	0.6681	1.2428	0.6777	1.2503	0.7978	2.8009
	1.6667	0.1968	1.1046	0.5099	1.4179	0.5671	1.4663	0.5734	1.4791	0.6690	3.1853
	2.0000	0.1616	1.3239	0.4221	1.7103	0.4689	1.7746	0.4734	1.7920	0.5483	3.7034
	2.5000	0.1274	1.6517	0.3355	2.1467	0.3728	2.2329	0.3761	2.2552	0.4326	4.4640
	3.3333	0.0941	2.1966	0.2501	2.8714	0.2781	2.9923	0.2806	3.0215	0.3206	5.7162
	5.0000	0.0617	3.2837	0.1658	4.3171	0.1845	4.5061	0.1863	4.5478	0.2114	8.2022
	10.0000	0.0303	6.5385	0.0824	8.6473	0.0919	9.0397	0.0929	9.1181	0.1046	15.6293
	Inf.	1.4826	1.0350	0.9134	0.9263	0.9061	0.9159	0.8654	0.8190	0.6502	0.2973
n	$1/R_s$	L_1	C_2	L_3	C_4	L_5	C_6	L_7	C_8	L_9	C_{10}

TABLE 11-54 Transitional Gaussian to 6-dB
Active Low-Pass Values

Order n	C_1	C_2
4	1.2594	0.8989
	1.5863	0.2275
6	1.8406	1.3158
	2.1404	0.3841
	4.5372	0.09505
8	2.3685	1.7028
	2.6089	0.5164
	3.4746	0.1870
	8.9127	0.05094
10	2.9551	2.1329
	3.1606	0.6564
	3.7355	0.2568
	5.4083	0.1115
	14.9120	0.03232

TABLE 11-55 Transitional Gaussian to 12-dB Active
Low-Pass Values

Order n	C_1	C_2
4	1.0778	0.2475
	1.0879	0.7965
6	1.4247	1.0330
	1.5000	0.3150
	2.2326	0.09401
8	1.8379	1.3309
	1.9324	0.4106
	2.3105	0.1557
	5.0556	0.04573
10	2.2051	1.5984
	2.2978	0.4965
	2.5733	0.1983
	3.4388	0.08903
	8.8028	0.02669

TABLE 11-56 Elliptic-Function LC Element Values

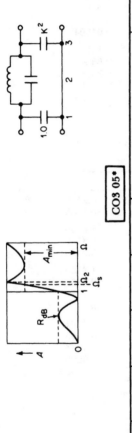

CO3 05*

θ	Ω_s	A_{min}	σ_0	σ_1	Ω_1	Ω_2	$K^2 = 1.0$			$K^2 = \infty$			
							$C'_1 = C'_3$	C_2	L'_2	C'_1	C'_2	L'_2	C'_3
1	57.2987	108.56	1.56379	0.78132	1.60724	66.1616	0.6395	0.0002	0.9786	0.3196	0.0003	0.7733	0.8092
2	28.6537	85.50	1.56503	0.78023	1.60733	33.0839	0.6390	0.0009	0.9776	0.3188	0.0012	0.7721	0.8090
3	19.1073	74.93	1.56708	0.77840	1.60748	22.0595	0.6381	0.0021	0.9761	0.3175	0.0027	0.7702	0.8087
4	14.3356	67.43	1.56997	0.77585	1.60768	16.5483	0.6370	0.0037	0.9739	0.3156	0.0048	0.7675	0.8083
5	11.4737	61.61	1.57370	0.77257	1.60793	13.2424	0.6354	0.0059	0.9711	0.3132	0.0075	0.7639	0.8077
6	9.5668	56.85	1.57828	0.76857	1.60822	11.0392	0.6336	0.0085	0.9676	0.3103	0.0108	0.7596	0.8071
7	8.2055	52.82	1.58373	0.76384	1.60854	9.4661	0.6314	0.0116	0.9636	0.3069	0.0148	0.7546	0.8063
8	7.1853	49.33	1.59006	0.75840	1.60887	8.2868	0.6289	0.0152	0.9589	0.3029	0.0195	0.7487	0.8055
9	6.3925	46.25	1.59730	0.75225	1.60922	7.3700	0.6261	0.0193	0.9536	0.2983	0.0248	0.7421	0.8045
10	5.7588	43.49	1.60546	0.74539	1.60955	6.6370	0.6229	0.0240	0.9477	0.2932	0.0309	0.7346	0.8035
11	5.2408	41.00	1.61458	0.73784	1.60986	6.0377	0.6194	0.0291	0.9411	0.2875	0.0378	0.7264	0.8024
12	4.8097	38.71	1.62467	0.72959	1.61013	5.5386	0.6155	0.0349	0.9339	0.2813	0.0454	0.7175	0.8012
13	4.4454	36.61	1.63579	0.72065	1.61033	5.1166	0.6113	0.0412	0.9261	0.2744	0.0540	0.7077	0.8000
14	4.1336	34.66	1.64795	0.71104	1.61046	4.7552	0.6068	0.0482	0.9177	0.2670	0.0634	0.6972	0.7987
15	3.8637	32.85	1.66121	0.70077	1.61048	4.4423	0.6020	0.0558	0.9087	0.2589	0.0739	0.6860	0.7974
16	3.6280	31.14	1.67561	0.68984	1.61037	4.1688	0.5968	0.0640	0.8991	0.2502	0.0854	0.6739	0.7961
17	3.4203	29.54	1.69120	0.67828	1.61011	3.9277	0.5913	0.0729	0.8888	0.2408	0.0980	0.6612	0.7949
18	3.2361	28.03	1.70803	0.66609	1.60967	3.7137	0.5855	0.0826	0.8780	0.2308	0.1120	0.6477	0.7936
19	3.0716	26.60	1.72616	0.65329	1.60903	3.5224	0.5793	0.0930	0.8665	0.2201	0.1272	0.6334	0.7925
20	2.9238	25.24	1.74565	0.63990	1.60815	3.3505	0.5728	0.1043	0.8545	0.2087	0.1440	0.6185	0.7914

θ	Ω_s	A_{min}	σ_0	σ_1	Ω_1	Ω_2	$L'_1 = L'_3$	L'_2	C'_2	L'_1	L'_2	C'_2	L'_3
21	2.7904	23.95	1.76659	0.62595	1.60701	3.1951	0.5661	0.1164	0.8418	0.1965	0.1625	0.6028	0.7905
22	2.6695	22.71	1.78903	0.61144	1.60558	3.0541	0.5590	0.1294	0.8286	0.1836	0.1828	0.5865	0.7897
23	2.5593	21.53	1.81308	0.59641	1.60383	2.9256	0.5515	0.1434	0.8148	0.1699	0.2052	0.5695	0.7891
24	2.4586	20.40	1.83881	0.58089	1.60172	2.8079	0.5438	0.1585	0.8004	0.1553	0.2298	0.5519	0.7887
25	2.3662	19.31	1.86632	0.56489	1.59923	2.6999	0.5358	0.1747	0.7855	0.1399	0.2571	0.5337	0.7887
26	2.2812	18.27	1.89572	0.54847	1.59633	2.6003	0.5275	0.1921	0.7700	0.1236	0.2873	0.5149	0.7889
27	2.2027	17.26	1.92713	0.53164	1.59298	2.5083	0.5189	0.2108	0.7540	0.1063	0.3208	0.4955	0.7896
28	2.1301	16.30	1.96066	0.51445	1.58916	2.4231	0.5100	0.2309	0.7375	0.0880	0.3580	0.4757	0.7908
29	2.0627	15.37	1.99644	0.49694	1.58485	2.3438	0.5009	0.2526	0.7205	0.0687	0.3997	0.4555	0.7924
30	2.0000	14.47	2.03461	0.47915	1.58000	2.2701	0.4915	0.2760	0.7031	0.0483	0.4463	0.4348	0.7947
31	1.9416	13.61	2.07532	0.46114	1.57461	2.2012	0.4819	0.3012	0.6852	0.0268	0.4986	0.4139	0.7977
32	1.8871	12.77	2.11873	0.44294	1.56865	2.1368	0.4720	0.3284	0.6669	0.0040	0.5577	0.3927	0.8014
33	1.8361	11.97	2.16500	0.42462	1.56210	2.0765	0.4619	0.3578	0.6482	-0.0201	0.6244	0.3714	0.8061
34	1.7883	11.20	2.21430	0.40622	1.55494	2.0199	0.4516	0.3896	0.6291	-0.0456	0.7003	0.3500	0.8117
35	1.7434	10.46	2.26682	0.38781	1.54717	1.9666	0.4411	0.4241	0.6097	-0.0725	0.7868	0.3286	0.8185

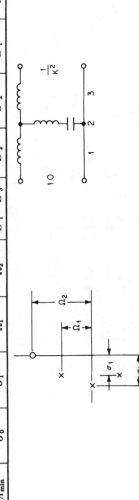

* Adapted from A. I. Zverev, *Handbook of Filter Synthesis*, John Wiley and Sons, New York, 1967.

11.69

TABLE 11-56   Elliptic-Function LC Element Values (*Continued*)

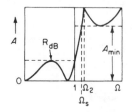   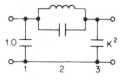

CO3 20°

θ	Ω_s	A_{min}	σ_0	σ_1	Ω_1	Ω_2	$K^2 = 1.0$			$K^2 = \infty$			
							$C'_1 = C'_3$	C'_2	L'_2	C'_1	C'_2	L'_2	C'_3
1	57.2987	115.77	0.84082	0.42027	1.13143	66.1616	1.1893	0.0002	1.1540	0.5946	0.0002	1.1713	1.1717
2	28.6537	97.70	0.84114	0.42001	1.13150	33.0839	1.1889	0.0008	1.1533	0.5940	0.0008	1.1704	1.1715
3	19.1073	87.13	0.84169	0.41958	1.13160	22.0595	1.1881	0.0018	1.1522	0.5932	0.0018	1.1690	1.1710
4	14.3356	79.63	0.84246	0.41899	1.13175	16.5483	1.1870	0.0032	1.1507	0.5920	0.0031	1.1670	1.1704
5	11.4737	73.81	0.84345	0.41822	1.13194	13.2424	1.1856	0.0050	1.1488	0.5904	0.0049	1.1645	1.1696
6	9.5668	69.05	0.84466	0.41728	1.13218	11.0392	1.1839	0.0072	1.1464	0.5885	0.0071	1.1614	1.1686
7	8.2055	65.03	0.84609	0.41617	1.13245	9.4661	1.1819	0.0098	1.1436	0.5862	0.0096	1.1577	1.1675
8	7.1853	61.54	0.84776	0.41489	1.13276	8.2868	1.1796	0.0128	1.1404	0.5836	0.0126	1.1535	1.1662
9	6.3925	58.46	0.84965	0.41344	1.13311	7.3700	1.1770	0.0162	1.1367	0.5807	0.0160	1.1487	1.1647
10	5.7588	55.70	0.85177	0.41182	1.13350	6.6370	1.1740	0.0200	1.1326	0.5773	0.0199	1.1434	1.1630
11	5.2408	53.20	0.85413	0.41003	1.13392	6.0377	1.1708	0.0243	1.1281	0.5737	0.0241	1.1374	1.1611
12	4.8097	50.92	0.85673	0.40807	1.13438	5.5386	1.1672	0.0290	1.1231	0.5696	0.0288	1.1310	1.1591
13	4.4454	48.82	0.85957	0.40593	1.13486	5.1166	1.1634	0.0342	1.1177	0.5653	0.0340	1.1239	1.1570
14	4.1336	46.87	0.86266	0.40363	1.13538	4.7552	1.1592	0.0398	1.1119	0.5605	0.0396	1.1163	1.1546
15	3.8637	45.05	0.86600	0.40115	1.13592	4.4423	1.1547	0.0458	1.1057	0.5554	0.0457	1.1082	1.1521
16	3.6280	43.35	0.86959	0.39851	1.13649	4.1688	1.1500	0.0524	1.0990	0.5500	0.0523	1.0994	1.1495
17	3.4203	41.75	0.87345	0.39569	1.13709	3.9277	1.1449	0.0594	1.0919	0.5441	0.0595	1.0902	1.1467
18	3.2361	40.23	0.87759	0.39270	1.13770	3.7137	1.1395	0.0669	1.0844	0.5379	0.0671	1.0803	1.1437
19	3.0716	38.80	0.88199	0.38954	1.13833	3.5224	1.1338	0.0749	1.0764	0.5314	0.0753	1.0700	1.1407
20	2.9238	37.44	0.88668	0.38621	1.13897	3.3505	1.1278	0.0834	1.0681	0.5244	0.0841	1.0590	1.1374
21	2.7904	36.14	0.89167	0.38272	1.13963	3.1951	1.1215	0.0925	1.0593	0.5171	0.0935	1.0475	1.1340
22	2.6695	34.90	0.89695	0.37905	1.14029	3.0541	1.1149	0.1021	1.0500	0.5094	0.1035	1.0355	1.1305
23	2.5593	33.71	0.90254	0.37521	1.14096	2.9256	1.1080	0.1123	1.0404	0.5013	0.1142	1.0229	1.1269
24	2.4586	32.57	0.90845	0.37120	1.14162	2.8079	1.1008	0.1231	1.0303	0.4928	0.1256	1.0098	1.1232
25	2.3662	31.47	0.91469	0.36702	1.14228	2.6999	1.0933	0.1345	1.0199	0.4839	0.1377	0.9961	1.1193
26	2.2812	30.41	0.92127	0.36268	1.14294	2.6003	1.0855	0.1466	1.0090	0.4746	0.1506	0.9819	1.1153
27	2.2027	29.39	0.92820	0.35817	1.14358	2.5083	1.0773	0.1593	0.9976	0.4649	0.1643	0.9672	1.1113
28	2.1301	28.41	0.93550	0.35349	1.14420	2.4231	1.0689	0.1728	0.9859	0.4548	0.1789	0.9519	1.1071
29	2.0627	27.45	0.94318	0.34864	1.14480	2.3438	1.0602	0.1869	0.9738	0.4443	0.1944	0.9362	1.1029
30	2.0000	26.53	0.95125	0.34364	1.14538	2.2701	1.0512	0.2019	0.9612	0.4333	0.2110	0.9199	1.0985

TABLE 11-56 Elliptic-Function LC Element Values (*Continued*)

θ	Ω_s	A_{min}	σ_0	σ_1	Ω_1	Ω_2	$K^2=1.0$ $C'_1=C'_3$	C'_2	L'_2	$K^2=\infty$ C'_1	C'_2	L'_2	C'_3
31	1.9416	25.63	0.95973	0.33847	1.14592	2.2012	1.0420	0.2176	0.9483	0.4219	0.2285	0.9030	1.0942
32	1.8871	24.76	0.96863	0.33313	1.14643	2.1368	1.0324	0.2343	0.9349	0.4101	0.2473	0.8857	1.0897
33	1.8361	23.92	0.97799	0.32764	1.14689	2.0765	1.0225	0.2518	0.9212	0.3978	0.2672	0.8679	1.0853
34	1.7883	23.09	0.98780	0.32199	1.14730	2.0199	1.0123	0.2702	0.9070	0.3851	0.2885	0.8496	1.0808
35	1.7434	22.29	0.99810	0.31619	1.14766	1.9666	1.0019	0.2897	0.8925	0.3719	0.3112	0.8308	1.0762
36	1.7013	21.51	1.00890	0.31023	1.14796	1.9165	0.9912	0.3103	0.8776	0.3582	0.3355	0.8116	1.0717
37	1.6616	20.74	1.02024	0.30412	1.14819	1.8692	0.9802	0.3320	0.8623	0.3441	0.3614	0.7919	1.0672
38	1.6243	20.00	1.03213	0.29786	1.14835	1.8245	0.9689	0.3549	0.8466	0.3294	0.3892	0.7718	1.0627
39	1.5890	19.27	1.04460	0.29147	1.14842	1.7823	0.9573	0.3791	0.8305	0.3142	0.4191	0.7512	1.0583
40	1.5557	18.56	1.05768	0.28493	1.14841	1.7423	0.9455	0.4047	0.8141	0.2985	0.4511	0.7303	1.0540
41	1.5243	17.86	1.07140	0.27825	1.14830	1.7044	0.9334	0.4318	0.7973	0.2823	0.4856	0.7089	1.0497
42	1.4945	17.18	1.08579	0.27145	1.14810	1.6684	0.9210	0.4605	0.7801	0.2655	0.5228	0.6872	1.0456
43	1.4663	16.52	1.10089	0.26452	1.14778	1.6343	0.9084	0.4909	0.7627	0.2481	0.5629	0.6651	1.0416
44	1.4396	15.86	1.11673	0.25747	1.14735	1.6018	0.8955	0.5232	0.7448	0.2301	0.6064	0.6427	1.0378
45	1.4142	15.22	1.13336	0.25031	1.14679	1.5710	0.8823	0.5576	0.7267	0.2115	0.6535	0.6200	1.0341
46	1.3902	14.60	1.15082	0.24304	1.14611	1.5415	0.8689	0.5942	0.7082	0.1923	0.7048	0.5971	1.0307
47	1.3673	13.98	1.16915	0.23567	1.14528	1.5135	0.8553	0.6331	0.6895	0.1725	0.7607	0.5739	1.0276
48	1.3456	13.38	1.18840	0.22821	1.14432	1.4868	0.8415	0.6747	0.6705	0.1519	0.8217	0.5505	1.0248
49	1.3250	12.79	1.20862	0.22067	1.14320	1.4613	0.8274	0.7192	0.6511	0.1307	0.8886	0.5270	1.0223
50	1.3054	12.22	1.22988	0.21306	1.14192	1.4369	0.8131	0.7668	0.6316	0.1087	0.9621	0.5034	1.0202
51	1.2868	11.65	1.25221	0.20539	1.14048	1.4137	0.7986	0.8179	0.6118	0.0860	1.0431	0.4797	1.0185
52	1.2690	11.10	1.27570	0.19766	1.13887	1.3914	0.7839	0.8728	0.5918	0.0625	1.1327	0.4560	1.0173
53	1.2521	10.56	1.30040	0.18990	1.13709	1.3702	0.7690	0.9319	0.5716	0.0382	1.2320	0.4323	1.0166
54	1.2361	10.03	1.32639	0.18211	1.13512	1.3498	0.7539	0.9958	0.5512	0.0130	1.3426	0.4088	1.0165
55	1.2208	9.51	1.35374	0.17431	1.13297	1.3303	0.7387	1.0648	0.5306	−0.0131	1.4662	0.3854	1.0171
56	1.2062	9.01	1.38253	0.16652	1.13064	1.3117	0.7233	1.1397	0.5100	−0.0401	1.6046	0.3622	1.0184
57	1.1924	8.51	1.41284	0.15873	1.12811	1.2938	0.7078	1.2210	0.4892	−0.0681	1.7605	0.3393	1.0205
58	1.1792	8.03	1.44478	0.15098	1.12540	1.2767	0.6921	1.3097	0.4684	−0.0971	1.9366	0.3168	1.0235
59	1.1666	7.57	1.47842	0.14328	1.12249	1.2603	0.6764	1.4065	0.4476	−0.1272	2.1364	0.2947	1.0274
60	1.1547	7.11	1.51387	0.13565	1.11939	1.2446	0.6606	1.5127	0.4268	−0.1584	2.3640	0.2731	1.0323
θ	Ω_s	A_{min}	σ_0	σ_1	Ω_1	Ω_2	$L'_1=L'_3$	L'_2	C'_2	L'_1	L'_2	C'_2	L'_3

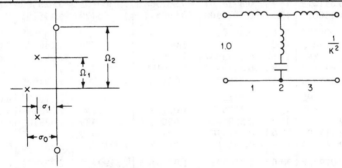

* Adapted from A. I. Zverev, *Handbook of Filter Synthesis,* John Wiley and Sons, New York, 1967.

TABLE 11-56 Elliptic-Function LC Element Values (*Continued*)

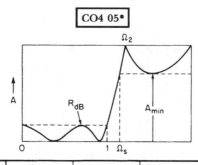

CO4 05*

θ	Ω_s	A_{min}	σ_1	σ_3	Ω_1	Ω_2	Ω_3
C	∞	∞	-0.4050275	-0.9778230	1.3452476	∞	0.5572198
6.0	10.350843	88.5	-0.4016789	-0.9797660	1.3444158	11.367741	0.5610746
7.0	8.876727	83.1	-0.4004697	-0.9804681	1.3441135	9.747389	0.5624723
8.0	7.771760	78.5	-0.3990745	-0.9812783	1.3437635	8.532615	0.5640888
9.0	6.912894	74.4	-0.3974934	-0.9821970	1.3433651	7.588226	0.5659256
10.0	6.226301	70.7	-0.3957264	-0.9832241	1.3429179	6.833109	0.5679847
11.0	5.664999	67.3	-0.3937735	-0.9843599	1.3424210	6.215646	0.5702682
12.0	5.197666	64.3	-0.3916348	-0.9856046	1.3418737	5.701423	0.5727782
13.0	4.802620	61.5	-0.3893103	-0.9869583	1.3412750	5.266618	0.5755174
14.0	4.464371	58.9	-0.3868003	-0.9884214	1.3406240	4.894214	0.5784885
15.0	4.171563	56.5	-0.3841047	-0.9899941	1.3399195	4.571732	0.5816946
16.0	3.915678	54.2	-0.3812237	-0.9916767	1.3391603	4.289813	0.5851389
17.0	3.690200	52.1	-0.3781575	-0.9934696	1.3383450	4.041300	0.5888249
18.0	3.490065	50.1	-0.3749063	-0.9953733	1.3374723	3.820626	0.5927565
19.0	3.311272	48.1	-0.3714704	-0.9973882	1.3365405	3.623399	0.5969377
20.0	3.150622	46.3	-0.3678500	-0.9995149	1.3355479	3.446101	0.6013728
21.0	3.005526	44.6	-0.3640455	-1.0017540	1.3344925	3.285888	0.6060665
22.0	2.873864	42.9	-0.3600572	-1.0041063	1.3333724	3.140431	0.6110236
23.0	2.753885	41.3	-0.3558857	-1.0065726	1.3321853	3.007807	0.6162494
24.0	2.644133	39.8	-0.3515315	-1.0091538	1.3309287	2.886413	0.6217494
25.0	2.543380	38.4	-0.3469952	-1.0118510	1.3296002	2.774903	0.6275294
26.0	2.450592	37.0	-0.3422776	-1.0146654	1.3281970	2.672139	0.6335958
27.0	2.364885	35.6	-0.3373795	-1.0175982	1.3267160	2.577149	0.6399549
28.0	2.285502	34.3	-0.3323020	-1.0206511	1.3251539	2.489103	0.6466138
29.0	2.211792	33.0	-0.3270460	-1.0238258	1.3235074	2.407283	0.6535797
30.0	2.143189	31.8	-0.3216130	-1.0271242	1.3217728	2.331070	0.6608602
31.0	2.079202	30.6	-0.3160044	-1.0305485	1.3199459	2.259921	0.6684634
32.0	2.019399	29.4	-0.3102219	-1.0341012	1.3180227	2.193363	0.6763979
33.0	1.963403	28.3	-0.3042674	-1.0377851	1.3159984	2.130982	0.6846724
34.0	1.910879	27.2	-0.2981431	-1.0416034	1.3138683	2.072410	0.6932966
35.0	1.861534	26.1	-0.2918515	-1.0455595	1.3116273	2.017322	0.7022800
36.0	1.815103	25.1	-0.2853955	-1.0496574	1.3092698	1.965429	0.7116332
37.0	1.771354	24.0	-0.2787783	-1.0539018	1.3067901	1.916475	0.7213667
38.0	1.730076	23.0	-0.2720036	-1.0582975	1.3041820	1.870229	0.7314921
39.0	1.691083	22.1	-0.2650754	-1.0628501	1.3014390	1.826485	0.7420210
40.0	1.654204	21.1	-0.2579985	-1.0675662	1.2985544	1.785057	0.7529658
θ	Ω_s	A_{min}	σ_1	σ_3	Ω_1	Ω_2	Ω_3

* Adapted from A. I. Zverev, *Handbook of Filter Synthesis*, John Wiley and Sons, New York, 1967.

TABLE 11-56 Elliptic-Function LC Element Values (*Continued*)

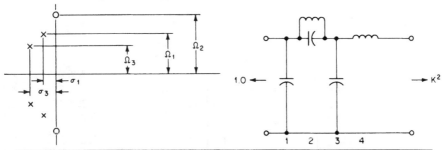

	$K^2 = 0.9048$					$K^2 = 0$			
C_1	C_2	L_2	C_3	L_4	C_1	C_2	L_2	C_3	L_4
0.7231	0.000000	1.207	1.334	0.6543	0.36157	0.000000	0.90444	1.16498	1.04995
0.7174	0.006461	1.198	1.330	0.6549	0.35333	0.00867	0.89233	1.16304	1.05291
0.7154	0.008813	1.194	1.329	0.6552	0.35034	0.01185	0.88795	1.16236	1.05398
0.7130	0.01154	1.190	1.327	0.6555	0.34687	0.01556	0.88290	1.16158	1.05522
0.7103	0.01464	1.186	1.325	0.6558	0.34293	0.01980	0.87717	1.16072	1.05662
0.7073	0.01814	1.181	1.323	0.6561	0.33851	0.02460	0.87076	1.15976	1.05820
0.7040	0.02202	1.176	1.321	0.6565	0.33360	0.02997	0.86368	1.15873	1.05993
0.7003	0.02630	1.170	1.318	0.6569	0.32819	0.03594	0.85592	1.15763	1.06184
0.6963	0.03100	1.163	1.316	0.6574	0.32227	0.04254	0.84748	1.15646	1.06391
0.6920	0.03612	1.156	1.313	0.6579	0.31584	0.04980	0.83836	1.15523	1.06616
0.6874	0.04166	1.148	1.310	0.6584	0.30888	0.05774	0.82856	1.15396	1.06857
0.6824	0.04766	1.140	1.306	0.6590	0.30139	0.06642	0.81808	1.15265	0.07115
0.6771	0.05411	1.132	1.303	0.6596	0.29334	0.07588	0.80692	1.15132	1.07390
0.6715	0.06103	1.122	1.299	0.6603	0.28473	0.08616	0.79508	1.14998	1.07682
0.6655	0.06845	1.113	1.295	0.6610	0.27554	0.09733	0.78256	1.14865	1.07991
0.6592	0.07637	1.103	1.291	0.6617	0.26575	0.10945	0.76935	1.14734	1.08316
0.6526	0.08482	1.092	1.286	0.6624	0.25534	0.12260	0.75547	1.14607	1.08658
0.6456	0.09383	1.081	1.282	0.6632	0.24428	0.13685	0.74091	1.14486	1.09016
0.6383	0.1034	1.069	1.277	0.6641	0.23257	0.15232	0.72568	1.14374	1.09391
0.6306	0.1136	1.057	1.272	0.6649	0.22015	0.16911	0.70977	1.14274	1.09780
0.6226	0.1244	1.044	1.267	0.6658	0.20702	0.18735	0.69320	1.14187	1.10185
0.6143	0.1359	1.030	1.262	0.6668	0.19313	0.20719	0.67596	1.14118	1.10605
0.6055	0.1481	1.017	1.256	0.6677	0.17844	0.22880	0.65807	1.14071	1.11038
0.5964	0.1611	1.002	1.250	0.6687	0.16291	0.25238	0.63954	1.14049	1.11485
0.5870	0.1748	0.9872	1.244	0.6698	0.14651	0.27816	0.62037	1.14057	1.11943
0.5772	0.1894	0.9717	1.238	0.6708	0.12916	0.30642	0.60057	1.14101	1.12412
0.5670	0.2049	0.9558	1.232	0.6719	0.11082	0.33749	0.58017	1.14186	1.12890
0.5564	0.2213	0.9393	1.226	0.6730	0.09142	0.37172	0.55919	1.14320	1.13375
0.5455	0.2388	0.9223	1.219	0.6742	0.07088	0.40959	0.53763	1.14511	1.13865
0.5341	0.2573	0.9048	1.212	0.6753	0.04911	0.45163	0.51554	1.14767	1.14358
0.5224	0.2771	0.8868	1.205	0.6765	0.02602	0.49848	0.49294	1.15100	1.14850
0.5103	0.2982	0.8683	1.198	0.6777	0.00149	0.55094	0.46988	1.15520	1.15338
0.4978	0.3206	0.8492	1.191	0.6789	−0.02462	0.60995	0.44638	1.16042	1.15818
0.4848	0.3446	0.8297	1.184	0.6801	−0.05244	0.67668	0.42250	1.16681	1.16286
0.4715	0.3702	0.8098	1.177	0.6813	−0.08216	0.75258	0.39830	1.17457	1.16735
0.4577	0.3976	0.7893	1.169	0.6825	−0.11399	0.83946	0.37385	1.18392	1.17160
L_1	L_2	C_2	L_3	C_4	L_1	L_2	C_2	L_3	C_4

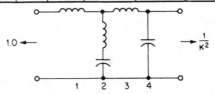

TABLE 11-56 Elliptic-Function LC Element Values (*Continued*)

CO4 20°

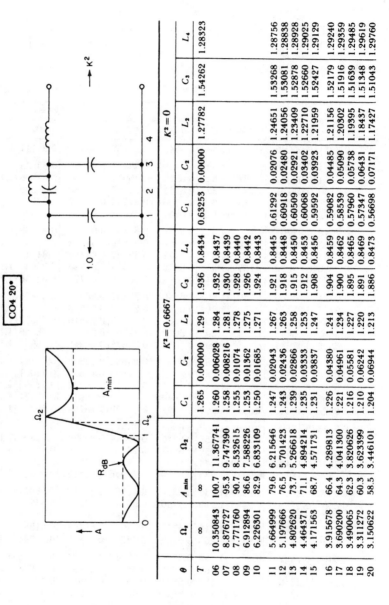

θ	Ω_s	A_{min}	Ω_2	C_1	C_2	L_2	C_3	L_4	C_1	C_2	L_2	C_3	L_4
					$K^2 = 0.6667$					$K^2 = 0$			
T	∞	∞	∞	1.265	0.000000	1.291	1.936	0.8434	0.63253	0.00000	1.27782	1.54262	1.28323
06	10.350843	100.7	11.367741	1.260	0.006028	1.284	1.932	0.8437					
07	8.876727	95.3	9.747390	1.258	0.008216	1.281	1.930	0.8439					
08	7.771760	90.7	8.532615	1.255	0.01074	1.278	1.928	0.8440					
09	6.912894	86.6	7.588226	1.253	0.01362	1.275	1.926	0.8442					
10	6.226301	82.9	6.833109	1.250	0.01685	1.271	1.924	0.8443					
11	5.664999	79.6	6.215646	1.247	0.02043	1.267	1.921	0.8445	0.61292	0.02076	1.24651	1.53268	1.28756
12	5.197666	76.5	5.701423	1.243	0.02436	1.263	1.918	0.8448	0.60918	0.02480	1.24056	1.53081	1.28838
13	4.802620	73.7	5.266618	1.239	0.02866	1.258	1.915	0.8450	0.60509	0.02921	1.23409	1.52878	1.28928
14	4.464371	71.1	4.894214	1.235	0.03333	1.253	1.912	0.8453	0.60068	0.03402	1.22710	1.52660	1.29025
15	4.171563	68.7	4.571731	1.231	0.03837	1.247	1.908	0.8456	0.59592	0.03923	1.21959	1.52427	1.29129
16	3.915678	66.4	4.289813	1.226	0.04380	1.241	1.904	0.8459	0.59082	0.04485	1.21156	1.52179	1.29240
17	3.690200	64.3	4.041300	1.221	0.04961	1.234	1.900	0.8462	0.58539	0.05090	1.20302	1.51916	1.29359
18	3.490065	62.3	3.820626	1.216	0.05581	1.227	1.895	0.8465	0.57960	0.05738	1.19395	1.51639	1.29485
19	3.311272	60.3	3.623399	1.210	0.06242	1.220	1.891	0.8469	0.57347	0.06431	1.18437	1.51348	1.29619
20	3.150622	58.5	3.446101	1.204	0.06944	1.213	1.886	0.8473	0.56698	0.07171	1.17427	1.51043	1.29760

θ	Ω_s	A_min	Ω_2	L_1	L_2	C_2	L_3	C_4	L_1	L_2	C_2	L_3	C_4
21	3.005526	56.8	3.285888	1.198	0.07689	1.205	1.881	0.8477	0.56014	0.07959	1.16365	1.50725	1.29908
22	2.873864	55.1	3.140431	1.191	0.08476	1.196	1.875	0.8481	0.55294	0.08798	1.15251	1.50394	1.30064
23	2.753885	53.6	3.007807	1.184	0.09309	1.187	1.870	0.8485	0.54537	0.09689	1.14085	1.50050	1.30227
24	2.644133	52.0	2.886413	1.177	0.1019	1.178	1.864	0.8490	0.53744	0.10634	1.12867	1.49694	1.30397
25	2.543380	50.6	2.774903	1.169	0.1111	1.169	1.858	0.8494	0.52913	0.11637	1.11597	1.49326	1.30575
26	2.450592	49.2	2.672139	1.161	0.1209	1.159	1.851	0.8499	0.52044	0.12700	1.10276	1.48947	1.30760
27	2.364885	47.8	2.577149	1.153	0.1311	1.148	1.845	0.8505	0.51136	0.13826	1.08902	1.48558	1.30952
28	2.285502	46.5	2.489103	1.145	0.1419	1.138	1.838	0.8510	0.50190	0.15018	1.07477	1.48159	1.31151
29	2.211792	45.2	2.407283	1.136	0.1532	1.126	1.831	0.8516	0.49203	0.16279	1.06001	1.47750	1.31358
30	2.143189	44.0	2.331070	1.127	0.1651	1.115	1.824	0.8521	0.48176	0.17615	1.04472	1.47333	1.31571
31	2.079202	42.8	2.259921	1.117	0.1775	1.103	1.816	0.8527	0.47107	0.19030	1.02893	1.46908	1.31792
32	2.019399	41.6	2.193363	1.108	0.1906	1.091	1.808	0.8533	0.45996	0.20527	1.01262	1.46476	1.32019
33	1.963403	40.5	2.130982	1.097	0.2043	1.078	1.800	0.8540	0.44842	0.22114	0.99580	1.46039	1.32253
34	1.910879	39.4	2.072410	1.087	0.2186	1.065	1.792	0.8546	0.43644	0.23796	0.97847	1.45596	1.32494
35	1.861534	38.3	2.017322	1.076	0.2337	1.051	1.784	0.8553	0.42400	0.25580	0.96063	1.45150	1.32740
36	1.815103	37.2	1.965429	1.065	0.2495	1.038	1.775	0.8560	0.41109	0.27473	0.94228	1.44701	1.32993
37	1.771354	36.2	1.916475	1.054	0.2661	1.023	1.766	0.8567	0.39771	0.29484	0.92344	1.44251	1.33251
38	1.730076	35.2	1.870229	1.042	0.2835	1.009	1.757	0.8574	0.38383	0.31623	0.90409	1.43801	1.33515
39	1.691083	34.2	1.826485	1.030	0.3017	0.9936	1.748	0.8581	0.36944	0.33899	0.88426	1.43352	1.33783
40	1.654204	33.3	1.785057	1.017	0.3208	0.9782	1.738	0.8589	0.35453	0.36326	0.86393	1.42908	1.34056

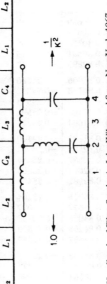

* Adapted from A. I. Zverev, *Handbook of Filter Synthesis*, John Wiley and Sons, New York, 1967.

TABLE 11-56   Elliptic-Function LC Element Values (*Continued*)

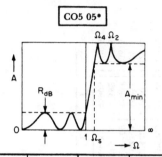

CO5 05°

θ	Ω_s	A_{min}	σ_0	σ_1	σ_3	Ω_1	Ω_2	Ω_3	Ω_4
C	∞	∞	0.80639	−0.24919	−0.65238	1.2218	∞	0.7551	∞
2.0	28.6537	167.86	0.80679	−0.24892	−0.65232	1.2216	48.7389	0.7554	30.1274
3.0	19.1073	150.25	0.80730	−0.24860	−0.65225	1.2214	32.4927	0.7559	20.0893
4.0	14.3356	137.74	0.80801	−0.24815	−0.65215	1.2212	24.3697	0.7566	15.0716
5.0	11.4737	128.04	0.80893	−0.24757	−0.65202	1.2210	19.4959	0.7575	12.0620
6.0	9.5668	120.11	0.81005	−0.24686	−0.65186	1.2207	16.2468	0.7588	10.0565
7.0	8.2055	113.40	0.81138	−0.24602	−0.65167	1.2203	13.9260	0.7599	8.6247
8.0	7.1853	107.59	0.81292	−0.24505	−0.65144	1.2199	12.1854	0.7613	7.5516
9.0	6.3925	102.45	0.81468	−0.24396	−0.65118	1.2194	10.8316	0.7630	6.7175
10.0	5.7588	97.86	0.81664	−0.24274	−0.65088	1.2188	9.7486	0.7649	6.0507
11.0	5.2408	93.69	0.81883	−0.24140	−0.65055	1.2182	8.8625	0.7670	5.5057
12.0	4.8097	89.89	0.82124	−0.23993	−0.65017	1.2176	8.1241	0.7693	5.0520
13.0	4.4454	86.39	0.82387	−0.23834	−0.64975	1.2168	7.4993	0.7718	4.6684
14.0	4.1336	83.14	0.82673	−0.23663	−0.64928	1.2160	6.9638	0.7744	4.3401
15.0	3.8637	80.11	0.82982	−0.23479	−0.64877	1.2152	6.4997	0.7774	4.0559
16.0	3.6280	77.27	0.83315	−0.23284	−0.64820	1.2143	6.0936	0.7805	3.8076
17.0	3.4203	74.60	0.83672	−0.23077	−0.64758	1.2133	5.7353	0.7838	3.5888
18.0	3.2361	72.08	0.84055	−0.22859	−0.64690	1.2123	5.4168	0.7873	3.3946
19.0	3.0716	69.69	0.84463	−0.22629	−0.64616	1.2112	5.1318	0.7911	3.2212
20.0	2.9238	67.41	0.84897	−0.22387	−0.64534	1.2100	4.8753	0.7950	3.0654
21.0	2.7904	65.25	0.85358	−0.22135	−0.64446	1.2088	4.6433	0.7992	2.9246
22.0	2.6695	63.18	0.85847	−0.21872	−0.64350	1.2075	4.4323	0.8036	2.7970
23.0	2.5593	61.20	0.86364	−0.21598	−0.64245	1.2061	4.2397	0.8082	2.6807
24.0	2.4586	59.29	0.86911	−0.21313	−0.64131	1.2047	4.0631	0.8131	2.5743
25.0	2.3662	57.46	0.87488	−0.21019	−0.64008	1.2032	3.9007	0.8181	2.4767
26.0	2.2812	55.70	0.88097	−0.20714	−0.63875	1.2016	3.7507	0.8234	2.3868
27.0	2.2027	54.00	0.88739	−0.20400	−0.63731	1.2000	3.6119	0.8289	2.3038
28.0	2.1301	52.35	0.89414	−0.20076	−0.63575	1.1983	3.4829	0.8347	2.2270
29.0	2.0627	50.76	0.90126	−0.19742	−0.63407	1.1965	3.3629	0.8407	2.1556
30.0	2.0000	49.22	0.90873	−0.19400	−0.63225	1.1947	3.2508	0.8469	2.0892

$$\theta = \sin^{-1}\left(\tfrac{1}{\Omega_s}\right)$$

$$\Omega_s = A_s = \frac{f_s}{f_c}$$

TABLE 11-56 Elliptic-Function LC Element Values (*Continued*)

θ	Ω_s	A_{min}	σ_0	σ_1	σ_3	Ω_1	Ω_2	Ω_3	Ω_4
31.0	1.9416	47.72	0.91660	−0.19049	−0.63029	1.1928	3.1460	0.8533	2.0274
32.0	1.8871	46.27	0.92486	−0.18690	−0.62818	1.1908	3.0476	0.8600	1.9695
33.0	1.8361	44.85	0.93355	−0.18322	−0.62590	1.1887	2.9553	0.8669	1.9154
34.0	1.7883	43.47	0.94267	−0.17947	−0.62345	1.1866	2.8683	0.8741	1.8646
35.0	1.7434	42.13	0.95225	−0.17565	−0.62081	1.1844	2.7864	0.8815	1.8170
36.0	1.7013	40.81	0.96232	−0.17175	−0.61798	1.1821	2.7089	0.8891	1.7722
37.0	1.6616	39.53	0.97290	−0.16778	−0.61493	1.1797	2.6356	0.8970	1.7299
38.0	1.6243	38.28	0.98402	−0.16375	−0.61166	1.1773	2.5662	0.9051	1.6901
39.0	1.5890	37.05	0.99571	−0.15966	−0.60815	1.1748	2.5003	0.9135	1.6525
40.0	1.5557	35.85	1.00800	−0.15552	−0.60438	1.1722	2.4377	0.9220	1.6170
41.0	1.5243	34.67	1.02092	−0.15132	−0.60034	1.1695	2.3781	0.9308	1.5833
42.0	1.4945	33.52	1.03453	−0.14707	−0.59601	1.1668	2.3213	0.9399	1.5515
43.0	1.4663	32.38	1.04885	−0.14277	−0.59137	1.1640	2.2672	0.9491	1.5213
44.0	1.4396	31.27	1.06395	−0.13844	−0.58641	1.1611	2.2154	0.9586	1.4926
45.0	1.4142	30.17	1.07986	−0.13407	−0.58110	1.1581	2.1660	0.9683	1.4654
46.0	1.3902	29.09	1.09665	−0.12967	−0.57542	1.1551	2.1187	0.9782	1.4396
47.0	1.3673	28.03	1.11439	−0.12524	−0.56935	1.1519	2.0733	0.9883	1.4150
48.0	1.3456	26.99	1.13313	−0.12079	−0.56287	1.1487	2.0299	0.9985	1.3916
49.0	1.3250	25.95	1.15297	−0.11632	−0.55595	1.1455	1.9881	1.0090	1.3693
50.0	1.3054	24.94	1.17399	−0.11184	−0.54858	1.1421	1.9480	1.0195	1.3481
51.0	1.2868	23.93	1.19628	−0.10735	−0.54072	1.1387	1.9095	1.0302	1.3279
52.0	1.2690	22.94	1.21995	−0.10286	−0.53235	1.1352	1.8724	1.0410	1.3087
53.0	1.2521	21.96	1.24513	−0.09838	−0.52344	1.1316	1.8366	1.0519	1.2903
54.0	1.2361	20.99	1.27194	−0.09390	−0.51398	1.1280	1.8021	1.0628	1.2728
55.0	1.2208	20.04	1.30055	−0.08944	−0.50393	1.1243	1.7689	1.0738	1.2561
56.0	1.2062	19.09	1.33113	−0.08500	−0.49326	1.1205	1.7368	1.0847	1.2402
57.0	1.1924	18.15	1.36386	−0.08058	−0.48196	1.1167	1.7057	1.0956	1.2250
58.0	1.1792	17.23	1.39898	−0.07620	−0.47000	1.1128	1.6757	1.1064	1.2104
59.0	1.1666	16.31	1.43673	−0.07186	−0.45737	1.1088	1.6467	1.1170	1.1966
60.0	1.1547	15.40	1.47740	−0.06757	−0.44404	1.1048	1.6185	1.1274	1.1834
θ	Ω_s	A_{min}	σ_0	σ_1	σ_3	Ω_1	Ω_2	Ω_3	Ω_4

* Adapted from A. I. Zverev, *Handbook of Filter Synthesis,* John Wiley and Sons, New York, 1967.

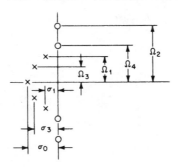

TABLE 11-56 Elliptic-Function LC Element Values (*Continued*)

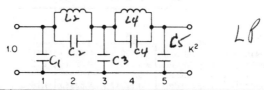

	$K^2 = 1.0$							$K^2 = \infty$						
θ	C_1	C_2	L_2	C_3	C_4	L_4	C_5	C_1	C_2	L_2	C_3	C_4	L_4	C_5
C	0.7664	0.0000	1.3100	1.5880	0.0000	1.3100	0.7664	0.3832	0.0000	0.9671	1.2835	0.0000	1.3983	1.2042
2.0	0.7661	0.0003	1.3099	1.5877	0.0008	1.3091	0.7656	0.3828	0.0004	0.9666	1.2827	0.0008	1.3971	1.2038
3.0	0.7658	0.0007	1.3095	1.5868	0.0018	1.3075	0.7646	0.3823	0.0010	0.9659	1.2818	0.0018	1.3955	1.2031
4.0	0.7654	0.0012	1.3088	1.5855	0.0033	1.3054	0.7633	0.3816	0.0017	0.9649	1.2804	0.0032	1.3934	1.2023
5.0	0.7648	0.0020	1.3080	1.5839	0.0052	1.3026	0.7615	0.3807	0.0027	0.9637	1.2787	0.0049	1.3907	1.2011
6.0	0.7641	0.0029	1.3070	1.5820	0.0076	1.2993	0.7594	0.3796	0.0039	0.9621	1.2766	0.0071	1.3874	1.1997
7.0	0.7632	0.0039	1.3058	1.5796	0.0103	1.2953	0.7569	0.3783	0.0054	0.9603	1.2741	0.0097	1.3835	1.1981
8.0	0.7623	0.0051	1.3044	1.5770	0.0135	1.2907	0.7540	0.3768	0.0070	0.9582	1.2713	0.0127	1.3789	1.1962
9.0	0.7612	0.0065	1.3028	1.5739	0.0172	1.2855	0.7507	0.3750	0.0089	0.9558	1.2680	0.0161	1.3738	1.1941
10.0	0.7600	0.0080	1.3011	1.5706	0.0213	1.2797	0.7470	0.3731	0.0110	0.9531	1.2644	0.0200	1.3681	1.1917
11.0	0.7586	0.0098	1.2991	1.5669	0.0259	1.2733	0.7429	0.3710	0.0134	0.9502	1.2604	0.0242	1.3618	1.1891
12.0	0.7572	0.0116	1.2970	1.5628	0.0309	1.2663	0.7384	0.3686	0.0160	0.9470	1.2561	0.0289	1.3548	1.1863
13.0	0.7556	0.0137	1.2947	1.5584	0.0364	1.2586	0.7335	0.3660	0.0188	0.9435	1.2513	0.0341	1.3473	1.1831
14.0	0.7538	0.0159	1.2922	1.5536	0.0424	1.2504	0.7283	0.3633	0.0219	0.9397	1.2462	0.0396	1.3392	1.1798
15.0	0.7519	0.0183	1.2895	1.5485	0.0489	1.2416	0.7226	0.3603	0.0253	0.9356	1.2408	0.0457	1.3305	1.1762
16.0	0.7499	0.0209	1.2866	1.5431	0.0559	1.2321	0.7165	0.3570	0.0289	0.9312	1.2349	0.0522	1.3212	1.1723
17.0	0.7478	0.0236	1.2836	1.5374	0.0635	1.2221	0.7101	0.3536	0.0328	0.9265	1.2287	0.0592	1.3113	1.1682
18.0	0.7455	0.0266	1.2803	1.5313	0.0716	1.2115	0.7032	0.3499	0.0370	0.9216	1.2222	0.0667	1.3009	1.1639
19.0	0.7431	0.0297	1.2768	1.5249	0.0802	1.2002	0.6959	0.3460	0.0414	0.9163	1.2153	0.0747	1.2898	1.1593
20.0	0.7406	0.0330	1.2732	1.5182	0.0895	1.1884	0.6883	0.3419	0.0462	0.9108	1.2080	0.0833	1.2782	1.1545
21.0	0.7379	0.0365	1.2694	1.5112	0.0994	1.1760	0.6802	0.3375	0.0513	0.9050	1.2004	0.0923	1.2660	1.1495
22.0	0.7350	0.0402	1.2653	1.5038	0.1099	1.1630	0.6717	0.3329	0.0566	0.8988	1.1924	0.1020	1.2532	1.1442
23.0	0.7321	0.0441	1.2611	1.4962	0.1210	1.1494	0.6628	0.3281	0.0623	0.8924	1.1841	0.1122	1.2399	1.1387
24.0	0.7290	0.0482	1.2567	1.4882	0.1329	1.1353	0.6534	0.3230	0.0684	0.8857	1.1755	0.1231	1.2260	1.1329
25.0	0.7257	0.0524	1.2520	1.4800	0.1454	1.1205	0.6437	0.3176	0.0748	0.8786	1.1666	0.1346	1.2115	1.1269
26.0	0.7223	0.0569	1.2472	1.4715	0.1588	1.1052	0.6335	0.3120	0.0816	0.8713	1.1573	0.1467	1.1964	1.1207
27.0	0.7187	0.0617	1.2421	1.4627	0.1729	1.0893	0.6229	0.3061	0.0888	0.8637	1.1477	0.1595	1.1809	1.1143
28.0	0.7150	0.0666	1.2369	1.4537	0.1879	1.0729	0.6118	0.2999	0.0963	0.8557	1.1377	0.1731	1.1647	1.1076
29.0	0.7112	0.0718	1.2314	1.4444	0.2038	1.0559	0.6003	0.2935	0.1043	0.8475	1.1275	0.1875	1.1480	1.1007
30.0	0.7072	0.0772	1.2257	1.4348	0.2206	1.0383	0.5884	0.2867	0.1128	0.8389	1.1170	0.2026	1.1308	1.0936

TABLE 11-56 Elliptic-Function LC Element Values (*Continued*)

	$K^2 = 1.0$							$K^2 = \infty$						
θ	C_1	C_2	L_2	C_3	C_4	L_4	C_5	C_1	C_2	L_2	C_3	C_4	L_4	C_5
31.0	0.7030	0.0828	1.2198	1.4250	0.2384	1.0201	0.5760	0.2797	0.1217	0.8300	1.1061	0.2186	1.1130	1.0863
32.0	0.6987	0.0887	1.2136	1.4150	0.2574	1.0015	0.5631	0.2723	0.1312	0.8208	1.0950	0.2355	1.0947	1.0788
33.0	0.6942	0.0948	1.2073	1.4048	0.2774	0.9822	0.5498	0.2647	0.1411	0.8112	1.0836	0.2534	1.0758	1.0710
34.0	0.6896	0.1012	1.2007	1.3943	0.2988	0.9625	0.5360	0.2567	0.1517	0.8013	1.0719	0.2722	1.0565	1.0630
35.0	0.6847	0.1078	1.1938	1.3837	0.3214	0.9422	0.5217	0.2484	0.1628	0.7911	1.0600	0.2922	1.0366	1.0549
36.0	0.6798	0.1148	1.1867	1.3729	0.3455	0.9214	0.5070	0.2397	0.1746	0.7806	1.0478	0.3134	1.0162	1.0465
37.0	0.6746	0.1220	1.1794	1.3619	0.3712	0.9001	0.4917	0.2306	0.1870	0.7697	1.0354	0.3357	0.9953	1.0379
38.0	0.6693	0.1295	1.1717	1.3508	0.3985	0.8782	0.4759	0.2212	0.2002	0.7585	1.0227	0.3595	0.9738	1.0291
39.0	0.6637	0.1374	1.1638	1.3396	0.4278	0.8559	0.4595	0.2114	0.2142	0.7469	1.0098	0.3847	0.9519	1.0202
40.0	0.6580	0.1456	1.1556	1.3282	0.4590	0.8331	0.4426	0.2012	0.2290	0.7350	0.9967	0.4115	0.9295	1.0111
41.0	0.6521	0.1541	1.1472	1.3168	0.4924	0.8099	0.4252	0.1905	0.2447	0.7227	0.9834	0.4399	0.9067	1.0017
42.0	0.6460	0.1630	1.1384	1.3053	0.5283	0.7862	0.4072	0.1794	0.2614	0.7100	0.9699	0.4703	0.8833	0.9923
43.0	0.6397	0.1722	1.1292	1.2937	0.5669	0.7620	0.3885	0.1678	0.2791	0.6970	0.9563	0.5027	0.8595	0.9826
44.0	0.6332	0.1819	1.1198	1.2822	0.6085	0.7375	0.3693	0.1558	0.2981	0.6836	0.9425	0.5374	0.8353	0.9728
45.0	0.6265	0.1920	1.1099	1.2706	0.6535	0.7125	0.3494	0.1432	0.3183	0.6697	0.9285	0.5745	0.8106	0.9629
46.0	0.6195	0.2025	1.0997	1.2591	0.7022	0.6871	0.3288	0.1300	0.3398	0.6555	0.9145	0.6143	0.7855	0.9528
47.0	0.6124	0.2135	1.0891	1.2478	0.7550	0.6614	0.3075	0.1163	0.3630	0.6409	0.9003	0.6572	0.7599	0.9426
48.0	0.6050	0.2251	1.0780	1.2365	0.8126	0.6354	0.2855	0.1019	0.3878	0.6259	0.8861	0.7035	0.7430	0.9323
49.0	0.5973	0.2372	1.0665	1.2254	0.8756	0.6090	0.2628	0.0869	0.4144	0.6104	0.8718	0.7536	0.7077	0.9219
50.0	0.5894	0.2498	1.0545	1.2145	0.9446	0.5824	0.2392	0.0712	0.4432	0.5946	0.8575	0.8079	0.6810	0.9114
51.0	0.5813	0.2632	1.0420	1.2039	1.0206	0.5556	0.2147	0.0548	0.4743	0.5783	0.8432	0.8671	0.6540	0.9008
52.0	0.5729	0.2772	1.0289	1.1937	1.1047	0.5285	0.1894	0.0375	0.5080	0.5615	0.8290	0.9317	0.6267	0.8903
53.0	0.5642	0.2920	1.0152	1.1838	1.1980	0.5013	0.1631	0.0194	0.5447	0.5443	0.8148	1.0027	0.5990	0.8797
54.0	0.5552	0.3076	1.0008	1.1744	1.3020	0.4740	0.1357	0.0004	0.5847	0.5266	0.8007	1.0808	0.5711	0.8691
55.0	0.5460	0.3242	0.9858	1.1656	1.4187	0.4467	0.1073	−0.0197	0.6285	0.5085	0.7868	1.1672	0.5430	0.8586
56.0	0.5364	0.3417	0.9700	1.1575	1.5502	0.4194	0.0777	−0.0408	0.6768	0.4899	0.7731	1.2633	0.5147	0.8482
57.0	0.5265	0.3605	0.9533	1.1501	1.6993	0.3921	0.0468	−0.0631	0.7301	0.4708	0.7597	1.3707	0.4862	0.8380
58.0	0.5163	0.3805	0.9358	1.1437	1.8693	0.3651	0.0145	−0.0867	0.7893	0.4512	0.7465	1.4914	0.4576	0.8280
59.0	0.5057	0.4020	0.9174	1.1382	2.0645	0.3382	−0.0191	−0.1117	0.8554	0.4312	0.7338	1.6279	0.4290	0.8182
60.0	0.4948	0.4251	0.8979	1.1340	2.2902	0.3117	−0.0545	−0.1382	0.9295	0.4107	0.7215	1.7833	0.4004	0.8087
θ	L_1	L_2	C_2	L_3	L_4	C_4	L_5	L_1	L_2	C_2	L_3	L_4	C_4	L_5

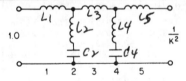

$L\,P$

TABLE 11-56   Elliptic-Function *LC* Element Values (*Continued*)

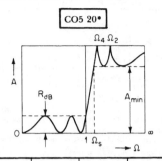

θ	Ω_s	A_{min}	σ_0	σ_1	σ_3	Ω_1	Ω_2	Ω_3	Ω_4
C	∞	∞	0.47472	−0.14670	−0.38406	1.0528	∞	0.6506	∞
1.0	57.2987	210.17	0.47476	−0.14667	−0.38405	1.0527	97.4775	0.6507	60.2470
2.0	28.6537	180.07	0.47489	−0.14659	−0.38404	1.0527	48.7389	0.6508	30.1274
3.0	19.1073	162.45	0.47511	−0.14646	−0.38402	1.0527	32.4927	0.6511	20.0893
4.0	14.3356	149.95	0.47542	−0.14628	−0.38399	1.0527	24.3697	0.6514	15.0716
5.0	11.4737	140.25	0.47582	−0.14605	−0.38396	1.0526	19.4959	0.6519	12.0620
6.0	9.5668	132.32	0.47631	−0.14577	−0.38392	1.0526	16.2468	0.6524	10.0565
7.0	8.2055	125.61	0.47689	−0.14543	−0.38387	1.0526	13.9260	0.6531	8.6247
8.0	7.1853	119.80	0.47757	−0.14505	−0.38381	1.0525	12.1854	0.6538	7.5516
9.0	6.3925	114.66	0.47833	−0.14461	−0.38375	1.0524	10.8316	0.6547	6.7175
10.0	5.7588	110.06	0.47918	−0.14412	−0.38367	1.0524	9.7486	0.6557	6.0507
11.0	5.2408	105.90	0.48013	−0.14358	−0.38359	1.0523	8.8625	0.6567	5.5057
12.0	4.8097	102.10	0.48117	−0.14299	−0.38349	1.0522	8.1241	0.6579	5.0520
13.0	4.4454	98.59	0.48231	−0.14235	−0.38338	1.0521	7.4993	0.6592	4.6684
14.0	4.1336	95.34	0.48355	−0.14166	−0.38327	1.0520	6.9638	0.6606	4.3401
15.0	3.8637	92.32	0.48488	−0.14092	−0.38314	1.0519	6.4997	0.6621	4.0559
16.0	3.6280	89.48	0.48631	−0.14013	−0.38299	1.0518	6.0936	0.6637	3.8076
17.0	3.4203	86.81	0.48785	−0.13929	−0.38283	1.0517	5.7353	0.6654	3.5888
18.0	3.2361	84.29	0.48949	−0.13840	−0.38266	1.0515	5.4168	0.6672	3.3946
19.0	3.0716	81.89	0.49123	−0.13746	−0.38247	1.0514	5.1318	0.6691	3.2212
20.0	2.9238	79.62	0.49308	−0.13647	−0.38227	1.0512	4.8753	0.6712	3.0654
21.0	2.7904	77.46	0.49503	−0.13543	−0.38204	1.0511	4.6433	0.6733	2.9246
22.0	2.6695	75.39	0.49710	−0.13434	−0.38180	1.0509	4.4323	0.6756	2.7970
23.0	2.5593	73.40	0.49929	−0.13320	−0.38153	1.0507	4.2397	0.6780	2.6807
24.0	2.4586	71.50	0.50159	−0.13201	−0.38125	1.0505	4.0631	0.6805	2.5743
25.0	2.3662	69.67	0.50401	−0.13078	−0.38093	1.0503	3.9007	0.6831	2.4767
26.0	2.2812	67.91	0.50655	−0.12950	−0.38060	1.0501	3.7507	0.6858	2.3868
27.0	2.2027	66.21	0.50922	−0.12817	−0.38023	1.0499	3.6119	0.6887	2.3038
28.0	2.1301	64.56	0.51201	−0.12679	−0.37983	1.0496	3.4829	0.6916	2.2270
29.0	2.0627	62.97	0.51494	−0.12536	−0.37941	1.0494	3.3629	0.6947	2.1556
30.0	2.0000	61.43	0.51801	−0.12389	−0.37895	1.0491	3.2508	0.6980	2.0892

TABLE 11-56 Elliptic-Function *LC* Element Values (*Continued*)

θ	Ω_s	A_{min}	σ_0	σ_1	σ_3	Ω_1	Ω_2	Ω_3	Ω_4
31.0	1.9416	59.93	0.52122	−0.12238	−0.37845	1.0488	3.1460	0.7013	2.0274
32.0	1.8871	58.47	0.52458	−0.12081	−0.37791	1.0486	3.0476	0.7048	1.9695
33.0	1.8361	57.06	0.52808	−0.11920	−0.37734	1.0483	2.9553	0.7084	1.9154
34.0	1.7883	55.68	0.53175	−0.11755	−0.37672	1.0479	2.8683	0.7122	1.8846
35.0	1.7434	54.33	0.53557	−0.11585	−0.37605	1.0476	2.7864	0.7160	1.8170
36.0	1.7013	53.02	0.53956	−0.11411	−0.37533	1.0473	2.7089	0.7200	1.7722
37.0	1.6616	51.74	0.54373	−0.11233	−0.37456	1.0469	2.6356	0.7242	1.7299
38.0	1.6243	50.49	0.54808	−0.11050	−0.37372	1.0465	2.5662	0.7285	1.6901
39.0	1.5890	49.26	0.55261	−0.10863	−0.37283	1.0461	2.5003	0.7329	1.6525
40.0	1.5557	48.06	0.55734	−0.10672	−0.37187	1.0457	2.4377	0.7375	1.6170
41.0	1.5243	46.88	0.56228	−0.10477	−0.37085	1.0453	2.3781	0.7422	1.5833
42.0	1.4945	45.72	0.56743	−0.10278	−0.36974	1.0448	2.3213	0.7471	1.5515
43.0	1.4663	44.59	0.57281	−0.10075	−0.36856	1.0444	2.2672	0.7521	1.5213
44.0	1.4396	43.47	0.57842	−0.09868	−0.36829	1.0439	2.2154	0.7573	1.4926
45.0	1.4142	42.38	0.58428	−0.09658	−0.36593	1.0434	2.1660	0.7626	1.4654
46.0	1.3902	41.30	0.59039	−0.09444	−0.36448	1.0429	2.1187	0.7681	1.4396
47.0	1.3673	40.23	0.59678	−0.09226	−0.36291	1.0424	2.0733	0.7738	1.4150
48.0	1.3456	39.19	0.60345	−0.09004	−0.36124	1.0418	2.0299	0.7796	1.3916
49.0	1.3250	38.15	0.61043	−0.08780	−0.35945	1.0412	1.9881	0.7856	1.3693
50.0	1.3054	37.13	0.61773	−0.08552	−0.35753	1.0406	1.9480	0.7917	1.3481
51.0	1.2868	36.12	0.62537	−0.08321	−0.35548	1.0400	1.9095	0.7980	1.3279
52.0	1.2690	35.13	0.63336	−0.08087	−0.35329	1.0393	1.8724	0.8045	1.3087
53.0	1.2521	34.14	0.64174	−0.07850	−0.35094	1.0387	1.8366	0.8112	1.2903
54.0	1.2361	33.17	0.65053	−0.07610	−0.34842	1.0380	1.8021	0.8180	1.2728
55.0	1.2208	32.20	0.65975	−0.07368	−0.34573	1.0373	1.7689	0.8250	1.2561
56.0	1.2062	31.25	0.66943	−0.07123	−0.34285	1.0365	1.7368	0.8322	1.2402
57.0	1.1924	30.30	0.67962	−0.06876	−0.33977	1.0358	1.7057	0.8395	1.2250
58.0	1.1792	29.36	0.69033	−0.06627	−0.33647	1.0350	1.6757	0.8470	1.2104
59.0	1.1666	28.42	0.70163	−0.06376	−0.33295	1.0342	1.6467	0.8547	1.1966
60.0	1.1547	27.49	0.71354	−0.06124	−0.32917	1.0333	1.6185	0.8626	1.1834
θ	Ω_s	A_{min}	σ_0	σ_1	σ_3	Ω_1	Ω_2	Ω_3	Ω_4

* Adapted from A. I. Zverev, *Handbook of Filter Synthesis*, John Wiley and Sons, New York, 1967.

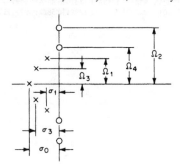

TABLE 11-56 Elliptic-Function LC Element Values (*Continued*)

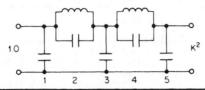

			$K^2 = 1.0$							$K^2 = \infty$				
θ	C_1	C_2	L_2	C_3	C_4	L_4	C_5	C_1	C_2	L_2	C_3	C_4	L_4	C_5
C	1.302	0.0000	1.346	2.129	0.0000	1.346	1.302	0.6510	0.0000	1.3234	1.6362	0.0000	1.6265	1.4246
1.0	1.30183	0.00008	1.34548	2.12835	0.00020	1.34532	1.30170	0.6509	0.0001	1.3233	1.6360	0.0002	1.6263	1.4244
2.0	1.30163	0.00031	1.34523	2.12770	0.00082	1.34459	1.30112	0.6507	0.0003	1.3229	1.6355	0.0007	1.6254	1.4240
3.0	1.30130	0.00070	1.34483	2.12660	0.00184	1.34339	1.30016	0.6503	0.0007	1.3223	1.6345	0.0015	1.6240	1.4233
4.0	1.30084	0.00125	1.34426	2.12507	0.00328	1.34170	1.29881	0.6498	0.0013	1.3215	1.6332	0.0027	1.6220	1.4224
5.0	1.30024	0.00196	1.34353	2.12311	0.00513	1.33954	1.29708	0.6491	0.0020	1.3205	1.6315	0.0042	1.6195	1.4211
6.0	1.29951	0.00282	1.34264	2.12070	0.00740	1.33689	1.29496	0.6483	0.0029	1.3193	1.6294	0.0061	1.6164	1.4196
7.0	1.29865	0.00384	1.34159	2.11786	0.01008	1.33376	1.29246	0.6473	0.0039	1.3178	1.6270	0.0083	1.6128	1.4178
8.0	1.29766	0.00502	1.34037	2.11459	0.01318	1.33015	1.28957	0.6462	0.0051	1.3161	1.6241	0.0109	1.6085	1.4158
9.0	1.29653	0.00637	1.33899	2.11088	0.01671	1.32607	1.28630	0.6450	0.0065	1.3141	1.6209	0.0138	1.6038	1.4135
10.0	1.29527	0.00787	1.33744	2.10675	0.02067	1.32150	1.28264	0.6436	0.0080	1.3120	1.6174	0.0171	1.5984	1.4109
11.0	1.29387	0.00953	1.33573	2.10217	0.02506	1.31646	1.27859	0.6420	0.0097	1.3096	1.6134	0.0207	1.5926	1.4080
12.0	1.29234	0.01136	1.33386	2.09717	0.02989	1.31094	1.27417	0.6403	0.0116	1.3069	1.6091	0.0247	1.5861	1.4048
13.0	1.29067	0.01335	1.33182	2.09172	0.03516	1.30495	1.26936	0.6384	0.0136	1.3041	1.6044	0.0291	1.5791	1.4014
14.0	1.28887	0.01551	1.32961	2.08588	0.04089	1.29848	1.26416	0.6364	0.0159	1.3010	1.5993	0.0338	1.5716	1.3977
15.0	1.28693	0.01783	1.32724	2.07959	0.04707	1.29154	1.25858	0.6343	0.0182	1.2976	1.5939	0.0389	1.5635	1.3938
16.0	1.28485	0.02033	1.32470	2.07288	0.05371	1.28413	1.25261	0.6319	0.0208	1.2941	1.5881	0.0444	1.5548	1.3895
17.0	1.28263	0.02300	1.32199	2.06574	0.06084	1.27625	1.24627	0.6295	0.0236	1.2903	1.5819	0.0502	1.5456	1.3850
18.0	1.28027	0.02584	1.31911	2.05819	0.06844	1.26790	1.23953	0.6268	0.0265	1.2862	1.5754	0.0565	1.5359	1.3803
19.0	1.27778	0.02885	1.31607	2.05021	0.07655	1.25909	1.23241	0.6240	0.0296	1.2820	1.5685	0.0632	1.5256	1.3753
20.0	1.27514	0.03205	1.31285	2.04182	0.08515	1.24981	1.22491	0.6211	0.0329	1.2774	1.5612	0.0703	1.5148	1.3700
21.0	1.27236	0.03542	1.30945	2.03301	0.09428	1.24007	1.21703	0.6180	0.0364	1.2727	1.5536	0.0778	1.5035	1.3644
22.0	1.26943	0.03898	1.30589	2.02379	0.10393	1.22987	1.20876	0.6147	0.0402	1.2677	1.5456	0.0857	1.4916	1.3586
23.0	1.26636	0.04272	1.30215	2.01416	0.11414	1.21921	1.20010	0.6112	0.0441	1.2624	1.5373	0.0941	1.4791	1.3525
24.0	1.26314	0.04666	1.29823	2.00412	0.12490	1.20809	1.19107	0.6076	0.0482	1.2569	1.5286	0.1029	1.4662	1.3461
25.0	1.25978	0.05079	1.29413	1.99368	0.13625	1.19652	1.18164	0.6038	0.0525	1.2512	1.5195	0.1122	1.4527	1.3395
26.0	1.25262	0.05511	1.28985	1.98283	0.14819	1.18450	1.17183	0.5998	0.0571	1.2452	1.5101	0.1220	1.4387	1.3327
27.0	1.25259	0.05963	1.28540	1.97159	0.16075	1.17203	1.16164	0.5957	0.0619	1.2389	1.5004	0.1323	1.4242	1.3256
28.0	1.24877	0.06436	1.28075	1.95995	0.17396	1.15911	1.15106	0.5914	0.0669	1.2324	1.4903	0.1431	1.4092	1.3182
29.0	1.22480	0.06930	1.27592	1.94792	0.18783	1.14576	1.14010	0.5869	0.0721	1.2256	1.4798	0.1544	1.3936	1.3105
30.0	1.24067	0.07446	1.27091	1.93550	0.20239	1.13196	1.12874	0.5822	0.0777	1.2186	1.4690	0.1663	1.3776	1.3027

TABLE 11-56 Elliptic-Function LC Element Values (*Continued*)

	$K^2 = 1.0$							$K^2 = \infty$						
θ	C_1	C_2	L_2	C_3	C_4	L_4	C_5	C_1	C_2	L_2	C_3	C_4	L_4	C_5
31.0	1.23638	0.07983	1.26570	1.92270	0.21768	1.11772	1.11700	0.5773	0.0834	1.2113	1.4579	0.1788	1.3610	1.2945
32.0	1.23192	0.08543	1.26030	1.90952	0.23371	1.10305	1.10487	0.5723	0.0894	1.2037	1.4464	0.1918	1.3439	1.2861
33.0	1.22731	0.09126	1.25470	1.89596	0.25054	1.08795	1.09235	0.5670	0.0957	1.1959	1.4346	0.2055	1.3264	1.2775
34.0	1.22252	0.09732	1.24890	1.88203	0.26819	1.07242	1.07944	0.5616	0.1023	1.1878	1.4225	0.2198	1.3083	1.2686
35.0	1.21757	0.10363	1.24290	1.86773	0.28671	1.05648	1.06614	0.5559	0.1092	1.1794	1.4100	0.2348	1.2898	1.2595
36.0	1.21244	0.11019	1.23669	1.85307	0.30614	1.04011	1.05244	0.5500	0.1164	1.1707	1.3972	0.2506	1.2707	1.2501
37.0	1.20714	0.11701	1.23028	1.83806	0.32654	1.02332	1.03835	0.5439	0.1239	1.1618	1.3841	0.2671	1.2512	1.2405
38.0	1.20166	0.12410	1.22364	1.82269	0.34795	1.00613	1.02386	0.5376	0.1318	1.1525	1.3707	0.2843	1.2313	1.2306
39.0	1.19600	0.13146	1.21679	1.80698	0.37044	0.98853	1.00897	0.5311	0.1400	1.1429	1.3570	0.3024	1.2108	1.2205
40.0	1.19015	0.13911	1.20971	1.79093	0.39408	0.97053	0.99368	0.5244	0.1485	1.1331	1.3429	0.3214	1.1899	1.2102
41.0	1.18411	0.14706	1.20241	1.77455	0.41894	0.95213	0.97798	0.5174	0.1575	1.1229	1.3286	0.3413	1.1686	1.1996
42.0	1.17787	0.15532	1.19486	1.75784	0.44510	0.93335	0.96187	0.5102	0.1668	1.1124	1.3139	0.3623	1.1467	1.1888
43.0	1.17144	0.16389	1.18708	1.74081	0.47265	0.91417	0.94535	0.5027	0.1766	1.1016	1.2989	0.3843	1.1245	1.1778
44.0	1.16480	0.17280	1.17904	1.72347	0.50170	0.89462	0.92841	0.4949	0.1868	1.0905	1.2837	0.4074	1.1018	1.1665
45.0	1.15794	0.18206	1.17075	1.70583	0.53236	0.87470	0.91105	0.4869	0.1975	1.0790	1.2681	0.4317	1.0787	1.1551
46.0	1.15088	0.19169	1.16219	1.68789	0.56476	0.85441	0.89326	0.4787	0.2087	1.0672	1.2523	0.4573	1.0551	1.1433
47.0	1.14359	0.20169	1.15336	1.66967	0.59903	0.83376	0.87504	0.4701	0.2205	1.0550	1.2362	0.4844	1.0311	1.1314
48.0	1.13607	0.21210	1.14425	1.65117	0.63534	0.81276	0.85638	0.4612	0.2328	1.0425	1.2198	0.5129	1.0068	1.1193
49.0	1.12831	0.22293	1.13484	1.63241	0.67386	0.79141	0.83727	0.4520	0.2457	1.0296	1.2032	0.5431	0.9820	1.1069
50.0	1.12031	0.23421	1.12513	1.61339	0.71481	0.76973	0.81771	0.4425	0.2593	1.0163	1.1863	0.5750	0.9568	1.0943
51.0	1.11206	0.24596	1.11509	1.59413	0.75841	0.74773	0.79768	0.4327	0.2736	1.0026	1.1691	0.6089	0.9313	1.0815
52.0	1.10354	0.25821	1.10473	1.57465	0.80492	0.72541	0.77717	0.4225	0.2886	0.9884	1.1517	0.6449	0.9053	1.0685
53.0	1.09476	0.27099	1.09401	1.55494	0.85465	0.70278	0.75619	0.4120	0.3044	0.9739	1.1341	0.6833	0.8790	1.0553
54.0	1.08569	0.28433	1.08293	1.53504	0.90794	0.67986	0.73470	0.4010	0.3211	0.9589	1.1162	0.7242	0.8524	1.0419
55.0	1.07633	0.29828	1.07147	1.51496	0.96518	0.65667	0.71270	0.3897	0.3388	0.9435	1.0981	0.7679	0.8254	1.0283
56.0	1.06666	0.31288	1.05960	1.49471	1.02684	0.63320	0.69016	0.3779	0.3574	0.9275	1.0798	0.8147	0.7981	1.0144
57.0	1.05668	0.32817	1.04731	1.47431	1.09344	0.60949	0.66709	0.3657	0.3772	0.9111	1.0613	0.8550	0.7705	1.0004
58.0	1.04636	0.34422	1.03456	1.45379	1.16561	0.58554	0.64344	0.3530	0.3983	0.8942	1.0426	0.9192	0.7425	0.9863
59.0	1.03570	0.36109	1.02134	1.43317	1.24407	0.56138	0.61920	0.3398	0.4207	0.8767	1.0237	0.9777	0.7143	0.9719
60.0	1.02467	0.37885	1.00760	1.41247	1.32969	0.53702	0.59435	0.3261	0.4446	0.8587	1.0046	1.0412	0.6858	0.9574
θ	L_1	L_2	C_2	L_3	L_4	C_4	L_5	L_1	L_2	C_2	L_3	L_4	C_4	L_5

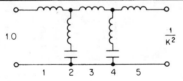

TABLE 11-56 Elliptic-Function LC Element Values (Continued)

CO6 20 b•

θ	Ω_s	A_{min}	C_1	C_2	L_2	Ω_2	C_3	C_4	L_4	Ω_4	C_5	L_6	θ
T	∞	∞	1.322	0.0000	1.373	∞	2.203	0.0000	1.469	∞	2.059	0.8816	T
16	3.751039	112.5	1.299	0.0250	1.344	5.452491	2.142	0.0468	1.412	3.888329	2.017	0.8828	16
17	3.535748	109.3	1.296	0.0283	1.341	5.133037	2.135	0.0530	1.405	3.664543	2.012	0.8830	17
18	3.344698	106.3	1.293	0.0318	1.337	4.849152	2.126	0.0596	1.397	3.465915	2.006	0.8831	18
19	3.174064	103.4	1.290	0.0355	1.333	4.595218	2.118	0.0666	1.389	3.288476	2.000	0.8833	19
20	3.020785	100.7	1.286	0.0395	1.328	4.366743	2.108	0.0740	1.380	3.129050	1.993	0.8835	20
21	2.882384	98.1	1.283	0.0436	1.324	4.160091	2.099	0.0818	1.371	2.985065	1.987	0.8837	21
22	2.756834	95.6	1.279	0.0480	1.319	3.972284	2.089	0.0901	1.362	2.854418	1.979	0.8839	22
23	2.642462	93.3	1.275	0.0527	1.314	3.800865	2.078	0.0989	1.352	2.735370	1.972	0.8841	23
24	2.537873	91.0	1.270	0.0576	1.309	3.643786	2.067	0.1081	1.341	2.626475	1.964	0.8843	24
25	2.441895	88.8	1.266	0.0627	1.303	3.499325	2.055	0.1177	1.331	2.526516	1.956	0.8845	25
26	2.353536	86.7	1.261	0.0680	1.297	3.366027	2.043	0.1279	1.320	2.434463	1.948	0.8848	26
27	2.271953	84.6	1.256	0.0736	1.291	3.242651	2.031	0.1385	1.308	2.349441	1.939	0.8850	27
28	2.196422	82.6	1.251	0.0795	1.285	3.128134	2.018	0.1497	1.296	2.270699	1.930	0.8853	28
29	2.126320	80.7	1.246	0.0857	1.279	3.021559	2.005	0.1613	1.284	2.197588	1.921	0.8855	29
30	2.061105	78.9	1.240	0.0921	1.272	2.922132	1.991	0.1735	1.271	2.129549	1.911	0.8858	30
31	2.000308	77.1	1.235	0.0988	1.265	2.829162	1.977	0.1863	1.257	2.066092	1.901	0.8861	31
32	1.943517	75.3	1.229	0.1057	1.258	2.742042	1.962	0.1996	1.244	2.006790	1.891	0.8864	32
33	1.890370	73.6	1.223	0.1130	1.250	2.660241	1.947	0.2136	1.230	1.951268	1.881	0.8867	33
34	1.840548	72.0	1.216	0.1206	1.243	2.583290	1.931	0.2281	1.215	1.899195	1.870	0.8870	34
35	1.793769	70.4	1.210	0.1285	1.235	2.510772	1.915	0.2433	1.200	1.850277	1.859	0.8873	35

36	0.8877	1.847	1.804254	1.185	0.2592	1.899	2.442318	1.226	0.1367	1.203	68.8	1.749781	36
37	0.8880	1.835	1.760893	1.169	0.2758	1.882	2.377598	1.218	0.1452	1.196	67.3	1.708362	37
38	0.8884	1.823	1.719987	1.153	0.2931	1.864	2.316318	1.209	0.1541	1.189	65.8	1.669312	38
39	0.8887	1.811	1.681350	1.137	0.3112	1.847	2.258212	1.200	0.1634	1.181	64.3	1.632449	39
40	0.8891	1.798	1.644814	1.120	0.3301	1.828	2.203043	1.191	0.1730	1.174	62.8	1.597615	40
41	0.8895	1.785	1.610227	1.103	0.3498	1.810	2.150595	1.181	0.1830	1.166	61.4	1.564662	41
42	0.8898	1.771	1.577454	1.085	0.3704	1.791	2.100673	1.172	0.1934	1.158	60.0	1.533460	42
43	0.8902	1.758	1.546370	1.067	0.3920	1.771	2.053102	1.161	0.2043	1.149	58.7	1.503888	43
44	0.8906	1.744	1.516862	1.049	0.4145	1.751	2.007720	1.151	0.2155	1.141	57.3	1.475840	44
45	0.8910	1.729	1.488829	1.030	0.4381	1.731	1.964382	1.140	0.2272	1.132	56.0	1.449216	45
46	0.8915	1.715	1.462178	1.011	0.4628	1.710	1.922953	1.130	0.2394	1.123	54.7	1.423927	46
47	0.8919	1.700	1.436822	0.9910	0.4888	1.689	1.883312	1.118	0.2521	1.113	53.4	1.399891	47
48	0.8923	1.684	1.412684	0.9711	0.5160	1.668	1.845347	1.107	0.2653	1.103	52.2	1.377032	48
49	0.8928	1.669	1.389693	0.9508	0.5446	1.646	1.808954	1.095	0.2791	1.093	50.9	1.355282	49
50	0.8932	1.653	1.367782	0.9302	0.5747	1.623	1.774040	1.083	0.2935	1.083	49.7	1.334577	50
51	0.8937	1.637	1.346891	0.9092	0.6063	1.600	1.740516	1.070	0.3084	1.073	48.5	1.314859	51
52	0.8942	1.620	1.326965	0.8878	0.6397	1.577	1.708301	1.057	0.3241	1.062	47.3	1.296076	52
53	0.8946	1.603	1.307952	0.8661	0.6749	1.554	1.677322	1.044	0.3404	1.050	46.1	1.278176	53
54	0.8951	1.586	1.289805	0.8440	0.7122	1.530	1.647510	1.031	0.3574	1.039	45.0	1.261116	54
55	0.8956	1.568	1.272479	0.8216	0.7517	1.506	1.618799	1.017	0.3752	1.027	43.8	1.244853	55
56	0.8961	1.551	1.255935	0.7989	0.7936	1.481	1.591131	1.003	0.3939	1.015	42.7	1.229348	56
57	0.8966	1.532	1.240135	0.7758	0.8382	1.456	1.564449	0.9881	0.4135	1.002	41.5	1.214564	57
58	0.8971	1.514	1.225044	0.7523	0.8857	1.431	1.538703	0.9732	0.4340	0.9894	40.4	1.200469	58
59	0.8976	1.495	1.210630	0.7286	0.9365	1.405	1.513843	0.9578	0.4556	0.9760	39.3	1.187032	59
60	0.8981	1.476	1.196863	0.7045	0.9909	1.379	1.489825	0.9420	0.4783	0.9623	38.1	1.174224	60
61	0.8987	1.456	1.183715	0.6801	1.049	1.353	1.466607	0.9258	0.5022	0.9481	37.0	1.162017	61
62	0.8992	1.436	1.171161	0.6554	1.112	1.326	1.444148	0.9091	0.5274	0.9335	35.9	1.150388	62
63	0.8997	1.416	1.159176	0.6304	1.181	1.299	1.422411	0.8920	0.5541	0.9184	34.8	1.139313	63
64	0.9002	1.395	1.147737	0.6051	1.255	1.272	1.401362	0.8743	0.5824	0.9028	33.7	1.128771	64
65	0.9008	1.374	1.136826	0.5795	1.335	1.244	1.380967	0.8562	0.6125	0.8867	32.6	1.118742	65
66	0.9013	1.352	1.126421	0.5536	1.424	1.216	1.361196	0.8374	0.6445	0.8700	31.5	1.109208	66
67	0.9018	1.330	1.116505	0.5274	1.521	1.188	1.342017	0.8182	0.6787	0.8528	30.4	1.100151	67
68	0.9023	1.308	1.107063	0.5010	1.629	1.160	1.323405	0.7982	0.7153	0.8349	29.3	1.091555	68
69	0.9028	1.285	1.098078	0.4744	1.748	1.131	1.305331	0.7777	0.7547	0.8163	28.2	1.083407	69
70	0.9032	1.261	1.089536	0.4475	1.883	1.102	1.287771	0.7564	0.7972	0.7970	27.1	1.075391	70

TABLE 11-56 Elliptic-Function LC Element Values (*Continued*)

θ	Ω_s	A_{min}	C_1	C_2	L_2	Ω_2	C_3	C_4	L_4	Ω_4	C_5	L_6	θ
T	∞	∞	1.322	0.0000	1.373	∞	2.203	0.0000	1.469	∞	2.059	0.8816	T
71	1.068397	26.0	0.7769	0.8433	0.7344	1.270700	1.073	2.034	0.4204	1.081425	1.237	0.9037	71
72	1.061511	24.9	0.7560	0.8936	0.7116	1.254095	1.044	2.206	0.3931	1.073732	1.213	0.9040	72
73	1.055024	23.7	0.7341	0.9487	0.6878	1.237933	1.015	2.405	0.3657	1.066446	1.188	0.9044	73
74	1.048925	22.6	0.7112	1.010	0.6631	1.222193	0.9860	2.634	0.3381	1.059558	1.162	0.9047	74
75	1.043207	21.5	0.6872	1.077	0.6374	1.206854	0.9568	2.905	0.3105	1.053059	1.135	0.9049	75
76	1.037860	20.3	0.6620	1.153	0.6104	1.191893	0.9278	3.226	0.2828	1.046940	1.107	0.9050	76
77	1.032878	19.1	0.6353	1.239	0.5822	1.177291	0.8991	3.615	0.2552	1.041196	1.079	0.9049	77
78	1.028255	17.9	0.6071	1.338	0.5525	1.163026	0.8706	4.093	0.2277	1.035818	1.050	0.9047	78
79	1.023985	16.6	0.5770	1.453	0.5211	1.149076	0.8427	4.695	0.2005	1.030804	1.019	0.9042	79
80	1.020064	15.4	0.5450	1.590	0.4879	1.135418	0.8156	5.471	0.1736	1.026148	0.9868	0.9033	80
81	1.016487	14.1	0.5105	1.755	0.4526	1.122029	0.7895	6.502	0.1473	1.021849	0.9529	0.9020	81
82	1.013253	12.7	0.4732	1.960	0.4149	1.108880	0.7650	7.925	0.1218	1.017905	0.9170	0.9001	82
83	1.010360	11.4	0.4325	2.223	0.3745	1.095939	0.7426	9.982	0.0974	1.014316	0.8784	0.8972	83
84	1.007808	9.9	0.3876	2.576	0.3309	1.083168	0.7234	13.14	0.0744	1.011085	0.8365	0.8930	84
85	1.005599	8.5	0.3377	3.075	0.2838	1.070517	0.7089	18.40	0.0535	1.008216	0.7898	0.8870	85
θ	Ω_s	A_{min}	L_1	L_2	C_2	Ω_2	L_3	L_4	C_4	Ω_4	L_5	C_6	θ

* Reprinted from R. Saal and E. Ulbrich, "On the Design of Filters by Synthesis," *IRE Transactions on Circuit Theory*, December 1958.

CO6 20 c°

θ/T	Ω_s	A_{min}	C_1	C_2	L_2	Ω_2	C_3	C_4	L_4	Ω_4	C_5	L_6	θ/T
∞	∞	∞	1.159	0.0000	1.529	∞	1.838	0.0000	1.838	∞	1.529	1.159	∞
16	3.878298	112.5	1.138	0.0209	1.500	5.644802	1.790	0.0350	1.769	4.020935	1.500	1.158	16
17	3.655090	109.3	1.135	0.0237	1.496	5.314073	1.784	0.0396	1.761	3.788961	1.496	1.158	17
18	3.456975	106.3	1.132	0.0266	1.492	5.020165	1.777	0.0445	1.751	3.583033	1.492	1.158	18
19	3.279996	103.4	1.129	0.0297	1.488	4.757266	1.770	0.0497	1.742	3.399040	1.488	1.158	19
20	3.120982	100.7	1.125	0.0330	1.483	4.520722	1.763	0.0552	1.731	3.233693	1.483	1.158	20
21	2.977369	98.1	1.122	0.0365	1.478	4.306769	1.756	0.0611	1.720	3.084330	1.479	1.158	21
22	2.847060	95.6	1.118	0.0401	1.473	4.112326	1.748	0.0673	1.709	2.948774	1.474	1.157	22
23	2.728322	93.3	1.114	0.0440	1.468	3.934847	1.739	0.0738	1.697	2.825225	1.469	1.157	23
24	2.619709	91.0	1.110	0.0480	1.463	3.772213	1.731	0.0807	1.685	2.712184	1.464	1.157	24
25	2.520009	88.8	1.106	0.0523	1.457	3.622641	1.722	0.0879	1.672	2.608393	1.458	1.157	25
26	2.428196	86.7	1.102	0.0568	1.451	3.484624	1.712	0.0955	1.658	2.512785	1.452	1.157	26
27	2.343395	84.6	1.097	0.0614	1.445	3.356877	1.702	0.1035	1.644	2.424454	1.446	1.156	27
28	2.264858	82.6	1.092	0.0663	1.439	3.238801	1.692	0.1118	1.630	2.342621	1.440	1.156	28
29	2.191939	80.7	1.087	0.0714	1.432	3.127945	1.682	0.1205	1.615	2.266617	1.433	1.156	29
30	2.124078	78.9	1.082	0.0767	1.425	3.024987	1.671	0.1297	1.599	2.195860	1.427	1.156	30
31	2.060787	77.1	1.077	0.0822	1.418	2.928712	1.660	0.1392	1.583	2.129845	1.420	1.155	31
32	2.001642	75.3	1.071	0.0880	1.410	2.838492	1.648	0.1492	1.567	2.068129	1.413	1.155	32
33	1.946266	73.6	1.065	0.0940	1.403	2.753776	1.636	0.1597	1.550	2.010323	1.405	1.155	33
34	1.894331	72.0	1.059	0.1003	1.395	2.674079	1.624	0.1706	1.532	1.956085	1.398	1.154	34
35	1.845543	70.4	1.053	0.1068	1.386	2.598969	1.611	0.1820	1.514	1.905110	1.390	1.154	35

11.87

TABLE 11-56 Elliptic-Function LC Element Values (*Continued*)

θ / T	Ω_s	A_{min}	C_1	C_2	L_2	Ω_2	C_3	C_4	L_4	Ω_4	C_5	L_6	θ / T
	∞	∞	1.159	0.0000	1.529	∞	1.838	0.0000	1.838	∞	1.529	1.159	
36	1.799643	68.8	1.047	0.1135	1.378	2.528063	1.598	0.1939	1.496	1.857129	1.382	1.154	36
37	1.756398	67.3	1.040	0.1206	1.369	2.461022	1.585	0.2063	1.477	1.811902	1.374	1.153	37
38	1.715603	65.8	1.033	0.1279	1.360	2.397538	1.571	0.2192	1.457	1.769212	1.365	1.153	38
39	1.677070	64.3	1.026	0.1355	1.351	2.337337	1.557	0.2328	1.437	1.728868	1.356	1.152	39
40	1.640634	62.8	1.019	0.1434	1.341	2.280174	1.543	0.2469	1.417	1.690696	1.348	1.152	40
41	1.608142	61.4	1.012	0.1516	1.332	2.225824	1.528	0.2617	1.396	1.654538	1.338	1.151	41
42	1.573460	60.0	1.004	0.1601	1.321	2.174087	1.513	0.2772	1.374	1.620254	1.329	1.151	42
43	1.542462	58.7	0.9963	0.1689	1.311	2.124779	1.498	0.2993	1.352	1.587714	1.319	1.150	43
44	1.513038	57.3	0.9882	0.1781	1.300	2.077734	1.482	0.3103	1.330	1.556804	1.309	1.150	44
45	1.485086	56.0	0.9798	0.1877	1.289	2.032800	1.466	0.3280	1.307	1.527416	1.299	1.149	45
46	1.458511	54.7	0.9712	0.1976	1.278	1.989839	1.450	0.3465	1.284	1.499453	1.289	1.148	46
47	1.433230	53.4	0.9624	0.2079	1.266	1.948725	1.433	0.3659	1.260	1.472828	1.278	1.148	47
48	1.409164	52.2	0.9533	0.2187	1.255	1.909340	1.416	0.3863	1.235	1.447459	1.267	1.147	48
49	1.386241	50.9	0.9439	0.2298	1.242	1.871578	1.399	0.4078	1.211	1.423273	1.256	1.146	49
50	1.364398	49.7	0.9343	0.2414	1.230	1.835340	1.381	0.4303	1.185	1.400200	1.245	1.146	50
51	1.343572	48.5	0.9244	0.2535	1.217	1.800536	1.363	0.4540	1.160	1.378179	1.234	1.145	51
52	1.323710	47.3	0.9142	0.2661	1.204	1.767082	1.345	0.4790	1.133	1.357152	1.222	1.144	52
53	1.304759	46.1	0.9037	0.2792	1.190	1.734901	1.327	0.5054	1.107	1.337064	1.210	1.143	53
54	1.286672	45.0	0.8929	0.2929	1.176	1.703919	1.308	0.5333	1.080	1.317868	1.197	1.142	54
55	1.269406	43.8	0.8819	0.3072	1.162	1.674071	1.289	0.5628	1.052	1.299518	1.185	1.141	55
56	1.252921	42.7	0.8705	0.3221	1.147	1.645294	1.269	0.5941	1.024	1.281971	1.172	1.140	56
57	1.237179	41.5	0.8587	0.3377	1.132	1.617530	1.249	0.6274	0.9957	1.265189	1.159	1.139	57
58	1.222145	40.4	0.8466	0.3541	1.116	1.590725	1.229	0.6629	0.9668	1.249136	1.145	1.138	58
59	1.207787	39.3	0.8342	0.3712	1.100	1.564828	1.209	0.7008	0.9375	1.233777	1.131	1.137	59
60	1.194077	38.1	0.8214	0.3892	1.084	1.539791	1.188	0.7413	0.9077	1.219083	1.117	1.136	60
61	1.180985	37.0	0.8081	0.4081	1.067	1.515571	1.167	0.7848	0.8775	1.205023	1.103	1.134	61
62	1.168486	35.9	0.7945	0.4280	1.049	1.492126	1.146	0.8317	0.8468	1.191572	1.088	1.133	62
63	1.156557	34.8	0.7804	0.4490	1.032	1.469414	1.125	0.8823	0.8157	1.178704	1.074	1.131	63
64	1.145175	33.7	0.7659	0.4712	1.013	1.447401	1.103	0.9372	0.7843	1.166396	1.058	1.130	64
65	1.134320	32.6	0.7509	0.4947	0.9940	1.426049	1.081	0.9970	0.7524	1.154626	1.043	1.128	65
66	1.123973	31.5	0.7354	0.5196	0.9744	1.405326	1.059	1.062	0.7201	1.143375	1.026	1.126	66
67	1.114116	30.4	0.7193	0.5462	0.9542	1.385199	1.037	1.134	0.6874	1.132624	1.010	1.125	67
68	1.104733	29.3	0.7027	0.5746	0.9332	1.365637	1.014	1.213	0.6543	1.122356	0.9932	1.123	68
69	1.095809	28.2	0.6854	0.6050	0.9115	1.346613	0.9915	1.301	0.6208	1.112555	0.9759	1.120	69
70	1.087329	27.1	0.6674	0.6377	0.8891	1.328096	0.9686	1.400	0.5870	1.103207	0.9582	1.118	70

θ	Ω_s	A_{min}	L_1	L_2	C_2	Ω_2	L_3	L_4	C_4	Ω_4	L_5	C_6	θ
71	1.079282	26.0	0.6488	0.6730	0.8657	1.310060	0.9456	1.511	0.5528	1.094297	0.9399	1.116	71
72	1.071656	24.9	0.6293	0.7114	0.8415	1.292478	0.9225	1.636	0.5184	1.085815	0.9211	1.113	72
73	1.064439	23.7	0.6089	0.7533	0.8162	1.275324	0.8994	1.780	0.4836	1.077747	0.9017	1.110	73
74	1.057623	22.6	0.5876	0.7994	0.7898	1.258571	0.8762	1.947	0.4486	1.070085	0.8816	1.107	74
75	1.051198	21.5	0.5652	0.8503	0.7621	1.242193	0.8530	2.141	0.4134	1.062820	0.8608	1.104	75
76	1.045158	20.3	0.5417	0.9073	0.7331	1.226164	0.8299	2.372	0.3781	1.055943	0.8393	1.100	76
77	1.039495	19.1	0.5168	0.9716	0.7025	1.210456	0.8071	2.650	0.3426	1.049447	0.8168	1.096	77
78	1.034204	17.9	0.4905	1.045	0.6701	1.195041	0.7845	2.990	0.3072	1.043327	0.7932	1.091	78
79	1.029281	16.6	0.4624	1.130	0.6358	1.179887	0.7625	3.415	0.2720	1.037578	0.7685	1.086	79
80	1.024722	15.4	0.4323	1.230	0.5991	1.164960	0.7411	3.961	0.2370	1.032198	0.7423	1.080	80
81	1.020525	14.1	0.3999	1.350	0.5598	1.150224	0.7206	4.677	0.2026	1.027183	0.7144	1.073	81
82	1.016691	12.7	0.3648	1.499	0.5174	1.135632	0.7016	5.659	0.1690	1.022536	0.6845	1.064	82
83	1.013219	11.4	0.3263	1.687	0.4715	1.121129	0.6845	7.062	0.1366	1.018256	0.6518	1.055	83
84	1.010114	9.9	0.2837	1.938	0.4214	1.106645	0.6702	9.190	0.1058	1.014351	0.6158	1.043	84
85	1.007381	8.5	0.2358	2.288	0.3664	1.092084	0.6603	12.67	0.0772	1.010827	0.5750	1.027	85

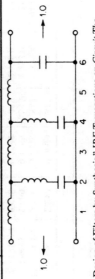

* Reprinted from R. Saal and E. Ulbrich, "On the Design of Filters by Synthesis," *IRE Transactions on Circuit Theory*, December 1958.

TABLE 11-56 Elliptic-Function LC Element Values (*Continued*)

CO7 20°

θ/T	Ω_s	A_{min}	C_1	C_2	L_2	Ω_2	C_3	C_4	L_4	Ω_4	C_5	C_6	L_6	Ω_6	C_7
	∞	∞	1.335	0.0000	1.389	∞	2.240	0.0000	1.515	∞	2.240	0.0000	1.389	∞	1.335
26	2.281172	105.4	1.310	0.0290	1.358	5.038750	2.100	0.1353	1.357	2.333900	2.049	0.0955	1.281	2.859592	1.247
27	2.202689	103.0	1.308	0.0314	1.355	4.848897	2.089	0.1465	1.345	2.253156	2.034	0.1034	1.272	2.756829	1.240
28	2.130054	100.7	1.306	0.0339	1.353	4.672457	2.078	0.1582	1.332	2.178409	2.019	0.1117	1.263	2.661529	1.233
29	2.062665	98.5	1.304	0.0364	1.350	4.508037	2.066	0.1704	1.319	2.109040	2.003	0.1204	1.254	2.572921	1.226
30	2.000000	96.3	1.302	0.0391	1.347	4.354434	2.054	0.1833	1.305	2.044515	1.987	0.1295	1.245	2.490337	1.218
31	1.941604	94.2	1.299	0.0420	1.344	4.210595	2.042	0.1966	1.292	1.984368	1.970	0.1390	1.235	2.413194	1.210
32	1.887080	92.2	1.297	0.0449	1.341	4.075602	2.029	0.2106	1.277	1.928190	1.952	0.1490	1.225	2.340984	1.202
33	1.836078	90.2	1.294	0.0479	1.338	3.948647	2.016	0.2252	1.262	1.875623	1.934	0.1593	1.214	2.273259	1.193
34	1.788292	88.3	1.292	0.0511	1.335	3.829016	2.002	0.2404	1.247	1.826351	1.916	0.1702	1.204	2.209625	1.184
35	1.743447	86.4	1.289	0.0544	1.332	3.716076	1.988	0.2562	1.232	1.780095	1.897	0.1815	1.193	2.149731	1.175
36	1.701302	84.6	1.286	0.0578	1.328	3.609267	1.973	0.2727	1.216	1.736606	1.878	0.1932	1.181	2.093268	1.165
37	1.661640	82.8	1.283	0.0614	1.324	3.508087	1.959	0.2900	1.199	1.695662	1.858	0.2055	1.169	2.039957	1.155
38	1.624269	81.0	1.280	0.0650	1.321	3.412086	1.943	0.3079	1.183	1.657065	1.837	0.2183	1.157	1.989552	1.145
39	1.589016	79.3	1.277	0.0689	1.317	3.320862	1.928	0.3267	1.165	1.620638	1.817	0.2317	1.145	1.941830	1.135
40	1.555724	77.6	1.274	0.0728	1.313	3.234050	1.912	0.3462	1.148	1.586220	1.795	0.2456	1.132	1.896591	1.124
41	1.524253	76.0	1.270	0.0770	1.308	3.151325	1.895	0.3666	1.130	1.553668	1.773	0.2601	1.119	1.853653	1.113
42	1.494477	74.3	1.267	0.0812	1.304	3.072388	1.879	0.3879	1.112	1.522851	1.751	0.2753	1.105	1.812855	1.102
43	1.466279	72.8	1.263	0.0857	1.300	2.996969	1.862	0.4101	1.093	1.493651	1.728	0.2911	1.092	1.774048	1.090
44	1.439557	71.2	1.259	0.0903	1.295	2.924824	1.844	0.4332	1.074	1.465961	1.705	0.3076	1.077	1.737098	1.078
45	1.414214	69.7	1.255	0.0950	1.290	2.855727	1.826	0.4575	1.055	1.439683	1.682	0.3248	1.063	1.701881	1.066

46	1.053	1.668286	1.048	0.3428	1.657	1.414728	1.035	0.4828	1.808	2.789476	1.285	0.1000	1.251	68.2	1.390164	46
47	1.040	1.636211	1.033	0.3617	1.633	1.391016	1.015	0.5093	1.789	2.725881	1.280	0.1051	1.247	66.7	1.367327	47
48	1.027	1.605563	1.017	0.3814	1.608	1.368471	0.9944	0.5370	1.770	2.664770	1.275	0.1105	1.243	65.2	1.345633	48
49	1.013	1.576255	1.001	0.4020	1.583	1.347026	0.9736	0.5661	1.751	2.605984	1.269	0.1160	1.238	63.7	1.325013	49
50	0.9992	1.548208	0.9850	0.4235	1.557	1.326618	0.9525	0.5965	1.731	2.549377	1.264	0.1217	1.234	62.3	1.305407	50
51	0.9848	1.521349	0.9684	0.4462	1.531	1.307190	0.9310	0.6286	1.711	2.494813	1.258	0.1277	1.229	60.9	1.286760	51
52	0.9699	1.495612	0.9514	0.4699	1.504	1.288687	0.9093	0.6622	1.690	2.442167	1.252	0.1339	1.224	59.5	1.269018	52
53	0.9547	1.470934	0.9340	0.4948	1.477	1.271063	0.8872	0.6977	1.669	2.391323	1.246	0.1404	1.219	58.1	1.252136	53
54	0.9391	1.447259	0.9163	0.5211	1.450	1.254270	0.8648	0.7351	1.648	2.342170	1.239	0.1471	1.213	56.8	1.236068	54
55	0.9230	1.424533	0.8981	0.5487	1.422	1.238269	0.8420	0.7745	1.626	2.294610	1.232	0.1541	1.208	55.4	1.220775	55
56	0.9065	1.402707	0.8796	0.5778	1.394	1.223020	0.8190	0.8163	1.604	2.248546	1.225	0.1614	1.202	54.1	1.206218	56
57	0.8896	1.381735	0.8607	0.6085	1.365	1.208487	0.7957	0.8605	1.581	2.203891	1.218	0.1690	1.196	52.7	1.192363	57
58	0.8722	1.361575	0.8414	0.6411	1.336	1.194638	0.7721	0.9075	1.558	2.160560	1.211	0.1770	1.190	51.4	1.179178	58
59	0.8543	1.342188	0.8217	0.6755	1.307	1.181442	0.7482	0.9576	1.535	2.118476	1.203	0.1853	1.183	50.1	1.166633	59
60	0.8360	1.323537	0.8016	0.7121	1.278	1.168869	0.7240	1.011	1.511	2.077565	1.195	0.1939	1.177	48.8	1.154701	60
61	0.8171	1.305587	0.7811	0.7510	1.248	1.156895	0.6995	1.068	1.487	2.037756	1.186	0.2030	1.170	47.5	1.143354	61
62	0.7976	1.288307	0.7602	0.7925	1.218	1.145494	0.6748	1.129	1.463	1.998983	1.177	0.2125	1.163	46.2	1.132520	62
63	0.7776	1.271668	0.7389	0.8369	1.188	1.134644	0.6498	1.195	1.438	1.961181	1.168	0.2225	1.155	44.9	1.122326	63
64	0.7570	1.255641	0.7171	0.8845	1.157	1.124323	0.6245	1.267	1.412	1.924292	1.159	0.2331	1.147	43.7	1.112602	64
65	0.7357	1.240200	0.6949	0.9357	1.126	1.114512	0.5990	1.344	1.386	1.888255	1.149	0.2441	1.139	42.4	1.103378	65
66	0.7138	1.225322	0.6722	0.9909	1.095	1.105192	0.5732	1.428	1.360	1.853014	1.138	0.2559	1.130	41.1	1.094636	66
67	0.6911	1.210984	0.6490	1.051	1.064	1.096346	0.5472	1.520	1.333	1.818515	1.127	0.2682	1.121	39.8	1.086360	67
68	0.6676	1.197165	0.6254	1.116	1.032	1.087959	0.5209	1.622	1.306	1.784703	1.116	0.2814	1.112	38.5	1.078535	68
69	0.6433	1.183845	0.6013	1.187	1.001	1.080016	0.4945	1.734	1.278	1.751526	1.104	0.2953	1.101	37.2	1.071145	69
70	0.6181	1.171007	0.5767	1.265	0.9689	1.072504	0.4678	1.859	1.250	1.718931	1.091	0.3102	1.091	35.9	1.064178	70
71	0.5920	1.158633	0.5516	1.351	0.9371	1.065409	0.4409	1.998	1.221	1.686865	1.077	0.3262	1.080	34.6	1.057621	71
72	0.5647	1.146708	0.5259	1.446	0.9051	1.058721	0.4138	2.156	1.192	1.655277	1.063	0.3433	1.068	33.3	1.051462	72
73	0.5363	1.135217	0.4997	1.553	0.8731	1.052428	0.3865	2.336	1.162	1.624111	1.048	0.3618	1.055	32.0	1.045692	73
74	0.5066	1.124147	0.4729	1.673	0.8412	1.046522	0.3591	2.543	1.131	1.593311	1.032	0.3818	1.042	30.7	1.040299	74
75	0.4754	1.113485	0.4455	1.810	0.8093	1.040993	0.3315	2.784	1.100	1.562818	1.014	0.4037	1.028	29.3	1.035276	75

TABLE 11-56 Elliptic-Function LC Element Values (*Continued*)

θ	T	Ω_1	A_{min}	G_1	C_2	L_2	Ω_2	G_3	C_4	L_4	Ω_4	G_5	C_6	L_6	Ω_6	G_7
		∞	∞	1.335	0.0000	1.389	∞	2.240	0.0000	1.515	∞	2.240	0.0000	1.389	∞	1.335
76	76	1.030614	27.9	1.013	0.4278	0.9953	1.532571	1.069	3.068	0.3038	1.035833	0.7776	1.968	0.4175	1.103221	0.4426
77	77	1.026304	26.5	0.9960	0.4544	0.9749	1.502499	1.036	3.408	0.2760	1.031035	0.7460	2.151	0.3888	1.093345	0.4079
78	78	1.022341	25.1	0.9782	0.4841	0.9527	1.472529	1.004	3.822	0.2483	1.026592	0.7148	2.368	0.3595	1.083849	0.3710
79	79	1.018717	23.6	0.9588	0.5177	0.9282	1.442574	0.9699	4.337	0.2205	1.022499	0.6841	2.628	0.3295	1.074724	0.3316
80	80	1.015427	22.1	0.9376	0.5562	0.9011	1.412537	0.9356	4.994	0.1929	1.018751	0.6540	2.946	0.2987	1.065966	0.2892
81	81	1.012465	20.6	0.9142	0.6011	0.8707	1.382299	0.9006	5.858	0.1656	1.015345	0.6248	3.346	0.2672	1.057569	0.2431
82	82	1.009828	18.9	0.8881	0.6545	0.8363	1.351718	0.8648	7.036	0.1387	1.012276	0.5968	3.863	0.2350	1.049533	0.1926
83	83	1.007510	17.3	0.8587	0.7197	0.7967	1.320610	0.8283	8.723	0.1125	1.009543	0.5706	4.559	0.2021	1.041856	0.1363
84	84	1.005508	15.5	0.8252	0.8023	0.7504	1.288733	0.7911	11.29	0.0873	1.007145	0.5470	5.545	0.1685	1.034542	0.0725
85	85	1.003820	13.6	0.7863	0.9121	0.6953	1.255747	0.7533	15.55	0.0636	1.005081	0.5275	7.042	0.1345	1.027600	−0.0016
θ	T	Ω_1	A_{min}	L_1	L_2	C_2	Ω_2	L_3	L_4	C_4	Ω_4	L_5	L_6	C_6	Ω_6	L_7

* Reprinted from R. Saal and E. Ulbrich, "On the Design of Filters by Synthesis," *IRE Transactions on Circuit Theory*, December 1958.

CO8 20 b*

θ	Ω_1	A_{min}	C_1	C_2	L_2	Ω_2	C_3	C_4	L_4	Ω_4	C_5	C_6	L_6	Ω_6	C_7	L_8	θ
T	∞	∞	1.343	0.0000	1.398	∞	2.261	0.0000	1.538	∞	2.307	0.0000	1.507	∞	2.097	0.8954	T
31	1.974165	111.4	1.289	0.0601	1.331	3.534655	2.051	0.1878	1.319	2.008837	2.028	0.1353	1.348	2.341711	1.977	0.8980	31
32	1.918381	109.1	1.285	0.0644	1.326	3.422880	2.037	0.2011	1.305	1.951720	2.010	0.1448	1.337	2.272128	1.969	0.8982	32
33	1.866186	106.8	1.281	0.0687	1.321	3.317819	2.023	0.2150	1.291	1.898264	1.992	0.1548	1.327	2.206887	1.961	0.8984	33
34	1.817268	104.6	1.277	0.0733	1.317	3.218876	2.008	0.2294	1.276	1.848149	1.973	0.1651	1.315	2.145605	1.952	0.8986	34
35	1.771347	102.4	1.273	0.0781	1.311	3.125526	1.993	0.2445	1.261	1.801092	1.953	0.1759	1.304	2.087945	1.943	0.8987	35
36	1.728178	100.3	1.268	0.0830	1.306	3.037300	1.978	0.2602	1.245	1.756840	1.933	0.1871	1.292	2.033606	1.934	0.8989	36
37	1.687539	98.3	1.264	0.0881	1.301	2.953780	1.962	0.2765	1.229	1.715168	1.912	0.1988	1.280	1.982320	1.925	0.8991	37
38	1.649233	96.3	1.259	0.0934	1.295	2.874592	1.946	0.2936	1.213	1.675876	1.891	0.2110	1.267	1.933848	1.916	0.8993	38
39	1.613085	94.3	1.255	0.0990	1.289	2.799400	1.929	0.3113	1.196	1.638784	1.869	0.2236	1.254	1.887974	1.906	0.8995	39
40	1.578935	92.4	1.250	0.1047	1.283	2.727903	1.912	0.3298	1.179	1.603728	1.847	0.2368	1.241	1.844505	1.896	0.8997	40
41	1.546640	90.5	1.245	0.1107	1.277	2.659827	1.895	0.3491	1.161	1.570563	1.824	0.2505	1.228	1.803267	1.885	0.9000	41
42	1.516070	88.7	1.239	0.1169	1.271	2.594925	1.877	0.3692	1.143	1.539156	1.801	0.2647	1.214	1.764103	1.875	0.9002	42
43	1.487108	86.8	1.234	0.1233	1.264	2.532974	1.859	0.3902	1.125	1.509989	1.777	0.2796	1.200	1.726867	1.864	0.9004	43
44	1.459648	85.1	1.228	0.1300	1.257	2.473768	1.840	0.4120	1.106	1.481151	1.753	0.2950	1.185	1.691432	1.852	0.9006	44
45	1.433592	83.3	1.222	0.1369	1.250	2.417121	1.821	0.4348	1.087	1.454344	1.728	0.3110	1.170	1.657678	1.841	0.9009	45
46	1.408853	81.6	1.217	0.1441	1.243	2.362865	1.801	0.4586	1.068	1.428878	1.703	0.3278	1.155	1.625498	1.829	0.9011	46
47	1.385348	79.9	1.210	0.1516	1.235	2.310842	1.781	0.4835	1.048	1.404670	1.677	0.3452	1.139	1.594793	1.817	0.9014	47
48	1.363006	78.2	1.204	0.1594	1.228	2.260911	1.761	0.5095	1.028	1.381645	1.651	0.3634	1.123	1.565471	1.805	0.9016	48
49	1.341757	76.5	1.197	0.1674	1.220	2.212939	1.740	0.5368	1.008	1.359734	1.624	0.3823	1.107	1.537451	1.792	0.9019	49
50	1.321539	74.9	1.191	0.1758	1.211	2.166805	1.719	0.5653	0.9869	1.338873	1.597	0.4021	1.090	1.510657	1.779	0.9021	50
51	1.302296	73.3	1.184	0.1845	1.203	2.122397	1.698	0.5951	0.9658	1.319003	1.569	0.4227	1.073	1.485017	1.766	0.9024	51
52	1.283974	71.7	1.177	0.1936	1.194	2.079568	1.676	0.6265	0.9444	1.300068	1.541	0.4443	1.055	1.460459	1.752	0.9028	52
53	1.266526	70.1	1.169	0.2030	1.185	2.038353	1.653	0.6594	0.9226	1.282028	1.512	0.4668	1.037	1.436948	1.738	0.9029	53
54	1.249906	68.6	1.161	0.2129	1.176	1.998531	1.630	0.6941	0.9006	1.264827	1.483	0.4904	1.019	1.414404	1.724	0.9032	54
55	1.234073	67.0	1.153	0.2231	1.167	1.960064	1.607	0.7306	0.8782	1.248426	1.453	0.5152	1.001	1.392784	1.710	0.9035	55

11.93

TABLE 11-56 Elliptic-Function LC Element Values (*Continued*)

θ	L_8	C_7	Ω_6	L_6	C_6	C_5	Ω_4	L_4	C_4	C_3	Ω_2	L_2	C_2	C_1	A_{min}	Ω_s	θ
T	0.8954	2.097	∞	1.507	0.0000	2.307	∞	1.538	0.0000	2.261	∞	1.398	0.0000	1.343	∞	∞	T
56	0.9038	1.695	1.372040	0.9816	0.5412	1.423	1.232786	0.8555	0.7691	1.583	1.922874	1.157	0.2338	1.145	65.5	1.218988	56
57	0.9041	1.680	1.352130	0.9622	0.5684	1.393	1.217872	0.8326	0.8098	1.559	1.886889	1.146	0.2450	1.136	64.0	1.204616	57
58	0.9044	1.664	1.333008	0.9425	0.5971	1.362	1.203647	0.8093	0.8529	1.535	1.852022	1.136	0.2566	1.128	62.5	1.190925	58
59	0.9046	1.648	1.314647	0.9223	0.6273	1.331	1.190084	0.7857	0.8986	1.509	1.818264	1.125	0.2688	1.119	61.0	1.177883	59
60	0.9049	1.632	1.297002	0.9017	0.6592	1.299	1.177152	0.7619	0.9472	1.484	1.785501	1.114	0.2816	1.109	59.5	1.165463	60
61	0.9053	1.615	1.280043	0.8808	0.6929	1.267	1.164824	0.7378	0.9990	1.458	1.753696	1.102	0.2950	1.099	58.0	1.153638	61
62	0.9056	1.598	1.263739	0.8593	0.7286	1.234	1.153075	0.7134	1.054	1.432	1.722794	1.090	0.3090	1.089	56.5	1.142384	62
63	0.9059	1.581	1.248062	0.8375	0.7665	1.201	1.141883	0.6887	1.114	1.405	1.692746	1.078	0.3238	1.079	55.0	1.131677	63
64	0.9062	1.563	1.232986	0.8152	0.8069	1.168	1.131225	0.6638	1.177	1.377	1.663502	1.065	0.3393	1.068	53.6	1.121498	64
65	0.9065	1.544	1.218485	0.7925	0.8499	1.134	1.121082	0.6387	1.246	1.350	1.635018	1.052	0.3557	1.056	52.1	1.111827	65
66	0.9068	1.526	1.204537	0.7693	0.8959	1.100	1.111435	0.6132	1.320	1.321	1.607250	1.038	0.3730	1.044	50.6	1.102644	66
67	0.9071	1.506	1.191121	0.7457	0.9452	1.065	1.102268	0.5876	1.401	1.292	1.580155	1.023	0.3913	1.032	49.2	1.093994	67
68	0.9075	1.487	1.178215	0.7215	0.9984	1.030	1.093563	0.5617	1.489	1.263	1.553693	1.008	0.4108	1.019	47.7	1.085681	68
69	0.9078	1.466	1.165802	0.6969	1.056	0.9947	1.085307	0.5356	1.585	1.233	1.527823	0.9929	0.4315	1.006	46.2	1.077870	69
70	0.9081	1.445	1.153865	0.6717	1.118	0.9590	1.077485	0.5092	1.692	1.202	1.502508	0.9766	0.4536	0.9917	44.8	1.070487	70
71	0.9084	1.424	1.142387	0.6460	1.186	0.9230	1.070085	0.4826	1.809	1.171	1.477710	0.9597	0.4772	0.9769	43.3	1.063520	71
72	0.9087	1.402	1.131353	0.6197	1.261	0.8867	1.063096	0.4559	1.941	1.140	1.453390	0.9419	0.5026	0.9614	41.8	1.056959	72
73	0.9091	1.379	1.120750	0.5928	1.343	0.8501	1.056506	0.4289	2.089	1.107	1.429511	0.9232	0.5300	0.9450	40.3	1.050791	73
74	0.9094	1.355	1.110565	0.5653	1.434	0.8131	1.050305	0.4017	2.257	1.074	1.406035	0.9036	0.5598	0.9277	38.7	1.045007	74
75	0.9097	1.331	1.100787	0.5371	1.537	0.7759	1.044487	0.3743	2.449	1.040	1.382921	0.8829	0.5922	0.9094	37.2	1.039599	75
76	0.9100	1.305	1.091406	0.5082	1.652	0.7384	1.039040	0.3468	2.671	1.006	1.360130	0.8611	0.6278	0.8899	35.6	1.034558	76
77	0.9103	1.279	1.082412	0.4785	1.784	0.7007	1.033960	0.3191	2.931	0.9701	1.337618	0.8379	0.6670	0.8691	34.0	1.029877	77
78	0.9105	1.251	1.073796	0.4480	1.936	0.6628	1.029240	0.2913	3.241	0.9337	1.315338	0.8131	0.7108	0.8469	32.4	1.025550	78
79	0.9108	1.222	1.065554	0.4166	2.114	0.6247	1.024824	0.2633	3.616	0.8964	1.293239	0.7866	0.7601	0.8228	30.7	1.021570	79
80	0.9110	1.192	1.057678	0.3843	2.326	0.5864	1.020857	0.2352	4.079	0.8579	1.271262	0.7581	0.8162	0.7968	29.0	1.017932	80
81	0.9111	1.159	1.050164	0.3509	2.584	0.5482	1.017188	0.2071	4.667	0.8183	1.249341	0.7271	0.8812	0.7683	27.2	1.014633	81
82	0.9111	1.125	1.043012	0.3162	2.907	0.5100	1.013862	0.1790	5.436	0.7774	1.227394	0.6931	0.9577	0.7368	25.3	1.011669	82
83	0.9110	1.088	1.036219	0.2803	3.323	0.4719	1.010878	0.1509	6.484	0.7351	1.205319	0.6555	1.050	0.7017	23.3	1.009036	83
84	0.9106	1.047	1.029789	0.2428	3.884	0.4342	1.008238	0.1231	7.989	0.6911	1.189984	0.6133	1.165	0.6619	21.3	1.006735	84
85	0.9098	1.003	1.023728	0.2036	4.688	0.3973	1.005943	0.0958	10.32	0.6453	1.160208	0.5649	1.315	0.6159	19.0	1.004764	85
θ	C_8	L_7	Ω_6	C_6	L_6	L_5	Ω_4	C_4	L_4	L_3	Ω_2	C_2	L_2	L_1	A_{min}	Ω_s	θ

CO8 20 c*

θ/T	Ω_s	A_min	C_1	C_2	L_2	Ω_2	C_3	C_4	L_4	Ω_4	C_5	C_6	L_6	Ω_6	C_7	L_8	θ/T
	∞	∞	1.215	0.0000	1.523	∞	1.963	0.0000	1.840	∞	1.840	0.0000	1.963	∞	1.523	1.215	
31	2.007273	111.4	1.159	0.0527	1.457	3.607866	1.782	0.1508	1.589	2.042921	1.628	0.1002	1.755	2.384868	1.442	1.210	31
32	1.950201	109.1	1.155	0.0564	1.452	3.494036	1.770	0.1614	1.573	1.984498	1.614	0.1073	1.741	2.313817	1.437	1.210	32
33	1.896788	106.8	1.151	0.0602	1.448	3.387051	1.758	0.1725	1.556	1.929808	1.600	0.1147	1.727	2.247191	1.431	1.210	33
34	1.846713	104.6	1.148	0.0642	1.443	3.286306	1.746	0.1841	1.539	1.878522	1.585	0.1223	1.713	2.184601	1.425	1.210	34
35	1.799694	102.4	1.143	0.0683	1.438	3.191263	1.733	0.1962	1.521	1.830353	1.570	0.1304	1.697	2.125700	1.420	1.209	35
36	1.755478	100.3	1.138	0.0726	1.432	3.101445	1.720	0.2088	1.503	1.785042	1.555	0.1387	1.682	2.070184	1.413	1.208	36
37	1.713841	98.3	1.134	0.0770	1.427	3.016426	1.706	0.2219	1.485	1.742360	1.539	0.1474	1.666	2.017779	1.407	1.208	37
38	1.674581	96.3	1.129	0.0816	1.421	2.935824	1.692	0.2355	1.466	1.702102	1.522	0.1565	1.650	1.968241	1.401	1.207	38
39	1.637519	94.3	1.124	0.0864	1.416	2.859298	1.678	0.2497	1.446	1.664085	1.506	0.1659	1.633	1.921349	1.394	1.207	39
40	1.602492	92.4	1.119	0.0914	1.410	2.786539	1.663	0.2645	1.426	1.628143	1.489	0.1757	1.616	1.876908	1.387	1.206	40
41	1.569355	90.5	1.114	0.0965	1.404	2.717269	1.648	0.2799	1.406	1.594127	1.471	0.1859	1.598	1.834738	1.380	1.206	41
42	1.537975	88.7	1.109	0.1018	1.397	2.651235	1.633	0.2959	1.385	1.561901	1.453	0.1965	1.580	1.794680	1.373	1.205	42
43	1.508233	86.8	1.103	0.1073	1.391	2.588210	1.617	0.3127	1.364	1.531345	1.435	0.2075	1.562	1.756586	1.365	1.205	43
44	1.480020	85.1	1.097	0.1131	1.384	2.527985	1.601	0.3301	1.342	1.502346	1.416	0.2190	1.543	1.720325	1.358	1.204	44
45	1.453236	83.3	1.092	0.1190	1.377	2.470370	1.585	0.3483	1.320	1.474804	1.397	0.2310	1.523	1.685775	1.350	1.203	45
46	1.427793	81.6	1.085	0.1251	1.370	2.415192	1.568	0.3673	1.297	1.448627	1.378	0.2435	1.503	1.652826	1.342	1.203	46
47	1.403607	79.9	1.079	0.1315	1.362	2.362292	1.551	0.3871	1.274	1.423730	1.358	0.2565	1.483	1.621377	1.334	1.202	47
48	1.380603	78.2	1.073	0.1381	1.355	2.311524	1.534	0.4078	1.251	1.400037	1.338	0.2701	1.462	1.591337	1.325	1.201	48
49	1.358712	76.5	1.066	0.1450	1.347	2.262754	1.516	0.4295	1.227	1.377477	1.317	0.2842	1.441	1.562620	1.317	1.200	49
50	1.337870	74.9	1.059	0.1521	1.339	2.215859	1.498	0.4521	1.203	1.355985	1.296	0.2990	1.419	1.535148	1.308	1.200	50
51	1.318020	73.3	1.052	0.1595	1.330	2.170723	1.479	0.4759	1.178	1.335501	1.275	0.3144	1.397	1.508850	1.299	1.199	51
52	1.299107	71.7	1.045	0.1672	1.322	2.127183	1.460	0.5008	1.153	1.315965	1.253	0.3305	1.374	1.483645	1.290	1.198	52
53	1.281092	70.1	1.037	0.1751	1.313	2.085317	1.441	0.5269	1.128	1.297345	1.231	0.3474	1.351	1.459515	1.280	1.197	53
54	1.263899	68.6	1.029	0.1834	1.304	2.044857	1.421	0.5543	1.102	1.279574	1.208	0.3651	1.328	1.436360	1.270	1.196	54
55	1.247516	67.0	1.021	0.1920	1.294	2.005778	1.401	0.5832	1.076	1.262617	1.186	0.3836	1.304	1.414144	1.260	1.195	55

11.95

TABLE 11-56 Elliptic-Function LC Element Values (*Continued*)

θ	T	L_8	C_7	Ω_6	L_6	C_6	C_5	Ω_4	L_4	C_4	C_3	Ω_2	L_2	C_2	C_1	A_{min}	Ω_s
∞	∞	1.215	1.523	∞	1.963	0.0000	1.840	∞	1.840	0.0000	1.963	∞	1.523	0.0000	1.215	∞	∞
56	56	1.194	1.250	1.392816	1.279	0.4030	1.162	1.246432	1.049	0.6137	1.381	1.967999	1.285	0.2010	1.013	65.5	1.231893
57	57	1.193	1.240	1.372332	1.254	0.4234	1.139	1.230984	1.022	0.6458	1.360	1.931448	1.274	0.2103	1.004	64.0	1.216995
58	58	1.192	1.229	1.352645	1.228	0.4449	1.115	1.216235	0.9944	0.6798	1.339	1.896030	1.264	0.2201	0.9956	62.5	1.202788
59	59	1.190	1.218	1.333732	1.202	0.4676	1.090	1.202161	0.9666	0.7159	1.318	1.861754	1.253	0.2302	0.9864	61.0	1.189241
60	60	1.189	1.207	1.315541	1.176	0.4914	1.066	1.188726	0.9384	0.7541	1.296	1.828485	1.242	0.2408	0.9770	59.5	1.176326
61	61	1.188	1.195	1.298043	1.149	0.5167	1.041	1.175903	0.9099	0.7948	1.274	1.796189	1.231	0.2519	0.9672	58.0	1.164014
62	62	1.186	1.183	1.281207	1.121	0.5434	1.015	1.163668	0.8810	0.8383	1.251	1.764813	1.219	0.2635	0.9570	56.5	1.152282
63	63	1.185	1.171	1.265004	1.093	0.5718	0.9897	1.151997	0.8517	0.8848	1.228	1.734303	1.206	0.2756	0.9465	55.0	1.141107
64	64	1.183	1.159	1.249405	1.064	0.6020	0.9636	1.140869	0.8220	0.9346	1.205	1.704611	1.193	0.2884	0.9356	53.6	1.130466
65	65	1.182	1.146	1.234386	1.035	0.6342	0.9373	1.130262	0.7921	0.9883	1.181	1.675689	1.180	0.3018	0.9243	52.1	1.120340
66	66	1.180	1.133	1.219923	1.005	0.6687	0.9106	1.120158	0.7617	1.046	1.157	1.647491	1.166	0.3159	0.9125	50.6	1.110711
67	67	1.178	1.120	1.205992	0.9744	0.7056	0.8835	1.110539	0.7311	1.109	1.132	1.619975	1.152	0.3308	0.9003	49.2	1.101561
68	68	1.176	1.106	1.192574	0.9433	0.7454	0.8561	1.101389	0.7000	1.178	1.107	1.593097	1.137	0.3465	0.8876	47.7	1.092874
69	69	1.174	1.091	1.179649	0.9115	0.7884	0.8285	1.092694	0.6687	1.253	1.082	1.566816	1.121	0.3632	0.8743	46.2	1.084636
70	70	1.172	1.077	1.167198	0.8791	0.8350	0.8005	1.084438	0.6370	1.335	1.056	1.541091	1.105	0.3810	0.8605	44.8	1.076833
71	71	1.170	1.061	1.155204	0.8460	0.8858	0.7722	1.076610	0.6049	1.426	1.029	1.515881	1.088	0.4000	0.8460	43.3	1.069453
72	72	1.167	1.046	1.143653	0.8121	0.9414	0.7435	1.069197	0.5726	1.528	1.002	1.491148	1.070	0.4202	0.8308	41.8	1.062484
73	73	1.165	1.029	1.132528	0.7775	1.003	0.7146	1.062190	0.5399	1.642	0.9745	1.466849	1.051	0.4420	0.8148	40.3	1.055915
74	74	1.162	1.013	1.121816	0.7421	1.071	0.6855	1.055577	0.5069	1.771	0.9464	1.442942	1.032	0.4655	0.7979	38.7	1.049736
75	75	1.159	0.9950	1.111505	0.7059	1.147	0.6560	1.049351	0.4735	1.918	0.9177	1.419386	1.011	0.4911	0.7801	37.2	1.043940
76	76	1.155	0.9767	1.101583	0.6684	1.233	0.6262	1.043503	0.4399	2.088	0.8884	1.396133	0.9886	0.5189	0.7613	35.6	1.038518
77	77	1.152	0.9576	1.092039	0.6306	1.330	0.5963	1.038027	0.4059	2.286	0.8584	1.373135	0.9650	0.5496	0.7412	34.0	1.033463
78	78	1.148	0.9374	1.082864	0.5914	1.442	0.5661	1.032917	0.3717	2.522	0.8276	1.350338	0.9398	0.5836	0.7197	32.4	1.028769
79	79	1.144	0.9162	1.074049	0.5510	1.573	0.5357	1.028167	0.3371	2.806	0.7961	1.327682	0.9127	0.6216	0.6967	30.7	1.024431
80	80	1.139	0.8937	1.065586	0.5094	1.729	0.5051	1.023774	0.3023	3.156	0.7638	1.305098	0.8833	0.6647	0.6717	29.0	1.020444
81	81	1.134	0.8697	1.057469	0.4664	1.918	0.4744	1.019736	0.2673	3.598	0.7305	1.282504	0.8513	0.7142	0.6445	27.2	1.016805
82	82	1.128	0.8438	1.049693	0.4217	2.152	0.4436	1.016050	0.2321	4.174	0.6961	1.259798	0.8160	0.7722	0.6146	25.3	1.013513
83	83	1.122	0.8156	1.042254	0.3753	2.453	0.4129	1.012717	0.1968	4.954	0.6606	1.236854	0.7767	0.8417	0.5813	23.3	1.010565
84	84	1.114	0.7845	1.035150	0.3268	2.856	0.3824	1.009739	0.1616	6.070	0.6238	1.213501	0.7321	0.9276	0.5436	21.3	1.007963
85	85	1.105	0.7494	1.028382	0.2758	3.428	0.3525	1.007120	0.1267	7.781	0.5856	1.189500	0.6805	1.039	0.5001	19.0	1.005708
θ	θ	C_8	L_7	Ω_6	C_6	L_6	L_5	Ω_4	C_4	L_4	L_3	Ω_2	C_2	L_2	L_1	A_{min}	Ω_s

11.96

CO9 20*

11.97

θ / T	C_9	Ω_8	L_8	C_8	C_7	Ω_6	L_6	C_6	C_5	Ω_4	L_4	C_4	C_3	Ω_2	L_2	C_2	C_1	A_{min}	Ω_s
∞	1.349	∞	1.405	0.0000	2.274	∞	1.551	0.0000	2.339	∞	1.551	0.0000	2.274	∞	1.405	0.0000	1.349	∞	∞
36	1.233	2.494683	1.263	0.1273	1.949	1.722454	1.247	0.2703	1.934	1.916452	1.310	0.2078	2.067	4.543865	1.367	0.0354	1.318	116.1	1.701302
37	1.226	2.428228	1.254	0.1352	1.931	1.682023	1.230	0.2873	1.912	1.869159	1.297	0.2207	2.055	4.414407	1.365	0.0376	1.316	113.8	1.661640
38	1.219	2.365290	1.246	0.1435	1.912	1.643916	1.213	0.3050	1.889	1.824497	1.283	0.2341	2.043	4.291507	1.362	0.0399	1.315	111.5	1.624269
39	1.212	2.305598	1.237	0.1521	1.893	1.607957	1.196	0.3234	1.866	1.782266	1.269	0.2481	2.030	4.174652	1.360	0.0422	1.313	109.3	1.589016
40	1.204	2.248907	1.228	0.1610	1.874	1.573989	1.178	0.3426	1.842	1.742285	1.254	0.2626	2.017	4.063382	1.357	0.0446	1.310	107.2	1.555724
41	1.197	2.194997	1.219	0.1703	1.854	1.541869	1.160	0.3626	1.817	1.704392	1.240	0.2777	2.004	3.957281	1.355	0.0471	1.308	105.1	1.524253
42	1.189	2.143669	1.209	0.1800	1.834	1.511468	1.142	0.3834	1.792	1.668439	1.224	0.2934	1.991	3.855969	1.352	0.0498	1.306	103.0	1.494477
43	1.180	2.094742	1.199	0.1901	1.813	1.482668	1.123	0.4052	1.767	1.634294	1.209	0.3097	1.977	3.759105	1.349	0.0525	1.304	100.9	1.466279
44	1.172	2.048051	1.189	0.2005	1.792	1.455364	1.104	0.4278	1.741	1.601835	1.193	0.3267	1.963	3.666376	1.346	0.0553	1.301	98.9	1.439957
45	1.163	2.003447	1.178	0.2114	1.770	1.429460	1.084	0.4515	1.714	1.570952	1.177	0.3444	1.948	3.577497	1.343	0.0582	1.299	97.0	1.414214
46	1.154	1.960793	1.168	0.2228	1.748	1.404867	1.064	0.4762	1.687	1.541544	1.160	0.3628	1.934	3.492207	1.340	0.0612	1.296	95.0	1.390164
47	1.145	1.919963	1.157	0.2346	1.725	1.381504	1.044	0.5020	1.659	1.513520	1.143	0.3820	1.918	3.410268	1.336	0.0643	1.294	93.1	1.367327
48	1.135	1.880842	1.145	0.2468	1.702	1.359299	1.023	0.5289	1.631	1.486796	1.126	0.4019	1.903	3.331459	1.333	0.0676	1.291	91.2	1.345633
49	1.126	1.843326	1.134	0.2596	1.679	1.338183	1.002	0.5571	1.603	1.461293	1.108	0.4227	1.887	3.255578	1.329	0.0710	1.288	89.3	1.325013
50	1.116	1.807315	1.121	0.2730	1.655	1.318096	0.9811	0.5867	1.574	1.436942	1.090	0.4444	1.871	3.182438	1.326	0.0745	1.285	87.5	1.305407
51	1.105	1.772722	1.109	0.2869	1.631	1.298979	0.9595	0.6176	1.544	1.413677	1.071	0.4671	1.854	3.111865	1.322	0.0781	1.282	85.7	1.286760
52	1.094	1.739462	1.096	0.3014	1.606	1.280780	0.9377	0.6501	1.514	1.391438	1.052	0.4908	1.837	3.043699	1.318	0.0819	1.279	83.9	1.269018
53	1.083	1.707460	1.083	0.3166	1.581	1.263452	0.9155	0.6843	1.484	1.370170	1.033	0.5155	1.820	2.977790	1.314	0.0858	1.275	82.1	1.252136
54	1.072	1.676644	1.070	0.3324	1.555	1.246949	0.8930	0.7202	1.453	1.349821	1.014	0.5414	1.802	2.914000	1.310	0.0899	1.272	80.4	1.236068
55	1.060	1.646949	1.056	0.3490	1.529	1.231230	0.8703	0.7580	1.421	1.330344	0.9939	0.5685	1.784	2.852198	1.305	0.0942	1.268	78.6	1.220775
56	1.048	1.618313	1.042	0.3664	1.502	1.216257	0.8472	0.7979	1.389	1.311695	0.9737	0.5969	1.765	2.792263	1.301	0.0986	1.265	76.9	1.206218
57	1.036	1.590678	1.028	0.3846	1.476	1.201995	0.8239	0.8401	1.357	1.293834	0.9531	0.6268	1.746	2.734079	1.296	0.1032	1.261	75.2	1.192363
58	1.023	1.563993	1.013	0.4037	1.448	1.188411	0.8003	0.8847	1.324	1.276723	0.9321	0.6582	1.726	2.677540	1.291	0.1080	1.257	73.5	1.179178
59	1.010	1.538206	0.9974	0.4238	1.420	1.175475	0.7764	0.9321	1.291	1.260327	0.9108	0.6912	1.707	2.622544	1.286	0.1131	1.253	71.8	1.166633
60	0.9959	1.513271	0.9816	0.4449	1.392	1.163158	0.7523	0.9825	1.257	1.244613	0.8891	0.7261	1.686	2.568993	1.281	0.1183	1.248	70.1	1.154701

TABLE 11-56 Elliptic-Function *LC* Element Values (*Continued*)

Handwritten note (top): resonant freq $= \dfrac{1}{\sqrt{L_2 C_2}},\ \dfrac{1}{\sqrt{L_4 C_4}},\ \dfrac{1}{\sqrt{L_6 C_6}}$

$\theta = T$	C_9	Ω_8	L_8	C_8	C_7	Ω_6	L_6	C_6	C_5	Ω_4	L_4	C_4	C_3	Ω_2	L_2	C_2	C_1	A_{min}	Ω_s
∞	1.349	∞	1.405	0.0000	2.274	∞	1.551	0.0000	2.339	∞	1.551	0.0000	2.274	∞	1.405	0.0000	1.349	∞	∞
61	0.9817	1.489144	0.9654	0.4671	1.363	1.151435	0.7279	1.036	1.223	1.229551	0.8670	0.7629	1.666	2.516797	1.275	0.1238	1.244	68.5	1.143354
62	0.9671	1.465786	0.9487	0.4906	1.334	1.140280	0.7033	1.093	1.189	1.215114	0.8446	0.8019	1.644	2.465867	1.269	0.1296	1.239	66.8	1.132570
63	0.9520	1.443156	0.9315	0.5155	1.305	1.129672	0.6785	1.155	1.154	1.201275	0.8217	0.8433	1.623	2.416121	1.263	0.1356	1.234	65.2	1.122326
64	0.9364	1.421219	0.9138	0.5418	1.275	1.119590	0.6534	1.221	1.119	1.188009	0.7985	0.8873	1.600	2.367476	1.257	0.1420	1.229	63.5	1.112602
65	0.9202	1.399940	0.8956	0.5698	1.244	1.110013	0.6281	1.292	1.083	1.175295	0.7749	0.9342	1.578	2.319854	1.250	0.1487	1.223	61.9	1.103378
66	0.9034	1.379288	0.8768	0.5995	1.213	1.100924	0.6026	1.369	1.047	1.163112	0.7509	0.9844	1.554	2.273180	1.243	0.1557	1.217	60.2	1.094636
67	0.8860	1.359230	0.8574	0.6313	1.182	1.092306	0.5769	1.453	1.011	1.151440	0.7265	1.038	1.531	2.227378	1.236	0.1631	1.211	58.6	1.086360
68	0.8679	1.339739	0.8374	0.6653	1.150	1.084144	0.5510	1.544	0.9738	1.140260	0.7017	1.096	1.506	2.182375	1.228	0.1710	1.205	56.9	1.078535
69	0.8491	1.320787	0.8167	0.7019	1.118	1.076422	0.5250	1.644	0.9367	1.129558	0.6764	1.159	1.481	2.138097	1.220	0.1793	1.198	55.2	1.071145
70	0.8294	1.302346	0.7953	0.7413	1.085	1.069128	0.4987	1.754	0.8992	1.119316	0.6507	1.227	1.455	2.094470	1.211	0.1882	1.191	53.6	1.064178
71	0.8089	1.284392	0.7732	0.7840	1.052	1.062248	0.4723	1.876	0.8614	1.109521	0.6245	1.301	1.429	2.051420	1.202	0.1977	1.184	51.9	1.057621
72	0.7875	1.266900	0.7503	0.8304	1.018	1.055772	0.4457	2.013	0.8233	1.100160	0.5979	1.382	1.401	2.008869	1.192	0.2078	1.176	50.2	1.051462
73	0.7650	1.249847	0.7265	0.8812	0.9841	1.049686	0.4190	2.166	0.7849	1.091222	0.5708	1.471	1.373	1.966738	1.182	0.2187	1.167	48.5	1.045692
74	0.7414	1.233209	0.7017	0.9370	0.9494	1.043989	0.3922	2.339	0.7463	1.082695	0.5432	1.571	1.344	1.924942	1.171	0.2305	1.158	46.8	1.040299
75	0.7165	1.216966	0.6760	0.9988	0.9141	1.038663	0.3652	2.538	0.7073	1.074570	0.5150	1.682	1.314	1.883393	1.159	0.2433	1.148	45.1	1.035276
76	0.6902	1.201093	0.6491	1.068	0.8782	1.033703	0.3381	2.768	0.6681	1.066839	0.4862	1.807	1.283	1.841992	1.146	0.2572	1.137	43.3	1.030614
77	0.6622	1.185571	0.6211	1.146	0.8418	1.029101	0.3110	3.036	0.6287	1.059494	0.4569	1.950	1.251	1.800631	1.132	0.2724	1.126	41.5	1.026304
78	0.6323	1.170376	0.5917	1.234	0.8048	1.024852	0.2838	3.355	0.5891	1.052550	0.4268	2.115	1.218	1.759188	1.117	0.2893	1.113	39.6	1.022341
79	0.6004	1.155487	0.5607	1.336	0.7669	1.020948	0.2564	3.741	0.5493	1.045943	0.3961	2.308	1.183	1.717524	1.100	0.3081	1.099	37.7	1.018717
80	0.5658	1.140881	0.5281	1.455	0.7286	1.017385	0.2291	4.216	0.5094	1.039728	0.3645	2.538	1.146	1.675471	1.082	0.3292	1.084	35.8	1.015427
81	0.5281	1.126534	0.4935	1.597	0.6895	1.014158	0.2019	4.817	0.4693	1.033885	0.3321	2.817	1.108	1.632828	1.061	0.3534	1.067	33.8	1.012465
82	0.4868	1.112418	0.4567	1.770	0.6497	1.011264	0.1746	5.599	0.4293	1.028414	0.2986	3.166	1.067	1.589344	1.038	0.3814	1.047	31.7	1.009828
83	0.4407	1.098505	0.4172	1.986	0.6090	1.008700	0.1476	6.660	0.3894	1.023319	0.2641	3.616	1.024	1.544692	1.011	0.4145	1.025	29.5	1.007510
84	0.3886	1.084760	0.3747	2.268	0.5676	1.006464	0.1208	8.175	0.3496	1.018605	0.2282	4.223	0.9782	1.498431	0.9794	0.4548	0.9995	27.1	1.005508
85	0.3281	1.071141	0.3283	2.655	0.5253	1.004554	0.0944	10.50	0.3103	1.014284	0.1909	5.093	0.9284	1.449932	0.9411	0.5054	0.9688	24.6	1.003820

Alternate (dual-ladder) column labels read along the bottom of the table: L_9, C_8, L_7, C_6, L_5, C_4, L_3, C_2, L_1, A_{min}, Ω_s, θ, T.

(Schematic at bottom: ladder network with series elements L_1, L_3, L_5, L_7, L_9 (paralleled by C_1, C_3, C_5, C_7, C_9) and shunt elements C_2, C_4, C_6, C_8 (with L_2, L_4, L_6, L_8); input/output ports labeled $10 \rightarrow$; nodes numbered 1 through 9.)

* Reprinted from R. Saal and E. Ulbrich, "On the Design of Filters by Synthesis," *IRE Transactions on Circuit Theory*, December 1958.

C10 20 b*

Filter schematic with termination resistances 1.0 and 0.6667; element sections numbered 1 2 3 4 5 6 7 8 9 10.

Response diagram labels: A, R_{dB}, A_{min}, $\Omega_2\ \Omega_4\ \Omega_6\ \Omega_8$, axis Ω with points 0, 1, Ω_s, 8.

θ	A_{min}	C_1	C_2	L_2	Ω_2	C_3	C_4	L_4	Ω_4	C_5	C_6	L_6	Ω_6	C_7	C_8	L_8	Ω_8	C_9	L_{10}	Ω_s	θ
T	∞	1.353	0.0000	1.410	∞	2.283	0.0000	1.559	∞	2.357	0.0000	1.571	∞	2.338	0.0000	1.522	∞	2.114	0.9019	∞	T
46	108.4	1.267	0.0953	1.304	2.837237	1.908	0.3703	1.158	1.526953	1.702	0.4577	1.092	1.414442	1.787	0.2327	1.258	1.848119	1.913	0.9056	1.402036	46
47	106.3	1.263	0.1002	1.298	2.772462	1.891	0.3898	1.141	1.494419	1.674	0.4823	1.072	1.390741	1.763	0.2448	1.246	1.810618	1.904	0.9058	1.378775	47
48	104.2	1.258	0.1053	1.293	2.710218	1.874	0.4102	1.123	1.473170	1.646	0.5079	1.052	1.368207	1.738	0.2574	1.233	1.774719	1.894	0.9059	1.356667	48
49	102.1	1.254	0.1106	1.287	2.650344	1.857	0.4315	1.105	1.448130	1.617	0.5347	1.031	1.346772	1.714	0.2705	1.221	1.740324	1.885	0.9061	1.335647	49
50	100.1	1.249	0.1161	1.282	2.592690	1.839	0.4536	1.087	1.424228	1.588	0.5628	1.010	1.326374	1.688	0.2841	1.208	1.707343	1.874	0.9063	1.315651	50
51	98.1	1.244	0.1218	1.276	2.537118	1.821	0.4767	1.068	1.401400	1.558	0.5921	0.9887	1.306956	1.663	0.2983	1.194	1.675693	1.864	0.9064	1.296624	51
52	96.1	1.239	0.1277	1.270	2.483501	1.802	0.5009	1.049	1.379588	1.528	0.6229	0.9670	1.288463	1.636	0.3130	1.180	1.645296	1.853	0.9066	1.278514	52
53	94.1	1.234	0.1339	1.263	2.431720	1.783	0.5262	1.029	1.358736	1.497	0.6552	0.9450	1.270848	1.610	0.3284	1.166	1.616083	1.842	0.9068	1.261271	53
54	92.2	1.229	0.1403	1.257	2.381665	1.763	0.5526	1.010	1.338794	1.466	0.6891	0.9227	1.254066	1.582	0.3444	1.151	1.587987	1.831	0.9069	1.244851	54
55	90.2	1.223	0.1470	1.250	2.333233	1.743	0.5803	0.9895	1.319714	1.434	0.7247	0.9002	1.238073	1.555	0.3611	1.136	1.560947	1.820	0.9071	1.229214	55
56	88.3	1.217	0.1539	1.243	2.286327	1.723	0.6093	0.9689	1.301455	1.402	0.7623	0.8773	1.222833	1.527	0.3786	1.121	1.534907	1.808	0.9073	1.214321	56
57	86.4	1.211	0.1612	1.236	2.240858	1.702	0.6398	0.9481	1.283976	1.369	0.8019	0.8541	1.208310	1.498	0.3969	1.105	1.509814	1.795	0.9075	1.200137	57
58	84.5	1.205	0.1687	1.228	2.196740	1.681	0.6719	0.9268	1.267239	1.336	0.8437	0.8307	1.194469	1.469	0.4160	1.089	1.485619	1.783	0.9077	1.186629	58
59	82.7	1.198	0.1767	1.220	2.153895	1.659	0.7056	0.9052	1.251211	1.303	0.8880	0.8070	1.181281	1.439	0.4360	1.073	1.462275	1.770	0.9079	1.173768	59
60	80.8	1.192	0.1849	1.212	2.112247	1.637	0.7412	0.8833	1.235859	1.269	0.9350	0.7830	1.168718	1.409	0.4570	1.056	1.439742	1.757	0.9081	1.161525	60
61	79.0	1.185	0.1936	1.204	2.071724	1.614	0.7789	0.8610	1.221153	1.234	0.9850	0.7587	1.156752	1.378	0.4790	1.038	1.417977	1.743	0.9083	1.149873	61
62	77.1	1.177	0.2026	1.195	2.032259	1.591	0.8187	0.8383	1.207066	1.199	1.038	0.7342	1.145359	1.347	0.5022	1.020	1.396945	1.729	0.9085	1.138790	62
63	75.3	1.170	0.2121	1.186	1.993787	1.567	0.8610	0.8153	1.193573	1.164	1.095	0.7095	1.134517	1.316	0.5267	1.002	1.376609	1.715	0.9087	1.128252	63
64	73.4	1.162	0.2221	1.176	1.956247	1.543	0.9059	0.7919	1.180648	1.129	1.156	0.6845	1.124204	1.284	0.5525	0.9831	1.356938	1.700	0.9089	1.118238	64
65	71.6	1.154	0.2327	1.166	1.919579	1.518	0.9538	0.7682	1.168271	1.093	1.221	0.6593	1.114401	1.251	0.5797	0.9636	1.337900	1.684	0.9091	1.108729	65

TABLE 11-56 Elliptic-Function LC Element Values (*Continued*)

θ	Ω_s	A_min	C_1	C_2	L_2	Ω_2	C_3	C_4	L_4	Ω_4	C_5	C_6	L_6	Ω_6	C_7	C_8	L_8	Ω_8	C_9	L_10	θ
T	∞	∞	1.353	0.0000	1.410	∞	2.283	0.0000	1.559	∞	2.357	0.0000	1.571	∞	2.338	0.0000	1.522	∞	2.114	0.9019	T
66	1.099707	69.8	1.145	0.2438	1.156	1.883725	1.493	1.005	0.7440	1.156420	1.056	1.292	0.6338	1.105088	1.218	0.6087	0.9437	1.319465	1.669	0.9093	66
67	1.091154	67.9	1.136	0.2555	1.145	1.848630	1.467	1.060	0.7195	1.145077	1.019	1.368	0.6082	1.096250	1.184	0.6394	0.9231	1.301607	1.652	0.9095	67
68	1.083056	66.1	1.127	0.2679	1.134	1.814240	1.440	1.119	0.6946	1.134223	0.9820	1.451	0.5823	1.087871	1.150	0.6721	0.9020	1.284300	1.635	0.9097	68
69	1.075399	64.3	1.117	0.2810	1.122	1.780499	1.413	1.183	0.6694	1.123842	0.9444	1.542	0.5562	1.079935	1.115	0.7071	0.8802	1.267519	1.618	0.9099	69
70	1.068167	62.4	1.106	0.2951	1.110	1.747356	1.385	1.252	0.6437	1.113920	0.9063	1.641	0.5299	1.072430	1.079	0.7446	0.8578	1.251241	1.600	0.9101	70
71	1.061350	60.5	1.095	0.3100	1.097	1.714757	1.356	1.327	0.6176	1.104442	0.8680	1.750	0.5034	1.065342	1.043	0.7850	0.8346	1.235443	1.581	0.9103	71
72	1.054935	58.7	1.084	0.3260	1.083	1.682648	1.327	1.410	0.5911	1.095394	0.8292	1.871	0.4768	1.058661	1.007	0.8287	0.8106	1.220106	1.562	0.9105	72
73	1.048912	56.8	1.071	0.3432	1.069	1.650973	1.297	1.501	0.5642	1.086767	0.7901	2.007	0.4500	1.052375	0.9696	0.8760	0.7859	1.205209	1.542	0.9107	73
74	1.043271	54.9	1.058	0.3618	1.054	1.619676	1.265	1.601	0.5368	1.078548	0.7506	2.159	0.4229	1.046476	0.9317	0.9277	0.7602	1.190733	1.521	0.9109	74
75	1.038003	52.9	1.045	0.3870	1.031	1.583010	1.245	1.716	0.5086	1.070450	0.7126	2.324	0.3972	1.040840	0.8909	0.9766	0.7408	1.175676	1.494	0.9111	75
θ	Ω_s	A_min	L_1	L_2	C_2	Ω_2	L_3	L_4	C_4	Ω_4	L_5	L_6	C_6	Ω_6	L_7	L_8	C_8	Ω_8	L_9	C_10	θ

Circuit (ladder network): input 1.0 — series inductors L_1, L_3, L_5, L_7, L_9 — shunt resonant arms L_2/C_2, L_4/C_4, L_6/C_6, L_8/C_8 and shunt capacitor C_{10} — output 1.500, nodes 0–10.

* Reprinted from R. Saal and E. Ulbrich, "On the Design of Filters by Synthesis," *IRE Transactions on Circuit Theory*, December 1958.

Ladder network schematic and attenuation response diagram (labels: Ω_6 Ω_4 Ω_8 Ω_2, A_{min}, A, R_{dB}, $1\ \Omega_s$, 0, ∞, $\Omega \rightarrow$, 1.0).

θ (T)	Ω_s	A_{min}	C_1	C_2	L_2	Ω_2	C_3	C_4	L_4	Ω_4	C_5	C_6	L_6	Ω_6	C_7	C_8	L_8	Ω_8	C_9	L_{10}	θ (T)
T		∞	1.248	0.0000	1.513	∞	2.033	0.0000	1.809	∞	1.957	0.0000	1.957	∞	1.809	0.0000	2.033	∞	1.513	1.248	T
46	1.414011	108.4	1.154	0.0853	1.413	2.880291	1.692	0.3083	1.364	1.542102	1.421	0.3593	1.367	1.426739	1.401	0.1712	1.669	1.870799	1.382	1.236	46
47	1.390318	106.3	1.149	0.0896	1.408	2.814916	1.677	0.3244	1.344	1.514114	1.398	0.3787	1.342	1.402604	1.383	0.1802	1.652	1.832802	1.375	1.235	47
48	1.367792	104.2	1.144	0.0941	1.403	2.752107	1.661	0.3412	1.325	1.487423	1.375	0.3988	1.317	1.379650	1.365	0.1895	1.635	1.796425	1.369	1.234	48
49	1.346366	102.1	1.139	0.0987	1.398	2.691699	1.645	0.3587	1.304	1.461955	1.352	0.4199	1.292	1.357807	1.346	0.1992	1.618	1.761569	1.363	1.233	49
50	1.325976	100.1	1.134	0.1035	1.392	2.633543	1.629	0.3769	1.284	1.437637	1.328	0.4419	1.266	1.337012	1.327	0.2093	1.600	1.728142	1.356	1.233	50
51	1.306565	98.1	1.129	0.1085	1.387	2.577498	1.613	0.3959	1.263	1.414404	1.303	0.4650	1.240	1.317206	1.308	0.2198	1.582	1.696060	1.349	1.232	51
52	1.288080	96.1	1.125	0.1137	1.381	2.523435	1.596	0.4157	1.241	1.392196	1.279	0.4891	1.213	1.298337	1.289	0.2307	1.563	1.665246	1.342	1.232	52
53	1.270472	94.1	1.118	0.1191	1.375	2.471234	1.579	0.4364	1.219	1.370959	1.253	0.5145	1.186	1.280355	1.269	0.2422	1.544	1.635627	1.335	1.230	53
54	1.253696	92.2	1.112	0.1247	1.369	2.420784	1.561	0.4580	1.197	1.350640	1.228	0.5411	1.158	1.263213	1.248	0.2541	1.524	1.607137	1.328	1.229	54
55	1.237711	90.2	1.106	0.1305	1.362	2.371980	1.543	0.4806	1.174	1.331192	1.202	0.5691	1.130	1.246870	1.228	0.2665	1.503	1.579712	1.320	1.228	55
56	1.222478	88.3	1.100	0.1365	1.356	2.324726	1.525	0.5043	1.151	1.312572	1.175	0.5986	1.102	1.231287	1.206	0.2795	1.483	1.553297	1.312	1.227	56
57	1.207961	86.4	1.093	0.1428	1.349	2.278929	1.506	0.5292	1.127	1.294738	1.149	0.6297	1.073	1.216427	1.185	0.2931	1.461	1.527838	1.304	1.226	57
58	1.194127	84.5	1.087	0.1493	1.342	2.234505	1.487	0.5553	1.103	1.277654	1.121	0.6626	1.044	1.202258	1.163	0.3074	1.440	1.503284	1.296	1.225	58
59	1.180946	82.7	1.080	0.1561	1.334	2.191372	1.467	0.5827	1.079	1.261283	1.094	0.6973	1.015	1.188747	1.141	0.3223	1.417	1.479589	1.287	1.224	59
60	1.168389	80.8	1.073	0.1632	1.326	2.149455	1.447	0.6116	1.054	1.245594	1.066	0.7342	0.9851	1.175867	1.118	0.3380	1.394	1.456709	1.278	1.223	60
61	1.156430	79.0	1.065	0.1706	1.318	2.108681	1.427	0.6420	1.029	1.230556	1.038	0.7733	0.9551	1.163590	1.095	0.3544	1.371	1.434604	1.269	1.221	61
62	1.145044	77.1	1.057	0.1783	1.310	2.068982	1.406	0.6743	1.003	1.216141	1.009	0.8150	0.9247	1.151891	1.072	0.3717	1.347	1.413236	1.260	1.220	62
63	1.134209	75.3	1.049	0.1864	1.301	2.030293	1.385	0.7084	0.9766	1.202323	0.9801	0.8595	0.8940	1.140748	1.048	0.3900	1.322	1.392568	1.251	1.219	63
64	1.123902	73.4	1.041	0.1949	1.292	1.992550	1.363	0.7446	0.9499	1.189078	0.9508	0.9073	0.8630	1.130139	1.024	0.4093	1.297	1.372567	1.241	1.217	64
65	1.114106	71.6	1.032	0.2038	1.283	1.955693	1.341	0.7831	0.9227	1.176383	0.9211	0.9585	0.8317	1.120044	0.9991	0.4297	1.271	1.353202	1.230	1.216	65
66	1.104800	69.8	1.023	0.2131	1.273	1.919665	1.318	0.8242	0.8951	1.164217	0.8911	1.014	0.8001	1.110444	0.9740	0.4514	1.244	1.334441	1.220	1.214	66
67	1.095969	67.9	1.014	0.2230	1.263	1.884408	1.295	0.8682	0.8670	1.152560	0.8607	1.073	0.7682	1.101323	0.9485	0.4744	1.217	1.316257	1.209	1.212	67
68	1.087597	66.1	1.004	0.2334	1.252	1.849867	1.272	0.9155	0.8384	1.141395	0.8300	1.138	0.7361	1.092664	0.9226	0.4989	1.189	1.298624	1.198	1.211	68
69	1.079669	64.3	0.9952	0.2444	1.241	1.815988	1.247	0.9664	0.8094	1.130704	0.7989	1.209	0.7036	1.084453	0.8962	0.5252	1.159	1.281515	1.186	1.209	69
70	1.072171	62.4	0.9823	0.2560	1.229	1.782715	1.223	1.021	0.7798	1.120472	0.7676	1.286	0.6709	1.076676	0.8693	0.5533	1.130	1.264906	1.174	1.207	70

Handwritten annotations (element labels): L_1 L_x C_0 · L_3 C_4 · L_5 L_6 C_6 · L_7 L_8 C_8 · L_9 C_{10}

TABLE 11-56 Elliptic-Function LC Element Values (*Continued*)

θ	Ω_s	A_min	C_1	C_2	L_2	Ω_2	C_3	C_4	L_4	Ω_4	C_5	C_6	L_6	Ω_6	C_7	C_8	L_8	Ω_8	C_9	L_10	θ
T	∞	∞	1.248	0.0000	1.513	∞	2.033	0.0000	1.809	∞	1.957	0.0000	1.957	∞	1.809	0.0000	2.033	∞	1.513	1.248	T
71	1.065092	60.5	0.9709	0.2684	1.216	1.749995	1.197	1.081	0.7496	1.110685	0.7358	1.371	0.6378	1.069320	0.8419	0.5836	1.099	1.248774	1.162	1.205	71
72	1.058418	58.7	0.9588	0.2817	1.203	1.717773	1.171	1.147	0.7189	1.101329	0.7038	1.465	0.6046	1.062375	0.8141	0.6163	1.067	1.233098	1.149	1.202	72
73	1.052141	56.8	0.9461	0.2958	1.189	1.685990	1.144	1.219	0.6877	1.092393	0.6715	1.570	0.5714	1.055828	0.7857	0.6518	1.034	1.217855	1.135	1.200	73
74	1.046250	54.9	0.9326	0.3110	1.174	1.654590	1.117	1.298	0.6558	1.083865	0.6887	1.692	0.5365	1.049671	0.7567	0.6906	1.000	1.203026	1.121	1.197	74
75	1.040737	52.9	0.9215	0.3329	1.151	1.615393	1.087	1.396	0.6196	1.075199	0.6033	1.848	0.4968	1.043669	0.7232	0.7369	0.9633	1.186858	1.101	1.194	75
θ	Ω_s	A_min	L_1	L_2	C_2	Ω_2	L_3	L_4	C_4	Ω_4	L_5	L_6	C_6	Ω_6	L_7	L_8	C_8	Ω_8	L_9	C_10	θ

1.0 →   ← 1.0   1:0

1 2 3 4 5 6 7 8 9 10

* Reprinted from R. Saal and E. Ulbrich, "On the Design of Filters by Synthesis," *IRE Transactions on Circuit Theory*, December 1958.

TABLE 11-56 Elliptic-Function LC Element Values (*Continued*)

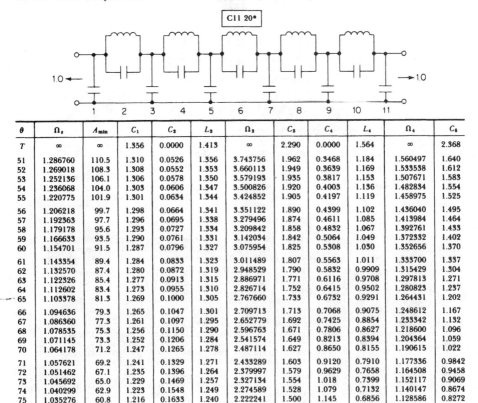

θ	Ω_s	A_{min}	C_1	C_2	L_2	Ω_2	C_3	C_4	L_4	Ω_4	C_5
T	∞	∞	1.356	0.0000	1.413	∞	2.290	0.0000	1.564	∞	2.368
51	1.286760	110.5	1.310	0.0526	1.356	3.743756	1.962	0.3468	1.184	1.560497	1.640
52	1.269018	108.3	1.308	0.0552	1.353	3.660113	1.949	0.3639	1.169	1.533538	1.612
53	1.252136	106.1	1.306	0.0578	1.350	3.579193	1.935	0.3817	1.153	1.507671	1.583
54	1.236068	104.0	1.303	0.0606	1.347	3.500826	1.920	0.4003	1.136	1.482834	1.554
55	1.220775	101.9	1.301	0.0634	1.344	3.424852	1.905	0.4197	1.119	1.458975	1.525
56	1.206218	99.7	1.298	0.0664	1.341	3.351122	1.890	0.4399	1.102	1.436040	1.495
57	1.192363	97.7	1.296	0.0695	1.338	3.279496	1.874	0.4611	1.085	1.413984	1.464
58	1.179178	95.6	1.293	0.0727	1.334	3.209842	1.858	0.4832	1.067	1.392761	1.433
59	1.166633	93.5	1.290	0.0761	1.331	3.142034	1.842	0.5064	1.049	1.372332	1.402
60	1.154701	91.5	1.287	0.0796	1.327	3.075954	1.825	0.5308	1.030	1.352656	1.370
61	1.143354	89.4	1.284	0.0833	1.323	3.011489	1.807	0.5563	1.011	1.333700	1.337
62	1.132570	87.4	1.280	0.0872	1.319	2.948529	1.790	0.5832	0.9909	1.315429	1.304
63	1.122326	85.4	1.277	0.0913	1.315	2.886971	1.771	0.6116	0.9708	1.297813	1.271
64	1.112602	83.4	1.273	0.0955	1.310	2.826714	1.752	0.6415	0.9502	1.280823	1.237
65	1.103378	81.3	1.269	0.1000	1.305	2.767660	1.733	0.6732	0.9291	1.264431	1.202
66	1.094636	79.3	1.265	0.1047	1.301	2.709713	1.713	0.7068	0.9075	1.248612	1.167
67	1.086360	77.3	1.261	0.1097	1.295	2.652779	1.692	0.7425	0.8854	1.233342	1.132
68	1.078535	75.3	1.256	0.1150	1.290	2.596763	1.671	0.7806	0.8627	1.218600	1.096
69	1.071145	73.3	1.252	0.1206	1.284	2.541574	1.649	0.8213	0.8394	1.204364	1.059
70	1.064178	71.2	1.247	0.1265	1.278	2.487114	1.627	0.8650	0.8155	1.190615	1.022
71	1.057621	69.2	1.241	0.1329	1.271	2.433289	1.603	0.9120	0.7910	1.177336	0.9842
72	1.051462	67.1	1.235	0.1396	1.264	2.379997	1.579	0.9629	0.7658	1.164508	0.9458
73	1.045692	65.0	1.229	0.1469	1.257	2.327134	1.554	1.018	0.7399	1.152117	0.9069
74	1.040299	62.9	1.223	0.1548	1.249	2.274589	1.528	1.079	0.7132	1.140147	0.8674
75	1.035276	60.8	1.216	0.1633	1.240	2.222241	1.500	1.145	0.6856	1.128586	0.8272
θ	Ω_s	A_{min}	L_1	L_2	C_2	Ω_2	L_3	L_4	C_4	Ω_4	L_5

* Reprinted from R. Saal and E. Ulbrich, "On the Design of Filters by Synthesis," *IRE Transactions on Circuit Theory,* December 1958.

TABLE 11-56   Elliptic-Function LC Element Values (*Continued*)

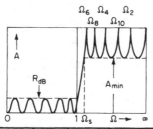

C_6	L_6	Ω_6	C_7	C_8	L_8	Ω_8	C_9	C_{10}	L_{10}	Ω_{10}	C_{11}	θ
0.0000	1.583	∞	2.368	0.0000	1.564	∞	2.290	0.0000	1.413	∞	1.356	T
0.6038	0.9877	1.294892	1.536	0.5121	1.045	1.367227	1.752	0.1984	1.198	2.051040	1.180	51
0.6351	0.9657	1.276846	1.505	0.5382	1.025	1.346576	1.730	0.2083	1.188	2.010050	1.172	52
0.6680	0.9434	1.259666	1.474	0.5656	1.004	1.326857	1.708	0.2185	1.179	1.970531	1.164	53
0.7025	0.9209	1.243308	1.441	0.5942	0.9837	1.308019	1.686	0.2292	1.168	1.932394	1.155	54
0.7388	0.8980	1.227731	1.409	0.6242	0.9628	1.290019	1.663	0.2403	1.158	1.895562	1.147	55
0.7770	0.8748	1.212897	1.376	0.6556	0.9415	1.272815	1.640	0.2520	1.147	1.859959	1.137	56
0.8173	0.8514	1.198770	1.342	0.6887	0.9198	1.256369	1.616	0.2641	1.136	1.825515	1.128	57
0.8599	0.8277	1.185319	1.308	0.7236	0.8979	1.240644	1.592	0.2769	1.125	1.792167	1.118	58
0.9050	0.8037	1.172513	1.274	0.7603	0.8756	1.225607	1.567	0.2902	1.113	1.759852	1.108	59
0.9528	0.7795	1.160324	1.239	0.7991	0.8530	1.211229	1.542	0.3042	1.100	1.728513	1.098	60
1.004	0.7551	1.148726	1.204	0.8402	0.8300	1.197480	1.516	0.3188	1.088	1.698097	1.087	61
1.058	0.7304	1.137695	1.169	0.8837	0.8067	1.184335	1.490	0.3342	1.075	1.668552	1.076	62
1.116	0.7055	1.127208	1.133	0.9300	0.7831	1.171767	1.463	0.3505	1.061	1.639830	1.065	63
1.178	0.6803	1.117245	1.096	0.9793	0.7592	1.159755	1.436	0.3676	1.047	1.611885	1.053	64
1.244	0.6549	1.107094	1.059	1.032	0.7349	1.148278	1.408	0.3857	1.032	1.584674	1.040	65
1.316	0.6294	1.098813	1.022	1.088	0.7103	1.137315	1.380	0.4049	1.017	1.558153	1.027	66
1.394	0.6036	1.090309	0.9849	1.149	0.6854	1.126849	1.351	0.4252	1.002	1.532284	1.014	67
1.478	0.5777	1.082259	0.9470	1.214	0.6602	1.116862	1.321	0.4468	0.9854	1.507028	0.9994	68
1.570	0.5515	1.074648	0.9089	1.285	0.6346	1.107340	1.291	0.4699	0.9685	1.482346	0.9846	69
1.671	0.5252	1.067462	0.8704	1.362	0.6087	1.098266	1.260	0.4946	0.9508	1.458204	0.9692	70
1.782	0.4988	1.060691	0.8316	1.446	0.5824	1.089629	1.228	0.5212	0.9323	1.434564	0.9530	71
1.905	0.4721	1.054321	0.7924	1.538	0.5558	1.081416	1.196	0.5498	0.9131	1.411392	0.9359	72
2.043	0.4454	1.048342	0.7530	1.640	0.5289	1.073617	1.162	0.5808	0.8929	1.388652	0.9179	73
2.198	0.4185	1.042744	0.7133	1.754	0.5016	1.066220	1.128	0.6145	0.8717	1.366309	0.8986	74
2.373	0.3914	1.037520	0.6733	1.881	0.4739	1.059218	1.093	0.6515	0.8493	1.344327	0.8788	75
L_6	C_6	Ω_6	L_7	L_8	C_8	Ω_8	L_9	L_{10}	C_{10}	Ω_{10}	L_{11}	θ

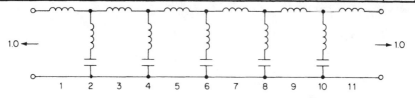

TABLE 11-56 Elliptic-Function *LC* Element Values (*Continued*)

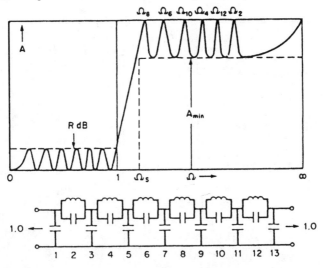

C13 05

Ω_s	A_{min}	C_1	C_2	L_2	Ω_2	C_3	C_4	L_4	Ω_4	C_5	C_6	L_6	Ω_6
1.0025	31.0	.61853	.26993	1.1251	1.8146	.92129	2.1719	.41706	1.0507	.35225	7.5421	.1312	1.0054
1.005	37.0	.64087	.22388	1.1728	1.9516	.99774	1.6854	.51699	1.0713	.42885	5.1475	.19059	1.0096
1.010	45.0	.67974	.18127	1.2246	2.1225	1.0950	1.2970	.63589	1.10113	.53277	3.5287	.27383	1.0173
1.015	50.3	.69701	.15876	1.2516	2.2433	1.1526	1.1098	.71228	1.1248	.60484	2.8432	.33510	1.0245
1.020	54.5	.70916	.14365	1.2702	2.3411	1.1953	.99005	.77013	1.1452	.66225	2.4383	.38553	1.0314
1.025	58.0	.71734	.13244	1.2839	2.4251	1.2286	.90388	.81694	1.1637	.71017	2.1632	.42895	1.0381
1.030	61.0	.72224	.12365	1.2942	2.4998	1.2553	.83747	.85635	1.1808	.75123	1.9603	.46742	1.0447
1.035	64.0	.73455	.11615	1.3057	2.5678	1.2841	.78305	.89143	1.1969	.79081	1.8007	.5026	1.0512
1.040	66.3	.73385	.11017	1.3115	2.6308	1.3013	.73867	.92134	1.2122	.82225	1.6739	.53417	1.0575
1.045	68.7	.74040	.10479	1.3190	2.6897	1.3218	.70024	.94890	1.2268	.85375	1.5671	.56384	1.0638
Ω_s	A_{min}	L_1	L_2	C_2	Ω_2	L_3	L_4	C_4	Ω_4	L_5	L_6	C_6	Ω_6

C_7	C_8	L_8	Ω_8	C_9	C_{10}	L_{10}	Ω_{10}	C_{11}	C_{12}	L_{12}	Ω_{12}	C_{13}
.15977	11.273	.088223	1.0028	.21860	4.7791	.20298	1.0153	.59824	1.4398	.49583	1.1835	.09888
.21320	7.2035	.13733	1.0054	.27866	3.4419	.27699	1.0242	.66555	1.1143	.59001	1.2333	.18466
.29301	4.6620	.21000	1.0117	.36511	2.4672	.37583	1.0385	.75813	.84247	.70324	1.2992	.29116
.35402	3.6504	.26543	1.0159	.42910	2.0369	.44461	1.0508	.81995	.71513	.76963	1.3479	.34621
.40548	3.0736	.31204	1.0211	.48202	1.7752	.49943	1.0620	.86844	.63416	.81800	1.3885	.38504
.45022	2.6910	.35283	1.0263	.52748	1.5936	.54545	1.0726	.90812	.57654	.85540	1.4240	.41364
.49007	2.4142	.38935	1.0314	.56739	1.4578	.58528	1.0826	.94133	.53275	.88535	1.4561	.43495
.52853	2.1990	.42323	1.0366	.60590	1.3479	.62191	1.0922	.97531	.49503	.91523	1.4857	.46207
.56134	2.0313	.45364	1.0417	.63778	1.2613	.65338	1.1016	.99915	.46692	.93520	1.5133	.47284
.59290	1.8911	.48252	1.0469	.66953	1.1867	.68315	1.1106	1.0251	.44111	.95665	1.5394	.49024
L_7	L_8	C_8	Ω_8	L_9	L_{10}	C_{10}	Ω_{10}	L_{11}	L_{12}	C_{12}	Ω_{12}	L_{13}

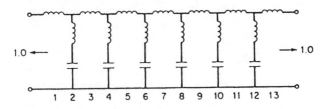

TABLE 11-56 Elliptic-Function LC Element Values (*Continued*)

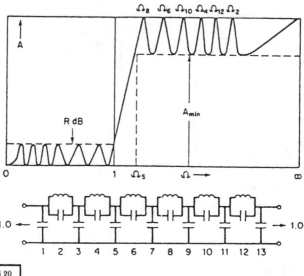

C13 20

Ω_s	A_{min}	C_1	C_2	L_2	Ω_2	C_3	C_4	L_4	Ω_4	C_5	C_6	L_6	Ω_6
1.0025	43.2	1.1344	.26614	1.1412	1.8146	1.2344	2.1026	.43081	1.0507	.45479	6.9790	.14176	1.0054
1.005	49.6	1.1682	.22184	1.1835	1.9516	1.3294	1.6860	.51682	1.0713	.55491	5.0110	.19578	1.0096
1.010	57.5	1.2018	.18144	1.2235	2.1225	1.4343	1.3391	.6159	1.1011	.68052	3.5964	.26868	1.0173
1.015	62.8	1.2210	.15952	1.2457	2.2433	1.5004	1.1617	.68043	1.1248	.76787	2.9549	.32244	1.0245
1.020	67.0	1.2328	.14467	1.2612	2.3411	1.5483	1.0452	.72950	1.1452	.83638	2.5644	.36658	1.0314
1.025	70.6	1.2428	.13361	1.2727	2.4251	1.5872	.96002	.76917	1.1637	.89399	2.2940	.40449	1.0381
1.030	73.7	1.2506	.12483	1.2819	2.500	1.6197	.89346	.80269	1.1808	.94396	2.0919	.43002	1.0447
1.035	76.4	1.2576	.11762	1.2894	2.5679	1.6479	.83927	.83172	1.1969	.98838	1.9329	.46822	1.0512
1.040	79.0	1.2629	.11149	1.2959	2.6308	1.6722	.79361	.85756	1.2122	1.0281	1.8032	.49587	1.0575
1.045	81.3	1.2673	.10620	1.3016	2.6897	1.6938	.75439	.88078	1.2268	1.0644	1.6943	.52150	1.0638
Ω_s	A_{min}	L_1	L_2	C_2	Ω_2	L_3	L_4	C_4	Ω_4	L_5	L_6	C_6	Ω_6

C_7	C_8	L_8	Ω_8	C_9	C_{10}	L_{10}	Ω_{10}	C_{11}	C_{12}	L_{12}	Ω_{12}	C_{13}
.19898	10.009	.099361	1.0028	.27500	4.2308	.22929	1.0153	.76950	1.1441	.62398	1.1835	.66583
.27115	6.8163	.14513	1.0054	.35662	3.2081	.29718	1.0242	.87123	.92605	.70996	1.2333	.74875
.37215	4.6685	.20970	1.0107	.46615	2.4216	.38291	1.0385	.99194	.73973	.80092	1.2992	.83448
.44829	3.7425	.25890	1.0159	.54644	2.0446	.44294	1.0508	1.0723	.64296	.85601	1.3479	.88544
.51159	3.1964	.30006	1.0211	.61161	1.8069	.49066	1.0620	1.1332	.57900	.89590	1.3885	.92041
.56646	2.8260	.33597	1.0263	.66770	1.6381	.53064	1.0726	1.1836	.53198	.92705	1.4240	.94844
.61591	2.5536	.36810	1.0314	.71725	1.5092	.56536	1.0826	1.2266	.49511	.95264	1.4561	.97128
.66084	2.3419	.39739	1.0366	.76196	1.4061	.59613	1.0922	1.2644	.46502	.94729	1.4857	.99093
.70282	2.1732	.42403	1.0417	.80263	1.3207	.62398	1.1016	1.2978	.43968	.99315	1.5133	1.0073
.73969	2.0318	.44909	1.0469	.84012	1.2483	.64942	1.1106	1.3278	.41788	1.0098	1.5394	1.0215
L_7	L_8	C_8	Ω_8	L_9	L_{10}	C_{10}	Ω_{10}	L_{11}	L_{12}	C_{12}	Ω_{12}	L_{13}

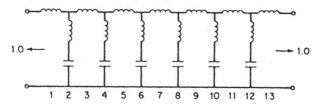

TABLE 11-56   Elliptic-Function *LC* Element Values (*Continued*)

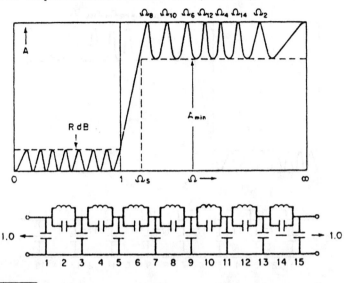

C15 05

Ω_s	A_{min}	C_1	C_2	L_2	Ω_2	C_3	C_4	L_4	Ω_4	C_5
1.0025	41.5	.66980	.20014	1.2044	2.0368	1.0506	1.4805	.57500	1.0838	.46533
1.005	49.0	.69772	.16589	1.2462	2.1994	1.1336	1.1861	.68057	1.1130	.55823
1.010	58.0	.72375	.13500	1.2851	2.4009	1.2214	.94181	.79778	1.1537	.67082
1.015	64.0	.73361	.11848	1.3051	2.5430	1.2720	.81727	.87149	1.1849	.74549
1.020	69.0	.74703	.10717	1.3211	2.6577	1.3136	.73507	.92685	1.2115	.80579
Ω_s	A_{min}	L_1	L_2	C_2	Ω_2	L_3	L_4	C_4	Ω_4	L_5

C_6	L_6	Ω_6	C_7	C_8	L_8	Ω_8	C_9	C_{10}	L_{10}	Ω_{10}
4.6650	.20991	1 0106	.19232	9.6185	.10341	1.0027	.14986	7.4719	.13263	1.0045
3.4198	.28253	1.0174	.25766	6.3927	.15478	1.0053	.20756	5.1678	.19035	1.0083
2.5089	.37660	1.0288	.34747	4.3004	.22773	1.0105	.28974	3.5936	.27000	1.0152
2.0883	.44366	1.0389	.41357	3.4183	.28358	1.0157	.35185	2.9074	.32942	1.0218
1.8272	.49802	1.0483	.46907	2.9009	.33081	1.0208	.40482	2.4963	.3789	1.0282
L_6	C_2	Ω_6	L_7	L_8	C_8	Ω_8	L_9	L_{10}	C_{10}	Ω_{10}

C_{11}	C_{12}	L_{12}	Ω_{12}	C_{13}	C_{14}	L_{14}	Ω_{14}	C_{15}
.28870	2.9883	.31625	1.0287	.70666	.95793	.65288	1.2645	.24946
.36392	2.2722	.40498	1.0425	.79002	.75627	.74959	1.3282	.33358
.46224	1.7246	.51269	1.0635	.88780	.59169	.84910	1.4108	.41380
.53168	1.4630	.58520	1.0907	.94966	.51005	.90593	1.4711	.45436
.58945	1.2985	.64242	1.0961	1.0006	.45515	.94997	1.5208	.49009
L_{11}	L_{12}	C_{12}	Ω_{12}	L_{13}	L_{14}	C_{14}	Ω_{14}	L_{15}

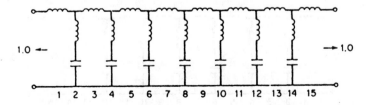

TABLE 11-56   Elliptic-Function *LC* Element Values (*Continued*)

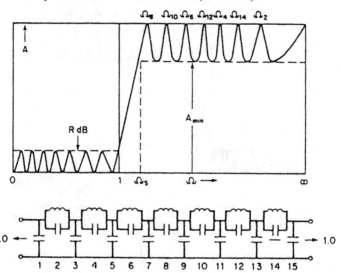

Ω_s	A_{min}	C_1	C_2	L_2	Ω_2	C_3	C_4	L_4	Ω_4	C_5
1.0025	53.8	1.1866	.20000	1.2055	2.0368	1.3802	1.5130	.56267	1.0838	.59582
1.005	61.3	1.2166	.16692	1.2385	2.1994	1.4737	1.2400	.65101	1.1130	.70799
1.010	70.3	1.2432	.13659	1.2701	2.4010	1.5724	1.0022	.74970	1.1537	.84179
1.015	76.4	1.2537	.11999	1.2887	2.5430	1.6300	.87593	.81313	1.1849	.93010
1.020	81.3	1.2662	.10891	1.3000	2.6577	1.6759	.79309	.85905	1.2115	1.0004
Ω_s	A_{min}	L_1	L_2	C_2	Ω_2	L_3	L_4	C_4	Ω_4	L_5

C_6	L_6	Ω_6	C_7	C_8	L_8	Ω_8	C_9	C_{10}	L_{10}	Ω_{10}
4.6915	.20872	1.0106	.24474	9.5079	.10461	1.0027	.18955	7.3373	.13507	1.0045
3.5500	.27217	1.0174	.32593	6.5701	.15060	1.0053	.26248	5.2695	.18667	1.0083
2.6686	.35405	1.0288	.43544	4.5542	.21503	1.0105	.36412	3.7708	.25730	1.0152
2.2442	.41285	1.0389	.51533	3.6653	.26448	1.0157	.44009	3.0885	.31010	1.0218
1.9798	.45962	1.0483	.58107	3.1403	.30558	1.0208	.50366	2.6791	.35305	1.0282
L_6	C_6	Ω_6	L_7	L_8	C_8	Ω_8	L_9	L_{10}	C_{10}	Ω_{10}

C_{11}	C_{12}	L_{12}	Ω_{12}	C_{13}	C_{14}	L_{14}	Ω_{14}	C_{15}
.36842	2.8793	.32822	1.0287	.92223	.82261	.75660	1.2645	.79310
.46306	2.2709	.40522	1.0425	1.0308	.67834	.83570	1.3282	.86834
.58392	1.7741	.49841	1.0635	1.1535	.54784	.91707	1.4108	.94187
.66836	1.5234	.56201	1.0807	1.2302	.47840	.96586	1.4711	.98059
.73748	1.3634	.61052	1.0961	1.2911	.43244	.99986	1.5208	1.0130
L_{11}	L_{12}	C_{12}	Ω_{12}	L_{13}	L_{14}	C_{14}	Ω_{14}	L_{15}

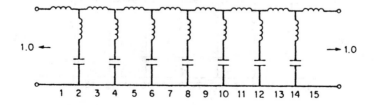

TABLE 11-56 Elliptic-Function *LC* Element Values (*Continued*)

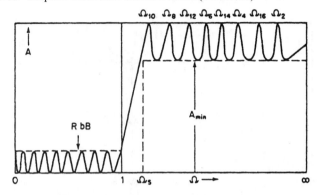

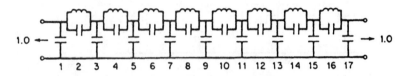

C17 05

Ω_s	A_{min}	C_1	C_2	L_2	Ω_2	C_3	C_4	L_4	Ω_4	C_5	C_6
1.001	42.5	.66324	.19395	1.2085	2.0655	1.0573	1.4295	.59091	1.0880	.47239	4.5935
1.0025	52.0	.70328	.15481	1.2593	2.2648	1.1597	1.1029	.71728	1.1243	.58427	3.2244
1.005	60.0	.71325	.12905	1.2884	2.4525	1.2285	.90180	.82048	1.1625	.68040	2.2768
1.01	70.5	.74209	.10490	1.3229	2.6844	1.3151	.72553	.93465	1.2144	.79977	1.8855
Ω_s	A_{min}	L_1	L_2	C_2	Ω_2	L_3	L_4	C_4	Ω_4	L_5	L_6

L_6	Ω_6	C_7	C_8	L_8	Ω_8	C_9	C_{10}	L_{10}	Ω_{10}	C_{11}	C_{12}
.21312	1.0107	.18029	11.636	.08564	1.0018	.09452	15.280	.065307	1.0011	.12014	7.8506
.29881	1.0188	.25348	7.2002	.13778	1.004	.14714	8.9932	.11061	1.0026	.17902	5.1532
.38130	1.0290	.32718	5.0584	.19478	1.0075	.20493	6.1080	.16202	1.0052	.24177	3.7777
.48547	1.0452	.42758	3.5444	.27444	1.0139	.29222	4.1694	.23493	1.0104	.33109	2.7502
C_6	Ω_6	L_7	L_8	C_8	Ω_8	L_9	L_{10}	C_{10}	Ω_{10}	L_{11}	L_{12}

L_{12}	Ω_{12}	C_{13}	C_{14}	L_{14}	Ω_{14}	C_{15}	C_{16}	L_{16}	Ω_{16}	C_{17}
.12636	1.0040	.28753	2.8937	.32570	1.0301	.71360	.92619	.66409	1.2751	.25125
.19097	1.0080	.37602	2.1074	.43275	1.0471	.81593	.69802	.78177	1.3537	.35696
.25762	1.0137	.45923	1.6658	.52759	1.0667	.89668	.56602	.86259	1.4311	.41230
.34718	1.0234	.56861	1.2987	.64190	1.0952	.99965	.44688	.95549	1.5304	.48828
C_{12}	Ω_{12}	L_{13}	L_{14}	C_{14}	Ω_{14}	L_{15}	L_{16}	C_{16}	Ω_{16}	L_{17}

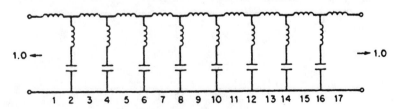

TABLE 11-56   Elliptic-Function LC Element Values (*Continued*)

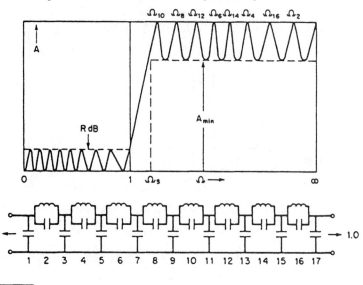

C17 20

Ω_s	A_{min}	C_1	C_2	L_2	Ω_2	C_3	C_4	L_4	Ω_4	C_5	C_6
1.001	55.2	1.1907	.19329	1.2126	2.0655	1.3951	1.4630	.57741	1.0880	.60710	4.6352
1.0025	64.4	1.2229	.15584	1.2510	2.2648	1.5032	1.1595	.68225	1.1243	.73846	3.3768
1.005	72.9	1.2479	.13013	1.2777	2.4525	1.5916	.96132	.76968	1.1625	.85763	2.6441
1.01	83.1	1.2694	.10648	1.3032	2.6844	1.6829	.78410	.86483	1.2144	.99483	2.0489
Ω_s	A_{min}	L_1	L_2	C_2	Ω_2	L_3	L_4	C_4	Ω_4	L_5	L_6

L_6	Ω_6	C_7	C_8	L_8	Ω_8	C_9	C_{10}	L_{10}	Ω_{10}	C_{11}	C_{12}
.21121	1.0107	.23055	11.597	.085923	1.0018	.12053	15.104	.066065	1.0011	.15313	7.7248
.28533	1.0188	.31974	7.4956	.13235	1.004	.18647	9.3341	.10657	1.0026	.22617	5.3000
.35718	1.0290	.41167	5.3817	.18308	1.0074	.25891	6.4810	.15269	1.0052	.30513	3.9711
.44675	1.0452	.53045	3.8493	.25270	1.0139	.36959	4.5437	.21558	1.0104	.41251	2.9541
C_6	Ω_6	L_7	L_8	C_8	Ω_8	L_9	L_{10}	C_{10}	Ω_{10}	L_{11}	L_{12}

L_{12}	Ω_{12}	C_{13}	C_{14}	L_{14}	Ω_{14}	C_{15}	C_{16}	L_{16}	Ω_{16}	C_{17}
.12842	1.0040	.36888	2.7916	.33762	1.0301	.93730	.79731	.77144	1.2751	.80538
.18569	1.0080	.47776	2.1247	.42922	1.0471	1.0644	.63165	.86392	1.3537	.89039
.24508	1.0137	.58347	1.7155	.51228	1.0667	1.1743	.52215	.93507	1.4311	.95636
.32322	1.0234	.71339	1.3681	.60935	1.0952	1.2948	.42410	1.0068	1.5304	1.0196
C_{12}	Ω_{12}	L_{13}	L_{14}	C_{14}	Ω_{14}	L_{15}	L_{16}	C_{16}	Ω_{16}	L_{17}

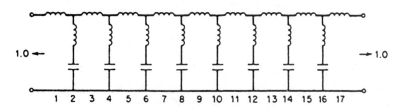

TABLE 11-57 Maximally Flat Delay with Chebyshev Stopband

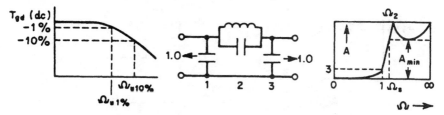

N = 3

A_{min}	Ω_s	T_{gd}(DC)	$\Omega_{\mu\,1\%}$	$\Omega_{\mu\,10\%}$	C_1	C_2	L_2	Ω_2	C_3
18	2.152	1.325	.9091	1.461	2.124	.2769	.5242	2.625	.001434
26	2.721	1.493	.8010	1.304	2.144	.1399	.6931	3.211	.1489
34	3.514	1.602	.7522	1.206	2.166	.07387	.8068	4.096	.2320
42	4.627	1.668	.7122	1.161	2.180	.03958	.8769	5.368	.2791
50	6.178	1.706	.6959	1.134	2.189	.02133	.9178	7.147	.3052
58	8.309	1.727	.6886	1.121	2.193	.01151	.9407	9.610	.3197
66	11.23	1.739	.6850	1.112	2.196	.006226	.9537	12.98	.3275
70	13.07	1.743	.6838	1.109	2.198	.004579	.9580	15.10	.3301

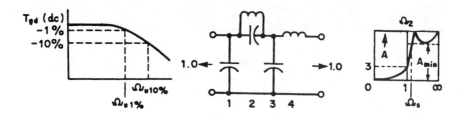

N = 4

A_{min}	Ω_s	T_{gd}(DC)	$\Omega_{\mu\,1\%}$	$\Omega_{\mu\,10\%}$	C_1	C_2	L_2	Ω_2	C_3	L_4
18	2.070	1.471	1.303	1.923	2.107	.3324	.5088	2.432	.1690	.1575
26	2.466	1.662	1.164	1.704	2.127	.1915	.6744	2.783	.3419	.1795
34	2.938	1.807	1.068	1.568	.1756	.1586	.5905	3.268	2.439	.4078
42	3.548	1.910	1.007	1.482	.2445	.09775	.6647	3.923	2.472	.4383
50	4.341	1.980	.9720	1.432	.1420	.08106	.5386	4.786	1.033	2.245
58	5.363	2.027	.9509	1.396	.1760	.04895	.5862	5.903	1.048	2.244
66	6.665	2.057	.9382	1.377	.1972	.03014	.6171	7.332	1.059	2.240
70	7.447	2.068	.9297	1.369	.2046	.02374	.6281	8.189	1.063	2.240

CHAPTER ELEVEN

TABLE 11-57   Maximally Flat Delay with Chebyshev Stopband (*Continued*)

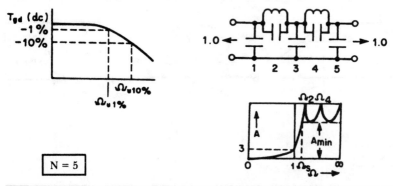

A_{min}	Ω_s	$T_{gd}(DC)$	$\Omega_{\mu\,1\%}$	$\Omega_{\mu\,10\%}$	C_1	C_2	L_2
34	2.6802	1.745	1.550	2.142	.02930	.3317	.3665
42	3.0263	1.904	1.408	1.968	.1338	.2216	.4381
50	3.4467	2.035	1.316	1.840	2.1836	.08543	.8830
58	3.9701	2.139	1.304	1.750	2.203	.06060	.9418
66	4.6213	2.218	1.215	1.688	2.218	.04274	.9872
70	5.0044	2.250	1.191	1.665	2.224	.03582	1.006

Ω_2	C_3	C_4	L_4	Ω_4	C_5
2.868	2.420	.07329	.5638	4.919	.1111
3.209	2.435	.05333	.6496	5.373	.1513
3.641	.5958	.08228	.3358	6.016	.07096
4.186	.6503	.05559	.3818	6.864	.1007
4.863	.6922	.03799	.4168	7.947	.1221
5.268	.7092	.03150	.4307	8.585	.1305

TABLE 11-57 Maximally Flat Delay with Chebyshev Stopband (*Continued*)

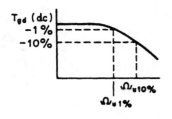

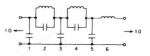

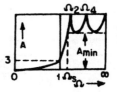

N = 6

A_{min}	Ω_s	T_{gd}(DC)	$\Omega_{\mu 1\%}$	$\Omega_{\mu 10\%}$	C_1	C_2	L_2
18	2.0530	1.415	2.096	—	.09332	.09400	1.907
26	2.3648	1.631	2.093	—	.1568	.07374	2.047
34	2.6429	1.820	1.910	2.604	2.128	.1820	.6982
42	2.9239	1.985	1.753	2.343	2.150	.1375	.7730
50	3.2353	2.129	1.643	2.190	2.172	.1047	.8371
58	3.6033	2.251	1.549	2.066	2.190	.07957	.8927
66	4.0446	2.352	1.485	1.982	2.206	.06014	.9396
70	4.2965	2.395	1.451	1.939	2.213	.05216	.9602

Ω_2	C_3	C_4	L_4	Ω_4	C_5	L_6
2.362	.4290	.2681	.2033	4.283	.08674	.1107
2.574	.5121	.2078	.2763	4.174	.1506	.1193
2.805	.4206	.2526	.2164	4.277	.08769	.09013
3.067	.4943	.1647	.2960	4.529	.1591	.09865
3.378	.5627	.1134	.3668	4.903	.2144	.1061
3.752	.6231	.08054	.4266	5.395	.2577	.1125
4.207	.6738	.05814	.4751	6.017	.2916	.1178
4.468	.6957	.04960	.4958	6.377	.3056	.1201

TABLE 11-57   Maximally Flat Delay with Chebyshev Stopband (*Continued*)

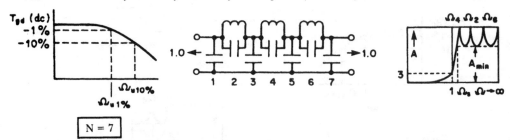

N = 7

A_{min}	Ω_s	$T_{gd}(DC)$	$\Omega_{\mu 1\%}$	$\Omega_{\mu 10\%}$	C_1	C_2	L_2	Ω_2
38	2.7259	1.839	2.357	—	.06065	.1724	.3777	3.919
42	2.8814	1.923	2.244	—	.07500	.1560	.4038	3.984
50	3.1288	2.080	2.087	2.704	.1064	.1259	.4543	4.181
58	3.3944	2.221	1.940	2.532	.1367	.1004	.5013	4.457
66	3.6959	2.348	1.839	2.395	.2557	.1169	.3703	4.806
70	3.8657	2.405	1.808	2.330	2.221	.04079	.9757	5.013

C_3	C_4	L_4	Ω_4	C_5	C_6	L_6	Ω_6	C_7
2.367	.2635	.4537	2.891	.2176	.09914	.1905	7.276	.01189
2.375	.2285	.4857	3.002	.2648	.08555	.2152	7.369	.02704
2.396	.1751	.5460	3.234	.3447	.06519	.2596	7.687	.05283
2.421	.1361	.6008	3.497	.4102	.05039	.2981	8.159	.07411
2.343	.07932	.8728	3.800	.5051	.04595	.2832	8.766	.06607
.6640	.1576	.4019	3.973	.3035	.05842	.2056	9.125	.03636

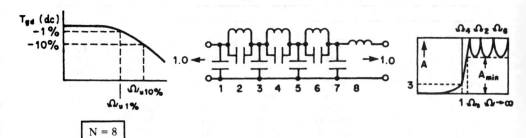

N = 8

A_{min}	Ω_s	$T_{gd}(DC)$	$\Omega_{\mu 1\%}$	$\Omega_{\mu 10\%}$	C_1	C_2	L_2	Ω_2
34	2.6318	1.798	2.660	—	.05238	.2052	.3371	3.802
42	2.8660	1.971	2.643	—	.06575	.1851	.3635	3.855
50	3.1053	2.128	2.434	—	2.198	.06844	.9184	3.987
58	3.3358	2.272	2.264	2.906	2.203	.06164	.9265	4.185
66	3.5839	2.403	2.152	2.738	2.209	.05407	.9386	4.439
70	3.7175	2.464	2.100	2.671	.1545	.09950	.4780	4.585

C_3	C_4	L_4	Ω_4	C_5	C_6	L_6	Ω_6	C_7	L_8
2.354	.3089	.4186	2.781	.1356	.1600	.1637	6.179	.07187	.06295
2.363	.2249	.4973	2.990	.2432	.1184	.2204	6.190	.1178	.07113
.5909	.5620	.1736	3.202	.09376	.1597	.1552	6.352	.06576	.06069
.5878	.3242	.2631	3.424	.2016	.1163	.1959	6.625	.1011	.06493
.6106	.2185	.3400	3.669	.2754	.08764	.2333	6.993	.1305	.06877
2.430	.1005	.6877	3.804	.4684	.05036	.3814	7.216	.2339	.09422

CHAPTER 12

INTRODUCTION TO DIGITAL FILTERS

12.1 RELATION TO ANALOG FILTERS

In the previous chapters, the art of analog filters was developed. Digital filters provide many of the same frequency selective services (low, high, bandpass) expected of analog filters. In some cases, digital filters are defined in terms of equivalent analog filters. Other digital filters are designed using rules unique to this technology. The hardware required to fabricate a digital filter are basic digital devices such as memory and arithmetic logic units (ALUs). Many of these hardware building blocks provide both high performance and low cost. Coefficients and data are stored as digital computer words and, as a result, provide a precise and noise-free (in an analog sense) signal processing medium. Compared to analog filters, digital filters generally enjoy the following advantages:

1. They can be fabricated in high-performance general-purpose digital hardware or with application-specific integrated circuits (ASIC).
2. The stability of certain classes of digital filters can be guaranteed.
3. There are no input or output impedance matching problems.
4. Coefficients can be easily programmed and altered.
5. Digital filters can operate over a wide range of frequencies.
6. Digital filters can operate over a wide dynamic range and with high precision.
7. Some digital filters provide excellent phase linearity.
8. Digital filters do not require periodic alignment and do not "drift" or degrade because of aging.

Because of these advantages, digital filters are penetrating a number of traditional analog markets including telecommunication, audio, speech, equalization, and communication.

12.2 DATA REPRESENTATION

In an analog filter, all signals and coefficients are considered to be real or complex numbers. As such, they are defined over an infinite range with infinite precision.

In the analog case, filter coefficients are implemented with lumped R, L, C, and amplifier components of assumed absolute precision. Along similar lines, the designs of digital filters typically begin with the manipulation of idealized equations. However, the implementation of a digital filter is accomplished using digital computational elements of finite precision (measured in bits). Therefore, the analysis of a digital filter is not complete until the effects of finite precision arithmetic have been determined. As a result, even though there has been a significant sharing of techniques in the area of filter synthesis between analog and digital filters, the analyses of these two classes of filters have developed separate tools and techniques.

Data, in a digital system, are represented as a set of binary valued digits. The process by which a real signal or number is converted into a digital word is called analog-to-digital conversion (ADC). The most common formats used to represent data are called *fixed* and *floating* point (FXP and FLP). Within the fixed-point family of codes, the most popular are binary-coded decimal sign magnitude (SM) and diminished radix (DR) codes. Any integer X such that $|X| < 2^{n-1}$ has a unique sign-magnitude representation, given by

$$X = X_{n-1}\colon\ (2^{n-2}X_{n-2} + \cdots + 2X_1 + X_0) \tag{12-1}$$

where X_i is the ith-bit and X_0 is referred to as the least significant bit (LSB). Similarly X_{n-2} is called the most significant bit (MSB) and X_{n-1} is the sign bit. The LSB often corresponds to a physically measurable electrical unit. For example, if a signed 12-bit analog-to-digital converter is used to digitize a signal whose range is ±15 volts (V), the LSB represents a quantization step size of $Q = 30$ V (range)$/2^{12}$ – bits = 7.32 mV/bit.

EXAMPLE 12.1

REQUIRED: Convert the integers $X = 10$ and $X = -10$ into a 5-bit sign-magnitude number.

RESULT: Using equation (12-1), obtain

$$X = 10 \rightarrow 0{:}1010$$
$$\text{or } X = (+)(1 \times 2^3 + 0 \times 2^2 + 1 \times 2^1 + 0 \times 2^0) = 10$$
$$X = -10 \rightarrow 1{:}1010$$
$$= (-)(1 \times 2^3 + 0 \times 2^2 + 1 \times 2^1 + 0 \times 2^0) = -10$$

where : denotes the sign-bit location.

Diminished radix cases are the 1's and 2's complement codes. The latter is by far the most common code used in signal processing. In this system, any integer $X\ \varepsilon$ $[-2^{n-1}, 2^{n-1})$ has the unique representation given by

$$\begin{aligned}X &= 2^{n-2}X_{n-2} + \cdots + 2X_1 + X_0 &&\text{if } X \geq 0\\ &= -2^{n-1} + 2^{n-2}\bar{X}_{n-2} + \cdots + 2\bar{X}_1 + \bar{X}_0 + 1 &&\text{if } X < 0\end{aligned} \tag{12-2}$$

where $\bar{X}_i$ denotes the complementing of the ith binary digit.

EXAMPLE 12.2

REQUIRED: Convert the integers $X = 10$ and $X = -10$ into a 5-bit 2's complement number.

RESULT: Using equation (12-2), obtain

$$X = 10 \rightarrow 0{:}1010$$
$$\text{or } X = 0 \times 2^4 + 1 \times 2^3 + 0 \times 2^2 + 1 \times 2^1 + 0 \times 2^0 = 10$$
$$X = -10; \; 0{:}1010 = 10$$

$$
\begin{array}{ll}
1{:}0101 & \leftarrow \text{complement} \\
+0{:}0001 & \leftarrow \text{add } 1 \\
\hline
1{:}0110 & \leftarrow -10 \text{ (result)}
\end{array}
$$

$$\text{or } X = -1 \times 2^4 + 0 \times 2^3 + 1 \times 2^2 + 1 \times 2^1 + 0 \times 2^0 = -10$$

Fractional numbers are also possible simply by scaling X by a power of 2. The value of $X' = X/2^m$ has the same binary representation of X except that the m LSBs are considered to be fractional bits.

EXAMPLE 12-3

REQUIRED: Scale the integers $X = 10$ and $X = -10$ by the power of 2 value $4 = 2^2$.

RESULT:

$$
\begin{array}{ll}
X = 10 & X' = 10/4 = 2.5 \\
\rightarrow 0{:}1010 & \rightarrow 0{:}10.10 \\
& \text{or } X' = 0 \times 2^2 + 1 \times 2^1 + 0 \times 2^0 + 1 \times 2^{-1} + 0 \times 2^{-2} = 2.5 \\
X = -10 & X' = -10/4 = -2.5 \\
\rightarrow 1{:}0110 & \rightarrow 1{:}01.10 \\
& \text{or } X' = -1 \times 2^2 + 0 \times 2^1 + 1 \times 2^0 + 1 \times 2^{-1} + 0 \times 2^{-2} = -2.5
\end{array}
$$

One of the significant attributes of the 2's complement system is its immunity to partial sum overflow provided that the final sum is a valid 2's complement number.

EXAMPLE 12-4

REQUIRED: Compute the 5-bit sum $S = X_1 + X_2 + X_3 + X_4$ for $X_i = \{7, 5, 5, -3\}$ or $S = 14$.

RESULT: The sum $S = 7 + 5 + 5 - 3$ when computed using 5-bit sign magnitude and 2's complement is

$$
\begin{array}{ccc}
7 & \text{SM} \quad 00111 & \text{2's} \quad 00111 \\
+\,5 & \text{SM} + 00101 & \text{2's} + 00101 \\
\hline
12 & 01100 & 01100 \\
+\,5 & + 00101 & + 00101 \\
\hline
17 & 10001 = -1 \neq 17 & 10001 \neq 17 \\
-\,3 & + 10011 & + 11101 \\
\hline
14 & 100100 = 4 \neq 14 & 101110 = 14
\end{array}
$$

Observe that an intermediate overflow was fatal to the sign-magnitude sum whereas the 2's complement accumulator was able to overcome its overflow and produce the correct results. This can be particularly important to the digital filter designer since knowledge that the final sum of products is a valid number is sufficient to ensure that no overflow error will occur.

Overflow can be detected in a 2's complement system, if necessary, by combining the "carry into" and "carry out of" the sign bit location using an exclusive OR operator, overflow $= C_{in} \text{ EXOR } C_{out}$.

The limited dynamic range of an FXP system can be overcome using an FLP code. Here, a number X is represented as

$$X = \pm m(x) r^{\pm e(x)} \qquad (12\text{-}3)$$

where $m(x)$ is called the mantissa or significand, $e(x)$ is an integer-valued exponent or characteristic, and r is the radix. The mantissa is usually considered to be a normalized fractional number $1/r < m(x) < 1$. For the case where $r = 2$, the normalized mantissa over $[0.5, 1.0]$ would have a most significant bit (MSB) of 1. Since this bit will always be 1 and thereby contributes no new information about the value of $m(x)$, it is often not explicitly displayed. In such cases it is called a *hidden bit*. In an attempt to provide some degree of structure to this field, the IEEE standard has been proposed and is summarized as follows [( ) denotes hidden bit].

Precision	Single	Double	Quad
Word length	32 bits	64 bits	128 bits
Sign	1 bit	1 bit	1 bit
Offset exponent	8 bits	11 bits	15 bits
Significand	(1) + 23 bits	(1) + 52 bits	112 bits
Max. positive no.	~1.7×10^{38}	~9×10^{307}	~1.2×10^{4932}
Min. positive no.	~1.2×10^{-38}	~2.2×10^{-308}	~1.6×10^{-4932}

The FLP code can represent numbers over a wide range but cannot explicitly represent zero or other exceptions such as the result of an invalid operation or *not a number* (NAN), overflow, division by zero, underflow, inexact result, and unnormalized result (QUAD only).

Between the fixed-point and the floating-point numbering systems the so-called block floating-point (BFP) code can be found. A block floating-point code is defined in terms of an array of data $\{x(n)\}$. The array is scanned to determine its maximum absolute valued entry, say M, such that $M \geq |x(n)|$ for all n. Once M is determined, all members of $\{x(n)\}$ are scaled by M to form a new array $\{x'(n)\}$ where $x'(i) = x(i)/M$. Alternatively, $x(i)$ 1 $x'(i) \times M$ where $|x'(i)| \leq 1.0$. In the BFP, arithmetic is performed over the $\{x'(n)\}$ data set where the magnitude corrective scale factor M is implicit to this operation. The BFP is essentially a fixed-point system with an overall scale factor applied to the final result. Examples of the commercial use of block floating-point are the analog device ADSP1101 16 by 16 multiplier with 40-bit accumulator chip and the Zoran ZR34161 16-bit DSP chip.

12.3 SIGNAL REPRESENTATION

An analog filter manipulates real signals of assumed infinite precision. In a discrete system, analog signals of assumed infinite precision are periodically sampled at a rate of f_s samples per second. The sample period is therefore given by $t_s = 1/f_s$ second(s). A string of contiguous samples is called a *time series*. If the samples are further processed by an analog-to-digital converter (ADC), a digital time series results. A digital filter can be used to manipulate this time series using digital technology. The hardware required to implement such a filter is the product of the recent microelectronics revolution. However, the mathematical tools used to analyze and synthesize such systems can be traced back to an earlier discrete or sample data era.

Shannon developed the mathematical connection between a real (analog) signal and its time series (see bibliography). Referred to as Shannon's "sampling theorem," it assumes that the highest frequency component in a sampled signal $x(t)$ is f_m Hz. The sampling theorem states that $x(t)$ can be reconstructed without error from its sample values (time series) provided that $f_s > 2f_m$. If this condition is violated, *aliasing errors* will occur. If, for example, $x(t) = \cos(2\pi f_x t)$ is sampled at a rate f_s samples per second, $x(n) = 1$ for all n. However, $\{x(n)\}$ now impersonates (alias) another signal $y(t) = 1$ for all time.

To reconstruct the original signal from its sample values, Shannon proposed an interpolation equation. Unfortunately, the elements of the interpolation formula are physically difficult to implement in hardware. As a result, interpolators have been developed to reconstruct the approximate version of $x(t)$ from the time series. The simplest interpolator is the *zero order hold,* or sample and hold, circuit, which is given by

$$x(t) \simeq x(nt_s) \text{ for } nt_s \le t < (n+1)t_s \tag{12-4}$$

Another popular interpolator is the *first-order hold* which uses a slope-intercept formula to produce

$$x(t) = x(nt_s) + [x((n+1)t_s) - x(nt_s)] \times t/t_s \tag{12-5}$$

These options are graphically summarized in figure 12-1.

EXAMPLE 12-5   see Computer-Based Instruction disk (CBI)

REQUIRED: Compute the discrete step response of a first-order low-pass filter if the sampling rate is 100 samples per second.

RESULT: The step response of a simple single-pole low-pass filter is given by $x(t) = 1 - e^{-t}$. The signal is sampled at a rate $f_s = 100$ samples per second. The resulting time series is reconstructed using a zero and first-order hold [equations (12-4) and (12-5)] and is shown in figure 12-2a. The resulting spectrum of the reconstructed signal is shown in figure 12-2b and 12-2c. It can be observed that the frequency response of the first-order hold is in better agreement with the low-pass theoretical ideal.

Discrete signals can be modeled in the time domain using a discrete difference equation of the type suggested in equation (12-5). Transforms are fundamentally important to the design of digital filters. Transform methods can also be used to model these signals. One approach would be to use the venerable Laplace transform and the delay theorem to represent difference equations. It may be recalled that the delay theorem of the Laplace transform states that if $x(t) \leftrightarrow X(s)$, then $x(t + \tau) \leftrightarrow e^{-s\tau}X(s)$. A notational simplification can be achieved if the exponential term is replaced by $z = e^{s\tau}$. This gives rise to the so-called z *transform*. The z transform of the time series $\{x(i)\}$ is formally given by

$$X(z) = \sum_{i=0}^{\infty} x(i)z^{-i} \tag{12-6}$$

which is simply a listing of the time series sample values. In some cases it is more convenient to represent $X(z)$ as a ratio of two polynomials. That is

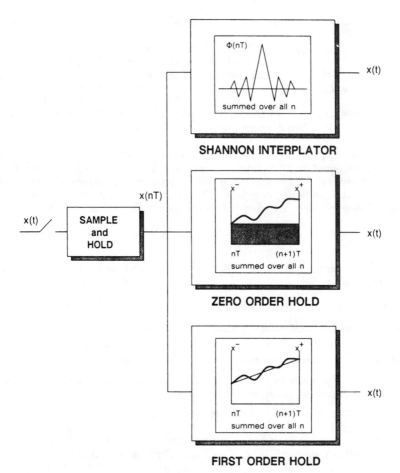

FIGURE 12-1   Interpolation of sample values.

$$X(z) = \sum_{i=0}^{\infty} x(i)z^{-i} = \sum_{i=0}^{M} a_i z^{-i} \Big/ \sum_{i=0}^{N} b_i z^{-i} = N(z)/D(z) \qquad (12\text{-}7)$$

where $X(z) = N(z)/D(z)$ is also referred to as a closed-form transform.

EXAMPLE 12-6

REQUIRED: Compute the z transform of a signal whose time response is $x(t) = e^{-t}$. Assume that the sample rate t_s is known.

RESULT: If $x(t) = e^{-t}$ is sampled at a rate t_s, then $\{x(n)\} = \{1, e^{-t_s}, e^{-2t_s}, \ldots\}$ or $X(z) = \Sigma\ (e^{-it_s})z^{-i}$, $i = 0, 1, 2, \ldots$ from equation (12-6). Using the useful relationship that $1/(1 - x) = 1 + x^1 + x^2 + x^3 + \cdots$ if $|x| < 1$, it follows that $X(z)$ can also be expressed using equation (12-7) as

$$X(z) = 1/(1 - e^{-t_s}z^{-1}) = z/(z - e^{-t_s}) = N(z)/D(z)$$

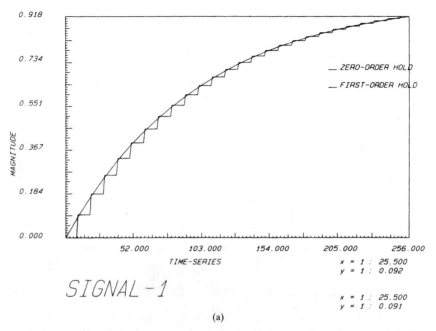

(a)

FIGURE 12-2 Step and frequency response of a single-pole low-pass filter using a zero and a first-order hold.

12.4 SPECTRAL REPRESENTATION

Besides representing signals in the continuous or discrete time domain, signals can also be modeled in the frequency domain. This condition is called *spectral representation*. The principal tools used to describe a signal in the frequency domain are:

Fourier transforms

Fourier series

Discrete Fourier transforms (DFT)

A Fourier transform will map an arbitrary transformable signal into a continuous frequency spectrum consisting of *all* frequency components from $-\infty$ to $+\infty$. The Fourier transform is defined by an indefinite integral equation whose limits range from $-\infty$ to $+\infty$. The Fourier series will map a continuous but periodic signal of period T [(i.e., $x(t) = x(t + kT)$ for all integer values of k] into a discrete but infinite spectrum consisting of frequency harmonics located at multiples of the fundamental frequency $1/T$. The Fourier series is defined by a definite integral equation whose limits are $[0, T]$. The discrete Fourier transform differs from the first two transforms in that it does not accept data continuously but rather from a time series of finite length. Also, unlike the first two transforms which produce spectra ranging out to $\pm\infty$ Hz, the DFT spectrum consists of a finite number of harmonics.

If $\{x(n)\}$ is a time series of N contiguous samples spaced t_s seconds apart, over a $T = Nt_s$ observation interval, the DFT is defined by:

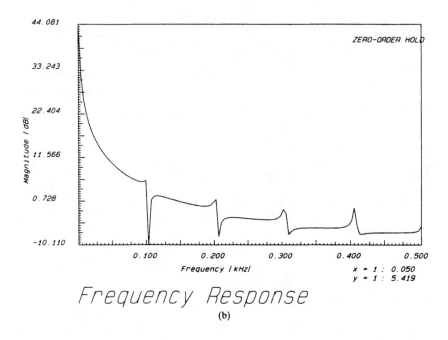

Frequency Response

(b)

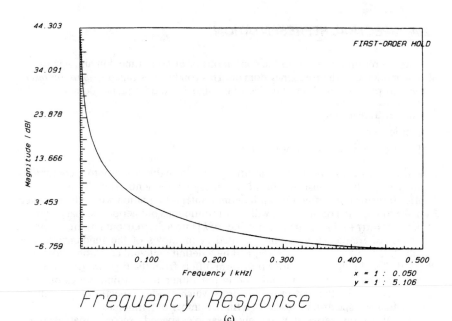

Frequency Response

(c)

FIGURE 12-2 (*Continued*)   Step and frequency response of a single-pole low-pass filter using a zero and a first-order hold.

$$X(k) = \sum_{n=0}^{N-1} x(n)W_N^{nk} \qquad k = 0, 1, \ldots, N-1 \qquad (12\text{-}8)$$

where $X(k)$ is the kth harmonic and W_N is the complex exponential; $W_N = \exp(-j2\pi/N) = \cos(2\pi/N) - j\sin(2\pi/N)$. The inverse DFT, IDFT, is given by

$$x(n) = \frac{1}{N} \sum_{k=0}^{N-1} X(k)W_N^{-nk} \qquad k = 0, 1, \ldots, N-1 \qquad (12\text{-}9)$$

The 0th harmonic, namely $X(0)$, corresponds to the DC strength of the signal and the first harmonic $[H(1)]$ is generally called the *fundamental*. Each harmonic is spaced $1/T = 1/Nt_s = f_s/N$ Hz from its neighbor. The frequency spectrum consists of a listing of N complex harmonics with $X(N/2)$ holding special significance. The $N/2$th harmonic is located at frequency location $f_s/2$ which is recognized to be the *Nyquist* frequency.

The DFT assumes that the signal being transformed satisfies certain side constraints. The most important of these are:

The signal is assumed to be periodic with period T.

The highest frequency component in the input signal is bounded from above by the Nyquist frequency ($f_s/2$).

Because of symmetry properties, the frequency spectrum is symmetrically "folded" about the Nyquist frequency $X(N/2)$. As a result, the Nyquist frequency is also referred to as the *folding* frequency. The first $N/2$ harmonics represent positive frequencies with the remaining $N/2$ harmonics corresponding to negative frequency components.

The relationship between the Fourier transform and discrete Fourier transform is summarized in figure 12-3. The production of negative harmonics, DFT equation, and data sampling are explicitly shown in this figure. However, because there are significant differences between the mathematical definitions and underlining assumptions used to implement these two transforms, the spectra can disagree at times. Some of the more commonly incurred errors associated with the DFT are aliasing and leakage. Aliasing occurs when a signal with a frequency above the Nyquist limit is transformed. This effect can be reduced by adding an antialiasing prefilter in front of the DFT. The prefilter is a low-pass, linear phase device whose cutoff frequency is set to the Nyquist frequency. Therefore, the potentially aliasing components of a signal would be severely attenuated before being presented to the DFT. The second error, leakage, is exemplified in figure 12-4. This error will occur whenever the periodic assumption is violated. Figure 12-4 describes what the DFT of a pure sinusoidal signal would be if it completed an integer (10) and noninteger (10.5) number of cycles within the data window interval T. The production of unwanted sideband harmonics in the latter case is the result of leakage. This condition can be reduced by increasing the window length (i.e., increase N).

The spectral resolution of a DFT is defined in terms of N, the number of samples, and f_s, the sample frequency. Sampling at a rate f_s for N consecutive samples will produce a time series of length $T = Nt_s$ s. This constitutes a T-second *uniform data window* of data which has been extracted from the original analog signal $x(t)$. The term T has been previously referred to as the *fundamental* period. The DFT of the N-sample time series will produce N harmonics where the kth harmonic $X(k)$ resides at frequency location $f_k = k/T = k/Nt_s = kf_s/N$ Hz. The incremental frequency change between harmonics is $\Delta(f) = 1/T = 1/Nt_s = f_s/N$ Hz. Since the sample rate f_s is limited by the Nyquist sampling theorem, increased frequency

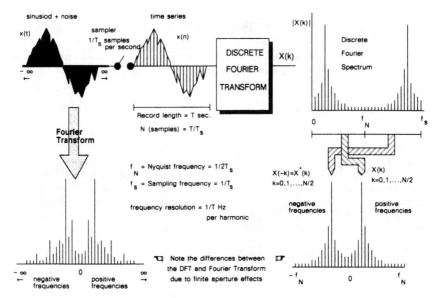

FIGURE 12-3   Comparison of Fourier and discrete Fourier spectra.

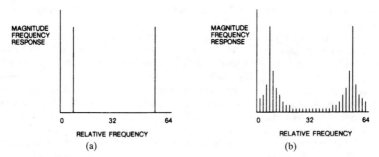

FIGURE 12-4   Spectra representing the DFTs of a sinusoid completing (*a*) 10 (no leakage) cycles and (*b*) 10.5 (leakage) cycles.

resolution is generally obtained through increasing the size of the window (i.e., increase *N*).

The DFT is an important and useful tool in the study of digital filters. The DFT can be used to both analyze and design digital filters. One of its principal applications is the analysis of a filter's impulse response. An impulse response database can be directly generated by presenting a one-sample unit pulse to a digital filter which is initially at a zero state (i.e., zero initial conditions). The output is the filter's impulse response which is observed for *N* contiguous samples. The *N*-sample database is then presented to an *N*-point DFT, transformed, and analyzed. The spectrum produced by the DFT should be a reasonable facsimile of the frequency response of the digital filter under test.

12.5 FILTER REPRESENTATION

A transfer function is defined by the ratio of output and input transforms. For digital filters, it is given by $H(z) = Y(z)/U(z)$ where $U(z)$ is the z transform of the input signal $u(n)$ and $Y(z)$ is for the output signal $y(n)$. The frequency response of a filter $H(z)$ can be computed using a discrete Fourier transform (DFT) of the filter's impulse response. Steady-state analysis $H(z = e^{j\omega t})$, $\omega t \in [-\pi, \pi]$, $\omega t = 2\pi f t$ where t is the sample period [i.e., $t = t_s$ in equation (12-4)].

EXAMPLE 12-7 (CBI)

REQUIRED: A linear filter possesses an impulse response $h(n) = \{1, -0.75, 0.5625, -0.421875, \ldots, (-3/4)^i, \ldots\}$ and is shown in figure 12-5a. Referring to example 12.6, it follows that $H(z) = \Sigma(-3/4)^i z^{-i} = 1/(1 - (-3/4)z^{-1}) = z/(z + 3/4)$. Compute the frequency response of the filter.

RESULT: The steady-state frequency response shown in figure 12-5 is produced by a DFT. It can be seen to be that of a high-pass filter. As a check, the DC (0th harmonic) gain is given by $H(z = e^{j0} = 1)$ or $H(z = 1) = 1.0/1.75 = 0.571 \sim -5$ dB. The high-frequency gain is defined as $\omega t = \pi$ r/s. The gain is given by $|H(z = e^{j\pi})|$ or

$$|H(z = -1.0)| = 4.0 \sim 12 \text{ dB}$$

Intermediate gains can be similarly computed.

Another transform tool which also is extensively used to study digital filters is the *bilinear z transform*. While the standard z transform can be related to the simple sample and hold circuit, the bilinear z transform is analogous to a first-order hold. The bilinear z transform is related to the familiar Laplace transform through

$$s = \frac{2(z - 1)}{t_s(z + 1)} \qquad z = \frac{(2/t_s) + s}{(2/t_s) - s} \tag{12-10}$$

Once an analog filter $H(s)$ is defined, it can be converted into a discrete filter $H(z)$ by using the variable substitution rule.

It is important to realize that the steady-state frequency response of a filter obtained using the bilinear z transform is different from that obtained using the standard z transform. This condition is related to the interpolation problem discussed in example 12-5. Here, it was noted that the frequency response associated with the zero-order hold circuit (z transform) was markedly different from the first-order circuit (bilinear z transform). If Ω denotes the frequency of an analog signal whose z transform is computed using equation (12-10), the corresponding discrete frequency, denoted ω, is given by

$$e^{j\theta} = \frac{(2/t_s) + j\Omega}{(2/t_s) - j\Omega} \qquad \theta = \omega t_s \tag{12-11}$$

Converting discrete to analog frequencies is accomplished using

$$\Omega = \frac{2}{t_s} \tan\left(\frac{\omega t_s}{2}\right) \tag{12-12}$$

The nonlinear relationship between the analog frequency range Ω and the discrete (digital) frequency range ω is called *warping*. The warping curve is shown in figure

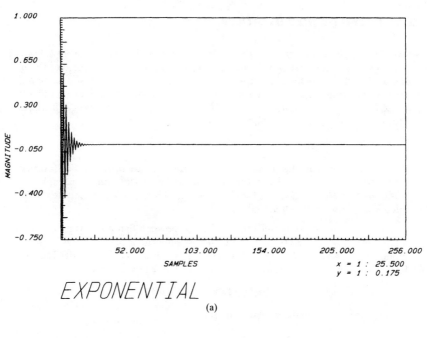

EXPONENTIAL

(a)

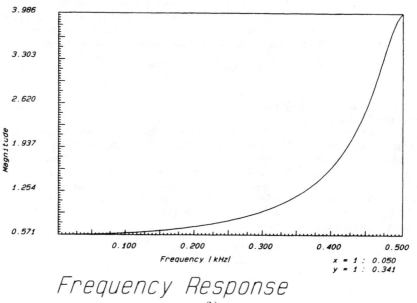

Frequency Response

(b)

FIGURE 12-5   Magnitude frequency response of a typical high-pass filter.

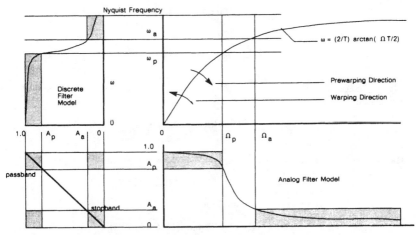

FIGURE 12-6 Relationship between the continuous frequency axis (denoted Ω) and the discrete frequency axis (denoted ω) using the bilinear z-transform.

12-6. Using this property, the following protocol can be used to establish a bilinear z transform model of a system or signal:

Given an analog filter $H(s)$ and a set of critical frequencies $\{\Omega_i\}$, design $H(z)$ as $H(z) = H[s = 2(z - 1)/t_s(z + 1)]$ where the critical frequencies of $H(z)$ are located at $\{\omega_i\}$ for $\omega_i = (2/t_s)\tan^{-1}(\Omega_i t_s/2)$.

Given a discrete (digital) filter $H(z)$ and a set of critical frequencies $\{\omega_i\}$, design $H(s)$ as $H(s) = H(z = [(2/t_s) + s]/[(2/t_s) - s])$ where the critical frequencies of $H(s)$ are located at $\{\Omega_i\}$ for $\Omega_i = (2/t_s) \tan (\omega_i t_s/2)$.

EXAMPLE 12-8

REQUIRED: A third-order Butterworth low-pass filter, discussed in chapter 2, is described by $H(s)$, where

$$H(s) = \frac{1}{4.03 \times 10^{-12}s^3 + 5.08 \times 10^{-9}s^2 + 3.18 \times 10^{-4}s + 1}$$

The filter's critical analog frequencies are located

$$-3 \text{ dB} \rightarrow \Omega_p = 6280 \text{ rad/s, or } 1000 \text{ Hz (end of passband)}$$

$$-18 \text{ dB} \rightarrow \Omega_a = 12560 \text{ rad/s, or } 2000 \text{ Hz (onset of stopband)}$$

Using the bilinear z transform and sample rate of 10K samples per second, compute the locations of the critical frequencies of the resulting third-order discrete Butterworth filter, and produce its transfer function.

RESULTS: The discrete filter version of $H(s)$, for $f_s = 10$ kHz, using the bilinear z transform is given by

$$H(s)\Big|_{s = 2(z - 1)/10^{-4}(z + 1)} = \frac{1}{A + B + C + D} = H(z)$$

$$A = 32.24(z - 1)^3/(z + 1)^3$$

$$B = 2.032(z - 1)^2/(z + 1)^2$$

$$C = 6.36(z - 1)/(z + 1)$$

$$D = 1$$

which simplifies to:

$$H(z) = \frac{0.02402(z^3 + 3z^2 + 3z + 1)}{z^3 - 2.1952z^2 + 2.1456z - 0.8543}$$

The critical frequencies of the discrete filter are given by equation (12-12).

$$-3 \text{ dB} \rightarrow \omega_p = (2 \times 10^4)\tan^{-1}(6280 \times 10^{-4}/2)$$

$$= 6087 \text{ rad/s} = 968.77 \text{ Hz}$$

$$-18 \text{ dB} \rightarrow \omega_a = (2 \times 10^4)\tan^{-1}(12560 \times 10^{-4}/2)$$

$$= 11215 \text{ rad/s} = 1784 \text{ Hz}$$

That is, 1 kHz (analog) is warped into 0.96877 kHz (digital) and 2 kHz (analog) is mapped to 1.784 kHz (digital).

BIBLIOGRAPHY

Oppenheim, A. V., and Schafer, R., *Digital Signal Processing,* Prentice-Hall, Englewood Cliffs, N.Y., 1975.

Taylor, E. J., *Digital Filter Design Handbook,* Marcel Dekker, New York, 1983.

——— and Stouraitis, T., *Digital Filter Design Using the IBM PC,* Marcel Dekker, New York, 1987.

CHAPTER 13

FINITE IMPULSE-RESPONSE FILTERS

13.1 INTRODUCTION

Linear constant coefficient filters can be categorized into two broad classes known as finite impulse-response (FIR) or infinite impulse-response (IIR) filters. An FIR filter can be expressed in terms of a simple discrete equation:

$$y(n) = c_0 x(n) + c_1 x(n-1) + \cdots + c_{N-1} x(n - N + 1) \qquad (13\text{-}1)$$

where the coefficients $\{c_i\}$ are called filter tap weights. In terms of a transfer function, equation (13-1) can be restated as

$$H(z) = \sum_{i=0}^{N-1} c_i z^{-i} \qquad (13\text{-}2)$$

As an example, a typical $N = 111$th-order FIR is shown in figure 13-1. Observe that the FIR exhibits several interesting features and they are:

1. The filter's impulse response exists for only $N = 111$ (finite) contiguous samples.
2. The filter's transfer function consists of zeros only (i.e., no poles). As a result, an FIR is sometimes referred to as an all-zero, or transversal, filter.
3. The filter has a very simple design consisting of a set of word-wide shift registers, tap-weight multipliers, and adders (accumulators).
4. If the input is bounded by unity (i.e., $|x(i)| \leq 1$ for all i), the maximum value of the output $y(i)$ is $\Sigma |c_i|$. If all the tap weights c_i are bounded, the filter's output is likewise bounded and, as a result, stability is guaranteed.
5. The phase, when plotted with respect to frequency (plot shown over the principal angles $\pm\pi/2$), is linear with constant slope.

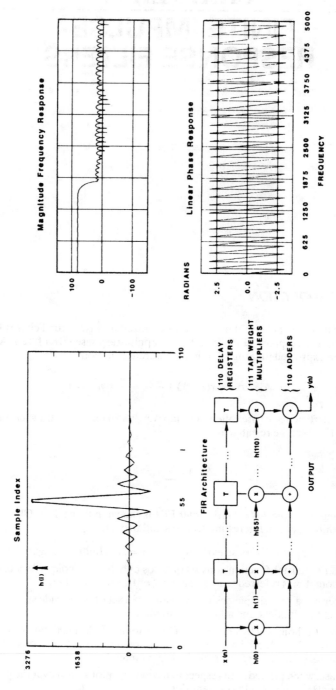

FIGURE 13-1 Typical FIR architecture, impulse response, and frequency response.

13.2 LINEAR PHASE BEHAVIOR

Observe that the FIR is basically a shift-register network. Since digital shift registers are precise and easily controlled, it may be expected that the FIR can offer the designer several interesting phase domain attributes which are difficult to achieve with analog filters. The most important of these are:

Potential for linear phase versus frequency behavior

Potential for constant group delay behavior

These properties are fundamentally important in the fields of:

Digital communication systems

Phase synchronization systems (e.g., phase-locked loops)

Speech processing

Image processing

Spectral analysis (e.g., Fourier analysis)

Other areas where nonlinear phase distortion cannot be tolerated

An Nth order FIR filter, having a transfer function given by

$$H(e^{j\omega}) = \pm |H(e^{j\omega})| e^{j\theta(\omega)} \tag{13-3}$$

is said to possess linear phase behavior if

$$\theta(\omega) = -a\omega + b$$

$$a = (N-1)/2 \qquad b = \pm \pi/2 \quad \text{or} \quad 0 \tag{13-4}$$

Group phase delay, denoted T_{gd}, has been defined to be the derivative of phase with respect to frequency. In this case it can be immediately seen that the group delay for the linear phase filter, given in equation (13-4), is

$$T_{gd} = -d(\theta(\omega))/d\omega = (N-1)/2 \tag{13-5}$$

In order for an FIR to be a linear phase filter, it is known that such a filter must possess a symmetric impulse response given by

$$h(n) = \pm h(N-1-n) \tag{13-6}$$

13.3 FIR DESIGN METHODS

The design of an FIR entails specifying the filter's impulse response, tap weights $\{c_i\}$. As a result, the design of an FIR can be as simple as prespecifying the desired impulse response. Other acceptable analytical techniques used to synthesize a desired impulse response are the inverse Fourier transform of a given frequency domain filter specification or the use of polynomial approximation techniques. These methods are summarized below.

Prespecified Impulse Response

On some occasions, the impulse response of a desired filter can be prespecified. This method is applicable to those cases where the use of a certain classically defined filter profile is desired. In such cases, the filter's tap-weight coefficients are assumed to be known a priori and cataloged. For example, the so-called Nth order *moving average* has an impulse response given by

$$h(n) = \begin{cases} 1 & \text{if } 0 \le n \le N - 1 \\ 0 & \text{otherwise} \end{cases} \tag{13-7}$$

or [refer to equation (13-2)] $H(z) = \Sigma\, z^{-i}, i = 0, 1, \ldots, N - 1$. The closed-form transfer function can be derived using the identity

$$\sum_{i=0}^{\infty} x^i = 1/(1 - x) \quad \text{if } |x| \le 1 \tag{13-8}$$

Upon applying equation (13-8), we obtain

$$H(z) = \sum_{i=0}^{N-1} z^{-i} = \sum_{i=0}^{\infty} z^{-i} - \sum_{i=N}^{\infty} z^{-i} \tag{13-9}$$

$$= 1/(1 - z^{-1}) - z^{-N}/(1 - z^{-1}) = (1 - z^{-N})/(1 - z^{-1})$$

The numerator of $H(z)$ contributes N uniformly spaced zeros, which are distributed along the periphery of the unit circle. One of these zeros is seen to be located at $z = 1$. The single pole of $H(z)$ resides at that location as well. As a result, they cancel each other. The resulting pole-zero pattern of the comb filter is displayed in figure 13-2.

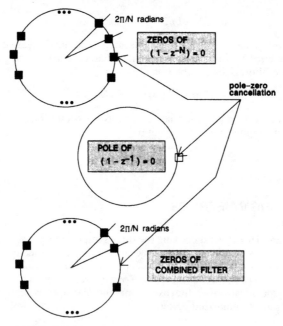

FIGURE 13-2   Pole-zero diagram of a comb filter.

An obvious feature of the comb filter is that all its coefficients are unity (i.e., $c_i = 1$). Therefore, the filter is technically multiplier-free. In practice, these coefficients are often assigned a value slightly less than unity. The comb filter's architecture and frequency response are displayed in figure 13-3. Observe that the magnitude frequency response repeats itself on multipliers of the sampling frequency. This is simply a manifestation of the Nyquist sampling theorem in that the comb filter treats a frequency component of f_0 Hz the same as it would be at $f_0 + kf_s$ Hz.

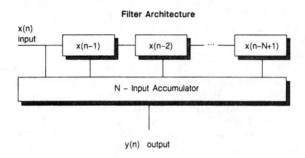

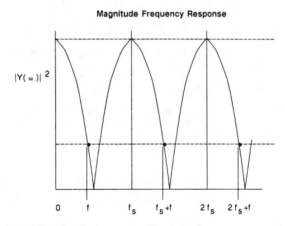

FIGURE 13-3 Moving average filter example.

Frequency Domain Techniques

A simple procedure for designing an FIR is to specify an acceptable frequency domain model, invert the filter's spectral representation using the inverse Fourier transform, and use the resulting time series to represent the filter's impulse response. In general, the inverse Fourier transform of a *desired* spectral waveshape would produce an infinitely long time domain record. However, from a hardware cost or throughput standpoint, it is unreasonable to consider the implementing of an infinitely or extremely long FIR. Therefore, a realizable FIR would be defined in terms of a truncated Fourier series. For example, the Fourier transform of the "nearly ideal" N=101 order low-pass filter, shown in figure 13-4a, is known to have a sin $(x)/x$ type impulse-response envelope. For a large value of N, the difference between the response of an infinitely long impulse response and its N-sample approximation would be small. However, when N is small, large approximation errors can occur. The impulse response of N=101 filter, shown in figure 13-4a, was produced using an inverse DFT and is presented in figure 13-4b. As expected, it is seen to possess the familiar $\sin(x)/x$ profile.

In general, a frequency-response shape can be chosen by the designer. The inverse DFT is used to produce a "long" representative impulse response. When a value of N is chosen (assume N is odd for purposes of discussion), the 0th and next $(N-1)/2$ sample values of the truncated impulse response are extracted from the inverse DFT database (i.e., impulse response). The 0th delay sample is assigned to be the center tap weight (i.e., $c[(N-1)/2]$) of the FIR under design. The remaining $(N-1)/2$ samples are appended to the right of the center tap. The tap weights ranging from delay 0 to $(N-3)/2$ are symmetric images of those to the right of the center tap location, as specified in equation (13-6). The resulting FIR is therefore of linear phase, with group delay $(N-1)/2$ (the location of the center tap), and provides frequency domain filtering services which approximate the original filter specifications. More specifically, the 31-point symmetric impulse response $[c(n)]$ of an ideal low-pass filter is shown in figure 13-4c. Here the filter is defined in terms of $h(0)$ and images of $h(1)$ through $h(15)$ in the manner previously described. The magnitude frequency and phase response are displayed in figure 13-4d and e. Observe that the distortion in the frequency response, due to the truncating of the impulse-response model to 31 samples, is immediately apparent upon comparing figure 13-4a with 13-4d. Finally, observe that the phase response remains linear.

EXAMPLE 13-1   (CBI)

REQUIRED: An ideal bandpass filter is to have a unity gain from 0.2 to 0.4 times the sampling frequency and zero gain elsewhere (see figure 13-5). Design a 31st-order FIR, which approximates the indicated "ideal" frequency response, using a 31-sample inverse discrete Fourier transform.

RESULTS: The inverse DFT has a $\sin(x)/x$ shape, which is interpreted in terms of filter coefficients $\{c_i\}, i = 0, 1, \ldots, 30$. The coefficients are symmetrically arranged about the mid-delay tap located at $(N-1)/2 = 15$. The coefficients are summarized below along with the computation of the filter's maximum output.

Filter Coefficients			Maximum Output Calculation
$c(0)$	$= c(30) =$	0.03820	
$c(1)$	$= c(29) =$	0.01551	Maximum output $|y(n)_{max}|$
$c(2)$	$= c(28) =$	0.08376	$= \Sigma \, |c(i)| \quad i = 0, \ldots, N-1$
$c(3)$	$= c(27) =$	-0.12525	$= 2 \Sigma \, |c(i)| + c(15)$
$c(4)$	$= c(26) =$	-0.05134	$\{i = 1, \ldots, M - 1\}$
$c(5)$	$= c(25) =$	0.01481	$= 2.5 \quad M = (N-3)/2$
$c(6)$	$= c(24) =$	-0.01461	
$c(7)$	$= c(23) =$	0.03616	
$c(8)$	$= c(22) =$	-0.08645	
$c(9)$	$= c(21) =$	-0.03592	Therefore, if the input is
$c(10)$	$= c(20) =$	0.00906	bounded by unit {i.e., $|x(n)|$
$c(11)$	$= c(19) =$	0.01462	≤ 1}, the data-word format
$c(12)$	$= c(18) =$	0.14963	should have at least a sign
$c(13)$	$= c(17) =$	-0.25786	and two integer bits to the
$c(14)$	$= c(16) =$	-0.12825	left of the binary-point.
$c(15) =$	$=$	0.41256	

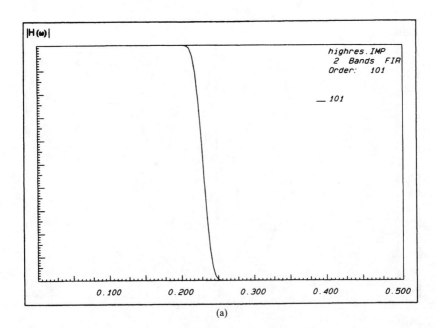

(a)

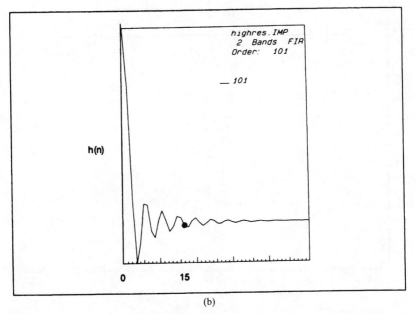

(b)

FIGURE 13-4 Relationship between infinite and finite impulse response: (a) original magnitude frequency response of a nearly ideal low-pass filter; (b) derived impulse response $h(n)$ when $h(n) = \text{IDFT}[H(\omega)]$.

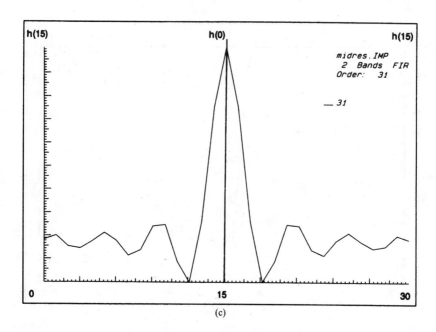

(c)

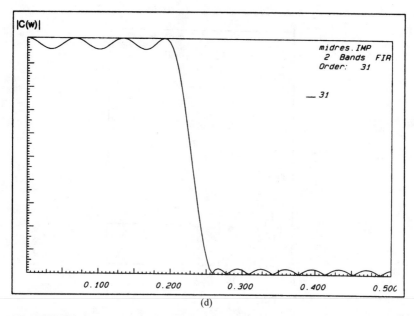

(d)

FIGURE 13-4 *(Continued)* Relationship between infinite and finite impulse response: (*c*) 31-point symmetric impulse response consisting of $h(0)$ and images of $\{h(1), \ldots, h(15)\}$ from figure 13-4*b*; (*d*) magnitude frequency response.

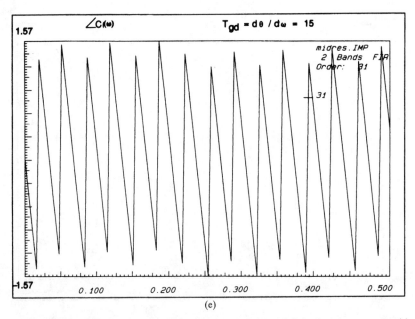

(e)

FIGURE 13-4 *(Continued)* Relationship between infinite and finite impulse response: *(e)* phase response.

The approximate ideal magnitude frequency response is reported in figure 13-5*b*, with the phase-response information plotted (modulo the principal angles $\pm\pi/2$) in figure 13-5*c* and in tabular form in figure 13-5*d*. At two adjacent frequency locations (shown as a fraction of the sampling frequency), the following phase angles, in radians, are found:

Frequency	Phase
0.10629921	−0.51541754
0.10236220	−0.14726216

which yields a group delay estimate of:

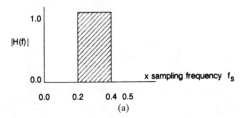

(a)

FIGURE 13-5 Approximation to an ideal FIR band-pass filter.

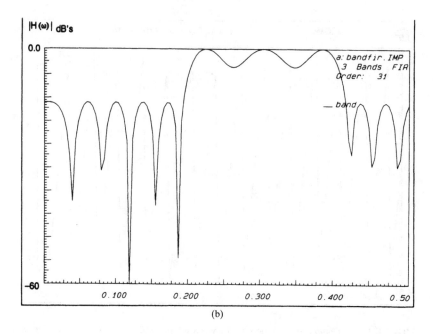

(b)

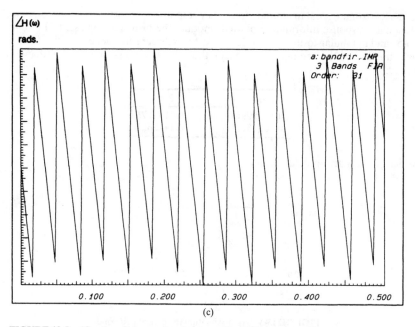

(c)

FIGURE 13-5 *(Continued)* Approximation to an ideal FIR bandpass filter.

Frequency	Phase
0.0000000000E+00	0.0000000000E+00
3.9370078740E-03	-3.6815538909E-01
7.8740157480E-03	-7.3631077818E-01
1.1811023622E-02	-1.1044661673E+00
1.5748031496E-02	-1.4726215564E+00
1.9685039370E-02	1.3008157081E+00
2.3622047244E-02	9.3266031904E-01
2.7559055118E-02	5.6450492995E-01
3.1496062992E-02	1.9634954085E-01
3.5433070866E-02	-1.7180584823E-01
3.9370078740E-02	-5.3996123726E-01
4.3307086614E-02	-9.0811662638E-01
4.7244094488E-02	-1.2762720155E+00
5.1181102362E-02	1.4971652490E+00
5.5118110236E-02	1.1290098599E+00
5.9055118110E-02	7.6085447085E-01
6.2992125984E-02	3.9269908176E-01
6.6929133858E-02	2.4543692695E-02
7.0866141732E-02	-3.4361169636E-01
7.4803149606E-02	-7.1176708536E-01
7.8740157480E-02	-1.0799224739E+00
8.2677165354E-02	-1.4480778643E+00
8.6614173228E-02	1.3253594005E+00
9.0551181102E-02	9.5720401152E-01
9.4488188976E-02	5.8904862244E-01
9.8425196850E-02	2.2089323336E-01
1.0236220472E-01	-1.4726215574E-01
1.0629921260E-01	-5.1541754486E-01
1.1023622047E-01	-8.8357293402E-01
1.1417322835E-01	-1.2517283233E+00
1.1811023622E-01	1.5217089716E+00
1.2204724409E-01	1.1535535530E+00
1.2598425197E-01	7.8539816365E-01
1.2992125984E-01	4.1724277451E-01
1.3385826772E-01	4.9087385403E-02
1.3779527559E-01	-3.1906800368E-01
1.4173228346E-01	-6.8722339275E-01
1.4566929134E-01	-1.0553787818E+00
1.4960629921E-01	-1.4235341707E+00
1.5354330709E-01	1.3499030965E+00
1.5748031496E-01	9.8174770382E-01
1.6141732283E-01	6.1359231501E-01
1.6535433071E-01	2.4543692599E-01
1.6929133858E-01	-1.2271846306E-01
1.7322834646E-01	-4.9087385212E-01
1.7716535433E-01	-8.5902924118E-01
1.8110236220E-01	-1.2271846302E+00
1.8503937008E-01	1.5462526369E+00
1.8897637795E-01	1.1780972451E+00
1.9291338582E-01	8.0994185601E-01
1.9685039370E-01	4.4178646693E-01
2.0078740157E-01	7.3631077849E-02
2.0472440945E-01	-2.9452431124E-01
2.0866141732E-01	-6.6267970032E-01
2.1259842519E-01	-1.0308350894E+00
2.1653543307E-01	-1.3989904785E+00
2.2047244094E-01	1.3744467860E+00
2.2440944882E-01	1.0062913969E+00
2.2834645669E-01	6.3813600781E-01
2.3228346456E-01	2.6998061872E-01
2.3622047244E-01	-9.8174770376E-02
2.4015748031E-01	-4.6633015947E-01
2.4409448819E-01	-8.3448554856E-01
2.4803149606E-01	-1.2026409377E+00

$$\Delta\phi(\omega)$$

(d)

FIGURE 13-5   *(Continued)* Approximation to an ideal FIR bandpass filter.

$$T_{gd} = -\Delta\theta(\omega)/\Delta\omega = -\frac{(-0.51541754 + 0.14726216)}{2\pi(0.10629921 - 0.10236220)}$$

$$= 14.88$$

This is in good agreement with the theoretical phase delay of $(N-1)/2 = 15$.

EXAMPLE 13-2   (CBI)

REQUIRED: We want to design an FIR having an ideal passband gain of unity and a stopband gain of zero.

RESULTS: Suppose the passband extends over $[0, cf_s]$ and the stopband over $[cf_s, f_N]$ for $0 < c < 0.5$ and $f_N = f_s/2$. The Fourier series representation of ideal low-pass filter model is

$$X(f) = 2c + (2/\pi) \sum_{i=1}^{\infty} [\cos(2\pi i f)\sin(2\pi i c)]/i$$

Suppose $c = 0.333$ and a filter with even coefficient symmetry about the center tap is desired (equation [13-6]). Then an Nth-order FIR could be specified by truncating the Fourier series after $(N + 1)/2$ terms with the retained values used as filter coefficients. If, for example, $N = 17$, then:

$$c(0) = -0.0254 = c(16)$$

$$c(1) = -0.0276 = c(15)$$

$$c(2) = 0.0276 = c(14)$$

$$c(3) = 0.0394 = c(13)$$

$$c(4) = -0.0551 = c(12)$$

$$c(5) = -0.0689 = c(11)$$

$$c(6) = 0.1378 = c(10)$$

$$c(7) = 0.2757 = c(9)$$

$$c(8) = 0.3333$$

The filter **architecture is shown in figure 13-6. It** makes direct use of the coefficient **symmetry property.**

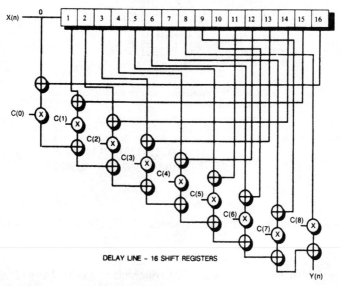

FIGURE 13-6 31st-order FIR.

Optimal Modeling Techniques

Weighted Chebyshev polynomials have been successfully used to design FIRs. In this application, Chebyshev polynomials are combined so that their combined sum minimizes the maximum difference between an ideal and the realized frequency response (i.e., mini-max principle). Because of the nature of these polynomials, they produce a "rippled" magnitude frequency-response envelope of equal minima and maxima in the pass- and stopbands. As a result, this class of filter is often called an *equiripple* filter. Much is known about the synthesis process, which can be traced back to McClellan et al. (see bibliography). Based on these techniques, a number of software-based CAD tools have been developed to support FIR design.

EXAMPLE 13-3 (CBI)

REQUIRED: A linear phase FIR is to be designed to provide an ideal constant gain from 0.125 to 0.225 times the sampling frequency and zero gain elsewhere. Three versions of the filter are to be designed using the weighted Chebyshev method. The three filters are of length $N = 127, 51$, and 15, respectively.

RESULT: Using the weighted Chebyshev method and the software presented in the Taylor and Stouraitis monograph (see bibliography), the filters were produced using a general-purpose computer. They are summarized in figure 13-7*a* through *d*. It can be noted that the filter's magnitude frequency response is a direct function of the filter order (i.e., N). That is, highly selective frequency-domain filtering requires a high-order FIR. It should also be appreciated that filter cost, complexity, and throughput are negatively related to the filter order. Therefore, the practical design of an FIR will always reflect a tradeoff between filter order and frequency-domain selectivity.

Finally, observe that in all cases the filter exhibits linear phase behavior regardless of its order. Phase contours are of a linear nature and given by $\theta(\omega) = -(N - 1)\omega/2 + b$, where $b = \{0, \pm\pi/2\}$. The basic difference between each phase profile is the slope (group delay) which has a theoretical value of $(N - 1)/2$.

13.4 WINDOWS

Digital filters usually are expected to operate over long, constantly changing data records. An FIR, while being capable of offering this service, can only work with a limited number of samples at a time. A similar situation presents itself in the context of a discrete Fourier transform. Refer to figure 13-8 and observe that the quality of the produced spectrum is a function of the number of transformed samples. Ideally, an infinitely long impulse response would be defined by an ideal filter. A *uniform window* of length T will pass N contiguous samples of data. The windowing effect may be modeled as a multiplicative switch which multiplies the presented signal by zero (open) for all time exclusive of the interval $[0, T]$. Over $[0, T]$, the signal is multiplied by unity (closed). In a sampled system, the interval $[0, T]$ is replaced by N samples taken at a sample rate f_s where $T = N/f_s$. Using 128- and 64-point discrete Fourier transforms, time series values of 128 and 64 contiguous samples of a low-pass filter (whose passband is defined over $[0.0, 0.2f_s]$ and stopband over $[0.21f_s, 0.5f_s]$) are transformed and displayed in figure 13-8. It can be seen that when the observation interval (i.e., N) becomes small, the quality of the spectral estimate begins to deteriorate. This consequence is called the *finite aperture effect*.

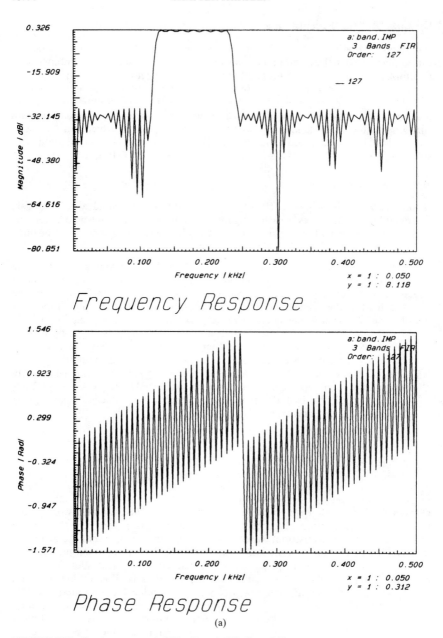

FIGURE 13-7   Band-pass example FIR of length 127, 51, and 15 taps.

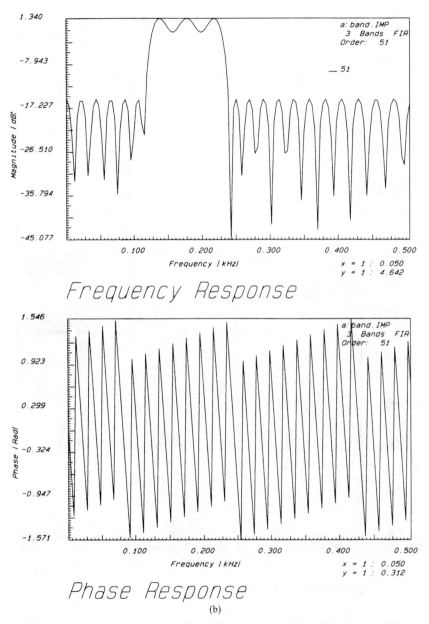

Frequency Response

Phase Response

(b)

FIGURE 13-7 *(Continued)* Band-pass example FIR of length 127, 51, and 15 taps.

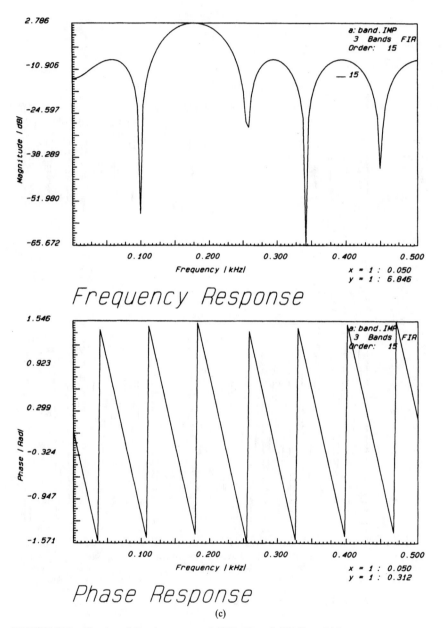

FIGURE 13-7 *(Continued)* Band-pass example FIR of length 127, 51, and 15 taps.

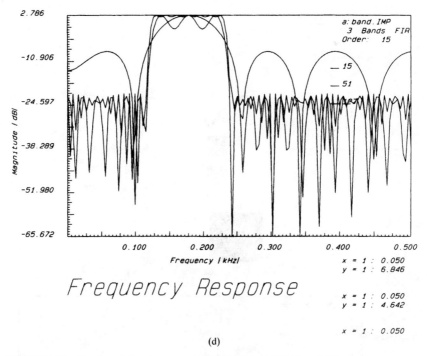

(d)

FIGURE 13-7 *(Continued)* Band-pass example FIR of length 127, 51, and 15 taps.

Windowing is a technique which tends to improve the quality of a spectrum obtained from a limited number of samples. The effect of a window can be analyzed in terms of the data presented in figure 13-9. Here, the time series used to produce the 128-point spectrum presented in figure 13-8 is reinterpreted in the context of windowing. The first spectrum, shown in figure 13-9*a,* shows the effect of applying a uniform window to the original time series. In figure 13-9*b* through *c,* significant spectral enhancements are obtained by applying to the original time series two common window functions (Hamming and Kaiser). These data suggest that when properly applied, windowing can reduce the effect of finite aperture effect found in DFTs or FIRs.

The mathematical effect of a window can be analyzed in a straightforward manner. The finite data record $s(t)$, of length T, is the result of presenting $x(t)$ to a multiplier (switch) which performs the indicated operation with respect to a specified window function $w(t)$. The window function $w(t)$ has an arbitrary value over $t \in [0, T]$ but is zero elsewhere. For purposes of analysis, let the spectral representations of $x(t)$, $w(t)$, and $s(t)$ be $X(f)$, $W(f)$, and $S(f)$, respectively. The object of the window is to place $S(f)$ in maximal agreement with $X(f)$. From the duality of theorem of Fourier transforms, it is known that

$$S(f) = X(f) * W(f) \qquad (13\text{-}10)$$

That is, the convolution of the spectral representations of $x(t)$ and $w(t)$ defines $S(f)$. Therefore, if $X(f) = S(f)$, it follows that $W(f) = \delta(f)$ (i.e., impulse frequency

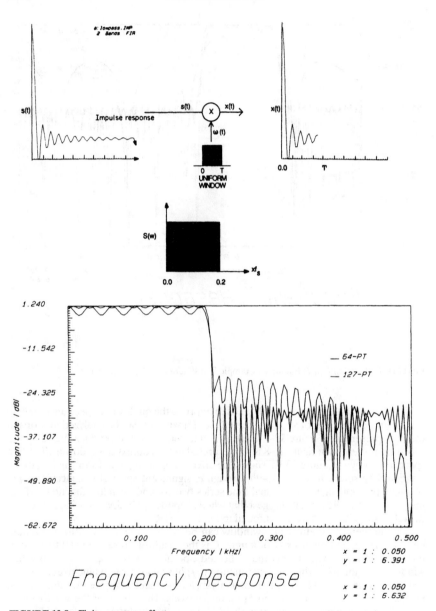

FIGURE 13-8 Finite aperture effect.

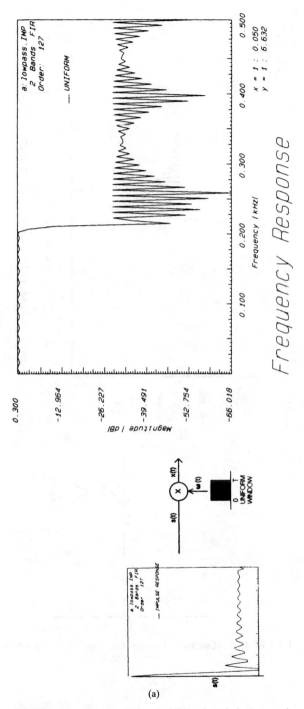

(a)

FIGURE 13-9 Uniform, Kaiser, and Hamming window comparison.

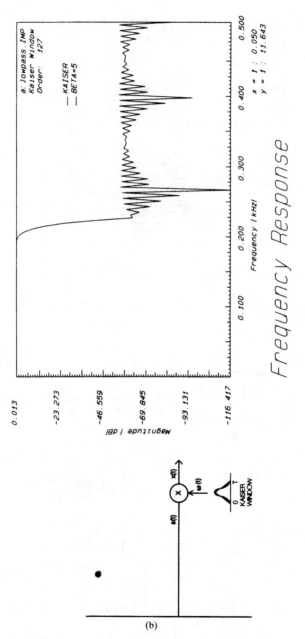

FIGURE 13-9 *(Continued)* Uniform, Kaiser, and Hamming window comparison.

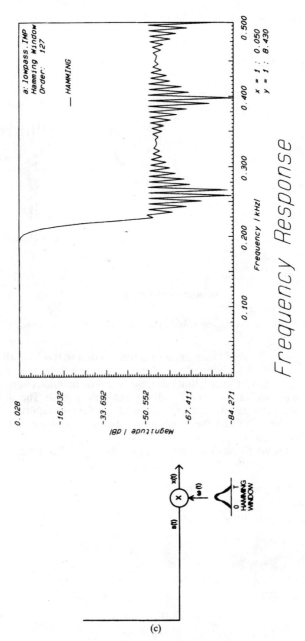

FIGURE 13-9 *(Continued)* Uniform, Kaiser, and Hamming window comparison.

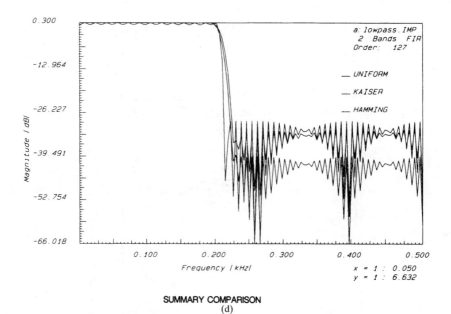

SUMMARY COMPARISON
(d)

FIGURE 13-9 *(Continued)* Uniform, Kaiser, and Hamming window comparison.

response). However, if $W(f)$ is an impulse, it follows that $w(t) = 1$ for all time. While mathematically correct, such a $w(t)$ would not qualify as a finite time duration window of aperture size T_s. Instead, finite duration window functions have been developed which have an impulse-like frequency response profile. The quality of the approximation can be parameterized in terms of the data set reported in figure 13-10. The *main-lobe* width and the *ripple ratio* (RR), are small for Dirac (impulse) approximating windows.

Over the last several decades a number of windows have been proposed. Some of the more popular windows found in contemporary use are the:

Rectangular or uniform window

Hamming window

Hann window

Blackman window

Kaiser window

More specifically
Rectangular window:

$$w(n) = \begin{cases} 1 \text{ if } |n| \le (N-1)/2 \\ 0 \text{ otherwise} \end{cases} \tag{13-11i}$$

Hamming/Hann window:

$$w(n) = \begin{cases} a + (1-a)\cos\left[2\pi n/(N-1)\right] & |n| \le (N-1)/2 \\ 0 \text{ otherwise} \end{cases} \tag{13-11ii}$$
$$a(\text{Hamming}) = 0.54 \qquad a(\text{Hann}) = 0.5$$

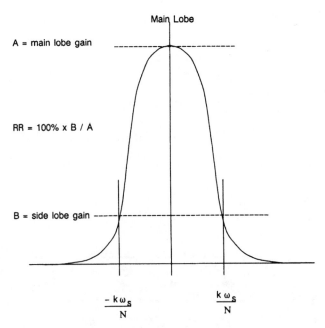

FIGURE 13-10 Typical data window comparison.

Blackman window:

$$w(n) = \begin{cases} 0.42 + 0.5 \cos\left[2\pi n/(N-1)\right] + 0.08 \cos\left[4\pi n/(N-1)\right] \\ |n| \le (N-1)/2 \\ 0 \text{ otherwise} \end{cases} \quad (13\text{-}11iii)$$

Kaiser window:

$$w(n) = \begin{cases} I_0(B\{1 - [2n/(N-1)]^2\}^{0.5})/I_0(B) \\ |n| \le (N-1)/2 \\ 0 \text{ otherwise} \end{cases} \quad (13\text{-}11iv)$$

$I_0(x) = $ 0th-order Bessel function

The spectral signatures of some of these windows are presented in figure 13-11. The spectrum is characterized by a main-lobe width and amplitude plus the side-lobe maximum amplitude. Different windows can be compared in terms of the main-lobe width and the so-called ripple ratio, or RR, where

$$RR\% = 100 \times (\text{max. side-lobe gain})/(\text{max. main-lobe gain}) \quad (13\text{-}12)$$

Several windows are interpreted below in terms of the RR figure of merit.

Type	Main Lobe	RR ($N = 11$)	RR ($N = 21$)	RR ($N = 31$)
Rectangular	$4w_s/N$	22.3	22.9	21.8
Hann	$4w_s/N$	2.6	2.7	2.7
Hamming	$4w_s/N$	1.5	0.9	0.8

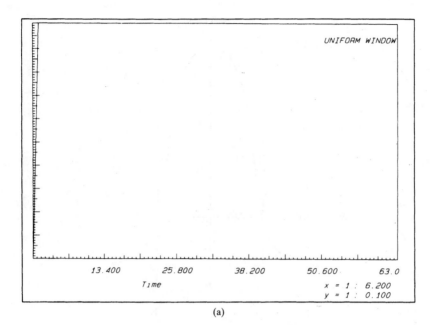

(a)

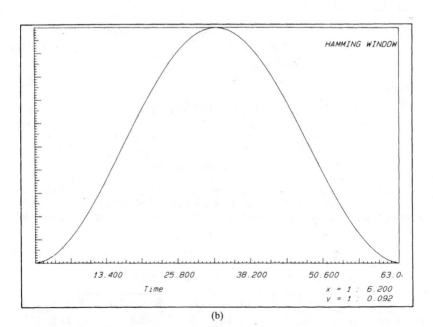

(b)

FIGURE 13-11 Typical window profiles.

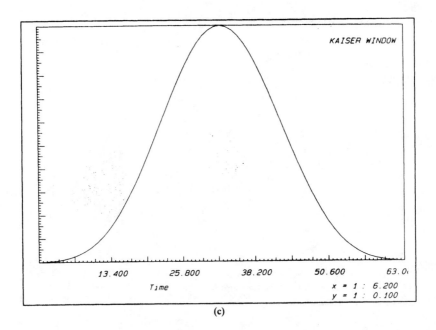

(c)

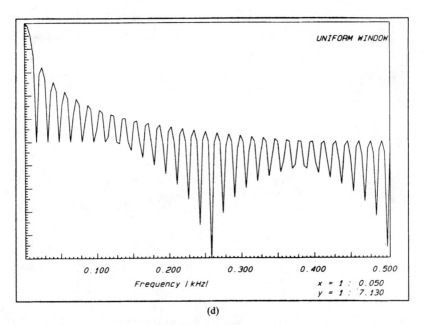

(d)

FIGURE 13-11 *(Continued)* Typical window profiles.

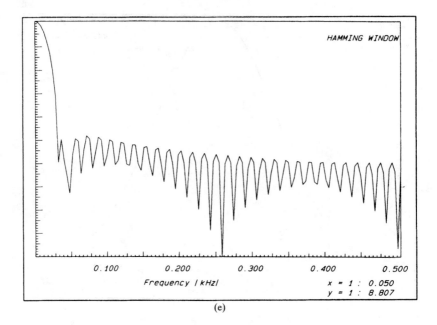

(e)

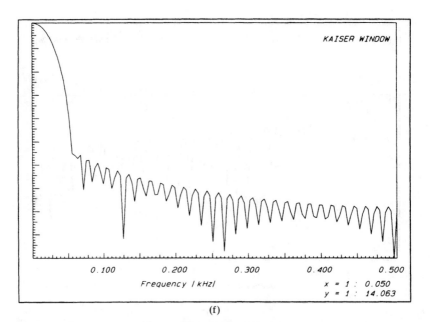

(f)

FIGURE 13-11 *(Continued)* Typical window profiles.

Windows can be directly applied to FIRs. To window an N-point FIR, simply multiply the tap weight coefficients c_i with the corresponding window weights w_i. Note that all of the standard window functions have even symmetry about the mid-sample. As a result, the application of such a window will not disturb the linear phase behavior of the original FIR.

EXAMPLE 13-4 (CBI)

REQUIRED: A dual bandpass FIR filter, having unity gain over the intervals $[0.1, 0.2]$ and $[0.3, 0.4]$ times f_s, is to be designed using the weighted Chebyshev method.

RESULTS: The resulting 61st-order FIR architecture is reported in figure 13-12 along with the computer-generated filter coefficient set. The filter shown in figure 13-12a requires 61 distinct multiplications by the tap weights $H(i)$. However, since a linear phase filter has been designed, there is known symmetry about the center tap. The symmetry condition can be used to reduce the number of distinct multiplications to 31 [in general, $(N + 1)/2$ as suggested in figure 13-12b. This device of trading off multiplications for additions essentially halves the number of multiplications required to complete an FIR cycle. For most designs, this action would normally result in a faster filter cycle.

The impulse response of the filter was then windowed using:

Uniform window
Hamming window
Blackman window
Kaiser window with $\beta = 2$
Kaiser window with $\beta = 5$
Kaiser window with $\beta = 10$

The windowed filter differs from that reported in figure 13-12 only in the specific values of the tap weights. More specifically, the coefficient $H(i)$ in figure 13-12 is replaced by $H(i) = H(i) \times W(i)$ where $W(i)$ is the window coefficient. Since the window weights have known symmetry about the central coefficient, the resulting windowed coefficient set maintains its original symmetry. Therefore, another linear phase filter is produced. The resulting time series, when presented to a DFT, gives the spectrum presented in figure 13-13. It can be observed that the windows have a "smoothing effect." The choice of which window to use, or not to use a window, is a design option. Numerical experimentation can often be used to examine this question.

13.5 MULTIRATE SIGNAL PROCESSING

Digital signal processing systems accept an input time series and produce an output time series. In between, a signal can be modified in terms of its time and/or frequency domain attributes. One of the important functions that a digital signal processing system can serve is that of sample rate conversion. As the name implies, a sample rate converter changes a system's sample rate from a value of f_{in} samples per second to a rate of f_{out} samples per second. Such devices are also called multirate systems since they are defined in terms of two or more sample rates. If $f_{in} > f_{out}$, then the system is said to perform decimation and is said to be decimated by an integer M if:

$$M = \frac{f_{out}}{f_{in}} \tag{13-13}$$

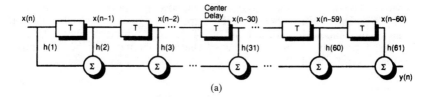

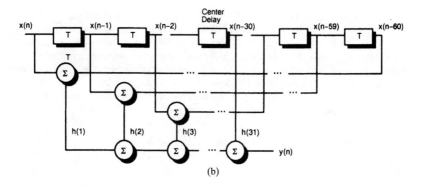

```
                        FILTER LENGTH= 61    BITS= 64

                              IMPULSE RESPONSE
                        H(  1 )= -.418772E-01   =H(  61 )
                        H(  2 )= -.691816E-02   =H(  60 )
                        H(  3 )= 0.202831E-01   =H(  59 )
                        H(  4 )= -.159539E-01   =H(  58 )
                        H(  5 )= 0.637023E-01   =H(  57 )
                        H(  6 )= -.196389E-01   =H(  56 )
                        H(  7 )= -.438400E-01   =H(  55 )
                        H(  8 )= -.168999E-01   =H(  54 )
                        H(  9 )= -.430768E-02   =H(  53 )
                        H( 10 )=-.202712E-01    =H(  52 )
                        H( 11 )=-.525528E-01    =H(  51 )
                        H( 12 )=-.184505E-01    =H(  50 )
                        H( 13 )=0.198650E-01    =H(  49 )
                        H( 14 )=-.625899E-02    =H(  48 )
                        H( 15 )=0.483218E-01    =H(  47 )
                        H( 16 )=0.451225E-02    =H(  46 )
                        H( 17 )=-.501234E-01    =H(  45 )
                        H( 18 )=-.326114E-04    =H(  44 )
                        H( 19 )=-.124289E-03    =H(  43 )
                        H( 20 )=-.829698E-03    =H(  42 )
                        H( 21 )=-.294351E-01    =H(  41 )
                        H( 22 )=0.887240E-02    =H(  40 )
                        H( 23 )=0.356960E-01    =H(  39 )
                        H( 24 )=0.117951E-01    =H(  38 )
                        H( 25 )=0.175192E+00    =H(  37 )
                        H( 26 )=0.145369E-02    =H(  36 )
                        H( 27 )=-.220598E+00    =H(  35 )
                        H( 28 )=0.520754E-05    =H(  34 )
                        H( 29 )=-.987576E-01    =H(  33 )
                        H( 30 )=0.102520E-01    =H(  32 )
                        H( 31 )=0.357111E+00    =H(  31 )
```

		LOWER BAND EDGE	UPPER BAND EDGE	DESIRED VALUE	DEVIATION	DEVIATION (IN dB)
BAND	1	0.000000D+00	1.000000D-01	0.000000D+00	1.367265D-01	-1.728295D+01
BAND	2	1.100000D-01	1.900000D-01	1.000000D+00	1.367265D-01	-1.728295D+01
BAND	3	2.000000D-01	3.000000D-01	0.000000D+00	1.367265D-01	-1.728295D+01
BAND	4	3.100000D-01	3.900000D-01	1.000000D+00	1.367265D-01	-1.728295D+01
BAND	5	4.000000D-01	5.000000D-01	0.000000D+00	1.367265D-01	-1.728295D+01

(c)

FIGURE 13-12 Dual pass-band filter.

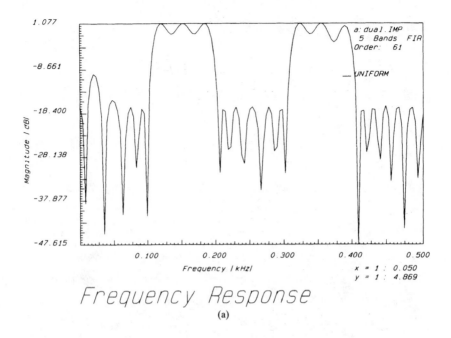

Frequency Response
(a)

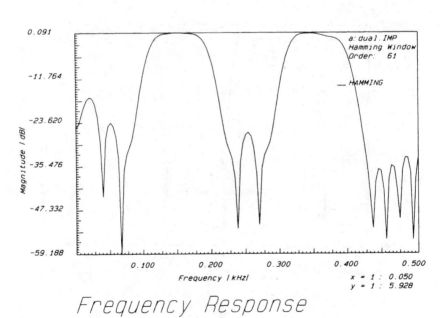

Frequency Response
(b)

FIGURE 13-13   Effect of windowing on a dual band-pass filter.

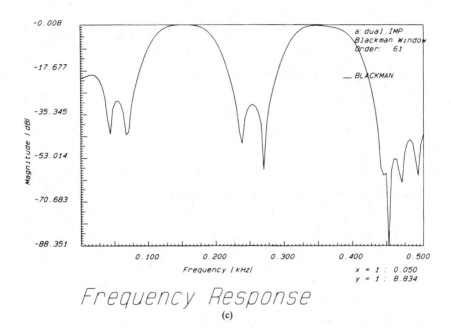

Frequency Response

(c)

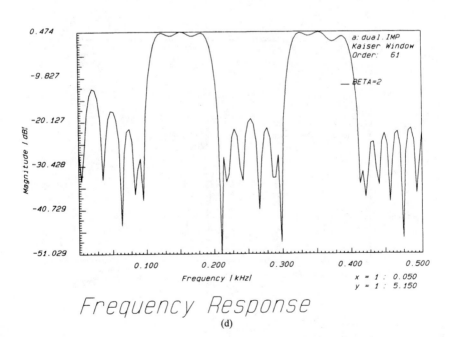

Frequency Response

(d)

FIGURE 13-13 *(Continued)* Effect of windowing on a dual band-pass filter.

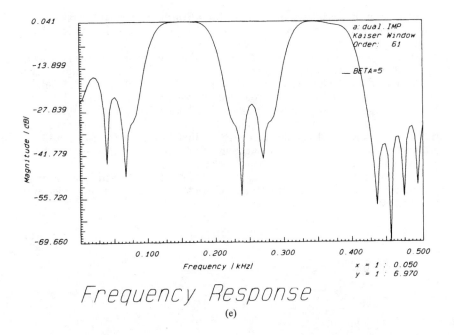

Frequency Response

(e)

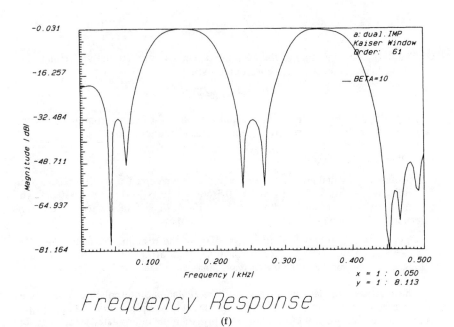

Frequency Response

(f)

FIGURE 13-13   *(Continued)* Effect of windowing on a dual band-pass filter.

In this case, the decimated time series $x_d[n] = x[Mn]$, or every Mth sample of the original time series is retained. Furthermore, the effective sample rate is reduced from f_{in} to $f_{dec} = f_{in}/M$ samples per second.

Applications of decimation include audio and image signal processing involving two or more subsystems having dissimilar sample rates. Other applications occur when a high data rate analog-to-digital converter (ADC) is placed at the front end of a system and the output is to be processed parameters which are sampled at a very low rate by a general-purpose digital computer. At other times, multirate systems are used simply to reduce the Nyquist rate to facilitate computational intensive algorithms, such as a digital Fourier analyzer (see FFT), to be performed at a slower arithmetic rate. Another class of applications involves processing signals, sampled at a high data rate, through a limited bandwidth channel.

The spectral properties of a decimated signal can be examined by exploring a decimated signal in the transform domain. Consider the decimated time series to be modeled as:

$$x_d[n] = \sum_{k=-\infty}^{\infty} x[k]\delta(n - kM) \tag{13-14}$$

which has a z transform given by

$$X_d[z] = \sum_{k=-\infty}^{\infty} z^{-k}\left(\sum_{n=-\infty}^{\infty} x[k]\delta(n - kM)\right) = \sum_{k=-\infty}^{\infty} x[k]\left(\sum_{n=-\infty}^{\infty} z^{-k}\delta(n - kM)\right)$$

$$= \sum_{k=-\infty}^{\infty} x[k]z^{-kM} = \sum_{k=-\infty}^{\infty} x[k](z^{-k})^M \tag{13-15}$$

or $$X_d(z) = X(z^M)$$

The frequency signature of the decimated signal, relative to the undecimated or parent signal, can therefore be represented by:

$$X_d(e^{j\phi}) = X(e^{jM\phi}) \tag{13-16}$$

which can be seen to be a frequency-scaled version of the original (parent) spectrum repeated on $2\pi/M$ centers relative to a normalized frequency axis.

EXAMPLE 13-5 (CBI)

REQUIRED: A signal given by $x(t) = \cos(2\pi f_s t/33)$ is sampled at a 1-kHz rate to form $\{x[n]\}$. The spectrum is given by $X(e^{j\omega}) = 0.5*\delta(\omega - 2\pi 10^3/33) + 0.5*\delta(\omega + 2\pi 10^3/33)$. The time series and spectrum are shown in figure 13-14. What is the spectrum of the decimated-by-3 version of $\{x[n]\}$?

RESULT: Equation (13-16) defines the shape of the resulting decimated spectrum which is given by $X_d(e^{j\omega}) = 0.5*\delta((\omega - 2\pi 10^3)/3) + 0.5*\delta((\omega + 2\pi 10^3)/3)$. The decimated time series and spectrum are also displayed in figure 13-14.

The antithesis of decimation is called *interpolation*. Interpolation attempts to reconstruct a facsimile of $\{x[n]\}$ from the sparse set of samples contained in $\{x_d[n]\}$. If $\{x_d[n]\}$ contains only every Mth sample of $\{x[n]\}$, then the interpolated signal is generally only an approximation of the original (parent) time series. Recall that signal

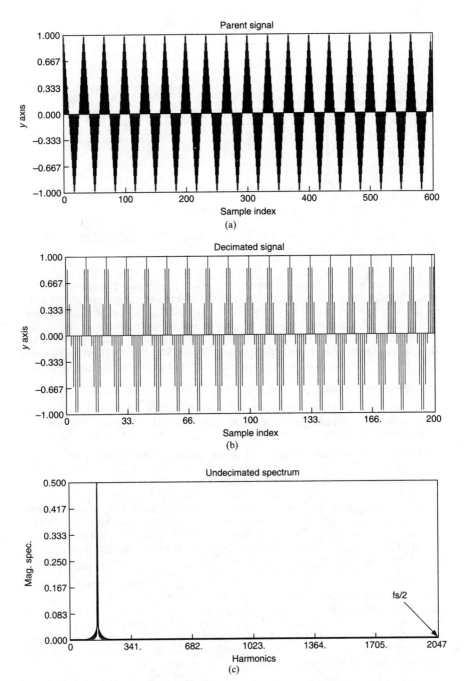

FIGURE 13-14 Shown are: (*a*) parent time series $x[n]$; (*b*) decimated-by-3 time series $x_d[n]$; magnitude frequency response $X[k]$; (*c*) magnitude frequency response of parent time series. *(Produced using SIGLAB, courtesy of The Athena Group)*

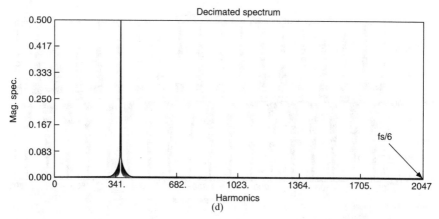

FIGURE 13-14 *(Continued)* Shown is: (*d*) Magnitude frequency response $X_d[k]$. *(Produced using SIGLAB, courtesy of The Athena Group)*

reconstruction was considered in section 12.3 when the Shannon sampling theorem was introduced. Shannon's sampling theorem stated that an analog signal $x(t)$ could be reconstructed, or interpolated, from the sample values of $x(t)$ if it is sampled at a sufficiently high rate. One should be aware that Shannon's sampling theorem also applies to decimation and interpolation. Suppose the highest frequency found in $x(t)$ is BHz. Then, aliasing is avoided if the original and decimated sampling rates are in excess of $f_s = 2*$BHz. This means that there is a practical upper bound to the decimation rate.

EXAMPLE 13-6   (CBI)

REQUIRED: The highest frequency found in the signal $x(t) = \cos(2*\pi*10^3 t)$ is $B = 10^3$ Hz. Suppose $x(t)$ is highly oversampled at a rate $f_s = 10^5$ Hz [see figure 13-15 *a* and *b*]. What is the maximum decimation rate that will ensure that no aliasing will occur?

RESULT: The minimum lower bound on the sampling rate, called the Nyquist frequency, is $2*10^3$ Hz. Therefore, the maximum decimation rate is $10^5/2*10^3 = 50$. The resulting time series produced by a decimation by $M = 8 < 50$ operation is shown in figure 13-15b. The spectra of the parent and decimated signals is reported in Figure 13-15c over the common frequency range $f \in [0,10^5/2)$. The production of aliased copies and frequency scaling of the parent is evident. To demonstrate what happens if the decimation rate is too high, consider the case where $M = 64 > 50$. The resulting time series is shown in figure 13-15d and is seen to impersonate (alias) a signal having a frequency equal to $(1/64 - 1/100)*10^3$ Hz.

Interpolating a decimated signal requires defining a procedure by which a signal $\{x_i[n]\}$ (the interpolated signal) can be constructed which *maximally* agrees with the original, or parent time series $\{x[n]\}$. Unfortunately, only every Mth sample of the parent is known. In the absence of any additional information, the most primitive interpolation formula assumes that an interpolated time series uses the sample value of $\{x_d[n]\}$ to restore selected values of $\{x_i[n]\}$ and sets all other values to zero. This technique is called zero-filling. That is,

$$x_i[n] = \begin{cases} x[n] \text{ if } n \bmod (M) = 0 \\ 0 \text{ otherwise} \end{cases} = \begin{cases} x_d[n/M] \text{ if } n \bmod (M) = 0 \\ 0 \text{ otherwise} \end{cases}$$

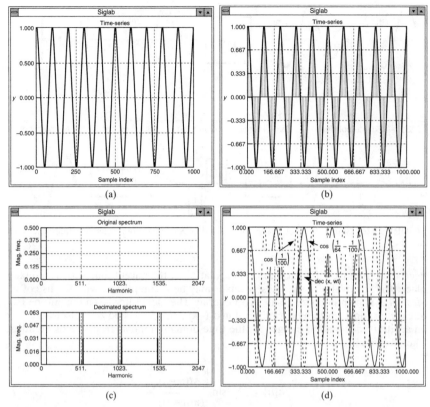

FIGURE 13-15 Shown are: (*a*) original $x(t)$; (*b*) decimated-by-8 time series; (*c*) magnitude frequency response (line spectrum) of the parent and decimated signal; and (*d*) the overlay of the parent, decimated-by-64 time series, and aliased image having a normalized frequency of $1/64 - 1/100$. (*Produced using SIGLAB, courtesy of The Athena Group*)

which is graphically interpreted in figure 13-16. It should be apparent that the zero-fill model produces a poor facsimile of the original (parent) time series. It can be seen, however, that the sample rate is restored to its original value. Therefore the zero-fill method is sometimes referred to simply as a sample rate converter.

Figure 13-16 also displays the interpolated results produced by zero and first-order hold models, which were introduced in figure 12-1. It can be noted that they represent a higher-quality interpolated formula when compared with the zero-filled model. Nevertheless, it can be seen that in all cases the sample rate is returned to $f_{in} = M f_{dec}$.

The question remains: *What is the ideal interpolator?* The answer can be found in the examination of spectra of decimated and interpolated signals. Consider the data presented in figure 13-17 which represents the outcome of a decimation and interpolation experiment. The baseband spectrum of a decimated-by-2 signal is shown in the top panel over the decimated Nyquist frequency range $f \in [-f_s/4, f_s/4]$, where f_s is the rate at which the parent signal was sampled. In the middle panel the zero-filled interpolated signal is found using an interpolation factor of $M = 2$. It can be seen that the interpolated signal spawns aliased copies of the baseband spectrum which will

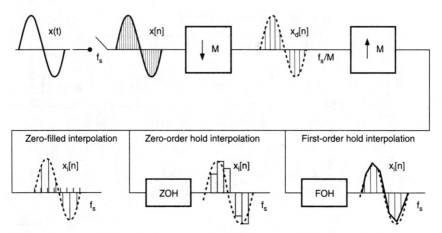

FIGURE 13-16 Simple interpolation models including zero-fill, *zero*th-order, and first-order hold circuits.

need to be removed if an accurate interpolation of the parent time series is to take place. The removal of these aliased copies may be accomplished with the use of an *ideal filter* shown in figure 13-17 as an overlay. The ideal filter has a magnitude frequency response given by $|H(\omega)| = 1$ if $\omega \in (-\pi f_s/M, \pi f_s/M)$ and zero elsewhere. For an arbitrary decimation integer M, the time domain impulse response of the ideal filter is given by:

$$h[n] = \sum_{i=-\infty}^{\infty} \sin \frac{\left(\dfrac{\pi}{M(n-i)} \right)}{(\pi(n-i))} \qquad (13\text{-}17)$$

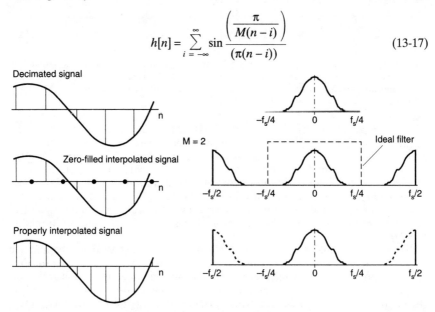

FIGURE 13-17 Spectra of decimated signal, zero-filled interpolated signal, and filtered baseband signal. Also shown is an overlay of an ideal anti-aliasing filter.

The filter has a classic $\sin(x)/x$ shape and is noncausal (i.e., persists for all time $n \in (-\infty, \infty)$ and is therefore not physically realizable. As a result, the ideal Shannon interpolation filter is generally approximated by a practical and realizable interpolator such as a zero or first-order hold circuit. Another approximate interpolation technique is a simple low-pass filter having a passband covering the range filter $f \in (-f_s/2M, f_s/2M)$.

A convenient mathematical modeling technique for multirate systems is called the *polyphase decomposition*. Polyphase models are defined in the z domain and are used to represent an arbitrary time series $\{x[k]\}$, sampled at a rate of f_s samples per second, satisfying

$$X(z) = \sum_{k=-\infty}^{\infty} x[k]z^{-k} \tag{13-18}$$

Suppose the time series $\{x[k]\}$ is partitioned into M sequences of data where the ith sequence is given by the sample values:

$$x_i[k] = \{\ldots, x[i], x[i+M], x[i+2M], \ldots\} \tag{13-19}$$

The ith block can be seen to be the original time series delayed by i samples and then decimating by M (i.e., retain every Mth sample beginning with $x[i]$). In terms of a z transform, noting that $Z(x[i+kM]) \Leftrightarrow z^{-(i+kM)} x[i+kM]$, the decomposed time series can be expressed as:

$$X(z) = \begin{cases} \ldots (x[0] + z^{-M}x[M] + z^{-2M}x[2M] + \ldots) \\ \ldots (x[1]z^{-1} + z^{-(M-1)}x[M+1] + z^{-(2M-1)}x[2M+1] + \ldots) \\ \ldots \qquad \ldots \qquad \ldots \qquad \ldots \qquad \ldots \\ \ldots (x[M-1]z^{-(M-1)} + z^{-(2M-1)}x[2M-1] + z^{-(3M-1)}x[3M-1] + \ldots) \end{cases} \tag{13-20}$$

Alternatively, the preceding expression can be grouped and factored to read

$$X(z) = \begin{cases} \ldots (x[0] + z^{-M}x[M] + z^{-2M}x[2M] + \ldots) \\ \ldots z^{-1}(x[1] + z^{-M}x[M+1] + z^{-2M}x[2M+1] + \ldots) \\ \ldots \qquad \ldots \qquad \ldots \qquad \ldots \qquad \ldots \\ \ldots z^{-(M-1)}(x[M-1] + z^{-M}x[2M-1] + z^{-2M}x[3M-1] + \ldots) \end{cases} \tag{13-21}$$

The ith row of equation (13-21) can now be defined in terms of the ith *polyphase function*

$$P_i(z) = \sum_{k=-\infty}^{\infty} x(kM-i)z^{-k} \tag{13-22}$$

which can be grouped together to synthesize $X(z)$ as follows:

$$X(z) = \sum_{i=0}^{M-1} z^{-i} P_i(z^M) \tag{13-23}$$

The resulting compact representation is called an M-component polyphase decomposition of a time series $\{x[n]\}$.

EXAMPLE 13-7

REQUIRED: Consider the time series $x[n] = \{\dots,0,1,2,3,4,3,2,1,0,1,2,3,4,3,2,1,0,1,2,3,4,$
$3,2,1,\dots\}$ where $x[0] = 0$, and $M = 4$. What is its polyphase representation?

RESULTS: From $P_0(z) = \{\dots + 0z^0 + 4z^{-1} + 0z^{-2} + 4z^{-3} + \dots\}$, $P_1(z) = \{\dots + 1z^0 + 3z^{-1}$
$+ 1z^{-2} + 3z^{-3} + \dots\}$, $P_2(z) = \{\dots + 2z^0 + 2z^{-1} + 2z^{-2} + 2z^{-3} + \dots\}$, and $P_3(z) = \{\dots + 3z^0$
$+ 1z^{-1} + 3z^{-2} + 1z^{-3} + \dots\}$, it follows that $X(z) = P_0(z^4)\ z^0 + P_1(z^4)\ z^{-1} + P_2(z^4)\ z^{-2}$
$+ P_3(z^4)\ z^{-3}$.

The mechanics of this polyphase decomposition are summarized in figure 13-18.
Notice that the solution consists of four parallel channels along with $M - 1 = 3$ shift
registers to properly phase the signals. Each channel consists of a 4:1 decimator and
a path from input to output which is being clocked at $f_s/4$. The bandwidth requirement of each individual channel, therefore, is $1/M = 1/4$th that of a direct input/out-
put path. This points out a possible utility of multirate systems which is channel
bandwidth compression.

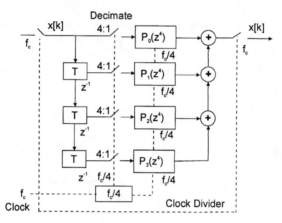

FIGURE 13-18   Example $M = 4$ polyphase multirate system.

A polyphase representation also can be used to explain decimation. First consider that a time series $\{x[n]\}$, being decimated by a factor M, produces a new time
series $\{x_d[n]\}$, where:

$$x_d[n] = x[Mn] \qquad (13\text{-}24)$$

and the z transform of the parent time series $\{x[k]\}$ is given by

$$X(z) = \sum_{k = -\infty}^{\infty} x[k]z^{-k} \qquad (13\text{-}25)$$

with respect to a sample delay of $T_s = 1/f_s$. The z transform of the decimated time
series is given by:

$$X_d(z) = \sum_{k = -\infty}^{\infty} x_d[k]z^{-k} = P_0(z) \qquad (13\text{-}26)$$

After some algebraic manipulation, the preceding equation can be expressed as

$$X_d(z) = P_0(z) = \frac{1}{M} \sum_{k=0}^{M-1} X(W_M^k z^{1/M}); \ W_M = e^{-j2\pi/M} \tag{13-27}$$

The term z^{-1} refers to the sample delay T_d. And $z^{-1/M}$ explicitly corresponds to a delay $T_s = T_d/M = 1/f_s$. This is illustrated in the following example.

EXAMPLE 13-8

REQUIRED: The time series $x[k] = a^k u[k]$, where $|a| < 1$, represents an exponential signal being sampled at a rate of f_s samples per second. Assume that the decimation rate is $M = 2$ (decimate by 2). From example 12-6, one knows that $X(z) = 1/(1 - az^{-1})$ where z^{-1} now corresponds to a delay of $1/f_s$ seconds. The decimated signal is given by $\{x_d[k]\} = \{x[2k]\} = \{1,a^2,a^4, \dots\}$. Therefore the z transform of the decimated signal satisfies that $X(z) = 1/(1 - a^2 z^{-1})$ where z^{-1} now corresponds to the delay of the decimated signal which is sampled every $2/f_s$ seconds. Verify this claim using polyphase techniques.

RESULTS: Evaluating equation (13-27), where $W_2^0 = 1$, $W_2^1 = -1$, it follows that

$$X_d(z) = \frac{1}{2}(X(W_2^0 z^{1/2}) + X(W_2^1 z^{1/2}))$$

where, at the sample rate of $f_d = f_s/2$, the component terms are, with respect to f_s,

$$X(W_2^0 z^{1/2}) = X(z^{1/2}) = \sum_{k=0}^{\infty} a^k z^{-k/2} = \frac{1}{1 - az^{-1/2}} \leftrightarrow \{1,a,a^2,a^3, \dots\}$$

$$X(W_2^1 z^{1/2}) = X(-z^{1/2}) = \sum_{k=0}^{\infty} (-1)^{-k/2} a^k z^{-k/2} = \frac{1}{1 + az^{-1/2}} \leftrightarrow \{1,-a,a^2,-a^3, \dots\}$$

It can immediately be seen that combining these terms in either the transform or time domain will synthesize $X_d(z)$ or $x_d[k]$.

EXAMPLE 13-9

REQUIRED: Consider again the problem considered in example 13-8, except now let $M = 4$.

RESULTS: Repeating the steps found in example 13-8, consider

$$X_d(z) = \frac{1}{4}(X(W_4^0 z^{1/4}) + X(W_4^1 z^{1/4}) + X(W_4^1 z^{1/4}) + X(W_4^1 z^{1/4}))$$

where, at the sample rate of $f_d = f_s/4$, the component terms are, with respect to f_s,

$$X(W_4^0 z^{1/4}) = X(z^{1/4}) = \sum_{k=0}^{\infty} a^k z^{-k/4} = \frac{1}{1 - az^{-1/4}} \leftrightarrow \{1, a, a^2, a^3, \dots\}$$

$$X(W_4^1 z^{1/4}) = X(-jz^{1/4}) = \sum_{k=0}^{\infty} (-j)^{-k/4} a^k z^{-k/4} = \frac{1}{1 + jaz^{-1/4}} \leftrightarrow \{1, -ja, -a^2, ja^3, \dots\}$$

$$X(W_4^0 z^{1/4}) = X(-z^{1/4}) = \sum_{k=0}^{\infty} (-a)^k z^{-k/4} = \frac{1}{1 + az^{-1/4}} \leftrightarrow \{1, -a, a^2, -a^3, \dots\}$$

$$X(W_4^1 z^{1/4}) = X(jz^{1/4}) = \sum_{k=0}^{\infty} (j)^{-k/4} a^k z^{-k/4} = \frac{1}{1 - jaz^{-1/2}} \leftrightarrow \{1, ja, -a^2, -ja^3, \dots\}$$

It can immediately be seen that combining these terms in either the transform or time domain will synthesize $X_d(z)$ or $x_d[k]$.

A logical question to pose relates to the location of the decimator. The two systems shown in figure 13-19 are equivalent. The topmost path of figure 13-19 consists of a decimator and a filter. The bottom path consists of a filter, which is identical to that found in the top loop, except its clock is running M times the rate of that found in the top loop. Both designs have the same number of coefficients and therefore the same arithmetic complexity. The major difference between the circuits is found in the rate at which the coefficient multiplication must be performed. The topmost filter has an internal data rate $1/M$th that of the bottom filter. Therefore, the top architecture is generally preferred due to its lower real-time computational requirement.

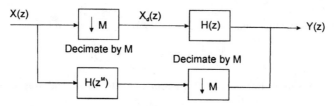

FIGURE 13-19   Equivalent decimated systems.

EXAMPLE 13-10

REQUIRED: Consider the case where the filter $H(z) = 1 + 2z^{-1} + z^{-2} + z^{-3}$ and $M = 2$. Implement $H(z)$ using the architectures shown in figure 13-19.

RESULTS: Observe that

$$H(z) = P_0(z^2) + z^{-1}P_1(z^2) = [1 + 2z^{-1}] + z^{-1}[2 + 1z^{-1}]$$

It then follows that the circuits shown in figure 13-20 are equivalent.

EXAMPLE 13-11   (CBI)

REQUIRED: Assume that an audio signal is band-limited to 20 kHz. This class of signal can be digitized above the Nyquist frequency using an industry standard 44.1 kHz ADC. Based on this sample rate, it can be seen that the audio spectrum is copied on 44.1-kHz centers. Between the spectrum centered at 0 and 44.1 Hz is a frequency band void of spectral energy of width

$$\Delta f = f_s - 2*20 \times 10^3 = 4.1 \text{ kHz}$$

To ensure that no aliasing errors occur, an anti-aliasing analog filter having a passband out to 20 kHz and a cutoff frequency of 24,100 Hz (i.e., transition band of Δf) will be required. This is generally considered to be a steep-skirt analog filter. To relax the design requirements of the analog anti-aliasing filter, an analog filter with a larger transition band is required. This immediately suggests that a higher sample rate be used.

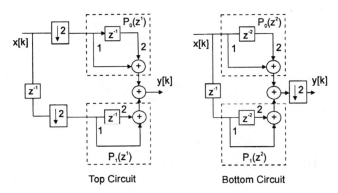

Top Circuit   Bottom Circuit

FIGURE 13-20   Equivalent third-order decimated filters.

RESULT: Suppose a four-times oversampling ADC is used (i.e., $f_s = 4*44.1 \times 10^3 = 176.4 \times 10^3$). Then the frequency range between the baseband audio spectrum and that centered about f_s is given by:

$$\Delta f = 176.4 \times 10^3 - 2*20 \times 10^3 = 136.4 \text{ kHz}$$

Now the anti-aliasing filter, with a passband of 20 kHz, need only have a transition band of 136.4 kHz, which is easily realized with a low-order analog filter.

To demonstrate the filter design differences, refer to figure 13-21 where the ±20-kHz baseband spectrum is displayed as the solid graph. The shape of the analog filter for $f_s = 44.1$ kHz and 136.4 kHz are also shown. The $f_s = 44.1$-kHz filter is seen to be a difficult-to-design steep-skirt filter, while the $f_s = 136.4$-kHz filter is a low-order easily implemented filter.

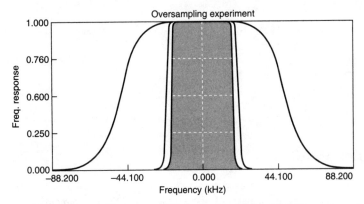

FIGURE 13-21   Oversample experiment. *(Produced using SIGLAB, courtesy of The Athena Group)*

A common problem is interfacing two systems having dissimilar rates, say f_{in} and f_{out}, respectively. Suppose they are related by the rational number $k = N/M$, where $f_{in} = kf_{out}$. If $k > 1$, then the sample rate is reduced, and the opposite if $k < 1$. The system described in figure 13-22, called a noninteger decimator, will perform this operation.

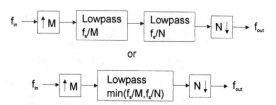

FIGURE 13-22 Noninteger decimation system.

13.6 QUADRATURE MIRROR FILTER

We have stated that multirate systems are often used to reduce the sample rate to a value which can be passed through a band-limited communication channel. Supposedly, the signal can be reconstructed on the receiver side. The amount of allowable decimation has been established by the Nyquist sampling theorem. What happens then when the bandwidth of the signal establishes a Nyquist frequency which exceeds the bandwidth of a communication channel? In such cases, the signal must be decomposed into subbands which can be individually transmitted across band-limited channels. This technique uses a bank of band-limited filters to break the signal down into a collection of subbands which all fit within the available channel bandwidths.

Quadrature mirror filters (QMF) are often used in the subband application described in figure 13-23. The basic architecture shown in figure 13-23 defines a QMF system and establishes two input-output paths which have a bandwidth requirement that is half the input or output requirements. Using this technique, the channels can be subdivided over and over, reducing the bandwidth by a factor of two

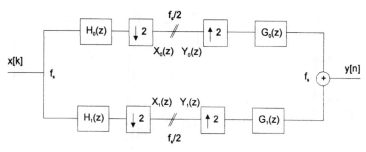

FIGURE 13-23 QMF filter.

each time. The top path consists of low-pass filters and the bottom path is formed by high-pass filters. Referring to equation (13-26) and example 13-8, it can be seen that:

$$X_0(z) = \frac{1}{2}\{X(z^{1/2})H_0(z^{1/2}) + X(-z^{1/2})H_0(-z^{1/2})\}$$

$$X_1(z) = \frac{1}{2}\{X(z^{1/2})H_1(z^{1/2}) + X(-z^{1/2})H_1(-z^{1/2})\} \qquad (13\text{-}28)$$

Noting that $Y_0(z)$ and $Y_1(z)$ are upsampled by 2, it follows that

$$Y(z) = G_0(z)Y_0(z^2) + G_1(z)Y_1(z^2) = \frac{1}{2}\{(H_0(z)G_0(z) + H_1(z)G_1(z))X(z)\}$$

$$+ \frac{1}{2}\{(H_0(-z)G_0(z) + H_1(-z)G_1(z))X(-z)\} \quad (13\text{-}29)$$

One would like the first term in equation (13-29) to reconstruct $X(z)$, which means that the second term should equal zero. Setting the second term to zero results in

$$\{(H_0(-z)G_0(z) + H_1(-z)G_1(z))X(-z)\} = 0 \quad (13\text{-}30)$$

which is satisfied if

$$G_0(z) = H_1(z) \text{ and } G_1(z) = H_0(z) \quad (13\text{-}31)$$

A special case often considered assumes that $H_0(z)$ and $H_1(z)$ are subband filters satisfying the following relationship

$$H_1(z) = H_0(-z) \quad (13\text{-}32)$$

which defines $H_1(z)$ to be the mirror image of $H_0(z)$. That is

$$H_1(e^{j\phi}) = H_0(e^{j(\phi - \pi)}) \quad (13\text{-}33)$$

From an implementation standpoint, the conversion of a filter having a z transform

$$H(z) = \sum_{i=-L}^{L} h_i z^{-i} \quad (13\text{-}34)$$

to its mirror image, given by

$$H_{\text{mirror}}(z) = H(-z) = \sum_{i=-L}^{L} h_i(-z)^{-i} = \sum_{i=-L}^{L} (-1)^i h_i z^{-i} \quad (13\text{-}35)$$

which simply states that the coefficients are modified by $(-1)^i$ (i.e., sign change).

EXAMPLE 13-12 (CBI)

REQUIRED: A 63rd-order low-pass FIR, having a transition band which is symmetric about the quarter sampling frequency (i.e., $f_{\text{transition}} = f_s/4 = f_{\text{Nyquist}}/2$) is called a *halfband* filter. A known property of a halfband filter is that, except for the center tap coefficient, every other FIR coefficient is zero. That is, the impulse response of a typical FIR is $h[n] = \{ \ldots h_{-5}, h_{-4}, h_{-3}, h_{-2}, h_{-1}, h_0, h_1, h_2, h_3, h_4, h_5, \ldots \}$. A halfband FIR has an impulse response given by $h_{\text{halfband}}[n] = \{ \ldots , h_{-5}, 0, h_{-3}, 0, h_{-1}, h_0, h_1, 0, h_3, 0, h_5, \ldots \}$ as shown in figure 13-24. As a result, compared with an arbitrary FIR, a halfband FIR needs approximately half the number of multiply coefficients per filter cycle. Use equation (13.35) to produce the mirror image of the example 63rd-order low-pass FIR.

RESULT: Upon multiplying the coefficients of the original filter by $(-1)^i$, a FIR filter has a magnitude frequency response shown in figure 13-25.

Under this condition, the z transform of the QMF system output is given by

$$Y(z) = [H_0^2(z) - H_0^2(-z)]X(z) \quad (13\text{-}36)$$

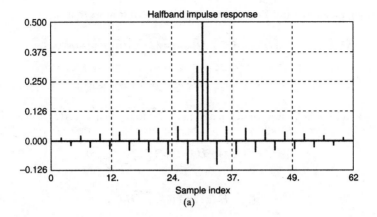

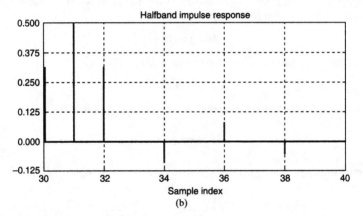

FIGURE 13-24 Original 63rd-order FIR halfband impulse response with zoom inspection of the coefficients showing it to be dense in zero-valued coefficients. *(Athena)*

Designing QMF is, unfortunately, not a trivial process. It is known that no meaningful flat response linear phase QMF filter exists. Most QMF designs represent some compromise. If the linear phase *or* perfect mirror condition [i.e., $H_1(z) = H_0(-z)$] is relaxed, then a magnitude and phase distortionless QMF system can be realized. A popular design paradigm is called the *perfect reconstruction QMF* (PRQMF). The output of a PRQMF system is equal to the input, with the addition of a known delay.

The PRQMF design procedure is given by the following recipe.

1. Define a linear phase FIR $F(z)$ to be a $2(N-1)$-order halfband FIR having a ripple deviation δ.

2. Add δ to the center tap weight of $F(z)$ to form $F_+(z) = F(z) + q\delta$ where $q > 1.0$, but close to unity. This action makes the minimum passband gain $F_+(z)$ bounded from below by unity. $F_+(z)$ is also halfband and the factors of $F_+(z)$ are moved slightly off the unit circle. This makes them easier to compute and interpret using a general-purpose digital computer.

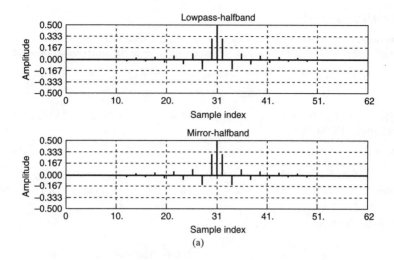

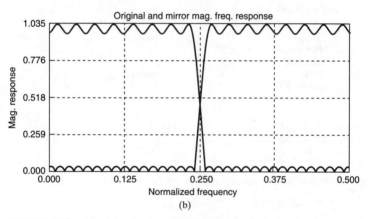

FIGURE 13-25 Original and mirror impulse and magnitude frequency responses. *(Produced using SIGLAB, courtesy of The Athena Group)*

3. Define an $(N-1)$-order FIRs $H_0(z)$ and $H_1(z)$ satisfying $F_+(z) = H(z)H(z^{-1})$. The zeros of $F_+(z)$ are found as complex conjugate reciprocal pairs. That is, if $z = re^{j\phi}$ is a zero of $F_+(z)$, then so are $z = re^{-j\phi}$ and $(1/r)e^{\pm j\phi}$. The zeros residing inside the unit circle are assigned to $H(z)$; those outside the unit circle belong to $H(z^{-1})$.

4.
$$H_0(z) = H(z)$$

$$H_1(z) = (-1)^{N-1}z^{-(N-1)}H(-z^{-1})$$

$$G_0(z) = H_1(-z)$$

$$G_1(z) = -H(-z)$$

The result is a PFQMF system having an input-output transfer function $T(z) = Kz^{-(N-1)}$ where K is a constant.

EXAMPLE 13-13 (CBI)

REQUIRED: Design a PRQMF system based on a 15th-order linear phase low-pass halfband filter having normalized critical frequencies of 0.2 and 0.3, and satisfying:

$$F(z) = -0.02648z^7 + 0.0441z^5 - 0.0934z^3 + 0.3140z^1 + 0.5 + 0.3140z^{-1} - 0.0934z^{-3}$$
$$+ 0.0441z^{-5} - 0.02648z^{-7}$$

The magnitude frequency response of $F(z)$ is shown in figure 13-25. Produce the required PRQMF system.

RESULT: Following the step-by-step processes,

Step 1: $F(z)$ is given and $\delta = 0.02377$.

Step 2: Let $q = 1.01$ and produce $F_+(z)$ such that $F_+(z) = F(z)$ except at $z = 0$ where $F_+(0) = F(0) + q\delta$.

Step 3: The factors of $F_+(z)$ are:

z_i	$|z_i|$	Interior/Exterior
$-0.968 \pm j0.441$	1.02	Exterior
$-0.875 \pm j0.371$	0.98	Interior
$-0.456 \pm j0.919$	1.01	Exterior
$-0.443 \pm j0.874$	0.98	Interior
$0.394 \pm j0.427$	0.58	Interior
0.561	0.56	Interior
$1.167 \pm j1.264$	1.72	Exterior
1.782	1.78	Exterior

Collecting the zeros residing within the unit circle (i.e., assigned to $H_{(z)}$) and multiplying them together, one obtains

$$H(z) = 1.0 + 1.3403z^{-1} + 0.6851z^{-2} - 0.2444z^{-3} - 0.3410z^{-4} + 0.0991z^{-5} + 0.2399z^{-6} - 0.1790z^{-7} = H_0(z)$$

$$H_1(z) = -0.1790 - 0.2399z^{-1} + 0.0991z^{-2} + 0.3140z^{-3} - 0.2444z^{-4} - 0.6851z^{-5} + 1.34030z^{-6} - 1.0z^{-7}$$

$$G_0(z) = -0.1790 + 0.2399z^{-1} + 0.0991z^{-2} - 0.3140z^{-3} - 0.2444z^{-4} + 0.6851z^{-5} + 1.34030z^{-6} + 1.0z^{-7}$$

$$G_1(z) = -1.0 + 1.3403z^{-1} - 0.6851z^{-2} - 0.2444z^{-3} + 0.3410z^{-4} + 0.0991z^{-5} - 0.2399z^{-6} - 0.1790z^{-7}$$

which are graphically reported in figure 13-26.

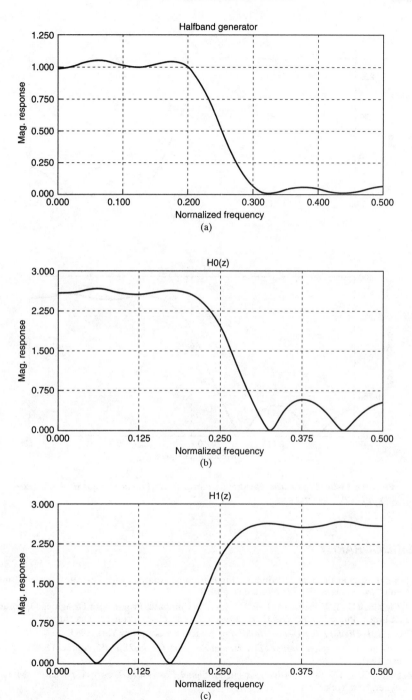

FIGURE 13-26 Quadrature mirror filter. *(Produced using SIGLAB, courtesy of The Athena Group)*

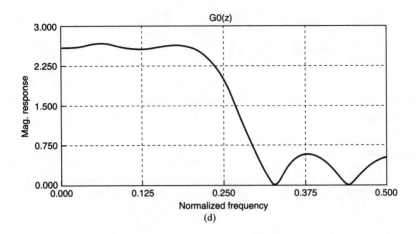

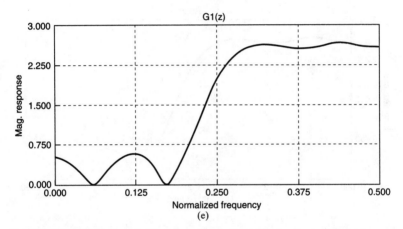

FIGURE 13-26 *(Continued)* Quadrature mirror filter. *(Produced using SIGLAB, courtesy of The Athena Group)*

BIBLIOGRAPHY

Harris, J. F., "On the Use of Windows for Harmonic Analysis with Discrete Fourier Transforms," *Proceedings of the IEEE,* January 1978.

McClellan, J. H., T. W. Parks, and L. R. Rabiner, "A Computer Program for Designing Optimum FIR Linear Phase Filters," *IEEE Trans. on Audio and Electroacoustics,* December 1973.

Taylor, F. J., *Digital Filter Design Handbook,* Marcel Dekker, New York, 1983.

——— and T. Stouraitis, *Digital Filter Design Software for the IBM PC,* Marcel Dekker, New York, 1987.

Zelniker, G. and F. Taylor, *Advanced Digital Signal Processing: Theory Applications,* Marcel Dekker, New York, 1994.

CHAPTER 14

INFINITE IMPULSE-RESPONSE FILTER

14.1 INTRODUCTION

In the previous chapter, the finite impulse-response filter, or FIR, was shown to exhibit superb linear phase behavior. However, it was observed that in order to achieve a high-quality (steep-skirt) magnitude frequency response, a high-order FIR was required. Compared to the FIR, the infinite impulse-response filter, or IIR,

1. Generally satisfies a given magnitude frequency-response design objective with a lower-order filter

2. Does not generally exhibit linear phase or constant group delay behavior

If the principal objective of the digital filter design is to satisfy the prespecified magnitude frequency response, an IIR is usually the design of choice. Since the order of an IIR is usually significantly less than that of an FIR, the IIR would require fewer coefficients. This translates into a reduced multiplication budget and an attendant saving in hardware and cost. Since multiplication is time consuming, a reduced multiplication budget also translates into potentially higher sample rates.

The impulse response of an IIR is an infinitely long data sequence $\{h(n)\}$. In terms of a monic (i.e., leading denominator coefficient equals unity) transfer function $H(z)$, it is represented as

$$H(z) = \frac{N(z)}{D(z)} = \sum_{n=0}^{\infty} h(n)z^{-n} = \frac{\displaystyle\sum_{i=0}^{M} b_i z^{-i}}{1 + \displaystyle\sum_{i=1}^{N} a_i z^{-i}} = K \times \frac{\displaystyle\prod_{i=1}^{M} (z - \alpha_i)}{\displaystyle\prod_{i=1}^{N} (z - \beta_i)} \tag{14-1}$$

From a practical viewpoint, a realizable filter must produce bounded outputs if stimulated by bounded inputs. The magnitude is bounded on an IIR's impulse response, namely

$$\sum_{n=0}^{\infty} |h(n)| < M \tag{14-2}$$

If M is finite (bounded), the filter is stable, and if it is infinite (unbounded), the filter is unstable. This condition can also be more conveniently related to the pole locations of the filter under study. It is well known that a causal discrete system with a rational transfer function $H(z)$ is stable (i.e., bounded inputs produce bounded outputs) if and only if its poles are interior to the unit circle in the z domain. This is often referred to as the circle criterion and it can be tested using general-purpose computer root-finding methods. Other algebraic tests—Schur-Cohen, Routh-Hurwitz, and Nyquist—may also be used. The stability condition is implicit to the FIR as long as all N coefficients are finite. Here the finite sum of real bounded coefficients will always be bounded.

14.2 DESIGN OBJECTIVES

The design of an IIR begins with a magnitude frequency-response specification of the filter. The filter's magnitude frequency response is specified as it would be for an analog filter design. In particular, assume that a filter with a magnitude-squared frequency response given by $|H(\omega)|^2$, having passband, transition band, and stopband behavior as suggested in figure 14-1, is to be synthesized. The frequency response of the desired filter is specified in terms of a *cutoff critical frequency* ω_p, a *stopband critical frequency* ω_s, and stop- and passband delimiters ε and A. The criti-

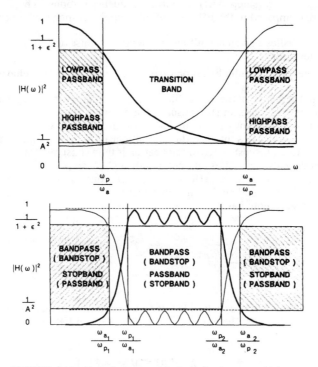

FIGURE 14-1 Typical design objectives for low-pass, high-pass, bandpass, and bandstop IIR filters.

cal frequencies ω_p and ω_a represent the end of the passband and the start of the stopband, respectively, for the low-pass example. In decibels, the gains at these critical frequencies are given by $-A_p = -10 \log (1 + \varepsilon^2)$ (passband ripple constraint) and $-A_a = -10 \log (A^2)$ (stopband attenuation). For the case where $\varepsilon = 1$, the common 3-dB passband filter is realized. Other classic design parameters found in general use are the *gain transition ratio* $\eta = \varepsilon/(A^2 - 1)^{1/2}$ and the *discrete transition frequency ratio* k_d which for a low-pass filter is given by $k_d = \omega_p/\omega_a$, $\omega_p < \omega_a$. The parameters η and k_d define the steepness of the filter's skirt. One often refers to the set of hybrid parameters defined as follows:

$$\varepsilon^2 = 10^{0.1A_p} - 1 \qquad [\text{from } 0.1A_p = \log (1 + \varepsilon^2)] \qquad (14\text{-}3)$$

$$\delta^2 = 10^{0.1A_a} - 1 \qquad [\text{from } 0.1A_a = \log (1 + \delta^2)]$$

where $\delta^2 = A^2 - 1$. Other hybrid parameters appearing in design tables are d and D, where

$$d = \frac{\delta}{\varepsilon} \qquad D = d^2 \qquad (14\text{-}4)$$

The metrics d and D are a measure of the depth of transition region. In terms of these parameters, classically defined filters such as Butterworth, Chebyshev, and elliptic can be designed. These filters form a very important class of discrete and digital filters since they possess outstanding magnitude frequency attributes. Furthermore, since they are defined in terms of well-known formulas, monographs (see chapter 2), and parametric design aids, it is generally considered advisable to relate the target digital filter to an equivalent analog of the same type.

14.3 REVIEW OF ANALOG DESIGN PRINCIPLES

In order to uniquely specify an analog filter whose transfer function satisfies

$$H(s) = \frac{KN(s)}{D(s)} = K \times \frac{\prod_{i=1}^{N} (s - \lambda_i)}{\prod_{i=1}^{N} (s - \sigma_i)} \qquad (14\text{-}5)$$

where N = filter order
             K = real gain adjustment
             $\{\lambda_i\}$ = analog filter zeros
             $\{\sigma_i\}$ = analog filter poles

the four tuple

$$T_4 = (N, K, \{\lambda_i\}, \{\sigma_i\}) \qquad (14\text{-}6)$$

must be completely specified. The process of designing an analog filter of a specified type begins with the translation of its frequency response into the filter's order. This process can be algebraically performed using the data presented in figure 14-2*a* through *c*. Here, the order of a low-pass Butterworth, Chebyshev, or elliptic filter is specified in terms of magnitude frequency response quantifiers:

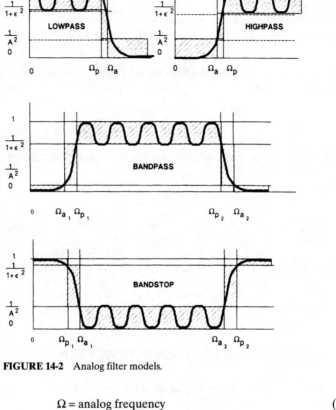

FIGURE 14-2 Analog filter models.

$$\Omega = \text{analog frequency} \tag{14-7}$$

$$\Omega_p = \text{end of passband}$$

$$\Omega_a = \text{beginning of attenuation band}$$

$$k = \text{analog transition ratio}$$

$$\Omega_r = 1/k = (\text{transition ratio})^{-1}$$

$$\varepsilon^2 = 10^{0.1A_p} - 1$$

$$\delta^2 = 10^{0.1A_a} - 1 = A^2 - 1$$

$$\eta = \varepsilon/(A^2 - 1)^{0.5} \quad (\text{gain transition ratio})$$

where the transition ratio is further qualified as (refer to figure 14-2)

$$\text{LP:} \quad k = \Omega_p/\Omega_a \tag{14-7i}$$

$$\text{HP:} \quad k = \Omega_a/\Omega_p \tag{14-7ii}$$

$$\text{BP:} \quad k = k_1 \text{ if } \Omega_u^2 \geq \Omega_v^2 \tag{14-7iii}$$

$$k = k_2 \text{ if } \Omega_u^2 < \Omega_v^2$$

$$\text{HP:} \quad k = 1/k_1 \text{ if } \Omega_u^2 \geq \Omega_v^2 \qquad (14\text{-}7iv)$$

$$k = 1/k_2 \text{ if } \Omega_u^2 < \Omega_v^2$$

where Ω_0 is the geometric mean frequency

$$\Omega_0 = \Omega_{p1}\Omega_{p2}/(\Omega_{p2} - \Omega_{p1})$$

and

$$k_1 = (\Omega_{a1}/\Omega_0)[1/(1 - \Omega_{a1}^2/\Omega_v^2)$$

$$k_2 = -(\Omega_{a2}/\Omega_0)[1/(1 - \Omega_{a2}^2/\Omega_v^2)]$$

$$\Omega_u^2 = \Omega_{a1}\Omega_{a2}$$

$$\Omega_v^2 = \Omega_{p1}\Omega_{p2}$$

Butterworth

An analog Butterworth low-pass filter is described in figure 14-3a. It represents a "smooth" transition between the passband and stopband with monotonically decreasing gain. The filter order can be estimated using the formula shown below:

$$n = \frac{\log\left[(A^2 - 1)/\varepsilon^2\right]}{2 \log (\Omega_r)} \qquad (14\text{-}8)$$

or

$$n = \frac{\log (d)}{\log (1/k)}$$

or

$$n = \frac{\log (\eta)}{\log (k)}$$

Chebyshev

An analog low-pass Chebyshev filter is displayed in figure 14-3b. It exhibits equiripple behavior in the passband and a smooth transition into the stopband. The order of this filter can be estimated as follows:

$$n = \frac{\log \{[1 + \sqrt{(1 - \eta^2)}]/\eta\}}{\log [\Omega_r + \sqrt{(\Omega_r^2 - 1)}]} \qquad (14\text{-}9)$$

or

$$= \frac{\cos h^{-1}(1/\eta)}{\ln\{[1 + \sqrt{(1 - k^2)}]/k\}} \qquad \ln = \log_e,$$

or

$$= \frac{\cosh^{-1}[\sqrt{(D)}]}{\cosh^{-1}(1/k)}$$

Elliptic

An analog elliptic low-pass filter is presented in figure 14-3c. A rippled passband and stopband results with a smooth transition in between. The order of an elliptic filter is approximated as follows:

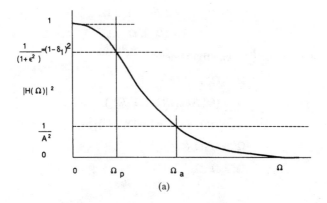

(a)

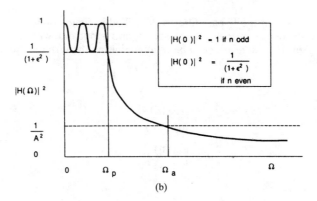

(b)

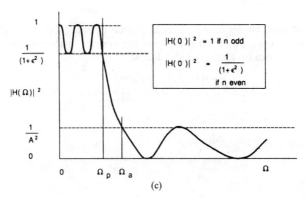

(c)

FIGURE 14-3 (*a*) Butterworth, (*b*) Chebyshev, and (*c*) elliptic low-pass filter's magnitude frequency-response profiles.

$$n = \frac{K(k)K[(1 - k_1^2)^{1/2}]}{K(k_1)K[(1 - k^2)^{1/2}]} \qquad (14\text{-}10)$$

where K is a complex elliptic integral of the form

$$\int_0^\Theta \frac{ds}{\sqrt{(1 - k^2 \sin^2 s)}}$$

To avoid tedious computation of n, based on evaluating this definite integral, use approximation methods. They are algebraic or nomograph. The order of an elliptic filter is approximately

$$n \geq \log (16D)/\log (1/q)$$

where $\qquad k = \Omega_p/\Omega_a \qquad k' = (1 - k^2)^{1/2}$

$$q_0 = \frac{0.5 \times [1 - (k')^{1/2}]}{[1 + (k')^{1/2}]}$$

$$q = q_0 + 2q_0^5 + 15p_0^9 + 150q_0^{13}$$

$$D = d^2$$

EXAMPLE 14-1

REQUIRED: A low-pass analog filter has an $A = 100$ (-40-dB attenuation band), $\varepsilon = 1$ (-3-dB passband), and an inverse transition ratio $\Omega_r = 1/k = 3.0$. Compute the estimated filter order for a Butterworth, Chebyshev, and elliptic design.

RESULTS:

Type	Order	
Butterworth	$n = \dfrac{\log (9999)}{2 \times \log (3)} = 4.2 \sim 5$	
		[after equation (14-8)]
Chebyshev	$1/\eta = (9999/1)^{1/2}$	
	$n = \dfrac{\log (999^{1/2} + 998^{1/2})}{\log (3 + 8^{1/2})} = 3.0057 \sim 4$	
		[after equation (14-9)]
Elliptic	$k = 1/3$ $\qquad\qquad\qquad\qquad$ $q = 7.3609 \times 10^{-3}$	
	$k' = [1 - (1/9)]^{1/2} \qquad\qquad + 2(2.16 \times 10^{-11})$	
	$\quad = .9428 \qquad\qquad\qquad\quad + 15(6.34 \times 10^{-20})$	
	$\qquad\qquad\qquad\qquad\qquad\qquad + 150(1.86 \times 10^{-28})$	
	$q_0 = \dfrac{0.5(1 - 0.9428)^{1/2}}{(1 + 0.9428^{1/2})} \qquad \sim 7.3609 \times 10^{-3}$	
	$\qquad\qquad\qquad\qquad\qquad\quad D = 9999$	
	$\quad = 7.3609 \times 10^{-3}$	
	$n \geq \dfrac{\log 159{,}984}{\log 135.85} = \dfrac{5.204}{2.133} \sim 3$	[after equation (14-10)]

EXAMPLE 14-2

REQUIRED: A low-pass analog filter has an $A = 100$ (-40-dB attenuation band), $\varepsilon = 1$ (-3-dB passband), and an inverse transition ratio $\Omega_r = 1/k = 3.0$. Compute the estimated filter order for a Butterworth, Chebyshev, and elliptic design.

RESULTS:

Type	Figure	Comment	
Butterwoth	2-34	$\Omega_r = 3$, stopband attentuation $= 40$ dB	
		Order estimate between 4 and 5	(check)
Chebyshev	2-45	$\Omega_r = 3$, stopband attenuation $= 40$ dB	
		Order estimate between 3 and 4	(check)
Elliptic	2-86	ϵ(eq. 2-34) $= \sqrt{(10^{R\ dB/10} - 1)}$	
		$= \sqrt{(10^{0.30} - 1)} \sim 1$	(check)
		ρ(eq. 2-52) $= \sqrt{(\epsilon^2/1 + \epsilon^2)}$	
		$= \sqrt{(1/2)} = 0.707$	
		$\rho\% = 70.7$	
		$A_{min} + A_p$ (fig. 2-86 for $\rho\% + 70.7$)	
		$= 40 + (A_p(70.7) < 4.78) < 44.78$	
		Order estimate between 2 and 3	(check)

To this point only the order N and transition ratio k of T_4 are known. It remains to compute the filter's poles and zeros $\{\lambda_i\}$ and $\{\beta_i\}$ or equivalently, in polynomial form

$$N(s) = \prod_{i=1}^{N} (s - \lambda_i) = \sum_{i=0}^{N} n_i s^i$$

$$D(s) = \prod_{i=1}^{N} (s - \beta_i) = \sum_{i=0}^{N} d_i s^i \qquad (14\text{-}11)$$

Fortunately, for the classic filters (Butterworth, Chebyshev, and elliptic), the pole/zeros, or polynomial coefficients (i.e., $\{n_i\}$, $\{d_i\}$), are tabled or precomputed for the 3-dB passband filter of critical frequency equal to 1 rad/s, $H^2(s = j1) = 0.5$ (see chapter 11). That is, the half-power frequency is 1 rad/s. Such filters are called *analog prototypes* and shall be denoted $H_p(s)$.

In the analog filter design exercise, a prototype filter $H(s)$ is mapped into its final form using frequency-to-frequency transforms (FTFT) as suggested in figure 14-4. The standard transforms are summarized below. They are predicated on knowledge of the order of prototype $H_p(s)$. The appropriate FTFT will map an Nth order prototype low-pass model $H_p(s)$ having a gain V at the critical frequency $s = j1$ rad/s into the desired analog final form. For low-pass and high-pass transforms, the order of the resulting final form filter remains unchanged. However, for a bandpass or bandstop design, the resulting filter is of order $2N$.

The choice of whether to implement a Butterworth, Chebyshev, or elliptic filter is, of course, the responsibility of the designer. However, it is generally accepted that, of the three, for a given filter specification, the elliptic filter will result in the lowest order design followed by Chebyshev and Butterworth. Typical magnitude response profiles are presented in figure 14-5.

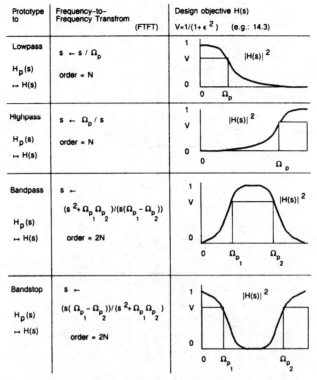

Prototype to	Frequency-to-Frequency Transfrom (FTFT)	Design objective H(s) $V=1/(1+\epsilon^2)$ (e.g.: 14.3)
Lowpass $H_p(s)$ ↦ H(s)	$s \leftarrow s/\Omega_p$ order = N	
Highpass $H_p(s)$ ↦ H(s)	$s \leftarrow \Omega_p/s$ order = N	
Bandpass $H_p(s)$ ↦ H(s)	$s \leftarrow$ $(s^2+\Omega_{p_1}\Omega_{p_2})/(s(\Omega_{p_1}-\Omega_{p_2}))$ order = 2N	
Bandstop $H_p(s)$ ↦ H(s)	$s \leftarrow$ $(s(\Omega_{p_1}-\Omega_{p_2}))/(s^2+\Omega_{p_1}\Omega_{p_2})$ order = 2N	

FIGURE 14-4 Frequency-to-frequency transformations based on knowledge of a low-pass analog model.

EXAMPLE 14-3

REQUIRED: A Butterworth low-pass filter, having a –3-dB gain at $\Omega_1 = 1034.5$ Hz (6500 rad/s) and a –10-dB gain at $\Omega_2 = 2069$ Hz $(2\Omega_1)$, is to be designed.

RESULTS: The order of the low-pass prototype model is given by equation (14-8) and it is

$$n = \frac{\log[(A^2-1)/\varepsilon^2]}{2\log(\Omega_r)}\bigg|_{\substack{\Omega_r=2\\ \varepsilon=1\\ A^2=10}} = 1.58 \to 2$$

From table 11-1

$$H_p(s) = \frac{1}{s^2+\sqrt{2}s+1} \qquad |H_p(\Omega)|^2$$

$$H(s) = H_p(s)\bigg|_{\substack{\text{low pass – to}\\\text{low pass FTFT}\\ s=s/6500}} \qquad |H_p(\Omega)|^2$$

$$= \frac{(6500)^2}{s^2+9192s+6500^2}$$

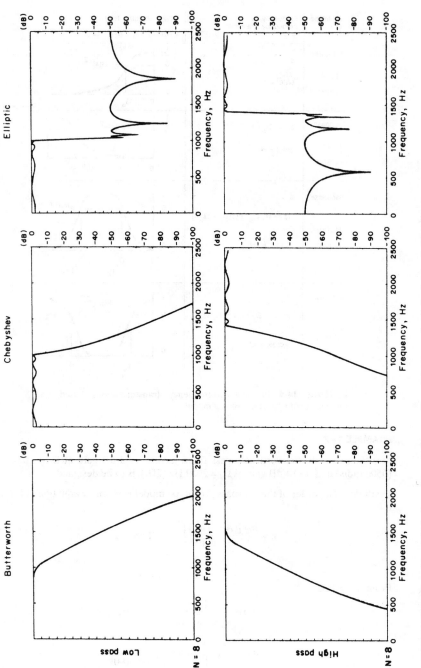

FIGURE 14-5 Typical magnitude frequency-response profiles of Butterworth, Chebyshev, and elliptic filters.

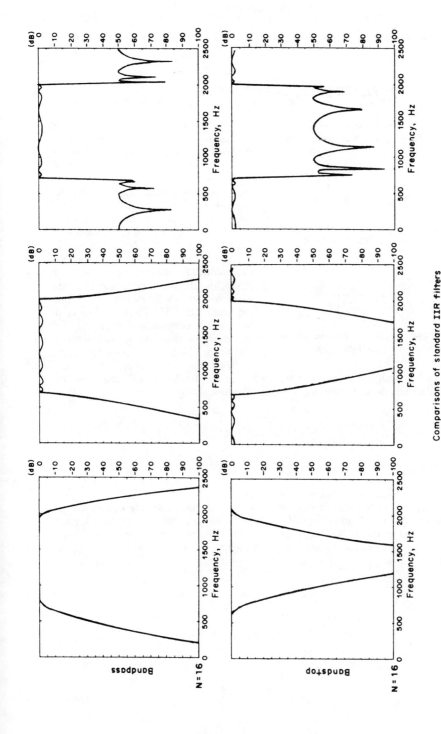

FIGURE 14-5 (*Continued*) Typical magnitude frequency-response profiles of Butterworth, Chebyshev, and elliptic filters.

The response and pole distribution of $H_p(s)$ and $H(s)$ are displayed in figure 14-6.

14.4 DIGITAL FILTER DESIGN PROTOCOL

In the previous section, the design of an analog Butterworth, Chebyshev, or elliptic filter was reviewed. It was noted that if the critical frequencies and gains were specified, an analog filter could be derived. However, it should be recalled that when the bilinear z transform is used to map an analog filter into its discrete equivalent, the frequency axis is distorted. This distortion is referred to as *warping* and is defined by $\Omega(\text{analog}) = (2/t_s) \tan (\omega(\text{digital})t_s/2)$ [equation (12-12)] with frequencies given in radians per second. To account for the warping effect, the digital filter frequencies are *prewarped* into a set of equivalent analog frequencies. The filter is designed in the analog domain and then mapped into a digital filter using the bilinear z transform which introduces a correcting warp to the analog filters' critical frequencies. The design process is summarized in figure 14-7. In general, an analog prototype filter has the structure presented in equation (14-5), namely

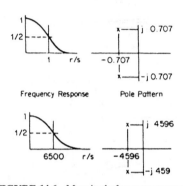

FIGURE 14-6 Magnitude frequency response and pole locations of $H_p(s)$ and $H(s)$.

$$H_p(s) = \frac{KN(s)}{D(s)} = K \times \frac{\prod_{i=1}^{N} (s - \tilde{\lambda}_i)}{\prod_{i=1}^{N} (s - \tilde{\sigma}_i)}$$

where $\tilde{\lambda}_i$ and $\tilde{\sigma}_i$ are the complex zeros and poles of $H_p(s)$. However, it is not advisable to implement complex coefficients since, in a digital computer, complex numbers occupy two words and the product of two complex numbers required four real multiplies and two adds. Since complex numbers come in complex conjugate pairs, second-order sections can be synthesized, which consist of real coefficients only. In this case,

$$H_p(s) = \prod_{i=1}^{L} H_i(s) \tag{14-12}$$

$$H_i(s) \equiv (s - \tilde{\lambda}_i)/(s - \tilde{\sigma}_i)$$

if $\tilde{\lambda}_i$ and $\tilde{\sigma}_i$ are real

$$H_i(s) = \frac{s^2 + a_i s + b_i}{s^2 + c_i s + d_i} \tag{14-13}$$

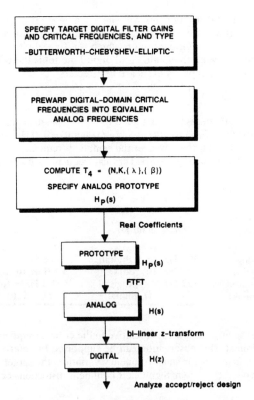

FIGURE 14-7 Digital filter design protocol based on knowledge of an analog prototype model and applicable frequency-to-frequency transforms.

if $\tilde{\lambda}_i$, $\tilde{\lambda}_i^*$, $\tilde{\sigma}_i$, and $\tilde{\sigma}_i^*$ are complex conjugate pairs, and

$$a_i = -(\tilde{\lambda}_i + \tilde{\lambda}_i^*) \qquad b_i = \tilde{\lambda}_i \tilde{\lambda}_i = |\lambda_i|^2$$
$$c_i = -(\tilde{\sigma}_i + \tilde{\sigma}_i^*) \qquad d_i = \tilde{\sigma}_i \tilde{\sigma}_i = |\sigma_i|^2$$

EXAMPLE 14-4

REQUIRED: Given

$$H(s) = \frac{1}{(s + 0.354)(s + 0.149 + i0.655)(s + 0.149 - i0.655)}$$

having complex coefficients, convert into a filter model consisting of only real coefficients.

RESULTS: Factor $H(s)$ as follows:

$$H(s) = \left[H_1(s) = \frac{1}{s + 0.354} \right]\left[H_2(s) = \frac{1}{s^2 + 0.298s + 0.451} \right]$$

The prewarping of digital frequencies will specify a new set of critical frequencies for an equivalent analog filter. It is the *prewarped* analog frequencies that must be used to synthesize the analog model upon which the final digital filter is premised. The only difference between the analog and digital model is the warping of the frequency axis. All critical gain parameters are unaffected.

EXAMPLE 14-5

REQUIRED: A digital filter is to be designed with given passband and stopband delimiters. Suppose that the critical frequencies are f_1(digital) = 480 Hz, f_2(digital) = 540 Hz, and Ω_r(digital) = 1.125. Furthermore, let the sampling frequency be f_s = 2 kHz and 20 kHz. Compute the equivalent prewarped critical frequencies using equation (12-12).

RESULT:

Prewarped Frequency	f_s = 2000 Hz	f_s = 20,000 Hz
Ω_1(analog)	3.756×10^3 rod/s	3.016×10^3 rod/s
f_1(analog)	597 Hz $\gg f_1$(digital)	480.2 Hz $\sim f_1$(digital)
Ω_2(analog)	4.537×10^3 rod/s	3.401×10^3 rod/s
f_2(analog)	722 Hz $\gg f_2$(digital)	541.3 Hz $\sim f_2$(digital)
Ω_r(analog)	$1.2094 > \Omega_r$(digital)	$1.127 \sim \Omega_r$(digital)

Observe that at the high sample rates, relative to the critical frequencies, the effects of warping are minimal. This observation can be supported by referring to figure 12-6. Here it can be noted that for small frequency variation, the target curve is approximately linear around the origin. Significant nonlinear distortions occur at higher frequencies.

A slightly simpler design protocol can be followed, which reduces the numerical complexity of the synthesis procedure. Recall that the analog prototype $H_p(s) = \Pi(s - \lambda_i)/\Pi(s - \beta_j); i \, \varepsilon \, [1, M], j \, \varepsilon \, [1, N]$, is defined in terms of prewarped analog frequencies. It is then mapped into an analog model using an appropriate frequency-to-frequency transform. The filter is then converted into a discrete filter $H(z)$ through the bilinear z transform. For example, in the case of an elementary low-pass design

$$H(z) = H_p(s) \Big|_{s = s/\Omega_p} = H(s) \Big|_{s = (2/T)(z - 1)/(z + 1)} \tag{14-14}$$

then

$$H(z) = g_p^{N - M} \frac{\prod_{i = 1}^{M} [(z - 1)/(z + 1) + g_p\lambda_i]}{\prod_{j = 1}^{N} [(z - 1)/(z + 1) + g_p\beta_j]} \tag{14-15}$$

$$g_p = \tan\left(\frac{\omega_p t}{2}\right) \qquad \Omega_p = \frac{2}{T} \tan\left(\frac{\omega_p t}{2}\right) \tag{14-16}$$

Observe that $H(z)$ is defined in terms of g, λ_i, and β_i but is not explicitly a function of $2/T$. As a result, a *modified z-transform prewarping* mapping can be used and is offered as a simplification of the formal prewarp mapping defined previously by equation (12-12). The modified prewarped analog model is then bilinearly z transformed using the modified formula

$$s = \frac{z-1}{z+1} \quad \text{and} \quad g_p = \tan\left(\frac{\omega_p t}{2}\right) \tag{14-17}$$

EXAMPLE 14-6

REQUIRED: A Butterworth filter has a –3-dB passband and a –10-dB stopband. Suppose $f_p = 1000$ Hz, $f_a = 2000$ Hz, and $f_s = 10{,}000$ Hz.

RESULTS: The prewarping of f_p and f_a are

$$\Omega_p = 1034.5 \text{ Hz} \qquad \Omega_a = 2069 \text{ Hz}$$

Then, as in example 14-3, $\Omega_r = 2$, and it follows that the filter has order $n = 2$. Referring to example 14-3, it is seen that

$$H_p(s) = \frac{1}{s^2 + 1.414s + 1}$$

with a critical frequency of $\Omega = 1$ rad/s. Using the modified prewarped mapping of equation (14-17) for $g_p = \tan(2\pi \times 10^3/2 \times 10^4) = \tan(0.1\pi) = 0.325$, it follows that

$$H(s) = H_p(s)\bigg|_{s\,=\,s/0.325} = \frac{(0.325)^2}{s^2 + 0.46s + 0.106}$$

Upon applying the modified bilinear z transform, $H(s)$ becomes

$$H(z) = H(s)\bigg|_{s\,=\,(z-1)/(z+1)} = \frac{0.0676(z+1)^2}{z^2 - 1.142z + 0.412}$$

$$= \frac{0.0676(z+1)^2}{(z - 0.57 + j0.295)(z - 0.57 - j0.295)}$$

14.5 BUTTERWORTH FILTER DESIGN

The nth-order prototype Butterworth filter, introduced in chapter 2, is characterized by the square response given by (see figure 14-3a)

$$|H_p(s)|^2 = 1/(1 + \varepsilon^2 s^{2n})$$

$$|H_p(0)|^2 = 1 \tag{14-18}$$

$$|H_p(1)|^2 = 1/(1 + \varepsilon^2)$$

The complex frequency response is given by

$$|H_p(s)|^2 = H_p(s)H_p(-s) \tag{14-19}$$

where the term $H_p(s)$ specifies what is referred to as the *realizable prototype filter.* The poles of $H_p(s)$ are located *entirely* in the left-hand s plane. The pole locations are well documented for a -3-dB (i.e., $\varepsilon = 1.0$) filter having a critical frequency $s = j\Omega = j1.0$ rad/s (see table 11-1). The poles are located on the periphery of the unit circle

$$Pi = \begin{cases} \exp(j\pi(2k-1)/2n) & \text{if } n \text{ even} \\ \exp(j\pi(k-1)/n) & \text{if } n \text{ odd} \end{cases} \Bigg\} k = n, n+1, \ldots, 2n \qquad (14\text{-}20)$$

If $\varepsilon \neq 1.0$, corrections must be made to these pole locations. Refer to figure 14-8 and note that there are two low-pass and one high-pass filters shown. Two are considered to be final analog models $H_f(\omega)$ and the third is an analog prototype model $H_p(\Omega)$. The filter $H_p(\Omega)$ is the nth-order filter having a -3-dB gain ($\varepsilon = 1.0$) at $j\omega = 1$ rad/s and poles given by equation (14-20). The critical frequency for the final low-pass filter, for the specified gain $|H(\Omega_\varepsilon)|^2 = 1/(1 + \varepsilon^2)$, can be directly computed to be

$$(1 + \varepsilon^2) = (1 + \Omega_\varepsilon^{2n}) \qquad (14\text{-}21)$$

or $$\Omega_\varepsilon = \varepsilon^{1/n} \qquad \text{rad/s}$$

The mapping of $H_p(\omega)$ into $H_f(\omega)$ is accomplished by the frequency-to-frequency transform $s = s/(\Omega_0/1.0) = s/(\Omega_p/\Omega_\varepsilon) = s/\Omega_{\text{LP}}$.

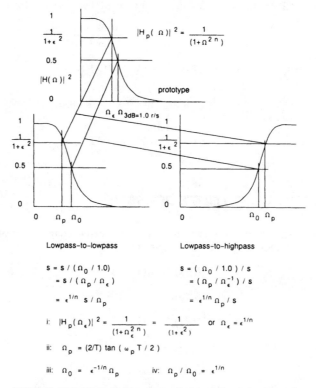

FIGURE 14-8 Critical frequency adjustment for low-pass and high-pass Butterworth filters given a low-pass prototype model.

A high-pass prototype filter $H_p^*(s)$ (not shown) is related to its low-pass parent through $s = 1.0/s$. The gain $|H_p^*(s)|^2$ is again $\frac{1}{2}$ (−3-dB) at $s = j1.0$ and $1/(1 + \varepsilon^2)$ at $s = j\varepsilon^{-1/n} = j\Omega_\varepsilon^{-1}$. This filter can in turn be mapped into the final high-pass model using the simple frequency translation

$$\frac{\Omega_{3\ dB} = 1.0}{\Omega_\varepsilon^{-1}} = \frac{\Omega_0}{\Omega_p} \tag{14-22}$$

or $\Omega_0 = \Omega_\varepsilon \Omega_p = \Omega_{HP}$. Therefore, the low-pass–to–high-pass frequency-to-frequency transform is given by $s = \Omega_{HP}/s$.

$$\text{Low-pass } s = \Omega_\varepsilon s/\Omega_p = s/\Omega_{LP} \qquad \Omega_\varepsilon = \varepsilon^{1/N} \tag{14-23i}$$

$$\text{High-pass } s = \Omega_\varepsilon \Omega_p/s = \Omega_{HP}/s \tag{14-23ii}$$

$$\text{Bandpass } s = \frac{s^2 + \Omega_0}{s\Omega_\delta} \tag{14-23iii}$$

$$\Omega_0 = \sqrt{\Omega_{p1}\Omega_{p2}}$$

$$\Omega_\delta = (1/\Omega_\varepsilon)(\Omega_{p2} - \Omega_{p1})$$

$$\Omega_{p1} = (2/T)\tan(\omega_{p1}T/2)$$

$$\Omega_{p2} = (2/T)\tan(\omega_{p2}T/2)$$

$$\text{Bandstop } s = \frac{s\Omega_\delta}{s^2 + \Omega_0^2} \tag{14-23iv}$$

EXAMPLE 14-7 (CBI)

REQUIRED: A Butterworth filter is to have a gain of −3 dB at 1.5 kHz with a sample frequency of 10 kHz. The stopband gain is equal to or less than −40 dB and begins at 2.5 kHz. Design the specified filter using the bilinear z transform.

RESULTS: The prewarped analog frequencies are:

$$\Omega_p(\text{analog}) = \frac{2}{t_s}\tan[\omega(\text{digital})t_s/2] \tag{12-7}$$

$$= 2 \times 10^4 \tan[\pi(0.15)]$$

$$= 10.19396 \text{ krad/s} = 1.62185 \text{ kHz}$$

$$\Omega_a(\text{analog}) = \frac{2}{t_s}\tan[\omega(\text{digital})t_s/2] \tag{12-7}$$

$$= 2 \times 10^4 \tan[\pi(0.25)]$$

$$= 20 \text{ krad/s} = 3.1831 \text{ kHz}$$

then $\Omega_r = 1.9625$ [equation (14-7i)], $\varepsilon = 1.0$, $A = 100$, and

$$n = \frac{\log(A^2 - 1)/\varepsilon}{2\log(\Omega_r)} = \frac{\log(9,999)}{2\log(1.9625)} \approx 6.83 \to 7$$

The value of 6.83 can also be deduced from figure 2-34. The seventh-order prototype filter satisfies (see table 11-1)

$$|H_p(s)| = \frac{1}{1 + s^{2n}} = H_p(s)H_p(-s)$$

The poles of $H(s)$ are reported in table 11-1 and are located at [equation (14-20)]

Real	Imaginary
-1.0	0
-0.9009688	± 0.43388374
-0.6234898	± 0.78183148
-0.2225209	± 0.97492791

or

$$H_p(s) = \frac{1.0}{s + 1.0} \times \frac{1.0}{s^2 + 1.809377s + 1.0} \times \frac{1.0}{s^2 + 1.246979s + 1.0} \times \frac{1.0}{s^2 + 0.4450418s + 1.0}$$

Observe, $|H_p(0)|^2 = 1$ and $|H_p(j1)|^2 = \frac{1}{2}$. The prototype filter's critical frequency is 1 rad/s. The low-pass-to-low-pass transformation is given by $s = s/\Omega_p = s/10.193966 \times 10^3$ [equation (14-23i) $\varepsilon = 1.0$ and $\Omega_e = 1.0$]. The resulting transformed analog filter is

$$H(s) = \frac{10193.96}{(s + 10193.96)} \times \frac{103916948.95}{(s^2 + 18368.89s + 103916948.95)}$$

$$\times \frac{103916948.95}{(s^2 + 12711.66s + 103916948.95)}$$

$$\times \frac{103916948.95}{(s^2 + 4536.74s + 103916948.95}$$

whose poles are located at

Real	Imaginary
-10193.96	0
-9184.44	± 4422.99
-6355.83	± 7969.96
-2268.37	± 9938.38

The discrete filter is defined by [equation (12-10)]

$$s = (2/t_s)[(z - 1)/(z + 1)] = 5 \times 10^3 (z - 1)/(z + 1)$$

or $$H(z) = H_0 \times H_1(z) \times H_2(z) \times H_3(z) \times H_4(z)$$

where $H_0(z) = 9.6449 \times 10^{-4}$

$H_1(z) = (z + 1.0)/(z - 0.3247679)$

$$H_2(z) = (z^2 + 2z + 1)/(z^2 - 0.67963923z + 0.156708)$$

$$H_3(z) = (z^2 + 2z + 1)/(z^2 - 0.7810668z + 0.329333)$$

$$H_4(z) = (z^2 + 2z + 1)/(z^2 - 0.9958199z + 0.694830)$$

The seven zeros are seen to all be located at $z = -1.0$ and the poles are found at

Real	Imaginary
0.3247679	0.0
0.3398196	±0.20305394
0.3905334	±0.4204951
0.4979099	±0.6685177

The magnitude frequency response of the realized filter is shown in figure 14-9.

EXAMPLE 14-8 (CBI)

REQUIRED: A Butterworth high-pass filter is to have −1-dB gain at 3000 Hz, at least 20-dB attenuation over [0, 2000] Hz, and be sampled at 10 kHz. Design the specified filter.

RESULTS: As such

$$\Omega_p(\text{analog}) = 27.527 \text{ krad/s} = 4.381 \text{ kHz} \tag{12-12}$$

$$\Omega_a(\text{analog}) = 14.531 \text{ krad/s} = 2.313 \text{ kHz} \tag{12-12}$$

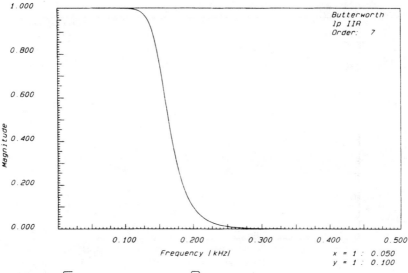

Frequency Response

FIGURE 14-9 Magnitude frequency response for example 14-8 low-pass filter.

$$k = \Omega_a / \Omega_p = 0.52786$$

$$n \equiv 5 \qquad \varepsilon^2 = 0.2589254 \qquad \varepsilon = 0.5088471$$

$$\Omega_\varepsilon = \varepsilon^{1/5} = 0.8736097$$

$$H_p(s) = \frac{1.0}{s + 1.0} \times \frac{1.0}{s^2 + 1.618034s + 1.0} \times \frac{1.0}{s^2 + 0.618034s + 1.0}$$

Use the frequency-to-frequency transform to obtain

$$H(s) = H_p(s) \Big|_{\substack{s = \Omega_\varepsilon \Omega_p / s = \Omega_{HP}/s \\ = 24048.4/s}} \tag{14-22}$$

$$= \frac{s}{s + 2.4048 \times 10^4} \times \frac{s^2}{s^2 + 3.891s \times 10^4 + 5.783 \times 10^8}$$

$$\times \frac{s^2}{s^2 + 1.4846 \times 10^4 s + 5.783 \times 10^8}$$

Finally, using the bilinear z transform

$$H(z) = 0.032423 \times \frac{(z - 1.0)}{(z + 0.091908)} \times \frac{(z^2 - 2.0z + 1.0)}{(z^2 + 0.20304z + 0.11391)}$$

$$\times \frac{(z - 2.0z + 1.0)}{(z^2 + 0.2796z + 0.53393)} \tag{14-17}$$

The magnitude frequency response is shown in figure 14-10.

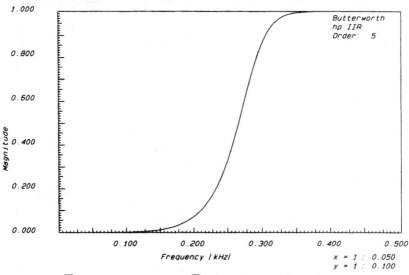

FIGURE 14-10 Magnitude frequency response for example 14-10 low-pass filter.

EXAMPLE 14-9 (CBI)

REQUIRED: A -1-dB bandpass Butterworth filter, having $f_s = 10$ kHz, $f_{a1} = 1$ kHz, $f_{p1} = 2$ kHz, $f_{p2} = 3$ kHz, $f_{a2} = 4$ kHz, and at least a -20-dB stopband, is to be designed.

RESULT: The prewarped frequency dataset [equation (12-12)] is:

$$\Omega_{a1} = (2/T)\tan(0.1\pi) = 6.498 \times 10^3 \text{ rad/s} \sim 1.03 \text{ kHz}$$

$$\Omega_{p1} = (2/T)\tan(0.2\pi) = 1.453 \times 10^4 \text{ rad/s} \sim 2.31 \text{ kHz}$$

$$\Omega_{p2} = (2/T)\tan(0.3\pi) = 2.753 \times 10^4 \text{ rad/s} \sim 4.38 \text{ kHz}$$

$$\Omega_{a2} = (2/T)\tan(0.4\pi) = 6.155 \times 10^4 \text{ rad/s} \sim 9.79 \text{ kHz}$$

$$[\text{bandwidth(analog)} = 2.07 \text{ kHz}]$$

from equation (14-7iii), it follows that

$$\Omega_{a1}\Omega_{a2} = 4.000 \times 10^8 \geq \Omega_{p1}\Omega_{p2} = 4.000 \times 10^8$$

$$k_1 = \frac{(\Omega_{p2} - \Omega_{p1})\Omega_{a1}}{(\Omega_{p1}\Omega_{p2} - \Omega_{a1}^2)} = \frac{8.447 \times 10^7}{3.578 \times 10^8} = 0.236$$

From k, $\varepsilon = 0.509$, $A = 10$, the order of the prototype can be determined to be $n = 3$. More specifically

$$H_p(s) = \frac{1}{(s+1)(s^2+s+1)}$$

Using low-pass to bandpass transform [equation (14-23iii)],

$$s = \frac{s^2 + \Omega_0^2}{s\Omega_\delta} = \frac{s^2 + 4.000 \times 10^8}{s(1.3 \times 10^4)/0.7986} = \frac{s^2 + 4.0 \times 10^8}{1.628 \times 10^4 s}$$

where

$$\Omega_0 = \sqrt{\Omega_{p1}\,\Omega_{p2}} = 2.000 \times 10^4$$

$$\Omega_\varepsilon = \varepsilon^{1/n(\text{prototype})} = (0.509^{1/3}) = 0.7986$$

$$\Omega_\delta = (\Omega_{p2} - \Omega_{p1})/\Omega_\varepsilon = 1.3 \times 10^4$$

The final analog model follows:

$$H_f(s) = K\,\frac{s}{s^2 + 1.628 \times 10^4 s + 4 \times 10^8} \times \frac{s}{s^2 + 1.089 \times 10^4 s + 8.084 \times 10^8}$$

$$\times \frac{s}{s^2 + 5.388 \times 10^3 s + 1.979 \times 10^8}$$

$$K = 4.3144 \times 10^{12}$$

Finally, the bilinear z transform, $s = (2/T)(z-1)/(z+1)$, produces

$$H(z) = K\,\frac{(z^2 - 1.0)}{(z^2 + 0.4215)} \times \frac{(z^2 - 1.0)}{(z^2 + 0.5727z + 0.6945)}$$

$$\times \frac{(z^2 - 1.0)}{(z^2 - 0.5727z + 0.6945)}$$

$$K = 3.047 \times 10^{-2}$$

The magnitude frequency response is reported in figure 14-11.

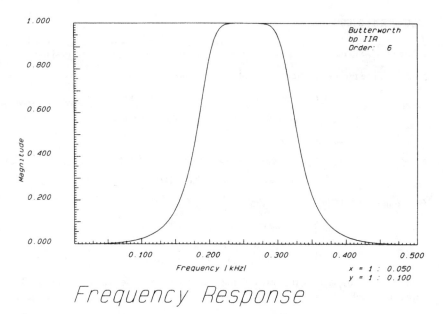

FIGURE 14-11   Magnitude frequency response for example 14-10 low-pass filter.

14.6 CHEBYSHEV FILTER DESIGN

The prototype filter is characterized by the squared magnitude response function

$$|H_p(s)|^2 = 1/[1 + \varepsilon^2 C_n^2(s)] \tag{14-24}$$

where $C_n(s)$ are the n-order Chebyshev polynomial reported in table 2-1. Observe that $|H_p(0)|^2 = 1$ if n is odd, $1/(1 + \varepsilon^2)$ if n is even, and $|H_p(1)|^2 = 1/(1 + \varepsilon^2)$ as shown in figure 14-3. If $\varepsilon = 1$, the response is said to be normalized. The complex frequency response is given in equation (14-24) where $H_p(s)$ is said to be the realizable filter. The poles of $|H_p(s)|^2$ are located along the periphery of an ellipse at coordinates $p_i = \sigma_i + j\omega_i$ for

$$\left. \begin{array}{l} \sigma_i = \pm \sinh[1/n \sinh^{-1}(1/\varepsilon)] \sin[(2k-1)\pi/2n] \\ \omega_i = \cosh[1/n \sinh^{-1}(1/\varepsilon)] \cos[(2k-1)\pi/2n] \end{array} \right\} k = 1,2,\ldots,n \tag{14-25}$$

Pole locations for Chebyshev filters of order $2 \le n \le 9$, for -0.01 to -1-dB passbands are reported in tables 11-22 to 11-26. Otherwise, equation (14-25) can be used.

The magnitude frequency response, reported in figure 14-12, is shown for two different passband attenuation values. Observe that equiripple passbands differ only in their depth and not in the locations of the external frequency. Therefore, the frequency-to-frequency transforms are invariant to ε. More specifically,

$$\text{Low pass } s = s/\Omega_p \tag{14-26i}$$

$$\text{High pass } s = \Omega_p/s \tag{14-26ii}$$

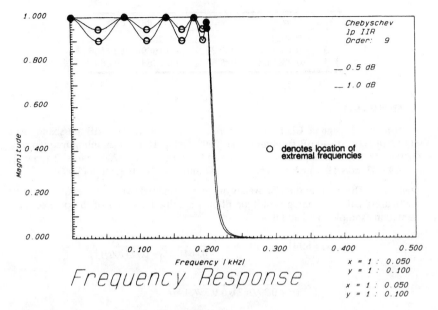

FIGURE 14-12   Chebyshev frequency response.

$$\text{Bandpass } s = \frac{s^2 + \Omega_0^2}{s\Omega_\delta} \qquad (14\text{-}26iii)$$

$$\Omega_0 = \sqrt{\Omega_{p1}\,\Omega_{p1}}$$

$$\Omega_\delta = \Omega_{p2} - \Omega_{p1}$$

$$\text{Bandstop } s = \frac{s\Omega_\delta}{s^2 + \Omega_0^2} \qquad (14\text{-}26iv)$$

EXAMPLE 14-10

REQUIRED: Compute the pole locations of a sixth-order 1-dB passband analog proto-type Chebyshev filter.

RESULTS: The pole locations are computed as follows:

let $e = 1/\varepsilon = 1.9646$

$$f = \sinh^{-1}(e) = \ln[e + \sqrt{(e^2 + 1)}] = 1.4279$$

$$g = \sinh(f/6) = 0.24023 \qquad k = \cosh(f/6) = 1.028454$$

$$\sigma_k = \pm g \sin\left[(2k - 1)\pi/12\right]$$

$$\omega_k = h \cos\left[(2k - 1)\pi/12\right]$$

k	σ_k	ω_k	Table 11-26	
1, 6	-0.062176	± 0.993411	-0.0607	± 0.9707
2, 5	-0.169882	± 0.727227	-0.1660	± 0.7106
3, 4	-0.232062	± 0.266184	-0.2268	± 0.2601

EXAMPLE 14-11

REQUIRED: Design a Chebyshev low-pass filter, having a -1-dB passband over [0, 1750] Hz and -40-dB stopband over [2500, 5000] Hz, for a sampling frequency of 10,000 Hz. The critical parameters are given by Ω_p (analog) = 12.256 rad/s, Ω_a (analog) = 19.99807 rad/s, Ω_r = 1.63, ε = 0.509, A = 100, and $\eta \sim \varepsilon/100$ [equation (14-7)].

RESULTS: The order of the Chebyshev model is estimated to be $n = 6$ [equation (14-9) or figure 2-24]. The analog prototype filter is specified in terms of the pole set presented in example 14-10 and it is

$$H(s) = 6.141333 \times 10^{-2} \times \frac{1.0}{(s^2 + 0.4641255s + 0.1247069)}$$

$$\times \frac{1.0}{(s^2 + 0.3397634s + 0.5577196)}$$

$$\times \frac{1.0}{(s^2 + 0.12436205 + 0.9907323)}$$

where $|H(0)|^2 = (6.141333 \times 10^{-2}/1.247069 \times 10^{-1} \times 5.577196 \times 10^{-2} \times 0.9907323)^2$
$$= 0.794328 \sim -1 \text{ dB}$$

The low-pass–to–low-pass transform is given by (14-26i)

$$s = s/\Omega_p = s/12.256 \times 10^3$$

which results in an analog model

$$H(s) = 2.0814144 \times 10^{23} \times \frac{1.0}{s^2 + 5688.33s + 18732212.74}$$

$$\times \frac{1.0}{s^2 + 4164.15s + 83775017.08}$$

$$\times \frac{1.0}{s^2 + 1524.18s + 148817821.42}$$

The final step is the application of the bilinear z transform

$$s = \frac{2}{T} \frac{(z-1)}{(z+1)} = 2 \times 10^4 \frac{(z-1)}{(z+1)}$$

which yields

$$H(z) = H_0 \times H_1(z) \times H_2(z) \times H_3(z)$$

$$H_0 = 1.189893 \times 10^{-3}$$

$$H_1(z) = \frac{z^2 + 2.0z + 1.0}{z^2 - 1.431995z + 0.572707}$$

$$H_2(z) = \frac{z^2 + 2.0z + 1.0}{z^2 - 1.11532z + 0.706263}$$

$$H_3(z) = \frac{z^2 + 2.0z + 1.0}{z^2 - 0.86719z + 0.894757}$$

The zeros are all located at $z = -1.0$ and the poles are found at

Real	Imaginary
0.715997	±0.245060
0.557659	±0.628713
0.433595	±0.8406858

The magnitude frequency response is displayed in figure 14-13.

EXAMPLE 14-12

REQUIRED: Design a −1-dB bandpass Chebyshev filter, having $f_s = 10$ kHz, $f_{a1} = 1$ kHz, $f_{p1} = 2$ kHz, $f_{p2} = 3$ kHz, $f_{a2} = 4$ kHz, and at least a −30-dB stopband.

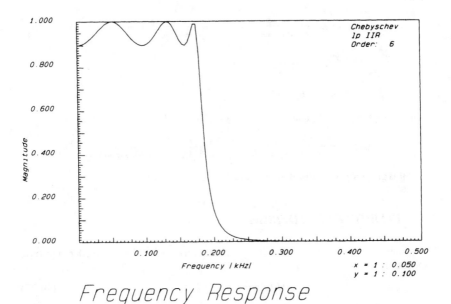

Frequency Response

FIGURE 14-13   Magnitude frequency response for example 14-12 low-pass filter.

RESULTS: The prewarped frequencies are [equation (12-10)]

$$\Omega_{a1} = (2/T) \tan(0.1\pi) = 6.498 \times 10^3 \text{ rad/s} \sim 1.03 \text{ kHz}$$

$$\Omega_{p1} = (2/T) \tan(0.2\pi) = 1.453 \times 10^4 \text{ rad/s} \sim 2.31 \text{ kHz}$$

$$\Omega_{p2} = (2/T) \tan(0.3\pi) = 2.753 = 10^4 \text{ rad/s} \sim 4.38 \text{ kHz}$$

$$\Omega_{a2} = (2/T) \tan(0.4\pi) = 6.155 \times 10^4 \text{ rad/s} \sim 9.79 \text{ kHz}$$

$$[\text{Bandwidth(analog)} = 2.07 \text{ kHz}]$$

From equation (14-7iii), it follows that

$$\Omega_{a1}\Omega_{a2} = 4.000 \times 10^8 \geq \Omega_{p1}\Omega_{p2} = 4.000 \times 10^8$$

$$k_1 = \frac{(\Omega_{p2} - \Omega_{p1})\Omega_{a1}}{(\Omega_{p1}\Omega_{p2} - \Omega_{a1}^2)} = \frac{8.447 \times 10^7}{3.578 \times 10^8} = 0.236$$

From k, $\varepsilon = 0.509$, $A^2 = 10^3$, the order of the prototype can be determined to be $n = 3$. More specifically

$$H_p(s) = \frac{0.4913}{(s + 0.4942)(s^2 + 0.4942s + 0.9942)}$$

The frequency-to-frequency transform is given by equation (14.26iii) and it is

$$s^2 = \frac{s^2 + \Omega_{p1}\Omega_{p2}}{s(\Omega_{p2} - \Omega_{p1})} = \frac{s^2 + 4.000 \times 10^8}{1.3 \times 10^4 s}$$

Therefore

$$H_f(s) = K \frac{s}{(s^2 + 6422s + 4 \times 10^8)} \times \frac{s}{(s^2 + 4175s + 7.433 \times 10^8)}$$

$$\times \frac{s}{(s^2 + 2247s + 2.153 \times 10^8)}$$

$$K = 1.0786 \times 10^{12}$$

Finally, applying the bilinear z transform $s = (2/T)(z + 1.0)/(z + 1.0)$, we obtain

$$H(z) = \frac{0.0115(z^2 - 1)^3}{(z^2 + 0.7233)(z^2 + 0.559z + 0.8638)(z^2 - 0.559z + 0.8638)}$$

and it is graphically interpreted in figure 14-14.

14.7 ELLIPTIC FILTER DESIGN

The low-pass prototype elliptic filter is characterized by the squared magnitude response function

$$|H_p(s)|^2 = 1/[1 + \varepsilon^2 E_n^2(s)] \tag{14-27}$$

where $E_n(s)$ is a rational Chebyshev function. For k (analog transition ratio) $= \Omega_p/\Omega_a$, and defining $\Omega_p = \sqrt{(k)}$ and $\Omega_a = \sqrt{(1/k)}$, then $E_n^2(s) = 1$ for $s = \pm j\sqrt{(k)}$. In particular [see equations (2-47, 2-48)],

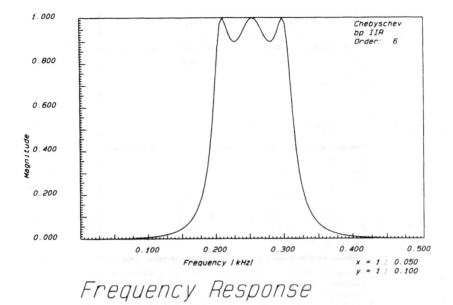

Frequency Response

FIGURE 14-14   Magnitude frequency response for example 14-13 low-pass filter.

$$E_n(s) = s^e \prod_{i=1}^{r} (a_{2i}^2 - s^2) / \prod_{i=1}^{r} (1 - a_{2i}^2 s^2) \tag{14-28}$$

$$e = 1 \qquad r = (n-1)/2 \qquad \text{if } n \text{ odd}$$
$$e = 0 \qquad r = n/2 \qquad \text{if } n \text{ even.}$$

The zeros are located at a_{2i} (and zero if n odd) with poles located at $1/a_{2i}$. The values of a_{2i} are defined in terms of the elliptic integral equation

$$\Lambda_k = \int_0^{\pi/2} \frac{d\theta}{\sqrt{(1 - k^2 \sin^2\theta)}} \tag{14-29}$$

Elliptic filter parameters, for some n, $p = \sqrt{[\varepsilon^2/(1+\varepsilon^2)]}$ and $\theta = \sin^{-1}(1/\Omega_s)$ (Ω_s given in figure 2-82) are reported in tables 11-56 and 11-57. Approximation methods can also be used. Antoniou (see bibliography) presents an efficient means of specifying the coefficients of $H_p(s)$ in factored form

$$H_p(s) = \frac{K_0}{D_0(s)} \prod_{i=1}^{V} \frac{s^2 + \alpha_{0i}}{s^2 + \beta_{1i}s + \beta_{0i}} \tag{14-30}$$

The procedure used to define K_0, D_0, α_{0i}, and β_{0i} is presented in figure 14-15.

The elliptic frequency-to-frequency transforms, like the Butterworth model, require modifications of the basic formulas shown in figure 14-7. Mathematically, the critical frequency of a low-pass prototype filter for a given $k = \Omega_p(\text{prototype})/\Omega_a(\text{prototype})$ is located at $\Omega_p(\text{prototype}) = \sqrt{(k)} = \Omega_a^{-1}(\text{prototype})$ rather than a normalized frequency of 1 rad/s. Therefore, the elliptic frequency-to-frequency transforms are given by

Enter A (Figure 14-1); n (Equation 14.10); q (Equation 14.10)
$k = \Omega_p / \Omega_a$; r (Equation 14.28); $\Omega_p = \sqrt{k} = \Omega_a^{-1}$

Compute intermediate parameters
$a_0 = [1/2n] \ln((A+1)/(A-1))$ $b_0 = \sum_{m=0}^{M} (-1)^m q^{m(m+1)} \sinh[(2m+1)a_0]$: M>3
$c_0 = 2 \sum_{m=0}^{M} (-1)^m q^{m^2} \cosh(2ma_0)$ $d_0 = 2q^{0.25} b_0 / (1+c_0)$
$e_0 = \sqrt{((1+kd_0^2)(1+d_0^2/k))}$

Computer parameter set
for i=1 to r
$\lambda[i] = i$ if n odd, else $i - 0.5$ $b_i = \sum_{m=0}^{M} (-1)^m q^{m(m+1)} \sin[(2m+1)\pi\lambda[i]/n]$
$c_i = 2 \sum_{m=0}^{M} (-1)^m q^{m^2} \cos[2m\pi\lambda[i]/n]$ $d_i = 2q^{0.25} b_i / (1+c_i)$
$h_i = \sqrt{((1-kd_i^2)(1-d_i^2/k))}$

Compute filter coefficients
for i=1 to r
$\alpha_{0i} = 1/d_i^2$ $\beta_{0i} = ((d_0 h_i)^2 + (e_0 d_i)^2)/(1+d_0^2 d_i^2)$
$\beta_{1i} = 2d_0 h_i / (1+d_0^2 d_i^2)$
$K_0 = d_0 \prod_{i=1}^{r} (\beta_{0i}/\alpha_{0i})$ if n odd and $= (1/A) \prod_{i=1}^{r} (\beta_{0i}/\alpha_{0i})$ if n even
$D_0(s) = s + \sigma_0$ if n odd and $= 1$ if n even

FIGURE 14-15   Elliptic filter design approximation technique.

Low pass	$s = s/(\Omega_p/\Omega_\varepsilon)$	(14-31i)
	$\Omega_p = (2/T) \tan(\omega_p T/2)$	
	$\Omega_\varepsilon = \Omega_p(\text{prototype}) = \sqrt{(k)}$	
High pass	$s = (\Omega_\varepsilon \Omega_p)/s$	(14-31ii)
Bandpass	$s = \dfrac{s^2 + \Omega_{p1}\Omega_{p1}}{s(\Omega_{p2} - \Omega_{p1})/\Omega_\varepsilon}$	(14-31iii)
Bandstop	$s = \dfrac{s(\Omega_{p2} - \Omega_{p1})/\Omega_\varepsilon}{s^2 + \Omega_{p1}\Omega_{p1}}$	

EXAMPLE 14-13 (CBI)

REQUIRED: Design an elliptic low-pass filter, having a –1-dB passband over [0, 1750] Hz and a –40-dB stopband over [2500, 5000] Hz, for a sampling frequency of 10,000 Hz.

RESULT: Following the method presented in figure 14-14, $\Omega_r = 1.63$, $k = 1/\Omega_r = 0.613$, $\varepsilon = 0.509$, $A = 100$. The order of the elliptic filter is approximated using

$$k' = \sqrt{(1 - k^2)} = 0.79023$$

$$q_0 = 0.5[1 - \sqrt{(k')}]/[1 + \sqrt{(k')}]$$

$$= 0.029395$$

$$q = q_0 + 2q_0^5 + 15a_0^9 + 150q_p0_p1_3 \sim q_0$$

$$D = (A^2 - 1)/\varepsilon^2 \sim 3.86 \times 10^4$$

It follows that [from tables 11-22 to 26, or equation (14-24)]

$$n \ge \log (16D)/\log (1/q) = 5.79/1.532 = 3.78 \rightarrow n = 4$$

$$H_p(s) = K_0 \frac{(s^2 + 9.1848)}{(s^2 + 0.56336s + 0.21221)} \times \frac{(s^2 + 1.85202)}{(s^2 + 0.17355s + 0.61084)}$$

$$K_0 = 6.7917 \times 10^{-3}$$

where $\quad H(0) = \dfrac{K_0(9.1848)(1.85202)}{(0.21221)(0.61084)} = 0.89125 = 10^{-0.05}(-1 \text{ dB})$ as a check

The low-pass–to–low-pass transform is given by

$$s = s/[\Omega_p/\sqrt{(k)}]$$

$$\Omega_p = 2/T \tan (.175\pi) = 1.2256 \times 10^4 = 1.95 \text{ kHz}$$

$$\sqrt{(k)} = 0.7829$$

or $\quad\quad\quad\quad\quad s = s/1.5654 \times 10^4$

then $\quad\quad\quad\quad H(s) = K_0 \dfrac{(s^2 + 2.251 \times 10^9)}{(s^2 + 8.820 \times 10^3 s + 5.202 \times 10^7)}$

$$\times \frac{(s^2 + 4.539 \times 10^8)}{(s^2 + 2.717 \times 10^3 s + 1.497 \times 10^8)}$$

Finally, using the bilinear z transform, namely

$$s = \frac{2}{T} \frac{(z - 1)}{(z + 1)} = 2 \times 10^{-4} \frac{(z - 1)}{(z + 1)}$$

then $\quad\quad\quad H(z) = \dfrac{K(z^2 + 1.396z + 1.0)}{(z^2 - 1.107z + 0.438)} \times \dfrac{(z^2 + 0.126z + 1.0)}{(z^2 - 0.828z + 0.820)}$

$$K = 4.051 \times 10^{-2}$$

Observe that the filter's DC gain, determined at $z = 1.0$, satisfies

$$H(1.0) = \frac{K(3.396)(2.126)}{(0.9915)(0.3316)} = 0.89 \sim -1 \text{ dB}$$

as before. The magnitude frequency response is presented in figure 14-16.

EXAMPLE 14-14 (CBI)

REQUIRED: Design a −1-dB bandpass elliptic filter, having $f_x = 10$ kHz $f_{a1} = 1$ kHz, $f_{p1} = 2$ kHz, $f_{p2} = 3$ kHz, $f_{a2} = 4$ kHz, and at least a least a −30-dB stopband.

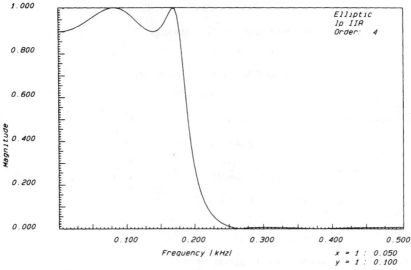

FIGURE 14-16 Magnitude frequency response for example 14-14 low-pass filter.

RESULT: The prewarped critical frequencies are [equation (12-7)]

$$\Omega_{a1} = (2/T)\tan(0.1\pi) = 6.498 \times 10^3 \text{ rad/s} \sim 1.03 \text{ kHz}$$

$$\Omega_{p1} = (2/T)\tan(0.2\pi) = 1.453 \times 10^4 \text{ rad/s} \sim 2.31 \text{ kHz}$$

$$\Omega_{p2} = (2/T)\tan(0.3\pi) = 2.753 \times 10^4 \text{ rad/s} \sim 4.38 \text{ kHz}$$

$$\Omega_{a2} = (2/T)\tan(0.4\pi) = 6.155 \times 10^4 \text{ rad/s} \sim 9.79 \text{ kHz}$$

$$[\text{Bandwidth (analog)} = 2.07 \text{ kHz}]$$

From equation (14-7*iii*), it follows that

$$\Omega_{a1}\Omega_{a2} = 4.000 \times 10^8 \geq \Omega_{p1}\Omega_{p2} = 4.000 \times 10^8$$

$$k_1 = \frac{(\Omega_{p2} - \Omega_{p1})\Omega_{a1}}{(\Omega_{p1}\Omega_{p2} - \Omega_{a1}^2)} = \frac{8.447 \times 10^7}{3.578 \times 10^8} = 0.236$$

From k, $\varepsilon = 0.509$, $A^2 = 10^3$, the order of the elliptic filter is determined to be $n = 2$. More specifically

$$H_p(s) = \frac{K(s^2 + 8.3524)}{(s^2 + 0.5247s + 0.2639)}$$

$$K = 2.816 \times 10^{-2}$$

The frequency-to-frequency transform is given by equation (14.31*iii*) and it is

$$s = \frac{s^2 + \Omega_{p1}\Omega_{p2}}{s(\Omega_{p2} - \Omega_{p1})/\sqrt{(k)}} = \frac{s^2 + 4.000 \times 10^8}{2.676 \times 10^4 s}$$

or
$$H_f(s) = K \frac{(s^2 + 6.753 \times 10^9)(s^2 + 2.369 \times 10^7)}{(s^2 + 9033s + 7.221 \times 10^8)(s^2 + 5004s + 2.216 \times 10^8)}$$

$$K = 2.816 \times 10^{-2}$$

The final filter, obtained by using the bilinear z transform $s = (2/T)(z - 1.0)/(z + 1.0)$, is

$$H(z) = \frac{K(z^2 + 1.776z + 1.0)(z^2 - 1.776z + 1.0)}{(z^2 + 0.4944z + 0.7226)(z^2 - 0.4944z + 0.7226)}$$

$$K = 9.079 \times 10^{-2}$$

with the magnitude frequency response presented in figure 14-17.

14.8 COMPARISON OF FIR AND IIR FILTERS

The principal attributes of FIR are its simplicity, phase linearity, and ability to decimate a signal. The strength of the IIR is its ability to achieve high-quality (steep-skirt) filtering with a limited number order design. Those positive characteristics of the FIR are absent in the IIR and vice versa.

The estimated order of an FIR, required to achieve an IIR design specification, was empirically determined by Rabiner. It was found that the approximate order n of an FIR required to meet a design objective

$$(1 - \delta_1)^2 = \frac{1}{1 + \varepsilon^2} \qquad \delta_1 \text{ (passband-ripple)} \qquad (14\text{-}32)$$

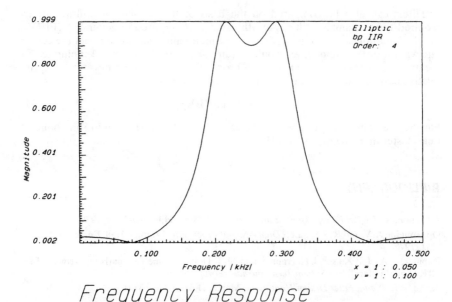

FIGURE 14-17 Magnitude frequency response for example 14-15 bandpass filter.

$$\delta_2^2 = \frac{1}{A^2} \quad \delta_2 \text{ (stopband bound)}$$

$$\Delta f \text{ (transition frequency range/} f_s)$$

was given by

$$n \sim \frac{-10 \log ((1 - \delta_1)\delta_2) - 15}{14\Delta f} + 1$$

EXAMPLE 14-15

REQUIRED: Compare the estimated order of a low-pass filter specified in terms of a −0.0873-dB passband, −80-dB stopband, f_s = 8000 Hz, a passband range of [0, 480] Hz, and a stopband range of [520, 4000] Hz.

RESULT: Given

$$\delta_1 = 0.99 \quad \text{or} \quad (1 - \delta_1) = 10^{-2}$$

$$\delta_2 = 10^{-4}$$

$$\Delta f = 40/8000 = 0.005$$

and

$$n = \frac{-10 \log (10^{-6}) - 15}{14(0.005)} + 1 = 644$$

or a 644th-order FIR is required to meet the design objectives. Analysis will reveal that a 12th-order elliptic FIR will also satisfy the design statement.

Filters can also be compared on the basis of the number of multiplications required to mechanize a filter. An nth order FIR requires, in general, M(FIR) = $(n + 1)/2$ multiplies if the tap weights are symmetrically distributed about the center tap. An nth-order elliptic filter would require about M(FIR) = $2n + 1$ multiplies on the average. If speed is assumed to be proportional to the multiplication rate, the relative data rate of the two filter classes can be expressed as

$$r = M(\text{FIR})/M(\text{IIR}) \tag{14-33}$$

For the previous example, $r = (645/2)/(25) = 12.9$. Or the IIR would run about 13 times faster than an equivalent FIR.

BIBLIOGRAPHY

Antoniou, A., *Digital Filters: Analysis and Design*, McGraw-Hill, New York, 1979.

Oppenheim, A. V. and R. S. Schafer, *Digital Signal Processing*, Prentice-Hall, Englewood Cliffs, N.J., 1975.

Rabiner, L. A., J. F. Kaiser, J. Herrmann, and M. T. Dolan, "Some Comparisons Between FIR IIR Digital Filters," *Bell System Tech. Journal*, February 1974.

Taylor, F. J., *Digital Filter Design Handbook*, Marcel Dekker, New York, 1983.

CHAPTER 15
FILTER ARCHITECTURE

15.1 INTRODUCTION

In the last chapter the infinite impulse-response filter, or IIR, was introduced. The transfer function for an IIR can be expressed as a polynomial model of the form

$$H(z) = \left(\sum_{i=0}^{N} a_i \, z^{-i} \right) \bigg/ \left(\sum_{i=0}^{N} b_i \, z^{-i} \right) \tag{15-1i}$$

$$= K \prod_{i=0}^{N} (z - z_i) \bigg/ \prod_{i=0}^{N} (z - p_i) \tag{15-1ii}$$

where $K = \lim H(z); z \to \infty$
$N =$ filter order
$\{a_i\} =$ real numerator coefficients
$\{b_i\} =$ real denominator coefficients
$\{z_i\} =$ complex zeros
$\{p_i\} =$ complex poles

The transfer function is said to be *monic* if $b_0 = 1.0$.

Standard design doctrine prescribes that complex poles and zeros should be grouped together as complex conjugate pairs to form second-order filter sections consisting only of *real* coefficients. Furthermore, it is generally accepted that complex zeros should be paired with nearby complex poles when forming first- or second-order sections of real coefficients. This policy generally reduces the undesirable effects of coefficient sensitivity caused by round-off or truncation errors. This is analogous to a 5 or 10 percent uncertainty of R, L, or C parameters in an analog design. As a result, equation (15-1) can be represented as a collection of M subfilters, of order 1 or 2, as follows:

$$H(z) = \sum_{i=1}^{M} H_i(z) \qquad N = \sum_{i=1}^{M} \text{degree}[H_i(z)] \tag{15-2}$$

$$H_i(z) = \begin{cases} (z + r_i)/(z + s_i) & \text{(if of degree one)} \\ \quad \text{or} \\ (z^2 + t_i z + u_i)/(z^2 + v_i z + w_i) & \text{(if of degree two)} \end{cases}$$

EXAMPLE 15-1

REQUIRED: A fifth-order high-pass Chebyshev filter having

$$f_s = 1K \text{ rad/s}$$

Stopband $= [0, 300]$ rad/s at -45 dB or less

Passband $= [400, 500]$ rad/s at -2 dB or greater

is to be designed where

$$H(z) = K(z-1)^5/(z^5 + 4.1z^4 + 7.133z^3 + 6.548z^2 + 3.16z^1 + 0.642z^0)$$

The poles and zeros are located at

Zeros	Poles
$+1 + i0$	$-0.867 + i0.0$
$+1 + i0$	$-0.829 + i0.338$
$+1 + i0$	$-0.829 - i0.338$
$+1 + i0$	$-0.786 + i0.553$
$+1 + i0$	$-0.786 - i0.553$

Convert $H(z)$ into a design having only real coefficients, using only first- and second-order sections.

RESULTS: The resulting filter consists of one first-order and two second-order subfilters satisfying the equation

$$H(z) = K[(z-1.0)/(z+0.867)]$$
$$\times [(z^2 - 2.0z^1 + 1.0)/(z^2 + 1.66z + 0.801)]$$
$$\times [(z^2 - 2.0z^1 + 1.0)/(z^2 + 1.57z + 0.923)]$$

In this case all the zeros are located at $z = 1.0$. As a result, the "pairing" of a zero with a nearby pole is arbitrary.

EXAMPLE 15-2

REQUIRED: The fourth-order elliptic bandpass filter, presented in example 14-14, is given by

$$H(z) = K(z^4 - 1.15z^2 + 1.0)/(z^4 + 1.756z^2 + 1.0)$$

The poles and zeros are located at

Zeros	Poles	
$-0.888 + i0.459$	$-0.247 + i0.813$	
$-0.888 - i0.459$	$-0.247 - i0.813$	1st pair
$0.888 + i0.459$	$0.247 + i0.813$	
$0.888 - i0.459$	$0.247 - i0.813$	2nd pair

Convert $H(z)$ into a design having only real coefficients using only first- and second-order sections with poles and zeros being locally paired.

RESULTS: The realized filter is given by

$$H(z) = K[(z^2 + 1.776z + 1.0)/(z^2 + 0.494z + 0.722)]$$
$$\times [(z^2 - 1.776z + 1.0)/(z^2 - 0.494z + 0.722)]$$

The production of an acceptable transfer function, namely $H(z)$, is only one part of the IIR design process. Another equally important step is to choose an architecture. Whereas the transfer function provides a mathematical description of the target filter, the architecture specifies its implementation. There is no unique architecture for a given transfer function, just as there is no unique design for a building or bridge. Different architectures offer contrasting attributes. Some are hardware intense, others are simple; some are sensitive of digital round-off and/or truncation errors, others are insensitive. The choice of what architecture to employ is dependent upon the application.

15.2 STATE-VARIABLE DESCRIPTION

The standard filter forms found in common use are:

1. Direct II
2. Standard
3. Cascade
4. Parallel

These basic filter cases are graphically interpreted in figure 15-1. The direct II and standard architectures are somewhat similar in their structure. Since both strategies possess information feedback paths ranging from one delay to n delays, their transfer functions are modeled by equation (15-1i). That is, the transfer function denominator is an nth-order polynomial. The cascade and parallel models are constructed using a system of low-order subsections or subfilters. In the cascade design, the low-order subsections are serially interconnected. In the parallel filter, these sections are simply connected in parallel. The low-order subfilters, in both cases, are the result of factoring the nth-order transfer function polynomial, given by equation (15-1), into lower-order polynomials. As a result, the transfer function is characterized by equation (15-1ii).

The design and analysis of all four classes of filters can be performed using manually manipulated equations or a digital computer. The most efficient method of formulating the filter design problem, whether using tables, calculators, or a computer, is called the *state-variable* technique. A state variable is a parameter which represents the information stored in a system. The set of state variables is called a *state vector*. For an analog system, information is stored on capacitors or in inductors. In earlier chapters, state variables were used to specify and facilitate the manipulation of the $R, L,$ and C components of an analog filter. In these cases, capacitive voltage and inductive current were valid state variables. Since resistors have no memory, they would not be the source of a state variable.

In general, for an analog system modeled by an nth-order ordinary differential equation

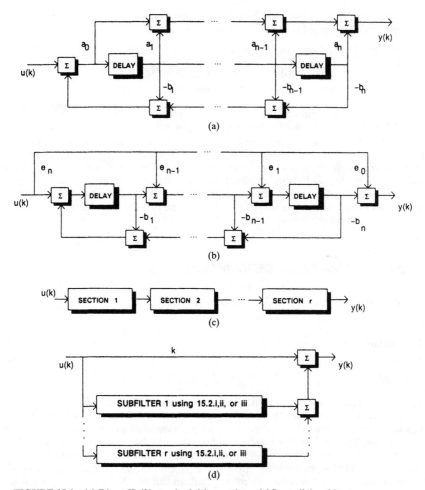

FIGURE 15-1 (*a*) Direct II, (*b*) standard, (*c*) cascade, and (*d*) parallel architectures.

$$d^n x(t)/dt^n + \cdots + a_2 d^2 x(t)/dt^2 + a_1 dx(t)/dt + a_0 x(t) = u(t) \qquad (15\text{-}3i)$$

The states can be assigned as follows:

$$x_1(t) = x(t)$$
$$x_2(t) = dx(t)/dt$$
$$x_3(t) = d^2 x(t)/dt^2 \qquad (15\text{-}3ii)$$
$$\cdots \qquad \cdots$$
$$x_n(t) = d^n x(t)/dt^n$$

with the *n*-dimensional state vector **x**(*t*) becoming

$$\mathbf{x}(t) = [x_1(t), x_2(t), \ldots, x_n(t)]^t \qquad (^t = \text{transpose}) \qquad (15\text{-}3iii)$$

A state-variable equation consists of several parts, and they are:

1. A vector of state variables

2. The *bonds of interaction* (i.e., a mathematical system of equations which relate a state-variable to the others)

3. Initial state information

Given an *initial* state vector, the bonds of interaction, and current and future inputs, all future states and outputs can be computed.

The study of digital filters concentrates on discrete equations rather than ordinary differential equations. For a discrete time system, given by the equation

$$x(k) + a_1x(k-1) + \cdots + a_{n-1}x(k-n+-1) + a_n \times x(k-n) = u(k) \qquad \text{(15-4i)}$$

the state assignment is given by

$$x_1(k) = x(k-1) \qquad \text{(15-4ii)}$$

$$x_2(k) = x(k-2)$$

$$\cdots \qquad \cdots$$

$$x_n(k) = x(k-n)$$

The memory element, which stores the state information, is simply a delay (shift) register. By interconnecting shift registers, coefficient multipliers, and adders, difference equations of the type shown in equation (15-4i) can be mechanized.

The state-variable representation of an nth-order digital filter, having an input time series $u(k)$ and output time series $y(k)$, is given by

$$x(k+1) = \mathbf{A}\,x(k) + \mathbf{b}\,u(k) \qquad \text{(15-5)}$$

$$y(k) = \mathbf{c}'x(k) + d\,u(k)$$

where $\mathbf{x}(k) = n$-dimensional vector of state variables
         $\mathbf{A} = n \times n$ coefficient matrix
         $\mathbf{b} = n$-dimensional vector of coefficients
         $\mathbf{c}' = n$-dimensional vector of coefficients
         d = scalar coefficient

The system defined by equation (15-5) is shown in block diagram form in figure 15-2. This format will be used to express the designs of direct II, standard, cascade, and parallel filter architectures. It shall also be assumed that the transfer function given by equation (15-1) is *monic*.

EXAMPLE 15-3

REQUIRED: Given a transfer function

$$H(z) = Y(z)/U(z) = N(z)/D(z)$$

$$= (z^3 - 0.5z^2 - 0.315z - 0.185)/(z^3 - 0.5z^2 + 0.5z - 0.25)$$

$$= [(z-1.0)(z^2 + 0.5z + 0.185)]/[(z-0.5)(z^2 + 0.5)]$$

$$= \frac{[(z-1.0)(z+0.25 - i0.35)(z+0.25 + i0.35)]}{[(z-0.5)(z - i0.707)(z + i0.707)]}$$

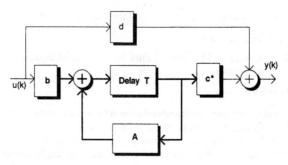

FIGURE 15-2   State-variable model.

Place the preceding equation in state-variable form.

RESULTS:

$$\text{Define } H(z) = H_1(z)H_2(z) \text{ where}$$
$$H_1(z) = X(z)/U(z) = z^3/D(z)$$
$$H_2(z) = Y(z)/X(z) = z^{-3}N(z)$$

This representation is not unique but will serve as a demonstration model. Concentrating on the first term, observe:

From $H_1(z) \rightarrow (z^3 - 0.5z^2 + 0.5z - 0.25)X(z) = z^3U(z)$

or $(1.0 - 0.5z^{-1} + 0.5z^{-2} - 0.25z^{-3})X(z) = U(z)$

or $x(k) - 0.5x(k-1) + 0.5x(k-2) - 0.25x(k-3) = u(k)$ [i]

From $H_2(z) \rightarrow z^{-3}(z^3 - 0.5z^2 - 0.315z - 0.185)X(z) = Y(z)$

or $(1.0 - 0.5z^{-1} - 0.315z^{-2} - 0.1875z^{-3})X(z) = Y(z)$

or $y(k) = x(k) - 0.5x(k-1) - 0.315x(k-2) - 0.185x(k-3)$ [ii]

Substituting $x(k)$ from [i] into [ii], we obtain

$$y(k) = [0.5x(k-1) - 0.5x(k-2) + 0.25x(k-3) + u(k)]$$
$$-0.5x(k-1) - 0.315x(k-2) - 0.185x(k-3)$$
$$= 0.0x(k-1) - 0.815x(k-2) + 0.065x(k-3) + u(k)$$ [iii]

To place the filter into state-variable form, define

$$x_1(k) = x(k-3) \qquad x_2(k) = x(k-2) \qquad x_3(k) = x(k-1)$$

or $x_1(k+1) = x_2(k)$

$$x_2(k+1) = x_3(k)$$

$$x_3(k+1) = 0.25x_1(k) - 0.5x_2(k) + 0.5x_3(k) + u(k)$$

$$= 0.25x(k-3) - 0.5x(k-2) + 0.5x(k-1) + u(k)$$

then

$$\mathbf{x}(k+1) = \begin{bmatrix} 0 & 1 & 0 \\ 0 & 0 & 1 \\ 0.25 & -0.5 & 0.5 \end{bmatrix} \mathbf{x}(k) + \begin{bmatrix} 0 \\ 0 \\ 1.0 \end{bmatrix} u(k)$$

and from [*iii*]

$$y(k) = [0.0x(k-1) - 0.815x(k-2) + 0.065x(k-3)] + u(k)$$
$$= [0.065x_1(k) - 0.815x_2(k) + 0.0x_3(k) + u(k)]$$

or $\qquad y(k) = [0.065, -0.815, 0.0]\mathbf{x}(k) + (1.0)u(k)$

At first glance, it may seem as though the state-variable approach is excessively mathematical and impractical. In fact the opposite is true. Indeed we can analyze a digital filter without using the state-variable approach, but this course of action generally requires more labor and time and can be generalized less easily. Furthermore, the state approach more readily lends itself to analysis using computer-aided engineering (CAE) tools than any other approach. This can be an enormous advantage when using a general-purpose computer to assist in the analysis of a filter as well as to investigate the time domain behavior of the system.

EXAMPLE 15-4

REQUIRED: Compute the response of the filter based on equation (15-5). Assume that a general-purpose digital computer can be used to perform the analysis.

RESULTS: The time response of the filter specified in example 15-3 can be coded as follows:

- Let $T = (T(1), T(2), T(3))$ be a temporary storage array configured as a stack (i.e., first in–first out).
- Let $A(3,3)$, $B(3)$, $B(3)$, and D be the matrix-vector four tuple (A, b, c, d).
- Let $U(i)$ be the ith input sample, $i = 1, \ldots, N$.
- Let $Y(i)$ be the ith output sample, $i = 1, \ldots, N$.

```
begin
  [initialize the state vector X(i)=0.0]
   for i=1 to N              ; N=time series length
     for j=1 to 3
        T(j)=B(j)*U(i) ; initialize accumulator
        for k=1 to 3
           T(j)=T(j)+A(j,k)*X(k) ; sum of products
        next k
     next j  ; next state variable stored in T(j)
     Y(i)=D*U(i)
     for j=1 to 3
        Y(i)=C(j)*X(j)+Y(i) ; compute output
     next j
     for j=1 to 3
        X(j)=T(j)  ; shift register stack
     next j
end
```

15.3 DIRECT II ARCHITECTURE

A filter whose transfer function is specified by equation (15-1) has a direct II realization as shown in figure 15-1. Another variation on this theme, which also qualifies as a direct II architecture, is displayed in figure 15-3. The transfer function is expressed as the ratio of two polynomials denoted $N(z)$ (numerator) and $D(z)$ (denominator). Since $H(z)$ is monic, it follows that a two-term continued fraction expansion of $H(z)$ satisfies

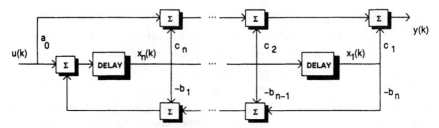

FIGURE 15-3   Direct II state-variable model.

$$H(z) = \sum_{i=0}^{N} a_i z^{-i} / D(z) = a_0 + \left(\sum_{i=1}^{N} (a_i - a_0 b_i) z^{-i} \right) / D(z) \qquad (15\text{-}6)$$

In particular, let $d = a_0$ and

$$c_1 = a_N - a_0 \times b_N$$
$$c_2 = a_{N-1} - a_0 \times b_{N-1} \qquad (15\text{-}7)$$
$$\cdots \quad \cdots$$
$$c_N = a_1 - a_0 \times b_1$$

Therefore, the state-variable definition of equation (15-5) is given by

$$\mathbf{x}(k+1) = \begin{bmatrix} 0 & 1 & 0 & \cdots & 0 & 0 \\ 0 & 0 & 1 & \cdots & 0 & 0 \\ 0 & 0 & 0 & \cdots & 0 & 0 \\ & & & \cdots & & \\ 0 & 0 & 0 & \cdots & 0 & 1 \\ -b_N & -b_{N-1} & -b_{N-2} & & -b_2 & -b_1 \end{bmatrix} \mathbf{x}(k) + \begin{bmatrix} 0 \\ 0 \\ 0 \\ \cdots \\ 0 \\ 1 \end{bmatrix} u(k) \qquad (15\text{-}8)$$

$$= \qquad\qquad\qquad \mathbf{A}\mathbf{x}(k) \qquad\qquad\qquad + \quad bu(k)$$

and

$$y(k) = (a_N - a_0 \times b_N, a_{N-1} - a_0 \times b_{N-1}, \ldots, a_1 - a_0 \times b_1)\mathbf{x}(k) + a_0 \times u(k)$$
$$= \mathbf{c}' \times \mathbf{x}(k) \qquad\qquad\qquad\qquad\qquad + du(k)$$

The direct II architecture for the state-variable filter given by equation (15-8) is diagrammed in figure 15-3. Comparing this architecture to the non-state-variable architecture presented in figure 15-1, it is seen that each filter consists of N shift registers (and N states) and $2N + 1$ coefficient multiplies and distributed summers.

EXAMPLE 15-5   (CBI)

REQUIRED: Place the low-pass Butterworth filter found in example 14-6, namely,

$$H(z) = 0.0676(z + 1)^2 / (z^2 - 1.142z + 0.412)$$
$$= (0.0676 + 0.1352z^{-1} + 0.0676z^{-2}) / (1 - 1.142z^{-1} + 0.412z^{-2})$$

into a direct II state-variable form.

RESULTS: For

$$a_0 = 0.0676 \qquad b_0 = 1.0 (\text{monic})$$
$$a_1 = 0.3152 \qquad b_1 = -1.142 \tag{15-1}$$
$$a_2 = 0.0676 \qquad b_2 = 0.412$$

Compute, using equations (15-7) and (15-8) for $N = 2$,

$$c_1 = a_2 - a_0 b_2 = 0.0397 \qquad c_2 = a_1 - a_0 b_1 = 0.1448$$

Then

$$\mathbf{x}(k+1) = \begin{bmatrix} 0.0 & 1.0 \\ -0.412 & 1.142 \end{bmatrix} \mathbf{x}(k) + \begin{bmatrix} 0 \\ 1.0 \end{bmatrix} u(k)$$
$$y(k) = [0.0397, 0.2124] \mathbf{x}(k) + 0.0676 u(k)$$

The circuit realization is shown in figure 15-4.

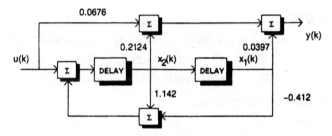

FIGURE 15-4   Second-order direct II filter.

15.4 STANDARD ARCHITECTURE

A filter having a transfer function given by equation (15-1) has a standard architecture as shown in figure 15-1b. Mathematically, the coefficient set $\{e_i\}$ is difficult to compute for high-order standard filters. For an $n = 2$ second-order filter, they are given by

$$e_0 = a_0 \tag{15-9}$$
$$e_1 = -b_1 a_0 + a_1$$
$$e_2 = (b_1^2 - b_2) a_0 - b_1 a_1 + a_2$$

For higher-order filters, a matrix state-variable definition is almost essential. The state definition of a standard filter is

$$\mathbf{x}(k+1) = \begin{bmatrix} 0 & 1 & \cdots & 0 & 0 \\ 0 & 0 & \cdots & 0 & 0 \\ & & \cdots & \cdots & \\ 0 & 0 & \cdots & 0 & 1 \\ -b_N & -b_{N-1} & & -b_2 & -b_1 \end{bmatrix} \mathbf{x}(k) + \begin{bmatrix} e_1 \\ e_2 \\ \cdots \\ e_{N-1} \\ e_N \end{bmatrix} u(k) \tag{15-10}$$

$$= \mathbf{Ax}(k) \qquad + bu(k)$$

and

$$y(k) = [-b_N, -b_{N-1}, \dots, -b_2, -b_1]\mathbf{x}(k) + e_0 u(k)$$
$$= \mathbf{c}'\mathbf{x}(k) \qquad + du(k)$$

where

$$
\begin{bmatrix} e_0 \\ e_1 \\ e_2 \\ \dots \\ e_N \end{bmatrix} =
\begin{bmatrix}
1 & 0 & 0 & \dots & 0 & 0 \\
b_1 & 1 & 0 & \dots & 0 & 0 \\
b_2 & b_1 & 1 & \dots & 0 & 0 \\
\dots & & & & \dots & \\
b_N & b_{N-1} & b_{N-2} & \dots & b_1 & 1
\end{bmatrix}
\begin{bmatrix} a_0 \\ a_1 \\ a_2 \\ \dots \\ a_N \end{bmatrix}
\qquad (15\text{-}11)
$$

A general-purpose digital computer can be readily programmed to solve equation (15-11). The standard architecture is shown in figure 15-1b. The complexity of the standard filter can be seen to be that of the direct II.

EXAMPLE 15-6

REQUIRED: Place the low-pass Butterworth filter found in example 14-6, namely,

$$H(z) = 0.0676(z + 1)^2/(z^2 - 1.142z + 0.412)$$
$$= (0.0676 + 0.1352z^{-1} + 0.0676z^{-2})/(1 - 1.142z^{-1} + 0.412z^{-2})$$

into a standard state-variable form.

RESULTS: For

$$a_0 = 0.0676 \qquad b_0 = 1.0(\text{monic})$$
$$a_1 = 0.3152 \qquad b_1 = -1.142 \qquad\qquad (15\text{-}1)$$
$$a_2 = 0.0676 \qquad b_2 = 0.412$$

Compute, using equation (15-9) and $N = 2$,

$$e_0 = a_0 = 0.0676$$
$$e_1 = -b_1 a_0 + a_1 = 0.238$$
$$e_2 = (b_1^2 - b_2)a_0 - b_1 a_1 + a_2 = 0.4879$$

or

$$\mathbf{x}(k+1) = \begin{bmatrix} 0.4 & 1.0 \\ -0.412 & 1.142 \end{bmatrix} \mathbf{x}(k) + \begin{bmatrix} 0.238 \\ 0.4879 \end{bmatrix} u(k)$$
$$y(k) = [-0.412, 1.142]\, \mathbf{x}(k) + 0.0676u(k)$$

The circuit realization is given in figure 15-5.

15-5   CASCADE ARCHITECTURE

A transfer function, given in factored form as shown in equation (15-1), has a cascade architecture as shown in figure 15-1c. One specific implementation is shown in

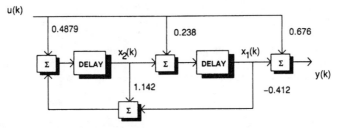

FIGURE 15-5 Second-order standard model.

figure 15-6. In this option, N first-order subfilters are serially connected through a system of unit and nonunity feed-forward gains (i.e., z_i), and simple feedback gains (i.e., p_i). If all the poles of the synthesized Nth-order filter are real, the design presented in figure 15-6a is viable. The matrix state representation of such a cascaded filter is shown below:

$$\mathbf{x}(k+1) = \begin{bmatrix} p_1 & 0 & \cdots & 0 & 0 \\ p_1 - z_1 & p_2 & \cdots & 0 & 0 \\ \cdots & & \cdots & & \\ p_1 - z_1 & p_2 - z_2 & \cdots & p_{N-1} & 0 \\ p_1 - z_1 & p_2 - z_2 & \cdots & p_{N-1} - z_{N-1} & p_N \end{bmatrix} \mathbf{x}(k) + K \begin{bmatrix} 1 \\ 1 \\ \cdots \\ 1 \\ 1 \end{bmatrix} u(k)$$

$$= \quad \mathbf{A}\mathbf{x}(k) \qquad\qquad\qquad + bu(k)$$

$$y(k) = [p_1 - z_1, \ldots, p_N - z_N] \qquad \mathbf{x}(k) + K u(k)$$

$$= \quad \mathbf{c}^t\mathbf{x}(k) \qquad\qquad + du(k)$$

(15-12)

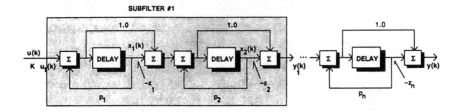

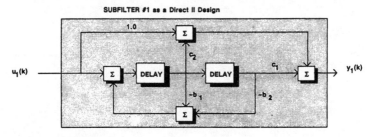

FIGURE 15-6 Cascade filter and subfilters.

For $H(z)$, a monic transfer function, $K = H(z \to \infty) = a_0$. If some or all of the poles are complex, they should be combined as complex conjugate pairs to form second-order subfilters consisting of only real coefficients. A logical choice for the architecture of a second-order subfilter of a cascade system is the direct II. Suppose, for example, that $p_1 = p_2^*$ where $*$ denotes complex conjugation. Let $H_1(z)$ represent the second-order subsection shown in figure 15-6b. More specifically,

$$H_1(z) = [(z - z_1)(z - z_1^*)]/[(z - p_1)(z - p_1^*)]$$
$$= (z^2 - 2\mathrm{Re}[z_1]z + |z_1|^2)/(z^2 - 2\mathrm{Re}[p_1]z + |p_1|^2)$$
$$= (z^2 + az + b)/(z^2 + cz + d) \tag{15-13}$$

can be realized, in direct II form, as

$$\mathbf{x}_1(k+1) = \begin{bmatrix} 0 & 1 \\ -d & -c \end{bmatrix} \mathbf{x}(k) + \begin{bmatrix} 0 \\ 1 \end{bmatrix} u_1(k) \tag{15-14}$$

$$y_1(k) = [c_1 = b - d, \; c_2 = a - c]\, \mathbf{x}_1(k) + 1\, u_1(k)$$

and is shown in figure 15-6b.

EXAMPLE 15-7   (CBI)

REQUIRED: Place the low-pass Butterworth filter found in example 14-6, namely,

$$H(z) = 0.0676(z + 1)^2/(z^2 - 1.142z + 0.412)$$
$$= (0.0676 + 0.1352z^{-1} + 0.0676z^{-2})/(1 - 1.142z^{-1} + 0.412z^{-2})$$

into a cascade state-variable form.

RESULTS: For

$$\begin{array}{ll} a_0 = 0.0676 & b_0 = 1.0(\text{monic}) \\ a_1 = 0.3152 & b_1 = 1.142 \\ a_2 = 0.0676 & b_2 = 0.412 \end{array} \tag{15-1}$$

Compute, using equations (15-1ii) and (15-13), for $N = 2$,

$$H(z) = 0.0676 H_1(z) \qquad \text{i.e., } K = 0.0676 \tag{i}$$
$$H_1(z) = Y(z)/U_1(z) = (z^2 + 2z + 1)/(z^2 - 1.142z + 0.412)$$

and from equation (15-14),

$$\begin{array}{ll} a = 2.0 & c = -1.142 \\ b = 1.0 & d = 0.412 \\ c_1 = b - d = 0.588 & c_2 = a - c = 3.142 \end{array}$$

Then

$$\mathbf{x}(k+1) = \begin{bmatrix} 0.0 & 1.0 \\ -0.412 & 1.142 \end{bmatrix} \mathbf{x}(k) + \begin{bmatrix} 0 \\ 1.0 \end{bmatrix} u_1(k)$$

$$y(k) = [0.588, 3.142]\mathbf{x}(k) + 1.0u(k)$$

However, from line $[i]$ preceding $u_1(n) = 0.0676u(n)$. Therefore the final state-variable equation is of the form

$$\mathbf{x}(k+1) = \begin{bmatrix} 0.0 & 1.0 \\ -0.412 & 1.142 \end{bmatrix} \mathbf{x}(k) + \begin{bmatrix} 0.0 \\ 0.0676 \end{bmatrix} u(k)$$

$$y(k) = [0.588, 3.142]\mathbf{x}(k) + 1.0u(k)$$

The circuit realization is shown in figure 15-7.

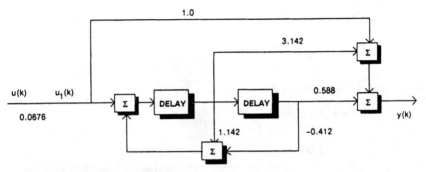

FIGURE 15-7   Direct II cascade subfilter.

15.6 PARALLEL ARCHITECTURE

A filter, having a factored transfer function as shown in equation (15-1), can be placed in parallel form. The N-poles, located at $z = p_i$ for $i = 1, 2, \ldots, N$, appear as either real or complex roots which are either nonrepeated or repeated. If, for example, $p_1 = p_2 = p_3, p_1$ is said to be a root of *multiplicity* three. The analysis of a parallel filter having nonrepeated roots is no more difficult than studying a cascade filter. However, the examination of a multiple-pole filter is significantly more complex. Therefore, unless the designer has access to CAD tools or is familiar with linear algebra, the adoption of a direct II, standard, or cascade architecture is recommended. As such, only the nonrepeated root case will be presented. For the analysis of the repeated root case, consult the referenced *Digital Filter Design Handbook* (F. Taylor).

Suppose the denominator of an Nth order $H(z)$ consists of R real poles (roots) $p_i = r_i$ and $M = (N-R)/2$ complex conjugate pole pairs p_j and $p_j{}^*$. Then using a *Heaviside* expansion of $H(z)$, we obtain

$$H(z) = q + \sum_{i=1}^{R} a_i/(z - r_i) + \sum_{j=1}^{M} (b_jz + c_j)/(z^2 + e_jz + f_j) \qquad (15\text{-}15)$$

where $q = H(z = \infty)$, $e_j = -(p_j + p_j{}^*) = -2\,\mathrm{Re}(p_j)$, $f_j = p_jpf_j{}^* = |p_j|^2$, and a_i, b_j, and c_j are the solutions to N equations in N unknowns. In a more compact form, the first and second terms can be collected in first- and second-order transfer functions denoted $H_1(z)$ and $H_2(z)$. Then equation (15-15) becomes

$$H(z) = q + \sum_{i=1}^{R} H_1i(z) + \sum_{j=1}^{M} H_2i(z) \qquad (15\text{-}16)$$

EXAMPLE 15-8 (CBI)

REQUIRED: Place the low-pass Butterworth filter found in example 14.6, namely,

$$H(z) = 0.0676(z+1)^2/(z^2 - 1.142z + 0.412)$$
$$= (0.0676 + 0.1352z^{-1} + 0.0676z^{-2})/$$
$$(1 - 1.142z^{-1} + 0.412z^{-2})$$

into a parallel state-variable form.

RESULTS: For

$$a_0 = 0.0676 \qquad b_0 = 1.0 \text{(monic)}$$
$$a_1 = 0.3152 \qquad b_1 = -1.142 \qquad\qquad (15\text{-}1)$$
$$a_2 = 0.0676 \qquad b_2 = 0.412$$

compute the Heaviside expansion of $H(z)$:

$$H(z) = q + H_2(z)$$
$$q = H(\infty) = 0.0676$$
$$H_2(z) = H(z) - q$$
$$= (0.0676z^2 + 0.1352z + 0.0676)/(z^2 - 1.142z + 0.412) - 0.0676$$
$$= (0.2124z + 0.0397)/(z^2 - 1.142z + 0.412)$$
$$= (0.2124z^{-1} + 0.0397z^{-2})/(1 - 1.142z^{-1} + 0.412z^2)$$

From equation (15-15), it follows that

$$b = 0.2124 \qquad c = 0.0397 \qquad e = -1.142 \qquad f = 0.412$$

Computing the state representation, using equation (15-8) for $N=2$, we obtain for $H_2(z)$

$$\mathbf{x}(k+1) = \begin{bmatrix} 0.0 & 1.0 \\ -0.412 & 1.142 \end{bmatrix} \mathbf{x}(k) + \begin{bmatrix} 0 \\ 1.0 \end{bmatrix} u(k)$$
$$y(k) = [0.0397, 0.2124]\mathbf{x}(k) + 0u(k)$$

The circuit realization is shown in figure 15-8. In this figure, all feed-forward gains, namely $q = 0.164$ and $a_0 = 0.097$, are combined to form $K = q + a_0 = 0.261$.

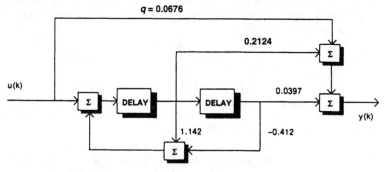

FIGURE 15-8 Parallel filter consisting of a direct II parallel subfilter.

15.7 COMPARISON

In this section, a comparison of the previously discussed designs will be presented for a common transfer function.

EXAMPLE 15-9

REQUIRED: Perform a comparative design of a filter whose transfer function is given by $H(z)$:

$$H(z) = 0.00183 \, (1 + z^{-1})^4/(1.0 - 1.499z^{-1} + 0.848z^{-2})$$
$$(1.0 - 1.5548z^{-1} + 0.649z^{-2})$$
$$= (0.00183 + 0.00732z^{-1} + 0.01098z^{-2} + 0.00732z^{-3} + 0.00183z^{-4})/$$
$$(1.0 - 3.054z^{-1} + 3.828z^{-2} - 2.291z^{-3} + 0.55z^{-4})$$

RESULTS: The filter coefficients are

$a_0 = 0.00183$	$b_1 = -3.0538$	$a_4 - a_0b_4 = 0.00082$
$a_1 = 0.00732$	$b_2 = 3.8281$	$a_3 - a_0b_3 = 0.01149$
$a_2 = 0.01098$	$b_3 = -2.2921$	$a_2 - a_0b_2 = 0.00399$
$a_3 = 0.00732$	$b_4 = 0.5507$	$a_1 - a_0b1_0 = 0.01288$
$a_4 = 0.00183$		

(a) **Direct II Architecture**
The direct II matrix definition becomes

$$\mathbf{A} = \begin{bmatrix} 0 & 1 & 0 & 0 \\ 0 & 0 & 1 & 0 \\ 0 & 0 & 0 & 1 \\ -0.5507 & 2.2921 & -3.8281 & 3.0538 \end{bmatrix} \quad \mathbf{b} = \begin{bmatrix} 0 \\ 0 \\ 0 \\ 1 \end{bmatrix}$$

$$\mathbf{c}^t = [0.00082, 0.01149, 0.00399, 0.01288]$$
$$d = 0.00183$$

and is graphically interpreted in figure 15-9.

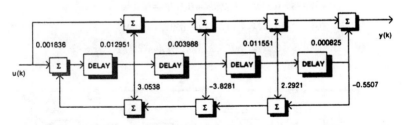

FIGURE 15-9 Fourth-order direct II filter.

(b) **Cascade Using Second-Order Subsections**
The example transfer function can be factored into two second-order sections denoted $H(z) = KH_1(z) H_2(z)$ where $H_i(z) = (a_{0i} + a_{1i}z^{-1} + a_{2i}z^{-2})/(b_{0i} + b_{1i}z^{-1} + b_{2i}z^{-2})$ and

$$K = 0.00183$$

$$H_1(z) = (1 + 2z^{-1} + z^{-2})/(1 - 1.499z^{-1} + 0.848z^{-2})$$

$$H_2(z) = (1 + 2z^{-1} + z^{-2})/(1 - 1.5548z^{-1} + 0.649z^{-2})$$

The matrix definition is given by

$$\mathbf{A}_1 = \begin{bmatrix} 0 & 1 \\ -b_{11} & -b_{21} \end{bmatrix} \quad \mathbf{b}_1 = \begin{pmatrix} 0 \\ 1 \end{pmatrix}$$

$$= \begin{bmatrix} 0 & 1 \\ -0.849 & 1.501 \end{bmatrix}$$

$$\mathbf{c}_1^t = [a_{21} - a_{01} \times b_{21}, a_{11} - a_{01} \times b_{11}] \qquad d_1 = a_{01}$$

$$= [0.1505, 3.5013] \qquad\qquad\qquad = 1.0$$

$$\mathbf{A}_2 = \begin{bmatrix} 0 & 1 \\ -b_{12} & -b_{22} \end{bmatrix} \quad \mathbf{b}_2 = \begin{pmatrix} 0 \\ 1 \end{pmatrix}$$

$$= \begin{bmatrix} 0 & 1 \\ -0.647 & 1.553 \end{bmatrix}$$

$$\mathbf{c}_2^t = [a_{22} - a_{02} \times b_{22}, a_{12} - a_{02} \times b_{12}] \qquad d_2 = a_{02}$$

$$= [0.3525, 3.5526] \qquad\qquad\qquad = 1.0$$

The schematic for the cascade design can be found in figure 15-10.

(c) **Parallel Using Direct II Second-Order Sections**

The example transfer function can also be factored as

$$H(z) = k_1 + (k_2 z^{-2} + k_3 z^{-1})/(1 - 1.499z^{-1} + 0.848z^{-2})$$
$$+ (k_4 z^{-2} + k_5 z^{-1})/(1 - 1.5548z^{-1} + 0.649z^{-2})$$

where $k_1 = 0.001836$. The values of $\{k_i\}$, for $i = 2, \ldots, 5$, can be computed in the following manner. Choose a set of z's which generate a system of four linearly independent equations of the form:

$$H(z) - k_1 = (k_2 z^{-2} + k_3 z^{-1})/D_1(z) + (k_4 z^{-2} + k_5 z^{-1})/D_2(z)$$

For example, let $z - \{1, -1, 2, -2,\}$; then

$$0.88544 = 2.865k_2 + 2.865k_3 + 10.62k_4 + 10.62k_5 \qquad z = 1$$

$$-0.00183 = 0.299k_2 - 0.299k_3 + 0.312k_4 - 0.312k_5 \qquad z = -1$$

$$0.05022 = 0.541k_2 + 1.081k_3 + 0.650k_4 + 1.299k_5 \qquad z = 2$$

$$-0.00179 = 0.217k_2 - 0.255k_3 + 0.129k_4 - 0.258k_5 \qquad z = -2$$

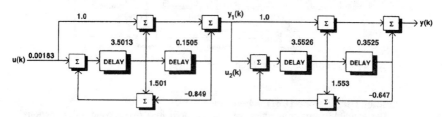

FIGURE 15-10   Fourth-order cascade filter.

Solving for the k's, we obtain

$$\{k_2, k_3, k_4, k_5\} = \{0.0629, -0.1381, -0.0473, 0.1509\}$$

Therefore, $H(z)$ is specified in factored (parallel) form. The last step in the design process is to architect each second-order section as a direct II filter. In this case (refer to the cascade example for details)

$$\mathbf{A}_1 = \begin{bmatrix} 0 & 1 \\ -0.849 & 1.501 \end{bmatrix} \quad \mathbf{b}_1 = \begin{pmatrix} 0 \\ 1 \end{pmatrix} \quad \mathbf{A}_2 = \begin{bmatrix} 0 & 1 \\ -0.647 & 1.553 \end{bmatrix} \quad \mathbf{b}_2 = \begin{pmatrix} 0 \\ 1 \end{pmatrix}$$

$$\mathbf{c}_1^t = [0.0640, -0.1394] \quad d_1 = 0 \quad \mathbf{c}_2^t = [-0.0478, 0.1522]$$

$$d_2 = 0$$

The filter is diagrammed in figure 15-11. Note that the memoryless feed-forward gains, namely q, equals $q = 0.00183$.

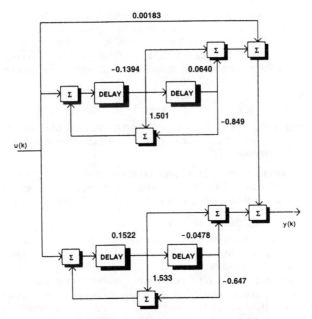

FIGURE 15-11 Fourth-order parallel filter.

15.8 FIXED-POINT DESIGN

An IIR, once designed and architected, often needs to be implemented in hardware. The choices are fixed- or floating-point. Of the two, fixed-point solutions generally provide the highest real-time bandwidth at the lowest cost. Unfortunately, fixed-point designs also introduce errors which are not found in more expensive floating-point IIR designs. The fixed-point error sources are either low-order inaccuracies, due to finite precision arithmetic and data (coefficient) roundoff effects, or potentially large errors due to run-time dynamic range overflow (saturation). To understand this phenomenon, consider a signed B bit number consisting of I integer bits and F fractional bits such that $B = I + F + 1$ (called a $[B,I,F]$ data format). In this number system representation, a number V would be symbolically expressed as $V \leftrightarrow [V_{B-1}:V_{B-2}, \ldots, V_{B-I+1} \Diamond V_{B-I}, \ldots, V_1, V_0]$ and is numerically equal to

$$V = -V_{B-1}2^I + V_{B-2}2^{I-1} + V_{B-3}2^{I-2} + \cdots$$
$$+ V_{B-I+1}2^0 + V_{B-I}2^{-1} + \cdots + V_1 2^{-(F-1)} + V_0 2^{-F} \qquad (15\text{-}17)$$

where $V_i = \{0,1\}$, and $\Diamond$ denotes the binary point location. The dynamic range of the $[B,I,F]$ numbering system is defined by $-2^I \leq V < 2^I - 1$ with a fractional precision given by $Q = 2^{-F}$, where Q is called the quantization step size and generally carries units of volts per bit. To eliminate run-time dynamic range overflow, I is chosen to be sufficiently large so as to ensure that each filter state is bounded by $|x_i| < 2^I$. Since $F = B - I - 1$, overspecifying I will result in reduced precision.

EXAMPLE 15-10

REQUIRED: A signal $x(t)$, having a ± 15 volt range, is digitized by a 16-bit analog-to-digital converter (ADC) to form a time series having sample values $x[n]$, where $|x[n]| < 1.0$. That is, the digitized data will be considered to be a fractional number. Suppose that the signal is to be "smoothed" by a simple filter which adds 16 consecutive samples together to form a new time series having sample values $y[n]$, where

$$y[i] = \sum_{j=0}^{15} x[i-j]$$

It immediately follows that $|y[n]| < 16 = 2^4$. Assume that the filter uses a $[16,I,F]$-data format. What is the minimum value of I which will guarantee overflow-free filtering? What is the corresponding Q?

RESULTS: Given that $|y[n]| < 2^4$, it follows that $B = 16$, $I = 4$, and $Q = 11$ bits. The analog-to-digital converter will therefore quantize the range $[0, 15]$ (equivalently $[-15, 0]$) volts into 11-fractional bits, which defines $Q = 15/2^{11} = 7.33$ milivolts/bit.

Additional precision can be gained by increasing the number of fractional bits assigned to the data and coefficients fields with an attendant decrease in dynamic range and an increased potential for run-time overflow. On the other hand, the overflow saturation problem can be reduced by enlarging the dynamic range of the system by increasing the integer bit field with an accompanying loss of precision. The problem facing the fixed-point filter designer, therefore, is achieving a balance between the competing desire to maximize precision and to simultaneously eliminate (or reduce) run-time overflow errors. This is called the *binary-point assignment problem* which is summarized in figure 15-12.

For IIR filters of arbitrary order and architecture, mathematically computing a meaningful bound on the dynamic range of a filter's states remains a challenging problem. Without such information, the dynamic range requirement of a filter's states cannot be estimated and, as a result, the binary assignment problem cannot be solved.

Recall from section 15.2, that a single-input single-output nth order proper and canonic IIR digital filter can be reduced to a state-variable model (see figure 15-2) which is repeated at this time for reader convenience.

$$\mathbf{x}[k+1] = \mathbf{A}\mathbf{x}[k] + \mathbf{b}u[k] - \text{state equation} \qquad (15\text{-}5)$$

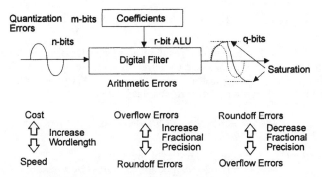

FIGURE 15-12 Binary-point assignment problem.

$$y[k] = c^T x[k] + du[k] - \text{output equation}$$

Classical methods have been developed which can bound the states of a digital filter in a ℓ_p sense. The ℓ_p norm of a causal time series $\{x[i]\}$, denoted $\|x\|_p$, is given by

$$\|x\|_p = \left(\sum_{i=0}^{\infty} |x[i]|^p \right)^{1/p} \tag{15-18}$$

where $p > 0$. For $p \to \infty$, $\|x\|_\infty = \max(|x[i]|, i \geq 0)$.

EXAMPLE 15-11 (CBI)

REQUIRED: A time series $\{x[i]\}$, having sample values $x[i] = 4*(u[i] - u[i - 1024)) = 4$ for $i \in [0, 1023]$ and 0 elsewhere is a causal pulse of duration 1024 samples. What is $\|x\|_p$ for $p = \{1/2, 1, 2, \text{and } \infty\}$?

RESULTS: Direct computation yields:

$$\|x\|_{1/2} = \left(\sum_{i=0}^{\infty} |x[i]|^{1/2} \right)^2 = (4^{1/2} 2^{10})^2 = 2^{22}$$

$$\|x\|_1 = \left(\sum_{i=0}^{\infty} |x[i]| \right) = (4 \times 2^{10}) = 2^{12}$$

$$\|x\|_2 = \left(\sum_{i=0}^{\infty} |x[i]|^2 \right)^{1/2} = (4^2 2^{10})^{1/2} = 2^7$$

$$\|x\|_\infty = (\max_{i \in [0,1023]} \{x[i]\})^2 = (4) = 2^2$$

It can therefore be seen that the value of norm of a time series is dependent on the choice of norm.

If the impulse response, measured at the ith state (or shift register location) is $\{x_i[k]\}$, then the forced response to an input $v[n]$, also measured at that location, is denoted $z_i[k] = x_i[k]*v[k]$ where * denotes linear convolution. From Holder's inequality,* it follows that:

---

* Holder inequality: $\Sigma |x_i y_i| \leq |x|_p |y|_q$ such that $1/p + 1/q = 1$.

$$|z_i[k]| = \sum_{m=0}^{\infty} |x_i[k-m]v[k]| \leq \|x_i\|_p \|v\|_q; \qquad \ni \frac{1}{p} + \frac{1}{q} = 1 \qquad (15\text{-}19)$$

Observe that if $\|v\|_q \leq 1$, the state resident in register location i will be bounded by $\|x_i\|_p$. This can serve as a measure to define dynamic range bound, namely $\|x_i\|_p \leq K_i \leq 2^I$. For $p = q = 2$ (i.e., ℓ_2 norms), the state bounds K_i can be defined to be the on-diagonal terms of an $n \times n$ matrix K which is given by:

$$K = xx^T = \|x\|_2^2 = \sum_{k=0}^{\infty} (A^k b)(A^k b)^T; \|x_i\|_2^2 = K_i \geq 0 \qquad (15\text{-}20)$$

That is, K_i is the (i,i) on-diagonal element of the $n \times n$ matrix K. The computing formula presented in equation (15-20) can be implemented by a general-purpose digital computer which can directly compute the ℓ_2 state bounds. Unfortunately, the ℓ_2 state bound is often referred to as a conservative bound. This can create difficulties when designing a high-order IIR since the integer field (i.e., I-bits) can be underassigned, leading to the possibility of dynamic range overflow during run time. The basic problem with the ℓ_2 norm is really found in the ℓ_2 assumption itself. From equation (15-19), it follows that $p = q = 2$. The input signal, therefore, must also be ℓ_2 bounded (assume $\|v\|_2 \leq 1$). This is generally an unrealistic requirement as the following example illustrates.

EXAMPLE 15-12

REQUIRED: Compute the ℓ_2 norms of a Kronecker impulse ($\delta[n]$), unit pulse of duration m samples $(x[n] = u[n] - u[n - m])$ and a decaying exponential $(y[n] = \{1, a, a^2, a^3, a^4, \ldots\}, 0 < a < 1$.

RESULT: Direct computation yields:

$$\|\delta[n]\|_2 = \sqrt{\sum_{n=0}^{\infty} \delta[n]^2} = 1 \qquad (i)$$

$$\|\mathbf{x}[n]\|_2 = \sqrt{\sum_{n=0}^{\infty} |\mathbf{x}[n]^2|} = \sqrt{\sum_{n=0}^{m-1} |\mathbf{x}[n]^2|} = \sqrt{\mathbf{m}} \qquad (ii)$$

Note, as $m \to \infty$, $\|x\|_2 \to \infty$ as well.

$$\|\mathbf{y}[n]\|_2 = \sqrt{\sum_{n=0}^{\infty} |a^{2n}|} = \sqrt{\frac{1}{1-a^2}} \qquad (iii)$$

Notice, for $a \to 1$, $\|y\|_2 \to \infty$. As a result, it can be seen that virtually any interesting long duration signal, such as $\cos(\omega k)$, would have an ℓ_2 norm which is extremely large, if not infinite.

Ideally, what is desired, is to produce a state bound on a sample-by-sample basis for all inputs having the physically meaningful requirement that $|v|_\infty = \max(\{v[k]\}) < 1$. This states that we simply require that the input be bounded by unity on a sample-by-sample basis. From Holder's inequality, it then follows that an ℓ_1 bound is to be computed on the ith state variable. The ℓ_1 norm is more pessimistic than the ℓ_2 bound in that $\|x\|_2 \leq \|x\|_1$. As a result, a more realistic estimate of the state bounds can be obtained.

The impulse response of an nth order linear shift invariant IIR filter, measured at the ith shift register location, has the general form:

$$x_i[k] = \sum_{j=1}^{n} \alpha_j k^{[g(j:i) - 1]} \lambda_{j:i}^k \qquad (15\text{-}21)$$

where $\lambda_{j:i}$ is the jth eigenvalue of the equation $e_i(\lambda \mathbf{I} - \mathbf{A})^{-1}b$, for $e_i = (0,0, \ldots , 1(i\text{th}$ location), $\ldots , 0)$, b given in equation (15-5), and $g[j{:}i] \geq 1$ corresponds to the multiplicity of the eigenvalue (root) $\lambda_{j:i}$. In general, $\lambda_{j:i}$ is complex and may appear with a multiplicity out to n. If the system is stable, the system's impulse response will decay to zero. That is, for a stable filter, $x_i[k] \to 0$ as $k \to \infty$. The ℓ_1 bound on $x_i[k]$ is given by:

$$|x_i|_1 = \sum_{k=0}^{\infty} | \sum_{j=1}^{n} \alpha_j k^{[g(j:i) - 1]} \lambda_{j:i}^k | < M \qquad (15\text{-}22)$$

which unfortunately does not, in general, have a simple closed form solution. Unlike steady-state analysis, where only the dominant eigenvalue trajectory is analyzed, the entire infinite sum needs to be accumulated for all sample values in the production of the ℓ_1 norm. A careful approximation, however, can be made. An estimate of the ℓ_1 state bound can be obtained by using a finite sum to approximate the infinite sum given in equation (15-22):

$$|\hat{x}_i|_1 = \sum_{k=0}^{k_1} |x_i[k]| \leq \sum_{k=0}^{\infty} |x_i[k]| = |x_i|_1 \qquad (15\text{-}23)$$

The problem, of course, is to estimate the indexing parameter k_1 so that the difference between the computed (estimated) and actual ℓ_1 norm is less than some acceptable value. A selection rule for k_1 can be based on the easily computed ℓ_2 norm of a filter state. For a stable IIR, there is a k_2 such that:

$$\sum_{k=0}^{k_2} |x_i[k]|^2 - K_i < \varepsilon \qquad (15\text{-}24)$$

where K_i is the ℓ_2^2 norm of $x_i[n]$ (i.e., $\|x_i\|2^2$) given by equation (15-20) and ε is an acceptable error threshold. The value of k_2 can be approximated by assuming that near convergence, the solution is defined only by a stable system's dominant eigenvalue (pole), assumed to be σ_{min}, where:

$$\sigma_{min} = \{\text{minimum}\{\sigma_i\}, \lambda_i = \sigma_i + j\omega_i, |\sigma_i| < 1.0, j \in [1,n]\} \qquad (15\text{-}25)$$

Under this assumption, the system's impulse response is convergent and has the form $x_i[k] = k^{s-1} \sigma_{min}^k \cos(k\omega + \phi)$, where s is the multiplicity of λ_i. For low multiplicity, as is generally the case:

$$\sum_{k=0}^{\infty} |x_i[k]|^p \leq (1 - |\sigma_{min}|^p)^{-s} \qquad (15\text{-}26)$$

where equality holds for $s = 1$. From this it follows that the relationship between k_1 and k_2 can be expressed as:

$$\text{scale factor} = \frac{k_1}{k_2} = \frac{\left(\dfrac{1}{1 - |\sigma_{min}|}\right)^s}{\left(\sqrt{\dfrac{1}{1 - |\sigma_{min}|^2}}\right)^{2s}} \qquad (15\text{-}27)$$

Notice that for $|\sigma_{min}| \rightarrow 1.0$, the scale factor correction term becomes unbounded. For a value $|\sigma_{min}|$ less than unity, a stopping rule for equation (15-23) can be defined which will result in an approximate ℓ_1 state bound.

The advantage of estimating an ℓ_1 bound can be appreciated when equation (15-19) (convolution) is interpreted in terms of a worst case ℓ_∞ input having a unit bound. The worst-case ℓ_∞ input, measured at state location i, is given by:

$$v[k] = \text{sign}(x_i[k - m]) \tag{15-28}$$

Convoluting the input defined by equation (15-28) with the filter's impulse response measured at state location i, namely $x_i[k]$, produces:

$$\sum_{m=0}^{\infty} x_i[k - m]v[k] = \sum_{m=0}^{\infty} x_i[k - m]\text{sign}(x_i[k - m])$$

$$= z_i[k] \leq \|x_i\|_1 \|v\|_\infty = \|x_i\|_1 \tag{15-29}$$

which is the actual ℓ_1 state norm which is assumed to be sufficiently well approximated by equation (15-23). Once the output has a computed estimate of the ℓ_1 bound, the filter's binary point can be defined.

EXAMPLE 15-13 (CBI)

REQUIRED: A 6th-order elliptic low-pass filter having the following specifications was designed and analyzed.

- –0.5-dB passband over $f \in [0,5]$ kHz
- –60-dB stopband over $f \in [7,22.05]$ kHz
- sample frequency = 44.1 kHz

The filter was implemented as the cascade system as shown in figure 15-13 and has a dominant eigenvalue $\sigma_{min} = 0.9646$. What is the approximate ℓ_1 worst-case state gain?

RESULT: The largest theoretical determined value of K_i was for states x_5 and x_6 and in particular $|x_5|_2^2 = |x_6|_2^2 = 17137.238$. Using a value of ε in equation (15-24) of 0.01 (~5 $\times$ 10^{-8} of $|x_5|_2^2$), the value of k_2 was found by using equation (15-26) and determined to be

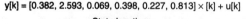

$$y[k] = [0.382, 2.593, 0.069, 0.398, 0.227, 0.813] \times [k] + u[k]$$

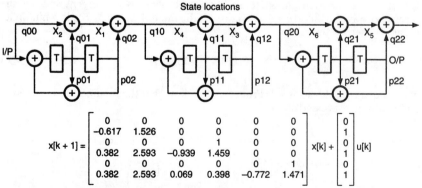

FIGURE 15-13 Cascade 6th-order IIR in state-variable form. (*Courtesy of the Athena Group*)

$k_2 = 50$. Given σ_{min}, this defines $k_1 \sim 370$ and $|x_5|_1 = 709.3$. Based upon the estimated ℓ_1 norm, the output would need to be bounded by $709.3 < 1024 = 2^{10}$ or 10 integer bits would be needed at the register level to ensure that no run-time overflow occurs. Testing this hypothesis with the known worst-case input [see equation (15-28)] results in the data shown in figure 15-14 where the maximal output achieves the computed ℓ_1 bound of 709.3. This corresponds to an integer bit assignment of $I = 10$ bits (i.e., $709.3 < 2^{10}$). In comparison, if one assumes that the worst-case input for a low-pass filter is a unit step, the maximum state value would have been bounded by 222.3 as shown in figure 15-14. This corresponds to an integer bit assignment of 8 bits. However, this is not the worst-case bound (which is 10 bits) and could result in run-time overflows.

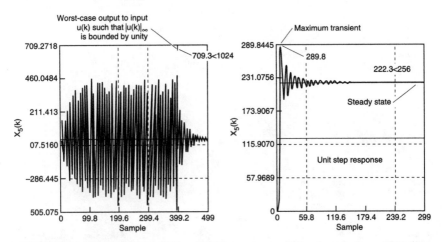

FIGURE 15-14 Worst-case bounded input and step response of filter shown in figure 15-13. (*Data produced using MONARCH, courtesy of the Athena Group*)

BIBLIOGRAPHY

The Athena Group, *MONARCH User Guide,* The Athena Group, Gainesville, Fla., 1994.

Oppenheim, A. V., and R. W. Schafer, *Digital Signal Processing,* Prentice-Hall, Englewood Cliffs, N.J., 1975.

Taylor, F. J., *Digital Filter Design Handbook,* Marcel Dekker, New York, 1983.

―――― and T. Stouraitis, *Digital Filter Design Software for the IBM PC,* Marcel Dekker, New York, 1987.

Werter, M. J., "Suppression of Parasitic Oscillations Due to Overflow and Quantization in Recursive Digital Filters," *Proefschrift,* Eindhover, 1989.

CHAPTER 16

DIGITAL FILTER TECHNOLOGY

Michael Lewis
The Athena Group

16.1 INTRODUCTION

Up to this point, our discussion of digital filters has emphasized the mathematical foundations. Having covered this, we now discuss the issues involved in implementing a digital filter with hardware and/or software. The types of systems that can be utilized for this vary broadly, but can be grouped into two categories. The first category relies on dedicated hardware such as specialized digital filtering chips and digital filters constructed from the basic building blocks of memory, adders, and multipliers. The other category utilizes a programmable processor which executes software that implements the digital filter.

Digital filter software can be run on general-purpose desktop computer processors (e.g., the 80X86 and 680X0 series); and it's possible to build filtering software for microcontrollers (e.g., the Intel 8051 and Motorola 68HC11 families). But there also exists another class of processor ideally suited for digital filtering applications: the *digital signal processing* (DSP) processors. This breed of processors, available from numerous manufacturers, has been specifically designed to perform DSP applications as efficiently and powerfully as possible. This chapter, therefore, will deal with some of the specifics of building software that will run on a DSP processor.

Given that numerous processor families are currently available and new chips appear daily, any attempt to detail *all* the available DSP processors will inevitably fail. In this chapter we will discuss several of the more typical available DSP processors, but, more importantly, we will cover some of the obstacles that must be overcome while learning to implement digital filters with DSP chips. Table 16-1 compares some popular DSP processors and their features.

Any attempt to describe how to implement a digital filter in software will be made much easier if the following fundamental structures are remembered. These were described in chapters 13 and 14, but they are worth repeating here. FIR filters have two common implementations, and IIR filters have many variations. The data flow and functionality of these algorithms can be more easily understood by representing them visually. Figure 16-1a shows the visual representation of an FIR of length 5, while figure 16-1b is a representation of a 5th-order IIR implemented as a DIRECT II architecture.

TABLE 16-1   Some Common DSP Processors

Manufacturer	Processor	Word Format
AT&T	DSP32C	32-bit floating-point
	DSP16	16-bit fixed-point
Analog Devices	ADSP2100	16-bit fixed-point
	ADSP21000	32-bit floating-point
	ADSP21060	32-bit floating-point
Motorola	56000	24-bit fixed-point
	96000	32-bit floating-point
Texas	TMS320C10	16-bit fixed-
Instruments	/20	point
	TMS320C30	32-bit floating-point
	TMS320C40	32-bit floating-point
	TMS320C50	16-bit fixed-point

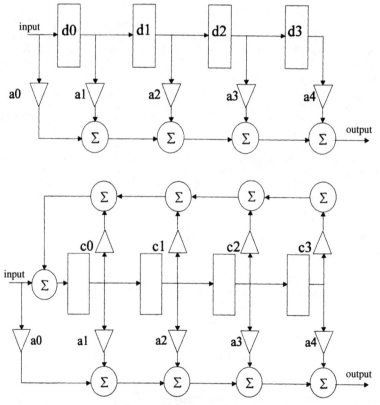

FIGURE 16-1   Block diagram of FIR of length 5 and 5th-order IIR filters.

An FIR consists of only feedforward data paths. The FIR, shown in figure 16-1a, consists of two elements. The first is the delay line, represented by d_0, d_1, d_2, d_3, which operates like an FIFO. The second element is the multiply-accumulate device, which performs the filter calculations. At the nth sample instant, the current sample, $x[n]$ is multiplied by filter coefficient a_0. This result is then summed with the product of $x[n-1]$ and a_1, and this result is then summed with the product of $x[n-2]$ and a_2. This multiply-accumulate operation is performed repeatedly for the remaining delay elements. The delay line is then linearly shifted one location, such that:

$$x[n] \rightarrow x[n-1], x[n-1] \rightarrow x[n-2], \ldots, x[n-(N-2)] \rightarrow x[n-(N-1)]$$

where N is the filter order and is equal to 5, in this case.

In other words, the output sample $y[n]$ is computed as the sum of products of the data samples with their corresponding filter coefficients, and then the data samples are linearly shifted one location.

An IIR filter consists of both feedforward and feedback data paths. The DIRECT II IIR structure is shown in figure 16-1b. The feedforward multiply-accumulate element and the delay line of the IIR are identical to that of the FIR. There is also an additional feedback multiply-accumulate element introduced which has a separate set of coefficients. Operation of the DIRECT II IIR then is to compute the output sample as a sum of the input sample and each of the data samples multiplied by their respective filter coefficients, identical to the FIR operation. The feedback term is then computed as the sum of the data elements multiplied by their respective feedback coefficients. The sum of the input sample with the accumulated feedback value is then used as the new d_0, while the remaining data elements are shifted, as in the FIR. While this implementation is called the DIRECT II architecture form of the IIR, all other forms of the IIR architecture also use the feedback element. This feedback element introduces the potential for arithmetic overflows, and variations of the DIRECT II IIR form have been created in the attempt to minimize these effects. The most common of these is the CASCADE architecture which will be discussed later. Keeping these structures in mind while authoring digital filter programs can assist in implementing and optimizing the programs.

As DSP techniques have been increasingly incorporated into electronics systems, manufacturers of processors have responded by creating new devices that are specialized to enhance their performance in executing DSP functions. The primary arithmetic function that is utilized in DSP is the multiply-accumulate function (MAC) and, in order to improve a processor's performance during MAC operations, manufacturers have designed processors which can have very unusual programming requirements and/or widely varied and complex internal elements which must be controlled by the programmer. These enhancements can be broadly grouped as follows:

- Alternative memory architectures
- Modulo addressing
- Pipelining
- Multi-instruction execution

It becomes the task of the engineer, then, to understand how to utilize the specialized properties of these varied products to implement digital filters. The next few sections will examine how these enhancements are implemented and how they affect the design and development of digital filtering software. We will then explore some of the differences between fixed-point and floating-point processors, detail FIR and IIR code, and, finally, discuss some of the tools that are required to develop a digital filtering program.

16.2 MEMORY ARCHITECTURE

Modifying the Von Neumann architecture computer model, shown in figure 16-2, is one method that DSP manufacturers have used to improve processor performance (e.g., the Harvard architecture). The Von Neumann architecture has a single block of memory to store both program code and data, which is connected to the processor through single address and data buses. The single address and data bus architecture limits access to the memory space creating the so-called *Von Neumann bottleneck*. The Harvard architecture, one version of which is shown in figure 16-3, has separate blocks of memory for storage of program code and data, which are connected to the processor through separate bus systems.

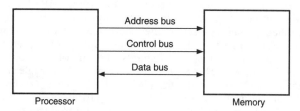

FIGURE 16-2 Von Neumann architecture.

Some DSP processors extend this scheme by further dividing the data memory space into separate areas which are also accessed through separate buses, allowing for multiple access of program and data memory spaces during a single instruction cycle. When used correctly, such architectural refinements can greatly increase the performance of digital filter programs. For example, consider an arbitrary n-tap FIR filter. For every sample instant, there are n multiples required of FIR coefficients with an N-sample time series. These coefficients and delay elements are traditionally stored in a linear array in memory. If an architecture can access memory several times during a single instruction cycle, then both the datum and filter coefficients can be retrieved from memory in a single cycle and dispatched to the multiplier. In addition, the memory access required for the instruction code fetch can be over-

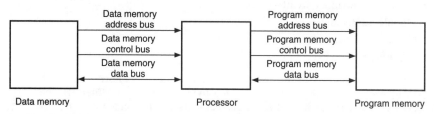

FIGURE 16-3 Harvard architecture.

lapped with data moves. The following figures show the memory architectures of several of the current DSP processors.

Figure 16-4 shows the Analog Devices ADSP210X family memory design, which uses separate program and data memory spaces. Both data and program memory spaces can be accessed during a single instruction as well as an additional program memory read to fetch the opcode.

Figure 16-5 shows the Motorola 56000 memory architecture. It consists of separate program and data memory spaces but also divides its internal data memory into two separate spaces known as the X and Y data spaces. With this method, a single opcode fetch and data access to both the X and Y memories can be performed in a single instruction cycle.

Figure 16-6 describes the Texas Instruments TMS320C3X memory architecture. It also utilizes two internal data memory devices which are denoted RAM Block 0 and RAM Block 1.

16.3 MODULO ADDRESSING

The delay element and coefficient arrays that have been discussed are known as *circular* arrays. On each sample instance, every data element in both arrays must be accessed during the digital filter computations. Modulo addressing techniques can assist the programmer in implementing these data structures. If a programmer had to maintain a circular array, s/he could keep a pointer to the base of the array, another pointer which indicates the current element being accessed, and a tertiary pointer which holds either the length of the array or the ending address of the array. On *every* access to the array, therefore, the programmer would have to access the data, increment the pointer, determine if the end of the array had been reached by comparison to a known length or ending address and, when appropriate, reset the pointer to the beginning of the array.

The overhead required to perform this is clearly substantial and must be performed for *every* circular array in use. Modulo addressing, however, can relieve the programmer of some or all of the burden of maintaining this style data structure. On-chip hardware has been designed to automatically perform most, if not all, of the address pointer generation and manipulation. The programmer then only needs to program the modular addressing hardware with the required information such as base address and length of the array. As long as the data is accessed through the modulo hardware, all address pointer maintenance is automatically handled.

An n-tap FIR or IIR filter requires that the last n data samples be accessed during calculation of the current output value. These samples are traditionally stored in a linear array in RAM, and the entire array is accessed and *shifted* on every sample interval. For each new sample, every data point d_x must be "pushed" to the succeeding element, $d_{(x+1)}$, with the final data element $d_{(n)}$ being replaced with the "old" $d_{(n-1)}$. Using general-purpose processors, the programmer must manage the array pointers to these different arrays, which requires a significant software overhead. As has been previously discussed, the modulo addressing hardware, if available, can relieve the programmer of maintaining these pointers but it can also be pressed into providing even more functionality. If the programmer were to attempt to program the FIFO functionality of the delay line, a great amount of processor resources would be wasted pushing data from one location to another. With proper programming and use of the modulo addressing, the FIFO function can be implemented with minimal software overhead. The key to implementing this is to allow the address of

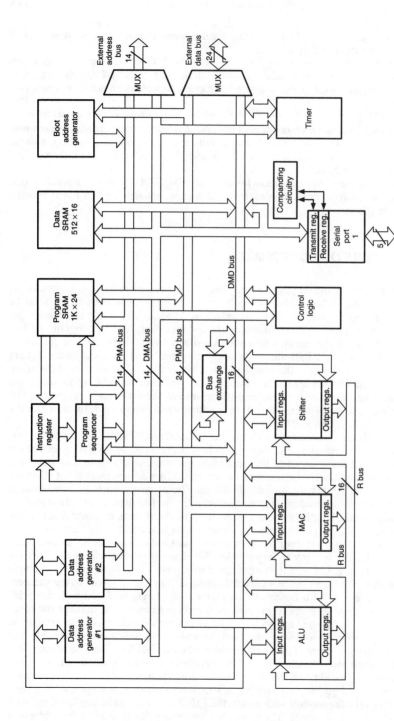

FIGURE 16-4 Analog Devices ADSP210X family.

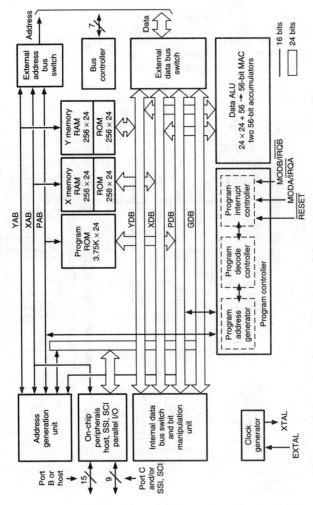

FIGURE 16-5 Motorola 56000 memory architecture.

16.7

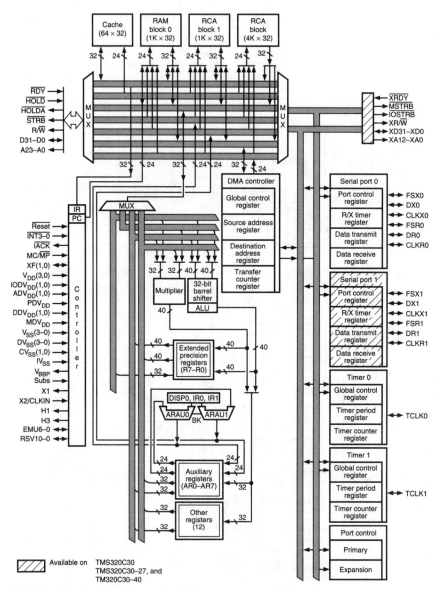

FIGURE 16-6   Texas Instruments TMS320C3X memory architecture.

data element 0 of the array to "float." Instead of moving the data around, modify the pointer that holds the address of data element 0. Refer to figure 16-7 for an example of this.

At $t = 0$, the base pointer is at the starting memory address of the array, d_0, and the other data elements are located sequentially in memory. By incrementing the base

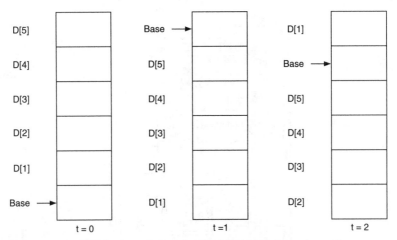

FIGURE 16-7 FIFO implementation using floating address of data element 0.

pointer, each element in the array can be accessed. Assuming that the pointer is initialized for a circular array of length 5, when the pointer is incremented the fifth time it will be reset to the beginning element in the array. Instead of performing the final increment, store the $t = 0$ input sample at the last location in the array. At $t = 1$, the base pointer will be pointing at the current d_0. To access the rest of the array, increment the base pointer, which will be automatically positioned by the modulo address hardware to the correct memory location. At the end of $t = 1$, again eliminate the fifth increment of the base pointer and store the $t = 1$ input sample where the base pointer indicates. When sample $t = 2$ occurs, the same set of operations takes place; each data element is accessed by incrementing the base pointer. As before, the base pointer will be automatically reset when it reaches the fifth memory address of the array, and each element of the delay can be accessed.

There are usually some address alignment restrictions such as mandatory beginning address boundaries as well as other operational restrictions which must be handled. Some processors also have restrictions as to when these subsystems can be initialized and/or modified. For example, a processor which uses a pipelining scheme may require that an address register not be considered valid until several instruction cycles after it has been loaded.

Figure 16-8 shows the address generation/manipulation hardware for the TMS320C3X DSP processor. Consisting of eight auxiliary registers, an auxiliary register pointer, and the block size or BK register, the "C3X" processor has provisions for eight indirection pointers, one of which can be utilized in a circular fashion.

Figure 16-9 shows the address generation/manipulation hardware for the Analog Devices ADSP210X DSP processors. It comprises two banks of four register sets which are used to access memory. Each register set consists of an index register, a length register, and an offset register. The index register holds the current address, the length register is used to determine when to roll over the current address back to the beginning, and the offset register determines how much to increment or decrement the index register when calculating the next address. These are named the I, L, and N registers and are further specified by a number, 0 through 7, such as the $I0$ index register or the $L7$ length register. Then any use of the Ix reg-

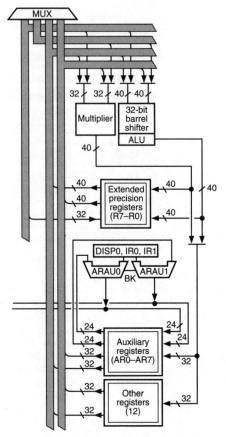

FIGURE 16-8 Address generation/manipulation for Texas Instruments TMS320C3X DSP processor.

ister causes it to be incremented by Nx. If Ix is now greater than the base address $+Lx$, Ix is reset to the base address.

16.4 PIPELINING

The CPU operations that are performed in the normal execution of a program can be roughly specified as follows. First a program *fetch* is performed; at this time the instruction is accessed from program memory. Then the instruction must be *decoded*; during this time the instruction is evaluated by the processor which determines what internal operations must be performed. Finally the instruction is *executed*; this phase is where the instruction is actually carried out. If the processor is designed accordingly, each of these phases can be performed independently and concurrently. While the execution phase of instruction n is being performed, instruc-

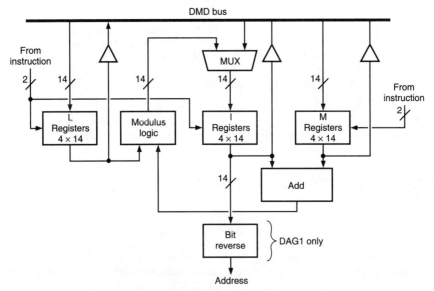

FIGURE 16-9 Address generation/manipulation for Analog Devices ADSP210X DSP processors.

tion $n + 1$ can be decoded, and instruction $n + 2$ can be fetched from program memory. This technique can dramatically improve the processor performance and is used in a number of popular DSP processors.

Performance improvements gained through pipelining, however, can place certain restrictions on the programmer. These are most obvious when program flow is altered by a branch or jump instruction. When the branch is executed, instructions which are currently in the process of being fetched and decoded may no longer be valid. This condition is referred to as a pipeline *flush* and forces the processor to reinitialize the pipeline hardware. During the period of pipeline initialization, normal program flow is suspended, causing a delay of several CPU cycles. Certain processors have specific instructions that allow the programmer to optimize the pipelining effect. Instructions such as the delayed branch permit the programmer to manually control aspects of the pipelining hardware, thereby permitting the design of programs which rarely cause a flush condition. These instructions are internally coded such that the instruction occurs in proper sequence for the pipelining mechanism to handle calculation of the branch address and begin the pipelining process at the correct branch address.

The TMS320C3X and the AT&T DSP32C represent a few of the DSP processors which incorporate pipeline techniques to enhance performance.

16.5 MULTI-INSTRUCTION EXECUTION

Another technique that has been exploited to optimize a DSP processor's performance is to design the various internal elements to operate independently. This technique, which is a form of pipelining, provides several independent internal units which can be programmed to operate in parallel. Consider an imaginary DSP processor which has been designed with four main independent units: the multiplier, adder, data memory load and store, and program memory load and store. With a traditional microprocessor, it would take four separate instructions to multiply two registers, add two other registers, move a word of data memory to a register, and fetch a data element from program memory. But a processor configured as previously described can be programmed to execute all four instructions simultaneously, resulting in a potential 400% increase in performance. There are a variety of ways to implement these independent units, but they consist primarily of multipliers, multiply-accumulators, barrel shifters, adders, data and program memory load and store, as well as the automatic modulo addressing capabilities.

16.6 FIXED-POINT VS. FLOATING-POINT PROCESSORS

The largest difference between DSP processors is in the method that they use to represent numbers which can be broadly categorized as either fixed-point or floating-point. A binary fixed-point representation is utilized in a fixed-point processor and traditionally uses 16, 24, or 32 bits which can represent either an integer or a fixed-point fraction. Both representations are illustrated in figure 16-10.

Each bit in the word is weighted with a value based on its position in the word, and if that bit is a 1, then its weight is used in constructing the value of the word. In other words, the sum of the weights of the 1 bits forms the numeric value of the word. Consider the unsigned nibble 1010; its decimal value is computed as $1*2^3 + 0*2^2 + 1*2^1 + 0*2^0$ which is equal to 10_{10}. For a fixed-point integer, the LSB, or bit 0, has a weight of $2^0 = 1$, bit 1 has a weight of $2^1 = 2$, bit 3 has a weight of $2^2 = 4$, and so on to bit n which has a weight of 2^{n-1}. The MSB is used as a sign bit, and, generally, if it is 0 the number is positive and if it is 1 the number is negative. For a fixed-point fractional format, the word is laid out similarly, but the weights are fractional values. The MSB is again the sign bit; bit $n-1$ has a weight of $1/2^1 = 1/2$, bit $n-2$ has a weight of $1/2^2 = 1/4$, and so on to bit 0 which has a weight of $1/2^{n-1}$. For example, the signed nibble 1011 has a decimal value that is computed as follows. Since the MSB is a 1, the number will be negative and the value is computed as $0*1/2^1 + 1*1/2^2 + 1*1/2^3$, which is equal to -0.625.

A floating-point processor will decompose the number into two parts, the exponent and the mantissa. The mantissa is a normalized value of the datum which will

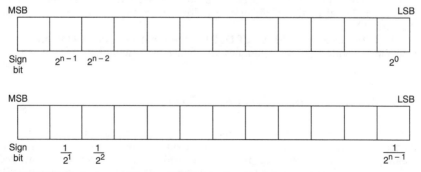

FIGURE 16-10   Integer and fixed-point fraction representations.

often range between 0 and 1, while the exponent holds the value to indicate the power to which to raise the number. The exponent can be stored in a variety of formats including base 10 or base 2 format. Many different methods have been designed to implement a floating-point representation, some of which were discussed in chapter 12. For processor-specific information, consult the DSP's data sheets. The advantage of a floating-point over a fixed-point processor is realized in enhanced dynamic range that can be symbolized in the same number of bits. Floating-point processors handle positive and negative integers and fractions equally and do not require the same level of programmer involvement as a fixed-point processor.

While floating-point processors offer the luxury of automatically handling practically every aspect of performing the desired mathematic operations, fixed-point processors are considerably more limited and require more attention by the programmer. The first obstacle usually encountered is the limited dynamic range available from a fixed-point processor, a 16-bit device offers a dynamic range of 96 dB and a 32-bit processor has a dynamic range of 192 dB, compared to floating-point processors which offer dynamic ranges well in excess of 1000 dB. The feedback element in the IIR can be particularly susceptible to creating intermediate results which can overflow the available dynamic range of a fixed-point processor.

Limited dynamic range is characterized by arithmetic overflow, and occurs when the results of a calculation cannot be represented by the number of bits available to store a number. Every fixed-point processor has some additional hardware to offer temporary assistance in the management of arithmetic overflow. Most incorporate one or more extended bits in the multiply-accumulate circuitry allowing for sustained sums-of-products operations which can exceed the intrinsic dynamic range of the chip. The programmer must, however, be aware of these overflows and handle them appropriately. As long as intermediate results don't overflow beyond the extended range, a calculation can be successfully completed and the results later scaled to conform to the system word size. As an example, the Motorola DSP56000 has eight extra bits in the accumulator hardware.

For certain applications, an extended precision scheme can be adopted. The programmer can use multiples of the intrinsic word size to implement larger dynamic range. On a 16-bit processor, the programmer can utilize 32, 48, 64, or more bits during arithmetic calculations, but it is normally the responsibility of the programmer to write the code required to implement this scheme. While nothing inherently prohibits performing multiword arithmetic, it requires more instruction cycles to execute and imposes larger data storage requirements. Multiword operations are performed by manipulating the datum in single-word portions. For example, consider a 32-bit add performed on a 16-bit processor. The first step involves any relevant setup operations such as clearing or setting the appropriate arithmetic status bits such as a carry bit or an overflow bit. Next, the least significant words are added together and the result is stored in the least significant word of the result variable. Then the two most significant words are summed along with the carry result from the previous add, and the result is stored in the most significant word of the result variable. Finally, the carry bit must be checked to ensure that there was not an overflow from the operation.

A similar sequence of events can also be used to perform multiword subtractions by replacing any addition instructions with subtraction instructions and replacing any references to the carry bit with the borrow bit. Figure 16-11 demonstrates graphically how these operations would be performed.

This same technique can be applied to integer multiplication as well, but it is performed in a somewhat different manner. It is important to remember when constructing multiword multiplication that the result of a multiplication of two n-bit

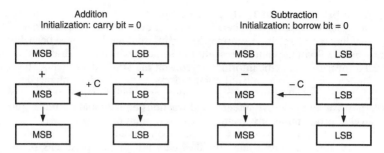

FIGURE 16-11 Multiword subtraction.

data produces a result which is of length $2*n$ bits, after accounting for sign bits. Thirty-two-bit multiplications therefore produce 64-bit results. Once again, consider two 32-bit data which are to be multiplied using a 16-bit processor. The least significant words are multiplied resulting in a 32-bit intermediate result. Then the least significant word of the multiplier is multiplied with the most significant word of the multiplicand, again resulting in a 32-bit intermediate result. This intermediate result must be shifted 16 bits to the left and summed with the first intermediate result, giving yet another temporary result which is now 48 bits in length. Next, the most significant word of the multiplicand is to be multiplied with the least significant word of the multiplier, again resulting in 32-bit data. This result must also be shifted 16 bits to the left and summed to the temporary result. Finally, both most significant words are multiplied, shifted 32 bits to the left, and summed, with the temporary result producing a final answer which is 64 bits in length.

The next limitation encountered when using multiword multiplication is caused by the fixed decimal point location. Fixed-point processors can usually handle data as either an integer or a fraction but not both. An application which does not exceed the dynamic range limitations of a processor may need to use data values which are both integer and fractional in nature. It is easy to envision scenarios which might require 4 bits of integer data along with 12 bits of fractional data. With a fixed-point processor, it is possible to perform arithmetic in this format, but the programmer must maintain the location of the decimal point in software where it is normally handled by the processor. This is exemplified by remembering the steps performed when multiplying decimal numbers. To multiply 2.5 by 3.4 requires performing the following steps: first the 5 and 4, and the 2 and 4 are multiplied. Next, the 3 and 5 and the 3 and 2 are multiplied. Then these two intermediate results are summed. Finally the decimal points are compensated for by shifting the decimal point over two places.

$$
\begin{array}{r}
2.5 \\
\times\,3.4 \\
\hline
100 \\
+\,75 \\
\hline
850 \\
\hline
8.50
\end{array}
$$

Using non-native decimal point placements is one method that can be implemented to "stretch" the usefulness of a fixed-point processor. This methodology is especially suited to DSP processors that have the capability to perform shifts in a single cycle. This way, different word formats can be implemented which don't require a large amount of overhead. Managing the decimal point is performed with a shift and can be implemented using the shift registers that are present on many DSP processors. Remember also that shifts to the left can be implemented with multiplies by powers of 2, limited, of course, by the number of bits available to represent the result. Multiplying by 2 is equivalent to shifting left one bit, multiplying by 4 is equivalent to shifting left 2 bits, and so on.

16.7   FINITE IMPULSE-RESPONSE FILTERS

The purpose of this section is to discuss the issues that are encountered during the coding of an FIR digital filter. As was previously discussed, the typical FIR architecture is implemented as in figure 16-1a. There are two data structures: the static array of coefficients and the dynamic circular array of past samples. An FIR filter can be quantified by the number of delay elements or taps used. An FIR of order 51 has 51 coefficients and a delay line with 50 elements. On every sample instance, each delay element must be multiplied by its coefficient and the sum of all these multiplications is the filtered output value. The delay line must also be altered such that the current sample is inserted into the d_0 element of the line, and each element is shifted one location. As was discussed earlier, this shifting is done by modifying the pointers to this array. In this way, only the address of d_0 is modified to simulate the effect of shifting each element. The following example should help to clarify this.

EXAMPLE 16.1

Consider a 3 tap FIR, with a coefficient set of $\{-0.5, 0.25, 0.3\}$. This system will have a delay line of two elements and three coefficients. At initialization, each element of the delay line is zero and is mapped into data memory at address 0 and 1. The *base address register* used for indirection is set to 0. On a given sample instance, the current sample is multiplied by coefficient 0 and summed with delay element 0 times coefficient 1 and delay element 1 times coefficient 2. This sum is the output of the filter. Next, the delay line must be updated. Using base address pointer manipulation, the base pointer is incremented to 1. This has the effect, considering modulo addressing, of moving d_0 to d_1. Now, using the new base address pointer, the current sample is stored at d_0. This same procedure is performed for each sample. It can be helpful to work out a complete paper simulation. Diagram the delay line and base address pointer especially.

Before presenting assembly language routines, it will be useful to examine the basic FIR code in C. This will allow us to examine the FIR operation at a high level. Note that circular addressing is not used in this example.

```
1    output = new_sample * coef[0];
2    for (i=1;i<num_taps;i++)
3            output = output + delay[i-1] * coef[i];
4    for (i=num_taps-1,i>0;i--)
5            delay[i]=delay[i-1];
6    delay[0] = new_sample;
```

Line 1 initializes the output variable with the value of the new data sample multiplied by its filter coefficient. Lines 2 and 3 compute the final output value, by calculating the sum of each of the coefficients multiplied by their corresponding delay element. Lines

4 and 5 shift the delay line up one element, and line 6 saves the new sample value in element 0 of the delay line.

The following two code listings are example FIR filters for the Motorola 56000 and the Texas Instruments TMS320C2X processors. Be sure to refer to the comments and the manufacturers' data books while examining this code. Pay particular attention to the use of modular address pointers and utilization of dedicated hardware units to enhance performance of the code.

```
* THIS SECTION OF CODE IMPLEMENTS THE FOLLOWING EQUATION:           *
* x(n-4)h(4) + x(n-3)h(3) + x(n-2)h(2) + x(n-1)h(1) + x(n)h(0) = y(n) *
*
NXTPT    IN XN,PA2        * GET THE NEW INPUT VALUE XN FROM PORT PA0 *
*
         ZAC             * ZERO THE ACCUMULATOR *
*
         LT XNM4         * x(n-4)h(4) *
         MPY H4
*
         LTD XNM3        * x(n-4)h(4) + x(n-3)h(3) *
         MPY H3
*
         LTD XNM2        * SIMILAR TO THE PREVIOUS STEPS *
         MPY H2
*
         LTD XNM1
         MPY H1
*
         LTD XN
         MPY H0
*
         APAC            * ADD THE RESULT OF THE LAST MULTIPLY TO *
*                        * THE ACCUMULATOR                        *
*
         SACH YN,1       * STORE THE RESULT IN YN *
*
         OUT YN,PA2      * OUTPUT THE RESPONSE TO PORT PA1 *
*
         B NXTPT         * GO GET THE NEXT POINT *

;
; ***********************************************************************
;
;            initialization
; ******************************
start          equ            $40
wddr           equ            $0
cddr           equ            $0
input          equ            $ffe0
output         equ            $ffe1
;
               org            p:start
```

```
            move            #wddr,r0              ;r0 → samples
            move            #cddr,r4              ;r1 → coefficients
            move            #n − 1,m0             ;set modulo arithmetic
            move            m0,m4                 ;for the 2 circular buffers
;
            opt             cc
;           filter loop :8+(n − 1) cycles
; ***************************************************************
            movep           y:1nput,x: (r0)      ;input sample in memory
            clr             a          x:(r0) + ,x0   y: (r4) + ,y0

            rep             #n − 1
            mac             x0,y0,a    x:(r0) + ,x0   y: (r4) + ,y0
            macr            x0,x0,a    (r0) −

            movep           a,y:output            ;output filtered sample
; ***************************************************************
            end
```

16.8 INFINITE IMPULSE-RESPONSE FILTERS

On the surface, IIR filters are merely an extension of the FIR filter. The programmer must implement a second sum-of-products code segment which calculates the feedback terms. The addition of the feedback element, as depicted in figure 16-1b, has an attendant performance penalty. As with any system incorporating feedback, there is a potential for overflow or oscillation, causing the IIR filter to be much more susceptible to arithmetic overflows than the FIR filter. To overcome this, several variations on the DIRECT II architecture, depicted in figure 16-1b, have been developed. The most popular form is the CASCADE architecture, which implements a filter transfer function as a set of first- and/or second-order sections which are serially interconnected to form the filter. Examples of both 1st-order and 2nd-order sections are diagrammed in figure 16-12a, b, and c are examples of a 4th-order CASCADE filter. A number of other architectures have been developed in an attempt to optimize an IIR architecture which will not exceed the dynamic range restrictions of fixed-point processors, some of which were discussed in chapter 15.

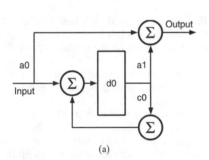

(a)

FIGURE 16-12 Examples of cascade architecture: (a) First-order cascade section.

16.9 TOOLS

So far, there has been no discussion of the actual types of systems that are likely to be encountered in the real world, nor have we discussed the actual operations

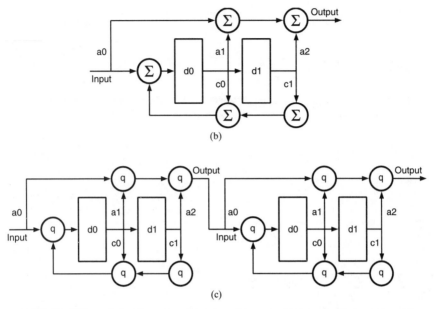

FIGURE 16-12 (*Continued*) Examples of cascade architecture: (b) Second-order cascade architecture; (c) Fourth-order cascade.

required to build a digital filter program that can be utilized by a DSP processor. The actual hardware that is likely to be encountered will fall into two broad categories. The hardware can be either a development system or the actual target DSP system.

A development system will connect to a host computer through either an internal card or an I/O port, and provides software tools to aid in debugging a program. A development system is usually the easiest way to create programs, because it will come with specialized programs to aid in developing your applications. This software can include program downloaders, debuggers, and, often, libraries of code which can be used in your application. The disadvantage of a development system is that it is not the final target hardware, and the program will have to be modified to run on the target hardware after the development process completes. A development system should be chosen so that it closely resembles the target hardware to ensure that porting to the final hardware is a minimal effort.

Attempting to develop programs on the target hardware can be considerably more difficult because it is rare when the target system provides enough interface hardware to allow for easy program development. There is usually no provision for any form of console I/O, nor any efficient method to install new versions of the program. It can also be difficult to run debugging software on the target system. These obstacles can be overcome through the use of an in-circuit-emulator, but an ICE is usually more expensive than a development system. However, the ICE will provide a very complete system that enables debugging both hardware and software elements of the target system.

The process of assembling and linking a program for a DSP processor differs slightly from the same process for a work station or a microcontroller but resembles

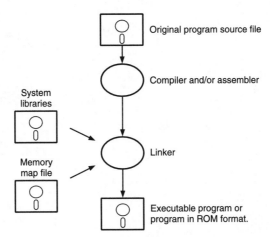

FIGURE 16-13 Assembling and linking a DSP program.

the usual compiling, assembling, and linking operations. The DSP program must be compiled and/or assembled like programs targeted for general-purpose computer systems, but the linking process is considerably more involved and requires greater effort on the part of the programmer. With a traditional computer system, the memory location of variables is of little concern to the programmer and, as such, that class of linker is designed to hide many of these details. When constructing programs for DSP processors, however, the memory location of variables is of extreme concern to the programmer. A variables location in memory may determine how often it can be accessed and whether or not it can be used by the modulo addressing hardware. Because of this, many assembler/linkers for DSP processors use some form of a MAP file while assigning variables to memory locations. The MAP file is how the programmer specifies where circular buffers are kept, ensures that critical data are placed correctly to allow access to or by specialized hardware, and possibly defines I/O locations to the external system such as A/D and D/A converters. The general method used has the programmer define different segments in memory by a unique name and, while creating the program, these segments are explicitly referred to when declaring variables. This gives the programmer the ability to exactly determine the memory mapping of critical variables. The general methodology for assembling and linking a DSP program is diagrammed in figure 16-13.

The final tool to be discussed is digital filter coefficient generating programs. A number of companies produce this software tool which allows for rapid and convenient generation of filter coefficients. These programs allow the user to specify filter parameters that characterize its frequency response, the number of taps, whether FIR or an IIR, and other parameters. Once these have been specified, the program calculates the filter coefficients and displays several facets of the filter's response, such as frequency and/or phase response. These tools are highly efficient and are recommended for use in any situation where even a modest number of filters is going to be created.

CHAPTER 17
SWITCHED-CAPACITOR FILTERS

17.1 INTRODUCTION

Switched-capacitor filters have gained widespread acceptance because they require no external reactive components, are precisely controlled by a clock derived from a crystal, and can be programmed easily. They come close to truly digital filters without requiring the mathematical complexity of computation and the sophistication required for implementation. Miniaturization is achieved by implementing these devices on a chip. Stability is a function of the external components which are typically low-temperature coefficient resistors and a crystal-derived clock. They can be used for frequencies ranging from a small fraction of a cycle to a few hundred kilohertz.

17.2 THEORY OF SWITCHED-CAPACITOR FILTERS

The theory of switched-capacitor filters is based on the ability to very closely match capacitor ratios on an MOS integrated circuit. The actual magnitudes of the capacitors can vary significantly from device to device due to differences in the dielectric constant of the MOS process. The ratios, however, between capacitors on the same device is very precise since the areas allocated to each capacitor are very closely controlled by the manufacturing process.

The Switched Resistor

Figure 17-1 illustrates a capacitor C connected to ground, two switches S_1 and S_2, and an applied voltage E. The charge on a capacitor is given by

$$Q = CE \qquad (17\text{-}1)$$

where Q is the charge in coulombs and E is the voltage applied to the capacitor.

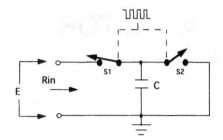

FIGURE 17-1   Resistor simulated by a switched capacitor.

The current through a capacitor is Q/T since an ampere is defined as a coulomb per second. The AC current through the capacitor of figure 17-1 is:

$$I_{ac} = \frac{\Delta Q}{\Delta T} = \frac{C \Delta E}{\Delta T} \qquad (17\text{-}2)$$

where ΔT is the time between closing of S_1 and S_2, which are operated alternately, and ΔE is the variation in voltage across the capacitor. The capacitor is switched between voltage E and ground during alternate parts of the switching cycle so ΔE is equal to E.

Since ΔT is determined by a clock frequency F_{clock}, we can say

$$I_{ac} = C \Delta E\, F_{clock} \qquad (17\text{-}3)$$

If we simply transpose and solve for the equivalent resistance R_{in}, in terms of voltage divided by current, we obtain:

$$R_{in} = \frac{1}{C F_{clock}} \qquad (17\text{-}4)$$

Equation (17-4) indicates that a capacitor can be made to behave like a resistor whose value is inversely proportional to the capacitance and to the clock-switching frequency. The switching rate should be much higher than any short-term variation in E.

Basic Integrator as a Building Block

Figure 17-1 illustrates how a resistor can be implemented using clock-controlled switches and a capacitor. This is exactly the technique used in monolithic switched-capacitor filters. The switches are actually MOSFETs and have relatively low resistance compared with the resistor values implemented. The capacitors are controlled by the geometry of surfaces on the substrate.

The circuit of figure 17-2a shows a conventional inverting integrator. The transfer function of this circuit is:

$$T(s) = \frac{1}{sRC} \qquad (17\text{-}5)$$

If we use a switched-capacitor resistor for R, the circuit of figure 17-2b is obtained. This is an inverting integrator implemented using a switched-capacitor approach. We can substitute equation (17-4) for R in equation (17-5) and obtain the following transfer function:

$$T(s) = \frac{1}{s\, C_b \dfrac{1}{C_a F_{clock}}} \qquad (17\text{-}5)$$

Simplifying equation (17-5) results in:

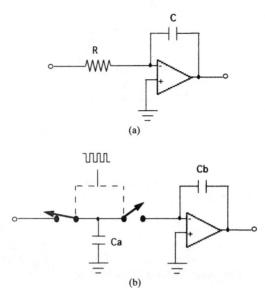

FIGURE 17-2   (a) Basic integrator; (b) switched-capacitor integrator.

$$T(s) = \frac{F_{clock}\, C_a}{s\, C_b} \tag{17-6}$$

Equation (17-6) indicates that the transfer function of a switched-capacitor integrator can be scaled proportionally by a clock frequency F_{clock} and is determined by a constant C_a/C_b, which is a ratio of two capacitors. Since this ratio can be very precisely determined by chip geometries, we can build a filter having properties that are directly proportional to an externally supplied clock and independent of absolute magnitudes of chip capacitors. Variations of the circuit of figure 17-2b are used as a basic building block for switched-capacitor filters.

Limitations of Switched-Capacitor Filters

Noise.   A complex switched-capacitor filter chip contains many capacitors within the device. In order to minimize the absolute magnitude of these capacitors to keep the device small, internal resistor values are relatively higher than in most CMOS ICs. As a result, the output noise of switched-capacitor filters is higher than that produced by a conventional active filter. Noise of switched-capacitor filters consists of two types: clock feedthrough and thermal noise. The clock of a switched-capacitor filter is normally 50 or 100 times the operating frequency range, so it can be easily filtered by a simple RC at the output. Thermal noise is in-band and is typically 80 dB below operating signal levels. It can be minimized by optimizing gain distribution for maximum signal-to-noise ratio. Careful PC layout and decoupling should occur as well.

Charge injection of the CMOS switches into the integrating capacitors and high internal impedance levels result in larger DC offsets than with active filters. However, there are some capacitive coupled architectures to eliminate this problem.

Frequency Limitations. Switched-capacitor filters have a limiting figure of merit which is the product of Q X center frequency. In other words, the higher the center frequency, the lower the realizable Q. For relatively low Qs, switched-capacitor filters are realizable for frequencies up to 200 kHz or so.

Since we are dealing with a sampled system, aliasing effects can occur. If input signals occur above $F_s/2$, where F_s is the internal sampling frequency (typically 50 or 100 times the cutoff), we get foldover, which could make the signals of interest unusable if the foldover components are significant in amplitude. Sometimes an input RC is useful to prevent this phenomenon, especially if the input signal consists of rectangular pulses.

17.3 UNIVERSAL SWITCHED-CAPACITOR SECOND-ORDER FILTERS

Figure 17-3 illustrates the basic architecture for a universal switched-capacitor building block. This was originally used in a device called an MF 5 developed by National and then a dual version called an MF 10. It has become the fundamental architecture for most complex switched-capacitor filters.

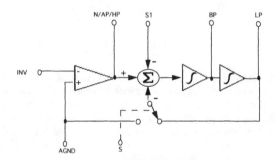

FIGURE 17-3 Block diagram of universal second-order filter.

This circuit realizes a second-order transfer function and can provide a bandpass, low-pass, high-pass, notch, or all-pass output by adding external resistors. Cascading of multiple sections results in switched-capacitor filters of very high complexity.

The basic configuration consists of an operational amplifier, a summing node, and two integrators. A MOS switch under control of input S connects one of the summing node inputs either to the second integrator or to ground. The output of the operational amplifier can either be a notch, all-pass, or high-pass response depending on how the device is configured. The two integrators can provide bandpass and low-pass outputs. In most cases, these outputs can be provided simultaneously.

Although not shown, a clock at either 50 or 100 times the center (pole) frequency must be provided. A logic input to the chip determines whether the clock is 50 or 100 times F_0.

Modes of Operation

The universal filter structure of figure 17-3 is quite flexible and can be reconfigured into various forms by adding external resistors. Each form or *mode* has unique properties which determine the filters' characteristics. Figures 17-4 through 17-10 show the most popular modes of operation. The design equations for each mode are given in Table 17-1.

Operating Mode Features

Mode 1.   The circuit of mode 1 provides simultaneous bandpass and notch outputs that are equal to each other and directly determined by $F_{clock} \div 50$ or $F_{clock} \div 100$. As a result we can design clock-tunable bandpass/bandstop networks with frequency

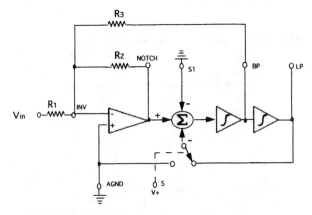

FIGURE 17-4   Mode 1: Bandpass, low-pass, $F_{notch} = F_0$.

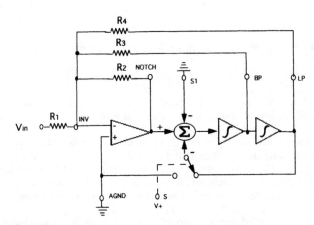

FIGURE 17-5   Mode 2: Bandpass, low-pass, $F_{notch} \leq F_0$.

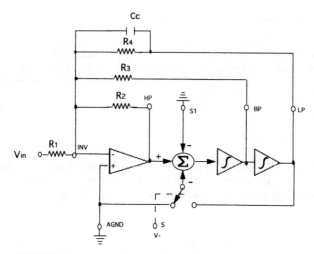

FIGURE 17-6 Mode 3: Bandpass, low-pass, high-pass.

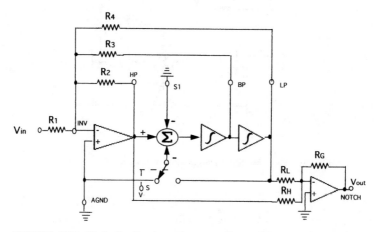

FIGURE 17-7 Mode 3a: Bandpass, low-pass, F_{notch} using external operational amplifier.

stability and accuracy as a direct function of the clock. Circuit Q is determined by the ratio R_3/R_2. A low-pass output is available as well.

Mode 2. The mode 2 configuration can provide bandpass and low-pass outputs as well as a notch output, providing that $F_{\text{notch}} \leq F_0$. Unlike the mode 1 configuration, center frequency F_0 can be different than F_{notch}. This circuit is useful for cascading second-order sections to create an elliptic-function high-pass, band-reject, or band-pass response requiring transmission zeros below the passband poles.

Mode 3. The circuit of mode 3 allows us to use a single resistor ratio (R_2/R_4) to tune F_0. Because the feedback loop is closed around the input summing amplifier, a

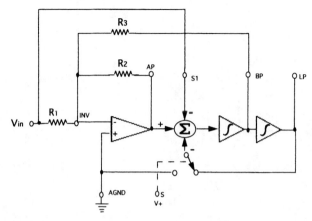

FIGURE 17-8   Mode 4: All-pass, bandpass, low-pass.

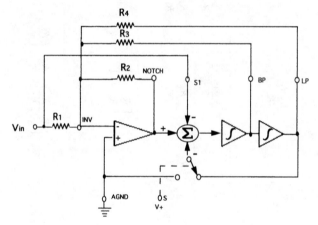

FIGURE 17-9   Mode 5: Numerator complex zeros, bandpass, low-pass.

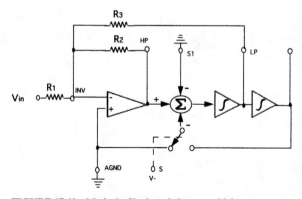

FIGURE 17-10   Mode 6a: Single-pole low-pass, high-pass.

TABLE 17-1 Design Equations for Modes of Operation

MODE	F_0	Q	F_{notch}	LP Gain	BP Gain	HP Gain	Notch Gain	All-pass Gain
1	$\dfrac{F_{clock}}{100(50)}$	$\dfrac{R_3}{R_2}$	F_0	$-\dfrac{R_2}{R_1}$	$-\dfrac{R_3}{R_1}$		$-\dfrac{R_2}{R_1}$ (as $F \to 0$)	
2	$\dfrac{F_{clock}}{100(50)} \times \sqrt{1+\dfrac{R_2}{R_4}}$	$\dfrac{\sqrt{\dfrac{R_2}{R_4}+1}}{R_2/R_3}$	$\dfrac{F_{clock}}{100(50)}$	$-\dfrac{R_2/R_1}{R_2/R_4+1}$	$-\dfrac{R_3}{R_1}$		$-\dfrac{R_2/R_1}{R_2/R_4+1}$ (as $F \to 0$)	
3	$\dfrac{F_{clock}}{100(50)} \times \sqrt{\dfrac{R_2}{R_4}}$	$\sqrt{\dfrac{R_2}{R_4}} \times \dfrac{R_3}{R_2}$		$-\dfrac{R_4}{R_1}$	$-\dfrac{R_3}{R_1}$	$-\dfrac{R_2}{R_1}$		
3a	$\dfrac{F_{clock}}{100(50)} \times \sqrt{\dfrac{R_2}{R_4}}$	$\sqrt{\dfrac{R_2}{R_4}} \times \dfrac{R_3}{R_2}$	$\dfrac{F_{clock}}{100(50)} \times \sqrt{\dfrac{R_H}{R_L}}$	$-\dfrac{R_4}{R_1}$	$-\dfrac{R_3}{R_1}$	$-\dfrac{R_2}{R_1}$	$Q\left[\dfrac{R_G R_2}{R_H R_1} - \dfrac{R_G R_4}{R_L R_1}\right]$ (at F_0)	
4	$\dfrac{F_{clock}}{100(50)}$	$Q_{pole}\ \dfrac{R_3}{R_2}$ $Q_{zero}\ \dfrac{R_3}{R_1}$		$-\left[\dfrac{R_2}{R_1}+1\right]$	$-\dfrac{R_3}{R_2}\left(1+\dfrac{R_2}{R_1}\right)$			$-\dfrac{R_2}{R_1}$ ($R_2 = R_1$ for all-pass)
5	$\dfrac{F_{clock}}{100(50)} \times \sqrt{1+\dfrac{R_2}{R_4}}$	$Q_{pole}\ \dfrac{\sqrt{1+\dfrac{R_2}{R_4}}}{R_2/R_3}$ $Q_{zero}\ \dfrac{\sqrt{1-\dfrac{R_1}{R_4}}}{R_1/R_3}$	$\dfrac{F_{clock}}{100(50)} \times \sqrt{1-\dfrac{R_1}{R_4}}$	$-\left(\dfrac{R_2+R_1}{R_2+R_4}\right) \times \dfrac{R_4}{R_1}$	$-\left(\dfrac{R_2}{R_1}+1\right) \times \dfrac{R_3}{R_2}$			
6a	$F_c = \dfrac{F_{clock}}{100(50)}\ \dfrac{R_2}{R_3}$			$-\dfrac{R_3}{R_1}$		$-\dfrac{R_2}{R_1}$		

slight Q enhancement occurs where the circuit Q is slightly above the actual design Q. A small capacitor across R_4 (10 to 100 pF) will result in a compensation phase lead which eliminates the Q enhancement.

Mode 3a. Mode 3a is probably the most versatile of all modes. An external operational amplifier sums together the low-pass and bandpass outputs of mode 3 to form a notch output which can be on either side of center frequency F_0. This is especially useful for elliptic-function low-pass, high-pass, band-reject, or bandpass response requiring transmission zeros both above and below the passband poles. Gains can be distributed between the internal circuitry and the external operational amplifier to achieve maximum dynamic range.

Mode 4. An all-pass output can be provided by using mode 4 in addition to low-pass and bandpass outputs. As in the case of mode 1, the center frequency F_0 is directly determined by $F_{clock} \div 50$ or $F_{clock} \div 100$. Resistor R_1 must be made equal to R_2 for all-pass characteristics.

Mode 5. This mode can be used for implementing complex numerator zeros for a transfer function and has low-pass and high-pass outputs as well.

Mode 6a. A single low-pass or high-pass real pole can be implemented using the mode 6a configuration. The major benefit of the added complexity of this implementation over a single RC is that the 3-dB cutoff F_c is clock dependent. This makes this approach very useful for filters requiring variable characteristics controlled by an external clock frequency. If the cutoff is fixed, an ordinary RC implementation of the real pole is more cost effective.

The MF-10 Dual Universal Second-Order Filter

The MF-10 is a very popular implementation of two universal second-order switched-capacitor filters within one substrate. The MF-10 was originally developed by National Semiconductor in the mid-1980s. A number of other devices are available that are pin-for-pin compatible with the MF-10 and offer a higher level of performance. These are listed in the selection guide of section 17.4 and more details are provided in the manufacturers' data books given as references.

Figure 17-11 is a block diagram of an MF-10 in a dual-in-line (DIP) 20-pin package. In addition to the pins that make up the basic switched-capacitor filter, other pin functions are provided as follows:

Power Supply Connections. Typically, the MF-10 operates from ±5-V supplies. Separate digital and analog positive and negative power supply pins are provided which are VD+ (pin 8), VA+ (pin 7), VD– (pin 13), and VA– (pin 14). Pins 7 and 8 can be tied together, providing that adequate bypassing exists. The same applies to pins 13 and 14. Analog ground (pin 15) is normally connected to ground, and the level shift function (pin 9) is also connected to ground.

The MF-10 is also capable of operating from a single positive supply. In that case, the VD– and VA– pins as well as level shift are connected to system ground. The analog ground (pin 15) should be biased at half of the positive rail and adequately decoupled to system ground.

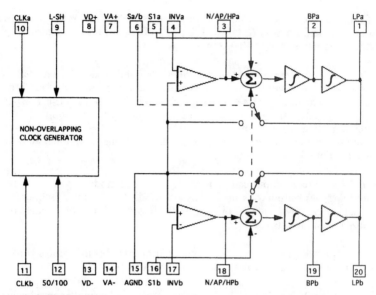

FIGURE 17-11   Block diagram of MF-10 dual universal second-order filter.

50/100 Clock Select.   The 50/100 function (pin 17) determines whether the clock is either in the 50:1 mode or the 100:1 mode. When pin 17 is connected to VD+ and VA+ the mode is 50:1. If pin 17 is connected to analog ground the mode is 100:1. Some devices also allow pin 17 to provide a sample-and-hold capability to freeze the outputs when connecting pin 17 to VD– and VA–.

Clock Input Pins.   Two separate TTL compatible clock input pins for the A section and B section filters are provided on pins 10 and 11, respectively. Clock duty cycle should be close to 50%.

$S_{a/b}$ Control.   This function controls the two CMOS switches that connect the summer input to either analog ground or the low-pass output function. When $S_{a/b}$ is connected to the negative rail, both switches go to analog ground. If $S_{a/b}$ is connected to the positive rail, both switches are connected to the two low-pass outputs. The switch positions are determined by the requirements of the operating mode.

EXAMPLE 17-1

REQUIRED: Design a switched-capacitor low-pass filter that has 0.5 dB maximum ripple below 100 Hz and greater than 18 dB rejection above 160 Hz. In addition, the filter should be programmable for a cutoff at any frequency in the range of 100 Hz through 10 kHz while maintaining the frequency ratio of 1.6 for greater than 18 dB of attenuation.

RESULT:

(a) Compute steepness factor:

$$A_s = \frac{160}{100} = 1.6 \qquad (2\text{-}11)$$

(b) Select a normalized elliptic-function filter from table 11-56 that makes the transition from less than 0.5 dB ripple to greater than 18 dB of rejection within a frequency ratio of 1.6.

(c) A filter corresponding to CO3 20 $\phi = 40°$ has the following parameters:

$$n = 3$$

$$R_{db} = 0.28 \text{ dB}$$

$$\Omega_s = 1.556$$

$$A_{min} = 18.56 \text{ dB}$$

The normalized poles and zeros are:

$$\alpha = 0.2849 \qquad \beta = 1.1484$$

$$\omega_\infty = 1.742$$

and the real pole is located at:

$$\alpha_0 = 1.0577$$

(d) To denormalize the pole-zero coordinates, first compute the frequency-scaling factor as follows:

$$\text{FSF} = 2\pi f_c = 2\pi 100 = 628.32$$

where the design cutoff frequency is 100 Hz.

The poles and zeros are denormalized as follows:

Complex Poles and Zeros:

$$\alpha = 0.2849 \qquad \alpha' = \alpha \times \text{FSF} = 178.9 \tag{3-46}$$

$$\beta = 1.1484 \qquad \beta' = \beta \times \text{FSF} = 721.2 \tag{3-47}$$

$$\omega_\infty = 1.742 \qquad \omega_\infty' = \omega_\infty \times \text{FSF} = 1,094 \tag{3-48}$$

Real Pole:

$$\alpha_0 = 1.0577 \qquad \alpha_0' = \alpha_0 \times \text{FSF} = 664.2 \tag{3-54}$$

Convert complex poles and zeros to frequencies and Q:

$$\omega_0' = \sqrt{(\alpha')^2 + (\beta')^2} = 743.1 \tag{3-49}$$

$$f_0 = \frac{\omega_0'}{2\pi} = 118.3 \text{ Hz} \tag{3-56}$$

$$Q = \frac{\pi f_0}{\alpha'} = 2.077 \tag{3-57}$$

$$f_\infty = \frac{\omega_\infty}{2\pi} = 174.1 \text{ Hz}$$

Convert real pole into 3-dB cutoff frequency:

$$f_c = \frac{\alpha_0'}{2\pi} = 105.7 \text{ Hz}$$

(e) Design a two-section switched-capacitor low-pass filter as follows:
   Section 1:

$$f_0 = 118.3 \text{ Hz}$$

$$Q = 2.077$$

$$f = 174.1 \text{ Hz}$$

Section 2:
Real pole where $f_c = 105.7$ Hz
   Use a single MF-10 dual second-order filter IC. The A section can be used to implement section 1 and the B section for section 2. The design proceeds as follows:
   Section 1 (A Section):

Use mode 3a

$$\text{Let } F_{\text{clock}} = 5000 \text{ Hz}$$

$$\text{Select 50:1 clock mode}$$

$$\text{Let } R_1 = R_4 = 10 \text{ k}\Omega$$

Using the f_0 equation for mode 3a from table 17-1 (where $f_0 = 118.3$ Hz):

$$R_2 = 13.99 \text{ k}\Omega$$

Using the Q equation for mode 3a from table 17-1 (where $Q = 2.077$):

$$R_3 = 24.57 \text{ k}\Omega$$

Using the f_{notch} equation for mode 3a from table 17-1 (where $f_{\text{notch}} = f = 174.1$ Hz):

$$\text{Let } R_L = R_G = 10 \text{ k}\Omega$$

$$\text{then } R_H = 30.31 \text{ k}\Omega$$

Section 2 (B Section):

Use mode 6a

$$\text{Let } F_{\text{clock}} = 5000 \text{ Hz}$$

Using the f_c equation for mode 6a from table 17-1 (where $f_c = 105.7$ Hz):

$$\text{Let } R_1 = R_3 = 10 \text{ k}\Omega$$

$$\text{then } R_2 = 10.57 \text{ k}\Omega$$

(f) The schematic of the resulting filter is shown in figure 17-12. The response curves for clock frequencies of 5000 Hz and 500 kHz are given in figure 17-13 where the cutoffs are 100 Hz and 10 kHz. For any clock frequency between 5000 Hz and 500 kHz, the filter cutoff will be exactly one-fiftieth of the clock frequency. All resistor values computed have been rounded off to their nearest 1% standard value.

17.4   TYPES OF SWITCHED-CAPACITOR FILTERS

Universal

Universal switched-capacitor building blocks consist of independent universal second-order filters using the configuration of figure 17-3. Anywhere from one to four sections

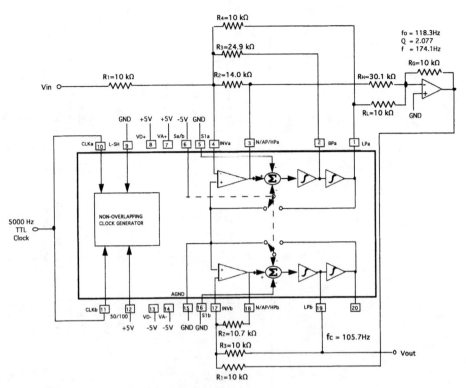

FIGURE 17-12 Low-pass filter of example 17-1.

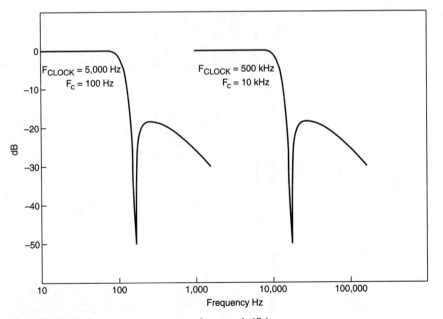

FIGURE 17-13 Frequency response curve for example 17-1.

17.13

TABLE 17-2 Switched Capacitor Filter Selection Guide

Device	Type	Response	Max. Order	Freq. Accur.	Max. Freq.	Ratio Clock: F_0	Special Features
LMF100	Universal	Universal	Dual $N=2$	±0.3%	100 kHz	50:1, 100:1	MF-10 pin-compatible
LMF120	Universal	Universal	12th	±1%	100 kHz	10:1 thru 500:1	Mask-programmable
LMF60	Low-pass	Butterworth	6th	±0.3%	25 kHz	50:1, 100:1	
LMF90	Notch	Elliptic	4th	±1%	30 kHz	33.33:1, 50:1, 100:1	built-in Xtal oscillator
LTC1059	Universal	Universal	2nd	±0.3%	40 kHz	50:1, 100:1	
LTC1060	Universal	Universal	Dual $N=2$	±0.3%	30 kHz	50:1, 100:1	MF-10 pin-compatible
LTC1061	Universal	Universal	Triple $N=2$	±1.2%	35 kHz	50:1, 100:1	
LTC1062	Low-pass	Butterworth	5th	±1%	20 kHz	100:1	Zero DC offset
LTC1064	Universal	Universal	Quad $N=2$	±0.6%	140 kHz	50:1, 100:1	Low noise
LTC1064-1	Low-pass	Elliptic	8th		20 kHz	100:1	Low noise
LTC1064-2	Low-pass	Butterworth	8th		140 kHz	50:1, 100:1	Low noise
LTC1064-3	Low-pass	Bessel	8th		95 kHz	75:1, 120:1, 150:1	Low noise
LTC1064-4	Low-pass	Elliptic	8th		100 kHz	50:1, 100:1	Low noise
LTC1164	Universal	Universal	Quad $N=2$	±0.5%	20 kHz	50:1, 100:1	Low power, low noise
MAX260	Universal	Universal	Dual $N=2$	±0.2%	10 kHz	Programmable	μC-programmable
MAX261	Universal	Universal	Dual $N=2$	±0.2%	57 kHz	Programmable	μC-programmable
MAX262	Universal	Universal	Dual $N=2$	±0.2%	140 kHz	Programmable	μC-programmable
MAX263	Universal	Universal	Dual $N=2$	±0.2%	57 kHz	Programmable	μC-programmable
MAX264	Universal	Universal	Dual $N=2$	±0.2%	140 kHz	Programmable	μC-programmable

Device	Function	Response	Order	Accuracy	Frequency	Ratio	Comments
MAX265	Bandpass	Universal	Dual $N = 2$	±0.2%	57 kHz	Programmable	µC-programmable
MAX267	Universal	Universal	Dual $N = 2$	±0.2%	140 kHz	Programmable	µC-programmable
MAX268	Bandpass	Universal	Dual $N = 2$	±0.2%	140 kHz	Programmable	µC-programmable
MAX270	Low-pass	Universal	Dual $N = 2$	±2.9%	25 kHz	Programmable	µC-programmable
MAX271	Low-pass	Universal	Dual $N = 2$	±2.9%	25 kHz	Programmable	µC-programmable, T/H
MAX275	Universal	Universal	Dual $N = 2$	±0.2%	57 kHz	Programmable	µC-programmable
MAX281	Low-pass	Bessel	5th		20 kHz	101:1, 202:1, 404:1	Built-in RC oscillator
MF-4	Low-pass	Butterworth	4th	±0.3%	20 kHz	50:1, 100:1	Built-in RC oscillator
MF-5	Universal	Universal	2nd	±0.2%	30 kHz	50:1, 100:1	Uncommitted amplifier
MF-6	Low-pass	Butterworth	6th	±0.3%	20 kHz	50:1, 100:1	Two uncommitted Op-amps
MF-8	Bandpass	Universal	4th	±0.3%	20 kHz	50:1, 100:1	Programmable Q up to 90
MF-10	Universal	Universal	Dual $N = 2$	±0.6%	30 kHz	50:1, 100:1	Industry standard
XR-1001	Low-pass	Butterworth	4th		15 kHz	100:1	
XR-1002	Low-pass	Butterworth	4th		30 kHz	50:1	
XR-1003	Low-pass	Bessel	4th		15 kHz	100:1	
XR-1004	Low-pass	Bessel	4th		30 kHz	50:1	
XR-1005	Low-pass	Cheb. 0.1 dB	4th		15 kHz	100:1	
XR-1006	Low-pass	Cheb. 0.1 dB	4th		30 kHz	50:1	
XR-1007	Low-pass	Cheb. 0.5 dB	4th		15 kHz	100:1	
XR-1008	Low-pass	Cheb. 0.5 dB	4th		30 kHz	50:1	
XR-1015	Low-pass	Elliptic	7th	±0.5%	25 kHz	100:1	
XR-1016	Low-pass	Elliptic	7th	±0.5%	50 kHz	50:1, 100:1	

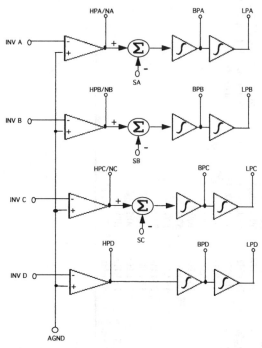

FIGURE 17-14 Block diagram of linear technology LTC1064.

can be contained within a single package. This architecture allows adjustment of filter parameters such as center frequency, Q, notch location, and gain. These parameters are all controlled by relationships between resistors and the applied clock frequency. Figure 17-14 shows a block diagram of the Linear Technology LTC1064 containing four second-order sections. Refer to the references for detailed applications information on these devices.

Filters of varying complexity can be designed using these building blocks. The design procedure consists of transforming a complex filter transfer function into individual first- or second-order sections as required. Each section is defined in terms of parameters, such as center or cutoff frequency, Q, and notch frequency and then implemented using cascaded ICs. This was illustrated in example 17-1 for a third-order elliptic function low-pass filter.

Dedicated

Dedicated switched-capacitor filters are already configured to provide a defined transfer function and as a result do not require external resistors. Typically they provide low-pass responses and are available with all standard shapes such as Butterworth, Chebyshev, Bessel, and elliptic-function. Designing with these devices is simply a matter of connecting a clock frequency that is either 50 or 100 times the cutoff frequency and connecting power and ground.

In some cases, the manufacturer simply customizes one of the universal filters by adding some components internally to the IC. A representative example of this approach is the Linear Technology LTC1064-1 which is shown in figure 17-15. This device is an eighth-order elliptic-function low-pass filter created from an LTC-1064 and requires no external components. It has a passband ripple of ±0.15 dB and makes the transition from passband to stopband within a steepness factor of 1.5, achieving over 68 dB of stopband attenuation. The clock-to-cutoff ratio is 100:1.

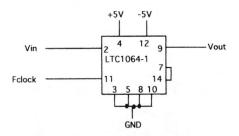

FIGURE   17-15   Eighth-order   elliptic-function low-pass filter using the LTC1064-1.

Selection Guide

Switched-capacitor filters offer circuit designers a solution to filtering needs while utilizing minimal printed circuit board area as compared with passive and active filters. They feature high stability and precision as well as the ability to change frequency characteristics under the control of an external clock. A selection guide to switched-capacitor filters is provided in Table 17-2.

BIBLIOGRAPHY

Exar Corporation, *Databook,* Exar Corporation, San Jose, Calif., 1992.

Linear Technology, *Monolithic Filter Handbook,* Linear Technology, Milpitas, Calif., 1990.

Linear Technology, *Linear Databook Supplement,* Linear Technology, Milpitas, Calif., 1990.

Maxim Integrated Circuit Products Inc. *New Releases Data Book,* Maxim Integrated Circuit Products Inc., Sunnyvale, Calif., 1992.

National Semiconductor Corporation, *Switched-Capacitor Handbook,* National Semiconductor Corporation, Santa Clara, Calif., 1985.

National Semiconductor Corporation, *Linear Databook, Rev 1,* National Semiconductor Corporation, Santa Clara, Calif., 1988.

CHAPTER 18

FILTER DESIGN FOR EMI SUPPRESSION

18.1 EMI

EMI (electromagnetic interference) is the generic term for the emission of electromagnetic fields that could cause interference in residential or business environments. The two major paths for EMI are *radiated* and *conducted*. Radiated fields are in the form of electromagnetic fields similar to those emitted by a radio or TV station antenna. Conducted signals travel down a power line in the form of current fluctuations and can be converted back to electromagnetic fields, which are then radiated.

There are a number of standards that define the limits of EMI and the methods of measurement. These are cited in the Bibliography. The purpose of this chapter is to discuss the various sources of EMI and indicate how filters can be used to minimize these effects. In the context of EMI, filters are defined in a very general sense and include components such as ferrite beads, inductors, feedthrough capacitors, bypass capacitors, and even resistors when used for band limiting.

The most efficient method for minimizing EMI is to limit it at its source. We will discuss some of the major sources of EMI and illustrate how filters can best be used to reduce the magnitude of these signals.

18.2 SOURCES OF EMI

Radiated

Every signal consists of both electric and magnetic fields. At low frequencies, the predominant field is magnetic. At frequencies above 50 kHz, the electric field begins to dominate. As the frequency increases, the tendency for radiated emissions increases as well. Most RF problems occur within the range of 30 to 300 MHz. Even though circuits may not have fundamental components in this band, digital signals are rich in harmonics which fall in the troublesome frequency range and frequently cause EMI.

Common-Mode Radiation. Digital signals such as clocks produce currents on a printed circuit board at fundamental operating frequencies and higher harmonics.

These currents are mainly the result of current drain from the power supply by digital integrated circuits and become a major source of EMI by interacting with PC board trace inductance.

The schematic in figure 18-1a is representative of a digital circuit containing a variety of different types of integrated circuit components located on a printed circuit board. The PC board contains trace inductances due to the length of conductors. Typically, we are dealing with numbers in the range of 25 nH per inch, which might not appear significant, but at frequencies such as 50 MHz this represents about 8 ohms per inch. Each digital device consumes power.

The current drain consists of two components: a quiescent DC level and a fluctuating or AC value determined by the clocking frequencies. It is these AC components of current that generate voltage drops across all the trace inductances.

The equivalent circuit of figure 18-1b lumps all these AC voltage drops into an equivalent source which consists of a complex signal containing not only the fundamental clocking frequencies but their harmonics as well. This source applies a common-mode RF signal to the traces on the PC board as well as to the cable connected to the board. Typically, the overwhelming source of radiated emission will be the cable. Both the center conductor and the shield of the cable will have this common-mode signal superimposed so the cable will act as an antenna.

Longitudinal Signal Radiation.   Not all radiation is due to common-mode signals. A clock signal at high frequencies and rich in harmonic content due to fast rise times can be a source of EMI radiation. This is especially true if this signal is permitted to occur over large areas of a printed circuit board. The area of the board containing these signals will function as an antenna and radiate RF energy.

Minimizing Radiated Signals

To minimize radiated EMI due to common-mode sources, the amplitude of the common-mode equivalent RF noise source depicted in figure 18-1b must be reduced.

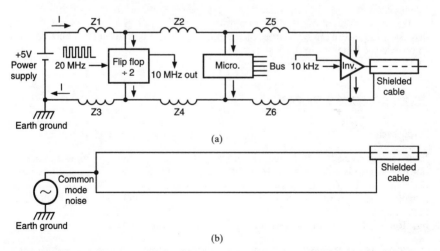

FIGURE 18-1 Common-mode RF noise: (*a*) typical digital circuit showing trace inductances; (*b*) equivalent circuit for common mode noise source.

This source is caused by the interaction of the power supply currents due to digital clock signals and the impedances due to traces on the PC board. These currents flow through both the power supply bus and its return. Longitudinal radiated signals are caused by clock signals interconnected between different points on the PC board. The longer the trace, the stronger will be the radiated signal. In either case (common-mode or longitudinal), the common denominator appears to be high-frequency timing signals.

Clock Decoupling from the Power Supply.   If each digital device had a power supply current waveform that was purely DC there would be no RF fluctuations occurring across the traces on the PC board. However, this is normally not the case since the current demand of the device follows the clock signals occurring within the chip itself. However, if we provided a "reservoir" of available charge directly at the power connections to the chip, this would prevent the RF fluctuations across the traces on the board. This can be accomplished using some of the methods shown in figure 18-2.

The simplest and most common approach is to place a ceramic capacitor as close as possible to the physical power supply connections of the chip itself. This is shown in figure 18-2*a*. Typically a 0.1-μF ceramic decoupling capacitor is used for this purpose. Each gate within the chip periodically generates current spikes from the power supply because of internal clocking. The capacitor filters or "short circuits" these spikes to ground directly at the chip itself, preventing voltage drops across the PC board traces.

Ceramic capacitors are used due to their excellent high-frequency properties so parasitic effects such as series inductance are minimized. Hence, they will represent a few ohms at a few hundred kilohertz. In order to filter lower-frequency components, larger capacitor values are required. A commonly used method is to combine a ceramic capacitor for good high-frequency properties and a tantalum capacitor for filtering lower frequencies. This approach is illustrated in figure 18-2*b*. Tantalum capacitors are superior to aluminum electrolytics since they are less inductive and have lower losses.

The impedance of a capacitor rolls off at 6 dB per octave at best. We can improve the filtering action of a decoupling network by adding another pole using an inductor. Depending on the frequency range being filtered, the inductor can be simply a ferrite bead using a single turn of wire which provides a few hundred nanohenries or higher inductance values using multiturn chokes if needed. This type of network is shown in figure 18-2*c* and eventually attains a rate of roll-off of 12 dB per octave.

We can carry this a step further using the network of figure 18-2*d*. By adding an additional 0.1-μF ceramic capacitor, a symmetrical PI network will result which rolls off at 18 dB per octave. A subtle advantage of this arrangement is the symmetry so that excellent decoupling occurs in both directions. Any noise on the supply is filtered from the chip as well as the current spikes from the chip being prevented from generating transients on the PC board traces.

Clock Wave Shaping.   Clocks are the major source of emissions either from coupling onto traces due to trace impedance or direct radiation from long traces. Therefore, reduction of the harmonic content of clock waveforms has a direct effect on EMI. Figure 18-3*a* shows a square wave and the accompanying spectrum. Fourier analysis will tell us that a square wave consists of an infinite train of odd harmonics having a magnitude inversely proportional to frequency. The harmonics roll off at a rate of 6 dB per octave (i.e., for a doubling of the frequency, the amplitude reduces by a factor of two). In many cases, it is these higher-order harmonics that contribute to EMI more significantly than the fundamental waveform.

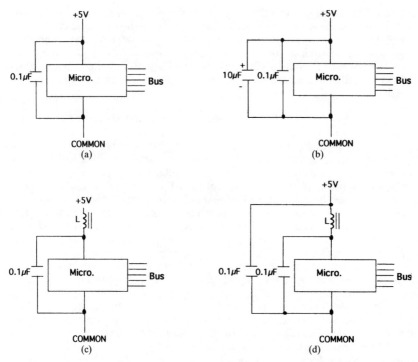

FIGURE 18-2   Methods for power supply decoupling: (*a*) conventional capacitive decoupling; (*b*) wideband capacitive decoupling; (*c*) LC decoupling; (*d*) PI filter decoupling network.

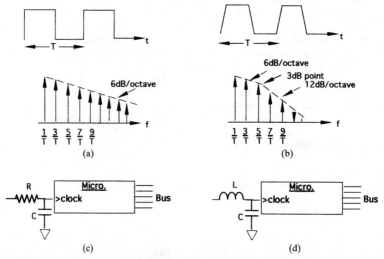

FIGURE 18-3   Adding wave shaping to clocks: (*a*) square wave and harmonic train; (*b*) effect of increased rise and fall time; (*c*) *RC* shaping; (*d*) *LC* shaping.

Figure 18-3*b* illustrates the effect of adding wave shaping using a single pole, as shown in figure 18-3*c*. The 3-dB breakpoint frequency is given by:

$$F = \frac{1}{2\pi RC} \tag{18-1}$$

Beyond the 3-dB point, the harmonics asymptotically approach a roll-off of 12 dB per octave rather than 6 dB, due to the added effect of the *RC* low-pass filter.

Care should be taken that excessive wave shaping does not occur, as this would cause marginal operation of the digital device. In addition, the value of *R* should not be excessive to avoid offsets that would violate trigger levels of the logic. No more than a few hundred ohms should be used with conventional CMOS logic. Waveforms should be examined with an oscilloscope to ensure that excessive shaping has not occurred.

If the shaping is introduced by an *LC* network as shown in figure 18-3*d*, a rate of roll-off of 18 dB per octave will be approached, as the *LC* network will contribute 12 dB per octave to the natural roll-off of the square wave of 6 dB per octave. The 3-dB break frequency would then be given by

$$F = \frac{1}{2\pi\sqrt{LC}} \tag{18-2}$$

Waveshaping Using Parasitics. Figure 18-4 illustrates how wave shaping can be introduced in conjunction with existing parasitic capacity and resistance. Parasitic or stray capacity results from the PC board traces and the conductor length inside the chip itself. This could amount to a few picofarads. Adding a resistor to interact with this capacity, as shown in figure 18-4*a*, will increase the wave shaping. The resistor should be physically located as close to the source of the clock as possible (near the inverter output for this example). An inductor in the form of a ferrite bead could be used instead of the resistor. In a similar manner, logic gates contain internal resistances. Adding an external capacitor as shown in figure 18-4*b* will result in additional wave shaping as well.

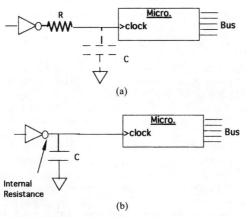

FIGURE 18-4 Wave shaping using parasitics: (*a*) adding resistance; (*b*) adding capacitance.

Good PC Design Practice. Good PC design techniques will minimize radiated interference. Previously, we indicated how trace inductance will result in common-mode voltage buildup which becomes a source of interference. By keeping trace lengths short, this effect will be kept to a minimum. When laying out a PC board, attention must be paid to component placement so that high-frequency clocks and buses travel the shortest distance possible. The impedances of power and ground traces should be kept low. This is usually achieved by using power and ground planes. In addition, layers containing signal traces should be filled in with ground and power grids. The object is to keep the power and ground impedances as low as possible.

Conducted Interference

Conducted emissions are signals that conduct back to the AC line cord and then radiate from the power lines which function as antennas. The most effective solution is to limit these signals at their source by decoupling, wave shaping, and grounding techniques, some of which were mentioned earlier in this chapter. However, the degree of improvement that can be achieved is sometimes limited unless a line filter is used.

Line Filters. Line filters are placed in series with the AC power line connections to the equipment. Typically an AC line filter is connected between the AC mains and the equipment power supply. Line filters consist of L or PI low-pass configurations and are balanced with respect to earth-ground.

Two types of capacitors are used in line filters and are called X and Y capacitors. An X capacitor is always connected line-to-line, whereas Y capacitors are connected between each side of the line to ground. An X capacitor behaves as a short circuit for high-frequency differential signals. A Y capacitor arrangement suppresses signals by short circuiting them to earth-ground and are more suited for common-mode signals than the differential type.

Common-mode chokes are used to remove the common-mode RF signals. Conventional chokes remove differential RF interference.

Two representative filter schematics are shown in figure 18-5. The circuit of figure 18-5*a* uses two conventional chokes, L1 and L2, along with both X and Y capacitors. An earth-ground connection is present which is used as a return for the Y capacitor. Both differential and common-mode filtering occurs since common-mode signals are suppressed to earth-ground through the Y capacitor earth connection.

Common-Mode Chokes. Common-mode chokes are wound in such a manner that differential AC currents create canceling magnetic fields and avoid saturation. This occurs because the chokes are both wound on the same magnetic core and the windings polarities are in opposition to each other relative to the direction of AC current flow. Current flow through one of the chokes produces a magnetic field that is canceled by that current returning to the source through the other choke.

Operation of a common-mode choke is shown in figure 18-6*a*. AC current entering via terminal 1 flows in the opposite direction as the current leaving through terminal 4, relative to the polarity (direction) of the windings which are on the same core. (The dots usually indicate the start of a winding.) Therefore, the magnetic fields cancel, and saturation of the core is avoided. Since the two inductances are in opposition in the loop consisting of terminals 1 through 4, the net inductance is zero; thus, no differential filtering occurs.

If we examine the effect of these inductances on a common-mode signal as shown in figure 18-6*b* the magnetic fields in both windings caused by this signal are in the

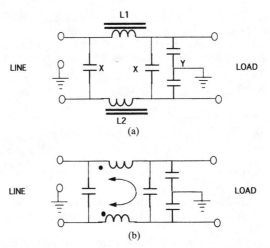

FIGURE 18-5 Line filters: (*a*) conventional low-pass; (*b*) use of common-mode chokes.

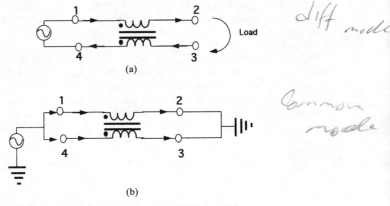

FIGURE 18-6 Common-mode choke: (*a*) differential current; (*b*) common-mode current.

same direction, so the net inductance will be finite (nearly four times the inductance of each individual coil due to the effect of mutual inductance).

Common-mode coils can provide common-mode filtering in circuits having high AC currents without having to go to physically large inductors to avoid saturation.

18.3 PARTS SELECTION FOR MINIMIZING EMI

Capacitors

Ceramic Capacitors. Because of their low-inductance construction, ceramic capacitors are best suited for RF bypassing.

Mainly, two parameters determine the operating characteristics of the capacitor: the temperature coefficient of the ceramic material and the dissipation factor d. Table 10-8 provides the three most readily available temperature characteristics and their associated dissipation factors. It is repeated here as Table 18-1.

TABLE 18-1   Properties of Ceramic Capacitor Materials

Material	Temperature Characteristic	Dissipation Factor
NPO	0 ± 30 ppm/°C −55 to +125°C	0.1% maximum
X7R	±15% from −55 to +125°C	2.5% maximum
Z5U	+22% to −56% +10 to +85°C	4% maximum

NPO-type material is intended for precision filter requirements. For EMI-type filter applications, either X7R or Z5U is adequate since neither stability nor tolerance is critical.

In order to minimize size, the voltage rating should not be excessive. For logic circuits operating from +5 V power, a voltage rating of 50 V DC is adequate. For AC mains, power filtering voltage ratings of 600 V or more are used.

Figure 18-7 illustrates the most common form of construction for ceramic capacitors. Ceramic capacitors in disc form have been used for many decades and are the traditional packaging format. However, chip capacitors offer better high-frequency characteristics since the capacitor leads which represent inductance have been eliminated.

The most effective construction for high-frequency bypass is in the form of a feedthrough capacitor, illustrated in figure 18-7c. A single insulated terminal going through the body of the capacitor represents one plate of the capacitor. This lead is isolated from the case by a ceramic dielectric. The other plate is the case itself which is normally soldered to a ground plane. The ends are typically sealed with glass or epoxy. This type of construction is used for passing signals from one physical compartment to another, such as signals leaving or entering a cabinet or equipment case.

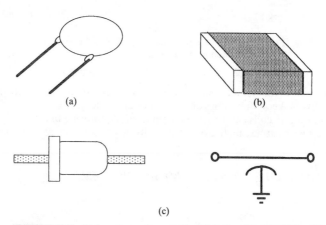

FIGURE 18-7   Styles of ceramic capacitors: (*a*) disc; (*b*) chip; (*c*) feedthrough.

Other Capacitor Types. Ceramic capacitors are limited in value to no more than about 0.47 µF without getting large and costly. Tantalum capacitors are best suited for low-frequency filtering where larger values are needed. Values up to 100 µF can be obtained with practical case sizes. Tantalum capacitors are preferred to aluminum electrolytics because they are less lossy at higher frequencies and are also less inductive. Typically, tantalum capacitors are paralleled with a ceramic to get wideband decoupling.

For AC applications, the polarization of tantalum capacitors becomes a limiting factor. Although a nonpolar tantalum can be configured by connecting two capacitors back-to-back, voltage ratings are limited to 50 V maximum. A polyester film (Mylar) capacitor is typically used in AC line filters, because these are nonpolar and can be obtained up to several hundred volts rating. A ceramic capacitor is paralleled for wideband filtering requirements.

Inductors

The three most common physical forms of inductors for EMI elimination are conventional radial leaded chokes, surface-mount chip inductors, and beads. The magnetic core material is generally ferrite. These three forms of construction are illustrated in figure 18-8.

A standard cylindrical choke, as shown in figure 18-8a, has been the traditional form for low- to medium-value inductors (from a few microhenries to a few hundred millihenries). The core consists of a cylinder of either iron or ferrite with insulated multiple turns of copper wire. For inductances of a few microhenries or less, the core can be ceramic.

A chip inductor is shown in figure 18-8b. A ferrite or ceramic chip has multiple turns of wire wound around the chip surface. The wire ends are attached to the end terminals for surface-mount contact. Inductances for ceramic cores range from a few nanohenries to a few hundred microhenries. Higher inductance values can be obtained using ferrite cores.

A ferrite bead consists of a cylinder of ferrite containing single or multiple holes drilled lengthwise through the cylinder. A wire lead is threaded through the hole or holes. Figures 18-8c and 18-8d show single-turn and double-turn configurations. The double-turn arrangement theoretically will have four times the impedance of the single-turn unit, with all other parameters identical.

Ferrite beads are generally specified in terms of their impedance at a test frequency such as 10, 25, 100, or 250 MHz. Factors such as material permeability varia-

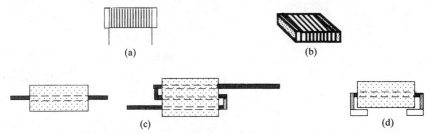

FIGURE 18-8   Ferrite inductors for EMI suppression: (*a*) choke; (*b*) chip inductor; (*c*) ferrite beads; (*d*) surface-mount ferrite bead.

tions with frequency and self-resonance of the inductor affect the impedance beyond the test frequencies. In addition, DC bias may cause saturation effects which reduce impedance. Refer to manufacturer catalogs and data sheets for detailed information.

BIBLIOGRAPHY

Compliance Design Inc., *Handbook of ECEMC Compliance, 1993 Edition,* Compliance Design Inc., Boxboro, Mass., 1993.

Compliance Engineering, *1994 Reference Guide,* vol. XI, no. 2, Compliance Engineering, Boxboro, Mass., 1994.

Coilcraft Catalog, "Surface Mount Products," Coilcraft, Cary, Ill., 1993.

Fair-Rite Products Corp., *Fair-Rite Soft Ferrites,* 12th ed., Fair-Rite Products Corp., Wallkill, N.Y., 1993.

US Microtech Filters Corp., *EMI Filters,* US Microtech Filters Corp., Sun Valley, Calif., 1992.

APPENDIX A

DISCRETE SYSTEMS MATHEMATICS

A.1 DIGITAL FILTER MATHEMATICS (THE z TRANSFORM)

The principal analysis tool for continuous or analog systems is the familiar Laplace transform. Unfortunately, digital filters cannot be efficiently modeled using Laplace transforms, but they do have a strong similarity to the study of discrete systems which have a well-known z-transform representation.

The z transform has historically been applied to the problem of analyzing and modeling the discrete system shown in figure A-1. The sampling circuit is considered to be an ideal *sample and hold* device which has the ability to instantaneously sample an analog signal and hold its value until the next sample instant. For δ_D denoting the Kronecker delta function (i.e., $\delta_D(i) = 1$ if $i = 0$ and 0 otherwise), it follows that

$$x(nT) = \sum_{n=-\infty}^{\infty} x(t)\delta_D(t - nT)$$

The "two-sided" Laplace transforms (positive and negative terms) of $\delta_D(t - nT)$ and $x(nT)$ are known to be

$$\mathcal{L}[\delta_D(t - nT)] = \exp(-nT)$$

and

$$X(s) = \mathcal{L}[x(nT)] = \sum_{n=-\infty}^{\infty} x(nT)\exp(-nsT)$$

where $\exp(-nsT)$ is often referred to as the *delay operator*. This term appears throughout discrete system equations and, as a result, has been given a shorthand representation, namely

$$z = \exp(sT) \qquad \text{or} \qquad z^{-1} = \exp(-sT)$$

Therefore, z^{-n} denotes a delay of n samples. It immediately follows that, using the z notation, the z transform of $x(nt_s)$ is

$$X(z) = X(s) \Big|_{z = \exp(sT)}$$

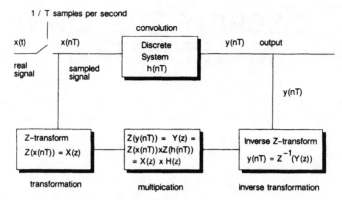

FIGURE A-1 Comparison of direct convolution calculation and that using the method of z transforms.

EXAMPLE A-1

Suppose $x(t)$ is a decaying exponential given by $x(t) = \exp(aT)$ for $t \geq 0$, 0 for $t < 0$, and $a < 0$. The trajectories of $x(t)$ are shown in figure A-2. Upon sampling $x(t)$ at a rate of $1/T$ samples per second, we obtain the time series given by

$$\{x(nT)\} = \{\exp(anT)\}$$

and it follows that

$$X(s) = \sum_{n=0}^{\infty} \exp(anT)\exp(-nsT)$$

and

$$X(z) = X(s)\bigg|_{z = \exp(sT)} = \sum_{n=0}^{\infty} \exp(anT)(z^{-n}) = \sum_{n=0}^{\infty} \exp(anT)(z^{-1})^n$$

The above equation can be placed in closed form by observing that

$$\sum_{i=0}^{\infty} x^i = 1 + x + x^2 + x^3 + \cdots = \frac{1}{1-x}$$

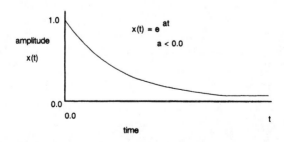

FIGURE A-2 Example exponential signal.

if $|x| < 1$ (proof is by long division), it follows that for this example

$$x = \exp(aT)z^{-1}$$

and

$$X(z) = \frac{1}{1 - \exp(aT)z^{-1}} = \frac{z}{z - \exp(aT)}$$

The methods by which z transforms are produced and manipulated are very similar to the techniques used in conjunction with Laplace transforms. Traditionally, the continuous signal $x(t)$ and system impulse response $h(t)$ were Laplace transforms using standard tables. In particular, if $x(t)$ [or $h(t)$] could be factored into recognizable exponential or sinusoidal terms, such that

$$x(t) = \sum_{i=1}^{L} \alpha_i x_i(t)$$

$$x_i(t) = \begin{cases} 1 & \text{constant} \\ \exp(-\lambda_i t) & \text{decaying exponential} \\ \exp(-\lambda_i t)\exp(j\omega_i t) & j = \sqrt{-1} \quad \text{decaying sinusoid} \end{cases}$$

then

$$X(s) = \sum_{i=1}^{L} \alpha_i X_i(s)$$

$$X_i(s) = \mathcal{L}[x_i(t)]$$

where $X_i(s)$ is not computed but obtained from a precomputed table of Laplace transforms of elementary functions. Once $X(s)$ and $H(s)$ are defined, the output transform, say $Y(s)$, is directly computed from the polynomial product $Y(s) = X(s)H(s)$. Finally, the time domain disruption of $Y(s)$, namely $y(t)$, is obtained again using standard tables. That is, upon factoring $Y(s)$ into first- or second-order terms, such that

$$Y(s) = \sum_{i=1}^{L} \beta_i Y_i(s)$$

$$Y_i(s) = \begin{cases} (n_0 s + n_1)/(s + p) & \text{if } p \text{ is real} \\ (n_0 s^2 + n_1 s + n_2)/(s^2 + p_1 s + p_2) & \text{otherwise} \end{cases}$$

the time domain response of $y(t)$ is given by

$$y(t) = \mathcal{L}^{-1} \sum_{i=1}^{L} \beta_i Y_i(s) = \sum_{i=1}^{L} \beta_i \mathcal{L}^{-1}(Y_i(s)) = \sum_{i=1}^{L} \beta_i y_i(t)$$

where $y_i(t)$ is determined from a table of Laplace transforms of elementary functions.

EXAMPLE A-2

Suppose $a < 0$ and $x(t) = \exp(at)$ for $t \geq 0$, 0 otherwise, is sampled at a rate of $1/T$ samples per second. The resulting time series then becomes $x(nT) = \exp(anT)$ for $n \geq 0$. Then, $X(z)$ is given by

$$X(z) = \sum_{n=0}^{\infty} [\exp(anT)z^{-n}]$$

which is recognized to be the 9th entry in Table A-1, or

$$X(z) = z/[z - \exp(aT)]$$

as found in example A-1.

EXAMPLE A-3

Suppose $x(t) = \exp(-j\omega_0 t)$ for $t \geq 0$, 0 otherwise, is sampled at rate $1/T$ samples per second. Then $x(nT) = \exp(-j\omega_0 nT)$ and $X(z)$ is given by (refer to example A-1)

$$X(z) = \sum_{n=0}^{\infty} \exp(-j\omega_0 nT)z^{-n}$$

$$= \frac{1}{1 - \exp(-j\omega_0 T)z^{-1}}$$

Using the standard trigonometric relationship

$$\exp(j\theta) = \cos(\theta) + j\sin(\theta)$$

it follows that

$$X(z) = \frac{1}{[1 - \exp(-j\omega_0 T)z^{-1}]}$$

$$= \frac{1}{[1 - \cos(\omega_0 T)z^{-1}] + j\sin(\omega_0 T)z^{-1}}$$

$$= \frac{1 - \cos(\omega_0 T)z^{-1} - j\sin(\omega_0 T)z^{-1}}{[1 - \cos(\omega_0 T)z^{-1}]^2 + [\sin(\omega_0 T)z^{-1}]^2}$$

$$= \frac{1 - \cos(\omega_0 T)z^{-1}}{D(z)} - \frac{j\sin(\omega_0 T)z^{-1}}{D(z)}$$

where

$$D(z) = 1 - 2\cos(\omega_0 T)z^{-1} + z^{-2}$$

Furthermore, the z transform of a pure sine and cosine signal can be extracted from the preceding equation. That is

$$Z[\cos(\omega_0 T)] = \frac{1 - \cos(\omega_0 T)z^{-1}}{D(z)}$$

$$= \frac{z^2 - \cos(\omega_0 T)z}{z^2 D(z)}$$

$$Z[\sin(\omega_0 T)] = \frac{\sin(\omega_0 T)z^{-1}}{D(z)}$$

$$= \frac{\sin(\omega_0 T)z}{z^2 D(z)}$$

where

$$z^2 D(z) = z^2 - 2\cos(\omega_0 T)z + 1$$

The same process is used to work with the z transform of an arbitrary signal $x(t)$. The signal $x(t)$ is first interpreted as a linear combination of elementary signals which have been summarized in table A-1.

TABLE A-1 Elementary Functions

$x(t)$ or $x(k)$	$X(z)$
δ_K (Kronecker delta)	1
$\delta(k - m)$	z^{-m}
1 (unit step)	$z/(z - 1)$
k (ramp)	$z/(z - 1)^2$
k^2	$\dfrac{z(z + 1)}{(z - 1)^3}$
k^3	$\dfrac{z(z^2 + 4z + 1)}{(z - 1)^4}$
k^4	$\dfrac{z(z^3 + 11z^2 + 11z + 1)}{(z - 1)^5}$
k^5	$\dfrac{z(z^4 + 26z^3 + 66z^2 + 26z + 1)}{(z - 1)^6}$
$\exp(at)$ (exponential)	$z/[z - \exp(aT)]$
$t \exp(-at)$	$\dfrac{zT\exp(-aT)}{[z - \exp(-aT)]^2}$
$t^2 \exp(-at)$	$\dfrac{T^2\exp(-aT)z[z + \exp(-aT)]}{[z - \exp(-aT)]^3}$
a^k (compare to exponential)	$\dfrac{z}{z - a}$
ka^k	$\dfrac{az}{(z - a)^2}$
k^2a^k	$\dfrac{az(z + a)}{(z - a)^3}$
k^3a^k	$\dfrac{az(z^2 + 4az + a^2)}{(z - a)^4}$
k^4a^k	$\dfrac{az(z^3 + 11az^2 + 11a^2z + a^3)}{(z - a)^5}$
k^5a^k	$\dfrac{az(z^4 + 26az^3 + 66a^2z^2 + 26a^3z + a^4)}{(z - a)^6}$
$(k + 1)a^k$	$\dfrac{z^2}{(z - a)^2}$
$\dfrac{(k + 1)(k + 2)a^k}{2!}$	$\dfrac{z^3}{(z - a)^3}$
$\dfrac{(k + 1)(k + 2)(k + 3)a^k}{3!}$	$\dfrac{z^4}{(z - a)^4}$
$\dfrac{(k + 1)(k + 2)\cdots(k + m)a^k}{m!}$	$\dfrac{z^{m+1}}{(z - a)^{m+1}}$
$\sin(\beta t)$	$\dfrac{z \sin (\beta T)}{(z^2 - 2z \cos (\beta T) + 1)}$

TABLE A-1   Elementary Functions (*Continued*)

$x(t)$ or $x(k)$	$X(z)$
$\cos(\beta t)$	$\dfrac{z(z - \cos(\beta T))}{(z^2 - 2z \cos(\beta T) + 1)}$
$\exp(at)\sin(\beta t)$	$\dfrac{z \exp(aT)\sin(\beta T)}{z^2 - 2z \exp(aT)\cos(\beta T) + \exp(2aT)}$
$\exp(at)\cos(\beta t)$	$\dfrac{z(z - \exp(aT)\cos(\beta T))}{z^2 - 2z \exp(aT) \cos(\beta T) + \exp(2aT)}$
$\sin(k\omega T)$ (compare to sin)	$\dfrac{z \sin(\omega T)}{z^2 - 2z \cos(\omega T) + 1}$
$\cos(k\omega T)$ (compare to cos)	$\dfrac{z[z - \cos(\omega T)]}{z^2 - 2z \cos(\omega T) + 1}$
$a^k \sin(k\omega T)$	$\dfrac{az \sin(\omega T)}{z^2 - 2az \cos(\omega T) + a^2}$
$a^k \cos(k\omega T)$	$\dfrac{z[z - a \cos(\omega T)]}{z^2 - 2az \cos(\omega T) + a^2}$
$\sin(k\omega T + \theta)$	$\dfrac{z[z \sin\theta + \sin(\omega T - \theta)]}{z^2 - 2z \cos(\omega T) + 1}$
$\cos(k\omega T + \theta)$	$\dfrac{z[z \cos\theta - \cos(\omega T - \theta)]}{z^2 - 2z \cos(\omega T) + 1}$
$ka^k \sin(k\omega T)$	$\dfrac{z(z - a)(z + a)a \sin(\omega T)}{[z^2 - 2az \cos(\omega T) + a^2]^2}$
$ka^k \cos(k\omega T)$	$\dfrac{az[z^2 \cos(\omega T) - 2az + a^2 \cos(\omega T)]}{[z^2 - 2az \cos(\omega T) + a^2]^2}$
$\sinh(k\omega T)$	$\dfrac{z \sinh(\omega T)}{z^2 - 2z \cosh(\omega T) + 1}$
$\cosh(k\omega T)$	$\dfrac{z[z - \cosh(\omega T)]}{z^2 - 2z \cosh(\omega T) + 1}$
$\dfrac{a^k}{k!}$	$\exp(a/z)$
$\dfrac{(\ln a)^k}{k!}$	$a^{1/z}$
$\dfrac{n!}{(n - k)!k!} a^k b^{n-k}$	$\dfrac{(bz + a)^n}{z^n}$
$\dfrac{1}{k}$ (for $k = 1, 2, 3, \ldots$)	$\ln\left(\dfrac{z}{z - 1}\right)$
$\dfrac{k(k - 1)}{2!}$	$\dfrac{z}{(z - 1)^3}$
$\dfrac{k(k - 1)(k - 2)}{3!}$	$\dfrac{z}{(z - 1)^4}$
$\dfrac{k(k - 1)(k - 2)\cdots(k - m + 1)}{m!}$	$\dfrac{z}{(z - 1)^m}$

In the highly possible event that the elementary signal representation of $x(t)$ does not coincide exactly with those shown in table A-1, agreement generally can be achieved by using one or more of the following relationships:

1. *Linearly.* If $x(t) = x_1(t) + x_2(t)$, then $X(z) = X_1(z) + X_1(z)$.
2. *Scaling.* If $x(t) = ax_1(t)$, then $X(z) = aX_1(z)$.
3. *Delay (left shifting).* If $x(t) = x_1(t + kT)$, then $X(z) = z^k X_1(z) - z^k x_1(0) - z^{k-1} x_1(T) - \cdots - zx(kT - T)$.
4. *Advance (right shifting).* If $x(t) = x_1(t - kT)$, then $X(z) = z^{-k} X_1(z) + z^{-k+1} x_1(-T) + \cdots + z^{-1} x_1(-kT + T) + x_1(-kT)$.
5. *Exponential scaling.* If $x(t) = \exp(-at)x_i(t)$, then $X(z) = X_1[\exp(aT)z]$
6. *Time bias.* If $x(t) = tx_1(t)$, then $X(z) = -Tz \, dX_1(z)/dz$.
7. *Reciprocal time bias.* If $x(t) = x_1(t)/t$, then $X(z) = (-1/T)\int (X_1(z)/z)dz$.
8. *Radix "a" bias.* If $x(t) = a^t x_1(t)$, then $X(z) = X_1(z/a^T)$.
9. *Summation.* If $x(t) = \Sigma y(iT), i = 1, \ldots, r$, then $X(z) = zY(z)/(z - 1)$.
10. *Periodic sequences.* If $x(t) = y(t + NT)$, then $X(z) = z^N Y(z)/(z^N - 1)$.
11. *Convolution.* If $z(t) = \Sigma x(t - nT)y(t)$, then $Z(z) = X(z)Y(z)$.

EXAMPLE A-4

Suppose $x(t) = t^2$. Given $x_1(t) = t$, then $x(t) = tx_1(t)$, and from property 6 and knowledge that $X_1(z) = Tz/(z-1)^2$,

$$X(z) = -TzdX_1(z)/dz$$

$$= -Tz \left[T \frac{1}{(z-1)^2} - 2T \frac{z}{(z-1)^3} \right]$$

$$= -T^2 z \left[\frac{(z-1) - 2z}{(z-1)^3} \right]$$

$$= T^2 z(z+1)/(z-1)^3$$

EXAMPLE A-5

Suppose $x(t) = t \exp(-at)$. Given $x_1(t) = t$, then $x(t) = \exp(-at) x_1(t)$ and from property 5 and knowledge that $x_1(t) = Tz/(z-1)^2$,

$$X(z) = X_1[\exp(aT)z]$$

$$= \frac{T[\exp(aT)z]}{[\exp(aT)z - 1]^2}$$

$$= \frac{T\exp(-aT)z}{[z - \exp(-aT)]^2}$$

It is often useful, as a test, to compute the initial and/or final value of a signal and compare them to known limiting cases. For example, if the initial value of an arbitrary signal is known, say $x(0)$, then

$$\lim_{t \to 0} x(t) = x(0) = \lim_{z \to \infty} X(z)$$

EXAMPLE A-6

From example A-5, let $x(t) = t \exp(at)$. It is readily apparent that $x(0) = 0$. This known value can be checked against

$$\lim_{z \to \infty} X(z) = \frac{T \exp(-aT)z}{[z - \exp(-aT)]^2} = 0$$

which is in agreement.

The final value of $x(t)$ can be similarly checked using the relationship

$$\lim_{t \to \infty} x(t) = \lim_{z \to 1} \left[\frac{(z-1)}{z} X(z) \right]$$

EXAMPLE A-7

Given $x(t) = \exp(-at)$ and $X(z) = z/[z - \exp(-aT)]$, then the final value satisfies

$$\lim_{z \to 1} \frac{(z-1) z'}{z' (z - \exp(-aT))} \to 0$$

as expected.

There also exists a systematic technique of converting a known Laplace transform $X(s)$ into its equivalent z transform $X(z)$. It makes use of the residue theory of calculus and is given by

$$X(z) = \sum_{k} \text{Res}(\{X(s)/[1 - \exp(sT)z^{-1}]\}, p_k)$$

where $\{p_k\}$ are the poles of $X(s)$. If $X(s)$ is expanded as a series (Laurent) of the form

$$X(s) = \frac{a_{-1}}{s} + \frac{a_{-2}}{s^2} + \cdots$$

the coefficient a_{-1} is called the residue of $X(s)$ at $s \to \infty$. Its value is computed by

$$a_{-1} = \lim_{s \to \infty} sX(s)$$

From the initial value theorem of Laplace transforms it can also be seen that $a_{-1} = X(0)$.

Suppose $X(s) = N(s)/D(s)$ and that $D(s)$ is an nth-order polynomial consisting of K distinct poles. Then $D(s)$ can be factored as

$$D(s) = \prod_{i=1}^{k} (s - p_i)^{n(i)}$$

where $n(i)$ is called the *multiplicity* of the root located at $s = p_i$ and $n = \Sigma n(i)$, $i = 1, \ldots, k$. The series expansion of $X(s)$ would then be given by

$$X(s) = \frac{a_{-11}}{(s - p_1)} + \frac{a_{-21}}{(s - p_1)^2} + \cdots + \frac{a_{-n(1)1}}{(s - p_1)^{n(1)}} + \frac{a_{-12}}{(s - p_2)} + \cdots$$

$$+ \frac{a_{-n(k)k}}{(s - p_k)^{n(k)}}$$

The residue of $X(s)$ at pole p_i is the coefficient a_{-1i}. That is, it is the coefficient associated with the simple (first-order) pole $(s - p_i)^1$. In general

$$a_{-1k} = \text{Res}(\{X(s)/[1 - \exp(sT)z^{-1}]\}, p_k)$$

$$= \frac{1}{(n(k) - 1)!} \lim_{s \to p_k} \frac{d^{n(k) - 1}(s - p_k)^{n(k)} X(s)/(1 - \exp(sT)z^{-1})}{d^{n(k) - 1}s}$$

If all the poles of $X(s)$ [roots of $D(s)$] are first order (simple), then the residues are

$$a_{-1k} = \lim_{s \to p_k} \left\{ \frac{(s - p_k)X(s)}{[1 - \exp(sT)z^{-1}]} \right\}$$

EXAMPLE A-8

Suppose $x(t) = \exp(-at)$ for $t \geq 0, 0$ otherwise. Then $X(s) = 1/(s + a)$ and

$$a_{-11} = \lim_{s \to -a} \frac{(s + a)[1/(s + a)]}{[1 - \exp(sT)z^{-1}]}$$

$$= \frac{1}{1 - \exp(-aT)z^{-1}} = \frac{z}{z - \exp(-aT)}$$

EXAMPLE A-9

Suppose $x(t) = t$ for $t \geq 0, 0$ otherwise. Then $X(s) = 1/s^2, n(1) = 2$, then

$$X(s) = \frac{a_{-11}}{(s - 0)} + \frac{a_{-21}}{(s - 0)^2}$$

and

$$a_{-11} = \lim_{s \to 0} \frac{d\{s^2(1/s^2)/[1 - \exp(sT)z^{-1}]\}}{ds}$$

$$= \lim_{s \to 0} \frac{d\{1/[1 - \exp(sT)z^{-1}]\}}{ds}$$

$$= \lim_{s \to 0} \frac{T\exp(sT)z^{-1}}{[1 - \exp(sT)z^{-1}]^2}$$

$$= \frac{Tz^{-1}}{(1 - z^{-1})^2} = \frac{Tz}{(z - 1)^2} = X(z)$$

EXAMPLE A-10

Suppose $x(t) = \cos(\omega_0 t)$ for $t \geq 0$ and 0 otherwise. Then $X(s) = s/(s^2 + \omega_0^2) = s/(s + j\omega_0)$ $(s - j\omega_0)$. For poles $p_1 = -j\omega_0$ and $p_2 = j\omega_0$, it follows that

$$a_{-11} = \lim_{s \to -j\omega_0} \frac{(s + j\omega_0)s}{(s + j\omega_0)(s - j\omega_0)[1 - \exp(sT)z^{-1}]}$$

$$= \frac{-j\omega_0}{-2j\omega_0[1 - \exp(-j\omega_0 T)z^{-1}]}$$

$$= \frac{1}{2[1 - \exp(-j\omega_0 T)z^{-1}]}$$

$$a_{-12} = \lim_{s \to j\omega_0} \frac{(s - j\omega_0)s}{(s - j\omega_0)(s + j\omega_0)[1 - \exp(sT)z^{-1}]}$$

$$= \frac{j\omega_0}{2j\omega_0[1 - \exp(j\omega_0 T)z^{-1}]}$$

$$= \frac{1}{2[1 - \exp(j\omega_0 T)z^{-1}]}$$

Finally

$$X(z) = \Sigma \, \text{Res}(\{X(s)/[1 - \exp(sT)z^{-1}]\}, p_k)$$

$$= a_{-11} + a_{-12}$$

$$= \frac{1}{2}\left[\frac{1}{1 - \exp(-j\omega_0 T)z^{-1}} + \frac{1}{1 - \exp(j\omega_0 T)z^{-1}}\right]$$

$$= \frac{1}{2}\left[\frac{1 - \exp(-j\omega_0 T)z^{-1} + 1 - \exp(j\omega_0 T)z^{-1}}{1 - (\exp(-j\omega_0 T) + \exp(j\omega_0 T))z^{-1} + z^{-2}}\right]$$

$$= \frac{1 - \cos(\omega_0 T)z^{-1}}{1 - 2\cos(\omega_0 T)z^{-1} + z^{-2}}$$

$$= \frac{z[z - \cos(\omega_0 T)]}{z^2 - 2\cos(\omega_0 T)z + 1}$$

A.2 INVERSE z TRANSFORM

The inverse of the z transform will convert a given z transform, say $X(z)$, into a parent time series $x(n)$. Formally,

$$x(n) = Z^{-1}(X(z)) = \frac{1}{2\pi j}\int_C X(z)z^{n-1}\,dz$$

where C is a close path found in the z plane. In general, the definition of the inverse z transform is too difficult and awkward to use on a routine basis. A similar condition exists in the study of Laplace transforms where integral definitions are also found. In the case of Laplace transforms, standard tables of transform pairs are used to bypass the formal integration process. In the case of z transforms, standard tables plus other short-cut techniques are used. The primary inversion methods are:

Long division
Partial fraction expansion
Residue calculus

Long Division

The first method, long division, converts a rational polynomial description of a z-transform signal, $X(z) = N(z)/D(z)$, into the fundamental defining z-transform equation $X(z) = \Sigma a_i z^{-i}; i = 0, 1, 2, \ldots$, using direct division. More specifically, if

$$X(z) = N(z)/D(z)$$

then

$$D(z) \overline{\left) N(z) \right.} \quad a_0 + a_1 z^{-1} + a_2 z^{-2} + \cdots$$

From the definition of the standard z transform of a time series $\{x(n)\} = \{x(0), x(1), x(2), \ldots\}$, it immediately follows that

$$\{x(n)\} = \{x(0) = a_0, x(1) = a_1, x(2) = a_2, \ldots\}$$

This method can prove useful if the time domain analysis can be restricted to a few sample values locally clustered around $t = 0$. An example of this is the transient analysis of a highly damped system.

EXAMPLE A-11

Consider again example A-4 for a given $X(z) = T^2 z(z + 1)/(z - 1)^3$. Now assume $T = 1$ for the purpose of simplification. Then

$$N(z) = z^2 + z$$

$$D(z) = z^3 - 3z^2 + 3z - 1$$

and $X(z) = N(z)/D(z)$ will yield

$$
\begin{array}{r}
z^{-1} + 4z^{-2} + 9z^{-3} \\
z^3 - 3z^2 + 3z - 1 \overline{\left) z^2 + z \right.} \\
\underline{z^2 - 3z + 3z^0 - z^{-1}} \\
4z - 3z^0 + z^{-1} \\
\underline{4z - 12z^0 + 12z^{-1} + 4z^{-2}} \\
9z^0 - 11z^{-1} + 4z^{-2}
\end{array}
$$

or $X(z) = 0z^0 + 1z^{-1} + 4z^{-2} + 9z^{-3} + \cdots$ and $x(n) = \{0, 1, 4, 9, \ldots\}$. From example A-4, it was shown that the inverse z transform of $X(z)$ should be $x(n) = n^2$. This agrees with the first four computed sample values of the long-division expansion of $x(n)$.

Partial Fraction Expansion

When working with Laplace transforms, the inversion of a given nth-order $X(s)$ usually begins with a partial fraction or Heaviside expansion. The form appears as follows:

$$X(s) = \Sigma a_i X_i(s), \text{ order } \{X_i(s)\} = n_i \le n$$

The order of the individual terms [i.e., $X_i(s)$] is generally lower than $X(s)$ itself. If the order of $X_i(s)$ is sufficiently low ($n_i = 1$ or 2), it is reasonable to assume that $X_i(s)$ can be matched to the transform of an elemental function. The same technique can be used to invert a given z transform $X(z)$. In this case, a given nth-order $X(z)$ would be factored into

$$X(z) = \Sigma a_i X_i(z), \text{ order } \{X_i(z)\} = n_i \leq n$$

where, if n_i is small (i.e., $n_i = 1$ or 2), the inversion of $X_i(z)$ can be accomplished using the table of elemental functions.

The difficulty associated with factoring a given $X(z)$ into low-order terms is a function of the locations of poles of $Z(z)$. For

$$X(z) = \frac{N(z)}{D(z)} \quad \begin{array}{l} \text{order } \{N(z)\} \leq n \\ \text{order } \{D(z)\} \leq n \end{array}$$

the poles are given by those values of z which set $D(z) = 0$ and the zeros are solutions to $N(z) = 0$. The poles, or roots of $D(z)$, can appear in one of two forms:

Distinct

Repeated

The distinct or nonrepeated root case is by far the easiest to analyze. In this case

$$D(z) = \prod_{i=1}^{N} (z - p_i)$$

where p_i is either real or complex. If it is complex, the poles must appear in complex conjugate pairs. That is, if p_i is a complex root, then so is p_i^*.

Suppose that the n roots of an nth-order $D(z)$ are found to be

$$z = r_i \quad \begin{array}{l} \text{if } r_i \text{ is real and } D(r_i) = 0 \\ i = 1, 2, \ldots, K \end{array}$$

$$z = p_i \quad \begin{array}{l} \text{if } p_i \text{ is complex and } D(p_i) = D(p_i^*) = 0 \\ i = K+1, K+2, \ldots, (N+K)/2 \end{array}$$

Under such conditions

$$X(z) = a_0 + \sum_{i=1}^{K} \frac{a_i z}{(z - r_i)} + \sum_{i=1}^{(N-K)/2} \frac{b_i z}{(z - p_i)} + \frac{c_i z}{(z - p_i^*)}$$

$$= a_0 + \sum_{i=1}^{K} a_i H_i[z{:}r_i] + \sum_{i=1}^{(N-K)/2} b_i H_i[z{:}p_i] + c_i H_i[z{:}p_i^*]$$

where the first-order factors $H_i[z{:}\alpha_i]$ are defined in the obvious manner. The coefficients $\{a\}, \{b\}$, and $\{c\}$ are given by

$$a_0 = \lim_{z \to 0} X(z)$$

$$a_1 = \lim_{z \to r_i} \frac{(z - r_i)X(z)}{z} \quad i = 1, 2, \ldots, K$$

$$b_i = \lim_{z \to p_i} \frac{(z - p_i)X(z)}{z} \quad i = 1, 2, \ldots, (N-K)/2$$

$$c_i = \lim_{z \to p_i^*} \frac{(z - p_i^*)X(z)}{z} \qquad i = 1, 2, \ldots, (N - K)/2$$

The inverse z transform of $H_i[z{:}r_i]$ is defined by the elementary function $x(t) = \exp(-a_i t)$ or from

$$Z(x(t)) = \frac{z}{z - \exp(-a_i T)} = H_i[z{:}r_i]$$

if $r_i = \exp(-a_i T)$. Similarly, if $x(t) = \exp(-j\omega_i t)$, then

$$Z[x(t)] = \frac{z}{z - \exp(-j\omega_i T)} = H_i[z{:}p_i]$$

if $p_i = \exp(-j\omega_i T)$ or $p_i^* = \exp(j\omega_i T)$. It follows that

$$x(nT) = Z^{-1}(X(z)) = a_0 + \sum_{i=1}^{K} a_i \exp(-r_i T)$$

$$+ \sum_{i=1}^{(N-K)/2} b_i \exp(-j\omega_i T) + c_i \exp(j\omega_i T)$$

EXAMPLE A-12

Suppose

$$X(z) = \frac{z^2}{(z - 1)[z - \exp(-T)]}$$

$$= a_0 + \frac{a_1 z}{(z - 1)} + \frac{a_2 z}{[z - \exp(-T)]}$$

where

$$a_0 = \lim_{z \to 0} X(z) = 0$$

$$a_1 = \lim_{z \to 1} (z - 1) \frac{X(z)}{z}$$

$$= \lim_{z \to 1} \frac{z}{[z - \exp(-T)]}$$

$$= \frac{1}{1 - \exp(-T)}$$

$$a_2 = \lim_{z \to \exp(-T)} [z - \exp(-T)] \frac{X(z)}{z}$$

$$= \lim_{z \to \exp(-T)} \frac{z}{(z - 1)}$$

$$= \frac{\exp(-T)}{\exp(-T) - 1}$$

$$= \frac{1}{1 - \exp(-T)}$$

Then $x(nT) = \begin{cases} a_1 + a_2\exp(-nT) & \text{for } n \geq 0, \\ 0 & \text{otherwise} \end{cases}$

For the repeated root case, the nth-order polynomial $D(z)$ can be factored in terms of L distinct roots such that

$$D(z) = \prod_{i=1}^{L} (z - p_i)^{n(i)}$$

$$n = \sum_{i=1}^{L} n(i)$$

where $n(i)$ is said to be the multiplicity of the root p_i. If p_i is a complex root, then so is its complex conjugate value p_i^*. If $n(i) = 1$ for all i, then the nonrepeated root case results. Otherwise, for

$$X(z) = N(z)/D(z)$$

then

$$X(z) = a_0 + \cdots + \frac{c_{i1}z}{z - p_i} + \frac{c_{i2}z}{(z - p_i)^2} + \cdots + \frac{c_{in(i)}z}{(z - p_i)^{n(i)}} + \cdots$$

Here

$$a_0 = \lim_{z \to 0} X(z)$$

$$c_{in(i)} = \lim_{z \to p_i} (z - p_i)^{n(i)} \frac{X(z)}{z}$$

$$c_{i1} = \lim_{z \to p_i} \frac{d[(z - p_i)^{n(i)}X(z)/z]}{dz}$$

$$\vdots$$

$$c_{ik} = \lim_{z \to p_i} \frac{1}{k!} \frac{d^{n(i) - k}[(z - p_i)^{n(i)}X(z)/z]}{dz^{n(i) - k}}$$

for $k \in [1, n(i)]$.

EXAMPLE A-13

Consider $X(z) = z^2/(z - 1)^2$, then the partial fraction expansion of $X(z)$ is given by

$$X(z) = \frac{a_{11}z}{z - 1} + \frac{a_{12}z}{(z - 1)^2} \qquad n(1) = 2$$

and

$$a_{12} = \lim_{z \to 1} \frac{(z - 1)^2 X(z)}{z}$$

$$= \lim_{z \to 1} z$$

$$= 1$$

$$a_{11} = \lim_{z \to 1} \frac{d[(z-1)^2 X(z)/z]}{dz}$$

$$= \lim_{z \to 1} (dz/dz)$$

$$= \lim_{z \to 1} 1$$

$$= 1$$

Then
$$X(z) = \frac{z}{z-1} + \frac{z}{(z-1)^2}$$

which consists of two elementary terms which can be inverted using standard tables:

$$Z^{-1}[z/(z-1)] = 1 \qquad \text{for } t \geq 0; \ 0 \text{ otherwise}$$

$$Z^{-1}[z/(z-1)^2] = nT \qquad \text{for } t \geq 0; \ 0 \text{ otherwise}$$

Therefore, $x(n) = 1 + nT$ for $t \geq 0$ and 0 elsewhere.

EXAMPLE A-14

Suppose

$$X(z) = \frac{3z^3 - 5z^2 + 3z - 0.5}{(z-1)^2(z-0.5)}$$

The partial fraction expansion of $X(z)$ has the form

$$X(z) = a_0 + \frac{a_{11}z}{(z-0.5)} + \frac{a_{12}z}{(z-1)} + \frac{a_{22}z}{(z-1)^2}$$

$$\quad\quad\quad\uparrow \quad\quad\quad\quad \uparrow \quad\quad\quad\quad \uparrow \quad\quad\quad\quad \uparrow$$

Kronecker   exponential   step function   ramp function

where
$$a_0 = \lim_{z \to 0} X(z)$$

$$= \frac{0.5}{0.5}$$

$$= 1$$

$$a_{11} = \lim_{z \to 0.5} \frac{(z-0.5)X(z)}{z}$$

$$= \lim_{z \to 0.5} \frac{(3z^3 - 5z^2 + 3z - 0.5)}{z(z-1)^2}$$

$$= \frac{(3/8 - 5/4 + 3/2 - 1/2)}{(1/2)(1/4)}$$

$$= 1$$

$$a_{12} = \lim_{z \to 1} \frac{(z-1)^2 X(z)}{z}$$

$$= \lim_{z \to 1} \frac{(3z^3 - 5z^2 + 3z - 1/2)}{z(z - 1/2)}$$

$$= \frac{(3 - 5 + 3 - 1/2)}{1/2}$$

$$= 1$$

$$a_{22} = \lim_{z \to 1} \frac{d(z - 1)^2 X(z)/z}{dz}$$

$$= \lim_{z \to 1} \left\{ \frac{9z^2 - 10z + 3}{z(z - 1/2)} - \frac{(3z^2 - 5z^2 + 3z - 1/2)((z - 1/2) + z)}{[z(z - 1/2)]^2} \right\}$$

$$= \left[\frac{9 - 10 + 3}{1(1/2)} \right] - \left\{ \frac{(3 - 5 + 3 - 1/2)(1/2 + 1)}{[1(1/2)]^2} \right\}$$

$$= 1$$

Therefore, upon collecting terms

$$x(nT) = \delta_K + (0.5)^{nT} + (1.0) + (nT)$$

The first few sample values of $x(nT)$ can be seen to be $\{x(n)\} = \{3, 5/2, 13/4, \ldots\}$ for $n = 0, 1$, and 2. As a check, consider the first several terms of $x(nT)$ produced by long division. Here

$$X(z) = \frac{N(z)}{D(z)} = \frac{3z^3 - 5z^2 + 3z - 1/2}{z^3 - 5/2z^2 + 2z - 1/2}$$

or

$$D(z) \overline{\smash{\big)}\, N(z)} \quad \frac{3 + (5/2)z^{-1} + (13/4)z^{-2} + \cdots}{}$$

which agrees with the derived time series.

If complex roots are encountered, the combining of first-order terms into second-order terms can be achieved using the following relationship:

1. Let $p_i = \alpha_i + j\beta_i$ and $n(i) = 1$ (nonrepeated) and $p_i^* = \alpha_i + j\beta_i$ and $n^*(i) = 1$ (nonrepeated)

$$X(z) = \frac{N(z)}{D(z)}$$

$$= \frac{N(z)}{D'(z)(z - \alpha - j\beta)(z - \alpha + j\beta)}$$

$$D'(z) = D(z)/(z - \alpha - j\beta)(z - \alpha + j\beta)$$

2. Partial fraction expansion

$$X(z) = \cdots + \frac{a_k z}{(z - \alpha - j\beta)} + \frac{a_{k+1} z}{(z - \alpha + j\beta)}$$

$$a_k = \lim_{z \to \alpha + j\beta} \frac{(z - \alpha - j\beta)N(z)}{zD(z)}$$

$$= \lim_{z \to \alpha + j\beta} \frac{N(z)}{zD'(z)(z - \alpha + j\beta)}$$

$$= \frac{N(\alpha + j\beta)}{(\alpha + j\beta)D'(\alpha + j\beta)(2j\beta)}$$

$$a_{k+1} = \lim_{z \to \alpha - j\beta} \frac{(z - \alpha + j\beta)N(z)}{zD(z)}$$

$$= \lim_{z \to \alpha - j\beta} \frac{N(z)}{zD'(z)(z - \alpha - j\beta)}$$

$$= \frac{N(\alpha - j\beta)}{(\alpha - j\beta)D'(\alpha - j\beta)(-2j\beta)}$$

3. Define

$$H_i(z) = \frac{a_k z}{z - p_i}$$

$$H_{i+1}(z) = \frac{a_{k+1} z}{z - p_i^*}$$

4. Define

$$H_k(z) \triangleq H_i(z) + H_{i+1}(z) = \frac{a_k z}{z - p_i} + \frac{a_{k+1} z}{z - p_i^*}$$

$$= \frac{(a_k + a_{k+1})z^2 + (-p_i^* a_k - p_i a_{k+1})z}{z^2 - 2\alpha_i z + (\alpha_i^2 + \beta_i^2)}$$

$$= \frac{c_i z^2 + d_i z}{z^2 + e_i z + f_i}$$

where c_i, d_i, e_i, and f_i are real and defined in the obvious manner.

5. Invert $H_k(z)$ using the table of elementary functions.

EXAMPLE A-15

Suppose

$$X(z) = \frac{z^3 - (\sqrt{2}/2)z^2 + z/2}{(z - \sqrt{2}/2)(z^2 - \sqrt{2}z + 1)}$$

The second-order polynomial $(z^2 - \sqrt{2}z + 1)$ can be factored into a pair of terms

$$z^2 - \sqrt{2}z + 1 = \left(z - \frac{\sqrt{2}}{2} - j\frac{\sqrt{2}}{2}\right)\left(z - \frac{\sqrt{2}}{2} + j\frac{\sqrt{2}}{2}\right)$$

$$\triangleq (z - p_1)(z - p_2)$$

where $p_2 = p_1^*$. The partial fraction expansion of $X(z)$ becomes

$$X(z) = a_0 + \frac{a_1 z}{z - \sqrt{2}/2} + \frac{a_2 z}{z - \sqrt{2}/2 - j\sqrt{2}/2} + \frac{a_3 z}{z - \sqrt{2}/2 + j\sqrt{2}/2}$$

where

$$a_0 = \lim_{z \to 0} X(z)$$

$$= 0$$

$$a_1 = \lim_{z \to \sqrt{2}/2} \frac{(z - \sqrt{2}/2)X(z)}{z}$$

$$= \frac{(1/2) - (1/2) + (1/2)}{(1/2) - 1 + 1}$$

$$= 1$$

$$a_2 = \lim_{z \to \sqrt{2}/2 + j\sqrt{2}/2} \frac{(z - \sqrt{2}/2 - \sqrt{2}/2)X(z)}{z}$$

$$= \lim_{z \to \sqrt{2}/2 + j\sqrt{2}/2} \frac{z^2 - (\sqrt{2}/2)z^1 + 1/2}{(z - \sqrt{2}/2)(z - \sqrt{2}/2 + j\sqrt{2}/2)}$$

$$= \frac{(1/2 + j1 - 1/2) - (1/2 + j1/2) + 1/2}{(j\sqrt{2}/2)(+j\sqrt{2})}$$

$$= \frac{j1/2}{-1} = -j/2$$

$$a_3 = \lim_{z \to \sqrt{2}/2 + j\sqrt{2}/2} \frac{(z - \sqrt{2}/2 + \sqrt{2}/2)X(z)}{z}$$

$$= \lim_{z \to \sqrt{2}/2 + j\sqrt{2}/2} \frac{z^2 - (\sqrt{2}/2)z^1 + 1/2}{(z - \sqrt{2}/2)(z - \sqrt{2}/2 - j\sqrt{2}/2)}$$

$$= \frac{(1/2 - j1 - 1/2) - (1/2 - j1/2) + 1/2}{(-j\sqrt{2}/2)(-j\sqrt{2})}$$

$$= \frac{-j1/2}{-1} = j/2 = a_2^*$$

Then, for $p_2 = -\sqrt{2}/2 - j\sqrt{2}/2$, it follows that

$$X(z) = a_0 + \frac{1z}{z - \sqrt{2}/2} + \frac{(-jz/2)}{(z + p_2)} + \frac{(jz/2)}{(z + p_2^*)} \qquad a_0 \to 0$$

$$= \frac{z}{z - \sqrt{2}/2} + j\frac{z}{2}\left(\frac{-p_2^* + p_2}{z^2 - \sqrt{2}z + 1}\right)$$

$$= \frac{z}{z - \sqrt{2}/2} + j\frac{z}{2}\left(\frac{-j\sqrt{2}}{z^2 - \sqrt{2}z + 1}\right)$$

$$= \frac{z}{z - \sqrt{2}/2} + \frac{\sqrt{2}z/2}{z^2 - \sqrt{2}z + 1}$$

Upon inspection of the table of elementary functions, we find that

$$Z^{-1}(z/(z - \sqrt{2}/2)) = \sqrt{2}/2)^{nT}$$

$$Z^{-1}[(\sqrt{2}z/2)/(z^2 - \sqrt{2}z + 1)] = \sin(\omega_0 nT)$$

for $\sin(\omega_0 T) = \sqrt{2}/2$.

Residue Calculus

The residue theorem was introduced earlier in this appendix. At that time, it was used to map the Laplace transform of a given $x(t)$, namely $X(s)$, into the z transform of the time series of $\{x(nT)\}$. The residue theorem can also be used to invert a z transform.

A function $X(z)$ is said to be analytic at a point $z = z_0$ if and only if it is single valued and uniquely differentiable at z_0. If $X(z)$ is analytic at z_0, it can be expanded as a Taylor series of the form

$$X(z) = \sum_{i=0}^{\infty} a_i(z - z_0)^i$$

$$a_0 = X(z_0)$$

$$a_n = \frac{1}{n!} \frac{d^n X(z)}{dz^n}\bigg|_{z = z_0}$$

If $X(z)$ is not analytic at z_0, a Laurent series is required and it is given by

$$X(z) = \sum_{i=1}^{\infty} a_{-1}/(z - z_0)^i$$

where a_{-1} is called the residue of $X(z)$ at z_0 and is given, in general, by

$$a_{-1} = \frac{1}{2\pi j} \int_{\substack{\text{closed} \\ \text{path}}} X(z)\, dz$$

Given knowledge of the residues of $X(z)$, the parent time series can be reconstructed as

$$X(n) = \sum_{K} \text{Res}\, (X(z)z^{n-1}, p_k)$$

where Res $[a, b]$ reads the residue of a at the point b.

EXAMPLE A-16

Suppose $X(z) = z^2/(z - 1)^2$. Using long division, it can be seen that

$$(z - 1)^2 = z^2 - 2z + 1 \overline{\big)\, z^2} \quad \frac{1 + 2z^{-1} + 3z^{-2} + \cdots}{}$$

Using a partial fraction expansion

$$X(z) = a_0 + \frac{a_{11}z}{(z - 1)} + \frac{a_{12}z}{(z - 1)^2}$$

where

$$a_0 = \lim_{z \to 0} X(z) = 0$$

$$a_{12} = \lim_{z \to 1} \frac{(z - 1)^2 X(z)}{z}$$

$$= \lim_{z \to 1} z$$

$$= 1$$

$$a_{11} = \lim_{z \to 1} \frac{d[(z - 1)^2 X(z)/z]}{dz}$$

$$= \lim_{z \to 1} (dz/dz)$$

$$= 1$$

Therefore,

$$X(z) = z_0 + \frac{z}{z - 1} + \frac{z}{(z - 1)^2}$$

and

$$x(n) = 1 + nT \qquad \text{for } n \geq 0; \ 0 \text{ otherwise}$$

Using the residue theorem

$$X(z)z^{n-1} = \frac{z^{n+1}}{(z - 1)^2}$$

$$= \frac{a_{-1}}{z - 1} + \frac{a_{-2}}{(z - 1)^2}$$

Computing a_{-1}, the residue, using the rules for repeating roots as presented in the partial fraction study

$$a_{-1} = \lim_{z \to 1} \frac{d(z - 1)^2 X(z) z^{n-1}}{dz}$$

$$= \lim_{z \to 1} \frac{dz^{n+1}}{dz}$$

$$= n + 1$$

which is in agreement with the other derivations.

Some care must be taken to ensure that all of the residues of $X(z)z^{n-1}$ are specified for all n. Example A-17 demonstrates this.

EXAMPLE A-17

Suppose $X(z) = (z + 1)^3/[(z + 1/2)(z - 1/2)^2]$. The term

$$X(z)z^{n-1} = \frac{(z + 1)^3 z^{n-1}}{(z + 1/2)(z - 1/2)^2}$$

has poles at $z = -1/2$ of multiplicity 1, and at $z = 1/2$ of multiplicity 2 for all $n > 1$. For the $n = 0$, an additional pole is created by $z^{n-1} = z^{-1}$ and it is seen to reside at the origin (i.e., $z = 0$). Therefore, the analysis must attend to these cases.

(a) For $n = 0$

$$X(z)z^{-1} = \frac{a_{-1}}{z} + \frac{b_{-1}}{z + 1/2} + \frac{c_{-1}}{z - 1/2} + \text{others}$$

$$\leftarrow \quad \text{residues} \quad \rightarrow$$

$$a_{-1} = \lim_{z \to 0} z[X(z)z^{-1}]$$

$$= \lim_{z \to 0} \frac{(z + 1)^3}{(z + 1/2)(z - 1/2)}$$

$$= \frac{1}{(1/2)(-1/2)^2}$$

$$= 8$$

$$b_{-1} = \lim_{z \to -1/2} (z + 1/2)[X(z)z^{-1}]$$

$$= \lim_{z \to -1/2} \frac{(z + 1)^3}{z(z - 1/2)^2}$$

$$= \frac{(1/2)^3}{(-1/2)(-1)^2} = -\frac{1}{4}$$

$$c_{-1} = \lim_{z \to 1/2} \left\{ \frac{d[(z - 1/2)^2 (X(z)z^{-1})]}{dz} \right\}$$

$$= \lim_{z \to -1/2} \left(\frac{d\{(z + 1)^3/[z(z + 1/2)]\}}{dz} \right)$$

$$= \lim_{z \to 1/2} \left\{ \frac{3(z + 1)^2}{z(z + 1/2)} - \frac{(z + 1)^3(z + z + 1/2)}{[z(z + 1/2)]^2} \right\}$$

$$= \frac{3(3/2)^2}{1/2(1)} - \frac{(3/2)^3(3/2)}{[(1/2)(1)]^2}$$

$$= \frac{27}{2} = -3 \, \frac{27}{4} = -6 \, \frac{3}{4}$$

Therefore

$$x(n = 0) = \sum_k \text{Res}(X(z)z^{-1}, p_k)$$

$$= a_{-1} + b_{-1} + c_{-1}$$

$$= 8 - \frac{1}{4} - 6 \, \frac{3}{4} = 1$$

As a check, the first team in a long division inversion of $X(z)$ yields

$$z^3 - z/2 - z/4 + 1/8 \,\overline{\left|\, z^3 + 3z^2 + 3z + 1 \right.}^{\textstyle 1z^0}$$

or $x(n = 0) = 1$ as derived.
Continuing, for the second case

(b) For $n > 0$

$$X(z)z^{n-1} = \frac{b_{-1}}{z+1/2} + \frac{c_{-1}}{z-1/2} + \text{others}$$

$$b_{-1} = \lim_{z \to -1/2} (z+1/2)[X(z)z^{n-1}]$$

$$= \lim_{z \to -1/2} \frac{(z+1)^3 z^{n-1}}{(z-1/2)^2}$$

$$= \frac{(1/2)^3(-1/2)^{n-1}}{-1^2}$$

$$= -(1/2)^2(-1/2)^n$$

$$= -(-1/2)^n/4$$

$$c_{-1} = \lim_{z \to 1/2} \frac{d(z-1/2)^2 X(z)z^{n-1}}{dz}$$

$$= \lim_{z \to 1/2} \frac{d[(z+1)^3 z^{n-1}/(z+1/2)]}{dz}$$

$$= \lim_{z \to 1/2} \left[\frac{(n-1)z^{n-2}(z+1)^3 + 3z^{n-1}(z+1)^2}{(z+1/2)} - \frac{(z+1)^3 z^{n-1}}{(z+1/2)^2} \right]$$

$$= (n-1)\left(\frac{1}{2}\right)^{n-2}\left(\frac{3}{2}\right)^3 + 3\left(\frac{1}{2}\right)^{n-1}\left(\frac{3}{2}\right)^2 - \left(\frac{3}{2}\right)^3\left(\frac{1}{2}\right)^{n-1}$$

$$= (n-1)\frac{27}{2}\left(\frac{1}{2}\right)^n + \left(\frac{27}{24} - \frac{27}{4}\right)\left(\frac{1}{2}\right)^n$$

$$= 27\left(\frac{n-1}{2} + \frac{1}{4}\right)\left(\frac{1}{2}\right)^n$$

$$= \frac{27}{2}\left(n - \frac{1}{2}\right)\left(\frac{1}{2}\right)^n$$

Then $$x(n) = \sum \text{Res}[X(z)z^{n-1}, P_k] \qquad n > 0$$

$$= b_{-1} + c_{-1}$$

$$= -\frac{1}{4}\left(-\frac{1}{2}\right)^n - \frac{27}{4}\left(\frac{1}{2}\right)^n + \frac{27}{2}n\left(\frac{1}{2}\right)^n$$

Using a partial fraction expression, as a check, one considers

$$X(z) = a_0 + \frac{a_1 z}{(z+1/2)} + \frac{a_2 z}{(z-1/2)} + \frac{a_3 z}{(z-1/2)^2}$$

$$a_0 = 0$$

$$a_1 = \lim_{z \to -1/2} (z+1/2)\frac{X(z)}{z}$$

$$= \lim_{z \to -1/2} \frac{(z+1)^3}{z(z-1/2)^2}$$

$$= \frac{(1/2)^3}{(-1/2)(-1)^2} = -\frac{1}{4}$$

$$a_3 = \lim_{z \to 1/2} \frac{(z+1)^3}{z(z+1/2)}$$

$$= \frac{(3/2)^3}{(1/2)(1)} = \frac{27}{4}$$

$$a_2 = \lim_{z \to 1/2} \frac{d[(z-1/2)^2 X(z)/z]}{dz}$$

$$= \lim_{z \to 1/2} \frac{d[(z+1)^3/z(z+1/2)]}{dz}$$

$$= \lim_{z \to 1/2} \left\{ \frac{3(z+1)^2}{z(z+1/2)} - \frac{(z+1)^3(z+z+1/2)}{[z(z+1/2)]^2} \right\}$$

$$= \frac{3(3/2)^2}{(1/2)(1)} - \frac{(3/2)^3(3/2)}{[(1/2)(1)]^2}$$

$$= \frac{27}{2} - \frac{27}{2}\left(\frac{3}{2}\right) = \frac{-27}{4}$$

Therefore

$$X(z) = -\frac{1}{4}\frac{z}{z+1/2} - \frac{27}{4}\frac{z}{(z-1/2)} + \frac{27}{4}\frac{z}{(z-1/2)^2}$$

referring to table A-1, it can be noted that every term except the last $[z/(z-1/2)^2]$ has a known inverse. The term in question will require the application of property 6 which results in the following analysis (for $T = 1$):

If
$$x(n) \longleftrightarrow X(z)$$

then
$$nx(n) \longleftrightarrow -z\,dX(z)/dz$$

Since $z/(z-1/2) \longleftrightarrow (1/2)^n$, it follows that

$$n(1/2)^n \longleftrightarrow -z\frac{d[z/(z-1/2)]}{dz}$$

where
$$-z\frac{d[z/(z-1/2)]}{dz} = -z\left[\frac{1}{(z-1/2)} - \frac{z}{(z-1/2)^2}\right]$$

$$= -z\left[\frac{-1/2}{(z-1/2)^2}\right]$$

$$= \frac{1}{2}\frac{z}{(z-1/2)^2}$$

which is seen to have the form of the unrecognized term. Therefore

$$X(z) = -\frac{1}{4}\left(\frac{z}{z+1/2}\right) - \frac{27}{4}\left(\frac{z}{z-1/2}\right) + \frac{27}{4}\left(\frac{z}{(z-1/2)^2}\right)$$

$$= -\frac{1}{4}\left(\frac{z}{z+1/2}\right) - \frac{27}{4}\left(\frac{z}{z-1/2}\right) + \frac{27}{2}\left[\frac{1}{2}\frac{z}{(z-1/2)^2}\right]$$

and
$$x(n) = -\frac{1}{4}\left(-\frac{1}{2}\right)^n - \frac{27}{4}\left(\frac{1}{2}\right)^n + \frac{27}{2}\left[n\left(\frac{1}{2}\right)^n\right]$$

for $n > 0$. This agrees with the result derived using the residue theorem.

A.3 DISCRETE SYSTEM STABILITY

It is generally assumed that a system is stable if and only if its outputs are bounded for every bounded input. There is no exclusion of time in the definition. Therefore, stability must be assured for all time ($t \rightarrow \infty$) if stability is to be generated at all.

If $\{h(nT)\}$ is the *impulse response* of a linear discrete system, the impulse response is stable if and only if

$$\sum_{n=-\infty}^{\infty} |h(nT)| < N < \infty$$

This condition will also guarantee that the filter is so-called *pulse* stable if the input to the system is given by $\{u(nT)\}$, where

$$|u(nT)| < M < \infty \qquad \text{for all } n$$

then the output of the filter, say $y(nT)$, where

$$y(nT) = \sum_{k=-\infty}^{\infty} h(kT)u(nT-kT)$$

is bounded by

$$|y(nT)| \le \sum_{k=-\infty}^{\infty} |h(kT)||u(nT-kT)|$$

$$\le MN \sum_{k=-\infty}^{\infty} |h(kT)|$$

$$\le MN$$

which is seen to be finite.

A system is said to be causal if $h(nT) = 0$ for all $n < 0$. A causal system, with a rational pulse transfer function $H(z)$, is stable if and only if all of its poles are contained within the unit circle in the z plane. This is often referred to as the *circle criterion*. If

$$H(z) = \sum_{n=0}^{\infty} h(nT)z^{-n}$$

where $|h(nT)| < N < \infty$, the sum converges for all $|z| < 1.0$.

This concept can be graphically interpreted as follows. It is well known that a continuous system having a transfer function $H(s)$ is stable if and only if the poles of $H(s)$ are in the left-hand plane. That is, the poles must reside in the restricted area shown in figure A-3. The poles will be mapped into the z plane using the standard z transform under the rule

$$z = \exp(sT)$$

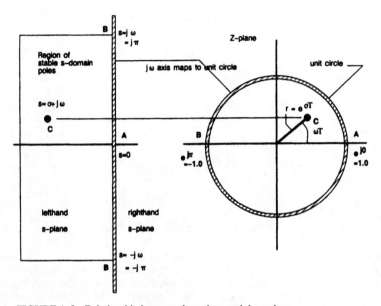

FIGURE A-3   Relationship between the s plane and the z plane.

Therefore, an arbitrary $s = \sigma + j\omega$, $\sigma < 0$ (for stability), is mapped into

$$z = \exp(\sigma T + j\omega T) = \exp(\sigma T)\exp(j\omega T)$$

where $\sigma T < 0$. It follows that $0 \leq \exp(\sigma T) < 1$. The mapping $z = \exp(\sigma T)\exp(j\omega T)$ can be viewed as a vector in the z plane of the form $r\exp(j\omega T)$. The length of the vector is r and it is oriented ωT radians from the real line. For all possible values of ωT, it is seen that $0 \leq r < 1.0$ and, as a result, the vector will reside within the unit circle.

In order to preserve uniqueness, the mapping $z = \exp[(s = \sigma + j\omega)T)]$ must remain single valued. Therefore, ϕ of $z = r\exp(j\omega T) = r\exp(j\phi)$ will be restricted to be a principal angle whose range is $-\pi < \phi \leq \pi$. Continuing, it follows that

$$|\omega T| < \pi$$

or, for $f_s = 1/T$ representing the sampling frequency in hertz, $\omega_s = 2\pi/T > 0$ in radians per second. Thus

$$|\omega T| = \frac{|\omega 2\pi|}{\omega_s} < \pi$$

and
$$|\omega| < \frac{\omega_s}{2}$$

where $\omega_s/2$ can be recalled to be the Nyquist frequency (i.e., one-half the sampling frequency).

The previous analysis was offered for the standard z transform. The bilinear z transform given by

$$z = \frac{1+s}{1-s}$$

is a one-to-one transfer of the s plane onto the z plane. The reverse mapping is given by

$$s = \frac{1-z}{1+z}$$

By letting $s = \sigma + j\omega$,

$$z = \frac{1 + \sigma + j\omega}{1 - \sigma - j\omega}$$

or

$$|z|^2 = zz^*$$

$$= \frac{(1+\sigma)^2 + \omega^2}{(1-\sigma)^2 + \omega^2}$$

For $\sigma < 0$, the demonstration is greater than unity, therefore $|z| < 1$. Once again, except this time using the bilinear z transform, the left-hand s plane is mapped into the interior of the unit circle. For $\sigma = 0$, it is noted that $|z| = 1$, or the mapping, is to the periphery of the unit circle in the z plane. Uniqueness was ensured for the standard z-transform map by restricting $|\omega T| < \pi$. No such restrictions are required for the bilinear z transform since for $\sigma = 0$

$$z = \frac{1 + j\omega}{1 - j\omega}$$

which is $z = 1.0$ for $\omega = 0$ and $z = -1.0$ for $\omega \to \infty$. Between $\omega = 0$ and infinity, z assumes unique values.

EXAMPLE A-18

Consider the fourth-order filter studied in example 15-9. Assume $T = 10^{-3}$ and

$$H(z) = \frac{0.001836(1 + z^{-1})^4}{(1.0 - 1.499z^{-1} + 0.848z^{-2})(1.0 - 1.5548z^{-1} + 0.649z^{-2})}$$

$$= \frac{0.00183 + 0.0073z^{-1} + 0.0110z^{-2} + 0.0073z^{-3} + 0.00183z^{-4}}{(1.0 - 3.054z^{-1} + 3.828z^{-2} - 2.291z^{-3} + 0.55z^{-4})}$$

$$= \frac{0.00183z^4 + 0.0073z^3 + 0.0110z^2 + 0.0073z^1 + 0.00183}{(z^4 - 3.054z^3 + 3.828z^2 - 2.291z^1 + 0.55)}$$

The stability of the filter is determined by the poles of $H(z)$ which are the roots to

$$z^2 - 1.499z + 0.848 = 0.0$$

$$z^2 - 1.5548z + 0.649 = 0.0$$

$$z = 0.7774 \pm j0.2113$$

or

$$z = 0.7495 \pm j0.535$$

which are all interior to the unit circle. Therefore, the filter is stable. Expanding

$$H(z) = H_0(z) + H_1(z) + H_2(z)$$

$$H_0(z) = H(z = 0) = 0.00336$$

$$H_1(z) = \frac{-0.07028z^2 - 0.03085z}{z^2 - 1.499z + 0.848}$$

$$= \frac{-0.07028(z^2 + 2.278z)}{z^2 - 1.499z + 0.848}$$

$$H_2(z) = \frac{0.06911z^2 + 0.04205z}{z^2 - 1.5548z + 0.649}$$

$$= \frac{0.06911(z^2 + 1.643z)}{z^2 - 1.5548z + 0.649}$$

The information in table A-1 can be used to invert some of the above terms directly. For instance,

$$h_0(z) = Z^{-1}[H_0(z)] = 0.00336\delta_K$$

The remaining two terms will be matched to the entries in the z transform tables. Two terms which have acceptable denominators are

$$\exp(at)\cos(\beta t) \longleftrightarrow \frac{z^2 - z\,\exp(aT)\cos(\beta T)}{D(z)} = H^1(z) \qquad \text{(A-1)}$$

and

$$\exp(at)\sin(\beta t) \longleftrightarrow \frac{z\,\exp(aT)\sin(\beta T)}{D(z)} = H^2(z) \qquad \text{(A-2)}$$

where $D(z) = z^2 - 2z\,\exp(aT)\cos(\beta T) + \exp(2aT)$. Matching the denominator of $H_1(z)$ to $D(z)$, we obtain

$$D(z) = z^2 - 2z\,\exp(aT)\cos(\beta T) + \exp(2aT)$$

$$= z^2 - 1.499z + 0.848$$

Therefore

$$\exp(2aT) = 0.848$$

or

$$aT = -0.08243$$

or

$$a = -82.43$$

and $-2\exp(aT)\cos(\beta T)$ $(\exp(aT) = 0.92087)$

$$= -1.84174\cos(\beta T)$$

$$= -1.499$$

or $\cos(\beta T) = 0.813905$

therefore $\beta T = 0.61995$ rad

or $\beta = 619.95$ rad/s

Equating the numerator of equations (A-1) and (A-2) to that of $H_1(z)$, it is seen that

$H^1(z)$:

$$K^1 N^1(z) = K^1(z^2 - z\,\exp(aT)\cos(\beta T)) = K^1[z^2 - z(0.749)] \neq N_1(z)$$

$H^2(z)$:

$K^2 N^2(z\,\exp(aT)\sin(\beta T)) \rightarrow$ not applicable due to absence of quadratic power of z

$H_1(z)$:

$$N_1(z) = -0.07028(z^2 + 2.2783z)$$

It is apparent that neither equation (A-1) or (A-2) can be used to model $H_1(z)$. However, a linear combination of these two can be tried. That is, let

$$H_1(z) = K^1 H^1(z) + K^2 H^2(z)$$

or $N_1(z) = (-0.07028z^2 - 0.03085z)$

$$= \{K^1 N^1(z) = K^1[z^2 - z\,\exp(aT)\cos(\beta T)]\}$$

$$+ \{K^2 N^2(z) = K^2[z\,\exp(aT)\sin(\beta T)]\}$$

$$= K^1(z^2 - 0.749z) + K^2(0.5349z)$$

Therefore,

$$K^1 = -0.07028$$

and $$K^2 = \frac{(0.749K^1 - 0.03085)}{0.5349}$$

$$= -0.15608$$

Finally, the inverse z transform of $H_1(z)$ becomes

$$h_1(z) = -0.07028\exp(-82.43t)\cos(619.95t)$$

$$-0.15608\exp(-82.43t)\sin(619.95t)$$

$$= \exp(-82.43t)[-0.07028\cos(619.95t) - 0.15608\sin(619.95t)]$$

$$= 0.1712\exp(-82.43t)[\cos(619.95t - 114.24°)]$$

The same procedure would be used to invert $H_2(z)$.

A.4 DISCRETE FOURIER TRANSFER

The representation of a signal by its frequency domain signature is called spectrum analysis. The decomposition of an arbitrary waveform into a set of sinusoidal components was known to Fourier in 1822. During the intervening century and a half, the techniques of Fourier have been used to develop new theory, focusing on the design of analog communication systems and engineering analyses. During this time, little was accomplished in the area of computing spectra. However, the advent of the digital computer provided the means by which efficient computer algorithms could be brought to bear on the problem. Initially, the availability of large-scale digital computers in the 1960s had little initial impact on spectral analysis. These software-based systems were slow and they consumed large amounts of computer memory. It was not until the Cooley-Tukey algorithm was published and accepted that spectral analysis harnessed the power of the modern digital computers. The Cooley-Tukey algorithm is a representative of a general class of discrete Fourier transforms, called the fast Fourier transform (FFT).

The continuous Fourier transform (CFT) transforms a class of time-domain signals, denoted $x(t)$, into the frequency domain. The inverse operation is called the inverse continuous Fourier transform (ICFT). These operations are mathematically defined as follows:

$$X(f) = \int_{-\infty}^{\infty} x(t)\exp(-j2\pi ft)\, dt \qquad \text{(CFT)}$$

$$X(t) = \int_{-\infty}^{\infty} X(f)\exp(j2\pi ft)\, dt \qquad \text{(ICFT)}$$

where $j = \sqrt{-1}$. Here, $X(f)$ is called the spectrum of $x(t)$. The spectrum $X(f)$ is a description of $x(t)$ in the frequency domain. It is characterized by a complex number representing magnitude and phase.

A special case of the Fourier transform is the Fourier series (FS). If $x(t)$ is periodic over some interval of time $[-T/2, T/2]$, it is possible to express the frequency-domain behavior of $x(t)$ as a discrete, rather than a continuous, series. A Fourier series can appear in either the trigonometric or the exponential form. The familiar trigonometric series is given by

$$x(t) = a_0 + \sum_{i=-\infty}^{\infty} a_i\cos(2\pi it/T) + b_i\sin(2\pi it/T) \qquad \text{(FS)}$$

where

$$a_0 = \frac{1}{T}\int_{-T/2}^{T/2} x(t)dt$$

$$a_n = \frac{1}{T}\int_{-T/2}^{T/2} x(t)\cos(2\pi nt)\, dt$$

$$b_n = \frac{1}{T}\int_{-T/2}^{T/2} x(t)\sin(2\pi nt/T)\, dt$$

For an exponential transform, use

$$\sin(a) = [\exp(ja) - \exp(-ja)]/2j$$
$$\cos(a) = [\exp(ja) + \exp(-ja)]/2$$

The result is that an exponential Fourier series is given by

$$x(t) = \sum_{i=-\infty}^{\infty} A_i \exp(j2\pi i t/T)$$

where $A_0 = a_0$

$$A_i = \begin{bmatrix} (a_i - jb_i)/2 \\ (a_i + jb_i)/2 \end{bmatrix} \quad \begin{array}{l} \text{for } i > 0 \\ \text{for } i < 0 \end{array}$$

The notable difference between a general CFT and the FS is resolution.

The CFT spectrum is a continuous image into the frequency domain, ranging from $-\infty$ to ∞ Hz. The spectrum generated by the Fourier series is a discrete cover of that interval. In fact, if the interval of signal repetition (called the fundamental period) is T, thereby defining the fundamental frequency of $x(t)$ to be f_0 where

$$f_0 = \frac{1}{T}$$

then the Fourier series exhibits spectral information at kf_0 Hz only, $k = (\ldots, 2, -1, 0, 1, 2, \ldots)$. In terms of harmonics,

$$|k| = 0 \qquad \text{implies the 0 harmonic (DC)}$$
$$|k| = 1 \qquad \text{implies the first harmonic (fundamental)}$$
$$|k| = 2 \qquad \text{implies the second harmonic}$$

The discrete Fourier transform (DFT) is conceptually similar to both the CFT and the FS. It is like the CFT in form, except integration is replaced by summation. It is also like the Fourier series in that it is a transformation of a time-domain record of length T into the discrete frequency domain. However, it differs from both in that it transforms a discrete time-domain record into the frequency domain. A principal difference is that the frequency spectrum of a DFT does not range from $-\infty$ to ∞ Hz but resides in a finite subinterval of that infinite interval. The hierarchy of Fourier transforms is diagrammed in figure A-4.

A time-series record of a signal $x(t)$ is generated by sampling. If a sample is taken every Δt s for a total of T s, the time series record of $x(t)$ would consist of N sample values, where

$$N = T/\Delta t$$

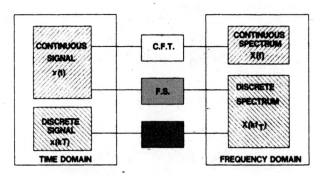

FIGURE A-4 Family of Fourier transforms.

The time series record

$$x(0\Delta t), x(1\Delta t)x(2\Delta t), \ldots, x[(N-1)\Delta t)]$$

is denoted

$$x(0), x(1), x(2), \ldots, x(N-1)$$

Again, let the fundamental frequency (first harmonic) of $x(t)$ be denoted f_0, where

$$f_0 = 1/T \text{ Hz}$$

or in radians per second,

$$\omega_0 = 2\pi f_0 \qquad \text{rad/s}$$

Then the discrete Fourier transform can be defined to be

$$X(i) = \frac{1}{N} \sum_{k=0}^{N-1} x(k)\, W_N^{ik} \qquad (i = 0, 1, \ldots, N-1) \qquad \text{(DFT)}$$

and the inverse discrete Fourier transform is given by

$$x(k) = \sum_{i=0}^{N-1} X(i)\, W_N^{-ik} \qquad (i = 0, 1, \ldots, N-1) \qquad \text{(IDFT)}$$

where

$$W_N^{ik} = \exp(-2\pi j i k/N) \qquad (j = \sqrt{-1})$$

The frequency components of the discrete Fourier transform are located at kf_0, $k = 0, 1, 2, \ldots, N-1$. This process is characterized in block diagram form in figure A-5. Here the sampling is assumed to be performed by a rotating switch completing a cycle every T s. The time interval between samples is the sampling rate Δt, where $\Delta t = T/N$ s.

One of the interesting features of the DFT is that both the time-series sample values and Fourier coefficients, namely $x(k)$ and $X(i)$, are periodic. That is, for m an integer

$$x(k) = x(mN + k) \qquad \text{time series}$$
$$X(i) = X(mN + i) \qquad \text{harmonics}$$

In addition, if $x(k)$ is a real sequence of sample values, there is symmetry in the transformation of the time series. This symmetry in the frequency domain is about the so-called folding frequency f_F, where

$$f_F = \frac{Nf_0}{2}$$

In addition, the real components of $X(f)$, $\text{Re}[X(f)]$, have even symmetry about f_F whereas the imaginary components, $\text{Im}[X(f)]$, have odd symmetry (antisymmetry). The symmetry properties of $X(f)$ allow the spectral components of $X(f)$, existing from $N/2$ to $N-1$, to be interpreted as negative frequency locations. The periodic behavior of $X(f)$ gives rise to the relation

$$X(-k) = X(N-k) \qquad (k = 0, 1, 2, \ldots, N-1)$$

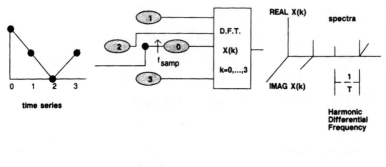

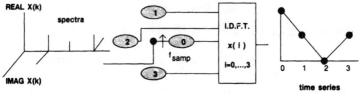

FIGURE A-5 Model of a DFT and IDFT transform for $N = 4$.

Then it follows that $X(k)$ and $X(-k)$ form a complex conjugate pair. That is,

$$X(k) = X(-k)*$$

where * denotes complex conjugation. The discussed symmetry properties are interpreted graphically in figure A-6.

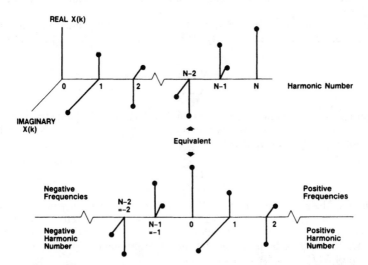

FIGURE A-6 Relationship between positive and negative frequencies of DFT harmonic database.

The Cooley-Tukey FFT algorithm is a numerically efficient method of producing discrete transforms. The generation of a spectra using the direct DFT equation would require approximately N^2 complex multiplications and additions. An FFT-produced spectra would require approximately $2N\log_2(N)$ complex multiply and add operations. The computational savings associated with the FFT method are shown in figure A-7. The increased efficiency is accomplished through the use of recursive operations on small groupings of data.

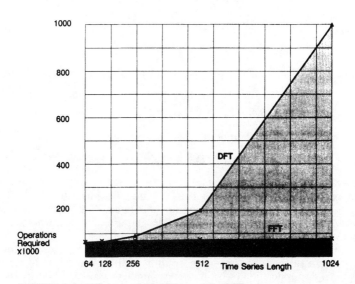

FIGURE A-7   Efficiency of the FFT versus the DFT.

The FFT of a time series input given by $x(k)$ $(k = 0, 1, 2, \ldots, N-1)$ begins with the times series further decomposed into two disjointed sequences, say $y(k)$ and $z(k)$, where

$$\left. \begin{array}{l} y(k) = x(2k) \\ z(k) = x(2k+1) \end{array} \right\} \quad k = 0, 1, \ldots, \frac{N}{2} - 1$$

That is, the sample values of $x(k)$ are alternately loaded into the array y and z. Let a discrete Fourier representation of the time series $y(k)$ and $z(k)$ be taken and denoted $Y(i)$ and $Z(i)$, respectively. In particular, $Y(i)$ and $Z(i)$ would satisfy

$$\left. \begin{array}{l} Y(i) = \displaystyle\sum_{k=0}^{(N/2)-1} y(k)\, W_N^{2ik} \\[2mm] Z(i) = \displaystyle\sum_{k=0}^{(N/2)-1} z(k)\, W_N^{2ik} \end{array} \right\} i = 0, 1, \ldots, \frac{N}{2} - 1$$

Noting

$$W^i Z(i) = W^i \sum_{k=0}^{(N/2)-1} x(2k+1) W^{2ik}$$

$$= \sum_{k=0}^{(N/2)-1} x(2k+1)\, W^{i(2k+1)}$$

the Fourier representation of $x(k)$ can be synthesized from the disjoint transforms $Y(i)$ and $Z(i)$ as follows:

$$X(i) = \sum_{k=0}^{(N/2)-1} x(2k)\, W_N^{2ik} + x(2k+1)\, W_N^{i(2k+1)}$$

$$i = 0, 1, \ldots, N-1$$

or $\qquad X(i) = Y(i) + W^i Z(i)$

A further simplification can be obtained if one recalls that $X(i)$ can be extended as

$$\left.\begin{array}{l} X(i) = Y(i) + W^i Z(i) \\ X(i+N/2) = Y(i) - W^i Z(i) \end{array}\right\} \quad i = 0, 1, \ldots, \frac{N}{2} - 1$$

Using these results, we may represent the negative frequency components as follows:

$$X(-i) = X*(i) = Y*(i) - W^i * Z*(i) = Y(-i) - W^{-i} Z(-i)$$

where * denotes complex conjugation.

Suppose, for example, that $N = 8$. The DFT and FFT generation of the spectra of $x(k)$, for this value of N, is block diagrammed in figure A-8. We note that the DFT required $N^2 = 64$ operations to produce the required spectra, whereas the FFT approach required only $2(N/2)^2 = 32$ operations.

If such savings can be reaped by partitioning the original time series into two sub-series, would a further decomposition result in additional savings? In general, yes. The optimal decomposition of N time series samples is known to satisfy the following equation:

$$N = \prod_{i=1}^{m} n_i = n_1 \times n_2 \times \cdots \times n_m$$

where n_i is a prime number. If all the n_i's have a value of 2 (for example, $8 = 2 \times 2 \times 2 = 2^3$), the algorithm is said to be radix (2) (radix means root). The example previously considered is reinvested using a radix (2) approach. The resulting mechanics of this operation can be found in figure A-9.

Error Sources

The utility of an FFT analysis is great. However, there are latent error sources embedded in this method that the user must be aware of. These error sources fall into three categories: aliasing, leakage, and the picket fence effect.

Aliasing. As the name implies, a signal may be impersonated (an alias) by another. It is the result of choosing the sample rate to be too slow to completely characterize the input signal. As a consequence, a bogus low-frequency signal impersonates the higher-frequency input signal. The aliasing problem can be removed by requiring that the sample rate chosen is to be at least twice that of the highest frequency residing in the signal to be sampled. This condition is often called the Nyquist condition. For example, suppose a signal $x(t)$ is bandwidth limited to a frequency

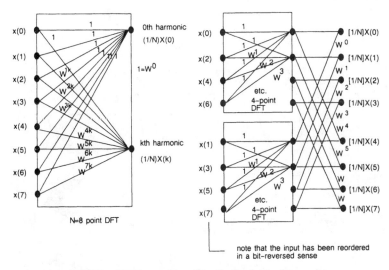

FIGURE A-8   DFT and FFT generation of an $N = 8$ point spectrum.

f_{max}. That is, there is a bandwidth limitation imposed on $x(t)$ in that all frequency components of $x(t)$ reside at frequencies less than or equal to f_{max} Hz; then a non-aliasing sample rate would be f_s where f_s is greater than or equal to $2f_{max}$ Hz. The effects of aliasing are shown in figure A-10.

Leakage.   Leakage is an undesirable harmonic distortion. The following example dramatizes the problem. Suppose a signal $x(t)$ is given by $x(t) = \sin(2\pi f_0 t)$; then only

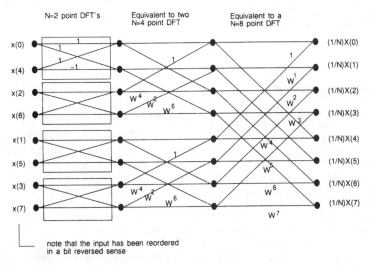

FIGURE A-9   Radix-2 FFT of length $N = 8$.

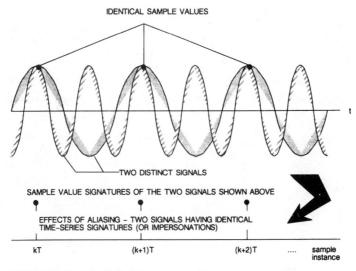

FIGURE A-10 Effects of aliasing.

one nontrivial DFT frequency component exists because the time series is periodic in the sampling interval. However, if $x(t) = \sin[(1.5)2\pi f_0 t]$, 1.5 periods are presented to the DFT. The resulting transform consists of a number of components which account for the energy in a signal not exactly at f_0 Hz. The problem of leakage is suggested in figure A-11.

The leakage problem can be minimized by establishing a sampling interval that is long compared to the fundamental period of the signal to be analyzed. The problem of leakage also may be reduced by a periodicity-inducing filter. Such a filter is used to make an aperiodic time series appear "nearly" periodic. For example, a popular periodicity-inducing filter is the Hamming filter. Over a period T_0, the Hamming filter, denoted $H(t)$, satisfies

$$H(t) = \frac{1}{2} [1 - \cos(2\pi f_0 t)]$$

The Hamming filter will alter an input process, say $x(t)$, as follows:

$$y(t) = H(t)x(t)$$

where $y(t)$ represents the filter output. Suppose the value of $x(0)$ is different from the value of $x(T_0)$. Then it is obvious that the process $x(t)$ is aperiodic. However, the output $y(t)$ will have identical end-point values, namely, $y(0) = t(T_0) = 0$. In addition, $y(t)$ will appear to be generally more periodic over the interval 0 to T_0. The effects of windowing are shown in figure A-12.

Picket Fence Effect. A third source of error is the picket fence effect. The DFT can be envisioned as a set of narrow bandpass filters whose center frequencies are located at k/T Hz, $k = 0, 1, 2, \ldots, N - 1$. The combined effect of these filters is graphically interpreted in figure A-13. The FFT filter response curve resembles a picket

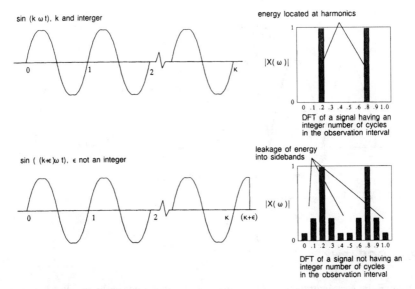

FIGURE A-11 Effects of leakage.

fence. The frequency components of an input signal $x(t)$ that reside at $k/T = kf_0$ Hz will be transformed without distortion. However, the frequency components of $x(t)$ that reside at noninteger multiples of f_0 are transformed with distortion.

Ensemble-averaging techniques can be used to minimize the effects of the picket fence effect. Interpolation methods, which minimize the effects of this error source, are also available.

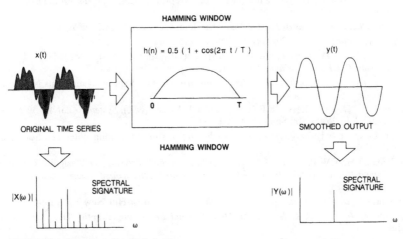

FIGURE A-12 Example of windowing.

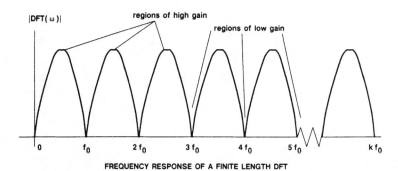

FREQUENCY RESPONSE OF A FINITE LENGTH DFT

FIGURE A-13   Picket fence effect.

BIBLIOGRAPHY

Blahut, R. E., *Fast Algorithms for Digital Signal Processing,* Addison-Wesley, Reading, Mass., 1985.

Bracewell, R., *The Fourier Transform and Its Applications,* McGraw-Hill, New York, 1978.

Brigham, E. O., *The Fast Fourier Transform,* Prentice-Hall, Englewood Cliffs, N.J., 1974.

Cadzow, J. A., *Discrete Time Systems,* Prentice-Hall, Englewood Cliffs, N.J., 1974.

Cheney, E. W., *Introduction to Approximation Theory,* McGraw-Hill, New York, 1966.

Childers, D. G. (ed.), *Modern Spectrum Analysis,* IEEE Press, New York, 1978.

Churchill, R. V., *Introduction to Complex Variables and Applications,* McGraw-Hill, New York, 1978.

Digital Signal Processing Committee of IEEE ASSPS, *Programs for Digital Signal Processing,* IEEE Press, New York, 1979.

Fourier, J., *Theorie analytique de la chaleur,* 1822, Reprint of English translation, Dover, New York, 1955.

Guillemin, E. A., *Synthesis of Passive Networks,* John Wiley and Sons, New York, 1957.

Haykin, S., *Communication Systems,* John Wiley and Sons, New York, 1983.

Heideman, M. T., D. Johnson, and C. S. Burrus, "Gauss and the History of the Fast Fourier Transform," *IEEE ASSP Magazine,* vol. 1, no. 4, October 1984, pp. 14–21.

Jury, E. I., *Theory and Application of the z-Transform Method,* John Wiley and Sons, New York, 1964.

Kaiser, J. F., "Digital Filters," in F. F. Kuo and J. F. Kasier (eds.), *Systems Analysis by Digital Computer,* John Wiley and Sons, New York, 1966.

Kuo, F. F., and J. F. Kaiser, *System Analysis by Digital Computer,* John Wiley and Sons, New York, 1966.

McClellan, J. H., T. W. Parks, and L. R. Rabiner, "A Computer Program for Designing Optimum FIR Linear Phase Digital Filters," *IEEE Trans. Audio Electroacoust.,* vol. AU-21, December 1973, pp. 506–526.

Papoulis, A., *The Fourier Integral and Its Applications,* McGraw-Hill, New York, 1962.

Oppenheim, A. V., and R. W. Schafer, *Digital Signal Processing,* Prentice-Hall, Engelwood Cliffs, N.J., 1975.

Rabiner, L. R., and B. Gold, *Theory and Application of Digital Signal Processing,* Prentice-Hall, Englewood Cliffs, N.J., 1975.

Roberts, A. R., and C. T. Mullis, *Digital Signal Processing*, Addison-Wesley, Reading, Mass., 1987.

Shannon, C. E., "Communicators in the Presence of Noise," *Proc. of the IRE*, vol. 30, no. 1, 1949.

————, *Digital Filter Handbook*, Marcel Dekker, New York, 1984.

———— and S. L. Smith, *Digital Signal Processing in Fortran*, Lexington Books, Lexington, Mass., 1965.

Tretter, S. A., *Introduction to Discrete Time Spectral Analysis*, John Wiley and Sons, New York, 1975.

Van Valkenburg, M. E., *Analog Filter Design*, Holt, Rinehart and Winston, New York, 1982.

Widrow, B., and S. D. Stearns, *Adaptive Signal Processing*, Prentice-Hall, Englewood Cliffs, N.J., 1985.

Wylie, C. R., Jr., *Advanced Engineering Mathematics*, McGraw-Hill, New York, 1966.

APPENDIX B
THE TMS320

Digital signal processing (DSP) is a rapidly expanding field. Much of the force behind this movement is the availability of powerful, low-cost applications-specific integrated circuits (ASIC) and DSP microprocessors. These devices are intended to serve the needs of a number of industries, each having its own performance objectives. For example, the sample rate requirements of typical applications are summarized below:

Control	1 kHz
Telecommunications	8 kHz
Speech	8–10 kHz
Audio	50 kHz
Video (frame rate)	30 Hz
Video (pixel rate)	14 MHz

Input data, in these applications, must be sampled or acquired, stored, manipulated, and exported at very high rates. Data conversion and memory technology have advanced to the point at which low-cost solutions are now commercially available. However, up until recently, low-cost data processors meant general-purpose microprocessors (e.g., INTEL 8086). It was found that the ALUs of these generic devices were generally too limited to support the high numeric data processing rates demanded by real-time DSP applications.

Digital signal processing is also a compute-bound operation. The atomic digital signal processing operation is the multiply-accumulate call. To overcome this problem, the semiconductor industry has introduced a number of digital signal processing microprocessors to the marketplace. Since the early 1980s, the Texas Instruments TMS320 series has been the most visible example of this technology. The TMS320C10 is a typical member of the family. It brings to the designer a 165-mW chip with a Harvard architecture, a 16- by 16-bit full-precision multiplier, input/output ports to memory and peripherals, 144-word on-chip RAM and 1.5K-word on-chip masked ROM. The TMS320C10 is rated at 5 million instructions per second (MIPS) and has a per-unit cost on the order of $50. A typical configuration is shown in figure B-1.

Normally, analog signal conditioning equipment is found at the front end of a DSP system. It normally performs several tasks including analog-to-digital conver-

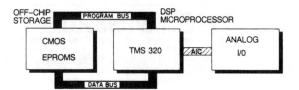

FIGURE B-1   TMS320 architecture.

sion (ADC) and antialiasing analog filtering. One device, for example, is the
TMC29C1X (X equals 8 or 9). This device encodes analog input to an 8-bit word
after the data have been passed through a μ-law compander. Mu-law (μ-law) companding has been effectively used to compress speech without significant loss of
intelligibility. As a rule of thumb, an 8-bit companded speech converter is equivalent
to a 12-bit uncompanded (linear) converter.

In front of the ADC are antialiasing filters. Generally these are analog devices.
They can be fabricated in many technologies. The filter cutoff frequency is set at or
near half the sampling frequency. It is important that the filters have good near-
linear phase behavior if precise filtering is to take place.

At the center of the system is the DSP microprocessor. It is interfaced to optional
off-chip programs and data storage devices. The analog interface chip (AIC) provides A/D, D/A, and I/O services. The AIC-TLC32040, for example, integrates an
antialiasing input filter, a 14-bit A/D, a 14-bit D/A, and a low-pass output filter on a
$20 chip.

The architecture of the TMS320 differs from traditional microprocessors in that it

Employs a Harvard architecture

Makes use of extensive pipelining

Possesses a dedicated multiplier

Incorporates a special DSP instruction set

Has a fast instruction cycle

A strict Harvard architecture would require that program and data memories be distinct, physically separate, and in command of their own bus. As such, full overlap of
instruction and data fetches can take place. In a traditional (non-Harvard) microprocessor, instructions and data are stored in common memory and share a common
bus. Here, no overlap takes place and, as a result, execution cycle times suffer. The
TMS320 uses a modified Harvard architecture which allows some transfers between
the program and data space to take place. This modification eliminates the need for
a separate coefficient ROM.

Pipelining is a standard technique used to increase the effective throughput of
the system. Currently, three levels of pipelining are being used which are called:

Prefetch

Decode

Execute

During any instruction cycle, all three states are active in the order indicated.

The instruction set of the TMS320 series was designed to provide support for the
following operations:

Digital signal processing
  Digital filtering
  Correlation
  Windowing
  Discrete Fourier transforms
  Radar, sonar, seismic processing
Instrumentation
  Spectrum (model) analysis
  Phase-locked loops
  Statistical signal processing
  Transient analysis
  Waveforms generation
Image processing
  Pattern recognition
  Image enhancement
  Image compression

Telecommunications
  Adaptive line equalizers
  Companding
  Tone generation
  Modems
  AM, FM, PM systems
  Encryption
  Spread spectrum
Speech processing
  Speech analysis
  Speech synthesis
  Vocoders
  Speaker verification
Numeric processing
  Multiply-accumulate
  Scaling
  Rotations
  Function generation

The TMS320 provides the user with approximately 60 instructions. These include branch instructions, table reads, table writes, subroutine calls, interrupt servers, and others. Direct, indirect, and immediate (i.e., instruction word contains the value of the immediate operand) memory addressing modes are provided.

The instruction set includes:

Mnemonic	Description
Accumulator Memory Reference Instructions	
ABS	Absolute value of accumulator
ADD	Add to accumulator with shift
ADDH	Add to high accumulator
ADDS	Add to low accumulator with sign extension suppressed
ADDT	Add to accumulator with shift specified to T register
ADLK	Add to accumulator long immediate with shift
AND	AND with accumulator
ANDK	AND immediate with accumulator with shift
CMPL	Complement accumulator
LAC	Load accumulator with shift
LACK	Load accumulator immediate short
LACT	Load accumulator with shift specified by T register
LALK	Load accumulator long immediate with shift
NEG	Negate accumulator
NORM	Normalize contents of accumulator
OR	OR with accumulator
ORK	OR immediate with accumulator with shift
SACH	Store high accumulator with shift
SACL	Store low accumulator with shift
SBLK	Subtract from accumulator long immediate with shift
SFL	Shift accumulator left
SFR	Shift accumulator right
SUB	Subtract from accumulator with shift
SUBC	Conditional subtract
SUBH	Subtract from high accumulator
SUBC	Subtract from low accumulator with sign extension suppressed

Mnemonic	Description
	Accumulator Memory Reference Instructions
SUBT	Subtract from accumulator with shift specified by T register
XOR	Exclusive-OR with accumulator
XORK	Exclusive-OR immediate with accumulator with shift
ZAC	Zero accumulator
ZALH	Zero low accumulator and load high accumulator
ZALS	Zero accumulator and load low accumulator with sign extension suppressed
	Auxiliary Registers and Data Page Pointer Instructions
CMPR	Compare auxiliary register with auxiliary register AR0
LAR	Load auxiliary register
LARK	Load auxiliary register immediate short
LARP	Load auxiliary register pointer
LDP	Load data memory page pointer
LDPK	Load data memory page pointer immediate
LRLK	Load auxiliary register long immediate
MAR	Modify auxiliary register
SAR	Store auxiliary register
	T Register, P Register, and Multiply Instructions
APAC	Add P register to accumulator
LPH	Load high P register
LT	Load T register
LTA	Load T register and accumulate previous product
LTD	Load T register, accumulate previous product, and move data
LTP	Load T register and store P register in accumulator
LTS	Load T register and subtract previous product
MAC	Multiply and accumulate
MACD	Multiply and accumulate with data move
MPY	Multiply (with T register, store product in P register)
MPYK	Multiply immediate
PAC	Load accumulator with P register
SPAC	Subtract P register from accumulator
SPM	Set P register output shift mode
SQRA	Square and accumulate
SQRS	Square and subtract previous product
	Branch and Call Instructions
B	Branch unconditionally
BACC	Branch to address specified by accumulator
BANZ	Branch on auxiliary register $\neq 0$
BBNZ	Branch if TC bit $\neq 0$
BBZ	Branch if TC bit $= 0$
BGEZ	Branch if accumulator ≥ 0
BGZ	Branch if accumulator > 0
BIOZ	Branch on I/O status $= 0$
BLEZ	Branch if accumulator ≤ 0
BLZ	Branch if accumulator < 0
BNV	Branch if no overflow
BNZ	Branch if accumulator $\neq 0$
BV	Branch on overflow
BZ	Branch if accumulator $= 0$
CALA	Call subroutine indirect
CALL	Call subroutine
RET	Return from subroutine

Mnemonic	Description
	Control Instructions
BIT	Test bit
BITT	Test bit specified by T register
CNFD	Configure block as data memory
CNFP	Configure block as program memory
DINT	Disable interrupt
EINT	Enable interrupt
IDLE	Idle until interrupt
LST	Load status register ST0
LST1	Load status register ST1
NOP	No operation
POP	Pop top of stack to low accumulator
POPD	Pop top of stack to data memory
PSHD	Push data memory value onto stack
PUSH	Push low accumulator onto stack
ROVM	Reset overflow mode
RPT	Repeat instruction as specified by data memory value
RPTK	Repeat instruction as specified by immediate value
RSXM	Reset sign-extension mode
SOVM	Set overflow mode
SST	Store status register ST0
SST1	Store status register ST1
SSXM	Set sign-extension mode
TRAP	Software interrupt
	I/O and Data Memory Operations
BLKD	Block move from data memory to data memory
BLKP	Block move from program memory to data memory
DMOV	Data move in data memory
FORT	Format serial port registers
IN	Input data from port
OUT	Output data to port
RTXM	Reset serial port transmit mode
RXF	Reset external flag
STXM	Set serial port transmit mode
SXF	Set external flag
TBLR	Table read
TBLW	Table write

The TMS320 series currently exists in two versions, Generations 1 and 2. The first generation is formed by the following devices:

TMS32010

TMS32011

TMS320C10

TMS320C15/E15

TMS320C17/E17

The family features are:

1. Instruction cycle time: 160, 200, and 280 ns
2. On-chip data RAM: 144 words and 256 words (TMS320C15/E15; 320C17/E17)

3. 4K words of on-chip program EPROM (TMS320E15, 320E17)
4. External memory expansion up to 4K words
5. 16- by 16-bit full precision parallel
6. Barrel shifter
7. Parallel shifter
8. 4- by 12-bit stack for context switching
9. Auxiliary registering for indirect addressing
10. Dual serial ports (TMS32011, 320C17, 320E17)
11. On-chip companding (TMS32011, 320C17, 320E17)
12. Coprocessor interface (TMS320C17, 320E17)

The second generation is represented by:

TMS32020
TMS320C25

It exhibits the following attributes:

1. Instruction cycle time: 100 ns (TMS320C25) and 200 ns (TMS32020)
2. 4K words of on-chip meshed ROM (TMS320C25)
3. 544 words of on-chip data RAM
4. 128K words of total program and data space
5. Eight-level stack
6. Doubly-buffer serial port
7. Wait states for off-chip memory
8. Serial port for multiprocessing and interfacing to codecs
9. DMA (TMS320C25)
10. Bit reversing for FFT (TMS320C25)
11. Extended precision arithmetic (TMS320C25)
12. High-speed MAC/MACD from external memory (TMS320C25)

The performance of the two generations are compared below for applications reported by Lin, Frantz, and Simar:

Applications	1st Generation	2d Generation
FIR filter tap	400 ns	100 ns
256-tap FIR	9.25 kHz	37 kHz
LMS FIR tap	700 ns	400 ns
256-tap LMS FIR	5.4 kHz	9.5 kHz
Biquad element (5 multipliers)	2 μs	1 μs
Echo canceler	8 ms	32 ms

B.1 FIR DESIGN USING THE TMS320

The TMS320 can be effectively used to implement finite impulse-response filters (FIRs). Fast convolution can be achieved through the use of a high-speed accumulator and a repeat instruction once the filter parameters are passed to the TMS320 from a data record which has the structure:

```
FIR Type = RECORD
    Filter_Order : integer;
    Real_Coefficients : array [1...128] of reals;
    Integer_Coefficients : array [1...128] of integers;
END
```

The program, shown in figure B-2, loads the required coefficient set as well as data. Initialization includes:

1. Disable interrupts
2. Set overflow mode
3. Set sign extension mode
4. Set no shift for product register
5. Load filter coefficients to on-chip memory
6. Clear block memory for storing temporary variables
7. Load filter control variable to on-chip locations

During execution, the filter operation sequences are as follows:

1. Initialize and move data to on-chip locations
2. Read input from host or port
3. Process the input
4. Return processed value to host or port
5. Shift state variables and wait for next input
6. Continue upon return to 2

EXAMPLE B-1

A 127th-order low-pass FIR, having a passband over [0, 250] Hz, sampling frequency of 1 kHz, was designed. The filter's impulse response is found in figure B-3, the magnitude frequency response is in figure B-4, and the phase response is in figure B-5. Note that the FIR exhibits linear phase behavior.

The filter was presented with a dual sinusoidal input (figure B-6). The input spectrum is shown in figure B-7. In figures B-8 and B-9, the output time series and spectrum, produced by the TMS320, are presented. It is observed that the output time series begins with a transient period and then enters a steady-state regime. At steady state, the output time series is not an exact replica of the input due to the FIR filter action. In figure B-9, it can be observed that the first tone, located at 75 Hz, appears at the FIR output with a larger gain (and different phase) than the second tone, which resides at 260 Hz.

```
*
*
***********************************************************************
*                                                                     *
*                    FIR  filter   File-to-File                       *
*                                                                     *
***********************************************************************
*                                                                     *
*                                                                     *
*              FIR IMPLEMENTATION FOR THE TMS2020                     *
*                                                                     *
*                                          Eric M. Dowling            *
***********************************************************************
A1       EQU       >490     ; Address of A coefficient matrix off-chip.
X1       EQU       >510     ; Address of state variables off-chip.
DEC1     EQU       >42A     ; Address of the decimal scale - 1 off-chip.
TVAL1    EQU       >42B     ; Address of the timer value off-chip.
FVAL1    EQU       >42D     ; Address of the Filter Order - 1 off-chip.
XP1      EQU       >37E     ; Location of the next to the last state var.
A        EQU       >FF00    ; Location of A coefficient matrix on-chip.
X        EQU       >300     ; Location of state variables on-chip.
DEC      EQU       >380     ; Location of the decimal scale -1  on-chip.
TVAL     EQU       >381     ; Location of the timer value  on-chip.
FVAL     EQU       >383     ; Location of the Filter Order - 1  on-chip.
*
*
*
PAGE0    EQU       0
PAGE3    EQU       3
PAGE6    EQU       6
PAGE8    EQU       8
*
*
XN       EQU       >480     ; Location of the Input to the filter.
YN       EQU       >480     ; Location of the Output from the filter.
*
*
         AORG >0            ; Reset from the host sets program count to 0000 H
         B INIT             ; Branch to Initialization.
*
*
         AORG >400          ; This is the location host sets the filter.
INIT     EQU  $             ; Label Initialization.
*
*
         DINT               ; No interrupts should occur in this program.
         LDPK PAGE8         ; Page pointer is now set to page 8.
         SSXM               ; Set sign extention mode when shifting.
         SOVM               ; Set overflow mode.
         SPM 0              ; Product register will not shift after operation.
         LRLK AR2,>200      ; A-coefficients will now have on-chip address.
         LARP 2             ; A-coefficient register pointer is set to 2.
         RPT  FVAL          ; Repeat next instruction of data move to Block 0.
         BLKD A1,*+         ; Block move of data coefficients to on-chip.
         CNFP               ; Reconfigurate Block 0 to program Ram.
         LDPK PAGE6         ; Page pointer is now set to page 6
         LRLK AR2,X         ; Auxiliary register 2 has location of state var.
         RPT  FVAL          ; Repeat the next load instruction (FVAL+1) times.
         BLKD X1,*+         ; Loads the state variables block into the chip RAMP.
         LRLK AR2,>380      ; Aux. reg. 2 now points to location of DEC on-chip.
```

FIGURE B-2

```
            RPTK 3           ; Repeat the next data load instruction 4 times.
            BLKD DEC1,*+     ; Loads DEC, Tval, (DVAL), FVAL into the chip.
            LRLK AR4,>385    ; On-chip address of Input and Output register (I/O).
            LRLK AR2,YN      ; Output location stored on auxiliary register 2.
LOOP1       BIOZ LOOP1       ; Wait for HOST to set BIO to 1.
            RXF              ; Reset XF field to 0, HOST will wait for XF  1.
            LARP 4           ; Points to on-chip input location.
            BLKD XN,*        ; Moves state var. input to on-chip location.
            LDPK PAGE0       ; Next direct address reside in page 0.
            ZAC              ; Zero out the accumulator.
            MPYK 0           ; Zero out the product register.
            LARP 3           ; Point to on-chip state variable.
            LRLK AR3,X       ; Auxiliary req. 3 now points to state var location.
            RPT FVAL         ; Repeat next instruction (FVAL+1) Times.
            MACD A,*+        ; Multiply and accumulate A-coeff. * State variables
            APAC             ; Add the last multiplicand to the accumulator.
            LARP 2           ; Points to on-chip output location.
            RPT DEC          ; Repeat next Shift instruction (DEC+1) times.
            SFL              ; Shift left the accumulator by one bit.
            SACH *,0         ; Store accumulator high with no shift.
            LARP 3           ; Points to the next state variable.
            LRLK AR3,XP1     ; AR3 now points to the next state variable.
            RPTK 127         ; Repeats 128 times the next Data move instruction.
            DMOV *-          ; Shift down all state variables, the last one out.
            SACH X,0         ; Accumulator has a newly created state variable.
            SXF              ; Set XF to establish handshake with HOST.
LOOP        BIOZ LOOP1       ; Wait for HOST to handshake BIO signal.
            B LOOP           ; Unconditional branch to LOOP1.
            LRLK AR0,>FFFF   ; Dummy statement.
*
```

FIGURE B-2   (*Continued*)

```
*
*
**********************************************************************
*                                                                    *
*               FIR    filter    Analog-to-Analog                    *
*                                                                    *
**********************************************************************
*                                                                    *
*               FIR IMPLEMENTATION FOR THE TMS32020                  *
*                                        Eric M. Dowling   *
**********************************************************************
A1        EQU        >490     ; Address of A coefficient matrix off-chip.
X1        EQU        >510     ; Address of state variables off-chip.
DEC1      EQU        >42A     ; Address of the decimal scale - 1 off-chip.
TVAL1     EQU        >42B     ; Address of the timer value off-chip.
FVAL1     EQU        >42D     ; Address of the Filter Order - 1 off-chip.
XP1       EQU        >31D     ; Location of the next to the last state var.
A         EQU        >FF00    ; Location of A coefficient matrix on-chip.
X         EQU        >300     ; Location of state variables on-chip.
DEC       EQU        >71      ; Location of the decimal scale -1  on-chip.
TVAL      EQU        >72      ; Location of the timer value  on-chip.
FVAL      EQU        >74      ; Location of the Filter Order - 1  on-chip.
FVAL2     EQU        >75      ; Location start of MACD loop variable.
TEMP      EQU        >76      ;
DEC2      EQU        >77      ;
*
*
*
PAGE0     EQU        0
PAGE3     EQU        3
PAGE6     EQU        6
PAGE8     EQU        8
*
*
XN        EQU        >79      ; Location of the Input to the filter.
YN        EQU        >78      ; Location of the Output from the filter.
TIM       EQU        >1
ADC       EQU        >2
DAC       EQU        >2
IMR       EQU        >4
IMASK     EQU        >FFC2
*
*
          AORG >0            ; Reset from the host sets program count to 0000 H
          B START            ; Branch to Start.
          AORG >4
          B    ISR
          AORG >400          ; This is the location host sets the filter.
START     EQU  $             ; Label Initialization.
*
*
          DINT               ; No interrupts should occur in this program.
          LDPK PAGE0         ; Page pointer is now set to page 0.
          LRLK 1,IMASK
          SAR 1,IMR
          LDPK PAGE8
          SSXM               ; Set sign extention mode when shifting.
          SOVM               ; Set overflow mode.
          SPM 0              ; Product register will not shift after operation.
          CNFD
```

FIGURE B-2 (*Continued*)

```
           LRLK AR2,>200      ; A-coefficients will now have on-chip address.
           LARP 2             ; A-coefficient register pointer is set to 2.
           RPT  FVAL          ; Repeat next instruction of data move to Block 0.
           BLKD A1,*+         ; Block move of data coefficients to on-chip.
           CNFP               ; Reconfigurate Block 0 to program Ram.
           LDPK PAGE0
           LRLK AR2,X         ; Auxiliary register 2 has location of state var.
           RPT  FVAL          ; Repeat the next load instruction (FVAL+1) times.
           BLKD X1,*+         ; Loads the state variables block into the chip RAMP.
           LRLK AR2,>71       ; Aux. reg. 2 now points to location of DEC on-chip.
           RPTK 3             ; Repeat the next data load instruction 4 times.
           BLKD DEC1,*+       ; Loads DEC, Tval, (DVAL), FVAL into the chip.
           LAR AR3,FVAL       ; Aux.req.3 contains Filter Order - 1.
           LRLK AR0,>300      ; Aux.req.0 points to beginning of State Var block.
           LARP 3             ; Pointer for next instruction ( $300+FVAL --> AR3 ).
           MAR *0+            ; Aux.reg.3 will now point to last state var.
           SAR AR3,FVAL2      ; Saves last reg. of State Var to be use in loop1.
           LRLK AR2,YN        ; Output location stored on auxiliary register 2.
           LAC DEC
           SBLK 1,0
           SACL DEC2
           LAR AR0,TVAL
           SAR AR0,TEMP
           OUT TEMP,TIM
           LRLK AR0,>300
           EINT
           NOP
LOOP       B LOOP
ISR        IN XN,ADC
           LAC XN,0
           RPT DEC2
           SFR
           LARP 0
           SACL *
           ZAC                ; Zero out the accumulator.
           MPYK 0             ; Zero out the product register.
           LARP 3             ; Point to on-chip last state variable.
           RPT FVAL           ; Repeat next instruction (FVAL+1) Times.
           MACD >FF00,*-      ; Multiply and accumulate A-coeff. * State variables
           APAC               ; Add the last multiplicand to the accumulator.
           RPT  DEC           ; Repeat next Shift instruction (DEC+1) times.
           SFL                ; Shift left the accumulator by one bit.
           RPT DEC2
           SFL
           SACH YN,0          ; Store accumulator high with no shift.
           OUT YN,DAC
           LAR AR3,FVAL2      ; Reset for MACD loop.
           EINT
           RET
*
```

FIGURE B-2   (*Continued*)

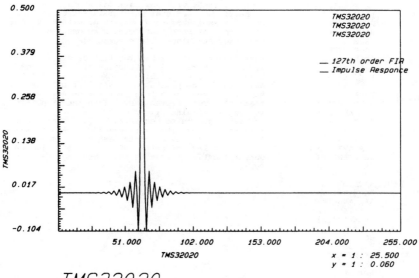

TMS32020

FIGURE B-3

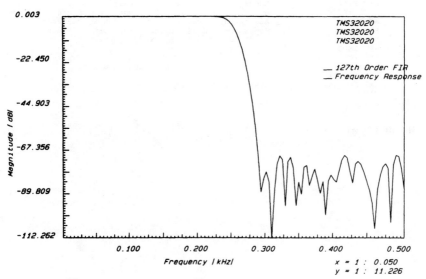

Frequency Response

FIGURE B-4

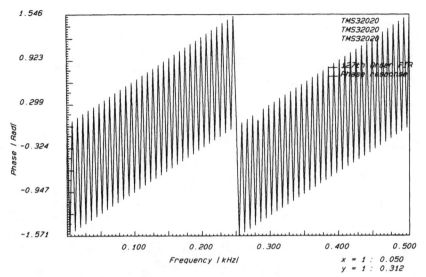

Phase Response

FIGURE B-5

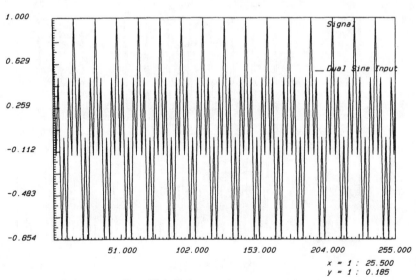

Signal Filtering

FIGURE B-6

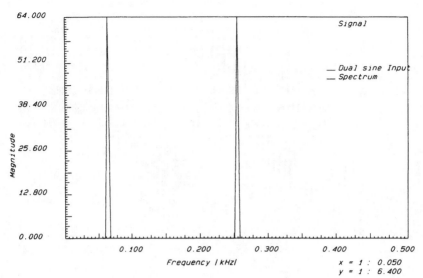

Frequency Response

FIGURE B-7

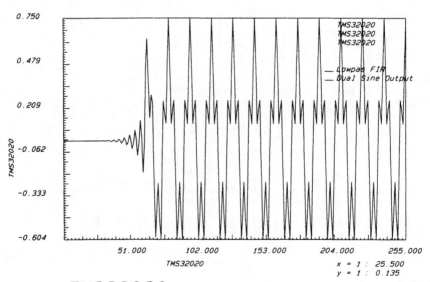

TMS32020

FIGURE B-8

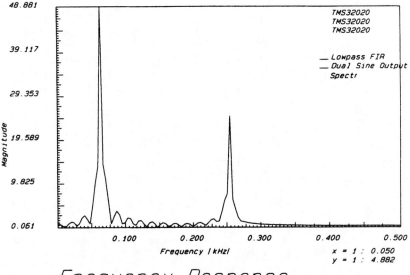

Frequency Response

FIGURE B-9

Technically, the second higher-frequency tone is outside of the passband. However, it is difficult for an FIR to implement a sharp transition (steep skirt) between passband and stopband. As a result, the unwanted output leaks into the output.

EXAMPLE B-2

Using the filter discussed in example B-1, and the piecewise continuous ramp input signal process shown in figure B-10, having the spectral signature shown in figure B-11, the output time series displayed in figure B-12 was produced using the TMS320 chip. Observe that there is a well-defined transient and steady-state behavior. The output spectrum is displayed in figure B-13. Finally, a mathematical model of the filter, being implemented by the TMS320, can be synthesized by ratioing the output and input complex signal spectra to produce a transfer function. From this, an impulse response can be realized.

B.2 IIR DESIGN USING THE TMS320

An IIR filter can also be implemented using a TMS320. A flowchart, for either file-to-file or analog-to-analog TMS320 processing, is presented in figure B-14. For example, a sixth-order cascade filter, consisting of three second-order sections, can be modeled as

$$\text{INPUT} * D_1 + X_1(1) * C_1(1) + X_2(1) * C_2(1) = \text{TEMP}$$

$$\text{TEMP} * D_2 + X_1(2) * C_1(2) + X_2(2) * C_2(2) = \text{TEMP1}$$

$$\text{TEMP} * D_3 + X_1(3) * C_1(3) + X_2(3) * C_2(3) = \text{OUTPUT}$$

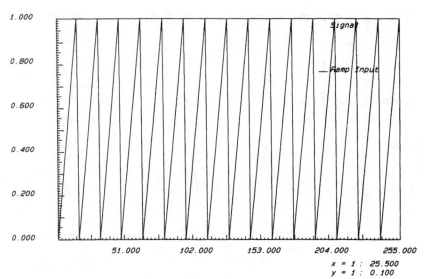

Signal Filtering

FIGURE B-10

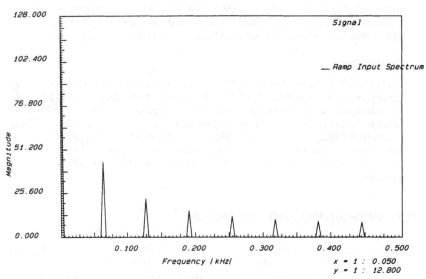

Frequency Response

FIGURE B-11

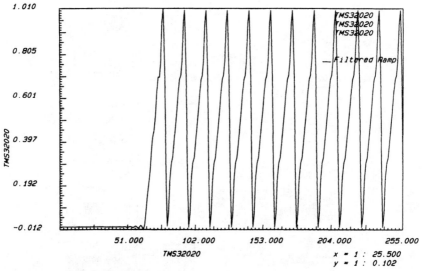

TMS32020

FIGURE B-12

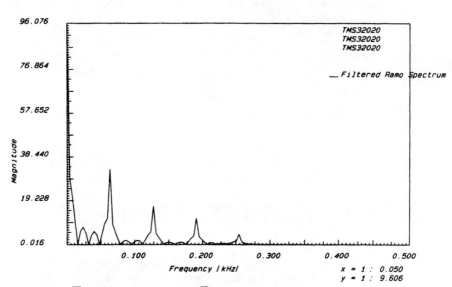

Frequency Response

FIGURE B-13

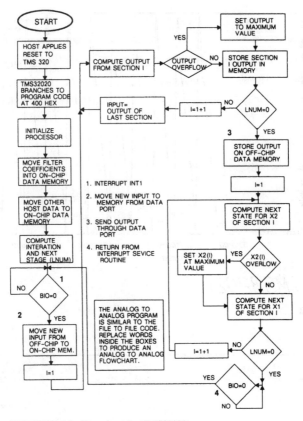

FIGURE B-14   Flowchart for TMS32020.

The *next state equations* calculate the new state variables of each section. These are computed after the output has been determined. The following equations compute the next state for section i.

$$\text{TEMP} = X_2(i)$$

$$X_2(i) = X_1(i) * A_i(21) + X_2(i) * A_i(22) + \text{OUTPUT}(i-1)$$

$$X_1(i) = \text{TEMP}$$

Handshaking between the host and the file-to-file TMS32020 programs must take place so that input and output sequence are properly managed. For example, suppose the host program supplies 256 inputs to the TMS32020 and then reads the 256 computed outputs. The required handshaking rules are:

1. The host must not write a new input to the TMS32020 until the host has read the output computed by the TMS32020 program using the last input.
2. The TMS32020 program must not read the next input before the host sends it.

Therefore, if the filter is specified by the four tuple (A, B, C, D) as defined in equation (15.5), access to the filter coefficient four tuple is shown by the pseudocode

```
for i = 1 to last section
    do begin
        get D(i)
        get X₁(i), C₁(i)
        get X₂(i), C₂(i)
    end
for i =1 to last section
    do begin
        get X₁(i), Aᵢ(21)
        get X₂(i), Aᵢ(22)
    end
```

As seen from the pseudocode, all filter coefficients are accessed in sequential order. Therefore, the coefficients should be stored in contiguous memory according to the data maps shown below:

$A_1(21)$	Section 1
$A_1(22)$	
$A_2(21)$	Section 2
$A_2(22)$	
.	
.	
.	
$A_8(22)$	

$C_1(1)$	Section 1
$C_2(1)$	
$C_1(2)$	Section 2
$C_2(2)$	
.	
.	
.	
$C_2(8)$	

$D(1)$	} Section 1
$D(2)$	} Section 2
$D(3)$	
$D(4)$	
.	
.	
.	
$D(8)$	

$X_1(1)$	Section 1
$X_2(1)$	
$X_1(2)$	Section 2
$X_2(2)$	
.	
.	
.	
$X_2(8)$	

The data are accessed by indirect register addressing which supports hardware autoincrement and decrement within an instruction. The next state variables, X, are initialized to zero and the unused filter section variables are filled with zeros.

Next, the two most important procedures are to generate the output and the next state variables. The output of a given section is calculated by (output of section $i-1$) $* D_i + X_1(i) * C_1(i) + X_2(i) * C_2(i) =$ (output of section i). The micro steps of this calculation are:

1. Get (output of last section)

2. Multiply (output of last section), D_i / Add product to ACC

3. Multiply $X_1(i)$, $C_1(i)$ / Add product to ACC
4. Multiply $X_2(i)$, $C_2(i)$ / Add product to ACC
5. Check overflow
6. Perform multiplication scaling
7. Store (output of section i)

These steps are repeated $LNUM$ (number of sections) times. The output of each section is stored in consecutive memory locations and then accessed sequentially for the purpose of computing the next state variables X_1 and X_2. In this procedure, the consecutive commands MPY and LTA are used to perform the multiply/accumulate operation in two cycles. The next state variables, X_1 and X_2, are generated as follows:

$$\text{TEMP} = X_2(i)$$

$$X_2(i) = X_2(i) * A_i(21) + X_2(i) * A_i(22) + \text{OUTPUT}(i-1)$$

$$X_1(i) = \text{TEMP}$$

The micro steps are

1. Multiply $X_1(i)$, $A_i(21)$ / Add product to ACC
2. Multiply $X_2(i)$, $A_i(22)$ / Add product to ACC
3. Check overflow
4. Add (output of last section) to ACC   ($\overline{\text{ACC}} = X_2(i)$)
5. Move old $X_2(i)$ into $X_1(i)$
6. Store ACC into $X_2(i)$

These steps are repeated $LNUM$ times.

Overflow detection and correction can be used to ensure that nonlinear distortion will not occur due to the input overdriving the system. However, it introduces a temporal overhead. For a sixth-order cascade IIR example, the maximum input frequencies of filters without overflow checking are:

$$[36 + 42 * (\text{filter order div 2})] * 200 \text{ ns} = 32.4 \text{ μs} \rightarrow 30.9 \text{ kHz}$$

With overflow checking they are:

$$[36 + 74 * (\text{filter order div 2})] * 200 \text{ ns} = 51.6 \text{ μs} \rightarrow 19.4 \text{ kHz}$$

It is shown that a 11.5-kHz penalty is paid for overflow detection. Overflow detection accounts for 37% of code execution time. Without overflow checking the analog-to-analog cascade program can operate for a higher frequency provided that the input is small enough that no overflow will occur.

EXAMPLE B-3

A sixth-order low-pass elliptic filter, having a −3-dB passband ranging over [0.0, $0.3f_{\text{Nyquist}}$] and a −65-dB stopband commencing at $0.4 f_{\text{Nyquist}}$, is given by

$$H(z) = \frac{(3.2z^6 + 2.3z^5 + 6.6z^4 + 4.9z^3 + 6.6z^2 + 2.3z^1 + 3.2) \times 10^{-3}}{(z^6 - 4.1z^5 + 8.2z^4 - 9.6z^3 + 6.9z^2 - 2.9z^1 + 0.6)}$$

$$= \frac{(3.2 + 2.3z^{-1} + 6.6z^{-2} + 4.9z^{-3} + 6.6z^{-4} + 2.3z^{-5} + 3.2z^{-6}) \times 10^{-3}}{(1.0 - 4.1z^{-1} + 8.2z^{-2} - 9.6z^{-3} + 6.9z^{-4} - 2.9z^{-5} + 0.6z^{-6})}$$

It can also be represented as

$$H(z) = K_0 + H_1(z) + H_2(z) + H_3(z)$$

$$K_0 = 0.005$$

$$H_1(z) = \frac{0.02z^2 + 0.07z}{z^2 - 1.6z + 0.7}$$

$$H_2(z) = \frac{0.02z^2 + 0.02z}{z^2 - 1.2z + 0.9}$$

$$H_3(z) = \frac{-0.05z^2 + 0.07z}{z^2 - 1.3z + 0.8}$$

The TMS320 code, which implements the parallel and direct II architectures, is presented in figure B-15. The results of implementing the sixth-order filter, using the TMS320 code, are displayed in figures B-16 and B-17. Superimposed on these figures are the actual magnitude spectra obtained from TMS320 implementation; the references are the ideal responses. The difference between the two spectra is due to finite word-length round-off errors effects.

The experiment was continued using a bandpass filter model. The results are reported in figures B-18 and B-19 where errors again can be attributed to finite word-length effects.

EXAMPLE B-4

For the filter defined in example B-3, a TMS320 cascade filter was designed. The impulse response shown in figure B-20 was produced. The magnitude frequency response is reported in figure B-21. The reason why the frequency response is not smooth is due to the distortion introduced by the finite word-length effects. The phase response is shown in figure B-22. It is observed that the highly irregular (nonlinear) phase behavior is the characteristic of the IIR filter.

Strengthening the test impulse by a factor of 20 would improve the signal to round-off error noise power ratio by a factor of $20^2 = 400$. The impulse, magnitude frequency, and phase response produced by the stronger test input are shown in figures B-23 through B-25. Comparing the frequency and phase responses (figure B-21 versus B-24 and figure B-22 versus B-25), it is seen that the quality of the spectrum is greatly improved. In general, we would like to adjust the amplitude of the input to be as large as possible, but it should not be so big as to cause dynamic range overflow. To illustrate this point, suppose the TMS320 16-bit word is set to have a binary point located at the fourth least significant bit. A real number x, in the range of $[1, 2]$, is then quantized into the TMS320 word X having a format as follows:

	16	15	14	13	12	11	10	9	8	7	6	5	4	3	2	1	0
$X =$	0	0	0	0	0	0	0	0	0	0	0	0	0	1	X	X	X	X

△
binary point

The difference between the real x and the quantized X is the round-off error ε and it is, on the average, equal to one-half of the least significant bit. Here the average round-

```
e          IDT          'F-TO-F'
*
*
***********************************************************************
*                                                                   *
*          DIRECT II IMPLEMENTATION FOR THE TMS32020                 *
*                                                                   *
*                                          Eric M. Dowling           *
***********************************************************************
*                                                                   *
*       This program implements the file to file DirectII            *
*     selection from the HOST program. The program                   *
*     initializes by placing all the coefficients in                 *
*     on chip memory. It then takes takes the summation of the       *
*     product of the state variables and C coefficients and          *
*     sends the result back to the HOST. It then takes the           *
*     the summation of the product of the state variables and        *
*     A coefficients and updates the sate variables. This            *
*     process finishes the algorithim of the DirectII filter.        *
*                                                                   *
***********************************************************************
X1         EQU          >420   ; Address of state variables off chip
DEC1       EQU          >42A   ; Address of the decimal scale off chip
TVAL1      EQU          >42B   ; Address of the timer value off chip
DVAL1      EQU          >42C   ; Location of D matrix from Host off chip
FVAL1      EQU          >42D   ; Location of the filter order-1 off chip
XP1        EQU          >6F    ; Location of the next to the last state var
X          EQU          >67    ; On chip location of the state variables
DEC        EQU          >71    ; Address of decimal scale on chip
TVAL       EQU          >72    ; Address of timer value on chip
DVAL       EQU          >73    ; Address of D matrix on chip
FVAL       EQU          >74    ; Location of the filter order-1 on chip
C1         EQU          >400   ; Address of C coefficient matrix off chip
A1         EQU          >40A   ; Address of A coefficient matrix off chip
C          EQU          >FF00  ; Location of C coefficient matrix on chip
A          EQU          >FF0A  ; Location of A coefficient matrix on chip
*
*
*
PAGE0      EQU          0
PAGE6      EQU          6
PAGE8      EQU          8
*
*
YN         EQU          >480   ; Location of the output from the filter
XN         EQU          >480   ; Location of the input to the filter
*
*
           AORG >0        ; Reset from the host sets program count to 0000H
           B INIT
*
*
           AORG >400      ; This is the location host sends the filter
INIT       EQU  $
*
*
           DINT           ; No interrupts should interfere with this program
           LDPK PAGE6     ; Page pointer is now set to page 8
           SSXM           ; Sign extension mode when shifting
           SOVM           ; Overflow mode
```

FIGURE B-15

```
          SPM 0           ;  Product register will not shift after operation
          LRLK AR2,>200   ;  Auxiliary register will now have on chip address
          LARP 2          ;  Auxiliary register pointer is set to 2
          RPTK 20         ;  Block move C and A coefficients to on chip
          BLKD C1,*+
          CNFP            ;  C and A coefficent now resides in program memory
          LDPK PAGE0      ;  page pointer points to page 0
          LRLK AR2,X      ;  Auxiliary register 2 has location of state variables
          RPTK 13         ;  Put state variables, filt. order, and dec shift on chip
          BLKD X1,*+
          LRLK AR4,>76    ;  On chip address of input and output
          LRLK AR2,YN     ;  Output location in auxiliary register 2
LOOP1     BIOZ LOOP1      ;  Wait for HOST to set BIO to 1
          RXF             ;  XF set to 0, Host will wait for XF 1
          LARP 4          ;  Point to on chip input location
          BLKD XN,*       ;  Move input to on chip
          LDPK PAGE0      ;  Next direct address reside in page 0
          ZAC             ;  Zero out the accumulator
          LT DVAL         ;  D matrix goes to temporary register for mult.
          MPY *           ;  D*Xn --> P reg.
          LARP 1          ;  Load aux pointer with 1
          LRLK AR1,X      ;  Aux reg. has state variable location
          RPT FVAL
          MAC >FF00,*+    ;  sum(State variables * C cofficients)--> acc.
          APAC            ;  add D*Xn to previous sum in acc.
          LARP 2          ;  Aux reg. pointer has 2
          RPT DEC         ;  scale the result in the accumulator
          SFL
          SACH *,0        ;  send the output to the HOST
          ZAC             ;  zero out the accumulator
          MPYK 0          ;  zero out the Product register
          LARP 1          ;  point to aux. reg. 1
          LRLK AR1,X      ;  load aux. reg. with state vaiable location
          RPT FVAL
          MAC >FF0A,*+    ;  sum(State variables * A coefficients)--> acc.
          APAC
          LARP 4          ; point to aux. reg. 4
          RPT DEC
          SFL             ;  scale the input signal and add it to next state var
          ADDH *          ;  put most significant digits added to accumulator
          LARP 3          ;  Point to aux. reg. 4
          LRLK AR3,XP1    ;  Point to next to the last state variable
          RPTK 8
          DMOV *-         ;  Starting with next state var, shift state var. out
          SACH X,0        ;  Accumulator has newly created state variable
          SXF             ;  XF handshake tells host processing is through
LOOP      BIOZ LOOP1      ;  Wait for host to handshake BIO signal
          B LOOP
          LRLK AR0,>FFFF  ;  dummy statement, assembler does not
*                            like to end on previous infinite loop
```

FIGURE B-15   (*Continued*)

```
          IDT        'DIRII'
*****************************************************************************
*                                                                          *
*           DIRECT II FILTER IMPLEMENTATION FOR THE TMS32020               *
*                                                  Eric M. Dowling         *
*****************************************************************************
*
*  The following variables will be initialized by the IBM-PC, through
*  the board interface.
*
X1       EQU        >420         * Off-Chip addresses (from interface)
DEC1     EQU        >42A
TVAL1    EQU        >42B
DVAL1    EQU        >42C
FVAL1    EQU        >42D
XP1      EQU        >70
X        EQU        >68          * on-Chip addresses (moved on chip by TMS)
DEC      EQU        >72
TVAL     EQU        >73
DVAL     EQU        >74
FVAL     EQU        >75
TEMP     EQU        >76
DEC2     EQU        >77
C1       EQU        >400
A1       EQU        >40A
C        EQU        >FF00
A        EQU        >FF0A
PAGE0    EQU        0            * Pages
PAGE6    EQU        6
PAGE8    EQU        8
YN       EQU        >78          * On-Chip I\O locations
XN       EQU        >79
TIM      EQU        1            * Analog - Digital Devices
ADC      EQU        2
DAC      EQU        2
IMR      EQU        4            * Interupt control
IMASK    EQU        >FFC2
         AORG >0
         B START                 * Reset control to program start
         AORG >4
         B    ISR
         AORG >400               * Interupt control to Int-service routine
START    EQU  $                  * start main program
         LDPK PAGE0              * Initialize system
         LRLK 1,IMASK
         SAR  1,IMR
         LDPK PAGE8
         SSXM
         SOVM
         SPM  0
         LRLK AR2,>200
         LARP 2
         RPTK 20
         BLKD C1,*+              * Move off-Chip variables on chip
         CNFP
         LDPK PAGE0
         LRLK AR2,X
         RPTK 13
         BLKD X1,*+
         LAC  DEC
```

FIGURE B-15 (*Continued*)

```
          SBLK 1,0
          SACL DEC2        * variable decimal point I/O control set-up
          LAR ARO,TVAL     * set sampling frequency
          SAR  ARO,TEMP
          OUT  TEMP,TIM
          LARP 1
          EINT
          NOP
LOOP      B LOOP           * Wait for interupt
ISR       IN XN,ADC
          LAC XN,0
          RPT DEC2         * shift input data into decimal point format
          SFR
          SACL XN
          ZAC
          LT DVAL
          MPY XN
          LRLK AR1,X
          RPT FVAL         * Process filter cycle
          MAC  >FF00,*+
          APAC
          RPT DEC          * Align decimal point
          SFL
          RPT DEC2         * Align Decimal point for DAC
          SFL
          SACH YN,0
          OUT YN,DAC
          ZAC
          MPYK 0
          LRLK AR1,X       * compute next state variable
          RPT FVAL
          MAC  >FF0A,*+
          APAC
          RPT DEC          * Align variable decimal point
          SFL
          ADDH XN
          LRLK AR3,XP1
          LARP 3
          RPTK 8           * Shift state variables over one place
          DMOV *-
          LARP 1
          SACH X,0         * Store new state variable
          EINT
          RET              * Go wait for another sample
```

FIGURE B-15 (*Continued*)

```
          IDT        'F-TO-F'
**********************************************************************
*                                                                    *
*            PARALLEL IMPLEMENTATION FOR THE TMS32020                *
*                                                                    *
*                              E.M. Dowling, K.A. Rowland *
**********************************************************************
*
*     This program implements a genreal parallel type filter.  The
*     coefficients are created by DF-PAK and down-loaded by the
*     HOST program.  This version does file to file I/O by taking its
*     input from the HOST and sending the output back to the HOST.
*
**********************************************************************
*
*     This section sets up the data areas needed by the program.
*
*     Data Area 1 - This area is written by the HOST program with the
*                   required data.  Values must be written to these
*                   locations.  (Data memory, off chip, page 8).
**********************************************************************

AOFF      EQU        >400     ; A matrix values for each section
COFF      EQU        >40A     ; C matrix values for each section
DOFF      EQU        >414     ; D matrix values for each section (0 fill !)
ICOFF     EQU        >419     ; Input constant
XOFF      EQU        >41A     ; Initial state
DSOFF     EQU        >42A     ; Decimal Scale
TVOFF     EQU        >42B     ; Timer value for analog to analog
UNSD1     EQU        >42C     ; not used
FOOFF     EQU        >42D     ; Filter order


**********************************************************************
*
*     Data Area 2 - On chip program memory for mac instruction.
*                   (Program memory, on chip).
*
**********************************************************************

CON       EQU        >FF00    ; C MATRIX ON CHIP

**********************************************************************
*
*     Data Area 3 - On chip data memory for program use.
*                   (Data memory, on chip, page 0).
*
**********************************************************************

AON       EQU        >63      ; A matrix values for each section
DON       EQU        >6D      ; D matrix values for each section (0 fill !)
ICON      EQU        >72      ; Input constant
XON       EQU        >73      ; Initial state
DSON      EQU        >7D      ; Decimal Scale
FOON      EQU        >7E      ; Filter order
INVAL     EQU        >7F      ; Input value

* I/O for HOST communication.

INPUT     EQU        >480     ; Input location
OUTPUT    EQU        >480     ; Output location
```

FIGURE B-15 (*Continued*)

```
*****************************************************************
*
*      This section does the initialization required to run the
*      program.  It moves coefficients on chip and sets required modes.
*
*****************************************************************

              AORG       >0
              B          INIT            ; Branch to start-up code

              AORG       >400
INIT          EQU        $               ; Start of program
              DINT                       ; Disable interupts
              SSXM                       ; sign extension mode when shifting
              SOVM                       ; saturating arithmetic
              SPM        0               ; no shift of P register
              CNFD                       ; make sure B0 is in data memory

*  Now move data on chip

              LARP       2               ; set aux reg ptr
              LDPK       8               ; page 8
              LRLK       2,>200          ; point to B0 in data memory
              RPTK       9               ; do 10 times
              BLKD       COFF,*+         ; move c matrix on chip
              CNFP                       ; configure as program memory
              LDPK       0               ; page 0, on chip B2
              LRLK       2,AON           ; point to on chip  A matrix location
              RPTK       9               ; do 10 times
              BLKD       AOFF,*+         ; move a on chip
              RPTK       15              ; do 15 times
              BLKD       DOFF,*+         ; move D, Input cons and X on chip
              LRLK       2,DSON          ; Address of decimal scale on chip
              BLKD       DSOFF,*         ; Move decimal scale
              LRLK       2,FOON          ; Address of filter order
              BLKD       FOOFF,*         ; Move filter order

*  Now begin filter operation.  Wait for input from host.
*  This is the start of the main loop.

WAITIN        BIOZ       WAITIN          ; wait for host to set BIO to 1
              RXF                        ; tell host to wait
              LRLK       4,INVAL         ; set reg 4 to pt to input loc. on chip
              LARP       4               ; set register pointer
              BLKD       INPUT,*         ; move input on chip

*  Now calculate the output.

              LDPK       0               ; make sure page pointer is set to 0
              LAR        2,FOON          ; load filter order
              LARP       2               ; set reg ptr.
              MAR        *-              ; decrement for repeat count
              SAR        2,FOON          ; restore filter order - 1
              ZAC                        ; zero accumulator
              MPYK       0               ; zero P register
              LRLK       3,XON           ; reg 3 points to state variables
              LARP       3               ; set register pointer
              RPT        FOON            ; do filter order number of times
              MAC        CON,*+          ; Acc <- X * C for all sections
```

FIGURE B-15   (*Continued*)

```
              APAC                      ; add last result
              LRLK    1,5               ; do 6 times, 6th is input constant
              LRLK    3,DON             ; register 3 pts to d values
    DLOOP     LARP    3                 ; set reg pointer
              LT      *+                ; load T
              MPY     INVAL             ; P <- Di * Input
              APAC                      ; accumulate to previous result
              LARP    1                 ; set register pointer
              BANZ    DLOOP,*-          ; loop until done

*  Accumulator now has output.  Scale result and save.

              RPT     DSON              ; decimal scale value
              SFL                       ; scale result
              LRLK    3,OUTPUT          ; load address
              LARP    3                 ; set pointer
              SACH    *,0               ; store value

*  Now we must calculate next states.

              LAR     1,FOON            ; load filter order ( -1)
              LARP    1                 ; set reg pointer
              MAR     *+                ; increment to old value
              SAR     1,FOON            ; restore old value
              LRLK    3,AON             ; address of A matrix
              LRLK    2,XON             ; address of state variables X
    NXLOOP    LRLK    0,1               ; load test value 1 into reg 0
              LARP    1                 ; point to reg 1
              ZAC                       ; clear acc.
              CMPR    0                 ; compare reg 1 = 1
              BBNZ    FSTORD            ; go do a first order section (last)

*  This is a second order section

              LARP    3                 ; set reg pointer
              LT      *+                ; T <- Ai(2,1) and point to Ai(2,2)
              LARP    2                 ; set ptr to X
              MPY     *+                ; P <- Xi(1) * Ai(2,1) & pt to next X
              APAC                      ; accumulate
              LARP    3                 ; point to A
              LT      *+                ; T <- Ai(2,2) & pt to next section
              LARP    2                 ; point to X
              LAR     4,*               ; load Xi(2) in 4 to save
              MPY     *                 ; P <- Xi(2) * Ai(2,2)
              APAC                      ; accumulate result
              RPT     DSON              ; scale value
              SFL                       ; scale result
              ADDH    INVAL             ; add input value
              MAR     *-                ; point to Xi(1)
              SAR     4,*+              ; Xi(1) <- Xi(2) & pt to Xi(2)
              SACH    *+,0              ; Xi(2) <- Acc & pt to next section
              B       NXTSCT            ; go do next section

*  This section of code does a 1st order section.  A 1st order section
*  will be the last section

    FSTORD    LARP    3                 ; set register pointer
              LT      *                 ; T <- Ai(2,2)
              LARP    2                 ; point to Xi(2)
              MPY     *                 ; P <- Xi(2) * Ai(2,2)
```

FIGURE B-15   (*Continued*)

```
          APAC                  ; put result in acc.
          RPT      DSON         ; scale value
          SFL                   ; scale result
          ADDH     INVAL        ; add input value to result
          SACH     *,0          ; store value back in Xi(2)
          B        NXTINP       ; go get next input. (last section)

NXTSCT    LRLK     0,2          ; index decrement value
          LARP     1            ; index register
          MAR      *0-          ; decrement by 2
          LRLK     0,0          ; compare value 0 to see if done
          CMPR     0            ; see if reg 1 = 0
          BBZ      NXLOOP       ; if not then go back

*  Done, tell host output is ready.  Go back and wait for host to send
*  next input.

NXTINP    SXF                   ; signal host done
WTHST     BIOZ     WAITIN       ; go back and wait
          B        WTHST        ; wait
          LRLK     0,>FFFF      ; dummy, assembler complains of last
*                               ; line infinite loop
```

FIGURE B-15 (*Continued*)

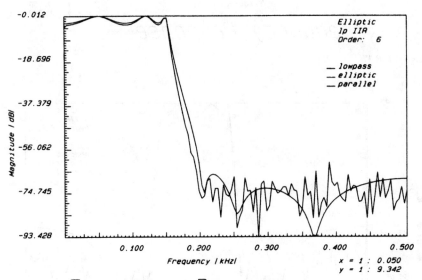

Elliptic
lp IIR
Order: 6

__ lowpass
__ elliptic
__ parallel

x = 1 : 0.050
y = 1 : 9.342

Frequency Response

FIGURE B-16

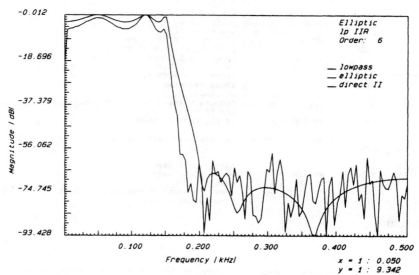

Frequency Response

FIGURE B-17

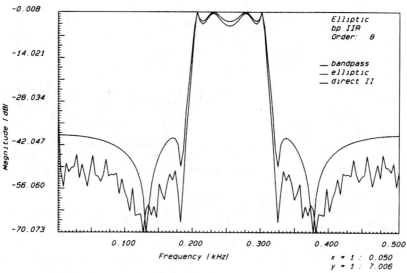

Frequency Response

FIGURE B-18

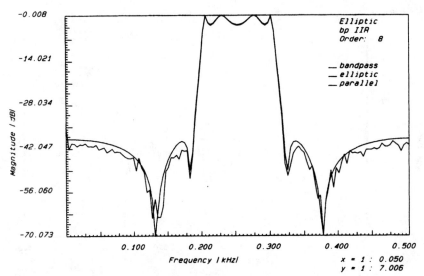

Frequency Response

FIGURE B-19

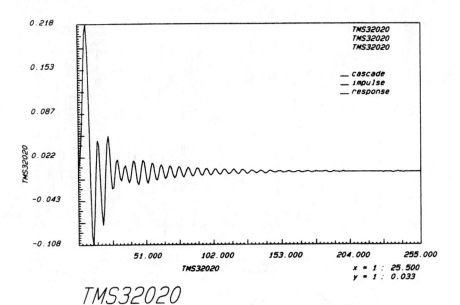

TMS32020

FIGURE B-20

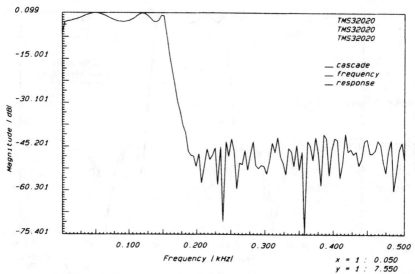

Frequency Response

FIGURE B-21

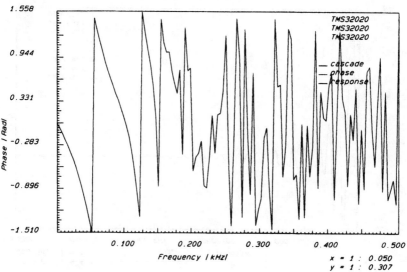

Phase Response

FIGURE B-22

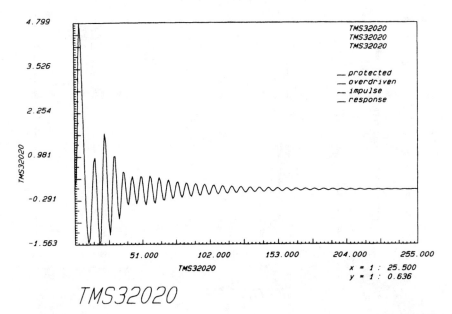

FIGURE B-23

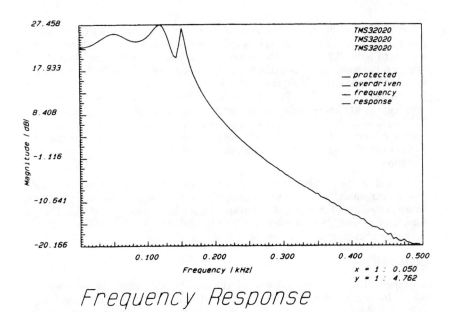

FIGURE B-24

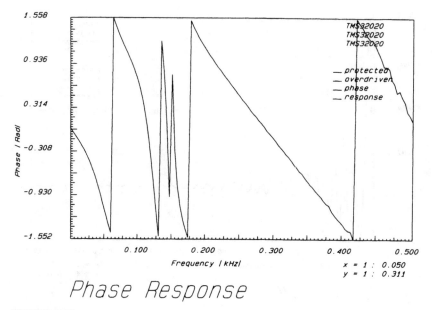

Phase Response

FIGURE B-25

off error is $E(\varepsilon) = 0.5Q$, where Q (the quantization step size) is given by $Q = 2^{-4}$ for this case. The error power, or variance, is usually modeled by $\sigma_\varepsilon^2 = Q^2/12$ which, in this case, is given by $\sigma_\varepsilon^2 = 2^{-8}/12 = 2^{-10}/3$. The signal-to-noise power ratio then becomes $(s/n)^2 = v^2/\sigma_\varepsilon^2$; v is the signal amplitude. If v is doubled, tripled, or quadrupled, etc., it can be seen that the $(s/n)^2$ ratio is improved by a factor of $2^2 = 4$, $3^2 = 9$, or $4^2 = 16$, and so on. For the case under study, a 20-fold increase of the input signal results in an $(s/n)^2$ advantage of 400. Therefore, it is advisable to increase the input signal such that the TMS word width is fully used. However, increasing the input signal beyond a certain point will cause overflow errors. These nonlinear overflow errors can be managed to some extent by using saturation arithmetic. Nevertheless, it still introduces unwanted distortion.

In figure B-26, the impulse response of an overdriven filter is presented. The steady-state low-amplitude oscillatory behavior is called *limit cycling*. The frequency response, shown in figure B-27, has a gross distortion over the desired low-pass profile. The output energy around 325 Hz is due to the limit cycling effect. Similar abnormal behavior can be found in the phase response as well (see figure B-28).

EXAMPLE B-5

In example B-1, a dual tone experiment with the TMS320 and an FIR filter was conducted. It was noted that a high-frequency tone persisted in the output as appearing in figure B-9. This contamination is due to the FIR's inability in implementing sharp frequency response (step skirt). The experiment conducted in example B-1 is repeated by using a sixth-order elliptic filter with a passband set to be [0, 150 Hz]. In figures B-29 and B-30, the input process is quantified. In figure B-31 the transient and steady-state

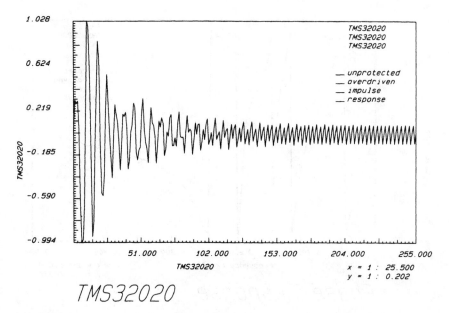

FIGURE B-26

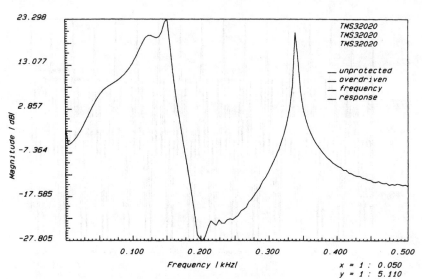

FIGURE B-27

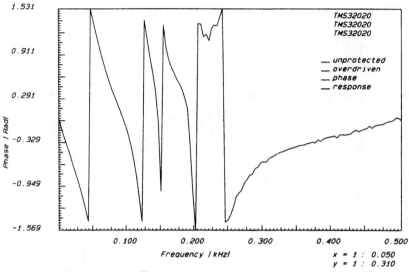

Phase Response

FIGURE B-28

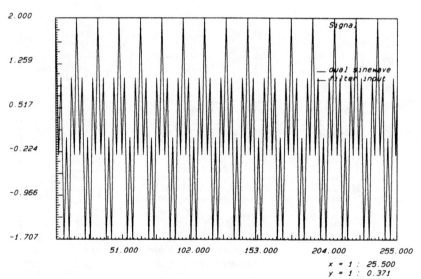

Signal Filtering

FIGURE B-29

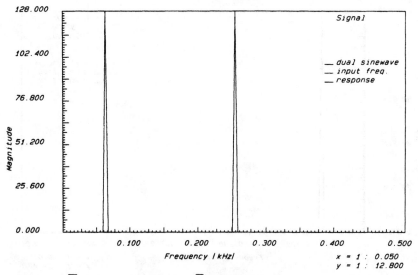

Frequency Response

FIGURE B-30

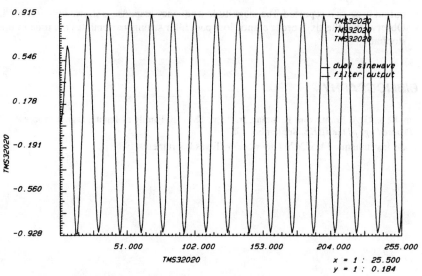

TMS32020

FIGURE B-31

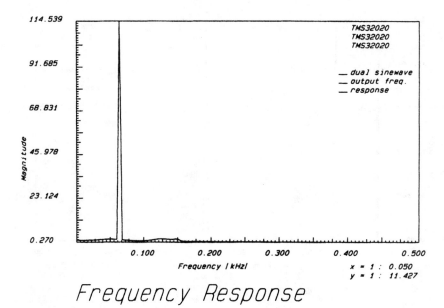

Frequency Response

FIGURE B-32

output process is reported. The magnitude frequency response is shown in figure B-32. Observe that the sixth-order elliptic low-pass filter strongly attenuates the tone in the stopband.

BIBLIOGRAPHY

Lin, K. S., G. A. Frantz, and R. Simar, Jr., "The TMS320 Family of Digital Signal Processors," *Proceedings of the IEEE,* September 1987.

Texas Instruments, *TMS32020 User's Guide,* Texas Instruments, 1986.

INDEX

ABOUT THE AUTHORS

Arthur B. Williams is vice-president for research and development at Coherent Communications Systems Corporation. He previously held design and engineering positions with the Telesignal Division of Singer Corp., Stelma Inc., and Burnell & Co. Mr. Williams is also the author of *The Designers Handbook of Integrated Circuits,* and *Active Filter Design.*

Fred J. Taylor is a professor of electrical engineering, professor of computer and information science, and director of the Institute for Advanced Computer Research at the University of Florida. His industrial experience includes positions at Texas Instruments and The Athena Group, as well as consultantships at Motorola, Harris, VTI, and others. He has been awarded three U.S. patents, authored 7 books, written two encyclopedia chapters, and has published over 100 technical papers.

WHAT IS THE MONARCH 2.0 DEMONSTRATION VERSION?

The MONARCH Version 2.0 demonstration software is a copy of the professional version with the following exceptions:

No data, filter, or any other information can be saved to the disk

The length of signals in SIGLAB and VIEW/2D is limited

Graphics hardcopy print-outs are disabled.

In addition to following the demonstration example below, feel free to enter any of the MONARCH design modules and design any filter you like. You can also enter "*.*" in the filename fields to look at example filters and signals which have been included with the demo version. Press <F1> for HELP. Press <F10> to QUIT.

SYSTEM REQUIREMENTS

IBM PC, XT, AT, PS/2 computer or 100% compatible; 640k RAM, MS/PC-DOS 3.0 or higher; hard disk drive (approx. 2Mb of space); EGA, VGA, Hercules, IBM8514, CGA, MCGA, AT&T 440, or PC 3270 graphics adapter; a math coprocessor is recommended and supported, but not required; a Microsoft compatible mouse is supported but not required.

INSTALLATION

(Note: The mouse may be used in place of the arrow keys, where the direction of movement corresponds to the relative arrow key, the left button is the <Enter> key, and the right button is the <Esc> key.)

1. Place the demonstration version of MONARCH in a floppy drive. If you are using the A drive, type a: followed by <Enter>, then type moninst followed by <Enter>. Press <Enter> to continue.

2. Verify or change the source and destination drives. Use the down arrow key to move to INSTALL MONARCH and press <Enter>. When the installation is completed, press <Enter> to continue.

3. From the MONDEMO directory, type monarch and press <Enter>.

4. When the MONARCH logo is displayed, press <Enter> to continue.

5. The MONARCH copyright screen is displayed next; when you are finished reading it press <Enter>. You are now in the MONARCH filter design and analysis environment.

DEMONSTRATION EXAMPLE

This demonstration example takes you through the design and analysis of a simple AM system used to transmit and receive an ECG (ElectroCardioGram) signal which is sampled at 500 Hz and contaminated with 60 Hz noise as shown in the figure below.

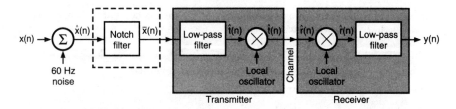

Files for this example have been presaved. You will design an FIR lowpass filter for your transmit and receive filters, and an IIR notch filter to remove noise. Then, you will use SIGLAB to complete and analyze your system design. Finally, you will see other methods by which the notch filter could have been designed or modified.

PART I (APPROX. 7 MIN.)

1. Using the arrow keys, highlight FIR under the DESIGN menu and press <Enter>. You will now generate the FIR lowpass filter used in the example. Enter "*.*" in the Filter File field and press <Enter>. Highlight the filter named ECG-FIR.FIR and press <Enter>. Notice that prespecified filter parameters appear in the appropriate fields. Press <Esc>, highlight GENERATE, and press <Enter>. This generates your FIR filter and displays the results. While the graphs are displayed, you may press z to zoom or c to use a crosshair for data location. Using the cursor arrows, move the zoom box or crosshair to the desired location and press <Enter>. The zoom box or crosshair can be sized using the keypad with NumLock ON (note that the upper left corner remains fixed in space). Press <Esc> three times, highlight QUIT, and press <Enter>. At the Save File? prompt, highlight NO and press <Enter>. *From now on , we simply instruct you to "select" an option, which means highlight it and press <Enter>. You can also "select" by typing the first letter of an option.*

2. Next, you will generate the IIR filter used in the example. Select IIR from the DESIGN menu. Enter "*.*" in the Filter File field and press <Enter>. Move to ECGIIR.IIR and press <Enter>. Press <Esc> and select GENERATE. This generates your IIR filter and displays the results. Press <Esc> twice and select QUIT. Select NO at the Save File? prompt.

3. Select ARC from the DESIGN menu. Since the last filter you designed was an IIR filter, MONARCH automatically loads the file ECGIIR.ARC. Move to the Architecture field and press <Enter> repeatedly to toggle through all of the options. Set the final architecture option to CASCADE. Press <Esc> and select GENERATE. This generates the architecture for the IIR filter. Press <Esc> and select QUIT.

4. Select SCHEMA from the DESIGN menu. Press <Esc> and select DISPLAY. This is a display of the architecture generated for the IIR filter. Press <Enter> to see the filter coefficients. Press <Esc> three times and select QUIT.

5. Use the right arrow key to move to the ANALYSIS menu, and select SIGLAB. At the Siglab> prompt, type include "ecg.s". This is a self running demo of the

analysis and design of an AM transmission system. The demo pauses before graphing and while graphs are displayed; *always press <Esc> to continue running the SIGLAB demo.* When the demo is finished, experiment with SIGLAB. Press <F1> to show SIGLAB's built-in functions. Press <F10> to exit SIGLAB.

PART II (APPROX. 3 MIN.)

6. We will now return to MONARCH's filter design modules. From the DESIGN menu, select POLEZERO. ECRIIR.ARC is automatically loaded. Press <Esc> and select VIEW. This displays the poles and zeros of your IIR filter. Press z to zoom in on the poles and zeros, move the box over the pole and zero locations, and press <Enter> to see a closer view of the poles and zeros. Continue to zoom in multiple times if you like. When you're finished, press <Esc> three times and select QUIT.

7. Select TRANSFER from the DESIGN menu. This displays the first 12 coefficients of the transfer function of the IIR filter. Highlight Page and press <Enter> to display the second page of coefficients. Press <Esc> and select QUIT.

8. Select STATEVAR from the DESIGN menu. Use the arrows keys to move around the matrices and display their elements. This is the state variable representation of the IIR filter with a cascade architecture. Press <Esc> and select EIGEN. This gives you the eigenvalues of the A matrix. Press <Esc> twice and select QUIT.

9. From the OSSHELL menu, select TYPE. Press <Enter>, press the backspace key one time, type RPT and press <Enter>. This displays all the report files. Move to ECGIIR.RPT and press <Enter>. This displays the engineering report for the IIR notch filter which was designed earlier. Press any key to scroll through the file, or press <Esc> to quit. When you finish viewing the report, press <Esc>.

This concludes the demonstration example. Remember, you can enter any of the MONARCH design menus and design any filter you like. You can enter "*.*" in the filename fields to look at filters and signals which have been included with the demo version of the software. Also, try exploring the FFT, 2D, and 3D modules.

(Please feel free to copy and distribute the demo software. It is free and is not copy protected.)